COMPUTER-AIDED ARCHITECTURAL DESIGN

William J. Mitchell

School of Architecture and Urban Planning
University of California, Los Angeles

COMPUTER-AIDED ARCHITECTURAL DESIGN

VAN NOSTRAND REINHOLD COMPANY
NEW YORK CINCINNATI TORONTO LONDON MELBOURNE

Library of Congress Catalog Card Number: 79-15641
ISBN: 0-442-80323-0
ISBN: 0-442-26248-5 pbk.

Manufactured in the United States of America

Published by Van Nostrand Reinhold Company Inc.
135 West 50th Street
New York, New York 10020

Van Nostrand Reinhold Company Limited
Molly Millars Lane
Wokingham, Berkshire RG11 2PY, England

Van Nostrand Reinhold
480 Latrobe Street
Melbourne, Victoria 3000, Australia

Macmillan of Canada
Division of Gage Publishing Limited
164 Commander Boulevard
Agincourt, Ontario M1S 3C7, Canada

15 14 13 12 11 10 9 8 7 6 5 4

Library of Congress Cataloging in Publication Data

Mitchell, William John, 1944-
Computer-aided architectural design.

Bibliography: p. 515.
Includes index.
1. Architectural design—Data processing. I. Title.
NA2728.M28 1979 721'.028'54 79-15641
ISBN 0-442-80323-0
ISBN 0-442-26248-5 pbk.

Contents

Preface

Computer-aided architectural design is now becoming a technologically and economically feasible reality. From simple beginnings in the early 1960's, the theory and practice of this field have developed to the point where it can be confidently predicted that, during the 1980s, everyday use of computer-aided design techniques will radically transform the practice of architecture. Several factors have contributed to the emergence of this potential: First, basic research conducted over the last decade has established some important theoretical foundations for the field. Second, an increasingly broad range of powerful and reliable computer software designed for use by architects is becoming available. Finally, the rapidly decreasing cost and widening availability of computer hardware are bringing acquisition of computing capabilities within the reach of even the smallest of architectural offices.

This book is intended to provide a comprehensive introduction to the fundamentals of computer-aided architectural design for the student of architecture, the architect in practice, and the computer professional who is interested in learning about this emergent application area. No detailed knowledge of programming is assumed, but some familiarity with a common programming language such as

FORTRAN, BASIC, APL or PL/1 will be helpful to the reader. A knowledge of elementary algebra and trigonometry should, in general, be sufficient mathematical preparation. For some of the more advanced topics covered, an acquaintance with matrix algebra and graph theory is a useful background.

The contents are organized into four parts: *Fundamental Concepts, Data Bases, Interfaces,* and *Problem-Solving.* Each part consists of several chapters. Part 1, *Fundamental Concepts,* introduces computers and their capabilities; discusses the theoretical foundations of computer-aided architectural design; and describes how computer-aided design techniques can be employed in practice. The following parts cover particular technical topics of importance in detail. Part 2, *Data Bases,* discusses methods for encoding and storing building and site description data in computer memory. Part 3, *Interfaces,* deals with communications between user and machine. Input and output hardware, alphanumeric communication techniques, and computer graphics techniques are covered. Part 4, *Problem-Solving,* discusses numerous computer-oriented techniques for solving specific types of problems involved in building programming, design, and evaluation. Finally, an extensive bibliography of the relevant research and professional literature is provided.

The selection and sequence of topics are based upon the author's experience in teaching courses in computer-aided architectural design at UCLA and Yale over the last seven years. For introductory, one-semester courses in design methodology and computer-aided design, Part 1, *Fundamental Concepts,* should be studied in detail, with the more technical chapters used as a reference source only. Part 2, *Data Bases,* is suitable for detailed study in the context of a one-semester course in architectural data base management. Part 3, *Interfaces,* is appropriate for a course in architectural computer graphics. Part 4, *Problem Solving,* can be used for an advanced course in computer-aided architectural design.

William J. Mitchell
Venice, California

Acknowledgments

My UCLA colleagues Robin Liggett and Murray Milne made such numerous and important contributions to this book that it is impossible to acknowledge them adequately. Charles Eastman, Jeff Hamer, Lawrence Harvey, Robin Liggett, Murray Milne, and Ched Reeder read various versions of the manuscript, and suggested improvements and corrections. Any errors that remain are my own. The illustrations were drawn by Diane Hertz, Wayne Johnson, Lucy Lichtblau, Tony Styant-Browne, and the author. Bill Jepson coded and ran a number of example programs. Photographs, drawings, and examples of output were kindly made available by Calcomp Inc., Frank Crow, Dynamic Graphics Inc., the Design Office Consortium, Charles Eastman, Donald Greenberg, Jeff Hamer, Leon Hoffman, Ed Hoskins, Peter Kamnitzer, Laser Scan Inc., Kaiman Lee, Murray Milne, Charles Moore, Nicholas Negroponte, Neville Quarry, Ron Resch, Tee Sasada, Tektronix Inc., Mathias Ungers, and Annette del Zoppo. Max Farrar prepared the bibliography. Shirley Nounnan typed the manuscript with particular care and skill. Dean Harvey Perloff of the School of Architecture and Urban Planning at UCLA provided important support for the project.

PART 1

FUNDAMENTAL CONCEPTS

This Part consists of three chapters which, together, provide an overview of the fundamental theoretical principles and important practical implications of computer-aided architectural design. Chapter 1, "Computers and Their Capabilities," gives a general introduction to computer technology, and briefly traces the historical emergence of computer-aided design. It may be quickly skimmed by those who have an up-to-date working knowledge of computing. Chapter 2, "The Computer's Role in Design," establishes some basic theoretical concepts which form the foundation for the remainder of the book. The reader must thoroughly understand this chapter before going further. Chapter 3, "Practical Application of Computer-Aided Architectural Design Techniques," analyzes architectural design processes from an information processing viewpoint; uses this analysis to show how computer-aided design techniques may be implemented in practice; and discusses some representative examples of working programs and systems.

1

Computers and Their Capabilities

ELEMENTS OF COMPUTER SYSTEMS

In the simplest terms, computers may be described as electronic devices which are capable of storing data in an internal memory, and of following stored sets of instructions (known as *programs*) to operate upon data in order to produce desired results. The fundamental elements of any computer system are items of computing machinery and associated devices, generally referred to as the *hardware,* the *data* to be operated upon, and the programs which are collectively known as the *software.*

Hardware

The hardware of a typical simple computer is diagrammed in *Figure 1.1.* Data entry to the system is via an *input device,* which might, for example, be a punch-card reader or an electric typewriter keyboard. The input device encodes data as electrical pulses; encoded information can then be stored in *memory.* Traditionally, computer memories have been constructed from ferrite *cores:* minute ceramic rings strung on a mesh of fine wires. Each core can be magnetized

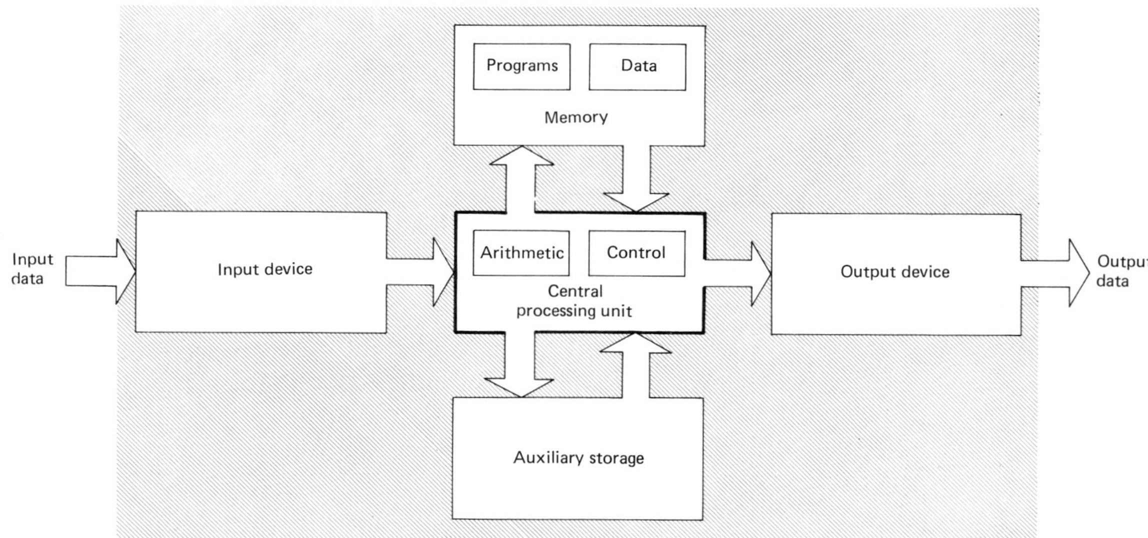

Figure 1.1
Schematic functional diagram of a simple computer

with either clockwise or counterclockwise polarity, and can thus store one *bit* (binary digit) of information. By passing pulses through the wires, polarities of cores can be sensed and changed as required. Some more recent computers employ semiconductor memories, fabricated upon small silicon chips. Information can be stored in, and retrieved from, core or semiconductor memory at very high speed. But these high speed memory media are expensive, and of limited capacity; cheaper but slower-operating *auxiliary storage units* such as magnetic disk or tape devices are usually employed to provide additional storage capacity. Information to be output is transmitted to the *output device* in the form of electrical pulses. The output device decodes this information, and expresses it as output data in a useful format, such as typed symbols or a picture displayed on a cathode ray tube.

The whole system is controlled by the *central processing unit* (CPU), which is composed of a *control section* and an *arithmetic and logical unit*. The control section retrieves, interprets, and executes (by sending signals to the appropriate devices) instructions from the program stored in memory. These instructions may require the input or output of data, storage or retrieval of data in memory, or performance of arithmetic and logical operations upon data. The arithmetic and logical operations are executed by the arithmetic and logical unit, a device consisting of electronic circuitry like that found in ordinary electronic calculators. The CPU's of early computers were fabricated using vacuum tubes; later computers employed transistors. Modern computers use integrated circuitry.

Numerous variations may be played upon the basic arrangement that has been described. For example, input and output devices are often combined into a single unit known as a *terminal*. A variety of *peripheral devices* (input and output devices, terminals, auxiliary storage units, etc.) may simultaneously be controlled by a single CPU. Several CPU's may operate simultaneously. A number of computers may be linked together to form a *network*. All the hardware might be grouped in a single compact unit, or it might be dispersed in widely separated locations. But the same fundamental principles of operation are followed in each case.

Data

Any device which converts any type of data into electrical signals, such as a card reader, a keyboard, a television camera, a microphone, or a laboratory sensing device, might potentially be used as a computer input device. Similarly, any machine which can be controlled by electrical signals, such as an electric typewriter, a cathode ray tube display device, a music synthesizer or even an elevator system, can potentially be used as an output device. The potential of encoding many different types of data for input, and of converting output signals into a wide variety of forms, means that computers are very flexible and general information processing devices. They can be mathematical machines, text-handling machines, graphics machines, talking and listening machines, music machines, mobile automata, feeling, tasting or smelling machines, and machines for controlling other machines, as the occasion demands.

Programs

The operations to be performed upon data by the CPU are specified by a *program* which, like the data, is stored in memory. A program consists of a sequence of instructions written in a computer language. In a simple program, these instructions are executed one-by-one in the sequence in which they occur (*Figure 1.2(a)*). More complex programs contain *loops* and *branches*. A loop is a sequence of instructions within the program, that is repeated a specified number of times (*Figure 1.2(b)*). A branch instruction chooses the next instruction to be executed, depending upon the result of some specified operation (*Figure 1.2(c)*). The use of loops and branches enables long and complex computations to be concisely described.

When a program is lengthy, it is usual to write it in separate parts known as *subroutines* or *functions*. (The technical distinction between subroutines and functions is a question of detail which need not concern us here.) A subroutine or function is a small program which is executed whenever *called* by an instruction in the main program. Upon completion of execution of the subroutine or function, execution of the main program is resumed. Subroutines and functions may themselves call other subroutines and functions, and a typical program thus has a hierarchical structure as shown in *Figure 1.3*.

It would make no sense for every programmer to separately develop subroutines for performing such standard operations as evaluating trigonometric functions, taking roots or logarithms, etc. Consequently, numerous standard *subroutine libraries* have been developed. The feasibility of programming complex and sophisticated computations usually depends upon the availability of adequate subroutine libraries.

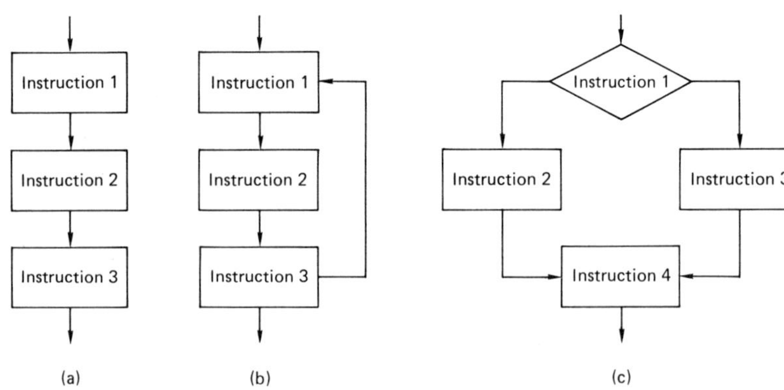

Figure 1.2
Program loops and branches. (a) Simple sequence. (b) Loop: instructions 1, 2 and 3 executed a specified number of times. (c) Branch: either instruction 2 or instruction 3 is executed, as chosen by instruction 1.

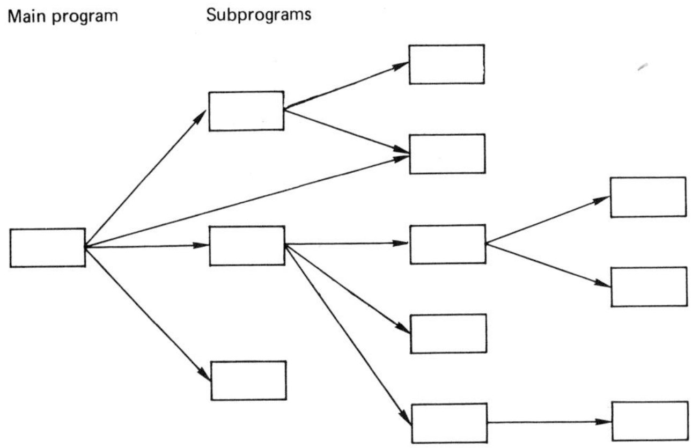

Figure 1.3
Hierarchical structure of a typical computer program.

Application software

The various types of programs utilized in a computer system are referred to collectively as the *software.* Programs written by computer users to solve specific problems are known as *application software.* Examples of architectural application software include programs to plot perspectives and working drawings, synthesize floor plans, perform engineering and cost analyses, and generate specifications.

For many common types of applications, programs are already developed and are available from various sources. Unusual, new, or highly specialized applications typically require the user to develop his or her own programs. It is not particularly difficult to acquire sufficient programming skill to write simple application programs, and in many professional fields this capability is now considered essential. Programming is still an unusual skill among architects, but many architectural curricula now include introductory courses in this area. These programs are written in some kind of appropriate *computer language.* The most primitive kind of computer language is the *machine language* of a particular computer. Machine language programs consist of sequences of binary * numbers, for example:

011011 000000 000000 000000 000001 000000

Machine language programs are very difficult to write and to understand. It is difficult to discover and eliminate errors in such programs. Furthermore, machine language programs cannot be transferred from one computer to another. To overcome some of these difficulties, *assembly languages* were introduced. An assembly language typically uses short mnemonics to describe operations, and allows the

* The base of the *binary* number system is 2, instead of 10 as used in the familiar *decimal* number system. The two binary digits are 0 and 1, rather than the ten decimal digits 0,1,2,3,4,5,6,7,8,9. In computing, it is often convenient to express numbers in binary rather than decimal form.

use of variable names to identify data to be operated upon. Typical assembly language instructions might be:

```
ADD A
CLA B
MPY X
```

However, assembly language programming is still quite difficult, and programs are still machine dependent. *Programming languages,* on the other hand, provide powerful and flexible notation for describing operations; they are designed to be relatively easy to write and understand; and they allow programs to be relatively easy to transfer from one machine to another. Familiar examples of programming languages are FORTRAN, BASIC, APL, ALGOL, COBOL, and PL/1. The vast majority of application programs are written in programming languages.

In order for a program written in a programming language to be executed, either a *compiler* or an *interpreter* (or in some cases both) must be employed to translate the program into a form which can be executed by the particular machine. A compiler is a program which accepts as input a *source program* written in a particular programming language, and produces an *object program* in machine or assembly language capable of being executed on a particular computer. An interpreter, by contrast, operates on a line-by-line basis. It accepts a line of source code, and produces the actual result of performing the specified actions. A skilled assembly language programmer can usually produce a program which executes somewhat more efficiently than a program which is written in a programming language and then compiled or interpreted. But this gain in efficiency only rarely justifies the added difficulty and expense of programming in assembly language.

In order to control and report on the sequencing, compilation or interpretation, loading, execution, and handling of input and output of programs in a computer, yet another type of program known as an *operating system* is employed.

Compilers, interpreters, operating systems, and other types of software required to support the execution of application programs are collectively referred to as *system software.* This system software is typically written and maintained by technical specialists known as *systems programmers.* At least some system software is usually provided with their equipment by hardware manufacturers. Normally system software is designed to support a wide variety of different types of applications. While an architectural user normally would not be called upon to design, program or even to understand the technical details of system software, he or she sometimes may be concerned with the choice of a language or operating system to support particular applications of interest.

Division of tasks between hardware and software

In designing a computer system, sometimes there is a choice to be made between performance of an operation by software and by hardware. For example, the CPU's of many early computers incorporated circuitry for performing additions, subtractions, and multiplications. But circuitry for division was complicated and expensive, so it was often eliminated and divisions were accomplished by executing a procedure of successive subtractions known as Newton's method (Perlis 1972).

In general, hardware costs have decreased over time, while software costs have increased. Early computer systems tended to be "software-intensive," i.e. oriented towards using extensive software to make the most out of a particular hardware investment. The tendency now is towards more "hardware-intensive" systems, in which special purpose hardware is widely employed to perform more efficiently certain common operations which would formerly have been accomplished by software.

A particularly important factor in this development has been the new technology of *microprocessors* and *microprogramming*. This technology allows the fabrication of special purpose logic circuits at very low cost on small silicon chips. Many elements of system software, for example, language interpreters, are now being replaced by microprogrammed chips in some new computer systems.

CAPABILITIES AND APPLICATIONS OF COMPUTERS

Computer systems have been put to a variety of different applications, with each of which exploiting somewhat different aspects of the computer's capabilities. Many of these applications were to some extent anticipated in earlier devices which the computer has now superseded. The following paragraphs briefly survey some of the main current areas of application.

Numerical computation in science, engineering, and operations research

The earliest and most obvious application of computer technology was to automation of complex, lengthy, and repetitive numerical computations, such as the generation of ballistic tables, astronomical tables, and tables of values for mathematical functions. The 19th century mathematician Charles Babbage conceived of a great mechanical "Analytical Engine" for this purpose, although it was never completed. ENIAC, which is generally regarded as the first modern electronic computer, was developed in the mid-1940's for the U.S. Army to compute ballistic tables.

Early in the 1950's, there began to emerge a first generation of programming languages which permitted the input of mathematical expressions in a notation resembling normal algebraic format. By the mid-1950's, the earliest versions of FORTRAN, the most famous and widely used of these languages, were released by the IBM Corporation. FORTRAN remains in widespread use today. In the late 1950's, as a result of international efforts, the ALGOL language emerged. This language embodied some important new concepts, which laid the foundation for subsequent rapid progress in the development of programming languages and techniques.

The increasing availability of computers, together with the development of languages like FORTRAN and ALGOL, led in the 1960's to a revolution in scientific, engineering, and operations research problem-solving. Computer-executed numerical techniques began to replace traditional analytic methods in many areas, and radically new problem-solving techniques which exploited the computer's power were developed. Among the most important of these were techniques for solving difficult optimization problems, for example, by use of linear programming methods, techniques for numerically simulating the behavior of complex systems, and matrix techniques for structural analysis. By the 1970's, the computer had become the indispensable partner of the scientist, the engineer, and the operations researcher.

Statistical and business data processing

A second important early application was statistical and business data processing. Whereas engineering and scientific computations characteristically involve relatively small quantities of input and output data, but require performance of extensive and complex sequences of operations, business data processing typically involves the handling of very large quantities of data and the performance of relatively simple operations such as storage, retrieval, sorting, tabulating, and printing out in specified formats.

Automated data processing techniques have a long history. In the 1880's Herman Hollerith devised a system for recording census data on punch cards, and an electric tabulating machine for compiling and tabulating the data. Hollerith's machines were first used in the U.S. census of 1890, and in 1896 he formed the Tabulating Machine Company which was one of the predecessors of IBM. An early application of the punch card technology to business data processing was made in 1895, when the Prudential Life Insurance Company introduced automatic card sorting machines for tabulating insurance premium data. In 1951, the U.S. Bureau of the Census once again pioneered the application of new automated data processing techniques when it installed a model of UNIVAC 1, the first commercially available computer. Today computers are very extensively employed in business and government for such data processing tasks as keeping accounts, inventories, employee and customer records, tabulating and manipulating census and other types of survey data, printing tabulated reports, orders, checks, and invoices, addressing envelopes, recording library accession and borrowing transactions, and so on. The COBOL programming language and special software packages known as *data base management systems* are widely utilized for these types of applications.

Data analysis

The computer's combination of numerical computation and data processing capabilities makes it extremely useful in the area of data analysis. Today, most data analysis computations in the social, behavioral, physical, and life sciences are routinely carried out by computers. Certain widely performed types of analysis, for example, factor analysis, cluster analysis, and multi-dimensional scaling, are true products of the computer era; they involve such extensive computation that manual processing (at least for problems of realistic scale) would be inconceivable.

Person-machine systems

Early computers (and many computers in use today) were designed primarily to solve preformulated problems or to process data according to predetermined procedures. However, there are many situations in which it may be desirable for a human operator to interact with a computer in a more immediate and continuous way. The concept of person-machine intellectual interaction can be traced back to the 1920's and the early teaching machines of Pressey, and later of Skinner (Lumsdaine and Glaser 1960). These machines presented a question to the pupil, then when an answer had been made, either checked it or displayed the correct answer for comparison, thus providing immediate reinforcement of understanding. A second important type of person-machine dialogue was proposed by Vannevar Bush (1945) in an article which discussed a hypothetical device called *memex:* a personalized, desk-sized, highly flexible, automated information storage and retrieval system. The potential advantages of person-machine dialogue in problem-solving were classically formulated, in a paper published by J. C. R. Licklider in 1960, as follows:

> . . . many problems which can be thought through in advance are very difficult to think through in advance. They would be easier to solve, and they could be solved faster, through an intuitively guided trial-and-error process in which the computer cooperated, turning up flaws in the reasoning or revealing unexpected turns in the solution. Other problems simply cannot be formulated without computing-machine aid. Poincare anticipated the frustration of an important group of would-be computer users when he said, "The question is not, 'What is the answer?' The question is, 'What is the question?' " One of the main aims of man-computer symbiosis is to bring the comput-

ing machine effectively into the formulative parts of technical problems.

The practical development of interactive computing was greatly facilitated by the commercial introduction, in the 1960's, of interactive cathode ray tube displays for text and graphics, and of the technique of *time-sharing* by means of which a computer can serve more than one user at a time. Interactive computer systems are now commonly employed for such purposes as entry, checking, storage, and retrieval of data, computer-aided instruction, writing and testing computer programs, performing psychological experiments, assisting in mathematical, scientific, and engineering problem solving, data analysis and hypothesis testing in the social and behavioral sciences, and computer-aided design (particularly in the aerospace and automobile industries).

Numerous very large networks of interactive terminals connected to time-sharing computer systems equipped with data base management facilities now exist in the commercial world, and it would be difficult for many modern businesses to operate without them. Airline reservations systems are a good illustration. It was reported in 1976, for example, that TWA's reservation system in the United States and Europe employed almost 3,000 interactive terminals, which communicated with the system approximately two million times per day.

Process control

As hardware technology advances and computing machinery generally becomes smaller, cheaper, and more robust, computers have physically moved out of research laboratories and specially-controlled environments where they were developed, and into the everyday environment of factory and office, into commercial ships and airplanes, and even into the rugged environment of military and space vehicles. It has become possible to employ computers to control complex mechanical and electrical systems such as industrial machinery and process plants, aircraft and spacecraft guidance systems, flows of vehicles in transportation networks, and elevator and air-conditioning systems for buildings. These applications are known as "process control" or "command and control" applications.

Computer graphics and image processing

Among the machines which a computer can be used to control are devices such as pen plotters and cathode ray tube displays which generate pictures. Over the last 15 years or so, graphics has been an increasingly extensive and important area of computer application. Typical applications of computer graphics techniques include engineering and architectural drafting, production of perspectives, mapping, and computer-aided design in various fields. Computer animation of scenes in perspective, a technique initially developed by the Boeing Company of Seattle in the early 1960's, allows sophisticated simulations of movement through an environment to be produced. Real-time visual simulation using a color television screen was introduced in the mid-1960's, and has been applied in the simulation of aircraft and spacecraft landing and ship docking.

A closely related field of application is *image processing,* i.e., computer analysis of photographs and other visual materials. Typical applications of image processing technology now include analysis of earth satellite photographs to extract data about crops, atmospheric and water pollution, mineral deposits, land use, etc., analysis of X-rays for medical diagnostic purposes, analysis of scientific data such as bubble-chamber photographs, and provision of visual perception capabilities for industrial robots.

Artificial intelligence

Even as the first modern computers were being constructed and put to work at numerical computation and data processing tasks around 1950, interest was developing in the even more exciting possibility of using computers to solve difficult intellectual problems of a non-numerical character. In 1950, the English logician A. M. Turing published a famous paper entitled "Computing Machinery and Intelligence," which posed and discussed the question, "Can machines think?" Within a few years, the first programs and systems which successfully solved significant non-numerical problems had appeared. For example, Dineen (1955) and Selfridge (1955) reported on systems which recognized visual patterns, Newell (1955) discussed a chess playing machine; and Newell, Shaw and Simon (1957) published a description of Logic Theorist, a system which most impressively proved theorems from Whitehead and Russell's *Principia Mathematica.* The name "artificial intelligence" was coined for this type of work.

Progress in artificial intelligence research over the last two decades has been extremely rapid, resulting in the design and implementation of systems possessing a bewildering variety of capabilities. Some of the main types of tasks for which at least partially successful artificial intelligence systems have been developed are:

Playing checkers, chess, go, and other complex games;

Recognizing printed and written characters and other two-dimensional patterns such as pictures of chromosomes, recognition of spoken words, automated analysis and interpretation of aerial and satellite photographs and other complex pictures and scenes;

Theorem-proving and other logical tasks;

Simulation of cognitive processes such as perception, learning, concept formation, and induction;

Natural language interpretation and translation, question answering, and conversation;

Performing complex physical manipulation tasks, and solving spatial problems such as path finding in complex physical environments;

Acting as highly sophisticated and flexible teaching machines;

Performing diagnosis and inference tasks in medicine and science;

Synthesizing music, poetry, painting, sculpture and architectural designs.

Although much of the work on artificial intelligence systems has so far been confined to the research laboratory, some sophisticated commercial products employing artificial intelligence techniques are now available. For example:

Industrial robots which perform complex assembly line operations;

Voice-operated supermarket checkout systems (to which clerks call out the prices of items) and voice-operated airport baggage routing systems;

Systems which scan printed text and speak words aloud, intended for use as reading machines by the blind;

Medical monitoring systems in the form of "biobelts," which transmit data on the user's bio-activity to a remote console for analysis.

Overviews of research in the field of artificial intelligence are provided in texts by Nilsson (1971), Slagle (1971), Uhr (1973), and Jackson (1974). Useful survey papers have been published by Minsky (1961), Feigenbaum (1963, 1969), and Newell (1973). Collections of important technical papers have been edited by Feigenbaum and Feldman (1963), and Minsky (1968). A Delphi survey, exploring views about the future of artificial intelligence held by workers in the field, has been published by Firschein, *et al* (1973).

Computer-aided design

The development of computer-aided design commenced in earnest in the early 1960's. Perhaps the most significant pioneering effort was Ivan E. Sutherland's Sketchpad system, implemented on the TX-2 computer at MIT's Lincoln Laboratory (Sutherland 1963). Sketchpad allowed an engineer to generate designs by sitting at an interactive graphics terminal, and manipulating drawings displayed on the screen by use of light-pen * and keyboard. The presentation of Sketchpad at the 1963 Spring Joint Computer Conference, and showings of a film on the system, generated intense interest among many engineers in the potentials of computer-aided design.

In parallel with the early work of Sutherland and others at MIT, IBM developed an elaborate system known as DAC-1 (Design Augmented by Computer), for use by General Motors in automobile design. The system was made public at the 1964 Fall Joint Computer Conference and was to be the forerunner of many interactive computer-aided design systems installed by automobile and aerospace firms by the end of the 1960's (Prince 1971). A third important early system was developed at around the same time by Itek Laboratories for lens design work. Since then, computer-aided design has been increasingly widely employed in various aspects of mechanical, civil, electrical, chemical, and industrial engineering (Gott 1973).

The application of computer-aided design in architecture lagged considerably behind applications in engineering. Hostility to the idea among architects, and ignorance of the potentials of computer technology, perhaps contributed to this; but the fundamental reason undoubtedly was economic. Automobile and aerospace firms tend to be very large, and capable of mobilizing capital to invest in expensive equipment, while architectural firms tend to be relatively small and unable to do so. Furthermore, in the automobile and aerospace industries the budget for the design of a product is usually quite large, often many times the cost of the individual product, whereas in architecture the design cost must usually be kept to a very small fraction of the cost of the product. Thus it is usually much more difficult for an architectural firm than for an automobile or aerospace firm to amortize the cost of expensive equipment. Since early computer-aided design systems required investments of hundreds of thousands or even millions of dollars, they were well beyond the means of architects.

However, interest in the potentials of computer-aided architectural design grew rapidly in the academic community during the 1960's. As the technology continued to develop, and as costs dropped spectacularly, it slowly became an increasingly widespread reality in practice during the early 1970's.

In the United States, discussions of the potentials of computer-aided architectural design began to be published in the early 1960's (see for example Dawson (1961), Eberhard (1962), and Souder and Clark (1963)). In 1964, Christopher Alexander published an influential book entitled *Notes on the Synthesis of Form,* which generated considerable enthusiasm for utilization of systematic, computer-based methods in architectural design. In that same year, a conference held at the Boston Architectural Center on "Architecture and the Computer" was able to attract nearly 600 attendees. Some very ambitious ex-

* See Interactive Graphic Input Devices in Chapter 9.

perimental interactive graphics computer-aided design systems were implemented during the 1960's, for example, Souder and Clark's CO-PLANNER (Souder and Clark 1964) and Negroponte's URBAN5 (Negroponte and Groisser 1970). In 1968, the Yale School of Architecture sponsored a major conference on computer graphics in architecture and design (Milne 1969). However, the first practical applications, which were mostly in the areas of structural and mechanical calculations, cost estimation and economic analysis, and specification production, were rather mundane in character and did not involve any elaborate graphics (see Harper 1968, Negroponte 1975). The first installations of interactive computer graphics systems in architectural offices began to appear in the early 1970's.

Basic research in computer-aided architectural design has been supported by a few government and private agencies and private foundations, most notably the National Science Foundation, the National Bureau of Standards, and the Graeme Foundation. Several universities have carried out quite extensive research programs. During the 1960's for example, departments of civil engineering at MIT and Pennsylvania State University pioneered various architectural engineering applications. Probably the most important centers during the seventies have been the Institute of Physical Planning at Carnegie-Mellon University, which has focused on building description and space planning issues, and the Architecture Machine Group at MIT, which has taken an artificial intelligence orientation. In addition to carrying out research activities, many schools of architecture now offer courses in computer-aided design (Mitchell 1974, Pohl 1975).

In Britain, the course of development has been somewhat different; the most important computer-aided design efforts have been very closely associated with large-scale, public-sector building programs, employing industrialized component building systems. In 1964, a demonstration program for housing design, using the IBIS industrialized component system, was shown at the Industrialized Building Systems and Components Exhibition in London (Fair *et al* 1966). Inspired by Sketchpad, a much more sophisticated interactive graphics program for assembly of IBIS-like components into building designs was implemented shortly afterwards by William M. Newman at the Cambridge University Mathematics Laboratory (Newman 1966). The West Sussex County Council installed an IBM computer graphics system at its architect's department in Chichester in 1967 for use with the SCOLA coordinated system of standard drawings for components and their assembly (Ray-Jones 1968). Since about 1970, several ambitious, large-scale computer-aided design systems for use in public sector system-building programs have been under development. Among these are (Campion and Reynolds 1974, Purcell 1975):

CEDAR, originally intended for design of post-office buildings using the SEAC component system, and later redeveloped for design of Property Services Agency office buildings in the PSA rationalized method of building.

HARNESS, a computer-aided design system sponsored by the Department of Health and Social Security for use in the HARNESS hospital building program.

OXSYS, sponsored by the Oxford Area Health Board for use with the Oxford Method of Building. The development of both HARNESS and OXSYS has been carried out by the firm of Applied Research of Cambridge.

CARBS (Computer-Aided Rationalized Building System), developed by the Liverpool University Computer-Aided Design Centre for use by the Clwyd County Council Architect's Department.

SSHA, systems for house design and site layout developed by Edinburgh University CAAD Studies for the Scottish Special Housing Association.

By 1977, most of these systems were either in the final stages of development or already in practical use.

The practical utilization of computer systems for assistance in quantity surveying and building documentation took place very early in Europe. In 1959, Bjorn Bindslev, a Danish architect and quantity surveyor, began investigation of the use of computers for building communication and contract documentation. This led to the development of a computer-oriented coding and classification system for construction data, known as CBC (Co-ordinated Building Communication). The first bills of quantities generated by computer using this system were produced in 1963 (*Architects' Journal* 1964). Since this pioneering work, however, developments in most parts of Western Europe seem to have lagged well behind those in the U.S. and U.K. (For summaries of developments in various Western European countries see Negroponte 1975.)

Available data on computer-aided architectural design research and applications in Russia and Eastern Europe is very sketchy. It is clear, though, that some activity is taking place. In July 1962, Moscow *Pravda* published an article entitled "Can a Machine Create a Design?" (Sinyakov 1965). Some applications to structural design and floor plan layout were discussed, and the question was answered in the affirmative. Since then, scattered reports on Russian and Eastern European developments in the field have appeared (e.g. Agabadian and Tshigogidze 1971, Aben 1975).

In Asia, Japan has been the clear leader in the field of computer-aided architectural design. Developments have been comparatively recent, mainly dating from the early 1970's (Tohmatsu 1974, Sasada 1975). Active research groups now exist at a number of locations, for example, Osaka University and the IBM Tokyo Scientific Center.

Large architectural and engineering firms like Nikken Sekkei make use of a wide variety of programs and systems, and Nippon Telegraph and Telephone offers programs for use via its time-sharing network.

In Australia, considerable research work has been carried out at the Department of Architectural Science at the University of Sydney, and at the CSIRO Division of Building Research since the late 1960's. A contract documentation system for use with a dimensionally coordinated method of building is under development by the Government Architect's Branch of the New South Wales Public Works Department (Blue 1974). This is somewhat similar in scope and character to the U.K. systems mentioned earlier.

By the mid-1970's, then, application of computer-aided design techniques had become commonplace in many fields of engineering and manufacturing, and a similar trend was becoming apparent in architecture in many parts of the world. The developing importance of the subject was reflected by its appearance in university curricula, by a proliferation of conferences and workshops (e.g., see Vlietstra and Wielinga 1973, IPC 1976), and by the emergence of a number of technical journals (e.g., *Computer-Aided Design*).

EVOLUTION OF COMPUTER TECHNOLOGY

Computers have improved enormously in performance while decreasing in cost and size since the first prototypes were constructed in the 1940's; and it seems clear that these trends will continue. When assessing the potential of computer-aided design in architecture, it is most important to understand that this process of technological development is continuously and rapidly expanding the realm of feasible applications. Many of the techniques which are discussed in this book have become clearly feasible in everyday practice only very recently; others are marginally practical, and yet others are still in the experimental stages. Almost all of these techniques, however, can be expected to become commonplace by the 1980's. The following paragraphs will briefly trace the evolution of computer capabilities over the last 20 years, and make some forecasts of expected developments during the next 20 years.

Computer generations

The evolution of computer technology has been cyclical in character, with each successive cycle commonly referred to as a new "computer generation." New generations are typically characterized by utilization of new component technologies, new system designs (system architecture), new types of software, and order-of-magnitude improvements in performance. There are variations in the ways that different authors identify the successive generations (see Turn 1974), but for our purposes they can be adequately described as follows:

Generation 1. The first commercially-marketed computers such as the UNIVAC I began to be introduced from 1951–52 onwards, and were employed for scientific computation and business data processing. These machines employed vacuum tubes, and were characterized by relatively low speeds, low reliability, limited memory capacity, and limited software.

Generation 2. This generation lasted from about 1959 to 1965. Transistors replaced vacuum tubes, permitting greater speed and reliability, and reduction in physical size, cost, power consumption and air-conditioning requirements for the machinery. Memories grew in capacity. Great advances were made in software. Computers became accessible to a much wider variety of users. Well-known examples of second generation computers were the IBM 7090, CDC 6600, and Philco 2000.

Generation 3. Solid state integrated circuits began to replace circuits assembled out of individual electronic components from about 1965. This permitted further significant improvements in performance and further miniaturization. Hardware components were assembled into increasingly complex and sophisticated systems. New types of terminals and other peripheral devices were introduced. Networks of remote terminals, combined with time sharing, began to make computers highly accessible to large numbers of users. Sophisticated new types of software were developed in order to take full advantage of these new hardware capabilities. Examples of third generation computers include the IBM 360 series, the UNIVAC 1108, and the Burroughs 6500.

Generation 4. Among the characteristics of the emerging fourth generation, which can be dated from 1971–72, are the interconnection of numerous computers to form large-scale computer networks, the introduction of very small and cheap minicomputers, and use of micro-programming. An example of a large computer which can be regarded as fourth generation is the University of Illinois' ILLIAC IV, and at the other end of the scale minicomputers like Digital Equipment Corporation's PDP-11, and very cheap systems like the MITS Altair 8800.

It can be seen that the average length of a generation cycle has been about 6 years. The improvement in performance appearing with each successive generation can be approximately summarized as follows (Joseph 1972):

Speed	increase × 10
Memory capacity	increase × 20
Reliability	increase × 10
Component cost	reduce × 10
Total system cost	reduce × 2.5

A typical first generation computer, the IBM 704, could process fewer than 10,000 bits of information per second, whereas the fourth generation ILLIAC IV can process close to 10,000,000. In cost effectiveness terms, a first generation IBM 704 could process about 1 bit/second/dollar, a second generation IBM 7094 about 10 bits/second/dollar, a third generation IBM 360/91 begins to approach 100 bits/second/dollar, and the fourth generation ILLIAC IV achieves nearly 1000 bits/second/dollar (Turn 1974). Sizes of processors were reduced by a factor of about 10 when transistors replaced vacuum tubes, and by another factor of 10 with the introduction of integrated circuits (Perlis 1972). Core memory capacities of early computers were measured in thousands of words, and by the third generation core memories of million-plus word capacity were being constructed. (A word typically stores 32 bits, or 4 characters, of information.) Physical size of core memories has been reduced by a factor of about 10 since their introduction around 1955 (Perlis 1972). Magnetic disk memories manufactured by IBM in 1956 could store approximately 2,000 bits of information in a cubic inch of space, and by 1970 this figure had risen to 800,000 bits/cubic inch (Hoagland 1972).

Minicomputers and microcomputers

Probably the most significant development in computer technology over the last decade has been the emergence of very small, cheap, and powerful minicomputers and microcomputers. The first minicomputers were the PDP-5 and PDP-8, introduced by Digital Equipment Corporation in 1963 and 1965, respectively. The PDP-8 was as powerful as many much larger machines, but was marketed at a fraction of the price. It was about the size of a two-drawer file cabinet. During the 1960's, a very active minicomputer industry developed. With the introduction of successive new models, sizes and costs have continued to decrease.

A major factor in the development of minicomputer technology was the development and continued refinement of techniques for fabricating miniature electronic circuits on small silicon chips. In 1971, the Intel Corporation introduced a single-chip "microprocessor," which was essentially equivalent to the CPU of a larger computer (Vacroux 1975). The entire circuit, containing 2,250 transistors, was fitted onto a single silicon chip measuring .117 by .159 inch. By the mid-1970's, microprocess or technology had developed to the point where tens of thousands of electronic components could be fabricated upon a chip less than a quarter of an inch square, at a cost of a fraction of a cent per component. Today, numerous cheap, compact, and powerful microcomputers are available. Computer hobby stores have appeared in major U.S cities, and enthusiasts are assembling small but useful home computers for little more than the price of a good stereo system. From an architectural viewpoint, a particularly important development has been the introduction in 1975, by Digital Equipment Corporation and Tektronix Corporation, of portable, desk-top computer graphics systems. These systems are powerful enough to perform many computer-aided design tasks but they, in some cases, sell for less than $10,000.

Anticipated future developments

Recent technological forecasts consistently predict that orders-of-magnitude increases in speed, capacity, and reliability, and reductions in size and cost can be expected to continue to emerge until the 1980's (Turn 1974). These continued improvements will result from predictable advances in component technology, particularly in the areas of integrated circuits and new types of memory devices, and from the introduction of new computer architectures.* Longer term (and thus somewhat less reliable) predictions are often quite startling. One recent study (Firschein, *et al* 1973) came to the following conclusions:

> It has been recently indicated by Foster (1972), that before 1980 a general purpose microcomputer complete with central processor and internal working memory (but no peripherals) will be available on a single chip in small quantities for a cost of between $1.00 and $10.00. About this time frame, magnetic bubble technology is expected to bring the cost of memory from the present $0.01 a bit to $0.001 a bit. In a recent article, Broers and Hatzakis (1972) predict 100,000 transistors and similar devices on a silicon chip a few millimeters square. In 25 years, it is predicted that a single-chip computer will be available capable of 20 million instructions a second with 65K (i.e. 65,000 words) of internal memory selling for *about $1.00.* Even if this estimate were off by an order of magnitude, the social significance is enormous.

It is unlikely that the cost of peripheral devices will drop as spectacularly as that of CPU's and memory, but even so, there is no doubt that computers are well on their way to becoming as cheap and ubiquitous as television sets.

The rapid drop in hardware costs is unlikely to be matched by a similar drop in software costs, since a program is hand produced by a skilled professional, and thus reflects the cost of that professional's time. Consequently, the projected future relations between hardware and software costs of computer systems can be shown in *Figure 1.4.*

Impact of technological evolution upon the feasibility of computer-aided architectural design

The impacts of improving performance and decreasing cost of computer systems on the feasibility of computer-aided architectural design are at least threefold. First, each major advance in speed makes possible the practical execution of new types of procedures

* The design of the hardware of a particular computer is referred to as its "architecture." "Computer architecture" is not to be confused with the subject of this book.

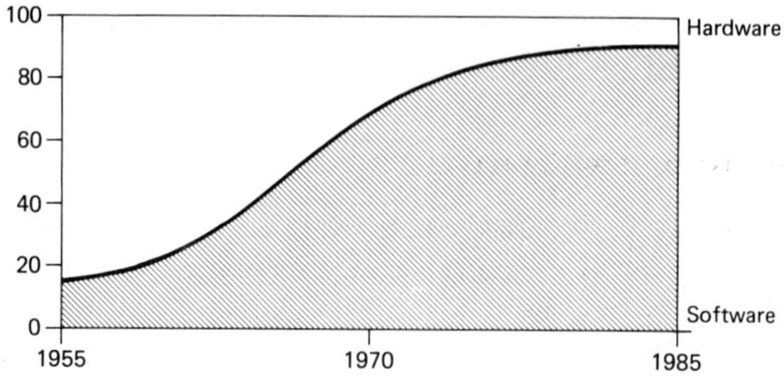

Figure 1.4
Projected relative costs of hardware and software, expressed as percentages of total computer system cost. The figures are from a study by Stanford Research Institute (*Voysey* 1974).

which could never be attempted before. Second, increases in memory capacity make it feasible to store and manipulate larger quantities of data. Both of these considerations are very important, since computer-aided architectural design techniques have, up until recently, consistently strained the limits of available computer technology. Third, the practical economics of implementation change. Computer-aided design, like other types of automation, replaces labor by capital. As it becomes cheaper and more effective, and as the cost of skilled professional labor rises, less capital is able to substitute for more labor.

The equation between capital and labor is not clearly defined, and its balance is constantly shifting. However, it is possible to gain some insight into the magnitudes involved by analyzing a practical case. The first comprehensive, commercially-marketed computer-aided architectural design system to appear in the United States was the ARK 2 system which appeared in the early 1970's. The hardware of ARK 2 consists of a Digital Equipment Corporation PDP 15/20 computer with 16,000 words of core memory, a Computek storage tube graphics terminal, and some other peripheral equipment. In 1974, the hardware was selling for approximately $122,000, and the associated architectural applications software package for about $38,000, making a total of about $160,000 for purchase of the complete system. When amortized over a period of 5 years, system purchase costs come to about $32,000 per year, *i.e.*, roughly the salary for one junior professional staff member plus 100% overhead at 1974 rates. (Of course, there are other costs and effects to consider.) By the end of 1974, several of these systems had been sold to architectural offices in the United States and elsewhere. This pioneering marketing effort indicates that, by the mid-1970's, the economic balance was beginning to tip in favor of the computer. The introduction in 1975 of desk-top computer graphics systems costing less than ten thousand dollars brought computer graphics capability within the range of almost any architectural office. Anticipated further decreases in hardware costs, combined with development of increasingly effective architectural applications software, seem likely to tip the economic balance strongly in the computer's favor by the late 1970's or early 1980's.

ACCESS TO COMPUTER FACILITIES

Over the last two decades it has progressively become easier and cheaper to obtain access to computer facilities; and it seems certain that this trend will continue. The basic alternative ways of obtaining access to computer facilities are:

Go to a computer center and run programs "over the counter";

Employ an in-house remote-access terminal;

Acquire a complete in-house computer system;

Employ a minicomputer system as an intelligent terminal.

Various combinations of these alternatives are also possible. The following paragraphs discuss each of these alternatives.

Use of a computer center

General-purpose computer centers are widely maintained by universities, large research organizations, and commercial computer service bureaus. Various different levels of service are usually available. A user may simply utilize the facilities of the center to run his own programs; he may make use of standard programs and computer processing services available through the center; or he may employ the services of the computer center staff to assist in developing and implementing a new program. Generally, jobs are submitted "over the counter," and are then run in batch mode by computer center technicians. The output is returned. Alternatively, the center may provide the user with access to the computer system via interactive terminals located at the center.

The costs to the user generally consist of charges for computer processing, royalties on any programs used, storage for programs and data, and fees for any staff consulting services.

Use of a computer center is most appropriate when the volume of computer usage in an organization is too low to justify acquisition of in-house facilities, and where the application is a discrete, well-defined task such as production of perspective renderings, or specifications. As the volume of computer usage rises, and as requirements for close integration of automated techniques into the ongoing work of an organization become more crucial, then it becomes reasonable to consider acquisition of in-house facilities.

Time-sharing systems and computer networks

One way to obtain an in-house computer facility at relatively low cost is to lease or buy a remote-access terminal connected to a large central computer, which simultaneously services many users by use of the technique of *time-sharing.* The terminal may be as simple as a Teletype or electric typewriter, or it may be a complex and sophisticated interactive graphics work station. It may be connected to the central time-sharing computer either via the switched telephone network, or via private lines.

There exist a large number of commercial time-sharing services, which enable a user to run his own program through his terminals, or to make use of standard programs maintained by the service. A particularly interesting example of a large time-sharing system serving remote terminals, in this context, is the Cambridge (U.K.) Computer-Aided Design Centre's system, which has been utilized by many of the large British computer-aided architectural design systems.

Early time-sharing systems basically utilized a single large, central computer, and many still do. But it has become increasingly common in recent years to link a number of computers together to form a computer network. Any computer in the network becomes potentially accessible to a user with a terminal connected to one of them. There are a number of advantages to this arrangement: hardware and software resources can be shared; data and programs can be rapidly transferred back and forth between nodes in the network; and the availability of back-up facilities guards against system breakdown are some of them. A survey of computer networks in the United States undertaken by the Mitre Corporation (Peterson and Veit 1971) identified 10 networks developed by that time, and many more have emerged since. Of these, the Advanced Research Project Agency (ARPA) network is the most extensive. The ARPA network links a great many of the large university and other research center computers in the U.S., and now even includes some overseas nodes. A number of large commercial networks are also in operation.

Costs to the user of a remote terminal connected to a time-sharing system generally include purchase or lease of the terminal itself, telephone line charges, storage charges for programs and data, and computer-processing charges, plus any royalties and consulting fees.

In-house systems

Until quite recently, few organizations could afford to consider acquiring in-house computer systems. But the availability of cheap, high performance hardware now makes this an attractive alternative in many cases.

It is usually possible either to lease the necessary equipment or to purchase it outright. Leasing normally tends to be more expensive than outright purchase in the long run, but it has the advantages that it does not require an initial large capital outlay, and does not entail such a firm commitment to particular equipment which may become obsolete. The relative advantages of lease and outright purchase should, in a particular context, be very carefully analyzed before a decision is made.

The balance between lease or purchase costs and the expected intensity of use is the central consideration in assessing the economics of in-house systems. If the system is to be in constant use, then over the long term, acquisition of an in-house system is likely to be a reasonable step. But if the system is to remain idle for a large part of the time, then it is probably more economical to buy computer time from a service bureau as required.

Intelligent terminals

Analysis of the computing needs of an organization often reveals that most, but not all, of these needs can be satisfied by a low cost minicomputer system such as a desk-top graphics system. In this case, it may be appropriate to employ the minicomputer system both as a stand-alone device and, when required, as an *intelligent terminal* connected to a time-sharing service. When it is necessary to perform a computation that is beyond the capabilities of the in-house machine, data is readied by the in-house machine and transmitted to the time-sharing machine for processing.

The future

In the past, computer facilities have been accessible only at high cost and at centralized locations. But the trend of development is very clearly in the direction of low cost and highly decentralized availability. The rapid development of microprocessor technology suggests that small, inexpensive, portable computers will soon become commonplace. The parallel development of large computer networks implies the possibility of plugging into a sophisticated nation-wide, or even world-wide, information utility at any telephone. This trend towards decentralized, low cost availability of computing capability and information has important implications for the feasibility of computer-aided architectural design, since architectural work is traditionally carried out by large numbers of relatively small offices rather than by a few giant organizations (as, for example, in the automobile industry).

SUGGESTED READINGS

Eames, C. *A Computer Perspective.* Cambridge, Mass.: Harvard University Press, 1973.

Goldstine, H. H. *The Computer from Pascal to von Neumann.* Princeton, New Jersey: Princeton University Press, 1972.

Milne, M. A. "Pencil Points to Computer Graphics." *Progressive Architecture,* June 1970, pp. 168–170.

Negroponte, N., ed. *Computer Aids to Design and Architecture.* New York: Petrocelli/Charter, 1976.

Nelson, T. H. *Computer Lib.* Chicago, Illinois: Hugo's Book Service, 1974.

Ralston, A., and Meek, C., eds. *Encyclopedia of Computer Science.* New York: Petrocelli/Charter, 1976.

Raphael, B. *The Thinking Computer.* San Francisco, California: W. H. Freeman and Company, 1976.

Sharpe, W. F. *The Economics of Computers.* New York: Columbia University Press, 1969.

Turn, R. *Computers in the 1980's.* New York: Columbia University Press, 1974.

von Neumann, J. *The Computer and the Brain.* New Haven, Connecticut: Yale University Press, 1958.

2
The Computer's Role in Design

In the previous chapter, the computer was characterized as a general-purpose machine, which could be programmed to play a wide variety of different roles. In this chapter, we consider in detail how a computer may be programmed to play a useful role in design.

For our purposes here, it is useful to regard architectural design as a special kind of problem-solving process, and to discuss design within the framework of a general theory of problem-solving. The view of problem-solving that will be introduced is one which has gained wide currency in recent years. It assumes that we can construct some kind of a *representation* of the system that interests us, and that problem-solving can be characterized as a process of *searching* through alternative *states* of the representation in order to discover a state that meets certain specified *criteria.* This view is not without its limitations, but it provides an appropriate starting point for discussion.

PROBLEMS

The existence of problems

To begin a discussion of problem-solving processes, we must define what we mean by a "problem." It is apparent, firstly, that problems begin with the existence of goals, and that problem-solving in general is purposeful behavior directed at the attainment of such goals as obtaining food, shelter, gratification, etc.

But not all goal-directed behavior involves problem-solving. If the action necessary to attain the goal is immediately obvious, then there is no problem. Typical examples of goal-directed behavior that we would not regard as problem-solving are a person picking up a pencil from the table to write, a frog striking at a fly, and a thermostat adjusting the temperature in a room. In other words, we usually say that a problem exists if something is desired but the actions necessary to obtain it are not immediately obvious.

This simple definition of a "problem" was utilized in Edward Lee Thorndike's pioneering experimental studies of animal and human problem-solving (Thorndike 1931), and continues to consistently reappear in the more recent literature on the subject. Karl Duncker's classic monograph "On Problem-Solving" (1945), for example, begins:

> A problem arises when a living creature has a goal but does not know how this goal is to be reached. Whenever one cannot go from the given situation to the desired situation simply by action, then there must be recourse to thinking. (By action we here understand the performance of obvious operations.) Such thinking has the task of devising some action which may mediate between the existing, and the desired situations. Thus the "solution" of a practical problem must fulfill two demands: in the first place, its realization must bring about the goal situation, and in the second place one must be able to arrive at it from the given situation simply through action.

The goal sought by a problem-solver is often some real or abstract *object,* for example, "a pen to write with," "the square root of 38," "an honest man," or "a better mousetrap." Alternatively, the goal might be a *state of the world,* for example, "an ambient temperature of 70°," "universal peace and love," or "no double-digit inflation." In some circumstances, rather than seeking an object or state, a problem-solver may want to find *path,* or *sequence of operations* that leads to some specified point such as the center of a maze, or a checkmate in chess.

Problem statements

To state a problem, then, we must provide some kind of a *description* of the object, state, path, or sequence of operations that is sought. Modern definitions of a "problem" usually incorporate the concept of the existence of some kind of goal description. For example, Reitman (1965) writes:

> In a sentence, we say a system has a problem when it has or has been given a description of something but does not yet have anything that satisfies the description.

In addition to a goal description, a problem statement usually includes further information such as a description of various *conditions* that must be met, the *tools* and *operations* that are available for use in attempting to find a solution, and limits on *resources* which may be utilized (Newell and Simon 1972).

The information which comprises a problem statement may be in verbal, graphic, or numerical form. It may include loose descriptions, examples, and analogies, or precise and rigorous specifications. It might be written on paper, or stored in the memory of the problem-solver (whether a living organism or a computer).

GENERATIVE SYSTEMS

Aristotle's concept of a generative system

If the goal of a problem-solver is to obtain some existing tangible object such as a pen, then problem-solving involves first obtaining an appropriate candidate object, and secondly verifying that it matches the given goal description. But if the goal is to obtain something that is as yet non-existent, such as the proof of a theorem, or the design for a building, then the question of how potential solutions may be produced for consideration arises.

An elegant answer, which can be traced back to Aristotle, is that we can construct a *generative system* which can then be operated to produce a variety of potential solutions. In his well-known discussions of the design of the constitution for a city (Politics, section 1290) Aristotle introduced the following biological analogy:

> If we were going to speak of the different species of animals, we should first of all determine the organs that are indispensable to every animal, as, for example, some organs of sense and instruments of receiving and digesting food, such as the mouth and stomach, besides organs of locomotion. Assuming now that there are only so many kinds of organs, but that there may be differences in them—I mean different kinds of mouths, and stomachs, and perceptive and locomotive organs—the possible combinations of these differences will necessarily furnish many varieties of animals. (For animals cannot be the same which have different kinds of mouths or ears.) And when all the combinations are exhausted there will be as many sorts of animals as there are combinations of the necessary organs.

In other words, he described a generative system for potential animals. He then continued on to argue that, in a similar way, designs for potential cities could be generated by analyzing cities into their essential constituent parts, listing the alternatives for each part, then taking various different combinations of alternatives.

Generative systems have had, since Aristotle, a long and varied history. They have played important roles in philosophy, in the evolution of literary and musical theory, and in the development of engineering and architectural design methodology. In the following paragraphs, some of the more interesting and important generative systems that have been developed are discussed.

Generative systems in philosophy

The 13th century Spanish scholar Ramon Lull developed generative systems consisting of concentric wheels inscribed with words and symbols (*Figure 2.1*). Spinning the wheels generated different combinations of symbols, and by means of this "combinatorial art" Lull apparently hoped to generate all possible knowledge (Yates 1954, Gardner 1958). Lull's concepts and methods had a major influence upon the medieval alchemists, who sought to synthesize desired materials by finding appropriate combinations of the elements. Renaissance philosophers such as Bruno were also influenced by Lull. Even as late as the 17th century, Lullian ideas exerted an important formative influence upon the philosophy of Leibniz. Although Lull is almost forgotten today, many scholars contend that the Lullian art can properly be regarded as the forerunner of modern symbolic logic.

Generative systems in literary composition

The Lullian art was savagely lampooned in Swift's *Gulliver's Travels*. When he visited the Academy of Lagado, Gulliver found, among other follies, a professor engaged in producing works of litera-

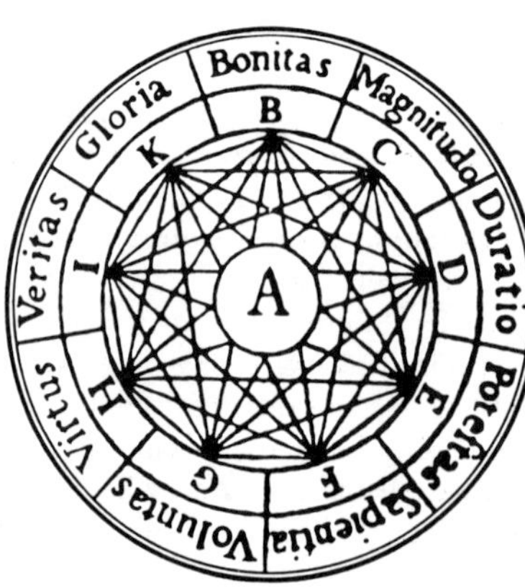

Figure 2.1
A Lullian wheel.

ture and science by randomly spinning wheels inscribed with words of the language and arranged within a frame (*Figure 2.2*). The scholar carefully explained that, "Everyone knew how laborious the usual method is of attaining to arts and sciences; whereas by his contrivance, the most ignorant person at a reasonable charge, and with a little bodily labor, may write books in philosophy, poetry, politics, law, mathematics, and theology, without the least assistance from genius or study."

The idea of a vast library, generated by exhaustive enumeration of combinations of letters and containing all possible books, has grasped the imagination of numerous authors. The German writer Kurd Lasswitz published a famous short story entitled, *The Universal Library,* which explored the dimensions of that library, and concluded by observing that the story itself could be regarded as "an excerpt from one of the superfluous volumes of the Universal Library." George Gamow's, *One, Two, Three . . . Infinity* also provided an estimate of the size of the library, and described the construction of a printing press to produce the volumes. In one of Jorge Luis Borges' arcane and subtle fables, *The Library of Babel,* the absolutely exhaustive character of the library was evoked with nightmarish vividness:

> Everything: the minutely detailed history of the future, the archangels' autobiographies, the faithful catalogue of the Library, thousands and thousands of false catalogues, the demonstration of the fallacy of those catalogues, the demonstration of the fallacy of the true catalogue, the Gnostic gospel of Basilides, the commentary on that gospel, the true story of your death, the translation of every book in all languages, the interpolations of every book in all books.

In addition to speculations about The Universal Library, there have been a number of serious attempts at poetic composition by means of generative systems. One of the earliest was described in a pamphlet by John Peters entitled, *Artificial Versifying: A New Way to Make Latin Verses* (1678). This incurred the critical scorn of Richard Steele, who wrote in *The Spectator* (no. 220):

> This virtuoso, being a mathematician, has, according to his taste, thrown the art of poetry into a short problem, and contrived tables by which anyone without knowing a word of grammar or sense may, to his great comfort, be able to compose, or rather to erect, Latin verses.

A haiku-generating system was exhibited at the Cybernetic Serendipity exhibition in London in 1968 (Masterman 1971). This system utilized a haiku "frame" as follows:

> I . . . the . . . in the . . .
> All . . . in the . . .
> Bang the . . . has . . .

In addition, there was a thesaurus of five short lists of words to be substituted into the seven blanks. For example, the list of choices for

Figure 2.2
The book-writing machine seen by Gulliver at the Academy of Lagado.

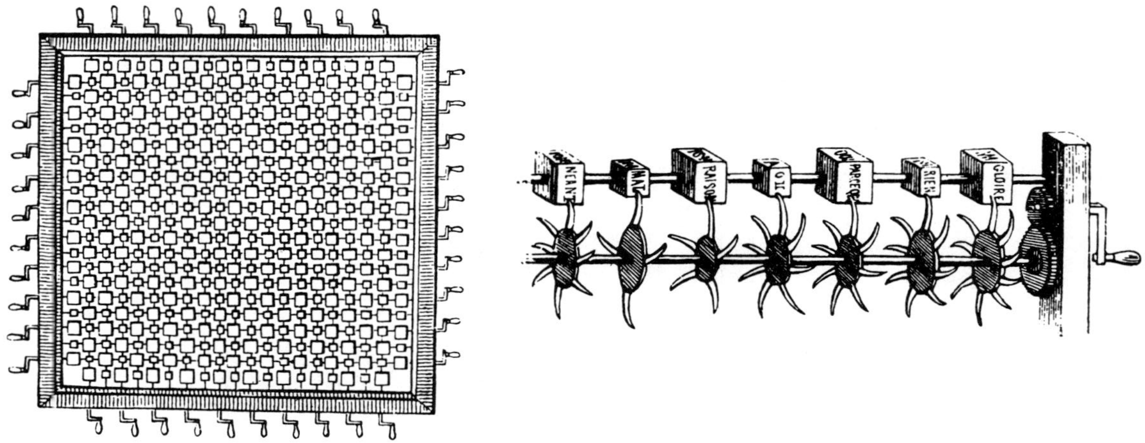

the first blank was "sense, paint, saw, heard, touched." The numbers of possible choices for each substitution were:

Blank	*Number of choices*
1	5
2	7
3	8
4	6
5	8
6	7
7	13

Therefore the number of different compositions which could be generated by the system was $(5 \times 7 \times 8 \times 6 \times 8 \times 7 \times 13) = 1,223,040$. The idea of a "frame" into which words are randomly inserted by computer has also been employed by Marie Boroff at Yale University in an investigation of poetic imagery and metaphor (Boroff 1971). In this case the vocabularies for substitution in each blank consisted of 50 words fitting appropriate grammatical, and in some cases semantic, specifications.

Generative systems in musical composition

The combinatorial aspect of musical composition has long been recognized. If a simple melody is to be made up from the 8 notes in a single octave, for example, it is clear that the number of different melodies of n successive notes must be 8^n (excluding the effect of varying rhythms). This number grows very rapidly, of course, with increasing values of n:

n	8^n
1	8
2	64
3	512
4	4,096
5	32,768
6	262,144
7	2,097,152
8	16,777,216

The 17th century Jesuit scholar Athanasius Kirchner, a follower of Ramon Lull, published a book on music which discussed composition as a combinatorial problem, and described a Lullian technique for generating combinations by sliding columns of symbols alongside each other. A Kirchner composition machine was actually built for Samuel Pepys around 1670. During the 18th and 19th centuries, numerous "mechanical composition" systems using tables, dice and mechanical contrivances to generate combinations were produced. The most famous was described in a pamphlet entitled *Musikalisches Wurfelspiel,* originally published in 1792, and attributed, probably

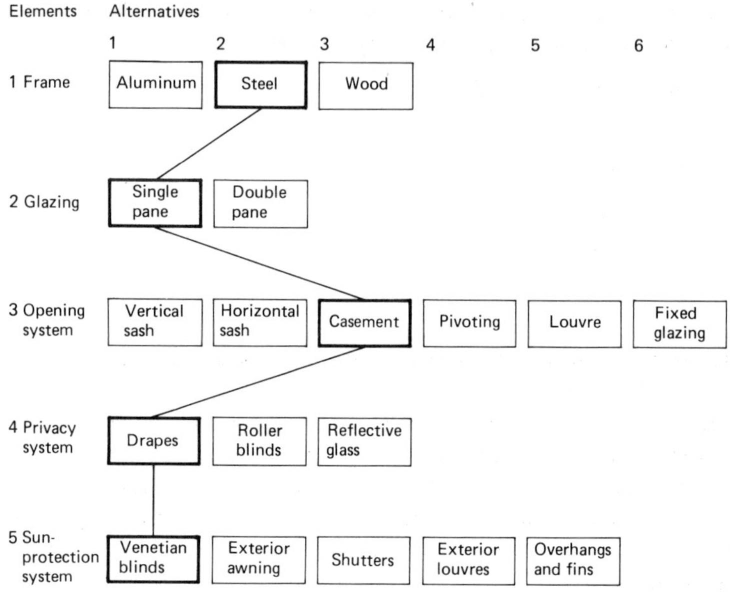

Figure 2.3
Example of a morphological chart (for design of a domestic window). A total of 540 different designs can be generated by connecting rows in different ways.

spuriously, to Mozart. This system employs charts and dice, and is capable of generating 11^{14} different waltzes. The extensive and curious history of mechanical composition techniques has been summarized in an article by Percy A. Scholes in *The Oxford Companion to Music* (1938) and in one of Martin Gardner's inimitable *Scientific American* columns (1974).

Generative systems in engineering design

The Lullian art was treated with considerable practical seriousness by the 17th century philosopher Leibniz, who wrote extensively on methods of invention and design by systematic generation of combinations. In a letter to the Duke Johann Friedrich, dated 1671, he claimed to have applied such methods successfully in the design of a wide variety of machines: an adding machine and a ready-reckoner, telescopes and microscopes, pumps, ships, and submarines. Leibniz grasped the essential point that exhaustive generation of possibilities can be practical and useful if the ranges of alternatives are carefully limited and well defined. This opened the way to widespread applications in engineering design.

In the 19th century, the mathematician Charles Babbage developed a notation system for description of the components of machinery. Influenced by Babbage's work, the engineer Franz Reuleaux (1876) wrote a very successful textbook in which the design of mechanical devices was systematically described as a process of generating combinations of fundamental "kinematic elements."

Much more recently, the astrophysicist Fritz Zwicky (1967) has popularized a similar exhaustive combinatorial approach to engineering design under the name of the "morphological" method. An example of use of the morphological method is illustrated in *Figure 2.3*. Alternatives for each essential element of the design are arranged in parallel rows, as shown. A potential design can then be generated by drawing a line connecting one alternative in each row.

Generative systems in architectural design

Systematic use of generative systems in architectural design can be traced back at least as far as Leonardo da Vinci. The historian Paul Frankl (1968) has described Leonardo's method as follows:

> Leonardo wanted to know in a general way what forms he could give to the central-plan church, and set out systematically to find the answer. He realized that if he began with the simplest spatial forms (square, octagon, circle, or dodecagon), he would arrive at every conceivable central-plan church, without taxing his imagination, by the mechanical addition of circular, semi-circular, or octagonal ancillary spaces to the principal and cross axes of his basic figures. A complete series of related central-plan churches could be developed from a basic schema. For example, he could begin with a Greek cross (four square arms added to the sides of a central square), and then either replace the square space by an octagon, a circle, or a dodecagon, or replace the square arms with rectangles, octagons, circles, semi-circles or dodecagons.

The 24 plans generated by this system are illustrated in *Figure 2.4*.

The classical approach to architectural design, as it was formalized in the textbooks of the Ecole Polytechnique and the Ecole des Beaux-Arts during the 19th century, was also based upon systematic exploration of alternative ways in which various elements from a fixed vocabulary could be assembled in different combinations to generate architectural forms (Banham 1960, Summerson 1963, Hernandez 1969). J. N. L. Durand's *Précis des Leçons d'Architecture* (1803) began with a profusely illustrated discussion of different ways in which building elements (columns, walls, etc.) could be assembled to generate sets of potential "combinaisons horisontales" (plans) and "combinaisons verticales" (elevations), then continued on to discuss urban design in analogous terms. ("De même que les murs, les colonnes, etc., sont les éléments dont se composent les édifices, de même les édifices sont les éléments dont se composent les villes." *) A typical plate from Durand's *Précis* is shown in *Figure 2.5*. Julien Guadet's later encyclopaedic compendium of Beaux-Arts design principles *Élé-*

* Just as walls, columns, etc., are the elements from which buildings are composed, so buildings are the elements from which towns are composed.

Figure 2.4
Leonardo's scheme for generation of central-plan churches, as described by Frankl (1968).

ments et Théorie de l'Architecture (1894), followed a similar scheme. As Reyner Banham (1960) has described it:

> The approach is particulate; small structural and functional members (elements of architecture) are assembled to make functional volumes, and these (elements of composition) are assembled to make whole buildings. To do this is to compose in the literal and derivational sense of the word, to put together.

Figure 2.5
An illustration from J. N. L. Durand's *Précis des Leçons d'Architecture* (1803) illustrating systematic combination of simple geometric elements to generate plan *partis*.

Although the ideology and specific formal devices of Beaux-Arts design have long since been rejected by architects, the concept of a *building system,* within which designs are generated by forming combinations of standard components, is still very widely utilized.

METHODS OF REPRESENTATION OF POTENTIAL SOLUTIONS BY GENERATIVE SYSTEMS

Representation and reality

Typically, a generative system does not directly produce the actual object which is sought. Instead, it produces some kind of *representation, model,* or *design* for the object, which can then be translated into reality. For example, a Kirchner musical composition machine produces a string of symbols describing a melody; Aristotle's system for enumerating varieties of animals produces verbal descriptions, not a zoo; and Durand's *Précis* consists of drawings, not actual buildings. There are exceptions, of course: when a potter works at the wheel, for instance, the processes of design and physical creation of an object are often combined.

Under most circumstances, the necessity of dealing with a representation, rather than directly with the real world, is obvious. A representation can be much quicker, easier, and cheaper to manipulate than the real object. Less obviously, representation in a particular way can give the designer special insights into a problem, and significantly aid the process of solution generation. For example, representation in terms of some particular mathematical formalism allows known theorems associated with that formalism to be exploited in the design process, while representation by means of orthographic projections facilitates understanding spatial relations.

When we say that a generative system "represents" potential solutions to a design problem, we mean that each particular potential *state* of the system corresponds in some definable and logically consistent sense to a particular potential solution. In other words, each specific state of the system *explicitly* represents one specific potential solution. Since the system can exist in many different states, we can also say that construction of the system *implicitly* establishes a set of potential solutions for exploration.

The concept of representation of a potential design solution by a state of a generative system will become clear as we examine some examples. Generative systems may be grouped into three broad categories, according to the ways in which they represent potential design solutions, as follows:

Analogue generative systems

Iconic generative systems

Symbolic generative systems

Analogue representation

Analogue generative systems often represent potential designs by settings of wheels, dials, sliding columns, etc. The operations per-

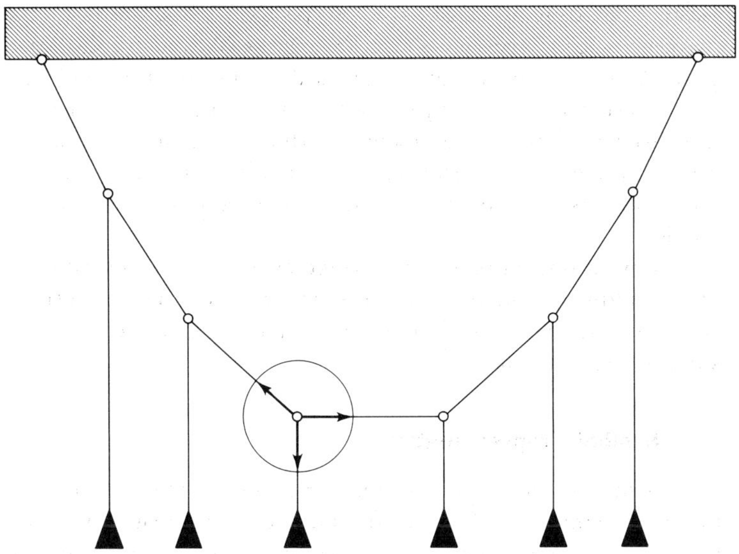

Figure 2.6
Analogue modeling technique employed by Antoni Gaudi for design of vaulting. Form taken by wire-frame suspension structure is inverted to give vault form.

formed to change the state of the system (*i.e.*, to describe a new potential design) are thus mechanical, *e.g.*, spinning wheels, setting dials, sliding columns alongside each other. Examples of analogue generative systems include the Lullian wheels and the Kirchner musical composition machine. These are, of course, of more historical than practical interest. A famous example of practical use of an analogue generative system in architectural design occurred in the work of the Catalan architect Antoni Gaudi (Sweeney and Sert 1960). In design of the church of the Sagrada Familia and the Guell Chapel in Barcelona, Gaudi employed a flexible, suspended wire frame covered in cloth and hung with weights (*Figure 2.6*). As the wires and weights were manipulated, the wire frame took up different forms, determined by the laws of statics governing suspension structures. The tension wires in the suspended frame were taken to represent the compression members in a vaulting system so that, if inverted, the form of the frame would represent an appropriate form for the vaulting.

In general, one set of properties in an analogue system is used to represent another, analogous set of properties of the item being designed. The analogue system may be a mechanical system, an electrical system, or any other type of system that proves convenient and appropriate.

Iconic representation

Iconic generative systems represent designs in a very literal way. A particular state of the system actually "looks like" the potential solution which it represents. For example, an interior designer might represent different furniture arrangements by arranging appropriately shaped cardboard cutouts on a plan drawing, an architect might represent a building by means of a perspective sketch, and a mechanical engineer might represent a part by means of orthographic views. In general, iconic representations are scale transformation (enlargements or reductions) of the objects which they describe. Where a two-dimensional drawing represents a three-dimensional object, some kind of projection transformation is involved. Occasionally, a transformation also occurs in the time dimension, as in a slow-motion movie.

Operations employed to change an iconic representation consist of the addition and deletion of elements, and the geometric operations of translation, scaling, rotation, and reflection of points, lines, surfaces, and volumes.

Symbolic representation

Symbolic generative systems represent potential solutions by means of symbols such as words, numbers, and mathematical operators. Mostly, linear formations of symbols such as lists, sentences or mathematical formulae are employed. However, tables, arrays, and other different types of formations may also be utilized. A typical example of a symbolic generative system was Aristotle's combinatorial scheme for generating descriptions of potential animals, where each different animal was represented by a different list of words or phrases describing its "essential organs." The operations performed to change a symbolic representation are arithmetic and logical, *e.g.*, addition, subtraction, multiplication, division, assignment, concatenation, substitution, etc. Thus the description of an animal, in Aristotle's system, is altered by substituting one word or phrase for another in the list.

The concepts of a *design variable,* and of the association of the design variables into *data structures,* are central to an understanding of the process of design by use of symbolic generative systems. A design variable may be thought of as a conceptual "mail box," possessing a name, to which different values may be assigned. We can symbolically model a system which is of interest to us by letting specific design variables represent specific properties of the system. For example, we might model a rectangular room by letting a variable named d_1 represent the length, d_2 the width, and d_3 the height (*Figure 2.7(a)*). A particular design proposal can then be represented by assigning numerical values to elements of the vector $D = [d_1, d_2, d_3]$, as shown in *Figure 2.7(b)*. The representation can be altered by performing various algebraic operations as illustrated in *Figure 2.7(c)*.

A structure is a relationship between the individual elements of a set, so such a collection of variables, associated in some specific way, may be referred to as a data structure. It is possible for a data structure to be very simple, as in the example above, or exceedingly large and complex. Data structures describing a practical building design

$D = [d_1, d_2, d_3]$

(a) Modeling the room by a vector.

$D = [12, 8, 8]$

(b) Assigning numerical values to represent one particular design.

$D = [12, 8, (8–4)]$

$D = 2.D$

(c) Performing algebraic operations to alter the design.

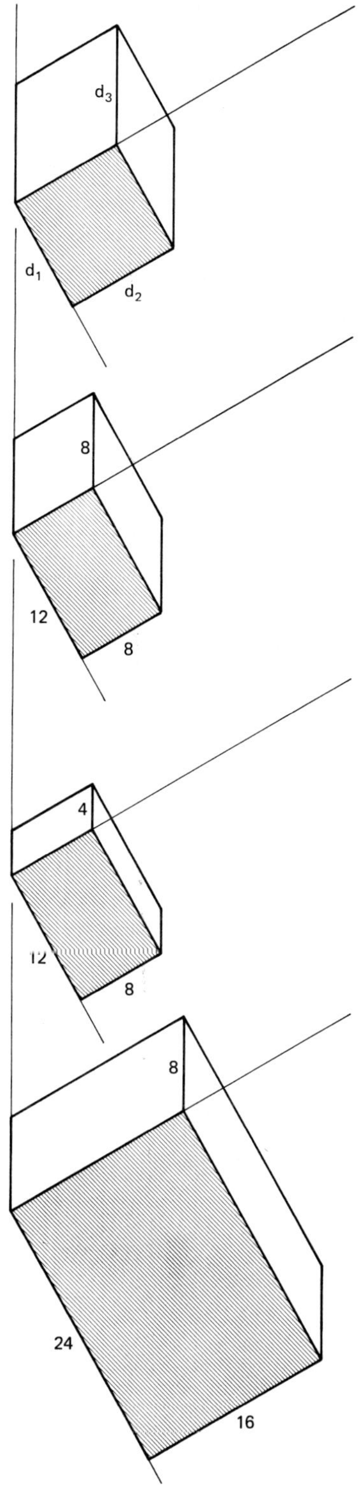

Figure 2.7
Representation of a rectangular room by a data structure.

might easily consist of many hundreds of thousands, or even millions of variables. Data structures can be stored in computer memory, and the arithmetic and logical operations necessary to change the states of data structures can be performed with great rapidity by the CPU. Thus a computer program operating upon a data structure which models a design can constitute a generative system. For example, the following simple FORTRAN program (flow diagrammed in *Figure 2.8*) embodies a generative system which produces potential solutions to the room dimensioning problem illustrated in *Figure 2.7.* For purposes of the example, it is assumed that d_1 has allowable values of 4, 8 and 12 ft., d_2 of 8, 9 and 10 ft., and d_3 of 8 and 9 ft.

```
      INTEGER D1, D2, D3
      DO 1 D1=4, 12, 4
      DO 1 D2=8, 10
      DO 1 D3=8, 9
      WRITE (6, 2) D1, D2, D3
    2 FORMAT (1X, 3I3)
    1 CONTINUE
      STOP
      END
```

The result produced by execution of this program is the following list of potential combinations of values for the design variables:

Figure 2.8
Flow diagram of a program which enumerates designs for a rectangular room.

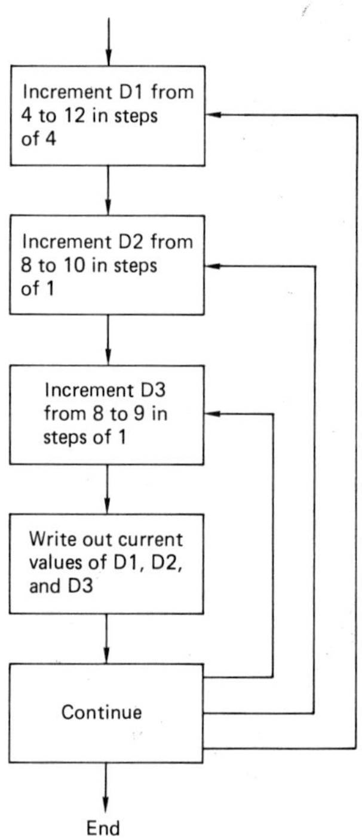

d_1	d_2	d_3
4	8	8
4	9	9
4	10	8
4	8	9
4	9	8
4	10	9
8	8	8
8	9	9
8	10	8
8	8	9
8	9	8
8	10	9
12	8	8
12	9	9
12	10	8
12	8	9
12	9	8
12	10	9

It seems likely that design which takes place "in the head" also utilizes a symbolic generative system, with the brain performing analogous functions to the memory and CPU of a computer (Craik 1943, von Neumann 1958, Newell and Simon 1972).

STATE-ACTION GRAPHS

The logic of fixed alternatives

The process of production of potential solutions using generative systems can be described by means of a diagram known as a *state-action graph.* The concept of a state-action graph is perhaps most easily understood by means of an analogy with exploration of a maze. *Figure 2.9(a)* illustrates the well-known Hampton Court maze. At each intersection, the explorer of the maze can take several alternative *actions, i.e.,* he can take several alternative paths. Execution of each action results in achievement of a new state, *i.e.,* a new location in the maze. The relations between states and actions may be described by means of a *state-action graph* as shown in *Figure 2.9(b)*. Each vertex * in this graph represents a potential state, and each edge a potential action. The entrance to the maze constitutes the *start-vertex,* and the center of the maze constitutes the *goal-vertex.* Viewed in this way, the problem-solver's task is to construct an appropriate chain of actions leading, like the thread trailed by Theseus in the Cretan labyrinth,

* The small circles in the graph are referred to as "vertices," and the lines connecting them as "edges."

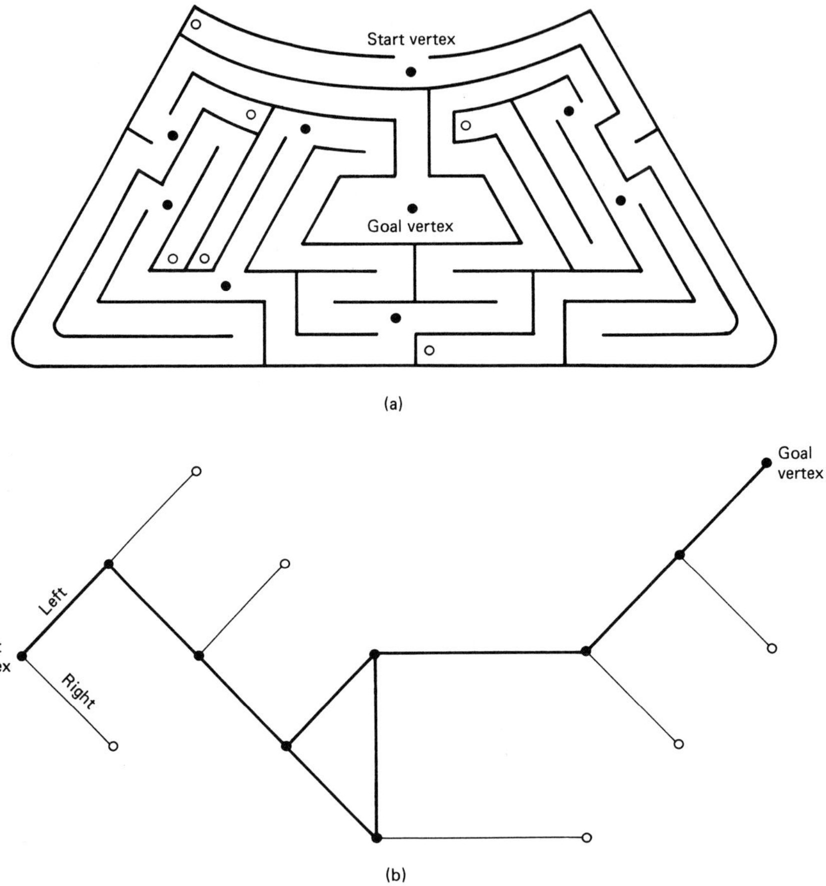

Figure 2.9
The state-action graph of a maze. (a) Hampton Court Maze. (b) Corresponding state-action graph.

from the start-vertex, through a sequence of intermediate vertices, to the goal-vertex.

Description of generative systems by state-action graphs

In a generative system, operations are performed one at a time, just as branches are chosen one at a time in the exploration of a maze.* At each step, a choice must be made between alternative allowable operations. Just as a maze may be described by means of a state-action graph, so a generative system may be described by a state-action graph in which each vertex represents a potential state of the system, and each edge an allowable operation which changes the state of the system. *Figure 2.10,* for example, illustrates the state-action graph for design of the rectangular room represented by the vec-

* Strictly speaking, *parallel* generative systems in which numerous operations are performed simultaneously are also possible. But we will not be concerned with parallel systems here.

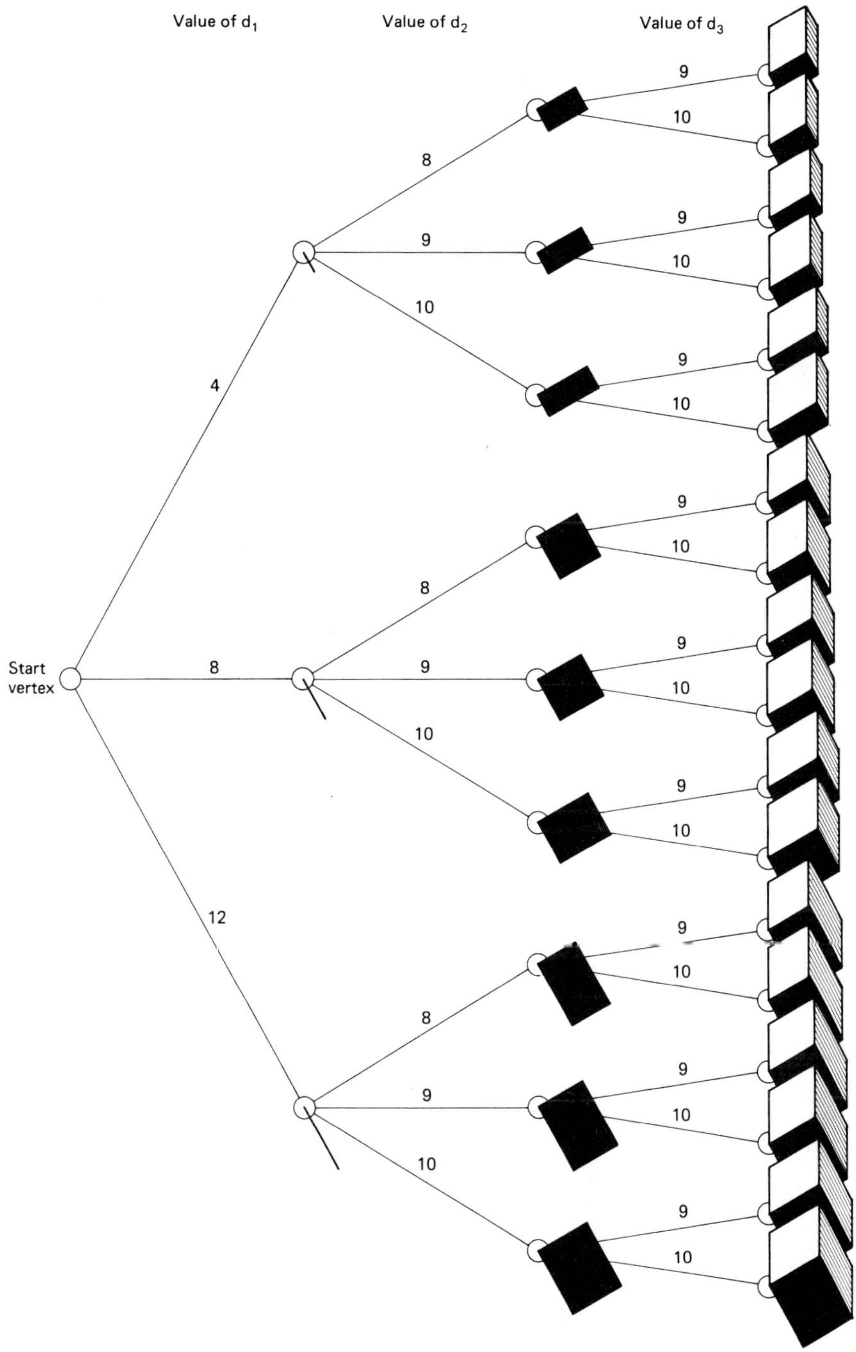

tor $D = [d_1, d_2, d_3]$ (see *Figure 2.7*). The FORTRAN program which enumerates the potential solutions actually performs an exhaustive search of this graph.

We can now more abstractly and formally describe a generative

Figure 2.10
State-action graph for design of a rectangular room.

system as consisting of a scheme for *representation* of potential solutions, together with a set of *operators* which enable us to *map* from one *state* of the system to another, and a set of *rules* concerning the selection and application of operators. In solving a problem we begin at an *initial state* of the system (*i.e.*, a start vertex of the state-action graph) and apply operators in order to move to a *goal state* (*i.e.*, a goal vertex in the state-action graph). In our room dimensioning example, the scheme for representation of potential solutions is the vector $D = \lfloor d_1, d_2, d_3 \rfloor$. The values of d_1, d_2, and d_3 are initially undefined. To map from one state of D to another we can apply the operator "assign a positive integer to any d." The relevant rules are: "d_1 takes value 4, 8 or 12," "d_2 takes value 8, 9, or 10" and "d_3 takes value 8 or 9." (Other types of operators, *e.g.*, "multiply any d by a constant" could in principle be included, but we have simply chosen not to do so.)

IDENTIFICATION OF ACCEPTABLE SOLUTIONS

The Meno paradox

The state-action graph representation of generative systems makes it clear that solving intellectual problems such as design problems can, quite literally, be regarded as a process of exploring a maze of alternative possibilities. The question of how to *recognize* an acceptable solution, once it has been found, now arises. The issue has been stated most dramatically in Plato's *Meno,* where the question is posed for Socrates:

> And how will you inquire, Socrates, into that which you do not know? What will you put forth as the subject of inquiry? And if you find what you want, how will you ever know that this is what you did not know?

Plato gave an ingenious, if somewhat unconvincing, answer, making reference to the previous existence of the soul. Finding an appropriate resolution of the so-called "*Meno* paradox" has occupied numerous philosophers since.

Tests for solutions

For our purposes here, we will make use of a resolution which has proven particularly important in the development of modern theories of problem-solving. It appears to have first been clearly proposed in a 1956 discussion of problem-solving machines by the computer scientist John McCarthy (McCarthy 1956, Minsky 1961, Simon 1967). McCarthy's resolution applies to a class of problems referred to as *well-defined* or *well-structured* problems. Drawing a clear distinction between proposed solutions which were not true solutions, and proposed solutions which were, McCarthy suggested that we can call a problem well-defined if there is a *test* which can identify a solution. "In case the proposed solution is a solution," McCarthy wrote, "the test must confirm this in a finite number of steps. If the proposed solution is not correct, we may either require that the test indicate this in a finite number of steps or else go on indefinitely."

A concrete example will make this clear. Consider the state-action graph illustrated in *Figure 2.10.* From examination of the terminal vertices, we can see that there are 18 potential solutions. Let us now impose the requirement that the total volume of the room should not be greater than 750 cubic feet. This requirement can be stated as a test for a solution as follows:

$v = d_1 \times d_2 \times d_3$
if $v \leqq 750$ then this potential solution is a solution

It could also be introduced into our FORTRAN program for generating solutions:

```
      INTEGER D1, D2, D3, VOLUME
      DO 1 D1=4, 12, 4
      DO 1 D2=8, 10
      DO 1 D3=8, 9
      VOLUME=D1*D2*D3
      IF (VOLUME.GT.750) GO TO 1
      WRITE (6, 2) D1, D2, D3, VOLUME
    2 FORMAT (1X, 3I3, I5)
    1 CONTINUE
      STOP
      END
```

(The flow diagram for this revised program is shown in *Figure 2.11.*) The program now produces the 12 of the 18 potential solutions that pass the test:

d_1	d_2	d_3	*Volume*
4	8	8	256
4	9	9	288
4	10	8	288
4	8	9	324
4	9	8	320
4	10	9	260
8	8	8	512
8	9	9	576
8	10	8	576
8	8	9	648
8	9	8	640
8	10	9	720

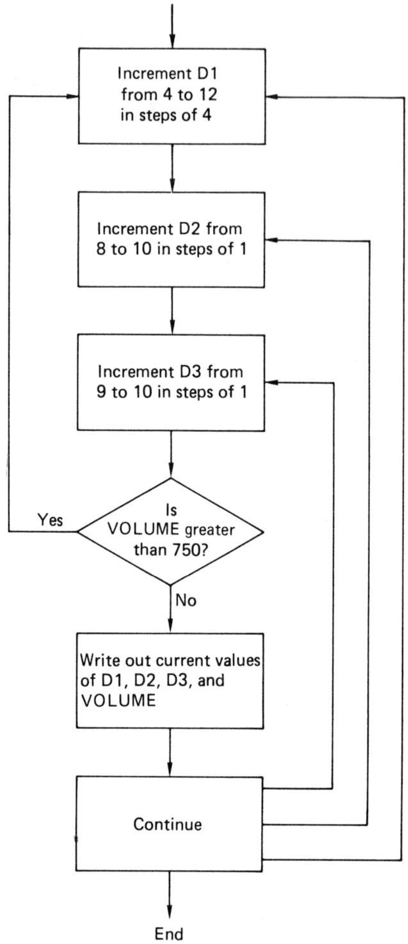

Figure 2.11
Flow diagram for revised room design program incorporating a test for satisfactory solutions.

Set-predicate description of design problems

We now have a way to describe design problems precisely and unambiguously, using a little elementary set theory. Let us call the set of potential solutions U. In the example shown in *Figure 2.12*, U has 18 members. The subset of U, which consists of potential solutions which pass the test, we will call the *goal set* G. In our example, G has 12 members. The designer's task is to search the state-action graph, producing members of U for consideration in order to find one that is a member of the goal set G. The subset of members of U actually produced for consideration in a design process will be called S. In our FORTRAN program example, $S \equiv U$, but this is not necessarily the case in general. The relations between U, G and S may be illustrated by a Venn diagram, for example, as shown in *Figure 2.12*.

The goal set G may be either large or small in relation to the set U of potential solutions. Several conceivable situations are shown in

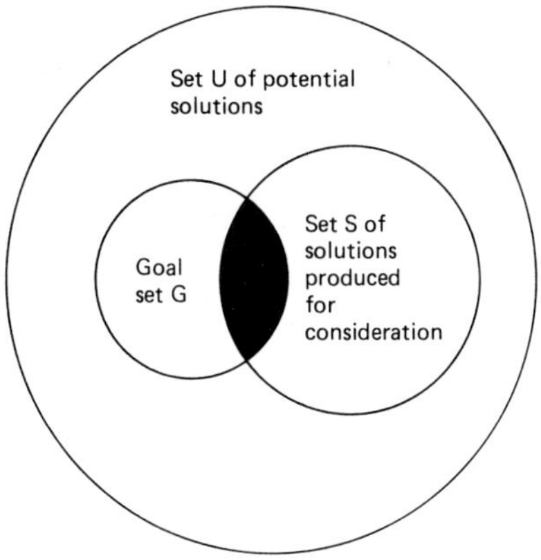

Figure 2.12
Venn diagram showing the relations between sets U, G and S.

Figure 2.13. If the solution criteria are very loose, then the goal set G may be identical with the set U of potential solutions (*Figure 2.13(a)*), *i.e.*, any potential solution is satisfactory. If the goal set is large in relation to the set of potential solutions, *i.e.*, there are many satisfactory solutions, then we say that the problem is *under-specified* (*Figure 2.13(b)*). In under-specified problems, the task may either be to find *one* satisfactory solution or to enumerate *all* satisfactory solutions. Sometimes the goal set has only one member; in this case we say that the problem is *uniquely-specified* (*Figure 2.13(c)*). Some examples of uniquely-specified problems are jigsaw puzzles, murder mysteries, and finding the owner of Cinderella's slipper. In some situations the solution criteria may define mutually exclusive conditions such that the goal set G contains no members at all, *i.e.*, the problem is *over-specified* (*Figure 2.13(d)*). It is often not obvious whether or not a

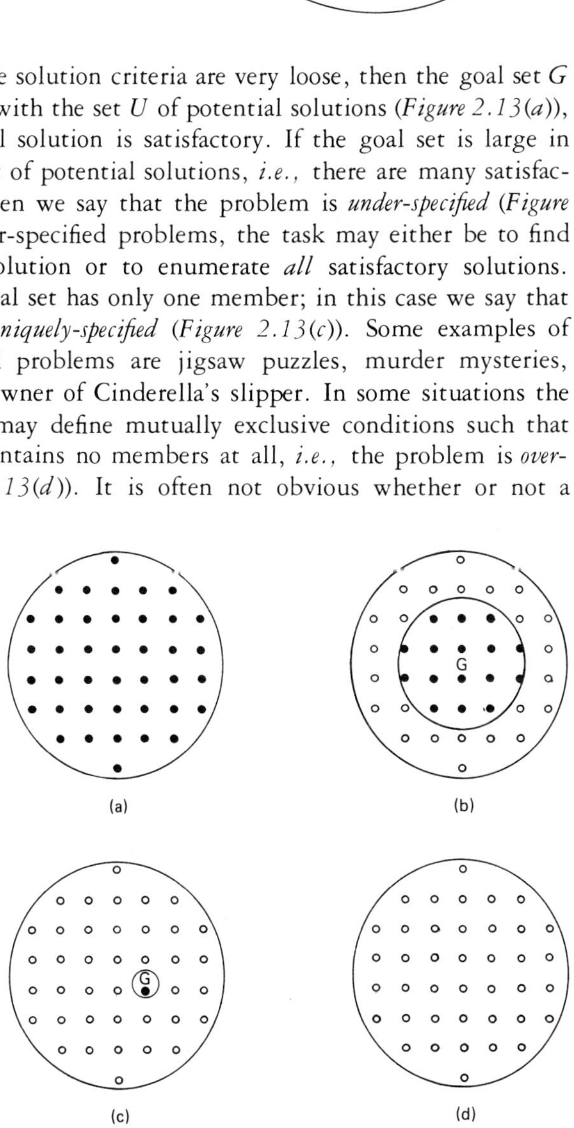

Figure 2.13
Possible relations between the set U of potential solutions and the goal set G. (a) $G \equiv U$. (b) Under-specified problem. (c) Uniquely-specified problem. (d) Over-specified problem.

problem is over-specified, and a designer may sometimes be required *either* to find a member of the goal set G *or* to demonstrate that the problem is in fact over-specified.

Constraints and objectives

Tests by means of which members of the goal set G are identified are most commonly defined by means of *constraints*. The following are typical examples of architectural design constraints:

Floor area must be greater than 80 sq. ft.

Floor area must be less than 120 sq. ft.

Cost must not exceed $100,000

Deflection must not exceed 1/180 of the span

Temperature must be held above 68°

Constraints may be thought of as defining the boundaries of the goal set G. This is shown graphically, for a very simple problem, in *Figure 2.14*. The problem is to dimension a rectangular room. A two-foot plan module is employed, so a set U of potential solutions can be generated by enumerating possible combinations of length and width as illustrated in *Figure 2.14(a)*. There are constraints on allowable room length (*2.14(b)*), width (*2.14(c)*), area (*2.14(d)*), and perimeter (*2.14(e)*). The combined effect of the constraints is shown in *Figure 2.14(f)*. If the dimensions of the room are allowed to vary continuously, rather than on a module, then both U and G become infinite (*Figure 2.14(g)*).

In addition to stating constraints, a second common method for specifying the design criteria which identify the goal set G is to state *objectives* to be minimized or maximized, for example:

Maximize usable floor area!
Minimize cost!

Objectives to be minimized or maximized are usually stated in conjunction with a set of constraints which must also be complied with. Considering our room dimensioning problem, for example, we might identify the goal set G by the statement:

Maximize the floor area *subject to* satisfying the length, width and proportion constraints (see *Figure 2.14(h)*).

The distinction between goal sets which are identified solely by means of constraints, and those whose specifications involve objectives to be minimized or maximized, is of considerable theoretical and practical importance. Sometimes it is possible to prove that a given potential solution under consideration represents the required minimum or maximum. For example, we might know that the optimum occurred where the first derivative of the objective function was zero. Where such a proof is not available, however, the requirement to

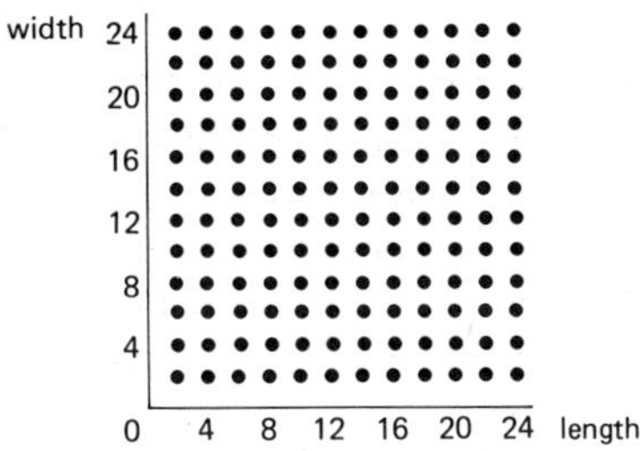

(a) Set U of potential combinations of length and width

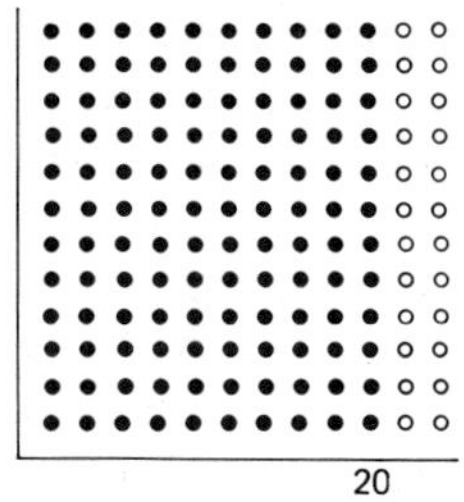

(b) Subset G_l of combinations meeting the constraint length $\leqslant$ 20

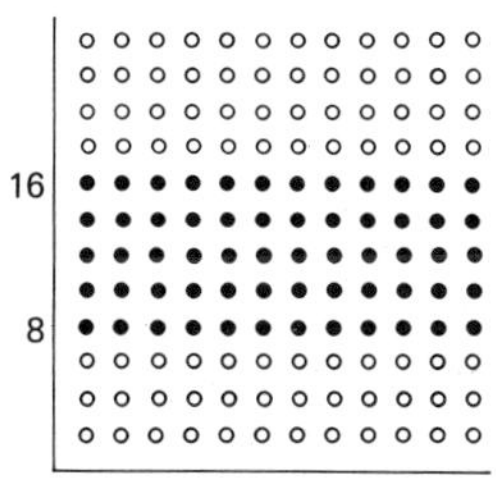

(c) Subset G_w of combinations meeting the constraints 8 $\leqslant$ width $\leqslant$ 16

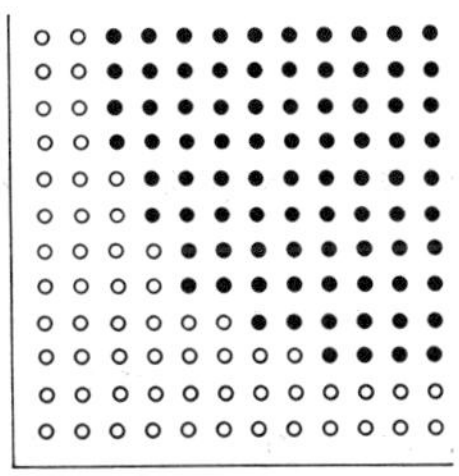

(d) Subset G_a of combinations meeting the constraint area $\geqslant$ 100

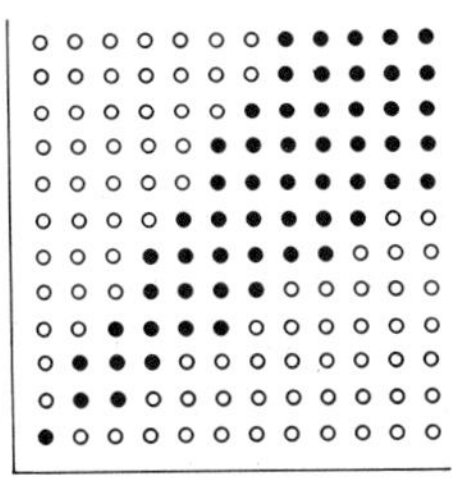

(e) Subset G_p of combinations meeting the constraint longest side $\leqslant$ 1.5 × shortest side

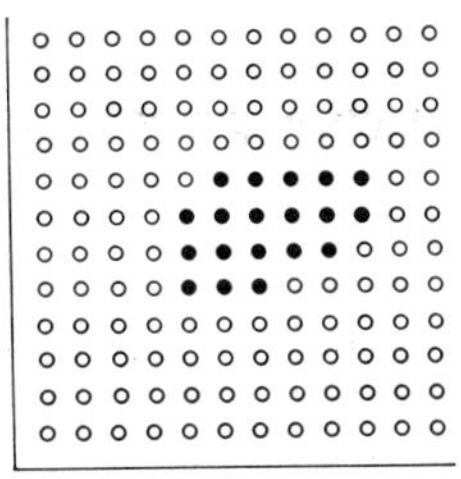

(f) Goal set $G \equiv G_l \cap G_w \cap G_a \cap G_p$ of combinations meeting all constraints

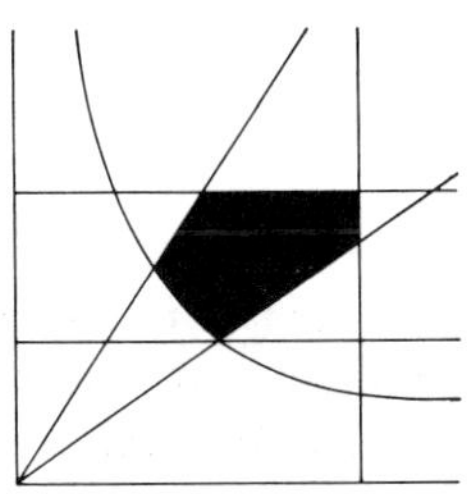

(g) Goal set G which results if length and width are allowed to vary continuously

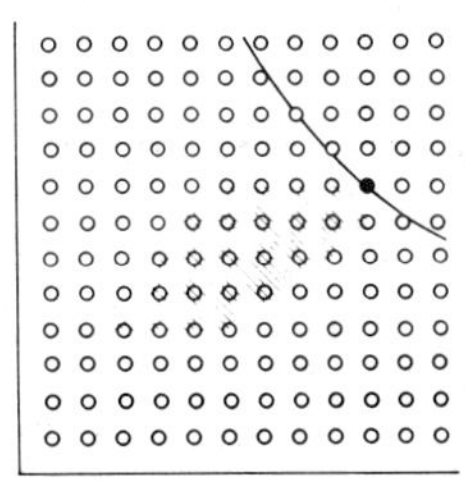

(h) Reformulation as an optimization problem: maximize area, subject to constraints length $\leqslant$ 20, 8 $\leqslant$ width $\leqslant$ 16, longest side $\leqslant$ 1.5 × shortest side

Figure 2.14 Constraints and objectives for a simple plan-dimensioning problem.

produce an optimum solution may introduce substantial difficulties. Consider for a moment an illustrative example given by Simon (1975). The task is to obtain a sewing needle. The set *U* of potential solutions consists of a set of needles located in some unknown pattern of distribution within a haystack. If the solution is identified by the constraint "Sharp enough to sew with," then the amount of searching required to find a solution is independent of the size of the haystack. It depends on the starting point of the search and the pattern of distribution of sharp needles within the haystack. If the solution is identified by the objective "The sharpest needle in the haystack," then it is necessary to search through the entire haystack before it can be shown that the solution has been found. The amount of searching involved then depends directly on the size of the haystack, and is independent of the starting position or the pattern of distribution of needles.

SOLUTION GENERATION PROCEDURES

A solution generation procedure may be thought of as a strategy for choosing particular paths through the state-action graph of a problem in search of members of the goal set G. In some cases, it is possible to specify procedures which can be shown to generate only members of the goal set G. In other cases it may be necessary to employ procedures which generate both members and non-members of G.

Analytical procedures

Certain fairly simple types of design problems can be solved by means of *analytical* procedures, *i.e.*, an acceptable solution can be deduced directly, without any trial-and-error exploration. The methods of elementary algebra and calculus, such as standard procedures for solving systems of simultaneous equations, optimization by setting first derivatives of functions to zero, and so on, are typical examples of analytical procedures. Few architectural design problems have analytical solutions.

Search procedures

A second major category of design procedures consists of those which require some kind of *search* of alternative paths through the state-action graph. A certain amount of trial-and-error is involved, and both satisfactory and unsatisfactory solutions may be produced for consideration. The simplest kinds of search procedures are exhaustive enumeration of alternatives (as for example in our FORTRAN program example) or random selection of alternatives. More sophisticated search procedures make use of some kind of information about the particular problem at hand to guide the search for a solution. The better the guiding information, the more efficient the search procedure is likely to be. Typical sources of guiding information are theoretical knowledge of the structure of the problem, previous experience with similar problems, and information gathered during the course of exploration of the state-action graph. Since computers operate at extremely high speed, they make practical the execution of very extensive searches. Many architectural design problems are amenable to solution by search procedures.

Usefulness of solution generation procedures

In order to have some ways of comparing the usefulness of the various different types of solution generation procedures, it is appropriate at this point to introduce the concepts of *algorithmic properties, heuristic power,* and *generality*.

If a procedure leads with complete certainty to a good solution (*i.e.*, a member of the goal set G) or else demonstrates that G is empty, then we refer to it as a algorithm. Examples of design algorithms include analytical solution generation procedures, exhaustive search of the state-action graph, and random search (if allowed to go on long enough). Not all useful design procedures are complete algorithms, however. In many practical situations we must be content with procedures which we believe are reasonably likely to produce a good solution, but which cannot be shown to be guaranteed to do so. The closer such a procedure approximates the certainty of a true algorithm, the better we say its algorithmic properties are.

We are not only interested in the certainty or otherwise that a procedure will produce a good solution, but also in the time and cost involved in generating a solution. It is well known, for example, that there is a straightforward algorithm for playing winning chess: simply consider all possible continuation sequences from the current board position, discover those that result in a win, and then work backwards from there to determine the next move. Due to the enormous size of the look-ahead tree that would be generated, this algorithm is completely impractical even if executed by the largest and fastest of computers. Failure to draw a clear distinction between the logical certainty that a procedure must eventually generate a good solution and the practical efficiency of the procedure leads to such apparent paradoxes as the spinning wheels at the Academy of Lagado producing works of scholarship, or the proverbial monkeys randomly pounding typewriters and eventually generating the works of Shakespeare. In these situations, generation of a solution by means of such a procedure is certain in principle but impossible in practice.

We say that a procedure which generates a good solution more quickly or cheaply than another has greater heuristic power. Analytical procedures and mathematical programming techniques are practically effective not only because they are algorithms, but also because they are heuristically powerful. Conversely, exhaustive search is generally ineffective in practice because it is heuristically very weak. Frequently (though not always) in practical problem-solving the utilization of powerful heuristics to guide the search for a solution means that algorithmic properties must be sacrificed. Many practical procedures can be characterized by saying that they are reasonably likely to produce a reasonably acceptable solution with reasonable expenditure of resources.

The practicality of a given solution-generation procedure in a given situation is determined not only by the inherent efficiency of the procedures, but also by the available resources for solving the problem. Where computers are employed, the development of increasingly powerful machines makes the practical execution of increasingly lengthy procedures possible. However there exist both practical and theoretical upper bounds to attainable computational capabilities. It has been estimated that advances in integrated circuit technology might increase the rate at which instructions can be processed by a factor of about one thousand (Jackson 1974). Use of coherent optical system technology might increase the rate beyond this by another factor of one thousand (Culver and Mehran 1971). From quantum theoretical considerations Bledsoe (1961) has suggested that an increase in processing rate of about 10^{15} over current computers is a theoretical limit for serial computers. Going a step further, Bremermann (1967) carried out some calculations which suggest that the maximum rate at which information can be processed in parallel in the universe is 7×10^{103} bits/year, representing a theoretical maximum attainable improvement in processing rate, over current computers, of 10^{91}. While these numbers are immense, it is not at all difficult to think of practical problems for which, if solution by exhaustive enumeration were attempted, even the bounds set by Bremermann's limit would be approached or exceeded.

In general, it appears that there is an inverse relation between the power of a solution generation procedure as measured by its capability to reliably and efficiently produce members of the goal set G and the generality of its applicability to different types of problems (Newell 1973). Procedures tend to be either general but weak, like exhaustive search which can be employed to solve any well-defined problem, or extremely powerful but very narrowly restricted in application, like specific analytical methods. This is not surprising when it is realized that powerful procedures gain much of their power by exploiting very specific knowledge about a particular problem domain.

It is worth reflecting that if powerful, general design algorithms existed, there would be little need for architects or engineers. We could simply mechanically apply the available algorithms to any design problems.

SOLUTION EVALUATION TECHNIQUES

Unless a solution generation procedure can be proved only to produce members of the goal set G, it is necessary to employ some kind of test procedure to determine whether in fact a proposed solution that has been generated is a member of the goal set G.

Tests for compliance with constraints, or for optimality of a proposed solution, may utilize either experimental, graphical, or mathematical techniques.

Experimental testing

The most straightforward approach to experimental evaluation is to actually build a prototype and test it under the appropriate conditions. Thus the structural adequacy of a building design might be tested by subjecting a prototype to appropriate loadings, the thermal performance by taking temperature readings, and so on. However, except in special circumstances, prototype testing is too lengthy and expensive a process to be practical in architectural design.

A more common approach is to perform laboratory experiments on some appropriate physical model. For example, the structural frame of a proposed building might be represented by a Plexiglas® scale model, to which appropriately scaled loads are applied, and readings taken from strain gauges. Techniques of architectural modeling for purposes of structural, thermal, acoustic, lighting, and visual evaluations of building designs are highly developed and widely applied (see Cowan *et al,* 1968 for a summary).

Graphical evaluation

In its simplest form, graphical evaluation merely involves inspection of, and perhaps taking a few measurements from, a drawing of the proposal. This is an extremely common procedure in architectural design. It is very effective for identifying spatial conflicts and inconsistencies. Less straightforward graphical evaluation techniques involve use of special graphs, nomograms, protractors, etc.

Mathematical modeling

The mathematical approach requires that constraints and objectives be expressed as functions of the design variables. The forms of these functions depend upon the laws which govern the behavior of the system under consideration. Thus models concerned with spatial properties reflect geometric theorems; models concerned with structural behavior incorporate functions reflecting the laws of statics and strength of materials; models concerned with acoustic behavior reflect the laws governing sound propagation; and so on. Where the relevant laws are not sufficiently well understood the mathematical modeling approach is not practical. If a mathematical model can be formulated, a computer can be employed to evaluate constraints and objectives.

Mathematical models are often categorized as either *static* or *dy-*

namic, and either *deterministic* or *stochastic.* A static model is either not concerned with the passage of time, or is concerned with the properties of the system at one moment of time; whereas a dynamic model is concerned with the behavior of the system over a period of time. Models of structural behavior under averaged load conditions are examples of static models; while thermal behavior models which take into account cycles of variation in external temperature are dynamic. In deterministic models all variables bear fixed mathematical or logical relationships to each other, while stochastic models incorporate an element of randomness. It is usually possible to determine likely system behavior from a stochastic model, but not to predict behavior with complete certainty. Most models for evaluating the spatial, structural, thermal, acoustic, and lighting performance of proposed building designs are deterministic. Models describing such properties as patterns of pedestrian circulation, elevator waiting times, etc., are invariably stochastic.

A further categorization distinguishes *analytical* and *simulation* models. In analytical models, values of relevant functions can be determined directly by performing algebraic operations. For example, the volume of a rectangular room can be found by multiplying its length, width, and height (as in our FORTRAN program example). With simulation models, values of functions are not so readily determinable; they can only be discovered by simulating and observing the behavior of the system in some appropriate way. Dynamic, stochastic models describing such properties as elevator waiting times, or dynamic thermal behavior typically are of this character.

Extensive comparative discussions of different types of mathematical models that might be employed in evaluation of architectural design proposals have been published by Echenique (1972) and March (1972).

Division of discriminatory power

Although it has been convenient, for purposes of exposition, to draw a clear distinction between solution generation and solution evaluation procedures, in practice the two are often very closely interrelated. The execution of a solution generation procedure results in production of a subset (S) of the set U of potential solutions. S may conceivably relate to U and to the goal set G in the following ways (*Figure 2.15*):

> S is identical with U, *i.e.,* the procedure is one of exhaustive enumeration. In this case we must rely entirely on the evaluation procedures to discriminate members of G from other members of U.
>
> G is a subset of S, *i.e.,* the generation procedure implicitly eliminates some unsatisfactory potential solutions from consideration by not producing them.

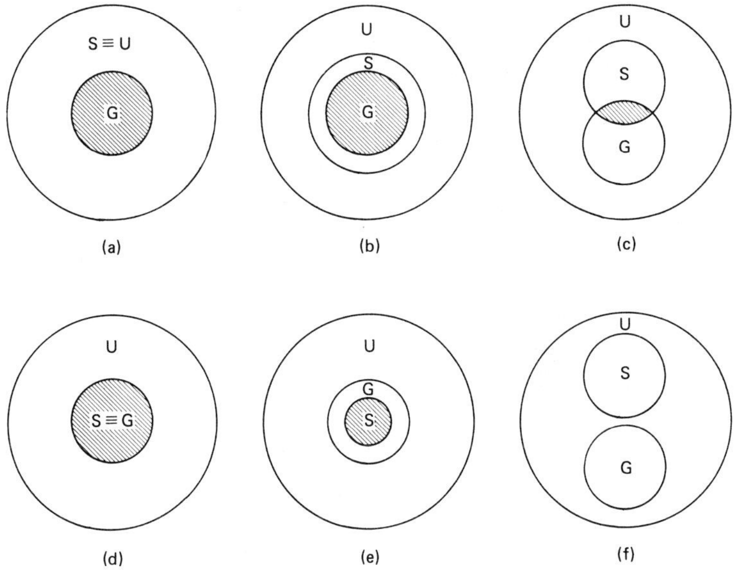

Figure 2.15
Possible divisions of discriminatory power between solution generation and solution evaluation procedures. Shaded areas indicate the satisfactory solutions that are actually produced.

S and *G* intersect, i.e., the generation procedure produces some, but not all good solutions, together with some unsatisfactory solutions.

S is identical with *G*, *i.e.*, the generation procedure exhaustively enumerates good solutions without producing any unsatisfactory solutions. If we know this to be the case, then separate evaluation procedures are not necessary. An important special case of this situation occurs in uniquely specified problems.

S is a subset of *G*, *i.e.*, the generation procedure produces only some of the satisfactory solutions, but no unsatisfactory solutions.

S and *G* are disjoint, *i.e.*, the generation procedure fails.

Thus we see that power to discriminate between potential solutions to a design problem can be divided between evaluation and generation procedures in different ways.

In general, the more discriminatory power a generation procedure has, the more expensive it tends to be to execute. Hence there are two contrasting types of design processes, both of which may prove effective in appropriate situations: either a large number of potential solutions are rapidly and cheaply generated for consideration by a relatively indiscriminate procedure, or a much smaller number of potential solutions are relatively slowly and carefully produced. Random generation of alternatives with selective retention is a characteristic example of the first approach, while analytical and mathematical programming methods are typical of the second.

PARADIGM FOR COMPUTER-AIDED ARCHITECTURAL DESIGN

The paradigm

We have seen that a design problem can be characterized in terms of:

A *data structure,* which consists of variables describing the relevant properties of potential solutions.

A set of *operators* which may be applied to variables to change the state of the data structure. These operators, together with the rules of their application, define a state-action graph, and implicitly establish a set U of potential solutions.

A set of *constraints* and/or *objectives* which define a *goal set* G of acceptable solutions.

A *solution generation procedure* which produces a set S of potential solutions for consideration. S may or may not intersect G.

This characterization indicates that a computer may be employed in design for any one, or a combination, of the following purposes:

Simply to *store and retrieve* data describing a design. In this case, the computer is used as a data processing machine. Its power is employed to retrieve required information efficiently, to sort data according to specified ordering schemes, and to generate alphanumeric or graphic displays. Thus it replaces or augments drawings, specifications, schedules, clerical, and drafting staff.

To *automatically generate solutions to well-defined problems* by executing a program which operates upon the data structure to compute and assign particular values to variables. In other words, the program traverses part of the state-action graph of the problem in order to produce a solution. In this case, the computer is used as an automated design synthesis machine, and replaces or augments some of the traditional functions of the design architect.

To *test potential solutions for membership of the goal set* G by executing a program which operates upon a mathematical model of a proposed design solution in order to compute value for constraints and objectives. In this role, the computer performs evaluative tasks traditionally undertaken by the architect or by specialist consultants.

A comprehensive computer-aided architectural design system performs all of these functions.

This is the paradigm which forms the foundation for the techniques described in the remainder of this book. It is a fruitful paradigm, which has led to a great deal of innovative work. But like any paradigm it has its limitations. Before going on it is worth taking note of these.

Lady Lovelace's objection

It has often been suggested that although it is clearly demonstrated that computers can solve well-defined problems in the ways that we have described, they cannot display anything corresponding to the original creative thought which we take to be characteristic of a good designer. One of the earliest and most famous statements of this position was made by Lady Lovelace, Lord Byron's only daughter. In describing Charles Babbage's Analytical Engine, a direct ancestor of the modern electronic computer, she remarked, "The Analytical Engine has no pretentions to originate anything. It can do whatever we know how to order it to perform." (Turing 1950.) More picturesquely, she also compared it to the Jacquard loom, an early 19th century invention that used sequences of punched cards describing woven designs to automatically control weaving processes: "We may say most aptly that the Analytical Engine weaves algebraical patterns just as the Jacquard loom weaves flowers and leaves." (Morrison and Morrison 1961.)

As Turing (1950) has pointed out, Lady Lovelace's argument appears to be based on the fallacious assumption that "as soon as a fact is presented to a mind all consequences of that fact spring into the mind simultaneously with it." Knowledge of a generative system defining a set of potential design solutions, solution criteria to be applied, and an automatically-executable procedure for generating potential solutions for consideration does not guarantee that the result produced by execution of that procedure will not appear original and surprising. The larger the set of potential solutions, the more complex the solution criteria, the more intricate and sophisticated the solution generation procedure, the more likely it is that we will ask in surprise of a computer system, "How did it 'think' of that?"

The question of stylistic variation

A creative designer will not only produce an "original" solution to a design problem, it is also likely that the solution will display certain recognizable stylistic properties. The idea of a solution possessing stylistic properties is meaningless if a problem is well-defined and there is one solution; there are no "stylistic differences" in solutions to a jigsaw puzzle, for example. But where the goal set G contains numerous acceptable solutions there is room for variation, and different solution generation procedures may tend to generate characteristically different subsets of G.* This holds whether the problem solver

* See the programs discussed in Chapter 13 for some examples.

is a human or a machine. So in principle we may expect that an automated design system might display not only originality, but a characteristic style as well. Simon (1975) has explored this concept of stylistic variation in design in some detail.

Ill-defined problems

In many practical problems, the condition of well-definedness which has been specified may not be met. The boundaries of the set of potential solutions may appear vague and fluid, and the solution criteria fuzzy, ambiguous, and largely implicit rather than explicit. It is often difficult to articulate exactly what the problem is, and it may be difficult to determine whether or not a design proposal is really a "solution" to a problem. Problems of this type have been widely discussed in the recent literature of problem-solving and design. They are often identified as "ill-defined" or "ill-structured" problems, as opposed to well-defined problems (Reitman 1965, Newell 1969, Eastman 1969, Uhr 1973). Some authors argue that all real design problems have this character, and that well-defined design problems should be referred to as "puzzles" (Van der Ryn 1966) or "exercises" (Mitroff and Featherinham 1974). Rittel and Webber (1973) draw a contrast between "tame" or "benign" problems which are amenable to solution by relatively straightforward systematic procedures, and more difficult "wicked" problems which must be dealt with in planning and design.

Although the concept of an ill-defined design problem is not itself very well-defined, it is possible to identify some typical characteristics, for example:

No complete and definitive formulation is "given" at the outset. An appropriate formulation must be abstracted out from a tangled, messy, and information-rich context. Many conditions and criteria may be assumed rather than explicitly stated.

No applicable model is provided. The problem solver must define variables and operations which establish an appropriate set U of potential solutions to be searched. There may be no way of guaranteeing that the set U which is defined is in fact "appropriate", i.e., that the problem solver is attempting to solve the "right" problem.

The formulation which is achieved is not rigorous. The set U of potential solutions to be explored and the solution criteria may be informally characterized rather than clearly and completely specified.

The formulation does not remain stable. Conditions and criteria may alter as the design process progresses, perhaps as a direct result of insights and knowledge gained by engaging in that process.

The formulation may embody conflicts and inconsistencies which must be resolved during the course of the design process. Furthermore, such conflicts and inconsistencies may only be brought to light by engaging in the process.

The problem-solver does not have all pertinent information available for consideration at any one time. Potential solutions may be overlooked or forgotten, and different subsets of potential solutions and criteria may be discovered or retrieved from memory at different stages in the design process.

Various normative and descriptive theories of problem-solving in ill-defined contexts have been developed. Each of these theories is concerned with different aspects of ill-definedness, and thus responds in a somewhat different way.

Perhaps the most common approach to dealing with ill-definedness is to formulate problems in probabilistic terms, and to make use of the concepts and techniques of *statistical decision theory* (see Raiffa 1968). This approach is useful where the consequences of decisions, constraints, and objectives cannot be described with certainty. Starr (1963) and Tribus (1969) and March (1976) have extensively discussed the utilization of statistical decision theory in the formulation and solution of engineering design problems.

An alternative approach is to employ the *theory of fuzzy sets, i.e.,* sets in which there may be grades of intermediate membership between full membership and non-membership (Zadeh 1965, Bellman and Zadeh 1970). Examples of fuzzy sets are the class of rooms of approximately 100 sq. ft., the class of well-designed buildings, or the class of small houses. Fuzzy sets of potential solutions, and fuzzy objectives and constraints may be employed in the formulation and solution of certain types of ill-defined design problems. Hormann (1972), for example, has described a computer-aided design system based upon the concept of formulation of problems in terms of fuzzy sets.

Where ill-definedness arises out of multi-person involvement in the problem-solving process, conflict of objectives between participants, processes of bargaining, coalition formation, etc., the very extensive literature of game theory provides some useful insights (see Luce and Raiffa 1957, Shubik 1964, Rapoport 1966, 1970). In particular, it clarifies the relationships between the different types of solutions which may be sought in such situations, *e.g.,* optimum solutions from the viewpoints of individual participants, and various types of cooperative solutions which are in some sense optimum from a group viewpoint, or from the viewpoint of some coalition of group members.

Ill-definedness arising out of modification of solution criteria during the process of problem-solving has been discussed in detail by Simon (1957). He argues that many real-world problem-solving processes are better described in terms of satisficing * behavior rather

* This new term was introduced by Simon.

than optimizing behavior, *i.e.,* in terms of seeking solutions which are merely "good enough" rather than "best." The level at which solutions are accepted as "good enough" may alter as the process of search for a solution progresses. For example, the "level of aspiration" may be lowered after an extensive and unsuccessful search.

Another way of looking at problem-solving processes in which criteria are modified by the problem solver, suggested by Reitman (1965), is to say that many of the solution-criteria are left "open" in the initial problem statement, and must be "closed" by the problem solver. To perform this "closing" of criteria, the problem solver must make use of general contextual knowledge. Architectural design problems, at least in their initial statement, typically contain a great many such open constraints.

The closing of constraints can take place prior to embarking on the search for a solution, or it can take place during the search. At the beginning of a design project, considerable time will typically be devoted to explicitly closing as many constraints as possible by conducting client interviews and questionnaire studies, use of criteria checklists, literature searches, and even by explicitly stating some arbitrary assumptions. But not all constraints can be closed in this way. Very often the only way to close some constraints is to actually engage in the process of design on the basis of incomplete criteria, to subject the resultant proposals to critical analysis, then to use the resulting clarified and more complete criteria as the basis for another design cycle. Criteria and solutions emerge concurrently, and the problem only begins to seem well-defined as the final solution is approached. Eastman (1970) has published a study of architecture students' approaches to a bathroom layout problem which clearly illustrates this type of process.

The existence of open constraints indicates the use of highly interactive computer-aided design systems, and of systems which are capable of automatically filling in "missing" information by asking appropriate questions of the user or by drawing upon an internal data base of architectural knowledge.

With a few notable exceptions, current computer-aided architectural design techniques are oriented towards the well-defined, rather than the ill-defined, aspects of design. It seems likely, however, that advances in artificial intelligence research over the next few years will result in implementation of systems capable of responding effectively to increasingly ill-defined problem situations. These developments should have important implications for automated architectural design.

SUGGESTED READINGS

Broadbent, G. H. *Design in Architecture.* New York: Wiley, 1973.

Eastman, C. M. "On the Analysis of Intuitive Design Processes," in *Emerg-*

ing Methods in Environmental Design and Planning, edited by G. T. Moore. Cambridge, Mass.: MIT Press, 1970.

Jones, J. C. *Design Methods.* London: Wiley, 1970.

Newell, A., and Simon, H. A. *Human Problem Solving.* Englewood Cliffs, New Jersey: Prentice-Hall, 1972.

Rittel, H. W., and Webber, M. M. "Dilemmas in a General Theory of Planning." *Policy Sciences,* vol. 4 (1973) pp. 155–169.

Rubinstein, M. F. *Patterns of Problem Solving.* Englewood Cliffs, New Jersey: Prentice-Hall, 1975.

Simon, H. A. *The Sciences of the Artificial.* Cambridge, Mass.: MIT Press, 1969.

Wickelgren, W. A. *How to Solve Problems.* San Francisco, California: W. H. Freeman and Co., 1974.

3 Practical Application of Computer-Aided Architectural Design Techniques

To discover the ways in which computer-aided design techniques can effectively be introduced into architectural practice, it is useful to examine the design and construction process from a special and rather unfamiliar viewpoint. In this chapter, we view design as an *information processing* task, and architectural design organizations as information processing systems. We are concerned for the moment with the mechanics of architecture, not with its soul: with "building as frozen data" rather than "architecture as frozen music."

As a first step in this analysis, the structure of the building team, and the roles of the various members, are examined. Next, the phases and tasks of a typical architectural project are described. It is argued that each project can be viewed as proceeding by the performance of various *functions,* each marking the achievement of some identifiable goal. Performance of each function requires the execution of some design *procedure,* which requires certain data as *input,* produces certain data as *output,* and consumes certain *resources.* As a design project progresses, the outputs from procedures accumulate, and an extensive, complex, *project data base* is built up. The project is complete when this data base contains a sufficiently complete, consistent, and detailed description of the proposed building to form a basis for a contract and for actual construction work.

When architectural design is viewed in this way, it becomes clear that computer-aided design techniques can potentially be introduced at a variety of levels. The most obvious and modest approach is to accept the general framework of a conventional design and construction process, but to develop various discrete application programs and systems which replace certain manual design procedures within that process. A more ambitious approach is to replace the traditional "paper format" design data bases by a comprehensive computer-based building description system. In other words, drawing boards are replaced by computer graphic terminals, and electronic processing of data substitutes for paper-and-pencil techniques. By integrating a wide variety of application programs with a building description system, an integrated computer-aided design system can be developed. A still more ambitious approach is to substantially reorganize the whole design and construction process in order to take fullest advantage of the potentials of computer-aided design. This is sometimes referred to as *computer-aided building.*

THE BUILDING TEAM

Evolution of the standard building team

The design and construction of a building typically involves a large number of different participants in the process: clients, architects, consultants, contractors, building materials suppliers, public agencies and officials of various kinds, and so on. The participants which are assembled together for a project may be described as the building team. As a result of a lengthy evolutionary process, a fairly standard make-up and organizational structure for building teams has emerged in Britain, the United States, and many other countries. This standard pattern has been recognized and codified by various professional societies of architects and engineers, and to a certain extent in law. It strongly influences the professional education of architects; and it forms the basis of professional fee structures. It also defines a particular pattern of information flow in a construction project, and must thus be taken into consideration when contemplating the introduction of computer-aided design techniques.

Perhaps the best way to understand this pattern is to trace its emergence out of the medieval guild system for design and construction. From the beginning of the 13th century, in Britain, the building industry was organized around a system of craft guilds (Salzman 1952, Harvey 1972). Masons, carpenters, smiths, tilers, plumbers, glaziers, and painters associated together in fraternities which took responsibility for the training, regulation, and supply of building craftsmen. Within the crafts certain individuals, having served their apprenticeship, rose to the status of *master*. Many masters, particularly master masons and master carpenters, became employers of groups of craftsmen and would enter into contracts with clients to undertake building construction work. These masters assumed a design, coordination, and supervision role. The structure of the medieval building team is illustrated in *Figure 3.1* and *Figure 3.2(a)*.

According to a study of the construction industry in Britain undertaken by the Tavistock Institute (Higgin and Jessop 1965), the guild system or organization of construction survived in Britain until about the time of the great fire of London in 1666. After the fire, it proved to be an inadequate structure for meeting the demands of speedy reconstruction of the city. Individual building craftsmen from the old guilds, such as bricklayers, carpenters, plumbers, etc., began to emerge as entrepeneurs operating small independent construction enterprises which competed for work. There was an increasing need for more centralized design control and coordination, so the role of the *architect* now began to separate out from that of craftsman as shown in *Figure 3.2(b)*. Architects tended to be educated gentlemen, rather than members of the artisan classes, since the London landlords on whose behalf they acted were mostly of the nobility. Since prices for work were based on piece-rates, a class of specialist *measurers* also emerged. Measurers were employed both by the craftsmen to negotiate their claims for payment and by the architect to check the claims and negotiate on his behalf. However, the distinction between different roles was by no means always clear and firm. Dr. Johnson's *Dictionary* of 1755 makes "architect" and "surveyor" synonymous terms; and individuals often combined the roles of carpenter and measurer or architect and measurer (Crook 1969).

Around the beginning of the 19th century, the emergent industrial revolution combined with the stresses of the Napoleonic wars resulted in further changes. In order to achieve greater speed and ef-

Figure 3.1
Structure of the medieval building team: the master builder plays an intermediate role between client and craftsmen (British Museum manuscript Cotton Nero D. I., reproduced by permission of the British Library Board).

ficiency, a system began to emerge whereby each job was under the control of one responsible *contractor,* as shown in *Figure 3.2(c)*. This contractor, usually a bricklayer, tended to incorporate some other trades within his own organization, while the rest would be handled by the responsible contractor letting *sub-contracts.* The modern system of competitive bidding on projects by contractors also began to develop. In order to find a common basis for comparison of bids of potential main contractors for a job, it became common to prepare a "bill of quantities" which measured the quantity of construction described in the drawings made by the architect. The measurers who prepared these bills of quantities became known in Britain as *quantity surveyors.*

With the increasing pace of industrialization through the 19th century, further changes soon became inevitable. Increasingly widespread use was made of new construction materials such as concrete, cast iron, and later steel, while industrialized mass-production of standardized components became common. Complex mechanical, and later electrical, systems began to be installed in buildings. Generally, new materials and techniques were introduced into the industry by specialist sub-contractors. This led to the emergence of specialist designers, distinct from the architect, who dealt with those aspects of the project involving their particular areas of expertise. Initially these specialists acted as designer/sub-contractors. Later the roles of specialist designers and specialist sub-contractors tended to separate, and the roles of structural, mechanical, and other *consultants* to the architect emerged. By the end of the 19th century, the quite complex pattern shown in *Figure 3.2(d)* had become established in Britain. Variations of this general arrangement still form the basis for the design and construction process in most developed western countries today.

One significant variation between different countries, which is worth noting, concerns responsibility for making quantity surveys and cost estimates. In Britain and other Commonwealth countries, it is the usual practice on substantial projects to employ a specialist quantity surveyor to prepare bills of quantities, make cost estimates and provide cost advice, negotiate pricing of variations, and so on. In the United States and many other countries, it is common for the architect to make estimates and for each contractor bidding on a job to take off his own quantities in order to price the work.

Institutionalization of the architect's professional role

At roughly the same time that the standard modern pattern of organization of the building team emerged, the modern distinction between professional and commercial activity was also crystallizing. This development had important implications for the definition and delimitation of an architect's design tasks, and for the economic framework within which those tasks are undertaken.

It has been convincingly argued (Carr-Saunders and Wilson

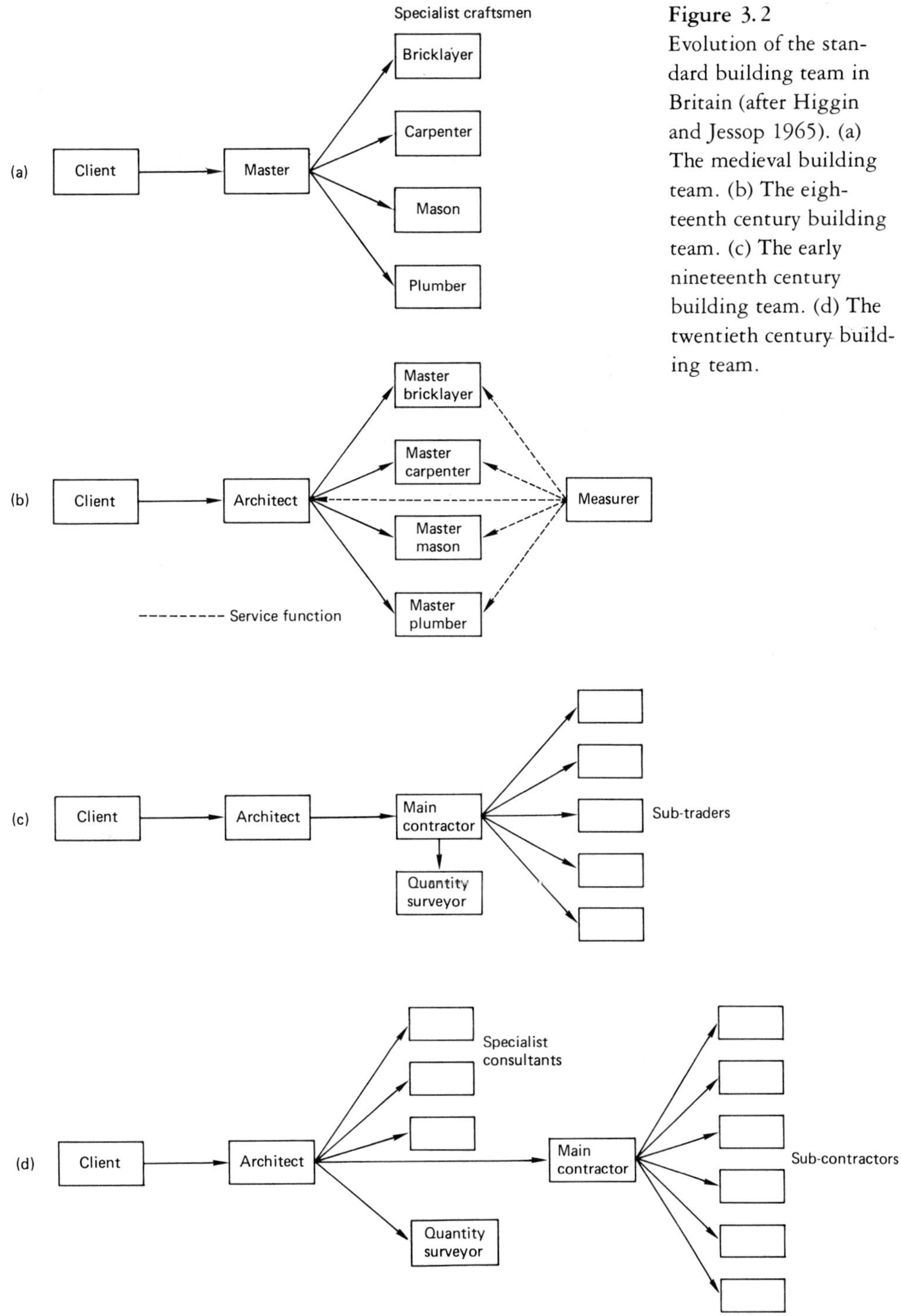

Figure 3.2
Evolution of the standard building team in Britain (after Higgin and Jessop 1965). (a) The medieval building team. (b) The eighteenth century building team. (c) The early nineteenth century building team. (d) The twentieth century building team.

1933, Kaye 1960) that in the laissez-faire economy of the mid-19th century, the motivation to distinguish clearly between professional and commercial services arose out of the inadequacy of the principle of *caveat emptor* in the professional marketplace. Acceptance of the principle of *caveat emptor* in the commercial marketplace was based upon the assumption that a buyer should know his needs and should be able to recognize those goods and services which fulfilled them. Neither assumption could be made with respect to increasingly complex and sophisticated professional services however. Thus to prevent chaos in the professional marketplace, voluntary professional organizations arose with the primary objectives of guaranteeing the independence, integrity and competence of their members. In England between 1818 and 1870, for example, organizations of civil engineers, architects, pharmacists, chemists, mechanical engineers, actuaries, accountants, dentists, surveyors, and teachers were added to those already existing in medicine and law. These developments were paralleled elsewhere.

The Royal Institute of British Architects was founded in 1834, and rapidly set about developing an effective guarantee mechanism. Its first step was to distinguish between the "profession" of design and the "trade" of building, as the opening address of the first meeting proclaimed (quoted by Kaye 1961):

> The Honorary Members shall consist of noblemen, who shall contribute a sum at one time of not less than twenty-five guineas, and of gentlemen *unconnected with any branch of building as a trade or business,* who shall contribute a like sum.

Similar steps were soon taken in other parts of the world. The Swiss Society of Engineers and Architects was formed in 1837, the Central Society of French Architects in 1840, and the American Institute of Architects in 1857.

By the second half of the 19th century in Europe and North America, the professional status of architects was firmly established, and architecture was clearly distinguished from the building trades, surveying, measuring, and engineering. Professional architects were required to abide by the provisions of codes of professional conduct which were specified by their institutes. These codes defined the extent and nature of professional duties, ethical professional conduct, and standard scales of remuneration.

ORGANIZATIONS

To fill the architectural design role within the building team, a wide range of different types of design organizations has emerged. Variation occurs in size, internal organizational structure, breadth of integration of activities, and building type specialization. Each one of these dimensions of variation has implications for the feasibility and manner of introduction of computer-aided design techniques.

Size

The traditional form of organization for architectural firms has been the small personal practice in which one principal (or a small group of principal partners) either works alone or is aided by a relatively small group of assistants. The principal makes most of the major decisions, and the assistants execute technical tasks under his direction. Obviously the size and complexity of projects which can be undertaken by such a firm is limited. However, in many parts of the world, there has been a long term trend towards the formation of increasingly larger firms which may have hundreds or even thousands of employees. These larger firms can potentially incorporate more diversified staff skills and capacities, achieve economies of scale, and undertake larger, lengthier and more complex projects.

In the governmental sector in most countries, very large architectural design organizations have also been developed in order to deal with extensive public building programs. Typically they are concerned with public housing, medical and educational facilities, and governmental buildings; and they may exist at national, state or regional, and local government levels. The United States is an important exception to this pattern; government architectural organizations play a relatively minor role.

Size is an important consideration in assessing the feasibility of introduction of computer-aided design systems into an organization. A large organization, with a large volume of work, may be in a better position than a smaller firm to acquire and amortize expensive equipment, and to absorb software development costs. It may be appropriate for smaller organizations to form consortia to acquire equipment and to spread development costs.

Internal organizational structure

The staff of a typical modern architectural design organization tends to be diversified in skills and experience. Different tasks on a project are undertaken by appropriate specialists, and the design which results is the product not of a single mind, but of the contributions of many. The principal of one very successful large U.S. firm has succinctly summarized the situation by stating, "The prima donnas have had their day. Now the architect is a team." (Caudill 1971.)

Design offices may be structured according to "vertical" or "horizontal" principles, or some combination of the two (Foxhall 1975). A typical vertical structure is shown in *Figure 3.3(a)*. The organization is hierarchically divided into specialized departments, each of

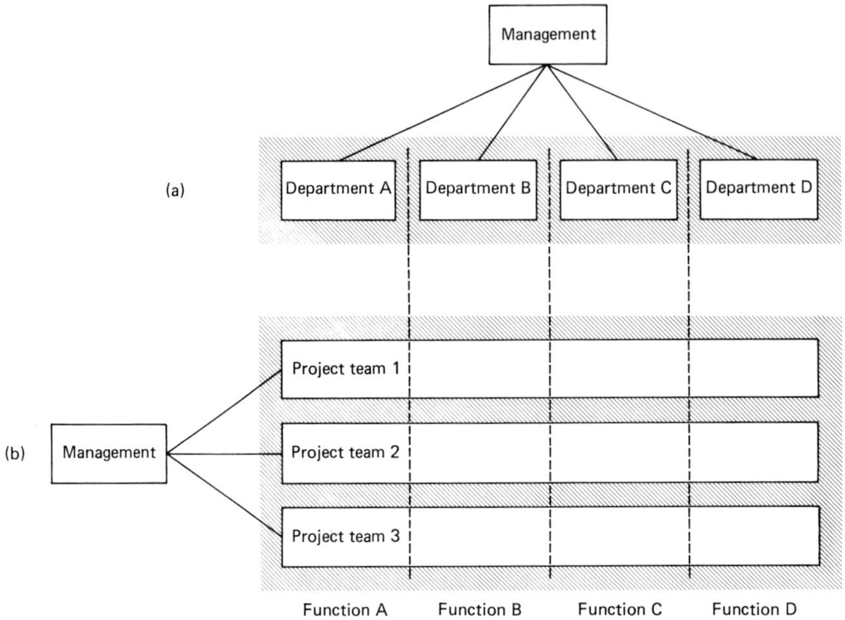

Figure 3.3
Vertical and horizontal structures for design offices. (a) Vertical structure. (b) Horizontal structure.

which is responsible for some particular aspect of each project. Typically, different departments are responsible for execution of successive phases of work, such as briefing, design, production of working drawings and specifications, and construction supervision. Specialist departments may also deal with particular aspects of projects such as structural and mechanical engineering, interiors, graphics, etc. Overall project direction and coordination are provided by a single project leader or small leadership group. This type of vertical departmental structure allows efficient utilization of specialist capabilities.

Alternatively, a horizontally integrated project team might be formed to carry a particular project through all stages from inception to completion, as shown in *Figure 3.3(b)*. The team would incorporate a variety of different specialist skills, and would usually shrink and grow according to the different demands of different phases of the project. This type of project team structure facilitates effective integration of different considerations into the overall design concept, and close coordination of work in the various different phases.

Many organizations attempt to incorporate both horizontal integration and vertical integration to achieve the advantages of each. For example, a project team may be formed for each job, but specialist departments may also exist to provide services as required.

Within a vertical organizational structure, it is a common pattern to introduce independent, highly specialized programs and systems for use by specialized departments. For example, the structural engineering department might have a structural analysis system; the mechanical engineering department might use heating and air-conditioning load programs, and so on. This may improve the performance of individual departments, but generally does little to facilitate overall coordination and integration of a project.

An alternative approach is to introduce a single computer system designed to handle the project data base throughout all phases, from inception to completion of a project. All specialized programs extract required input data from this common computer-stored data base, and return results to it. This type of arrangement provides an opportunity to achieve very effective horizontal integration.

Breadth of integration of activities

A variety of pressures are now calling into question the traditional scopes of activities (which evolved in response to 19th century conditions) of actors in the design and construction process. Among these pressures are demands for greater speed and tighter cost control, more complex briefs, and the growing sophistication of construction technology. In particular, there has been a widespread tendency to attempt to integrate broader ranges of skills and resources under centralized control within single organizations, in the hope of achieving better coordination and greater efficiency. This may take place in several ways: a large client organization may acquire in-house design and construction capabilities; an architectural firm may integrate specialist consultants such as structural and mechanical engineers; architects may begin to take active, risk-taking roles in development (Griffin 1972); contractors and manufacturers may offer design-and-build services. Public agencies in Britain and elsewhere often encompass close to the full spectrum of design and construction activities under centralized coordination and control.

There is considerable evidence that this tendency towards broader integration will eventually result in disappearance of the traditional architectural firm's role. A recent study sponsored by the American Institute of Architects (McCue *et al* 1970), foresaw numerous major changes in the U.S. construction industry over the coming decades, and the significant entry of many new actors, such as non-profit research and development groups, into the process. It was suggested that the traditional small- to medium-sized architectural firms will play a decreasing role in the detailed design and documentation phase, and will tend to be more concerned with project inception, research, programming, feasibility, and conceptual design work. Detailed design and documentation will be increasingly closely related to the manufacturing and construction processes, and are likely to be undertaken by giant design/manufacturing/construction organizations.

When attempting the introduction of new technologies and methods into the design and construction process, breadth of integration of the organizations involved is a critically important consideration. It has long been recognized, for example, that the highly fragmented character of the construction industry in the United States makes it extremely difficult to generate and implement needed major innovations in construction technology, industrialized production, design methods, and management techniques (Schon 1967). The situation has been summarized as follows:

> It is a risky, Balkanized industry in which no organization has a dominant position. It is highly competitive, though it engages in *ad hoc* collaborative efforts; and it is passive in nature, *i.e.*, it responds to external stimuli on a short-term time scale. It has not internalized technology for the purpose of management and it has invested little in research on itself, its products, and its future. (Midwest Research Institute 1970)

Conversely, the broadly integrated control often exerted by government agencies concerned with design and construction in Europe has greatly facilitated the development and practical implementation of such innovations as industrialized building methods, coordinated building information systems, new forms of relationships with builders such as serial contracting (an understanding with a contractor that there will be a series of future contracts for similar buildings), and of computer-aided design techniques.

Building type specialization

Since the 19th century, the types of building that are constructed have become increasingly diverse and specialized. The historian Nikolaus Pevsner (1976) has identified about 20 basic modern building types. This diversity is reflected in the organization of architectural practice. Due to the highly specialized knowledge and capabilities often necessary for design of specific building types, few but the largest architectural firms today attempt to deal with the full range of different types of building. Most tend to specialize in one or a small number of particular areas such as commercial and industrial buildings, educational facilities, medical facilities, and residential construction of various types. Larger firms, which do deal with a wide variety of building types, usually include specific building type specialists on their staff, or even have divisions oriented towards particular building types. Architectural design divisions of government agencies usually deal exclusively with the particular facilities that are of concern to that agency, most commonly public housing, educational facilities, schools, postal, and transportation facilities.

Many of the computer-aided architectural design systems that have been developed were produced for use by specialized organizations, and are quite specifically oriented towards a particular building type. Typical examples are the Harness * hospital design system and the SSHA * housing design system. Very few systems are completely general in their scope of application.

* See Integrated Systems below for descriptions.

FUNCTIONS, PROCEDURES, AND PROCESSES

A typical architectural project can be broken down into several fairly standard and well-defined phases. Within each phase, various functions are performed by the execution of design procedures. The sequence in which functions are performed is not arbitrary, since the output from one design procedure may be required as input to another. The execution of design procedures, in appropriate sequence, constitutes a design process. The following paragraphs analyze the structure and sequencing of a typical architectural project, and discuss the potentials for automation of functions.

Phases

The institutionalization of the architect's role within the building team has resulted in considerable standardization of tasks and phases. The architect's normal responsibilities and remuneration are fairly clearly established at each step. Although details and terminology vary somewhat in different areas, the four major phases of a typical project may be summarized as follows:

1. The *briefing* phase, in which feasibility and other preliminary research studies are conducted, and a program of requirements for the proposed building is produced and agreed upon.
2. The *sketch design* phase, in which design alternatives are explored, and a final design is developed and agreed upon.
3. The *construction documents* phase, in which detailed design decisions are made, and working drawings and specifications for the proposed building are produced. This phase normally concludes with the calling of bids from construction contractors to undertake the work described in the drawings and specifications, and the award of the contract to the successful bidder.
4. The *construction supervision* phase, in which the architect monitors the contractor's operations.

Normally one phase does not begin until the previous phase has been completed. However, under increasing pressure to shorten design and construction time on projects, there has recently been considerable interest in the possibility of partial overlapping of design and construction. This is sometimes known as "fast-track scheduling" (Caudill 1971). It is accomplished by dividing a project into several separate bid packages, for example, site work and foundations, the building shell, and interior systems, then allowing bids to be called and construction to begin on the earlier packages while design still continues on the later packages.

Functions and procedures

For purposes of description and analysis, it is useful to assume that each architectural project proceeds by the performance of various functions, each marking the achievement of some identifiable goal. Examples of functions might be the generation of a site-plan alternative, the design of a beam, the selection of a plumbing fixture, the making of a cost estimate, and so on. Functions may be conveniently grouped into four categories depending on whether they occur at the briefing, sketch design, construction documents, or construction supervision phases. In addition, we can define a fifth category of management functions: the overall coordination and control of the design and construction process.

Design functions are performed by the execution of design procedures. A design procedure may be defined, for our purposes here, as a describable sequence of operations having identifiable beginning and end points. Certain information is required as input, and certain results are produced as output. Design procedures may be precisely and accurately specified, or they may be loose, changeable, and informal. They may be executed by individuals, teams, computers, or person-machine systems. For performance of a given function, there may be a variety of different possible procedures.

Traditional architectural design procedures are usually highly labor-intensive; they are executed by architects or technicians working with very simple equipment, often no more than pencil and paper and perhaps one or two reference manuals. Consequently, large architectural offices are among the few places where one may still experience the Dickensian spectacle of rows of poorly paid junior staff bent over desks and engaged in tracing, copying, measuring, checking, annotating, calculating, and other manual operations of a routine and repetitive character.

An alternative to performance of a function by execution of a traditional manual design procedure is to employ a computer system to perform that function by execution of an appropriate program. In many cases, this approach can produce higher quality results, and can do so at lower cost and higher speed. Of course it is not feasible to automate all design functions (at least at present), but the range of functions for which useful programs have now been developed is impressive. Here is a representative list, based upon the results of several recent surveys (Hoskins 1973, Lee 1974).

Briefing phase

Feasibility study	Economic feasibility analysis
	Housing type mix analysis
Programming	Problem structuring
	Activity data analysis
	Space need projection

Accommodation schedule production
Circulation analysis
Cluster and bubble diagram generation

Sketch design phase

Site planning	Site mapping
	Slope analysis
	Drainage analysis
	Cut and fill analysis
	View analysis
	Accessibility analysis
	Overlay mapping analyses
	Site plan synthesis
Schematic design synthesis	
	Floor plan layout
	Three-dimensional spatial synthesis
Performance and cost analysis of proposals	
	Checking for compliance with the brief
	Circulation analysis
	Preliminary structural computations
	Heat gain computations
	Heat loss computations
	Insolation and shadow pattern analyses
	Natural lighting computations
	Artificial lighting computations
	Sound transmission computations
	Reverberation time computations
	Preliminary cost estimation
Presentation	Plotting sketch plans, elevations, sections
	Plotting perspectives

Production documents phase

Detail design	Building products data retrieval
	Automated detailing
	Structural member selection and sizing
	Mechanical and electrical system detail design
	Duct, pipe, and electrical network layout

Costing	Generation of bills of quantities
	Pricing of bills of quantities
	Cost analyses
Production	Generation of schedules
	Generation of specifications
	Plotting of working drawings

Construction supervision phase

Network analysis
Precedence diagramming
Project cost control

Management functions

Job costing
Time and payroll functions
Invoicing

Sequencing and scheduling of functions

Sequential dependencies exist between architectural design functions. In other words, some design procedures cannot be executed until others have been completed, since output from the earlier procedures is required as input for the later. The pattern of sequential dependencies is most clearly illustrated by means of a network diagram, as shown in *Figure 3.4*. Typically there exist a number of parallel "paths" through the network. One of these paths will be "critical" in the sense that any delay in completion of a function on the critical path will result in a delay in completion of the project. Conversely, a certain amount of "slack" exists for completion of functions which do not lie on the critical path.

Automation of a procedure for performing a function which lies upon the critical path, and consequent reduction of the time taken in performance of that function, will reduce the time taken to complete the project. But this may also cause another path to become critical, and thus the gains may not be as great as expected. If a function does not lie upon the critical path, introduction of a quicker automated

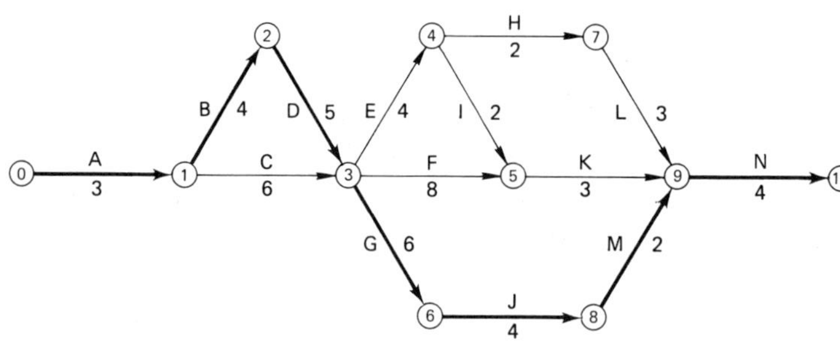

Figure 3.4
An example of a simple network diagram for a design project. Arrows represent functions, and circles represent "events," i.e. the beginnings and endings of functions. The duration of each function is shown, and the heavy line represents the critical path through the network.

procedure will not reduce total project time (though it may have other benefits).

DATA BASE MANAGEMENT

As a design project progresses, outputs from various procedures accumulate and an extensive, complex, *project data base* is built up. Some of the information in this data base is simply temporary working data, *i.e.*, the output of one procedure (or step of a procedure) temporarily recorded in some way so that it can be used as input to another procedure. Sketches, notes, and mental notes fall into this category. Other information must be recorded more permanently, and is eventually incorporated in the working drawings, specifications, etc., which constitute the final design. In one sense, a design project may be thought of as the building up of a body of data which consistently and completely describes a proposed building.

In addition to project-specific data, many design procedures require data of a general, non-project-specific type. Typical examples of non-project-specific design data include catalogues of building materials and components, libraries of standard design details, and description of previous buildings. This may be referred to as *library* data, as distinguished from specific *project* data.

Size of project data bases

The quantity of information in a project data base can be quite large. Few precise studies have been conducted, but some indicative figures can be cited. Scher (1972), for example, studied two typical medium-sized projects completed in Britain in 1969, a 100,000 square foot school extension and an 80,000 square foot hospital maternity unit, and found that both required about 1,000 production drawings. Slightly more than a third of these were produced by the architect, and the remainder by consultants and contractors.

A number of estimates of the amount of computer storage required for a typical project data base have been made. Jackson (1970) estimated that a detailed and comprehensive computer-stored description of a typical twenty-story U.S. office building would require a minimum of 10,000,000 characters of data, and that an estimate of 100,000,000 characters would not be at all unreasonable. A study by the consulting firm Bolt Beranek and Newman (1965) estimated, somewhat less generously, that a computer-stored description of a 188-bed hospital at a sufficient level of detail for automated checking for compliance with building codes would require about 100,000 18-bit words of computer storage (*i.e.*, roughly 40,000 to 50,000 characters). Eastman *et al* (1974) calculated that a typical 10-story office building of about 120,000 square feet consists of about 150,000 separate parts which need to be described (*i.e.*, about 1.25

parts/square foot). A conservative estimate of 100 characters per part implies that a description would require about 15,000,000 characters. They also suggested that design variations could lead to at least an order of magnitude variation in this number for a building of the same size. Teague and Davis (1972) estimated that a furniture and equipment schedule for a large teaching hospital can contain 1,500,000 or more characters of information. For comparison, a typical book of 250 pages, 50 lines per page, 80 characters per line, contains 1,000,000 characters.

These estimates should all be treated with caution, since little experience has been gained as yet with comprehensive, computer-stored project data bases. Furthermore, different techniques for structuring data in computer storage can produce large variations in the amount of storage required. But they do at least give an indication of the orders of magnitude involved. They suggest that it is impractical to consider storing complete project data bases in computer core memories, but that there should be no difficulty in storing such data bases in auxiliary disk or tape storage units.

Size of library data bases

Library data bases tend to be larger than project data bases. A survey conducted by the U.K. Department of the Environment (1971) concluded, for example, that about 360,000 different building products were currently in use in that country. Based on the International Council for Building Research (CIB) Master List of Properties for building products (Eldridge 1968), it can be roughly estimated that about 50 items of information need to be recorded to adequately describe the properties of each product. Assuming about 10 characters per item of information, this means that a comprehensive building products catalogue for Britain would contain about 180,000,000 characters of data. Of course any practical catalogue is selective, but it can be seen that a data base giving reasonably comprehensive coverage must amount to some significant fraction of 180,000,000 characters. While data bases of this magnitude are large by any standard, they can successfully be handled using existing computer technology. (Commercial and governmental computer data bases of over one billion characters are not unusual today.)

Updating

Both project and library data bases require frequent updating and correction. As a design is being developed, of course, the project data base is in a continuous state of flux. However, even after the design has supposedly been finalized at the working drawings stage, a large number of amendments and revisions normally must still be made. Amendment or revision may be prompted by the necessity to correct errors, to add detail, or to respond to new conditions which may have arisen during progress of the job. In a study of two typical projects (a hospital and a school) conducted by Scher (1972) it was estimated that at any given moment approximately one third of the architect's staff were engaged in amending production drawings rather than making new ones. A count of indexed revisions on the drawings indicated that a total of 1,602 revisions were made to the 1,150 drawings on the school project, and 877 revisions on the 992 drawings for the hospital project. Although the majority of the drawings had very few revisions, some were amended as many as 10 or 15 times. After completion of a building, it is widespread practice to prepare a set of "as-built" drawings, which incorporate all revisions and corrections and record the final state of the project data base.

Some library data requires little updating, but much of it changes very rapidly, particularly building materials and components information. One indicative estimate (Pennington 1967) is that about 20,000 new construction products were at that time appearing on the market each year in Canada, while about 5,000 were going off the market in the same period. It seems likely that the figures would be higher for the U.S. and Britain, and would be increasing.

Maintaining data base consistency

Alteration of one part of a project data base typically requires other parts to be altered as well if data base consistency is to be maintained. For example, alteration of a dimension on a plan may require elevation and section drawings to be altered in addition. The situation arises in this case because the data base is *redundant,* i.e., the same information is repeated in several different places. Consistency problems may also arise due to logical *dependence* of data. For instance, shifting the location of a beam may imply that a duct should also be shifted in order to avoid a spatial conflict. The essentially clerical task of maintaining simple consistency relations in the project data base as a design develops absorbs a great deal of staff time and effort. Furthermore, it rarely proves possible to avoid incorporating some inconsistencies, which may not become evident until construction time.

Inconsistencies due to complex logical interdependencies of design decisions may be very difficult to identify and resolve, and the "consistency problem" in this sense is a central issue of design methodology (see Baer and Eastman, 1976, for an extensive discussion).

Querying and reporting operations

A large amount of effort, in a typical design project, is expended in *querying* and *reporting* operations. A querying operation involves search of a data base to extract needed information, for example, search of a building products catalogue to find a product suitable for use in a particular situation, or examination of a plan to find the location of a column. Reporting involves systematic examination of a data base in order to extract certain information and to present it in a special format for some special purpose. Production of a bill of quantities from working drawings and specifications is a typical example of a reporting operation. Less obviously perhaps, the production of a perspective from plans and elevations can also be considered to be a form of reporting.

Privacy and security

In a very direct sense, project and library data bases represent a design organization's most valuable assets. Thus, it is vital to protect them from damage and destruction. In addition, it is often important to prevent unauthorized alteration or disclosure of their contents. Security issues arise not only in relation to outsiders, but also within the design team itself, where different members may be authorized to access different parts of a data base. For example, only the structural engineer may be authorized to enter or alter structural data, while only the mechanical engineer may be authorized to enter or alter information concerning mechanical systems, and so on.

Where conventional drawings, etc., are employed as the data base media, privacy and security are achieved by physical protection of documents, and by instituting appropriate management controls. Where data bases are stored in computer memory, quite sophisticated technology may need to be employed in order to insure privacy and security, especially if the computer system employed is part of a network.

Building description systems

In a traditional architectural design process, the data bases typically consist of information existing in one or another of the following formats (Bolt Beranek and Newman 1965):

Arrangement drawings (plans, elevations, sections, perspectives, utility network layouts, etc.) which describe a building's geometry and topology.

Schedules of accommodation requirements, quantities, finishes, doors, windows, etc.

Detail drawings, illustrating details of jointing, etc., not included in the main arrangement drawings.

Narrative text, for example, specification clauses.

It is now technologically and economically feasible to consider replacing drawings and text on paper as the primary media of building description by computer data base management systems. In these systems, project and library data bases are maintained in computer memory, and updating, interrogation, and reporting operations are performed via computer graphics terminals.

Eastman (1975) has specified the basic capabilities required of an effective comprehensive building description system as follows:

> A means to store a "complete" description of any building element, including, minimally, its spatial description, materials, weight, cost, and source of supply;
>
> A means to spatially organize the elements into a configuration representing a building, *e.g.*, apply the geometric transformations to their spatial description;
>
> Means to directly interrogate the data base in order to answer directly a limited range of questions;
>
> Analytic routines that allow answers to more complex questions, such as structural integrity, thermal properties, lighting levels and capital and operating costs;
>
> Means of display and output portions of the resulting data base in particularly meaningful formats for visual inspection.

Implementation of a comprehensive building description system having these capabilities is a difficult and expensive task. Some of the important technical problems involved still remain without fully satisfactory resolution. However, intensive research has been conducted in this area over the last 10 years or so, and some very powerful systems are now emerging.

A pioneering analysis of the requirements for a comprehensive building description system, together with a prototype for a comprehensive system, was developed by Bolt Beranek and Newman under contract to the U.S. National Bureau of Standards in the mid-1960's (Clark 1967). At around the same time, a system known as ICES (Integrated Civil Engineering System) was developed at MIT (Roos 1967). As the name implies, ICES is not restricted to architectural applications, but does include a structural analysis and design subsystem called STRUDL, and an architectural design subsystem called BUILD (Teague 1970). ICES was conceived as a large set of computer programs, united by a common system for data storage and communication. Although many of the sophisticated data handling capabilities projected for ICES have never been implemented, considerable research on the problems of data management in this type of system was carried out, and some useful concepts were established.

Following on from the early work on ICES, Jackson (1970) suggested a design for a very comprehensive computer-based building data management system. Jackson's system is built up from basic facilities provided in ICES. It comprises a large number of different computer files, each holding data that is relevant to particular aspects of building design. Central to the organization of the system are files for general project data, site data, the basic geometry of the building, and assignments of activities to locations. Specialized files contain data on building structure, heating, ventilation, and air conditioning, communications, pipe systems, walls, occupancy and circulation, elevators, electrical systems, power distribution, and lighting.

At the time of this writing, the most sophisticated building description system yet to be developed in the United States was BDS (Building Description System) produced by a team under the leadership of Charles Eastman at Carnegie-Mellon University (Eastman, Lividini and Stoker 1975, Eastman 1975). BDS was initially implemented on a DEC PDP-11/20 computer with extended disk memory and graphics capabilities. It is designed to provide a facility for storing and manipulating design information at the level of detail and accuracy necessary for performance of virtually any practical design, construction, or operational analysis task.

In BDS, a building design is treated as the spatial composition of a set of elements. Designs described in this way can be stored on disk, and displayed in various ways on a CRT screen as required. Application programs can be interfaced with the data base. To provide an appropriate interface with the user, the following capabilities are provided:

A means for easy graphic entering of arbitrarily complex element shapes.

An interactive graphic language for editing and composing element arrangements.

Hardcopy graphic capabilities that can produce perspective or orthographic drawings of high quality.

A sort and format capability allowing sorting of the data base by attributes, *e.g.,* material type or supplier.

Another very interesting prototype building description system known as IDAS (Integrated Designer's Activity Support System) has been implemented on an experimental basis by IBM's Tokyo Scientific Center (Matsuka, Kawaie and Uno 1975). IDAS is notable for its use of a sophisticated technique known as *relational data structuring* (Codd 1970) for organizing storage of the building description, and for its capability to preserve a historical record of the sequence of design decisions as they are made, and of alternative schemes which are considered. A designer can return, at any point, to any previously-considered scheme. The interactive graphics display system associated with IDAS allows drawings to be generated and displayed at different levels of detail.

Computer-based building descriptions potentially have many important advantages. The most obvious is flexibility; data can be retrieved, and reports in any required format can be produced rapidly and efficiently. The computer representation is also much more compact than a typical "paper" representation; a complete description of a complex building can be stored on a reel of tape. Updating and consistency problems arising out of the redundancy of conventional architectural drawings are avoided. In drawings, the same data must often be represented several times at different scales and levels of detail, for example, in site plans, floor plans, and wall details. Furthermore, the practice of employing plans, elevations, and sections requires each part of the building to be represented twice, once projected on a horizontal plane and once on a vertical plane. Problems of maintaining consistency inevitably arise, and when design changes are made a number of different drawings may need to be altered. Often, different members of the design team must work with different sets of drawings, some of which may be obsolete or inaccurate, leading to communication problems and to abortive work. All of these problems can be minimized, and perhaps eliminated altogether, in a building description system where a single, definitive, up-to-date description is stored in the computer. A building description system can also provide members of the building team with greatly improved capabilities to visualize the design and to identify spatial conflicts, since sections and perspectives can be generated as required at any location.

PATTERNS OF RESOURCE ALLOCATION

Conventional design processes

A number of studies have shown that, when traditional design techniques and procedures are employed, there is a consistent and characteristic pattern of distribution of effort over the duration of an architectural project. A survey of over 3,000 U.S. offices conducted by the American Institute of Architects in 1950 (Bannister 1954) reported that the average distribution of total staff time to different activities was as follows:

Working drawings	17.9%
Design	15.2%
"Overall activities"	11.5%
Administration	10.7%
Field supervision	9.7%
Client relations	9.2%
Specifications	6.4%

The remaining 19.4% was thinly distributed over 21 miscellaneous activities. It can be seen that production of construction documents (working drawings and specifications) directly accounted for nearly 25% of total time, compared with about 15% for design and less than 10% for supervision.

A more recent AIA survey (quoted by McCue 1970), based upon analysis of billings for nearly 500 projects, showed some shifts in emphasis but confirmed the continued dominance of production of construction documents. Between 25% and 40% of total cost and effort was reportedly devoted to work by outside engineering consultants, and the remainder was distributed as follows:

Design services	5–10%
Construction documents	15–18%
Engineering services (in house)	5%
Client communications	2–5%
Construction supervision	7–10%
General activities	15–30%

A similar pattern has been observed in Britain. A study conducted by the Department of the Environment (quoted by Cross 1974) investigated total man-hours devoted to projects at different stages, and produced graphs plotting effort against time as illustrated in *Figure 3.5*. The "hump" in the effort curve at the stage of detailed design and production of construction documents is evident.

Within each phase of a project, characteristic patterns of distribution of effort can also be observed. From time-lapse camera data, Evans, Wood and Purcell (1971) developed "activity profiles" for architects' work on different types of drawings. A typical profile for production of an early sketch was:

Activity	*Percentage total time*
Writing and annotation	2%
Drawing	56%
Reviewing	14%

Figure 3.5
Design effort over several stages of a typical project, from a study by the Building Economics Research Unit, University College London (Cross 1974).

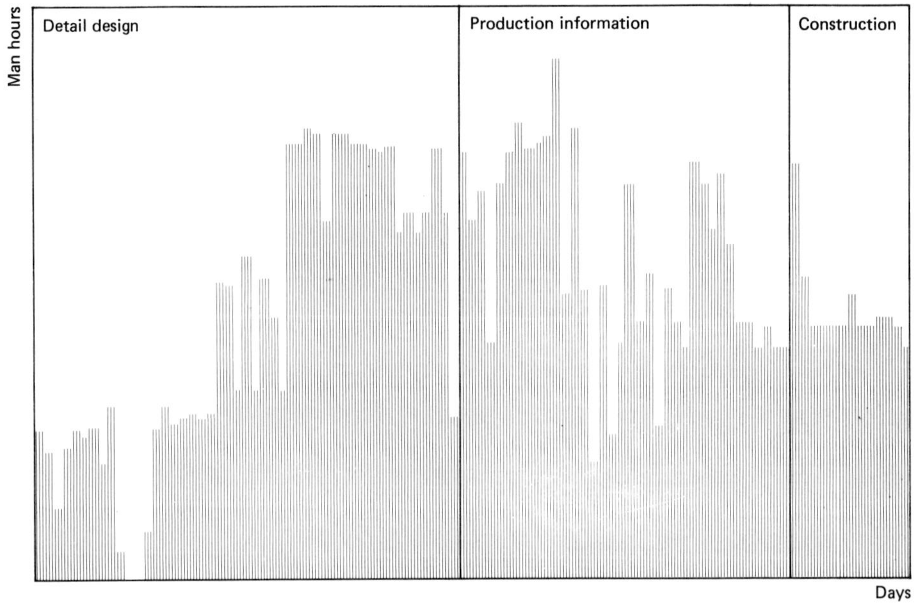

Measuring	5%
Miscellaneous other	23%

A typical profile for a much more formalized later sketch, however, was quite different:

Activity	*Percentage total time*
Referencing manuals, previous drawings, etc.	23%
Writing and annotation	14%
Drawing	17%
Erasing	3%
Reviewing	18%
Measuring	4%
Miscellaneous other	21%

Examination of these statistics clearly reveals where greatest economies in time and effort could potentially be achieved by introduction of automated techniques. But since professional fee structures are usually based upon these standard patterns of resource allocation in the design process, achievement of such economies in practice may not be a simple matter.

Computer-aided design processes

One of the most striking effects of the large-scale introduction of computer-aided architectural design techniques in practice is likely to be a very substantial reduction in the total length of the design and construction process. A case study reported by Thompson and Hughes (1974) showed that use of CEDAR, a comprehensive computer-aided architectural design system, reduced the elapsed time for design of a building structural frame from 38 days for a typical manual process to 2 days. Use of the SSHA housing design system is claimed to increase design team productivity by about 25% for detail design and documentation tasks, and by about 40% for site planning tasks (Applied Research of Cambridge 1975). It has been estimated that the use of a comprehensive computer-aided design system in conjunction with the Harness hospital building program in Britain would reduce design time for a large hospital from a normal 5 years to about 9 months.

Not only will total time spent be reduced, there will also be a significant redistribution of total effort spent in the various phases. As was shown in *Figure 3.5,* use of traditional manual procedures results in a large "hump" in the effort curve at the stages of detailed design and generation of construction documents. These are precisely the stages at which currently available computer-aided design systems effect their greatest time savings, resulting in a reversed effort curve as

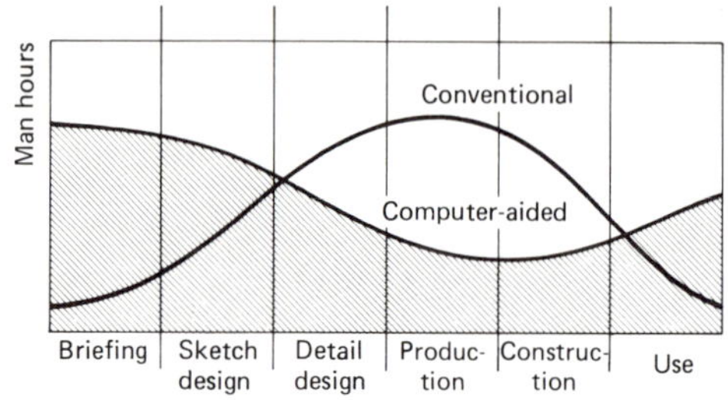

Figure 3.6
Redistribution of design effort with use of computer-aided design methods.

shown in *Figure 3.6.* Some systems, like that used in conjunction with the Harness hospital program, also potentially allow considerable reduction in the time spent at general scheme design. This redistribution of effort should allow greater resources to be allocated to the tasks of pre-design research and post-construction evaluation.

An important consequence of this redistribution of effort is likely to be that the staffing requirements for a typical design team will change considerably. It has been widely reported (*e.g.,* Mumford and Banks 1967) that the introduction of large-scale computerized systems into organizations typically results in a flattening of the management pyramid. Many time-consuming semi-skilled tasks are automated; in addition, much of the need for middle management staff may be eliminated as computer systems make wider spans of control possible for senior management. Understandably, in view of the very recent development of effective large-scale architectural computer systems, there is little available data on whether this pattern will be followed in architectural offices. However, a recent study by Auger (1972), a principal of an architectural office, strongly suggests that it will be. Cooley (1972) has published an extremely interesting analysis of the likely impacts of computer-aided design systems on the employment of engineering technicians and draftsmen, written from the point of view of a union leader and coming to a somewhat similar conclusion.

STRATEGIES FOR INTRODUCTION OF COMPUTER-AIDED DESIGN TECHNIQUES IN PRACTICE

Discrete application programs

The most straightforward and obvious way to introduce computer-aided architectural design techniques in practice is to replace certain manual procedures with *discrete application programs* which perform the same functions.

Such programs are available from a variety of sources. Many have been developed by universities, research organizations, computer manufacturers, etc., and may be obtained free or at little cost. Numerous specialized consulting firms and computer service bureaus actively market architectural application programs. A considerable number of architectural firms have been able to develop extensive in-house program libraries. Among the first firms to do this on a fairly large scale were Ellerbe Associates, Skidmore Owings and Merrill, and Caudill Rowlett and Scott in the United States, Cusdin Burden and Howitt, and Turner Lansdown Holt and Partners in the U.K., and Nikken Sekkei in Japan. Several consortia have been set up to develop, maintain, and distribute programs to their members. For example, the Design Office Consortium (DOC) based in Cambridge, U.K., is an association for promoting the use of computers in the building industry. It provides both programs and consulting services. Membership consists of architectural, structural, mechanical, and electrical engineering, quantity surveying, and contracting firms, and local government design offices. A more specialized consortium is Automated Procedures for Engineering Consultants (APEC), a U.S. group which has developed many programs for use by services engineers.

It is often not necessary to make any investment at all in hardware or program development in order to employ discrete application programs in design. For occasional or intermittent running of discrete application programs, use of bureau services is usually adequate. Some bureaus even process data submitted by mail, and send back the results. Where usage is more intensive, it may become worthwhile to install a terminal connected to a time-sharing service; constant, heavy usage may eventually justify installation of an in-house system.

The principal advantages of the strategy of introducing discrete application programs may be summarized as follows:

1. Many such programs have already been developed, and are widely available;
2. Costs of development are usually relatively low;
3. They can often be developed and implemented relatively quickly;
4. Major investment in computer hardware is not necessarily required;
5. They can be introduced incrementally, without substantially disrupting established organizational frameworks and procedures (at least initially).

For many small- and medium-sized architectural offices, these considerations are of overriding importance, and the use of discrete application programs is the only feasible way to introduce computer-aided design techniques. In many cases, program development and implementation costs must be covered by the short-term ability of computerized methods to achieve cost savings over conventional methods.

There is, however, a fundamental disadvantage inherent in use of discrete application programs within the framework of a traditional design and construction process. The data preparation step usually involves substantial time and effort, and the output produced by the program may also require some time to be spent in interpretation. Very often the economies and advantages resulting from successful automation of a design function are detracted from, or even outweighed by, the time spent at these tasks. For example, time spent in preparing data for input to a perspective plotting program can easily exceed the time which would be taken by a skilled renderer to complete the drawing.

Repeated use of data for different computations

The inefficiency inherent in use of discrete application programs can be overcome if data, once prepared in machine-readable form, can be used repeatedly for different computations. For instance, perspective plotting programs become much more cost-effective if many different views are generated from a set of input data, rather than just one. A typical relation between costs of automated and manual production of multiple perspective views is illustrated in *Figure 3.7.* For one or a small number of views, the high fixed cost of data input to the perspective plotting program may place it at a disadvantage; but as the number of views increases, the much lower cost per view gives the program an increasingly substantial cost advantage. Thus automated perspective plotting programs have been most effectively used for such purposes as comprehensive visual documentation of projects, generation of animated sequences, and production of sequential views along paths of movement such as highways and amusement park rides.

The same set of input data may also sometimes be used within a program for a variety of quite different purposes. The Cambridge Environmental Model (Hawkes and Stibbs 1969) is an excellent example of this approach. To use this program, a description of the building to be analyzed (plus other necessary data) is first prepared and input.

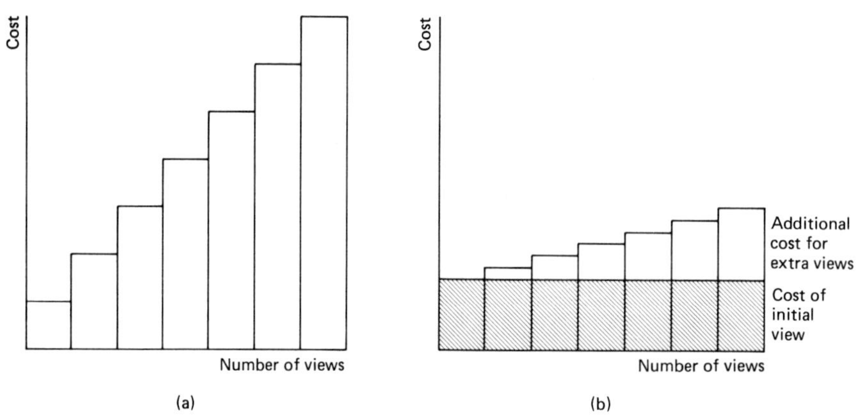

Figure 3.7

Typical comparative costs of manual and automated perspective production. (a) Manual production. (b) Computer production.

This data is then utilized by the program in performance of the following calculations:

Daylight factors within the spaces;

Power required by lighting installations in order to achieve specified illumination levels;

Heating and cooling loads;

Noise levels in spaces.

The flow of data is schematically illustrated in *Figure 3.8.* The advantages of this arrangement over separate programs for performing the analyses are obvious.

By extension of this concept, special *mapping programs* can be written to take input and/or output data from one program and re-express it in a format suitable for input to another program (*Figure 3.9*). While this approach can sometimes be useful, mapping programs tend to be difficult to implement, and the resultant interlinked system of programs is often cumbersome and inflexible.

Integrated systems

Most effective and economical use is made of the computer's capabilities if application programs and a computer-based building description system are combined into a comprehensive *integrated system* (*Figure 3.10*). Since the central project and library data bases are potentially accessible to all the various programs, data need only be entered into the data base once, and expensive and time consuming manual data preparation and input is minimized. The whole system

Figure 3.8
Re-use of data in an integrated sequence of analyses performed by the Cambridge Environmental Model.

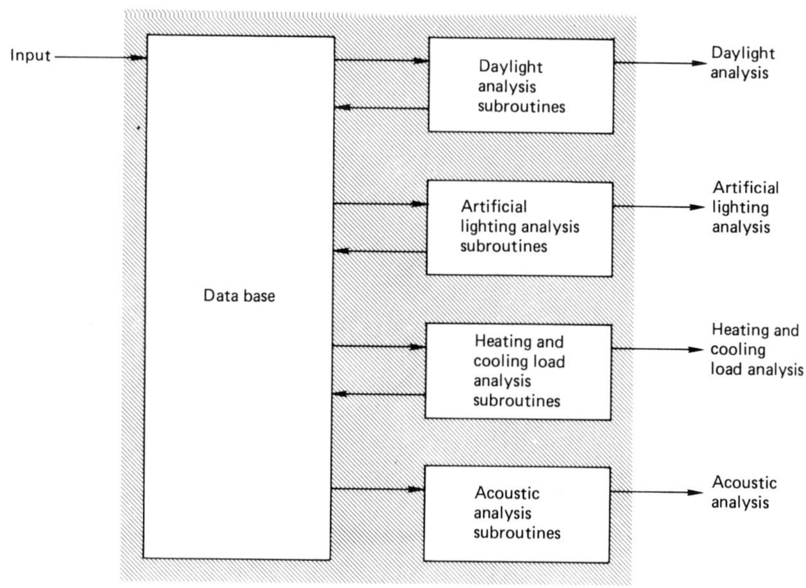

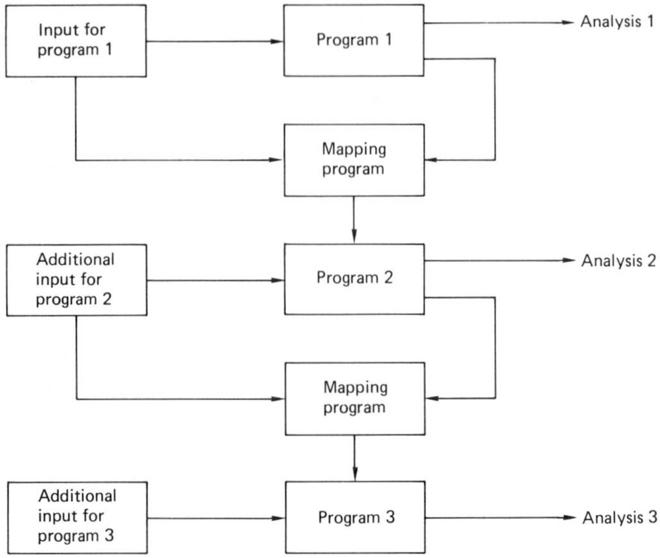

Figure 3.9
Use of mapping programs to re-format data for use in different analyses.

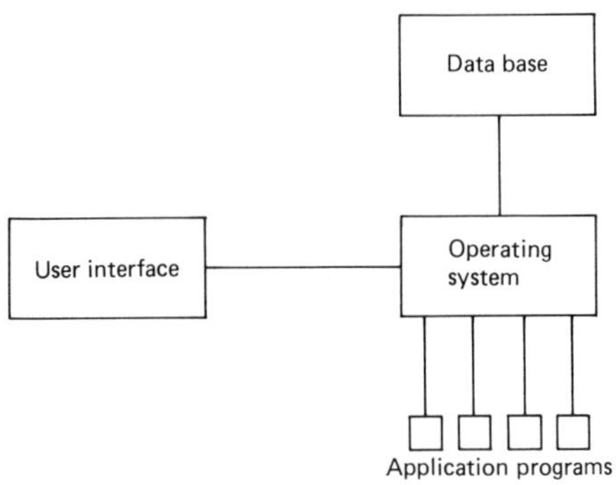

Figure 3.10
Schematic diagram of an integrated computer-aided design system.

may be controlled by a specially developed operating system (Applied Research of Cambridge 1975, 1976). Facilities are provided for users to manipulate the design, interrogate the data base, produce required reports (both alphanumeric and graphic) and call for application programs to be executed as required.

Numerous integrated computer-aided architectural design systems have been proposed, and in many cases implemented. The earlier systems to be developed were severely limited in their capacities and capabilities by inadequacies in their building description facilities, and weaknesses in the programs which they incorporated. Many were nothing more than demonstration systems, capable only of handling very restricted "toy" problems. But some of the more recent systems are sufficiently powerful to have achieved a high level of practical usefulness.

One well-known early integrated system was URBAN-5 (Negroponte 1970). This system utilized a computer graphics console,

Figure 3.11
The URBAN-5 system.

equipped with keyboard and light-pen (*Figure 3.11*), which allowed the user to generate a design proposal by locating elements from a standard menu displayed on the screen. A constantly-updated representation of the design proposal was stored in computer memory, and operated upon by a wide variety of procedures to produce simple evaluations of structural feasibility, compliance with geometric constraints, environmental performance, etc. URBAN-5 was notable for its incorporation of many highly innovative features, in particular, facilities for encouraging a very fluid and natural dialogue between user and machine. It was eventually abandoned when the limitations inherent in its basic design began to severely limit further development. Other early integrated systems, which reached varying stages of implementation, have been described by Teague and Hershdorfer (1967), Elms (1972), Cole (1972), and Hamer *et al* (1973).

The first commercially marketed integrated system in the United States is a system known as ARK-2, which is sold as a complete hardware and software package (Stewart 1975). It employs a minicomputer and low cost storage tube interactive graphics terminals. Facilities are provided for storing project and library data bases on disk and tape; and there is a repetoire of graphics, data analysis, design evaluation, and design synthesis programs. The user controls the system by typing in simple verbal commands at a keyboard.

In the U.K., a fairly general and comprehensive integrated system for housing design, developed initially by Ed CAAD for use by the Scottish Special Housing Association, is now available (Bijil 1971, 1972, Applied Research of Cambridge 1975). The system is not tied to any particular standard plan types, methods of construction, or materials. However, there is a restriction to single and two-story orthogonal houses with level floor plans. It consists of two parts: software for detailed design and documentation of housing units and software for site layout, and appraisal and costing of site plan alternatives. It relies upon the use of a library of standard construction details, which is established by the user organization.

To design a housing unit, the architect begins by defining an arrangement using a storage tube interactive graphics terminal. Next, materials, surfaces, fittings, electrial layout, plumbing, and other services are specified. As these detailed decisions are made, cross-references to standard construction details are automatically established. It is not necessary to start every design from scratch: facilities are provided for storing a library of standard designs, and for recalling designs from the library and modifying them.

To aid the designer, the system includes the following features (see *Figure 3.12*):

A floor structure analysis program which locates and sizes timber beams, and calculates joist direction and sizing, given the configuration of structural support from below.

A daylight contour program, which will produce plots for each room. (Daylight computations are often required by building codes in the U.K.)

A heat loss computation program.

Programs for producing area and volume summaries.

Programs to allow the designer to position and revise furniture layouts within rooms.

The production information that can be automatically generated by the system includes:

Dimensioned plans, sections, and elevations.

Surface finish and component specifications.

Furnishing and fitting layouts.

Cross references to construction details at junctions.

Electrical layouts.

Plumbing isometrics.

Bills of quantities.

The site description software allows the architect to describe dimensions and locations on a site of housing and garage blocks, roads, drainage networks, site services, landscapes areas, and linear features such as fences and walls. Facilities are provided for automatically establishing levels and alignments, for costing alternative layouts, for performing certain evaluations such as computing areas of

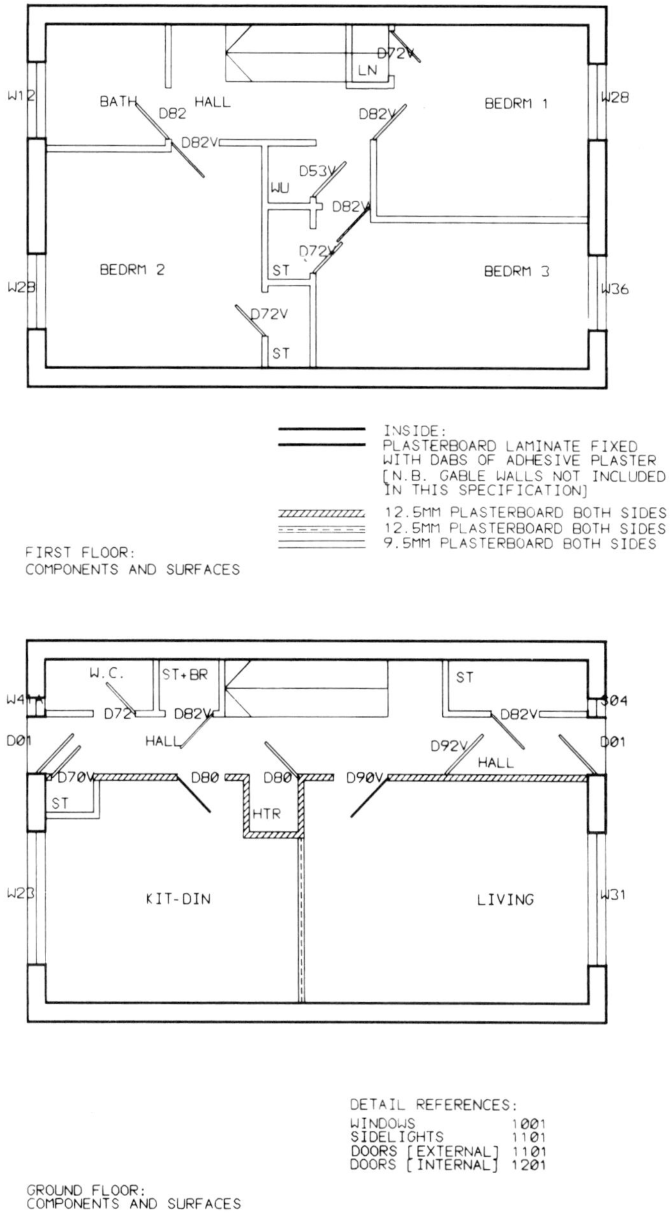

(a)

Figure 3.12
A typical example of working drawings for a house generated by the SSHA system.
(a) Plans. (b). Elevations. (c) Sections. (d) Joist layouts. (e) Area and thermal analyses. (f) Plumbing isometrics.

open space, and for performing cut and fill, foundation, and sewer and drain calculations.

In addition to time and cost savings, the system provides an opportunity to achieve other important benefits. The use of libraries of standard details, and of previously developed designs, encourages rationalization of the design and construction process, and the use of

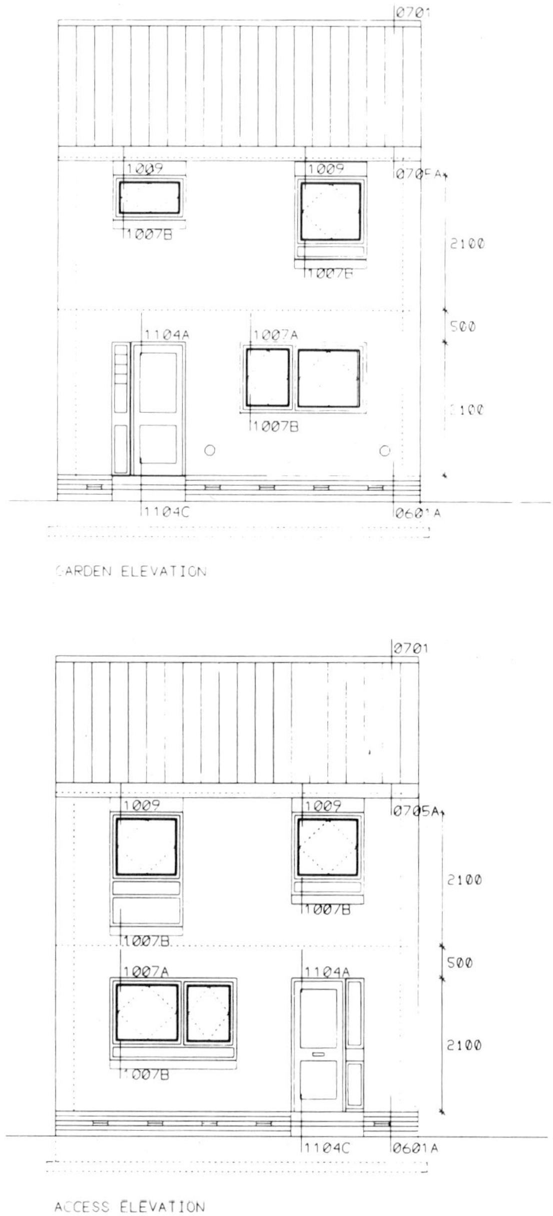

(b)

feedback information to improve design quality. Interchangeable libraries of standard details for different methods of construction may be developed, thus providing great flexibility in responding to changing cost and availability of materials and labor. The ability to perform rapid cost and other analyses enables the architect to maintain very ef-

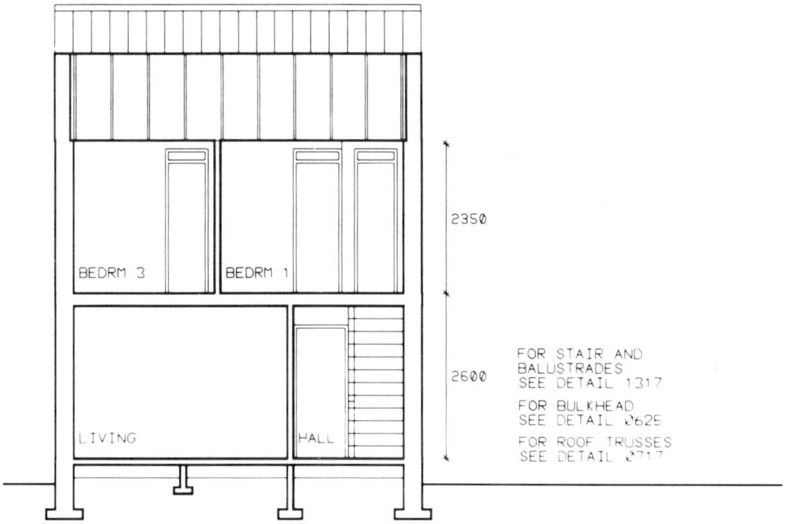

SECTION BETWEEN GABLES

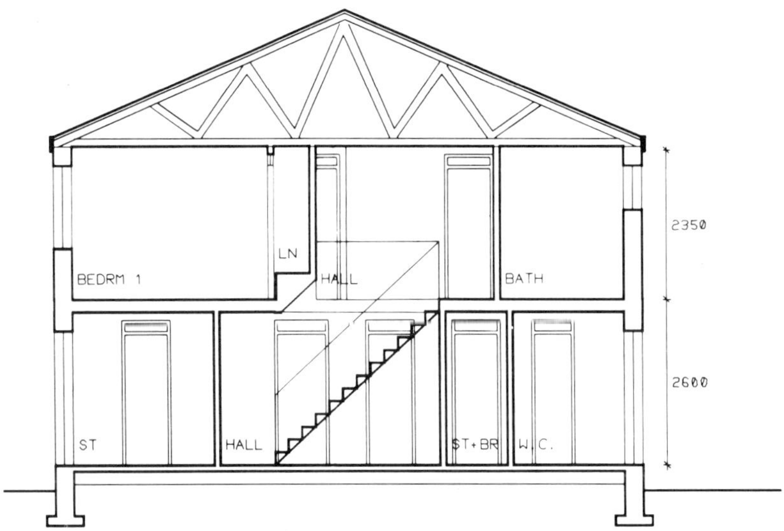

SECTION FROM FRONT TO BACK

(c)

fective cost and quality control. Automatic production of documentation assures consistency, accuracy, and compatibility between different documents.

As increasingly sophisticated building description systems are developed, it seems likely that numerous different integrated computer-aided architectural design systems will be built around them.

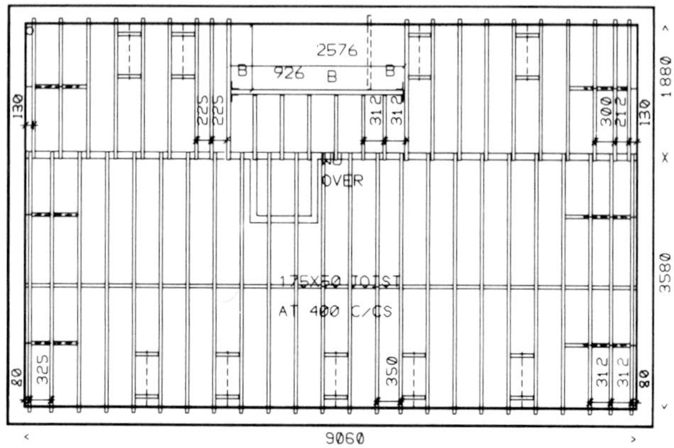

B = 1/175MM X 63MM
DWANGS 150MM X 50MM

SEE DETAIL 0621 FOR JOIST HANGERS
SEE DETAILS 0211 AND 0212 FOR WALL ANCHORS
NOTE: ANCHORS ON MUTUAL WALLS ARE OMITTED

FIRST FLOOR

(d)

GROUND FLOOR
ST+BR = 0.80 SQ.M
HTR = 0.64 SQ.M
KIT-DIN = 13.35 SQ.M
LIVING = 16.45 SQ.M
HALL = 2.07 SQ.M
ST = 1.84 SQ.M
ST = 0.40 SQ.M
HALL = 9.18 SQ.M
W.C. = 1.44 SQ.M

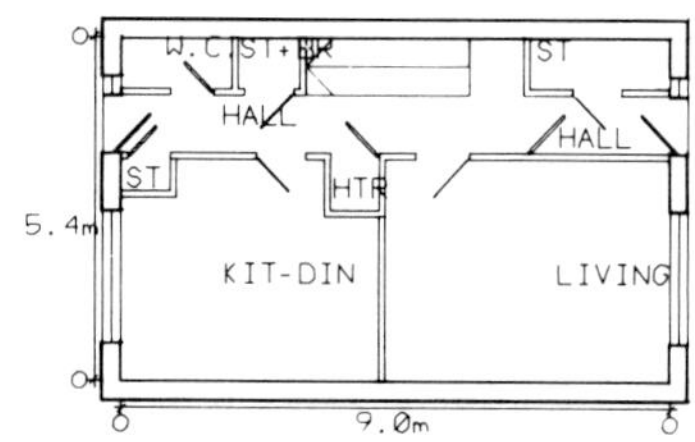

FIRST FLOOR
LN = 0.54 SQ.M
BEDRM 3 = 10.53 SQ.M
BEDRM 1 = 10.20 SQ.M
WU = 0.63 SQ.M
ST = 0.77 SQ.M
ST = 0.91 SQ.M
BEDRM 2 = 12.39 SQ.M
HALL = 6.44 SQ.M
BATH = 3.80 SQ.M

GROUND FLOOR STORAGE = 2.82 SQ.M
FIRST FLOOR STORAGE = 1.68 SQ.M
TOTAL STORAGE = 4.50 SQ.M

NETT SPACE = 92.70 SQ.M

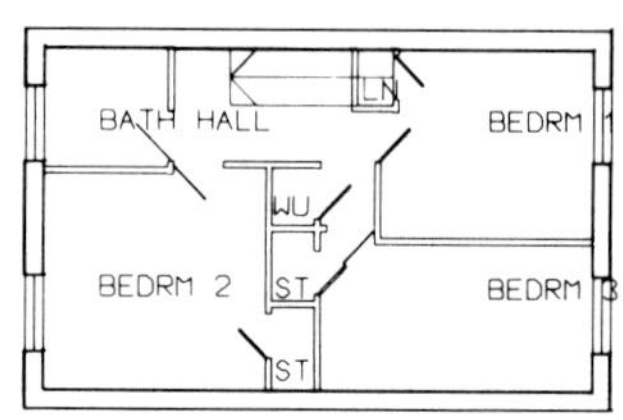

KITCHEN STORAGE
UNITS = 1.80 CU.M. (INCLUDES 0.49 CU.M. LARDER)
BROOMS = 0.53 CU.M. (0.22 SQ.M. FROM ST+BR)
TOTAL = 2.33 CU.M.

LINEN STORAGE = 1.30 CU.M.

HEAT LOADING IF DETACHED (NO FINES)
ROOF = 48.60 SQ.M X 0.550 W/SQ.MoC = 26.7 W/oC
WALL =133.56 SQ.M X 0.735 W/SQ.MoC = 98.2 W/oC
FLOOR = 48.60 SQ.M X 1.056 W/SQ.MoC = 51.3 W/oC
OPENINGS= 16.20 SQ.M X 5.678 W/SQ.MoC = 92.0 W/oC
TOTAL = 268.2 W/oC
AVERAGE U-VALUE FOR EXTERNAL WALL = 1.270 W/SQ.MoC

HEAT LOADING IF DETACHED (FCD BRWK)
ROOF = 48.60 SQ.M X 0.550 W/SQ.MoC = 26.7 W/oC
WALL =133.56 SQ.M X 0.688 W/SQ.MoC = 91.9 W/oC
FLOOR = 48.60 SQ.M X 1.056 W/SQ.MoC = 51.3 W/oC
OPENINGS= 16.20 SQ.M X 5.678 W/SQ.MoC = 92.0 W/oC
TOTAL = 261.9 W/oC
AVERAGE U-VALUE FOR EXTERNAL WALL = 1.228 W/SQ.MoC

(e)

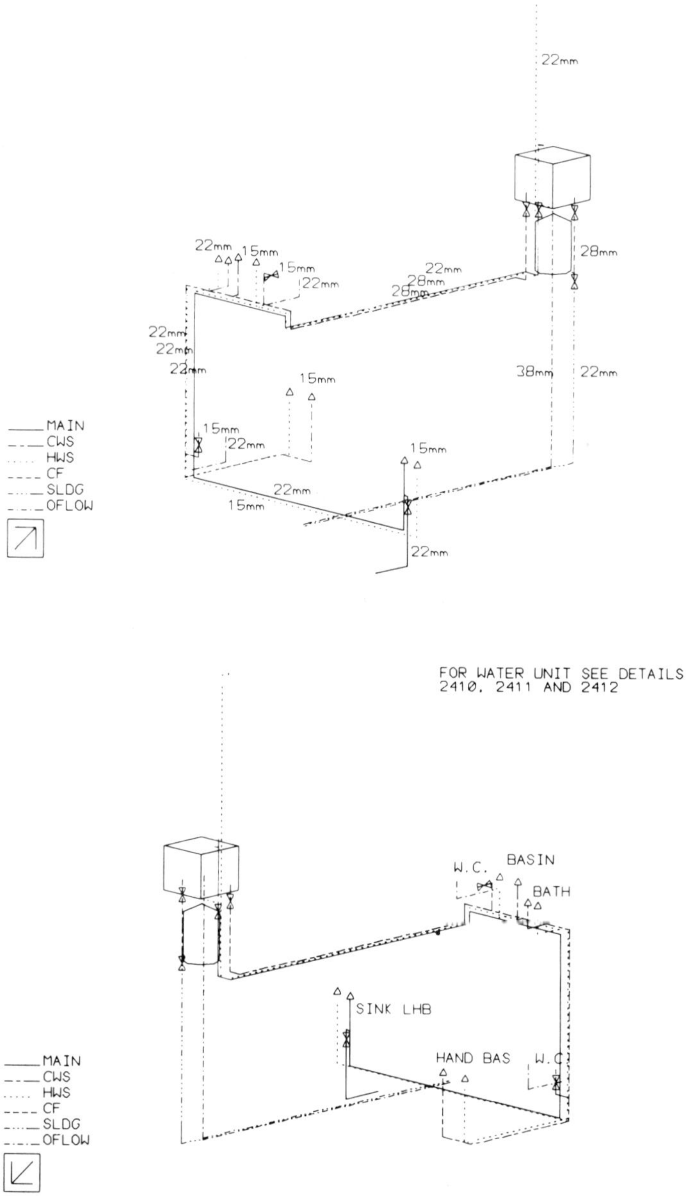

(f)

Computer-aided systems building

Under certain circumstances it may be very useful to consider a further level of integration: the integration of a computer-aided design system with a building system to produce a comprehensive building design and construction system. There are several potential advantages to this approach. The use of a consistent, rationalized building system, where choices of components are well and narrowly defined and where precise rules of assembly are specified, vastly simplifies the technical problems of computer software development. Not only is it possible to successfully implement automated analysis and documentation routines, it is also possible to develop quite powerful and sophisticated automated design synthesis routines for use in certain circumstances. The context of large-scale, repetitive building programs, in which economy and speed of construction are emphasized, is where industrialized building systems have shown themselves to be most effective; it is also likely to be where computer-aided design systems can have their greatest immediate impact.

A recent analysis of requirements for the development of such integrated systems (Hoskins 1973) concluded that the following are required, on the building system side, for full realization of the benefits of a comprehensive integrated system:

A manageable data base of components whose performance standards are known and assembly conditions pre-defined;

Design rules for location of components;

Design rules for arrangement of spaces;

Activity data for specification of spaces, fittings, and finishings;

Establishment of criteria for evaluation and optimization.

Basic requirements on the computer system side are:

A data base structure for ease of accessing and storage;

An ergonomically suitable user-command system;

Ergonomically suitable peripherals and terminals.

The organizational and economic implications of these requirements, according to the analysis, are very significant:

> It appears that such a system can most usefully be developed within a multiprofessional organization which has a large ongoing program of single-function buildings, or which makes use of a single building system and can therefore support development costs. Such an organization is likely to combine either "client and design" functions under one roof . . . such as a hospital board . . . or "design and build" functions . . . such as a package dealer. Individual professions or organizations concerned with a single aspect of the building process are unlikely to develop an integrated system themselves, although they might participate in development.

Thus the concept of comprehensive integrated systems does not appear to be very compatible with the traditional fragmentation of the construction industry or the traditional pattern of allocation of functions to members of the building team.

The most advanced work in development of large-scale computer-aided building systems appears to be taking place in the public sector in Britain, for the design offices of national authorities such as the Property Services Agency (PSA) and Department of Health and Social Security (DHSS), or for local and regional authorities. These public sector design organizations tend to have very large-scale ongoing building programs based on repetitive facility types (*e.g.*, hospitals, schools, etc.) and/or use of a particular building system. Hence they can provide the type of organizational and economic framework within which the development of highly integrated systems becomes most feasible. In addition, there has been a tradition of fairly substantial government support of computer-aided design research and development, beginning with the establishment of the Computer-Aided Design Centre at Cambridge in 1969, and leading to substantial funding for a series of prototype architectural systems in the early 1970's.

The pioneering integrated system in Britain was developed by the West Sussex County Council design offices in Chichester (Ray-Jones 1968, Paterson 1972, 1974). It was an interactive graphics system, employing refreshed cathode ray tube graphics terminals equipped with light pens and driven by an in-house IBM System/370 computer. West Sussex employs the SCOLA industrialized component building system, and utilizes a serial tendering relationship with contractors whereby bids are made to produce a certain volume of construction of a certain type for a certain price before the buildings to be produced have actually been designed. This allows prices to be accurately known at the design stage. The computer system provided facilities for interactive graphic descriptions of buildings, and cost analyses of SCOLA building designs (based on the known unit prices), plus environmental and structural evaluations, and automatically generated construction documentation. The building types handled included libraries, schools, and health care buildings. For a number of years the system was in everyday practical use, but by 1974 a change in policy had led to its discontinuation.

A more recent system, which also operates within the context of an unconventionally organized design and construction process, is the Harness hospital design system (Hoskins and Bott 1972, Meager 1972, 1973), sponsored by the U.K. Department of Health and Social Security. A Harness hospital is assembled by arranging standardized, pre-designed hospital departments along a circulation spine, as shown in *Figure 3.13*. Rules of assembly are defined for this kit-of-parts, so that the range of potential arrangements suitable for a given situation is well-defined and relatively small. Several different component building systems may be used for construction of Harness hospitals. The computer system, which is not dependent upon interactive graphics, performs tasks of structural, environmental and cost evaluation, automated generation of layouts, and production of documents. Due to the high level of standardization of Harness hospitals, the design process can be almost completely automated. The system is intended to deal with a hospital building program involving approximately $125,000,000 worth of building per year, although changes in the U.K. economic situation since the system was conceived now make the carrying out of this program very unlikely.

Several other large-scale systems, all using interactive graphics terminals and oriented towards the type of rectilinear post-beam-and-panel industrialized component building system shown in *Figure 3.14*, have recently been developed in Britain. The CEDAR 2 system (Chalmers 1972), sponsored by the Department of the Environment, was oriented toward construction of post office buildings using the SEAC (South East Architects Collaboration) component system. A pilot version was implemented in 1973. It provided capabilities for cost estimation, daylight, thermal, and acoustic analysis, detailed design of framing and external walling, and production of documentation. Another example is CARBS (Computer-Aided Rationalized Building System), developed by the Liverpool University Computer-Aided Design Center in collaboration with the Clwyd County, Architects Department (Daniel 1973). A typical design developed with the aid of CARBS is illustrated in *Figure 3.15*. CEDAR 2 and CARBS are basically design evaluation and documentation systems; the principal responsibility for design synthesis is allocated to human designers.

Conceptually one of the most advanced of these systems is OXSYS (Hoskins 1972), developed for design of hospitals in the Oxford Method of Building (*Figure 3.16*). It incorporates capabilities for cost estimation from early sketch designs, performing structural and environmental analyses, semi-automatic design and detailing, and production of documentation. The system was put into production in 1974. OXSYS is designed so that it is not restricted to one particular building system; component descriptions and assembly rules for different systems of the same general type may be loaded into the computer as data. The OXSYS approach appears to be an intelligent compromise between the immediate practical advantages of assuming a specific, narrow context of building type and construction system as exemplified by Harness and CEDAR 2, and the ultimate goal of achieving a high degree of generality and flexibility in automated architectural design systems.

Another fairly general system is CEDAR 3. Development work on this successor to CEDAR 2 was begun in 1975. It is intended for use in conjunction with the U.K. Government Property Services Agency's *Method of Building* (MOB). The MOB is not a component-based system, but a set of rules concerning dimensions, a set of ranges of preferred components, and a set of standard details. It is expected to deal with a wide range of building types. CEDAR 3 is intended for use at the sketch design stage, and its primary aim is to facilitate the comparison of alternative building geometrics and site layouts with respect to capital and running costs. It provides facilities for building description input and editing, cost analysis, elevator selection, thermal analysis, daylight calculations, and energy cost calculations.

A documentation-oriented system under development in Australia (Blue 1975) also avoids orientation towards any one particular

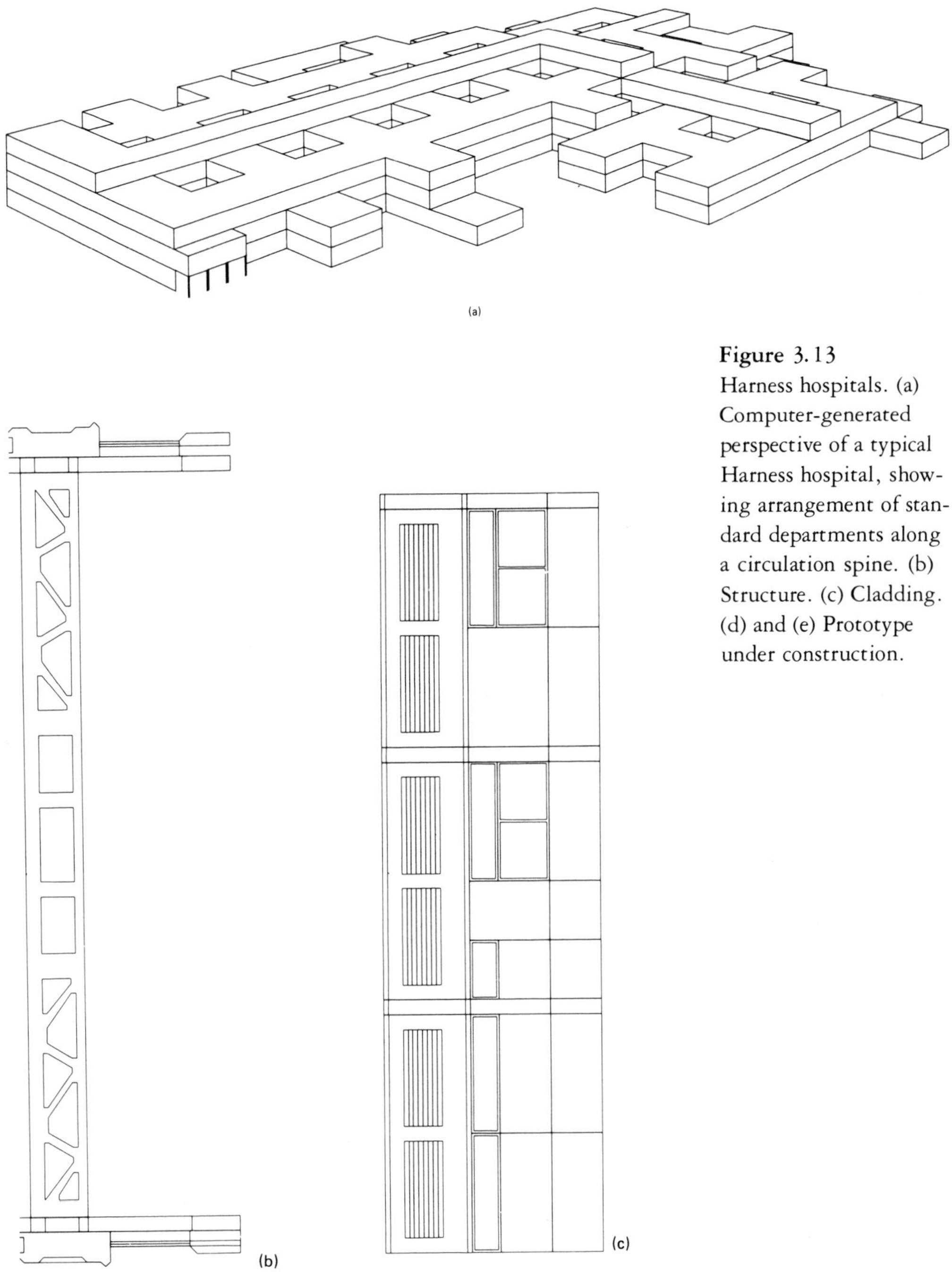

Figure 3.13
Harness hospitals. (a) Computer-generated perspective of a typical Harness hospital, showing arrangement of standard departments along a circulation spine. (b) Structure. (c) Cladding. (d) and (e) Prototype under construction.

building system. It relies instead upon use of a dimensionally coordinated method of building, which utilizes preferred dimensions for materials, components, and spaces, and thus limits the variety of potential assemblies to be dealt with.

(d)

(e)

The various systems discussed in this section have mostly been designed, implemented, and put into production in the period 1970–1977. They are very similar to one another, and may be regarded as a "first generation" of such systems. It can be expected

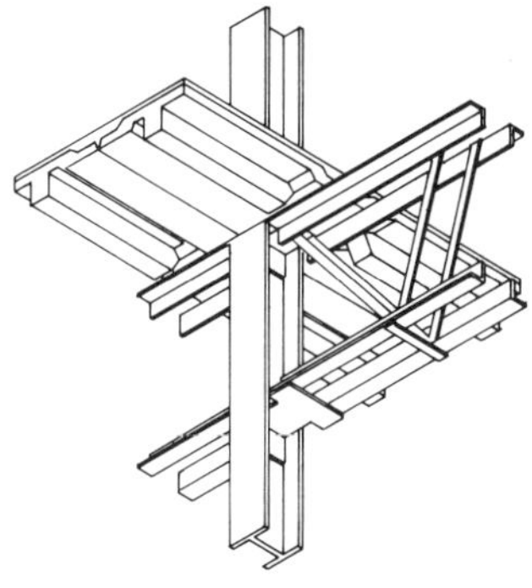

(a)

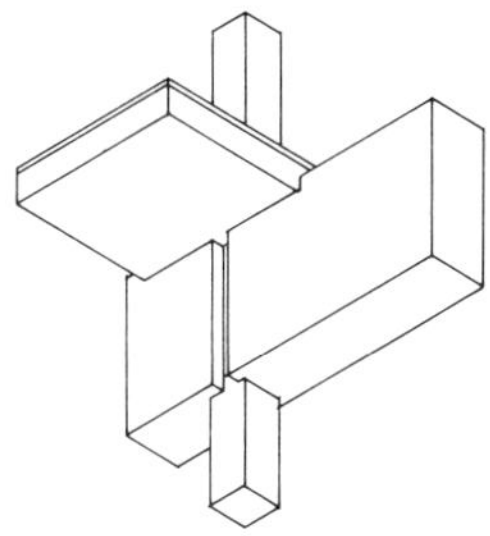

(b)

Figure 3.14 Post-beam-and-panel system. (a) Post-beam-and-panel system of construction. (b) Approximate representation of system geometry by orthogonal rectangular parallelepipeds.

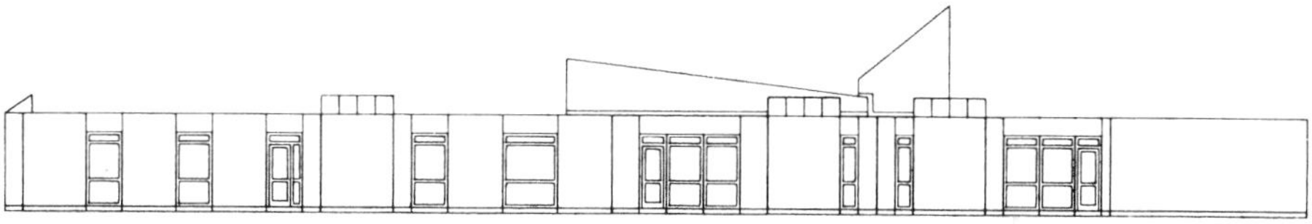

Cornist, south elevation

Figure 3.15 Drawing, produced by the CARBS system, of an industrialized component building.

that future systems will draw on knowledge gained during development of members of this first generation, and on experience gained of their use in practice, so that the second generation will incorporate a variety of new ideas.

Computer-aided design and future patterns of architectural practice

The continued development of cheap and powerful interactive computer graphics systems, together with the development of computer-based building description techniques, will shortly make it possible for almost any architect to work with sophisticated integrated computer-aided design systems. The effect of this development on the pattern of architectural practice will be revolutionary. Graphics terminals will largely replace drawing boards, and tape cassettes (or similar media) will largely replace drawings. It will be possible to undertake projects within much more compressed time frames. The ability

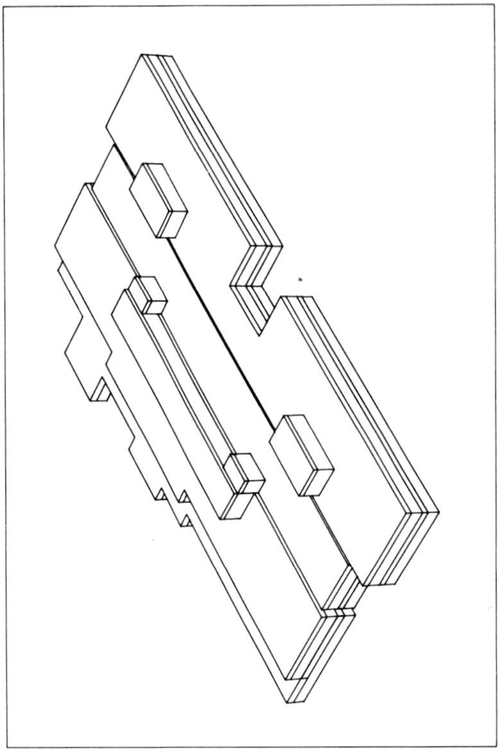

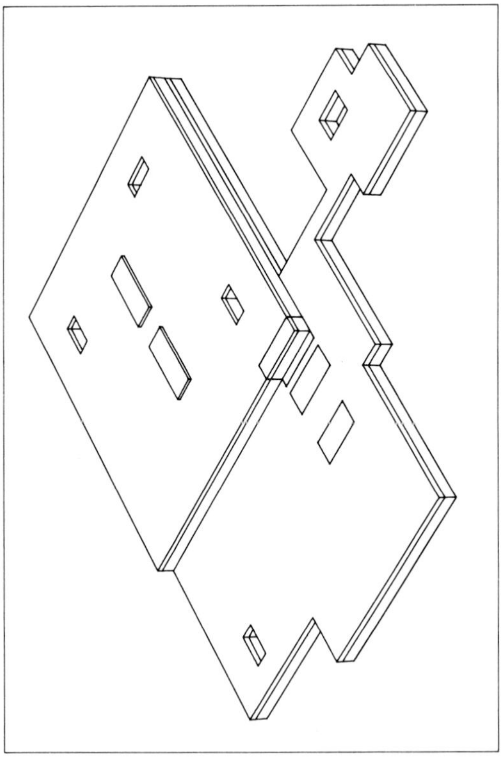

to integrate sophisticated analysis and optimization techniques into the design processes will make it possible to maintain much more effective cost control, and to respond more effectively to complex and subtle design constraints. Wider ranges of alternatives will be explored. Highly complex and sophisticated projects will be dealt with by comparatively small design teams. As some architectural firms begin to develop these new capabilities, clients will begin to demand them, and those firms which cannot provide them will find it very difficult to compete.

An important new professional role will emerge: that of the designer of design systems. People filling this role will need to combine a sound general knowledge of architecture with competence in computer science and technology. They will be responsible for design and implementation of architectural data base management systems, development of application programs, and integration of computer-aided design techniques into the design and construction process.

A second new professional role within design offices will be that of the data base manager. The data base manager role is now well-established within the many areas of business and industry that make extensive use of data base management systems, and increasing use of building description systems will certainly lead to a similar development within architectural offices. To perform this role, both architectural skills and substantial technical knowledge of data base technology will be required. Responsibilities of the data base manager will include selection, implementation, and maintenance of building description and other data base management systems, management control of data entry and report generation, and control of data quality and security.

The traditional patterns of use of specialist consultants are likely to alter. Many routine specialist tasks involved in structural and mechanical system design and evaluation, cost estimating, and so on, will be automated. Use of a centralized computer-based project file will enable much closer coordination of the work of specialists, and will allow specialists to collaborate on a continuous rather than an intermittent basis throughout the project (Building Research Station, 1969). The net effect of this development is likely to be that design teams will often be composed of relatively small groups of specialists working closely together within a single organization, with many of the management and coordination functions traditionally performed by the architect being taken care of by the computer system. Just as the building team structure which had emerged in the seventeenth and eighteenth centuries was superseded in the new context set by the industrial revolution of the nineteenth century, so it seems that the present essentially nineteenth-century structure will in turn be replaced as computer-aided building continues to develop.

In the long run, the utilization of cheap and powerful integrated computer-aided design systems may lead to disappearance of the role of the professional architectural designer as we know it. Just as the

Figure 3.16 *(opposite)* Several alternative designs generated using OXSYS, for a hospital in the Oxford Method.

introduction of printed books meant that literacy and learning would no longer be the exclusive domain of a few priests and scribes, so the introduction of widely available, powerful design aids will mean that the ability to design will no longer be confined to those with specialized technical knowledge and skills.

SUGGESTED READINGS

Auger, B. *The Architect and the Computer.* New York: Praeger, 1972.

Carter, J. "Computers and the Architect." Series of four articles. *Architects' Journal,* 3 October 1973; 10 October 1973; 24 October 1973; and 31 October 1973.

Foxhall, W. B. *Techniques of Successful Practice for Architects and Engineers.* New York: McGraw-Hill, 1975.

Higgin, G., and Jessop, N. *Communications in the Building Industry.* London: Tavistock Publications, 1965.

Krauss, R. I., and Myer, J. R. "Design: A Case History," in *Emerging Methods in Environmental Design and Planning,* edited by G. T. Moore. Cambridge, Mass.: MIT Press, 1970.

Lee, K. *Computer Programs in Environmental Design.* Boston, Mass.: Environmental Design Research Center, 1974.

McCue, G. M.; Ewald, W. R.; and The Midwest Research Center. *Creating the Human Environment.* Urbana, Illinois: University of Illinois Press, 1970.

PART 2

DATA BASES

In this Part, we turn to consideration of a centrally important technical issue: techniques for encoding, structuring, and storing in computer memory the data to be operated upon in computer-aided architectural design applications. Chapter 4: *Data Structures,* provides an introductory analysis of the problem and discusses general principles of data structure design and implementation. Chapters 5, 6, 7 and 8 extend the analysis to specific types of data bases and data structures that have proven useful in computer-aided architectural design, and critically discuss numerous examples. Although some illustrative examples of applications are included here, detailed consideration of the problem solving programs which operate upon architectural data bases is postponed to Part 4: *Problem Solving.*

4 Data Structures

This chapter introduces some fundamental principles of data structure design. Broadly speaking, a data structure is a relationship between a collection of data items. Such a relationship can be defined in many ways, for example, by means of diagrams on paper, mathematical expressions, or statements in a programming language. In this chapter, we first consider in a general way the types of data items and relations on those data items that may be useful in building description. Then computer data storage technology is introduced, and tools for constructing data structures in computer memory are described. In subsequent chapters, the structures of various different types of computer implemented data bases that may be employed in computer-aided architectural design are considered in detail: non-geometric building descriptions, descriptions of building geometry, standard element and detail library files, and site descriptions.

SYMBOLIC DESCRIPTION OF BUILDING DESIGNS

Elements

In order to develop a systematic method for symbolic description of a building, it is first necessary to conceive of the building as divisible into a collection of discrete *elements,* and to devise a notation for identifying and describing the relevant properties of each of these elements. The elements employed as the basis for a description might, for example, be abstract geometric entities such as square or cubic modules, functional elements such as rooms, or physical components such as columns, beams, and slabs. For different purposes, it is appropriate to utilize descriptions based upon different types of entities. Thus a circulation analysis might employ a description of a building as a set of rooms, while a structural analysis would employ a description in terms of physical components.

Attributes

The next step is to decide which *attributes* of an element should be described. Attributes might be geometric (*e.g.,* dimensions, location), physical (*e.g.,* weight, thermal conductivity), economic (*e.g.,* cost, availability) or of any other kind relevant to the applications for which the description is being developed.

There is often a choice to make between explicit storage of an attribute and calculations from other data as required. For example, the area of a rectangular room is indirectly represented if the length and width are stored; it can be calculated as required. But if an algorithm repeatedly is to require area data, it may be appropriate to store it explicitly, thus saving computation at the cost of increased storage requirements.

Relations

In addition to describing elements, it may also be necessary to describe various *relations* which may exist between elements. The types of relations that need to be described depend upon the task at hand. For a circulation analysis, for instance, it would be important to express the adjacencies and circulation connections of rooms in the plan, while for a structural analysis the types of structural connections between members might need to be described.

Relations may either be expressed explicitly, *i.e.,* by storing some data, or implicitly by virtue of location within the data structure. For example, an explicitly stored attribute of a room might be a list of adjacent rooms. Alternatively, adjacency between rooms might be implicitly represented by storing descriptions of adjacent rooms at adjacent locations in memory.

Just as there is often a choice to be made between storage and calculation of attributes, so there is often a choice between storage and calculation of relations. For example, a floor plan layout algorithm might require data indicating the distances between centroids of rooms located in plan. Where there are n rooms, there are $(n^2 - n)$ such distance relations to be considered. One possible approach would be to store these distances in the form of a n x n matrix. Another approach, requiring less storage but more computation during execution of the algorithm, would be to store coordinates of centroids and to calculate distances as required.

Subsets and hierarchies

It is often useful to conceive of a building as consisting of a hierarchy of subsets of entities. For example, we might say that a building consists of (*owns*) a set of major departments, each department owns a set of suites, each suite owns a set of rooms, each room owns a set of surfaces, each surface owns a set of components, and so on. Different design algorithms may utilize descriptions at different levels in such a hierarchy. For instance, a site plan layout algorithm might appropriately treat a building as a set of major wings to be located, while a detailed cost analysis algorithm would treat it as a set of components. For this reason, comprehensive building descriptions which are intended to be operated upon by a variety of different algorithms are typically structured in hierarchical fashion.

Factoring of data

Buildings typically include many standard elements. For example, a particular window unit might be repeated hundreds of times on the facade of an office building. It would clearly be uneconomically repetitive to give detailed descriptions of that unit hundreds of times. Instead, it would probably be more appropriate to store *one* detailed description, plus a list of locations of *instances* which occur in the building. This type of factoring of data to eliminate repetition in stored building descriptions is very commonly utilized in the design of data structures for building description.

Use of mathematical and logical formalisms *

Very often, it is useful to express building descriptions in terms of the conventions of some established mathematical or logical formalism. For example, the dimensions and locations of elements might be expressed in terms of x, y, and z coordinates, in a Cartesian coordinate system, of the vertices of forms. To express interrelations between elements of a building, some form of interaction matrix

* See Chapter 6 for more detailed discussion of these techniques.

might be employed. If topological properties are an important concern, then the formalism of graph theory might be utilized.

Associated with the various different formalisms are developed bodies of theory which can often be exploited to great advantage in problem solving. For example, if geometric data can be expressed in terms of Cartesian coordinates, then all the theorems and techniques of analytical geometry, of transformation by means of homogeneous coordinate techniques, and so on, become applicable. Similarly, expression of data in matrix form allows the techniques of matrix algebra to be applied, expression in terms of graph theory allows utilization of the extensive body of theorems associated with that branch of mathematics, etc. Usually the choice of a formalism for expression of data is guided by the intent to employ some particular theorems or algorithms associated with that formalism to the problem at hand.

Access and updating requirements

In execution of a particular program, some of the information stored in a building description may be accessed frequently, and other information infrequently. Data may be accessed either in random sequence, or in some predetermined order. Questions asked of the description may be of several different types. For example, "What is the *n*th element?", "What are the attributes of a given element?", "What elements have a given attribute?", "What elements are related to a given element in a given way?", or "What relation exists between a given pair of elements?" In developing a description for a particular purpose, it is necessary to consider the expected pattern of data access, and to organize the structure of the description in such a way that the most frequent access operations are facilitated.

A particularly important requirement in most architectural applications is to have the ability to access data by *spatial* properties, *i.e.,* to ask such questions as "Which columns fall within room *n*?" "Does element *a* intersect element *b*?", or "Is element *a* located within *n* feet of element *b*?". Techniques of access by spatial property are known as methods of *spatial search* (Eastman and Lividini, 1976).

In some applications, for example in interactive computer graphics systems, it is often necessary to insert data into the description and delete data from the description. Thus the organization of the data structure must allow for rapid and efficient performance of these operations. In other situations, updating of the description may only occur at relatively infrequent intervals, and thus ease of updating may not be a major determinant of data structure design. In the extreme case, the description may be completely static.

When an item of information is inserted, deleted, or altered, other information in the building description may need to be altered in order to maintain consistency. For example, altering the "length" attribute of a room may require alteration of the "area" and "volume" attributes as well. This update information might be manually entered by the user, or automatically generated by the program. In either case, facilitation of the task of maintaining consistency is likely to be a consideration in structuring the building description.

Level of sophistication required

Some computer-aided design tasks require very complex and sophisticated building descriptions for operation upon. For other tasks, very simple descriptions will suffice. In general, the simplest type of description that is adequate should be employed.

A discussion by Clark (1967) has usefully distinguished several different categories of computer-aided design tasks, classified according to the level of complexity and sophistication required of the stored building description:

> Simple tasks of counting, grouping and tabulating building elements or calculating quantities of material do not require much more than consistent formats for input data and punch card machines or simple computer programs. We will refer to such tasks as representative of the *enumeration* type.
>
> More difficult tasks may require information on locations, areas, or distances to be derived. These we will label as the *spatial reference* type . . .
>
> For some types of analysis tasks the information on connectivity and shared elements is of major importance. Examples include some kinds of structural frame analysis and circulation studies. This we will call the *relational* type.
>
> Finally, some analyses require information on the flow of a process, the level of use of a connecting link, the relationships that determine distribution and equilibrium in a network, etc. We will lump all such requirements together as the *performance* type . . .
>
> These types of requirements have been stated roughly in order of increasing complexity and information content. They are not exclusive, and requirements for several together are obvious. Generally, the more complex requirements subsume the lesser ones, in the sense that requirements for *relational* data also imply *spatial reference* and *enumeration* needs.

PHYSICAL ORGANIZATION OF DATA IN COMPUTER MEMORY

In considering how to store a symbolic building description in computer memory, it is useful to draw a clear distinction between *physical* and *logical* structures of the organization of data. A physical structures describes the actual pattern of data in computer memory, and its representation by means of physical devices such as core memory, disks, tapes, etc. A logical structures is concerned with the way in which data and relations on data are expressed using the facilities of a programming language or data base management system. Many different physical structures may usually be employed to implement a specified logical structure. It is usually desirable for the logical structure to be as independent as possible from particular physical structures, and for the operations employed to perform physical manipulations to be "transparent" to the application programmer. (For further discussion of the distinction between physical and logical organization see Mealy (1968), Engles (1970), Gray (1970), and Martin (1975).) Although we will primarily be concerned here with the logical description of data structures, a brief discussion of the physical organization of data in computer memory will first be necessary.

Types of storage media

Most computer systems employ a combination of several different types of storage media: high-speed core memory for *primary storage,* plus magnetic disks (or cylinders), and magnetic tape for *auxiliary storage.* These different media may be conveniently classified into three categories: *high-speed random access, lower-speed random access,* and *serial access,* depending upon the ways in which items of data can be accessed by the central processing unit.

High-speed random access memory

High-speed random access memory usually employs magnetic cores as the storage media. Each core can take two states, denoted 0 and 1. Thus each memory element can represent one *bit* of information. However, the items of information that computers manipulate are normally represented by groups of bits, so it is convenient to have some larger units of storage. It has been common, since the introduction of IBM 360 computers, to use a unit composed of 8 bits, known as a *byte* for this purpose. A byte can have $2^8 = 256$ different states. By use of a suitable coding scheme, these 256 states can be used to represent all the digits, letters, and symbols found on a normal keyboard. Generally, the smallest unit in memory that can be addressed in a computer is a byte. For most programming purposes though, it is convenient to utilize a larger unit of storage than the byte, called a *word.* Typically, a word contains 4 bytes, *i.e.,* 32 bits. (It should be noted, however, that terminology and conventions are not consistently used. On some computers 6-bit bytes are used, and words of 8, 12, 16, 18, 24, 36, and 64 bits are employed.) Minicomputers and microcomputers usually have smaller words than larger machines.

Associated with each location in core memory is a number referred to as its *address.* Given the address of a location, the CPU can access its contents in an extremely short period of time. The time taken to access the contents of a location in this way is very short, and is not dependent on its address. Hence the name "random" access.

An increasingly popular alternative to core memory is semiconductor memory, composed of numerous minute transistors and fabricated on tiny silicon chips. Semiconductor memories are less bulky than core memories, require less power, and are less expensive. They are of two basic types: *read-only memories* (ROM's) and *read-write memories* (RAM's). ROM's, as the name implies, are employed for permanent storage of programs and data tables. They cannot be altered during operation of the computer. ROM's are usually programmed by a chip manufacturer, using a process of permanently "burning" the required bit pattern. This process is quite expensive, so it is normally only used for large-quantity production. Special types of ROM's, known as PROM's (programmable random access memory), may be reprogrammed using special equipment, and are used for lower quantity production. Semiconductor RAM's are employed in a similar way to core RAM's.

Memory capacity is usually described in units of 1024 (2^{10}) words, referred to as a "K". Small computers typically have memories of 4, 8, 16 or 32K, while larger machines may have up to 1000K or more.

Lower-speed random access memory media

The most common lower-speed random access device is the *magnetic disk.* A disk is a flat circular plate coated with ferromagnetic oxide, as illustrated in *Figure 4.1.* The surface of the disk is divided into concentric circular *tracks,* upon which information is represented by small polarized spots, and each track is subdivided into *sectors.* A sector is the smallest practically addressable unit on a disk, and is thus analogous to a byte in core memory. However, a sector typically stores 512 or 1,024 bytes of information.

Disks are usually stacked in packs. These packs are rotated at high speed by a disk drive, and read/write heads can move in and out between the disks in the pack to access any particular track. All the tracks which can be accessed from a given position of the read/write

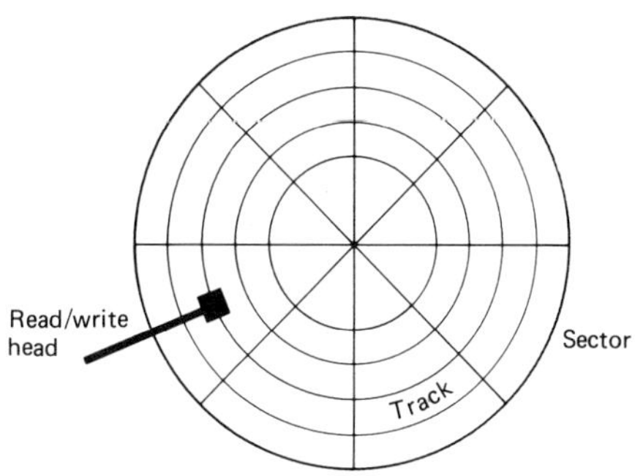

Figure 4.1
Schematic diagram of a magnetic desk.

heads constitute a *cylinder*. Thus cylinders, tracks, and sectors form a hierarchy of physical storage units.

Each cylinder, track, and sector has an identifying number. Data stored at a particular address on disk can thus be accessed by means of the following process:

1. Move the read/write heads to the specified cylinder.
2. Activate the head corresponding to the specified track.
3. Begin reading from or writing on the sector when its starting point rotates beneath the head.

The time taken to access a sector depends upon the time taken to move the heads to the required position (the *seek time*), and the time taken for the starting point of the sector to rotate around to the head (the *rotational delay*). Clearly there will be some variation in access time, depending upon the previous position of the heads, and the position of the starting point of the sector.

A number of variations upon this basic principle of disk storage are possible. Instead of moving read/write heads from cylinder to cylinder, for example, a separate head may be provided for each cylinder. This is a more expensive arrangement, but results in faster access times. Occasionally, rotating drums equipped with multiple heads are used in place of disks. An important recent innovation has been the introduction of "floppy" disks. These are small, flexible plastic disks which look rather like gramophone records. They have the advantages of being cheap, robust, and portable; and it seems likely that they will find increasingly extensive applications.

Disk memories allow much larger quantities of data to be stored much more cheaply than in core memory, but the time taken to access an item of information is considerably greater.

Serial access media

As the name implies, serial access media, such as magnetic and paper tapes, must be read strictly serially. This is a great disadvantage unless the order of access of data is either immaterial or can be predicted in advance and the order of data on the tape arranged accordingly. However, serial storage media are very cheap, their capacity is essentially unlimited, and they are robust, compact, and portable.

Traditionally, computer tapes have been kept on reels, which can be mounted on reel-to-reel tape drives as required. More recently, computer tape cassettes of various kinds have been introduced. These are very convenient to store and handle, and are finding wide application in minicomputer systems.

Comparative advantages and disadvantages

The comparative advantages and disadvantages of the different types of storage media may be summarized as follows:

Medium	*Access time*	*Cost per byte*	*Capacity*
High-speed random access	Fast (millionths of seconds)	High	Low (thousands or millions of bytes)
Lower-speed random access	Slower (hundredths of seconds)	Lower	Higher (tens of millions of bytes)
Serial access	Very slow (seconds or minutes)	Very low	Essentially unlimited (hundreds of millions of bytes)

Most computer systems employ a hierarchy of storage media in order to exploit the advantages and minimize the disadvantages. Data currently needed for execution of programs can be kept in core. Data for which the need is less immediate can be kept in auxiliary disk storage, ready to be read into core as required. Data needed only relatively infrequently can be kept on tape which is loaded and read as required.

THE DATA STRUCTURING PRIMITIVES OF PROGRAMMING LANGUAGES

Fortunately, in order to create a building description in computer memory, it is not necessary for an application programmer to describe directly how the information is to be physically organized in memory. Instead, the data structure may be expressed using statements in a programming or data description * language. It is then the function of the software to automatically translate the programmer's logical description into an appropriate physical storage organization.

In this section, we will discuss the storage and retrieval of data in high-speed random access memory, using the data structuring primitives of programming languages. We will consider the different types of *primitive data items* that are operated upon by a computer program, how these items are *named,* and how they may be combined into more complex *structures.*

Primitive data items

Words in core memory may be employed to store the primitive data items, *i.e.,* values of individual variables, upon which programs

* See Data Base Management Systems in this chapter.

operate. Variables are classified according to the *type* of data which their values represent, *i.e.*, *integer* (or *fixed-point*) numbers, *real* or (*floating-point*) numbers, *logical* values (.TRUE.or.FALSE.), and *character strings* (*e.g.*, 'CHAR').

For various computational purposes *binary* (base 2), *octal* (base 8) and *hexadecimal* (base 16) number systems are employed. But common programming languages like FORTRAN allow all numerical values to be expressed in the conventional *decimal* (base 10) number system, and we will not be concerned here with values of variables expressed in any other system.

Since the number of bits in a word is limited, there are limitations upon the sizes of numbers and character strings which can be assigned to variables. For example, the 32-bit words of an IBM 370 computer allow storage of integers in the range -2^{31} to $(2^{31}-1)$, *i.e.*, -2147483648 to 2147483647 (one of the 32 bits is used to represent the sign of the number). Floating-point numbers ranging in magnitude from $0.5397605 \times 10^{-78}$ (approximately) to 0.7237005×10^{76} (approximately) can be represented to a precision of seven significant decimal digits. By use of more than one word to store a number, however, higher precision can be achieved. Strings of up to four characters can be stored in a single word.

Names and structures

When a program is written in a low-level language like machine code or some assembly codes, primitive data items are referred to by specifying the actual address of the item in memory. A programming language, on the other hand, normally allows an item to be referred to by *variable name*. When the name is given in a statement, the computer automatically establishes the corresponding address and accesses the item. This facility enables the writing of very concise statements like the following:

A = B + C

which may be interpreted as, "Take the number in the location named B, add it to the number in the location named C, and store the result in the location named A."

Often it is convenient to refer to a collection of related variables (*i.e.*, a data structure) by using a common name in conjunction with a numeric index. For example, it may be convenient to refer to the rooms of a building as ROOM(1), ROOM(2) . . . etc. Most programming languages allow for the use of such arithmetically constructed variable names in programs. The facilities provided for naming and manipulating these collections of variables are the data structuring primitives of the language. Different languages provide primitives for dealing with different types of data structures, organized according to different principles. The following paragraphs discuss some of the more common and important types.

Arrays *

The most common and familiar type of data structure, for which almost all common programming languages make provision, is known as an *array*. An array consists of individual words occupying successive locations in memory, and identified by array name and subscript (*Figure 4.2*). For example, the FORTRAN † programming language provides a primitive known as the DIMENSION statement for creation of arrays. Thus the FORTRAN statement

DIMENSION X(10)

creates an array called X, consisting of 10 consecutive words in memory (*Figure 4.2(a)*). FORTRAN arrays must be defined before the program actually begins execution, and are of fixed size. However some other languages *e.g.*, PL/1, EULER (Wirth and Weber 1966), allow for creation and dimensioning of arrays during execution of the program. For example, execution of the EULER statement ‡

X ← ARRAY [Y];

results in creation of an array called X of a dimension determined by the current value of the integer variable Y.

To access an item of data stored in an array, the subscript is given. Thus X (5) refers to the fifth word in the array, and execution of the FORTRAN statement

A = X(5)

results, for example, in the value of X(5) being assigned to A.

If the subscript of an item is not known, then the array must be *searched* in order to access that item. The simplest search method is simply to scan through the array in sequence. If the entries in the array are ordered in some way (*e.g.*, alphabetically), some more efficient procedure may be possible. (Knuth (1973) has published a definitive discussion of search methods.)

* For some examples of practical applications of arrays, see Representations Based on Regular Grids and Lattices in Chapter 6.

† Descriptions of all languages discussed in this chapter will be found in Sammet (1969) unless otherwise noted.

‡ The symbol "←" (read as "gets") signifies the operation of assignment. Use of parentheses ( ) as in FORTRAN or brackets [ ] as in EULER is simply a matter of different conventions adopted in the two languages.

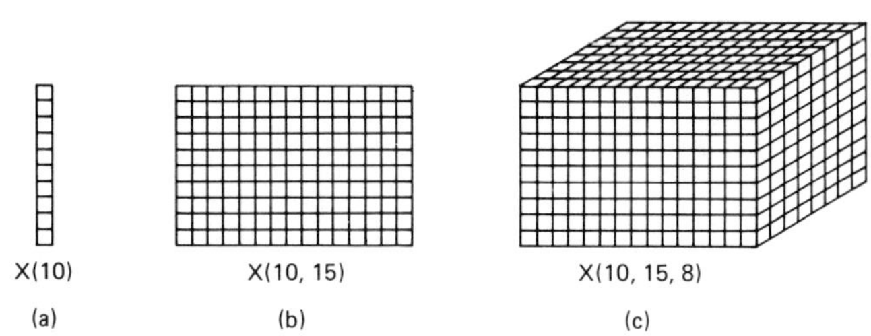

Figure 4.2 Arrays. (a) One-dimensional. (b) Two-dimensional. (c) Three-dimensional.

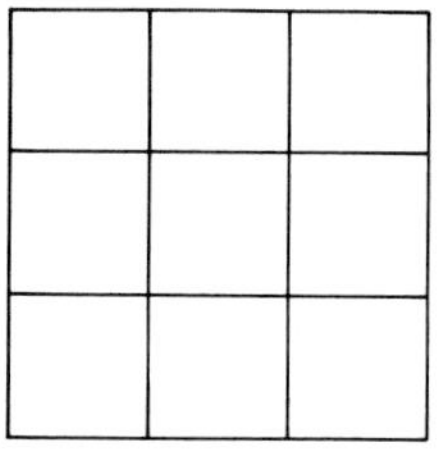

X←ARRAY[3, 3];

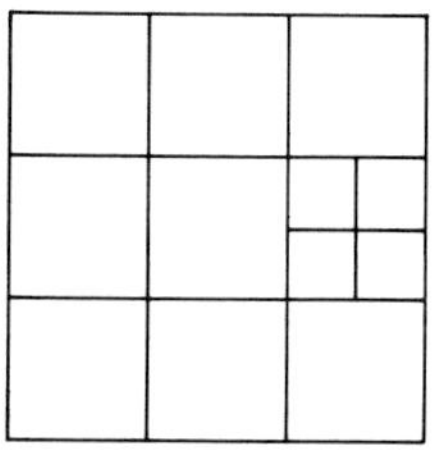

X[2, 3] ←ARRAY[2, 2];

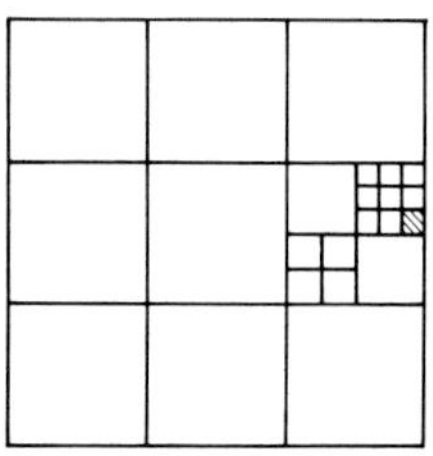

X[2, 3] [1, 2] ←ARRAY[3, 3];
X[2, 3] [2, 1] ←ARRAY[2, 2];

Figure 4.3
Hierarchical arrays.

The types of arrays which have been discussed so far are useful for storage of linearly-related collections of data, for example, a list of room areas. But some collections of data, for example, the entries in a matrix, are ordered in two dimenisons. In this case, a two-dimensional array, in which two subscripts are employed, could be utilized. For example, the FORTRAN DIMENSION statement

```
DIMENSION X(10,15)
```

created an array suitable for storing a 10×15 matrix (*Figure 4.2(b)*). Similarly, three-dimensional arrays employing three subscripts, four-dimensional arrays employing four subscripts, and so on, can be created (*Figure 4.2(c)*).

A few languages also allow for construction of hierarchical arrays as illustrated in *Figure 4.3*. For example, execution of the sequence of EULER statements

```
X ← ARRAY [3,3];
X [2,3]←ARRAY [2,2];
X [2,3][1,2] ← ARRAY [3,3];
X [2,3][2,1] ← ARRAY [2,2];
```

produces the result (in conceptual terms) shown. An extended subscripting technique is used to refer to particular words in the array, thus the element which is cross-hatched in the figure is referred to as X [2,3][1,2][3,3].

Lists *

A second common and important type of data structure is a *list*. The concept of a list is based on drawing a distinction between the *physical* and *logical* sequence of words in memory. The elements of a list may be thought of as cells, each of which is divided into two parts as shown in *Figure 4.4(a)*. The first part contains an item of information, as in a word in an array, and the second part contains a number which gives the address in memory of the next item in logical sequence. These numbers are referred to as *pointers,* since they may be thought of as "pointing" to locations of items of information in memory, and lists are commonly diagrammed on paper by representing the pointers as arrows (*Figure 4.4(b)*). An additional pointer is required to indicate the location of the *head* (beginning) of the list. The pointer from the *tail* (end) contains a special null value.

Drawing this distinction between physical and logical sequence allows for much greater flexibility in inserting, deleting, and rearranging items of information in data structures. If, for example, an item is to be inserted into a one-dimensional array, it is necessary

* For some examples of practical applications of lists, see Breadth-First and Depth-First Search Methods, and Shortest Path Calculations in Chapters 13 and 14, respectively.

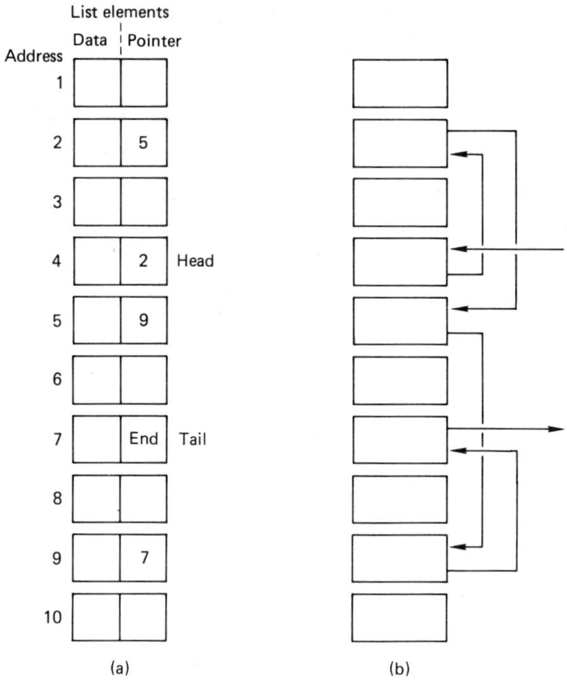

Figure 4.4
Use of pointers to create a list structure. (a) Logical sequence of data indicated by pointers. (b) Pointers illustrated by arrows.

to "open up a space" by "pushing down" items by the procedure shown in *Figure 4.5(a)*. This is cumbersome, and can involve considerable computation if the array is lengthy. But the insertion of an item in a list merely involves assigning values to two pointers (*Figure 4.5(b)*). No currently stored data need be shifted to accommodate the new item. The price which must be paid for this flexibility is that, in order to discover the address of a required item of information in a list, it is necessary to "follow the pointers" in sequence from the beginning of the list. (In an array, it will be recalled, the address is directly determined from the subscripts.) This means that, especially if the list is lengthy, it is likely to take significantly longer for the CPU to access an item of information held in a list rather than an array. Furthermore, storage of pointers of course consumes additional memory.

Important special types of lists are *stacks, queues,* and *deques.* A stack is a list in which entries are inserted and deleted on a last-in-first-out (LIFO) basis, as in a stack of trays at a cafeteria. A queue is maintained on a first-in-first-out (FIFO) basis. In a deque, entries and deletions are made at both ends.

Not all popular programming languages have list processing primitives. FORTRAN for example does not, although there is a subroutine package known as SLIP (Weizenbaum 1963) which may be used to add list-processing capabilities to standard FORTRAN. Some languages, such as IPL-V, and LISP are specifically oriented towards use of lists, and are known as *list-processing* languages for that

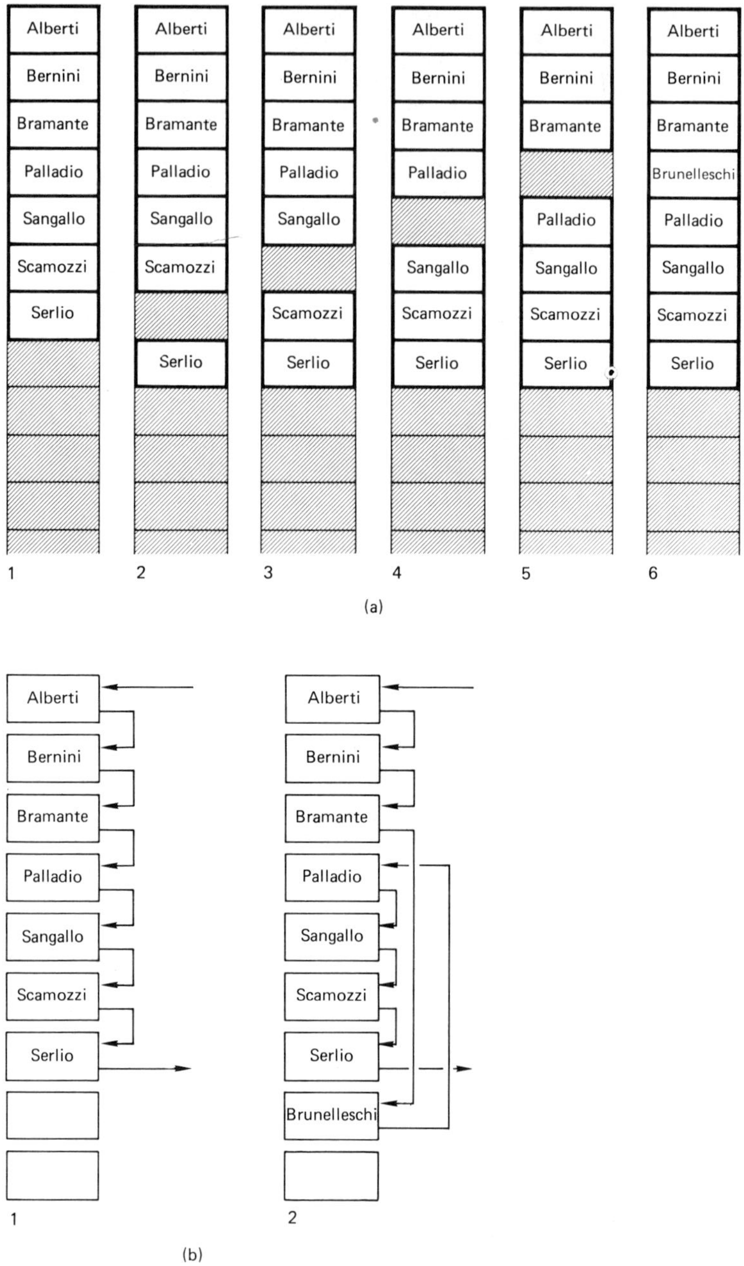

Figure 4.5
Insertion of new items into lists and arrays. (a) Procedure for opening up a space and inserting a new item in an alphabetized sequence of names stored in array. (b) Insertion of the item into a list.

reason. Some general purpose languages incorporate list-processing along with other types of data structuring primitives.

A variety of types of statements are employed to construct and manipulate lists. In the EULER language, for example, the statement

X ← LIST [20];

constructs a list called X consisting of 20 cells;

X ← LIST [Y];

constructs a list of size determined by the current value of the variable Y;

X ← LIST [ ];

constructs a list of undefined length; and

X ← [A,B,C,D,E];

constructs a list of length 5 containing the current values of the variables A,B,C,D,E. Items of information stored in lists may be referred to by giving subscripts, as in arrays. Statements are also available for performing a variety of useful operations on lists. For example

INSERT I1 AFTER X[3];

inserts an item called I1 after the third element of X;

REMOVE 2 : X;

deletes the second element of X, and

Z ← X & Y;

concatenates lists X and Y to form a new list Z.

Trees

Slightly more complex structures, known as *trees,* may be built up by assigning lists to the elements of lists. Thus the EULER statements

X ← LIST [3];
X [1] ← LIST [2];
X [2] ← LIST [3];
X [1] [2] ← LIST [2];

create the tree structure shown in *Figure 4.6.*

Other pointer-implemented structures

In addition to simple list and trees, a wide variety of other data structures make use of pointers. Some examples are illustrated in *Figure 4.7. Two-way threaded lists* (*Figure 4.7*(*a*)) allow pointers to be followed in both directions. *Multi-linked lists* (*Figure 4.7*(*b*)) allow several different sequences to be followed. *Rings* * (*Figure 4.7*(*c*)) are lists connected head-to-tail, which may be entered at any point. *Networks*

* See Sparse Matrix Techniques in Chapter 6 for an interesting application of a ring structure.

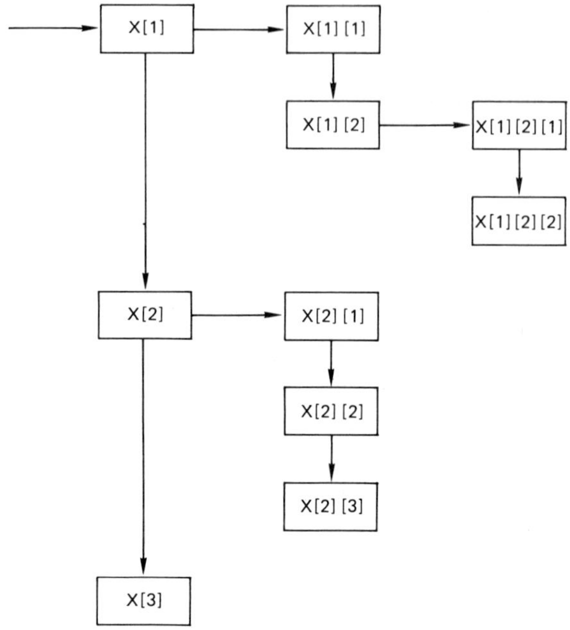

Figure 4.6
A tree structure.

(*Figure 4.7(d)*) of various types can be used to define very complex patterns of association between items of information. A few specialized languages provide primitives for dealing with these types of structures.

Figure 4.7
Examples of pointer-implemented data structures. (a) Two-way threaded list. (b) Multi-linked list. (c) Ring. (d) Network.

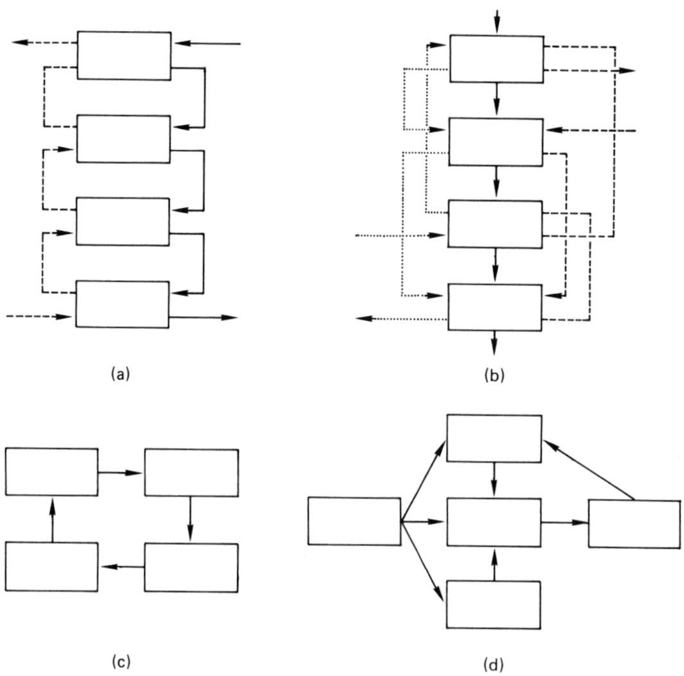

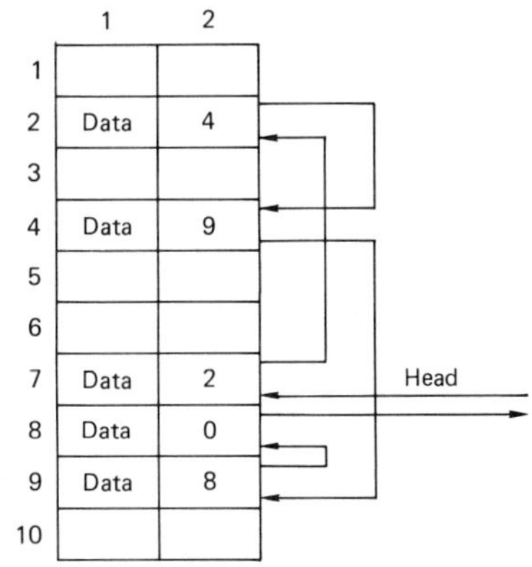

Figure 4.8
Simulation of a list using an array.

Simulation of pointer-implemented structures using arrays

If a language does not include primitives for handling pointer-implemented structures, it may be possible to simulate them using arrays. Simple list structures may be simulated using FORTRAN arrays, for example, as shown in *Figure 4.8.* An n × 2 array is treated as a "memory" in which each row is an element of a list. The first word in each row contains an item of information, and the second word contains a "pointer" giving the subscript of the next row in logical sequence. The "pointer" from the last element in the "list" contains a special null value, indicating the end. Simple FORTRAN subroutines can be written for manipulation of this type of "list." Since FORTRAN is very widely used, the subject of how to simulate more sophisticated data structures using FORTRAN arrays is of considerable practical interest. An extensive discussion of techniques for this purpose has been published by Brillinger and Cohen (1972).

TECHNIQUES AND FACILITIES FOR HANDLING DATA IN AUXILIARY STORAGE

Unlike data in primary memory, data in auxiliary storage cannot be directly accessed by the CPU, so special software is necessary to transfer data to and from primary memory for processing. In this section, software for handling data in auxiliary storage is considered. First, the standard terminology for describing data in auxiliary storage is introduced. Next, common methods of organizing and accessing data are discussed. Finally, specific types of software that can be used for this purpose are described.

Elementary data items, fields, records and files

Data in auxiliary storage is customarily described in terms of *elementary data items, fields, records,* and *files.* In accordance with standard usage, we may describe these elements as follows:

An elementary data item is any useful piece of information which cannot be broken down, separated, mathematically reduced, etc., into a "smaller" useful piece of information. Elementary data items may be single numbers, words, logical values, etc., or larger but irreducible formations of symbols.

A field is the unit of storage of an elementary data item on disk, tape, etc. In general a field may consist of as many bytes as are necessary to represent the corresponding elementary data item.

Related fields are concatenated into *records,* with a common identifier (the *record number*). For example, a record describing a room in a building might contain fields for length, width, height, floor area, enclosed volume, type of floor finish, type of wall finish, etc. Within a record, one of the fields is usually designated as the *key,* by means of which the record may be identified. For example, a field for room number, or name of occupant might be employed for this purpose. Sometimes more than one key may be employed. In this case, a distinction is normally drawn between primary and secondary keys.

A file is a collection of records with a common logical structure, identified by number or name. A collection of related files is commonly referred to as a *data base.**

Bytes, fields, records, and files thus form a logical hierarchy of data units of increasing size, as illustrated in *Figure 4.9.*

* This is the narrow technical sense of the term. More broadly, any coherent collection of information often is referred to as a "data base."

Figure 4.9
The logical hierarchy of data units in auxiliary storage.

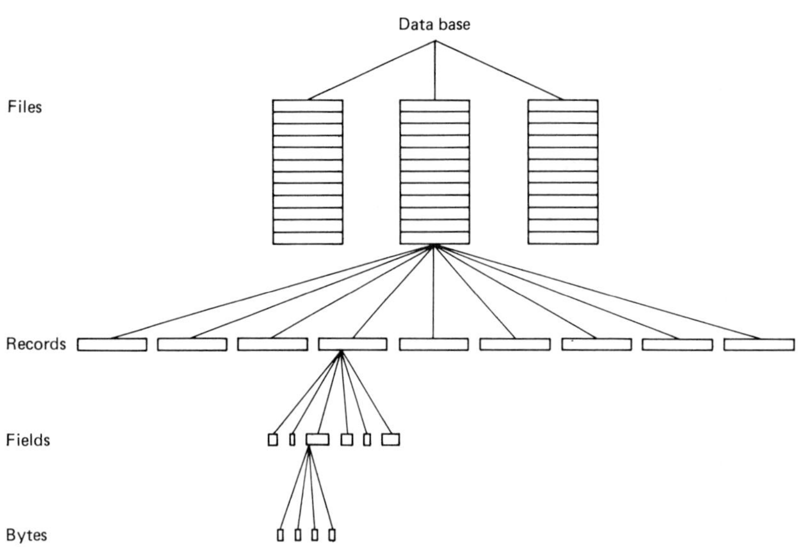

Fixed and variable formats for records and files

Records within files may have either fixed or variable formats. In a fixed format file, each record contains the same fields in the same sequence. Thus the fields of a record are *implicitly* identified by virtue of their locations within the record. Fixed format files are relatively straightforward to implement, and are widely employed in business data processing applications. However, they are not suitable for use in situations where it is desirable to allow different records to contain different fields, for example, in a building products data file where different properties may be relevant in describing different types of products.

In this case, variable format records can be utilized. A variable format record contains an *explicit* description of its own structure, *i.e.*, fields which describe the formats and identify the contents of fields employed to store the actual data. Such records are *self-describing.*

Another approach to self-description of files, which is widely employed, is to include some initial records in the file which describe the format of the following records.

Methods of file organization

There are three basic methods of organizing records within a file: *sequential organization, random organization,* and *list organization* (Dodd 1969). The choice of a particular organization depends upon both the application and the storage medium to be employed. Sequential organization may be utilized with either disk or tape, but random and list organizations are restricted to random access storage media such as disk. The following three subsections discuss each of these methods in turn.

Sequential organization

Sequential organization is the simplest and most widely employed method for organizing records within files. In a sequential organization, records are simply stored in consecutive locations on disk or tape.

Many programming languages provide facilities for creation of sequential files by execution of WRITE statements addressed to the appropriate device. Whenever such a WRITE statement is executed, a record in the specified format is added to the file. For example, the FORTRAN statements

```
  WRITE (11, 1) I, J, K
1 FORMAT (3I6)
```

cause the values of the integer variables I, J, and K to be written in a record consisting of three fields, each of which is six characters long.

The number immediately following the left-parenthesis in the WRITE statement specifies the device to be addressed. In this case, device 11 might be either a disk unit or a tape drive.

Similarly, to read a sequential file into core memory, READ statements addressed to the appropriate device are executed. Thus the FORTRAN statement

```
READ (11, 1) I, J, K
```

would read back the values for these variables. Every time such a READ statement is executed, the file advances one record. To reposition a file at its start, so that it can be read once more from the beginning, the FORTRAN statement

```
REWIND 11
```

can be employed.

The sequence of records is a sequential file may either be arbitrary, or determined by key. For example, a file of accommodation requirements data might be alphabetically ordered according to employee name, or numerically ordered according to room number. To order a sequential file into a particular sequence according to some chosen key, a *sort* program is employed. Since sorting of sequential files probably accounts for more use of computer time than any other operation, the topic of sorting has received considerable attention from computer scientists and programmers, and some very efficient sorting procedures and systems have been developed (Martin 1971, Knuth 1973, Page and Wilson 1973).

Where the order in which records will be required for processing is known, very efficient access of records is possible. The file is simply sorted into the appropriate sequence, then records are accessed one-by-one as required. Where the order is not known, access is much less efficient. Typically, the file must be searched in sequence from the beginning until the specified key is found. On average (if the order of records is random), half the records in the file must be read to access a particular record in this way. Where the records are stored in some ordered sequence on disk, more efficient search strategies such as the well-known *binary search* technique may be employed. In binary search, the file is first sampled in the middle. This eliminates half the records from contention. The process is repeated for the remaining half, and so on.

It is difficult to alter, insert, or delete records in a sequential file. Updating is normally accomplished by copying records into a new file, making required alterations, insertions, and deletions in appropriate sequence. This process is relatively time-consuming and expensive, so updating is usually only carried out when a number of records must be dealt with. Numerous special *merge programs* have been written for updating sequential files (see Gildersleeve 1971 for examples).

To summarize, sequential files have the advantages of simplicity and efficiency in the case where the order of access of records is known. They can be implemented on magnetic tape as well as disk, and can often be created and read using standard facilities of common programming languages. The disadvantage is that updating is usually difficult, and accessing particular records is likely to be costly in the case where the sequence in which they will be required is not known.

Random organization

Random organization overcomes the disadvantages of sequential organization. It has been defined by Dodd (1969) as follows:

> In random data organization, records are stored and retrieved on the basis of a predictable relationship between the key of the record and the direct address of the location where the record is stored. The address is used when the record is stored and used again when the record is retrieved.

Of course, random organization can only be implemented using a random-access memory medium, like disk. A randomly organized file on disk is directly analogous to an array in core memory.

The details of implementation of random files need not concern us here (see Dodd 1969 for further information). However, it is worth noting briefly that three different methods are employed for accessing records in random files:

Direct address

Dictionary look-up

Calculation

Direct address means that the address of a record is directly employed for its storage or retrieval. Using *dictionary look-up,* an index is searched to find the address of the desired record. With the *calculation* technique, addresses are found by the application of a mathematical formula to keys.

List organization

Just as random files are analogous to arrays, list organized files are analogous to lists in core memory. Each record contains one or more *pointer fields.* A pointer field gives the address of the next record in logical sequence. In addition to simple list organizations, pointer fields may also be employed to produce other pointer-implemented file organizations, such as trees, two-way threaded lists, multi-linked lists, rings, and networks.

A special type of list organization, which is of growing importance, is the *inverted list structure* (Dodd 1969, Cardenas 1975, Martin 1975). Often it is desired to extract from a file all the records having particular values for some specified attribute. For example, it might be desired to extract from the file shown in *Figure 4.10(a)* all the

	Room	Floor	Walls
1	Bath	Tile	Tile
2	Bed 1	Carpet	Plaster
3	Bed 2	Carpet	Paper
4	Bed 3	Carpet	Paper
5	Carport	Tile	Brick
6	Dining	Wood	Brick
7	Kitchen	Tile	Plaster
8	Living	Wood	Plaster
9	Passage	Carpet	Plaster
10	Patio	Tile	Brick

(a)

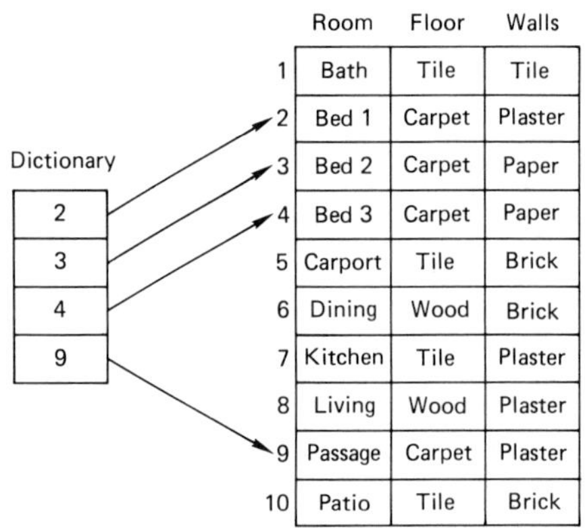

(b)

Figure 4.10
Inverted list structure. (a) A file of room data. (b) Inverted on attribute *Floor* and value *Carpet.* (c) Fully inverted. (d) Inverted on logical combination of attributes.

rooms which require carpet on the floor. This could obviously be done by exhaustive search. But more efficient access of the required records becomes possible if there is available a dictionary file of the addresses of those records for which the attribute *Floor* has the value *Carpet,* as shown in *Figure 4.10(b).* We say that this file is *inverted* on the attribute *Floor* and the value *Carpet.* The original file and the dictionary file are collectively referred to as a *file set.* Files can be inverted on any number of attributes and values, and on logical combinations of values. *Figure 4.10(c)* shows an inverted file structure on all attributes and values for our example, and *Figure 4.10(d)* shows a file structure inverted on a combination of values.

The inverted list organization greatly facilitates efficient retrieval of records by attribute. However it has the disadvantage that large dictionary files must be stored (they may in fact be larger than the data files), and storage and updating of records are relatively difficult and costly due to the need to maintain dictionaries.

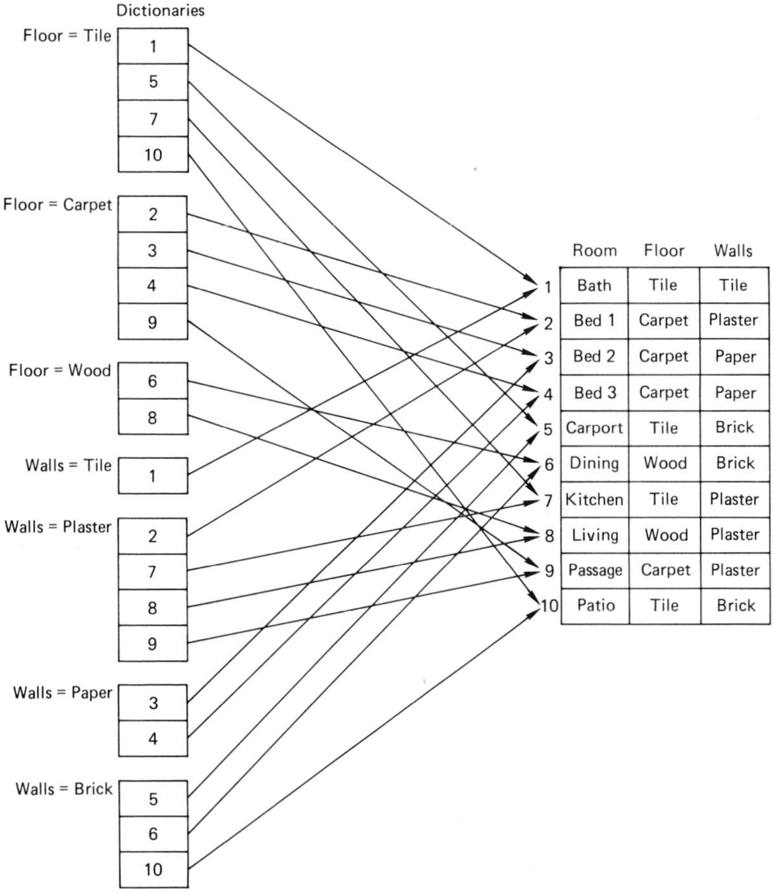
Dictionaries
Floor = Tile
1
5
7
10
Floor = Carpet
2
3
4
9
Floor = Wood
6
8
Walls = Tile
1
Walls = Plaster
2
7
8
9
Walls = Paper
3
4
Walls = Brick
5
6
10
Room Floor Walls
1 Bath Tile Tile
2 Bed 1 Carpet Plaster
3 Bed 2 Carpet Paper
4 Bed 3 Carpet Paper
5 Carport Tile Brick
6 Dining Wood Brick
7 Kitchen Tile Plaster
8 Living Wood Plaster
9 Passage Carpet Plaster
10 Patio Tile Brick

(c)

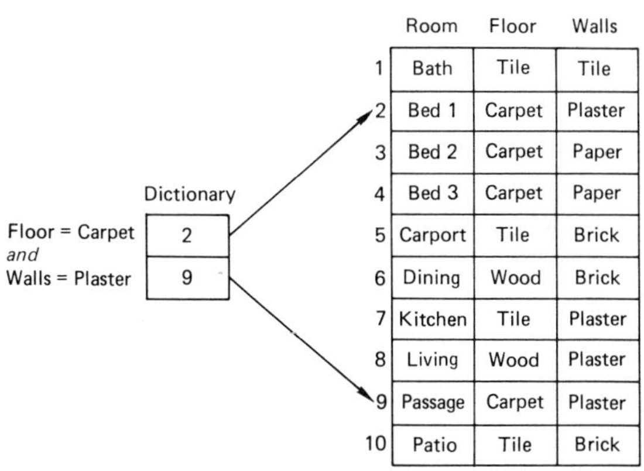
Dictionary
Floor = Carpet
and
Walls = Plaster
2
9
Room Floor Walls
1 Bath Tile Tile
2 Bed 1 Carpet Plaster
3 Bed 2 Carpet Paper
4 Bed 3 Carpet Paper
5 Carport Tile Brick
6 Dining Wood Brick
7 Kitchen Tile Plaster
8 Living Wood Plaster
9 Passage Carpet Plaster
10 Patio Tile Brick

(d)

Data base management systems

Software for organization and management of data kept in auxiliary storage has evolved considerably over the last decade. In the early 1960's, typical file handling software consisted of programs written in COBOL, FORTRAN or assembly language to perform input, output, sorting and merging operations. Data organization was defined in the code of these programs. To change the organization, the program had to be modified. Implementation of sophisticated organizations of data was difficult, since the available languages provided only a few simple primitives for performing file operations.

As the commercial data processing industry evolved, more sophisticated software was developed. Random and list-organized files came into use. Some programming languages, for example, the ICETRAN language used in the ICES civil engineering system (Goodman 1967), began to provide more powerful primitives for performing file operations. The idea of *physical data independence,* meaning it should be possible to change storage hardware without changing application programs, began to be implemented in file management software. More advanced software even allowed a certain amount of *logical data independence, i.e.,* the possibility of changing the logical organization of data without altering application programs.

By about 1970, the idea of a comprehensive and flexible *data base management system* had emerged. Central to the modern concept of a data base management system is the following carefully restricted definition of a data base (Martin 1975):

> A data base may be defined as a collection of interrelated data stored together without harmful or unnecessary redundancy to serve one or more applications in an optimal fashion; the data are stored so that they are independent of programs which use the data; a common and controlled approach is used in adding new data and in modifying and retrieving existing data within the data base.

A data base management system may be defined (Cagan 1973) as a set of programs which enable the user of such a data base to:

- Create files
- Maintain files
- Sort files
- Perform computations upon fields
- Process queries, or requests for information
- Produce reports

and perform these functions in a generalized fashion, *i.e.,* source data input formats, file formats, report formats, and field, group, record, and file designations may vary without requiring changes to the programs in the system.

There are now literally hundreds of different data base management systems in use in the U.S. Some are offered by software companies as proprietary products, some were implemented by computer manufacturers, and some were developed by organizations for their own internal use. They may be divided into two basic types: *host language* systems, and *self-contained* systems.

Host language systems are designed to provide programmers using COBOL, PL/1, etc., with additional primitives for performing data base operations. For example, the IDS (Integrated Data Store) system (Katzan 1975) is designed as an extension to COBOL. It provides for construction of more complex structures than is possible with standard COBOL, and also provides additional primitives for performing retrieval, update, and modification operations.

The operation of a typical self-contained data base management system is schematically illustrated in *Figure 4.11*. Inputs to the system consist of *file definitions, transactions,* and *information requests.* A file definition is a description of the format and structure of the records and files which constitute a data base. Transactions are operations performed to input data or to update an existing data base. Information requests specify information to be printed out, and perhaps the format in which it is to be given.

A key concept in data base management systems is the use of several different types of languages for structuring and manipulating data. In particular, many systems employ a *data definition language* (DDL) in order to specify the logical structure of data as viewed by the application programmer. In accordance with the concept of data independence, the logical structure may be implemented physically in many different ways, but the details of physical implementation need not concern the application programmer.

In host language systems, operations upon data are programmed using a *data manipulation language* (DML) embedded in the host languages. In self-contained systems, special very high level languages are employed for describing transactions. (In this context, "very high level language" means a language which does not require the user to

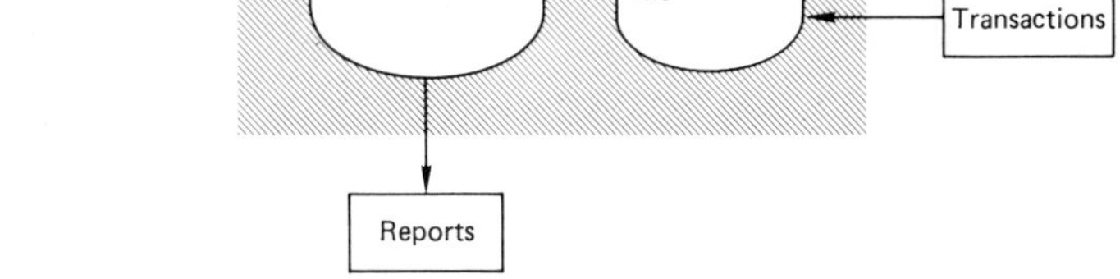

Figure 4.11
Schematic diagram of a typical self-contained data base management system.

describe the sequence of detailed steps the system uses to process his requirements. Instead, execution of a statement causes a preprogrammed procedure to be executed.)

Most self-contained systems provide powerful facilities for report generation. These enable the user to describe the information that is required, to request that it be sorted, totalled, etc., as required, and to be printed out in a specified format. Thus a wide variety of special reports can be produced from a data base as needed without the necessity to write special programs to generate them.

The principles of data base management systems and their uses are discussed in several recent texts (Cagan 1973, Katzan 1975, Martin 1975). Trade journals such as *Computerworld, Datamation* and *Computer Decisions* often carry discussions of new developments in the field, and advertisements for various systems on the market. The authoritative CODASYL Systems Committee, composed of data base management professionals, has published an extensive *Feature Analysis of Generalized Data Base Management Systems* (1971).

It is worth noting that a building description system used to maintain a project data base is in fact a special type of data base management system. But in this case file updates are produced by performing operations upon a graphic display, and "reports" may be in the form of plans, elevations, sections, perspectives, etc.

SUGGESTED READINGS

Gray, J. C. "Fundamental Concepts in Computer-Aided Architecture: Storage and Data Structure." Working Paper 49. Cambridge, England: Martin Center for Architectural and Urban Studies, University of Cambridge, December 1970.

Hawkes, D., and Stibbs, R. "Computer Descriptions of Built Forms," in *The Architecture of Form,* edited by L. March. Cambridge, England: Cambridge University Press, 1976.

Lewis, T. G., and Smith, M. Z. *Applying Data Structures.* Boston, Mass.: Houghton Mifflin Co., 1976.

Martin, J. *Computer Data-Base Organization.* Englewood Cliffs, New Jersey: Prentice-Hall, 1975.

Mitchell, W. J. "Vitruvius Computatus," in *Models and Systems in Architecture and Building,* edited by D. Hawkes. Hornby, England: The Construction Press, 1975.

Page, E. S., and Wilson, L. B. *Information Representation and Manipulation in a Computer.* Cambridge, England: Cambridge University Press, 1973.

Preparata, F. P., and Yeh, R. T. *Introduction to Discrete Structures for Computer Science and Engineering.* Reading, Mass.: Addison-Wesley, 1973.

Special issue. "Data-Base Management Systems." *Computing Surveys* 8, no. 1 (March 1976).

5 Non-Geometric Building Descriptions

A useful distinction can be drawn between two types of building descriptions that are commonly employed in architectural design:

> *Geometric* descriptions, such as plans, elevations, sections, and perspectives, which describe the dimensions, shapes, and locations of elements;
>
> *Non-geometric descriptions,* such as accommodation, door, and window schedules, bills of quantities, etc., which describe quantities, costs, and other mostly non-spatial attributes of elements.

These two types of descriptions play different and complementary roles in a traditional design process. Geometric descriptions are usually primary, and non-geometric descriptions are used in three kinds of supplementary ways:

> To describe a building *before* form decisions have been made, and thus before any geometric descriptions exist. The initial schedule of accommodation requirements is an example of a non-geometric description in this role.

To record component *selection* decisions. Door, window, and furniture and fitting schedules are examples of this application.

To facilitate tasks of *tabulating, aggregating,* and *checking* quantities, costs, areas, etc. Bills of quantities, and to a certain extent accommodation schedules, are used in this way.

The types of operations that are typically performed upon non-geometric descriptions are:

Sorting elements into sequences and subsets;

Taking *sub-totals* and *totals,* and performing other simple arithmetic tasks;

Combining data from different sources (for example applying unit costs to a bill of quantities);

Producing *reports* in various required formats.

These are all standard data-processing tasks, which are very straightforward to automate using well-established existing technology. In this chapter, techniques for non-geometric building description are discussed, then the more difficult issue of geometric description is taken up in the following chapter.

CONSTRUCTION DATA CLASSIFICATION AND CODING SCHEMES

Construction of a useful non-geometric building description presupposes the existence of an appropriate scheme by means of which elements can be uniquely identified and unambiguously classified. Considerable effort has been devoted to the development of classification and coding schemes for this purpose, particularly in Europe, and before considering specific computer applications it will be worthwhile to make a brief analysis of some of the better known architectural data classification and coding methods.

Hierarchical versus faceted classification

The Dewey Decimal, Universal Decimal, and Library of Congress systems are well known examples of general purpose classification schemes. They are *hierarchical* in character; *i.e.,* they first divide the entire field of human knowledge into broad categories, which in turn are broken down into sub-categories, which may themselves be further subdivided, and so on. Each sub-category is assigned a unique numeric or alphanumeric identifying code. The length of an identifying code depends upon the level at which the corresponding sub-category occurs in the hierarchy. Because of their generality, these schemes are not particularly useful for classifying architectural data. However, special purpose hierarchical classification schemes can also be constructed for architectural data, as shown by the simple example illustrated in *Figure 5.1*.

An alternative approach is to use a *faceted* system of classification. Under faceted systems, an item is simultaneously classified according to each of several different attributes (facets). This is equivalent to assigning to the item being classified coordinates in a multi-dimensional space, with each dimension corresponding to a particular facet. To illustrate the principle, a simple three-facet classification for structural members is illustrated in *Figure 5.2(a)*. A concise alphanumeric code for each category in the system can be constructed as shown in *Figure 5.2(b)*. Position of a symbol indicates the facet referred to, and each symbol identifies a particular subdivision of a facet. If faceted codes are employed to identify records in computer files, sorting and grouping may then be carried out according to any specified facet or combination of facets.

The SfB system and its successors

In Europe, since the 1940's, considerable effort has been devoted to the development of special faceted classification systems for building information. In 1948 the Swedish Council for Building Research developed a classification scheme for building product data known as SfB (Green 1966). (The initials SfB derive from the Swedish name for the Institute, *Samarbetskommitten for Byggnadsfragor.*) This is a three-faceted system. The facets are: *Functional element* (door, window, etc.); *form* (tubing, plate, wire, etc.); *material* (wood, steel, concrete, etc.). An alphanumeric code is assigned to a product for each of the three facets. SfB has been quite widely and successfully used in the construction industry in Europe since the 1950's. Several successor schemes based on the same general concept have been developed and put into operation. In the early 1960's the Royal Institute of British Architects, the well-known English journal, the *Architects' Journal,* and others began to promote the use of a variant known as SfB/UDC. This employs seven instead of three facets, and incorporates the Universal Decimal Classification general subject classification system. It is more general in scope, and can be used as a complete library classification scheme for all kinds of architectural data. In the late 1960's, a still more elaborate and refined system known as CI/SfB was published (Ray-Jones 1969).

Meanwhile, in Denmark a proprietary classification system known as *CBC* (Coordinated Building Communication) was developed by the brothers Bjorn and Knud Bindslev (Bindslev 1964). A typical CBC code is illustrated in *Figure 5.3*. CBC is also directly derived from SfB, but its intended uses are wider. Not only can it be used as a product data and library classification scheme, it can also be used as a coding technique for identifying particular components and materials in working drawings, specifications, and bills of quantities, and for facilitating cross-referencing between different documents.

Figure 5.1
A simple hierarchical classification and coding scheme. (a) Coding and classification system for elements of the classical orders. (b) Drawing with elements identified by code.

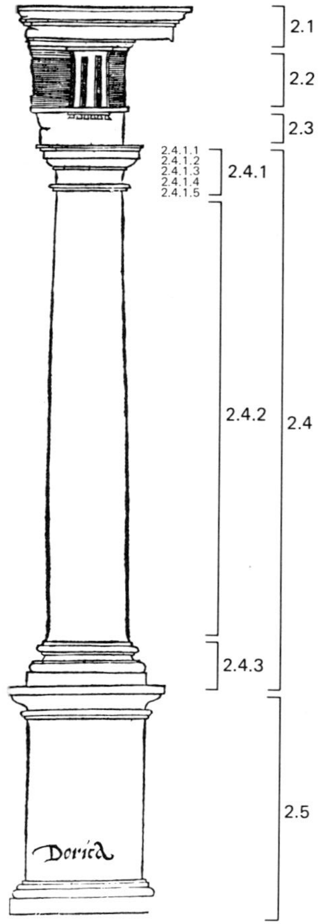

(b)

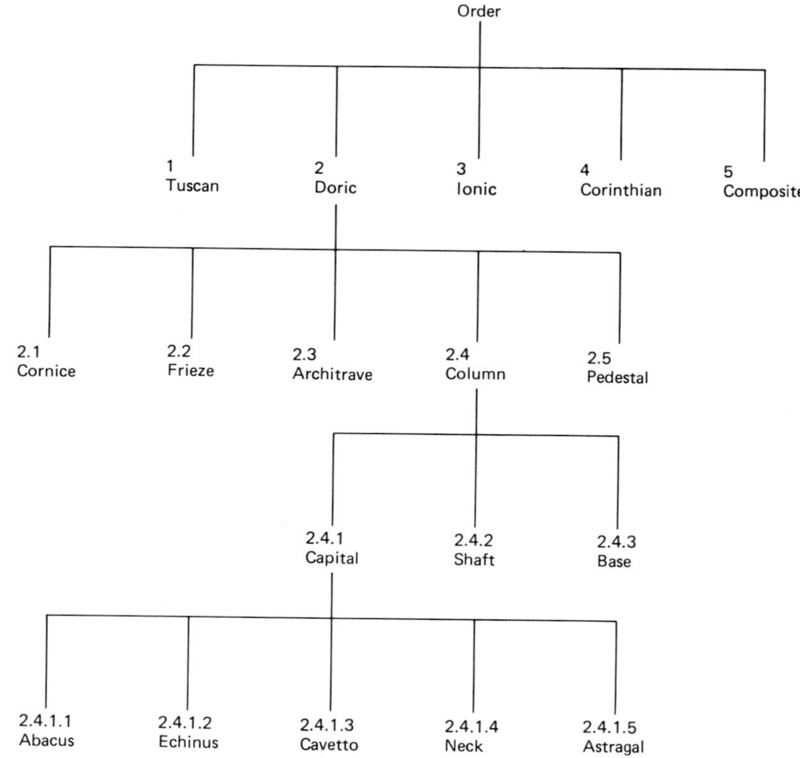

(a)

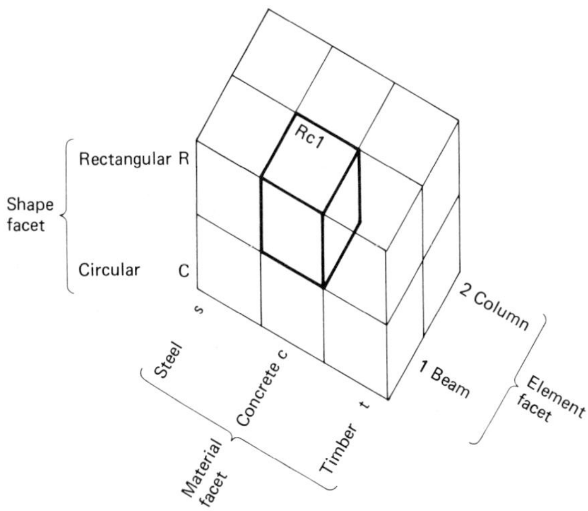

(a)

Code	Interpretation
Rs1	Rectangular steel beam
Rs2	Rectangular steel column
Rc1	Rectangular concrete beam
Rc2	Rectangular concrete column
Rt1	Rectangular timber beam
Rt2	Rectangular timber column
Cs1	Circular steel beam
Cs2	Circular steel column
Cc1	Circular concrete beam
Cc2	Circular concrete column
Ct1	Circular timber beam
Ct2	Circular timber column

(b)

Figure 5.2
A simple faceted classification and coding scheme. (a) Three-faceted classification and coding scheme for structural members. (b) Interpretation of codes.

Furthermore, it was specifically designed to form a suitable basis for development of computerized construction information management and document production systems. The Bindslevs have developed and marketed a set of proprietary computer programs for this purpose.

In Sweden, a system very closely based on CBC, known as BDC (Birgerson 1967), has also been developed. This is intended to introduce standardized, computer-produced contract documentation at a national scale. It employs a comprehensive "central catalogue,"

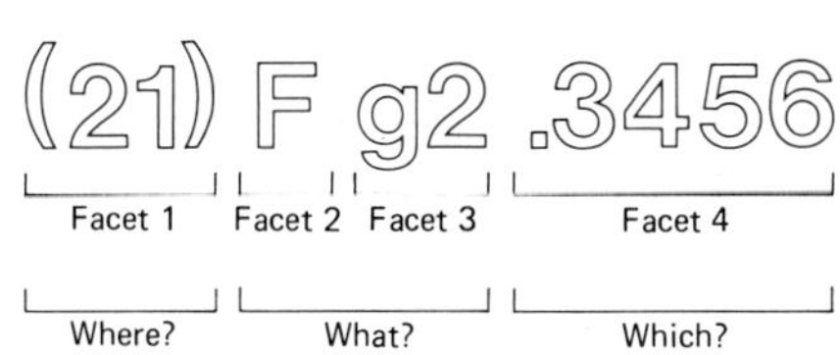

Interpretation:

Facet 1 = (21) = External walls
Facet 2 = F = Brickwork and blockwork
Facet 3 = g2 = Clay
Facet 4 = .3456 = Pointer to a detailed description or specification contained in a library file

Figure 5.3
An example of a CBC code (for a clay brick external wall).

which lists unique codes for all commonly used building materials and components.

U.S. developments

There have also been efforts to implement a standard construction coding system in the United States and Canada (Rosen 1974). The first major step towards this goal was the publication, in 1963, of the Construction Specifications Institute's *CSI Format for Construction Specifications.* This suggested standard section titles, with associated code numbers, for construction specifications. It soon became apparent that this scheme could be extended into a more general system for filing product data and for construction cost accounting. A Joint Industry Conference Committee was set up, and published a *Uniform System for Construction Specifications, Data Filing, and Cost Accounting, Title One Buildings* in 1966. In 1972 this was revised into the now widely-employed *Uniform Construction Index.*

Attempts at standardization

Unfortunately, despite all the efforts and studies that have been made, surprisingly little standardization of building information coding schemes has been achieved in practice. A conference on classification and coding for computer use, held by the International Council for Building Research in 1968, revealed that dozens of different systems were in use in different parts of the world, many of which adhoc and proprietary in nature (CIB 1968).

APPLICATIONS OF SIMPLE SEQUENTIAL FILE TECHNOLOGY

Very simple data processing techniques, employing sequential tape or disk files usually in conjunction with a faceted classification and coding scheme like CBC, have proven quite successful for handling accommodation and component schedules and bills of quantities. Although this approach is now being rendered obsolete by the introduction of modern data base management systems, it is historically important, since it produced some of the earliest successful applications of computer technology in architectural practice. Some representative examples of these applications are discussed in the following paragraphs.

Component schedules and bills of quantities

The capacity of a computer to store, sort, merge, perform arithmetic upon, and print out large sequential files was recognized very early as a powerful aid in design documentation and cost estimation. Since the early 1960's, systems which manipulate sequential files for this purpose have been in widespread everyday use.

The basic procedure generally followed in use of these systems is roughly as follows:

> The architect prepares working drawings and schedules in the normal way. However, each item (*i.e.*, product or building element) in the drawings and schedules is identified by a standard alphanumeric code.
>
> Coded items are "taken off" from the drawings and schedules, usually by a quantity surveyor, and recorded on coding sheets.
>
> Data on the coding sheets is then key-punched, and a magnetic tape file of items is produced.
>
> The computer is employed to sort the file into different sequences and subsets, to tabulate quantities, and to print out reports in different formats as required for different purposes for different members of the building team. Additional library files of cost data, detailed descriptions, specification clauses, etc., corresponding to item codes may be employed in this process. (The topic of library files will be taken up in Chapter 7.)

Typical reports produced in this way might be: bills of quantities sorted according to trade subdivisions; cost analyses broken down in any desired way; purchase documents for components and materials; and so on.

Programmatic data

Similar sequential file techniques to those which have been employed in building documentation and cost estimation have also been utilized for handling programmatic data on large projects. Burgess and Leather (1968) have described one such application: the production of accommodation and equipment schedules for a hospital project. A file of accommodation and equipment requirements can be developed, and from this, a schedule giving the contents of each room can be printed out. As the brief is developed and modified during the project, the new data can be merged into the file and updated schedules printed out. Reports and summaries broken down in different ways can be produced as required. On completion of the project the file might be retained in a historical data base, to be used for reference in generating programs for future projects.

Space management data

Accommodation and equipment files of this type can also be used as the basis for *space management systems*. For a large and complex facility such as a university, school, or hospital, a space management system can be a valuable tool for use in allocation and scheduling, management of maintenance, etc. With the inclusion of fields giving dimensions and locations of spaces, graphic output in the form of simple floor plans may be produced in addition to alphanumeric reports. *Figure 5.4* illustrates a typical example.

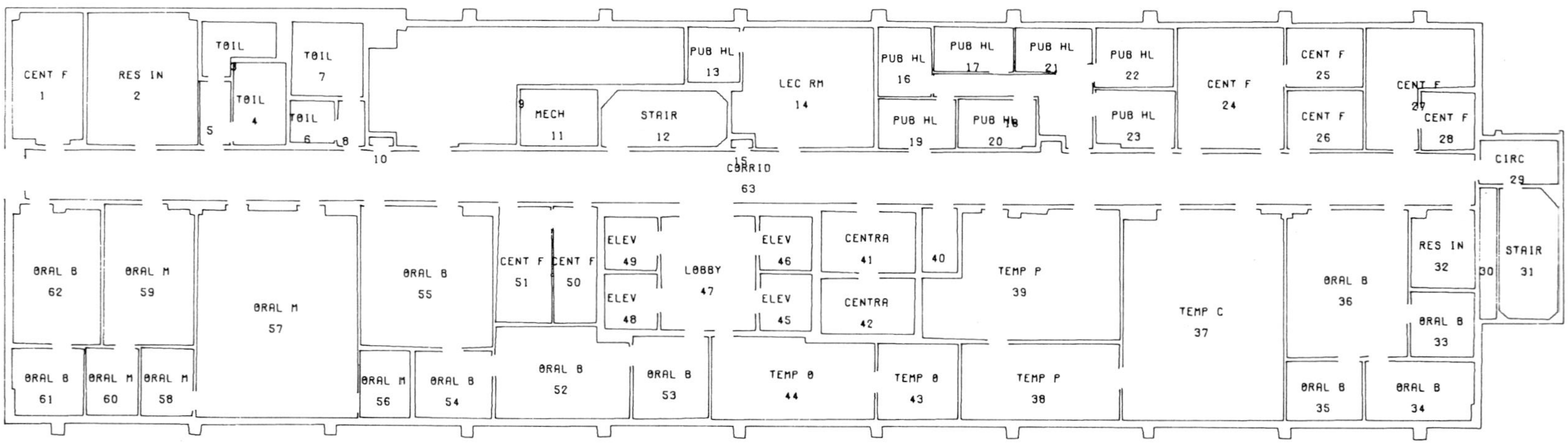

Figure 5.4
Typical graphic output from a space management system (Leon Hoffman Associates, Los Angeles, California).

APPLICATIONS OF GENERAL PURPOSE DATA BASE MANAGEMENT SYSTEMS

The systems which have been described so far employ special programs, written in languages like COBOL or FORTRAN, to perform the required data processing tasks. An alternative and more powerful approach, which is now feasible, is to employ the facilities of a general purpose data base management system. This approach confers the advantage of at least some degree of system independence from particular physical implementations, allows required special programs to be relatively simply and quickly written in very high-level languages, and provides more sophisticated and flexible file manipulation and report generation capabilities.

An example of a relatively simple data structure employed in a programmatic data base management application by the Chicago architectural firm of Skidmore, Owings and Merrill is shown in *Figure 5.5* (Teague and Davis 1972). It was implemented using TABLE II, a data base management subsystem of the ICES integrated civil engineering system (Logcher and Jackson 1969). The user conceptualizes TABLE files as *tables,* in which the rows are called *items* and the columns are called *headings.* To create a data structure for a particular purpose, the user defines heading names and the types of data each heading may contain: character, integer, and single or double precision floating point numbers. Each cell in the table may contain either a single value or a list of values. Internally, a table is stored as an indexed file accessed by the item names. Facilities are provided by TABLE II for creating, modifying, and deleting tables, sorting tables and columns, extracting data, totalling columns, and printing out reports.

Another type of data structure, in this case hierarchical in character to reflect a hierarchical classification of data, is illustrated in *Figure 5.6.* This example is from the IBES space and equipment inventory system employed by the East Anglia Regional Hospital in Cambridge, England (Applied Research of Cambridge 1974, Hayward 1975).

This hierarchical type of structure, which is very suitable for many applications, can be implemented in several different ways. *Fig-*

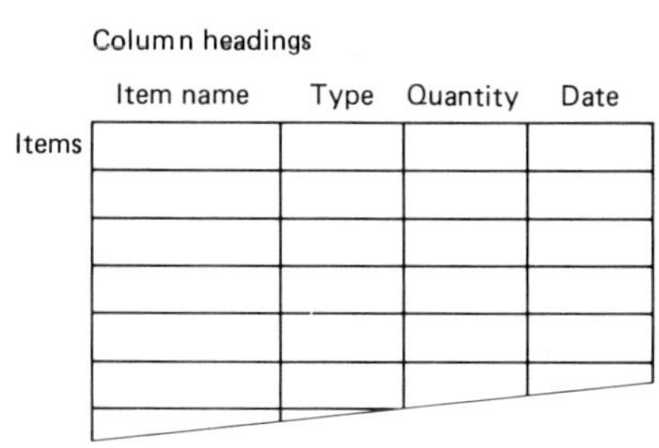

Figure 5.5
An example of a TABLE data structure for storing work station requirements data (after Teague and Davis 1972).

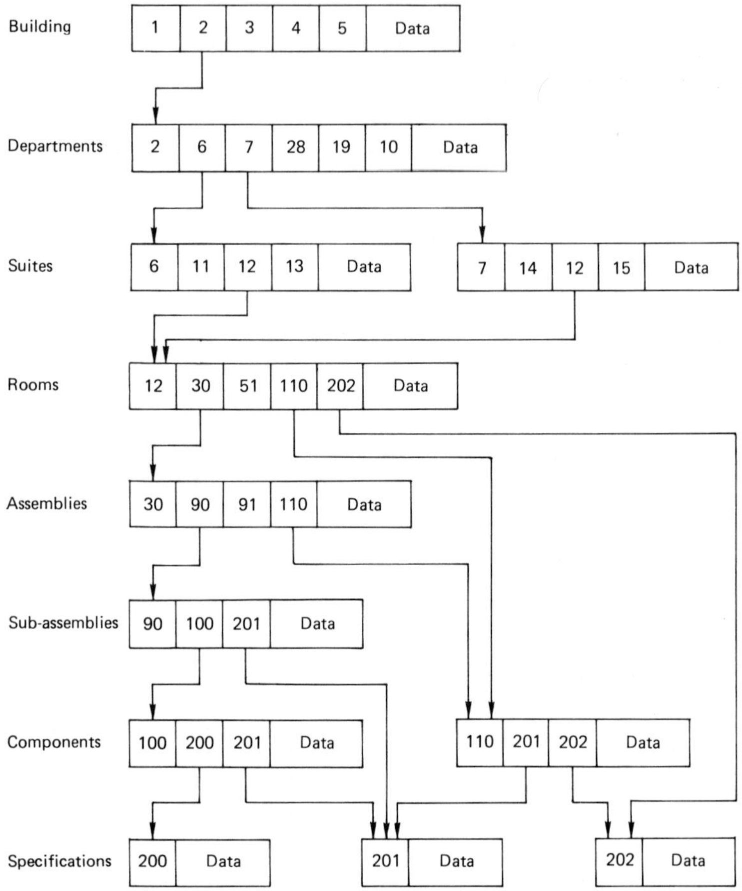

Figure 5.6
An example of a hierarchical data structure for storing non-geometric building descriptions (after Hayward 1975). The left hand part of each record contains pointer fields, and the right hand part contains data.

ure 5.7(a), for example, illustrates an implementation in which all records are contained within a single file. This type of implementation is commonly referred to as an *integrated data base.* While relatively straightforward, an integrated hierarchically-structured data base has the distinct disadvantage that queries and updates may always be entered with high-level keys. For example, a query to the data base illustrated in *Figure 5.7(a)* would have to be stated, "Tell me about room e, in sector 3, of building A" rather than simply "Tell me about room e." An alternative, which overcomes this problem, is *modular* organization of the data base into several files, each one of which represents a single level of the hierarchy, as shown in *Figure 5.7(b)*. Records in each file contain pointer fields, providing necessary cross-referencing between levels. Although it is generally more difficult to implement than an equivalent integrated organization, a modularized data base has several important advantages: updates can be processed more efficiently, queries can be stated more simply and directly, and processing time for simple queries tends to be lower. Often, a particular application is most efficiently dealt with

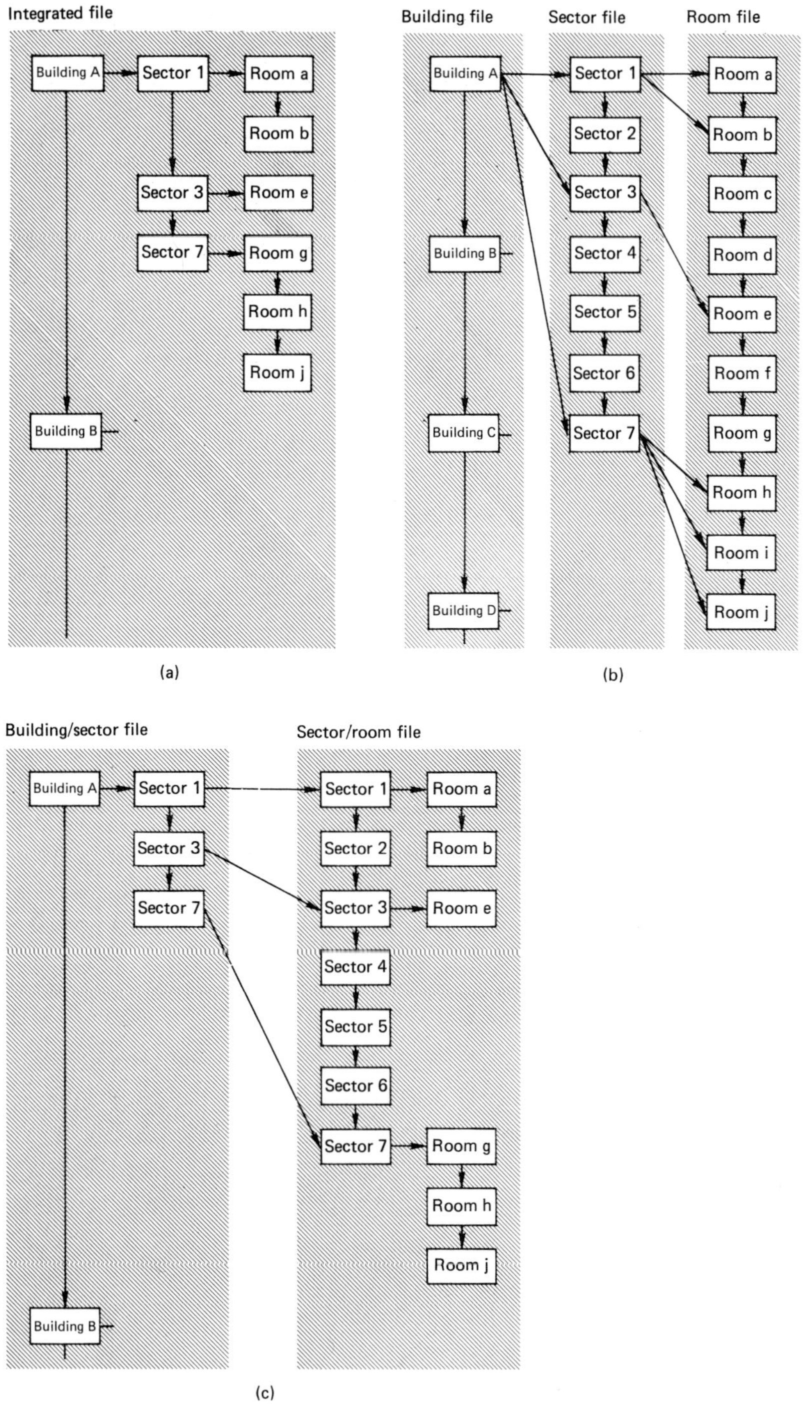
Integrated file
Building A
Sector 1
Room a
Room b
Sector 3
Room e
Sector 7
Room g
Room h
Room j
Building B
(a)
Building file
Sector file
Room file
Building A
Building B
Building C
Building D
Sector 1
Sector 2
Sector 3
Sector 4
Sector 5
Sector 6
Sector 7
Room a
Room b
Room c
Room d
Room e
Room f
Room g
Room h
Room i
Room j
(b)
Building/sector file
Sector/room file
Building A
Sector 1
Sector 3
Sector 7
Building B
Sector 1
Sector 2
Sector 3
Sector 4
Sector 5
Sector 6
Sector 7
Room a
Room b
Room e
Room g
Room h
Room j
(c)

by some combination of the integrated and modular approaches, for example as shown in *Figure 5.7(c)*.

When designing a hierarchically-structured data base for a particular application, the hierarchy of data items must be very carefully considered. It is usually relatively easy, in a typical data base management system, to make minor changes in data base organization such as the addition or deletion of fields within a record; but the addition or deletion of an entire level in an implemented data base is likely to prove difficult and costly.

Collecting and entering data

Use of data base management system requires systematic organization of the data gathering process. The basic steps of the process are:

Preparation of *source documents;*

Keypunching and *verifying;*

Input of the data to the system;

Editing and *updating* the data base.

Examples of source documents include employee questionnaires used to determine space and equipment needs, coding sheets used to record the results of furniture and equipment inventories, and work

Figure 5.8
Example of a questionnaire form designed for use in conjunction with a space and equipment data base management system.

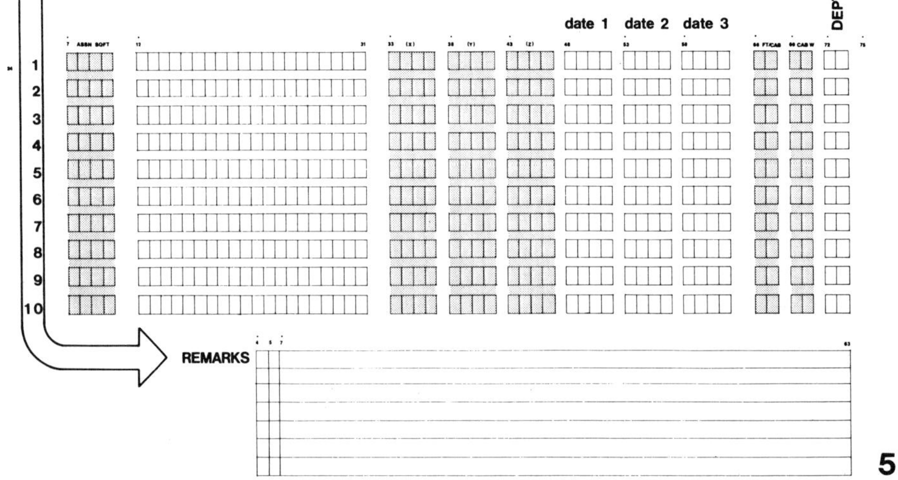

sheets used in taking off quantities from drawings. Source document formats must be designed with considerable care to minimize ambiguities and chances of respondent error. The format should also be arranged to facilitate the keypunching of data directly from the source documents, without the need to translate information manually into some intermediate form. An example of a questionnaire form designed for use in conjunction with a space and equipment data-base management system is shown in *Figure 5.8.*

Keypunching * of data to convert it to machine-readable form can be carried out either by clerical staff within the organization or by a commercial keypunching service. It is usually advisable to verify the punched data in order to eliminate as many as possible of the errors which are inevitably introduced during the keypunching process. Verification is accomplished by repunching the data using a special machine which indicates any discrepancy between a symbol as originally punched and the verification key-stroke. During the mid-1970's, the cost of keypunching and verification was around fifty cents per thousand characters. Thus a typical architectural data base of one or two million characters might cost $500 to $1000 to input.

* Keypunch machines and similar devices are discussed in Chapter 9.

Figure 5.9
Example of a transaction form.

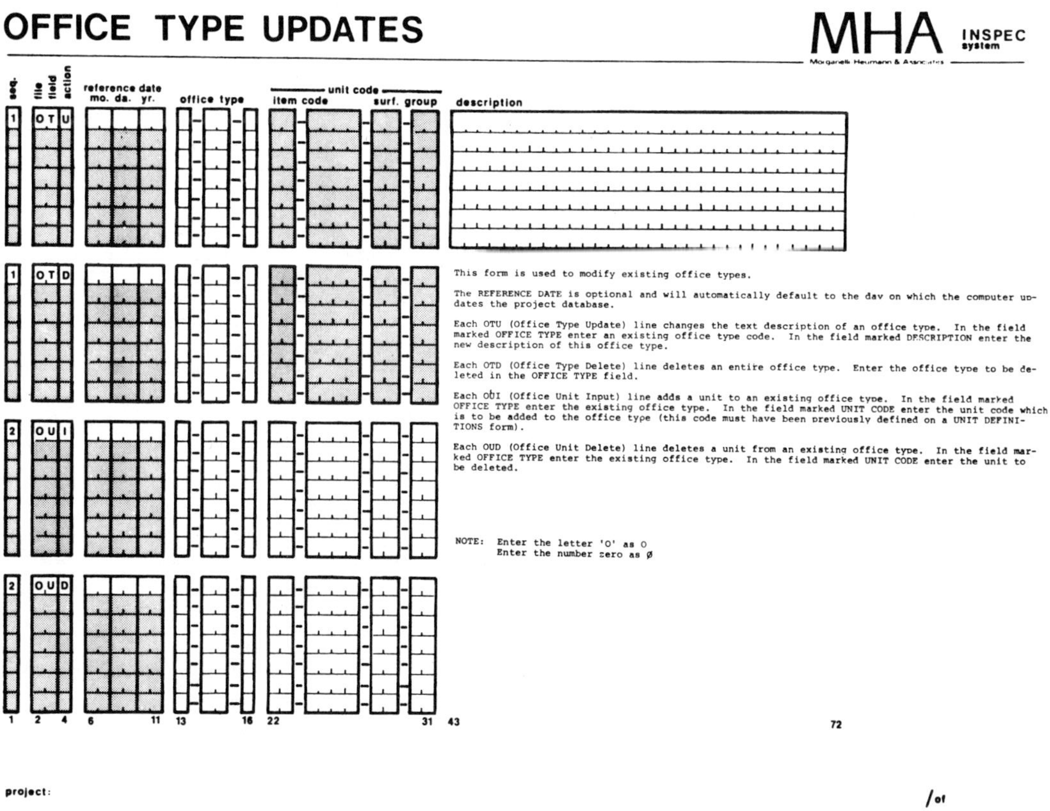

OFFICE TYPE UPDATES

MHA INSPEC system

Morganelli Heumann & Associates

seq. | file | field | action | reference date mo. da. yr. | office type | unit code: item code, surf. group | description

1 O T U

1 O T D

2 O U I

2 O U D

1 2 4 6 11 13 16 22 31 43 72

This form is used to modify existing office types.

The REFERENCE DATE is optional and will automatically default to the day on which the computer updates the project database.

Each OTU (Office Type Update) line changes the text description of an office type. In the field marked OFFICE TYPE enter an existing office type code. In the field marked DESCRIPTION enter the new description of this office type.

Each OTD (Office Type Delete) line deletes an entire office type. Enter the office type to be deleted in the OFFICE TYPE field.

Each OUI (Office Unit Input) line adds a unit to an existing office type. In the field marked OFFICE TYPE enter the existing office type. In the field marked UNIT CODE enter the unit code which is to be added to the office type (this code must have been previously defined on a UNIT DEFINITIONS form).

Each OUD (Office Unit Delete) line deletes a unit from an existing office type. In the field marked OFFICE TYPE enter the existing office type. In the field marked UNIT CODE enter the unit to be deleted.

NOTE: Enter the letter 'O' as O
Enter the number zero as Ø

project:

/of

MAY 14, 1975 INSPEC: INVENTORY & SPECIFICATIONS SYSTEM—MORGANELLI-HEUMANN & ASSOCIATES
FURNITURE INVENTORY BY DEPARTMENT AND OFFICE TYPE
ATLANTIC RICHFIELD CORPORATION

		DEPARTMENT NUMBER	OFFICE TYPE	UNIT CODE	SHORT DESCRIPTION		ID
		3244500	C2RG	DK103R-	RIGHT HAND REFERENCE DESK	10-5C	00000311
				WP102A-VYTN	SPANNER PANEL (1 SIDE)	10-11C	00000312
				WP102B-VYTN	SPANNER PANEL (2 SIDES)	10-11C	00000313
OFFTYPE	COUNT	3244500	C2RG	9			
			EALB	CH103-FAPT	SECRETARIAL POSTURE CHAIR	10-18	00000492
				DK101L-PATN	LEFT HAND 'SINGLE PED'	10-14E	00000493
				TR101L-	LEFT HAND TYPING RETURN	10-15E	00000494
OFFTYPE	COUNT	3244500	EALB	3			
			EARG	CH103-FAG	SECRETARIAL POSTURE CHAIR	10-18	00000522
				DK101R-PATN	RIGHT HAND 'SINGLE PED'	10-14E	00000523
				TR101R-	RIGHT HAND TYPING RETURN	10-15E	00000524
OFFTYPE	COUNT	3244500	EARG	3			
			EBLY	CH103-FAAG	SECRETARIAL POSTURE CHAIR	10-18	00000567
				CR102L-PATN	LEFT HANDED CREDENZA	10-26E	00000568
				DK101L-PATN	LEFT HAND 'SINGLE PED'	10-14E	00000569
				TR102L-PATN	TYPING RETURN LEFT	10-25E	00000570
OFFTYPE	COUNT	3244500	EBLY	4			
DEPT	COUNT	3244500		55			
		3246000		FI104-SG2	FILE CABINET	10-36	00000006
				FI104-SG2	FILE CABINET	10-36	00000007
OFFTYPE	COUNT	3246000		2			
			BARY	CH104-FAAG	CHAIR	10-19	00000156
				CH101-FAAG	SWIVEL/TILT CHAIR	10-16	00000157
				TB101-SG5	CYLINDER TABLE	10-23	00000158
				FI101R-	RIGHT HAND FILE/STORAGE	10-3B	00000159
				WR102R-	RIGHT HINGED WARDROBE	10-2B	00000160
				CR101R-	RIGHT HAND REF. CREDENZA	10-1B	00000161
				DK102-	TABLE DESK	10-4B	00000162
OFFTYPE	COUNT	3246000	BARY	7			
			EALP	CH103-FAPR	SECRETARIAL POSTURE CHAIR	10-18	00000501
				DK101L-PATN	LEFT HAND 'SINGLE PED'	10-14E	00000502
				TR101L-	LEFT HAND TYPING RETURN	10-15E	00000503
OFFTYPE	COUNT	3246000	EALP	3			
DEPT	COUNT	3246000		12			
		3246100		FI104-SG2	FILE CABINET	10-36	00000008

(a)

MAY 14, 1975 INSPEC: INVENTORY & SPECIFICATIONS SYSTEM—MORGANELLI-HEUMANN & ASSOCIATES PAGE 19
FURNITURE INVENTORY BY IDENTIFIER
ATLANTIC RICHFIELD CORPORATION

ID	UNIT CODE	OFFICE TYPE	-INVENTORY-- DATE & NUMBERS	-LOCATIONS-- DATE & PLACE	-CONDITIONS-- DATE & CONDTN.
00000460	DK105-	D2RG	*	04/30/75..1..20.........3246500	04/30/75.NEW........
00000461	CH101-FAG	D2RG	*	04/30/75..1..20.........3246500	04/30/75.NEW........
00000462	CH102-FAG	D2RG	*	04/30/75..1..20.........3246500	04/30/75.NEW........
00000463	WP103A-VYTN	D2RG	*	04/30/75..1..20.........3246500	04/30/75.NEW........
00000464	WR101R-	D2RP	*	04/30/75..1..20.........3246500	04/30/75.NEW........
00000465	FI102-	D2RP	*	04/30/75..1..20.........3246500	04/30/75.NEW........
00000466	DK105-	D2RP	*	04/30/75..1..20.........3246500	04/30/75.NEW........
00000467	CH101-FAPR	D2RP	*	04/30/75..1..20.........3246500	04/30/75.NEW........
00000468	CH102-FAPR	D2RP	*	04/30/75..1..20.........3246500	04/30/75.NEW........
00000469	WP103A-VYTN	D2RP	*	04/30/75..1..20.........3246500	04/30/75.NEW........
00000470	WR101R-	D2RP	*	04/30/75..1..20.........3246500	04/30/75.NEW........
00000471	FI102-	D2RP	*	04/30/75..1..20.........3246500	04/30/75.NEW........
00000472	DK105-	D2RP	*	04/30/75..1..20.........3246500	04/30/75.NEW........
00000473	CH101-FAPR	D2RP	*	04/30/75..1..20.........3246500	04/30/75.NEW........
00000474	CH102-FAPR	D2RP	*	04/30/75..1..20.........3246500	04/30/75.NEW........
00000475	WP103A-VYTN	D2RP	*	04/30/75..1..20.........3246500	04/30/75.NEW........
00000476	WR101R-	D2RY	*	04/30/75..1..20.........3246500	04/30/75.NEW........
00000477	FI102-	D2RY	*	04/30/75..1..20.........3246500	04/30/75.NEW........
00000478	DK105-	D2RY	*	04/30/75..1..20.........3246500	04/30/75.NEW........
00000479	CH101-FAAG	D2RY	*	04/30/75..1..20.........3246500	04/30/75.NEW........
00000480	CH102-FAAG	D2RY	*	04/30/75..1..20.........3246500	04/30/75.NEW........
00000481	WP103A-VYTN	D2RY	*	04/30/75..1..20.........3246500	04/30/75.NEW........
00000482	WR101L-	D4RB	*	04/30/75..1..20.........3246204	04/30/75.NEW........
00000483	WR101R-	D4RB	*	04/30/75..1..20.........3246204	04/30/75.NEW........
00000484	CH101-FAPT	D4RB	*	04/30/75..1..20.........3246204	04/30/75.NEW........
00000485	DK105-	D4RB	*	04/30/75..1..20.........3246204	04/30/75.NEW........

(b)

MAY 14, 1975 INSPEC: INVENTORY & SPECIFICATIONS SYSTEM—MORGANELLI-HEUMANN & ASSOCIATES
FURNITURE INVENTORY BY LOCATION
ATLANTIC RICHFIELD CORPORATION

	LOCATION			LOCATION DATE	SHORT DESCRIPTION		ID	UNIT CODE	
	1	17	3244500	04/30/75	LEFT HAND 'SINGLE PED'	10-14E	00000569	DK101L-PATN	
					TYPING RETURN LEFT	10-25E	00000570	TR102L-PATN	
LOCATION COUNT	1	17	3244500						55
	1	20	3246000	04/27/75	FILE CABINET	10-36	00000006	FI104-SG2	
					FILE CABINET	10-36	00000007	FI104-SG2	
				04/30/75	CHAIR	10-19	00000156	CH104-FAAG	
					SWIVEL/TILT CHAIR	10-16	00000157	CH101-FAAG	
					CYLINDER TABLE	10-23	00000158	TB101-SG5	
					RIGHT HAND FILE/STORAGE	10-3B	00000159	FI101R-	
					RIGHT HINGED WARDROBE	10-2B	00000160	WR102R-	
					RIGHT HAND REF. CREDENZA	10-1B	00000161	CR101R-	
					TABLE DESK	10-4B	00000162	DK102-	
					SECRETARIAL POSTURE CHAIR	10-18	00000501	CH103-FAPR	
					LEFT HAND 'SINGLE PED'	10-14E	00000502	DK101L-PATN	
					LEFT HAND TYPING RETURN	10-15E	00000503	TR101L-	
LOCATION COUNT	1	20	3246000						12
	1	20	3246100	04/27/75	FILE CABINET	10-36	00000008	FI104-SG2	
					FILE CABINET	10-36	00000009	FI104-SG2	
				04/30/75	CHAIR	10-19	00000100	CH104-FAPR	
					SWIVEL/TILT CHAIR	10-16	00000101	CH101-FAPR	
					CYLINDER TABLE	10-23	00000102	TB101-SG5	
					LEFT HAND FILE/STORAGE	10-3B	00000103	FI101L-	
					LEFT HINGED WARDROBE	10-2-B	00000104	WR102L-	
					LEFT HAND REF. CREDENZA	10-1B	00000105	CR101L-	
					TABLE DESK	10-4B	00000106	DK102-	
					FILE-STORAGE UNIT	10-7C-D	00000215	FI102-	
					SPANNER PANEL	10-10-C-D	00000216	WP101-	
					SWIVEL/TILT CHAIR	10-16	00000217	CH101-FAAG	
					TABLE DESK	10-9C	00000218	DK104-	
					CHAIR	10-19	00000219	CH104-FAAG	
					LEFT HINGED WARDROBE	10-6-C-D	00000220	WR101L-	
					LEFT HAND REFERENCE DESK	10-5C	00000221	DK103L-	
					SPANNER PANEL (1 SIDE)	10-11C	00000222	WP102A-VYTN	
					SPANNER PANEL (2 SIDES)	10-11C	00000223	WP102B-VYTN	
					FILE-STORAGE UNIT	10-7C-D	00000251	FI102-	
					SPANNER PANEL	10-10-C-D	00000252	WP101-	
					SWIVEL/TILT CHAIR	10-16	00000253	CH101-FAPT	
					TABLE DESK	10-9C	00000254	DK104-	
					CHAIR	10-19	00000255	CH104-FAPT	
					RIGHT HINGED WARDROBE	10-6-C-D	00000256	WR101R-	
					RIGHT HAND REFERENCE DESK	10-5C	00000257	DK103R-	
					SPANNER PANEL (1 SIDE)	10-11C	00000258	WP102A-VYTN	
					SPANNER PANEL (2 SIDES)	10-11C	00000259	WP102B-VYTN	
					SECRETARIAL POSTURE CHAIR	10-18	00000516	CH103-FAPT	
					RIGHT HAND 'SINGLE PED'	10-14E	00000517	DK101R-PATN	
					RIGHT HAND TYPING RETURN	10-15E	00000518	TB101R-	

(c)

Figure 5.10
(a) Page from a furniture inventory sorted by *department number* (primary key) and *office type* (secondary key). (b) A second report generated from the same data base. Different information is printed out, and the format also differs. Records have been resorted by identifier. (c) A third report generated from the same data base. Records sorted and counted by *location*.

In most applications the initial data base does not remain static; transactions must be executed at intervals to edit and update the data. Formats for transactions can be defined using the transaction definition facilities of the data base management system. Special printed forms, for example as shown in *Figure 5.9,* are a useful aid to the system user in preparing data for these transactions.

Generating reports

The reports that are required from a data base are likely to be of two types: *standard reports,* the need for which can be anticipated in advance, and *special* reports, which are not anticipated in advance. The contents and formats for required reports can be specified using the report generation facilities of the data base management system. The production of standard reports can be a routine task, carried out by clerical staff using pre-written programs. However, the production of a special report requires a technically competent programmer or data base manager to write the necessary special program.

Some typical examples of reports generated from an architectural data base are illustrated in *Figure 5.10.* These were produced by the INSPEC (INventory and SPECifications) system employed by Morganelli-Heumann and Associates of Los Angeles to maintain furniture and fittings data for large interior design projects. INSPEC is implemented using the facilities of the widely-used MARK-IV data base management system. In the first report shown (*Figure 5.10(a)*) a furniture inventory is sorted by department number (the primary key) and office type (the secondary key). The second report (*Figure 5.10(b)*) shows the same inventory resorted by furniture item identification number, and the third report (*Figure 5.10(c)*) shows items sorted and counted by location.

Examples of applications

Data base management systems which can handle non-geometric descriptions of buildings are now finding wide application throughout all phases of design and construction, particularly in organizations which undertake large hospital, school or commercial projects. Typical data bases dealt with include schedules of space and equipment needs, existing space and equipment inventories, finish, furniture, equipment, and component schedules.

Not only are these data bases used during the design and construction phases of a project, but in many cases they also continue in use after occupancy as an element in the client organization's space management system. Furthermore, where a design organization repeatedly deals with buildings of a similar character, it is often not necessary to generate new data for each new project; relatively minor editing of an existing data base from an earlier project may be all that is necessary. Thus a library of data bases from previous projects can be a valuable resource.

SUGGESTED READINGS

Bindslev, B. and Bindslev, K. "The Computer and CBC." *Architects' Journal,* May 27, 1964, pp. 1193–1200.

Burgess, D., and Leather, G. "Information Scheduling by Computer." *Royal Institute of British Architects Journal,* 75, no. 1 (January 1968), pp. 36–38.

Campion, D. "Computer-Aided Handling of Briefing and Design Information for Building Projects." *Proceedings of the Second International Conference on Computers in Engineering and Building Design.* Guildford, Surrey, England: IPC Science and Technology Press, 1976.

CIB (International Council for Building Research, Studies, and Documentation). *Information Flow in the Building Process: Classification and Coding for Computer Use.* Oslo, Norway: Norwegian Building Research Institute, 1968.

Teague, L. C., and Davis, C. F. "Information Systems for Architectural Programming," in *Environmental Design: Research and Practice,* edited by W. J. Mitchell. Los Angeles, California: Proceedings of the EDRA3/AR8 Conference, School of Architecture and Urban Planning, 1972.

6 Descriptions of Building Topology and Geometry

In a traditional design process, drawings (principally plans, elevations and sections) are employed to represent the shapes, dimensions, locations, connections, and relations of components and spaces in the building. Drawings are normally employed in performance of those design functions which require spatial reference, relational, and performance data, and which require the designer to check for spatial consistency. If these functions are to be automated, some way must be found to incorporate sufficient shape, dimensional, locational, and relational information into data structures used to describe buildings in the computer.

One obvious expedient is merely to add extra fields for geometric data of various kinds to the types of data structures used for non-geometric representation, as discussed in the previous chapter. For example, fields for room shape, dimension, and location could be added to the records of a programmatic data file. Indeed in one rather simple-minded sense, the task of building planning in response to a given brief is a task of generating the information to fill these extra fields. But although such a straightforward technique for describing building geometry may be suitable for some purposes, it tends to prove inadequate as a basis for automated performance of the complex spatial synthesis and evaluation functions involved in architectural design. This chapter discusses various alternative approaches which may be taken to the design of data structures capable of representing building topology and geometry for these purposes.

TYPES OF GEOMETRIC DESCRIPTION

Different types of geometric description can be distinguished according to:

The type of geometric *element* upon which the description is based,

The particular geometric and topological *attributes* of entities to be described,

The types of geometric and topological *relations* between entities to be represented,

The *level of detail* at which the description is made,

The *geometric assumptions* upon which the description method is based.

Elements

A fishing net, according to the old joke, can be regarded either as a pattern of strings or as a pattern of holes. It depends upon how you look at it. Similarly, there are many different ways of looking at a building. We might choose to regard it as an assemblage of physical components, like columns, beams, etc., or of bounding surfaces like the planes of walls, floors, and ceilings, or (as in a conventional architectural drawing) of bounding lines marking edges and intersections of surfaces, or of enclosed functional volumes like rooms, or of abstract building blocks like square or cubic modules. Descriptions based upon different types of *elements* are suitable for different purposes. But the choice of geometric elements is not simply a technical question. In a very direct sense, the choice of elements begins to establish a language of architectural design.

Attributes

For most applications, it is necessary to describe the primary geometric properties of overall length, width, height, and orientation, and location in the building, of each element. Sometimes it is necessary to include detailed descriptions of shape properties. It may be worthwhile to explicitly store some secondary geometric data, like volume, surface area, etc. For engineering computations, it is often necessary to store non-geometric physical attributes like weight, U-value, etc.

Relations

For many applications, it is necessary to be able to determine which elements are adjacent to any specified element. Adjacency data may either be explicitly stored, implicitly represented by location of elements in the data structure, or computed as required from element dimension and location data. Other types of relations that it may be important to have the capability of determining are distances between elements, alignment, symmetry, intersection, visibility of one element from another, etc. Sometimes relations other than adjacency are explicitly stored, but it is more usual to compute them as required.

Level of detail

In a traditional design process, a general progression in level of detail of drawings tends to take place as design decisions are made. Early sketches may be at 1″ : 32′ or 1″ : 16′, and show very little detail. Walls may be indicated by a single line, openings may be omitted, etc. More developed sketches and working drawings may move up to 1″ : 8′ or even 1″ : 4′. Wall thicknesses are indicated, locations of openings are now shown, individual construction elements are more carefully differentiated, and so on. For details, a scale of 1″ : 2′ or greater is employed, and more information still is included. *Figure 6.1* illustrates this progression.

When considering techniques for computer representation of building geometry, the stage of the design process for which the representation is intended must be kept in mind. A representation which incorporates too much or too little geometric information, or data at too high or too low a level of detail, will not be successful.

Geometric assumptions

Considerable efficiencies can be achieved in geometric description if some general geometric assumptions can be made, for example, that all angles are 90°, that dimensions vary in modular increments, that all curves are segments of circles, or that all objects are convex polyhedra. Conversely, unless building form is developed within the framework of a disciplined geometry, it becomes very difficult both to describe and to construct. Jørn Utzon's Sydney Opera House (*Figure 6.2*) is a striking illustration of this point. This building was originally sketched with free-form curved shells, but it was found necessary at the detail design stage to redefine the shells as segments of spherical surfaces. In developing techniques for storage of geometric descriptions of built form in computer memory, it is necessary to make trade-offs between the efficiencies that can be attained by adopting particular geometric disciplines and the restrictions on the range of representable forms that result.

A more subtle consideration is that a given method of structur-

Figure 6.1
Comparison of initial sketches and developed drawings for a design project, illustrating changes in levels of detail and precision in representation. (Moore house, Orinda, California, architect Charles W. Moore, 1961.) (a) Initial sketches. (b) Developed drawings.

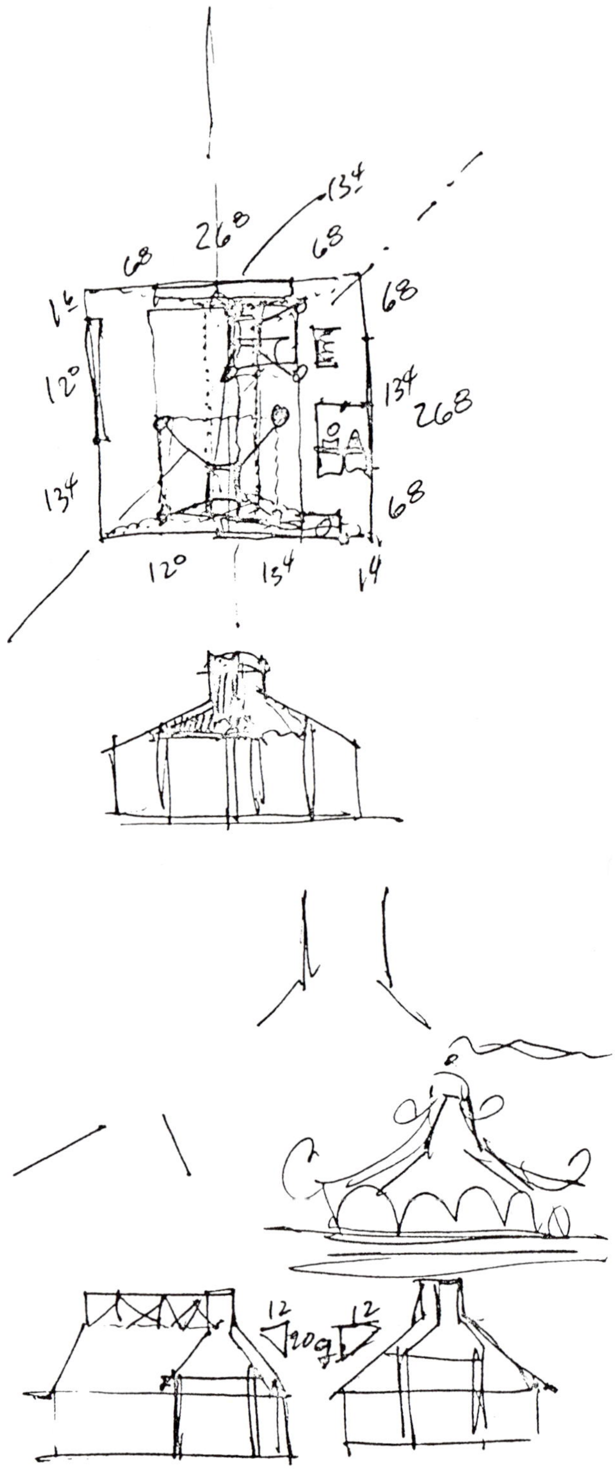

(a)

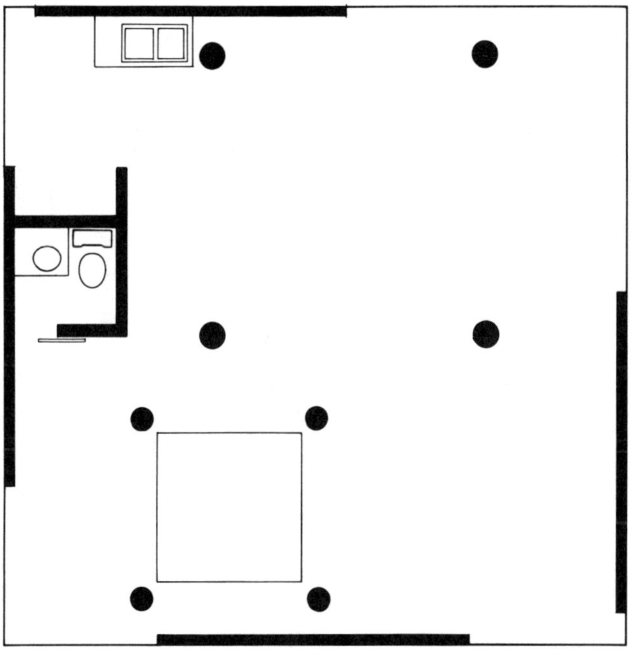

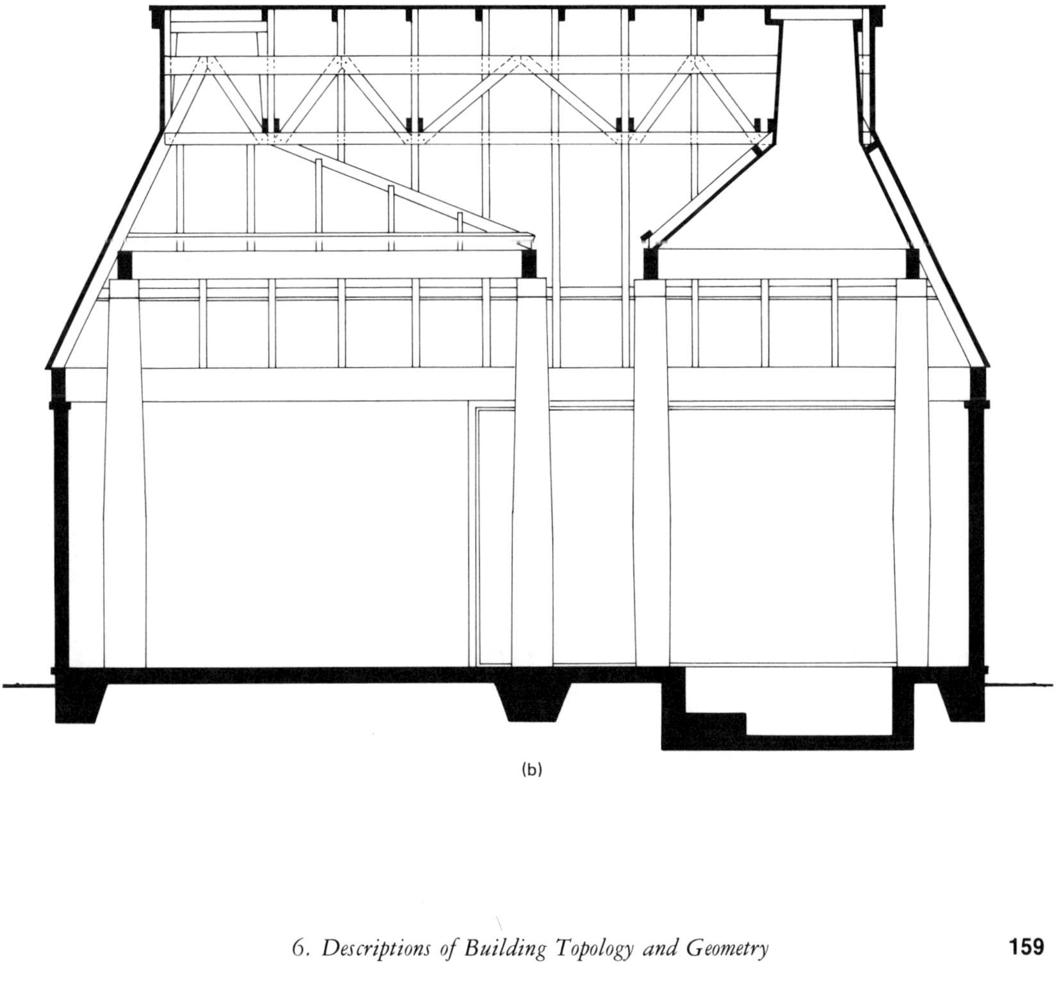

(b)

(a)

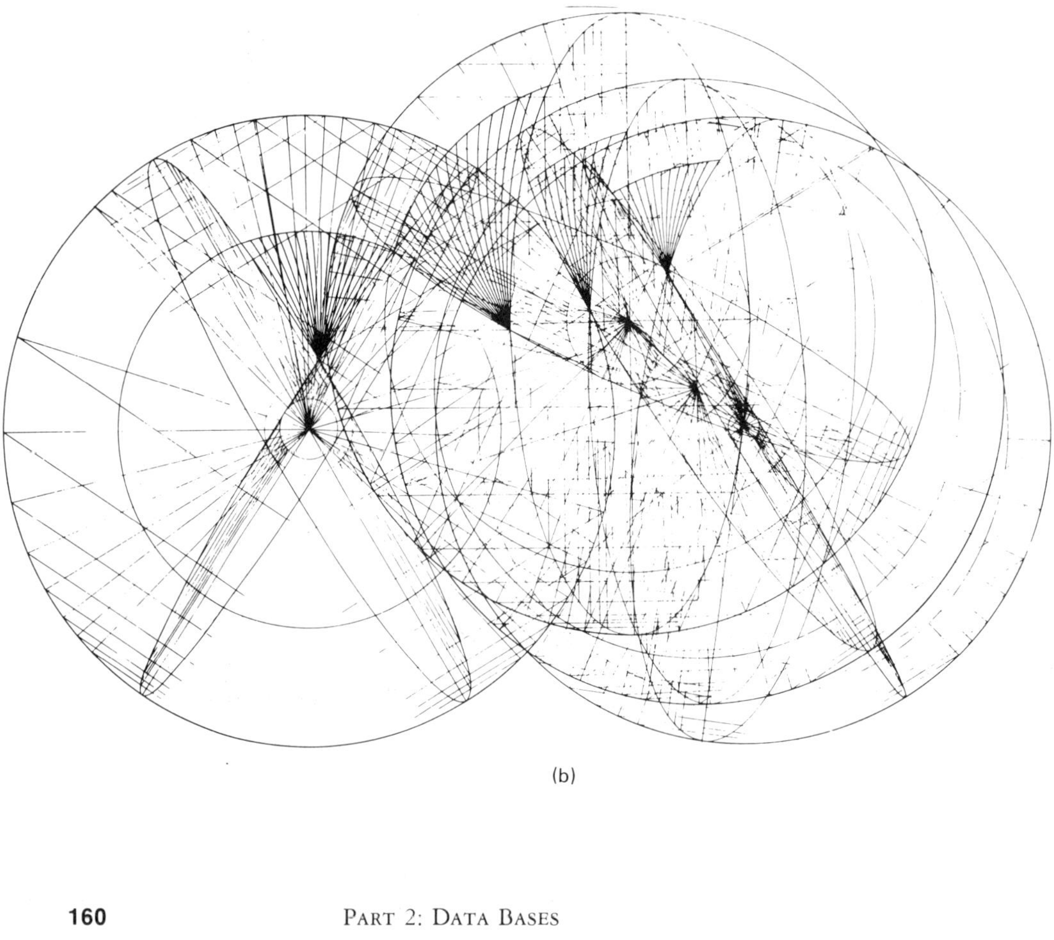

(b)

ing a geometric building description may make it easy to compute some types of relations and difficult to compute others. Most types of data structures that are commonly employed for storing geometric building descriptions, for instance, make it difficult or impossible to detect whether a design is symmetrical about some axis. Thus, they would be unsuitable for use in a design analysis or synthesis task which involved symmetry criteria.

Figure 6.2 *(opposite)* Geometric discipline of the Sydney Opera House. (a) Sydney Opera House, Sydney, Australia, architect Jørn Utzon (photo by David Moore). (b) Spherical geometry of the shells.

Range of approaches

In response to the considerations discussed above, diverse approaches to structuring geometric descriptions of buildings have evolved. These can be grouped into five broad categories:

Representations based upon regular grids and lattices.

Representations based upon variably-dimensioned grids and lattices.

Polygon and polyhedron representations.

Dual-graph representations.

Smith diagram representations.

The remaining sections of this chapter discuss and compare these various approaches.

REPRESENTATIONS BASED ON REGULAR GRIDS AND LATTICES

Geometric representations based upon regular and semi-regular grids and lattices are among the easiest to understand and the most straightforward to implement. Hence they form an appropriate starting point for discussion of geometric description techniques.

Plans of buildings are often constructed within square or rectangular modular grids (*Figure 6.3*), and less commonly within triangular, hexagonal, or more complex grids (*Figure 6.4*). Extending this concept to three dimensions, lattices composed of cubes or rectangular parallelepipeds are often employed in the generation of architectural forms. A famous example is Albert Farwell Bemis' (1936) proposal for use of a four-inch cube as a universal module for building design. A more recent example, a project by O. Mathias Ungers, is illustrated in *Figure 6.5*. A few architects have also worked with non-orthogonal three-dimensional lattices. The identical spatial modules formed by regular grids and lattices make very convenient elements upon which to base geometric descriptions. The following paragraphs describe some typical examples of descriptions produced in this way.

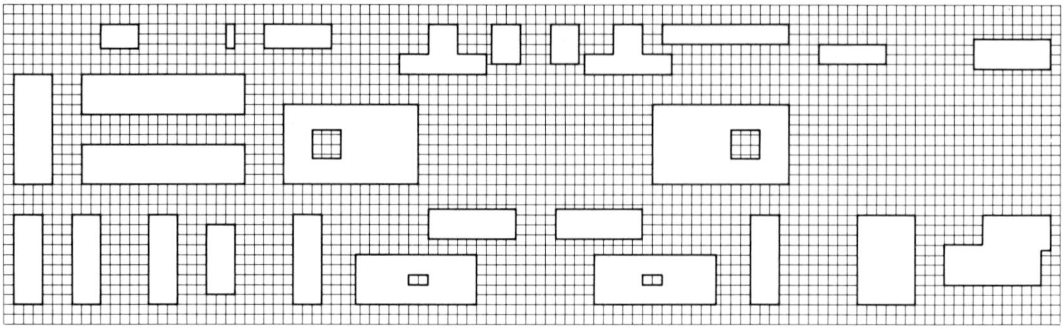

Figure 6.3
Use of a square grid in building design: site plan for the Illinois Institute of Technology, architect Ludwig Mies van der Rohe, 1940.

Square grids

Any arbitrary two-dimensional shape can be represented to any required level of accuracy by a pattern of binary elements (black and white squares, or 1's and 0's) within a two-dimensional square grid, as shown in *Figure* 6.6. Each cell of the grid contains 1 bit of infor-

Figure 6.4
Plan forms of two projects by Walter Netsch, illustrating use of complex grids.

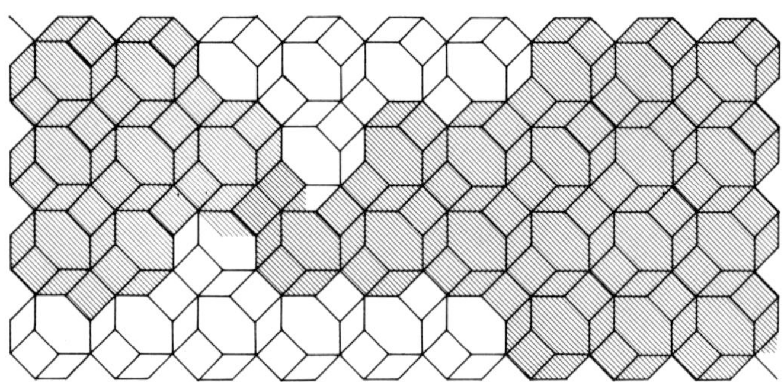

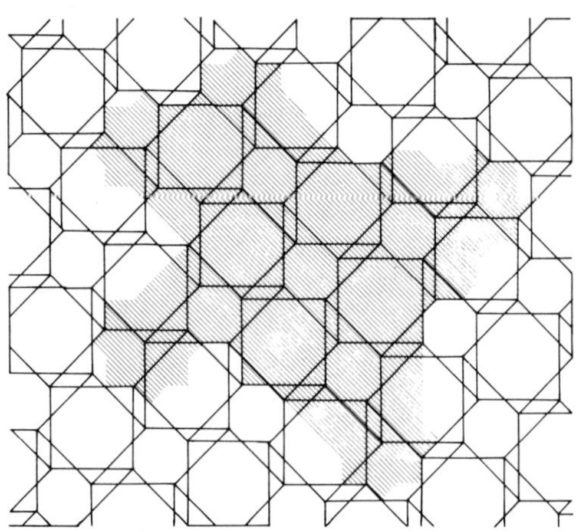

Figure 6.5 *(opposite)*
Project by O. Mathias Ungers for the Roosevelt Island housing competition, New York, 1974, illustrating use of a cubic module.

LOFT TYPE
OPEN PLAN
FLEXIBLE APARTMENTS
WAREHOUSE SPACE
FIXED CORE & FLEXIBLE FLOOR AREA · SKELETAL STRUCTURAL SYSTEM IN STEEL OR CONCRETE · PREFABRICATED SOLID & GLASS WALLS · INFILL EXTERIOR WALLS LIGHT WEIGHT MOVABLE PARTITION

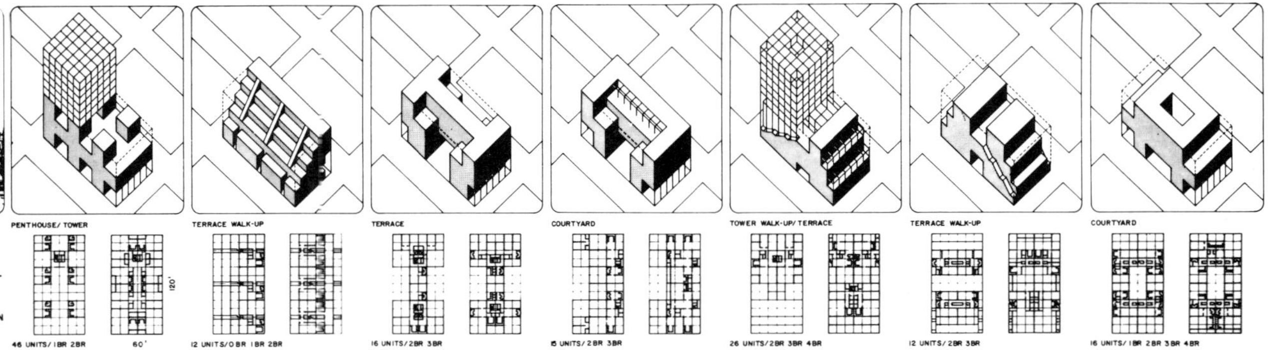

STANDARD TYPE
FIXED PLAN
SET OF ALTERNATIVE APARTMENTS
TYPICAL URBAN BLOCK TYPE
TERRACE, COURTYARD, WALK-UP
BEARING WALL CONSTRUCTION IN BRICK OR CONCRETE BLOCK WITH PAINT OR PLASTERED, GLOSSY FINISH · PARTITION WALLS IN STANDARD MATERIALS

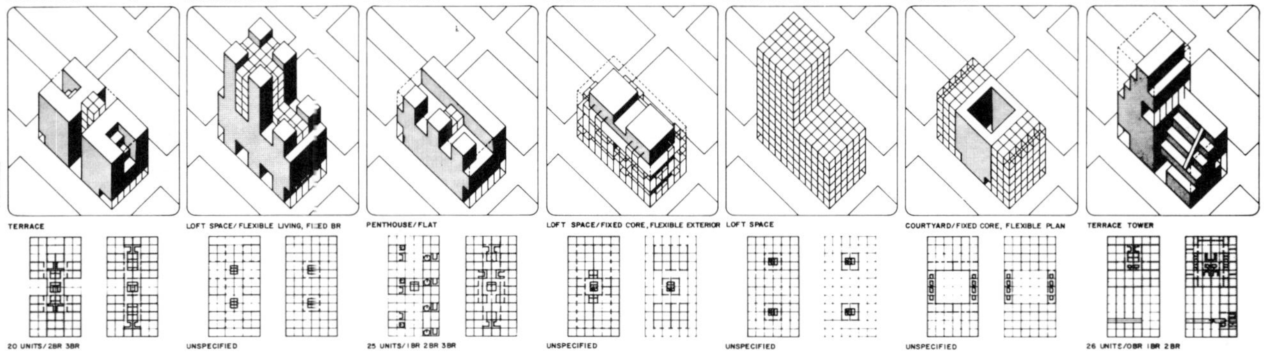

PALAZZO TYPE
SPECIAL PLAN
URBAN PALACE
PENTHOUSE, GARDEN APARTMENT
CONVENTIONAL CONSTRUCTION · MIXED STRUCTURAL SYSTEM · EXTERIOR WALLS WITH TILE COVERING · ELABORATED FACADE DETAILS · FIXED INTERIOR SPACES WITH WIDE PLAN VARIATION

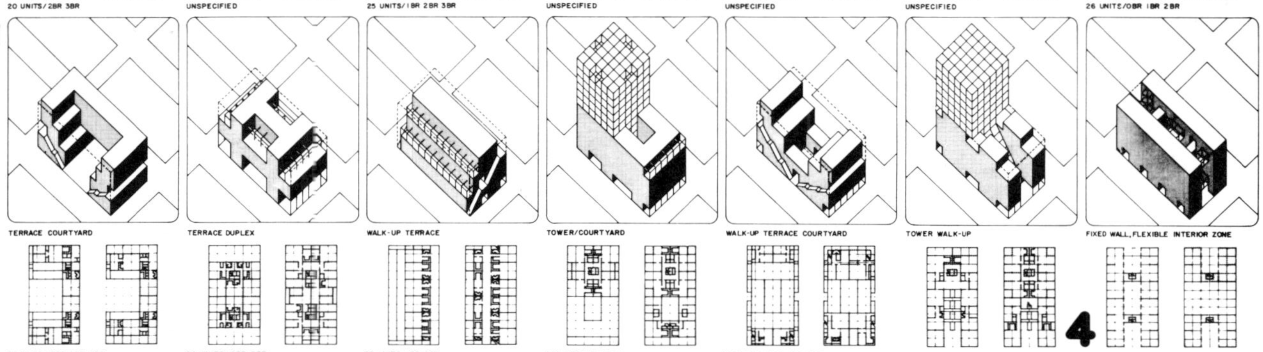

mation, so the amount of information required to represent a form in this way is equal to m × n bits, where m is the number of rows in the grid and n the number of columns. The amount of information required rises exponentially as the level of accuracy is increased; if, for example, the width of a cell is halved, the number of cells in the grid is quadrupled.

Further data can be recorded by utilizing different numbers to represent different properties of the surface, for example, tone, as shown in *Figure 6.7(a)*. This technique has been very widely employed for the numerical encoding of two-dimensional graphic data of various kinds, for example, earth satellite photographs. It provides a direct and obvious method for the numerical representation of building floor plans; a different integer is simply employed for each different space in the plan, as shown in *Figure 6.7(b)*. Walls and other bounding elements are usually not explicitly represented. A boundary is implicitly defined when adjacent cells contain different integers.

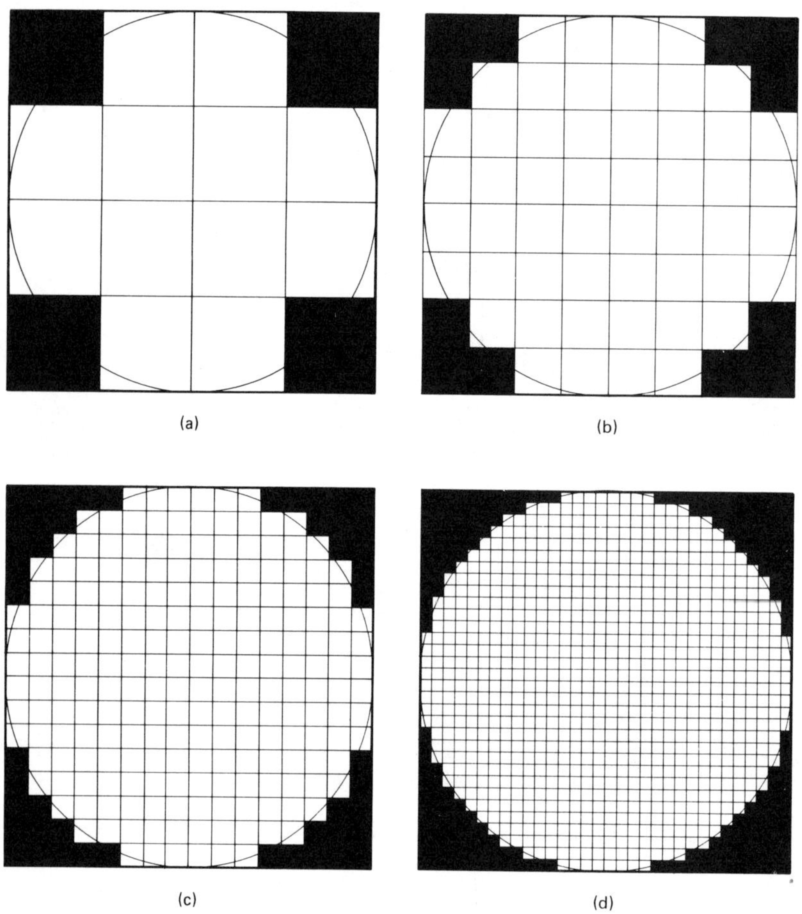

Figure 6.6
Representations of a circle within a square grid. (a) 16 bits. (b) 64 bits. (c) 256 bits. (d) 1024 bits.

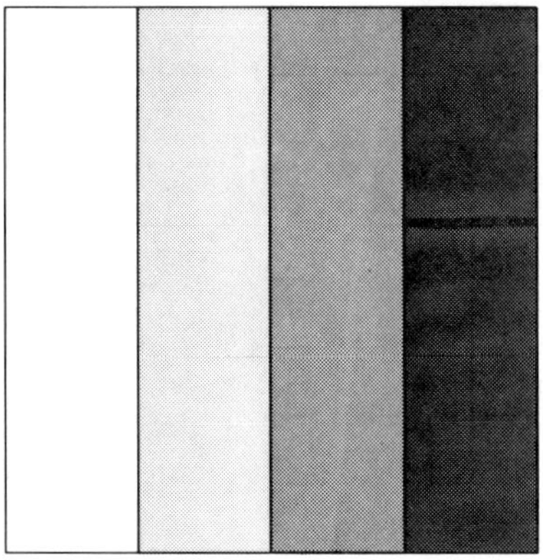

0	0	20	20	40	40	60	60
0	0	20	20	40	40	60	60
0	0	20	20	40	40	60	60
0	0	20	20	40	40	60	60
0	0	20	20	40	40	60	60
0	0	20	20	40	40	60	60
0	0	20	20	40	40	60	60
0	0	20	20	40	40	60	60

(a)

Project from Serlio's The Book of Architecture (London, 1611)

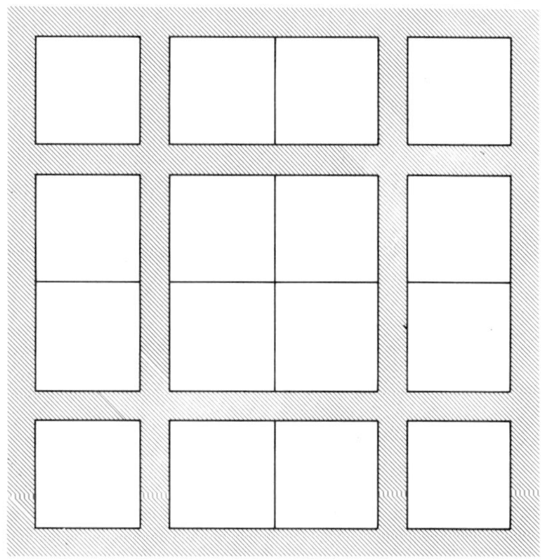

Schematized representation of the layout

1 2 2 3
4 5 5 6
4 5 5 6
7 8 8 9

Schematized representation encoded

(b)

Figure 6.7
Encoding forms as integer arrays. (a) Encoding a grey scale picture as an integer array. (b) Encoding a floor plan as an integer array.

Over the last decade or so numerous automated floor plan synthesis programs employing this type of representation have been developed (Armour and Buffa 1963, Whitehead and Eldars 1964, Beaumont 1967, Lee and Moore 1967, Seehof and Evans 1967, Spillers 1970, Willoughby 1970, Fullenwider 1972, Liggett 1972, Mitchell and Dillon 1972). Most of the programs employing this representation have been written in FORTRAN, ALGOL, PL/1 or other high-level general purpose languages. The array handling facilities of these languages make it very straightforward and convenient to store plans encoded in this way as simple two-dimensional integer arrays, and this has almost invariably been the approach taken.

A rather more sophisticated use of a square-grid representation stored in a two-dimensional array occurs in the Harness hospital integrated computer-aided design system (Jacobsberg 1975). A Harness hospital is a highly modular building. Although minor variations occur, it is essentially laid out on a 5.4m square grid (*Figure 6.8*). Furthermore, each department is composed from 16.2m structural bays. The contents of each 5.4m module are represented by a special 48-bit code (the computer which is used has 48-bit words) and the codes for each floor level are stored in two-dimensional arrays (referred to as *plan matrices*). The first 24 bits describe the cladding, if the module happens to have an external face. The next 21 bits indicate which department, circulation area, etc., occupies the location. The final 3 bits define the phase at which the area will be constructed. A further identically dimensioned matrix (called the *height matrix*) is used to store data indicating the ground level at each point, the presence or absence of floors at each level, a marker indicating the presence of any non-standard construction, and a phase number as before. Since the structural grid for departments is also based upon a square module, and the range of possible layouts of columns and beams in bays is strictly limited, a similar approach is taken to description of the structure.

The two-dimensional array approach to representation of building plans is simple but powerful, because it effectively utilizes the structure of the array itself to implicitly represent positions and adjacencies of spatial elements.

The principal disadvantage of the simple two-dimensional integer array representation of floor plans is that it consumes a great deal of storage. A 100 module x 100 module grid, for example, requires

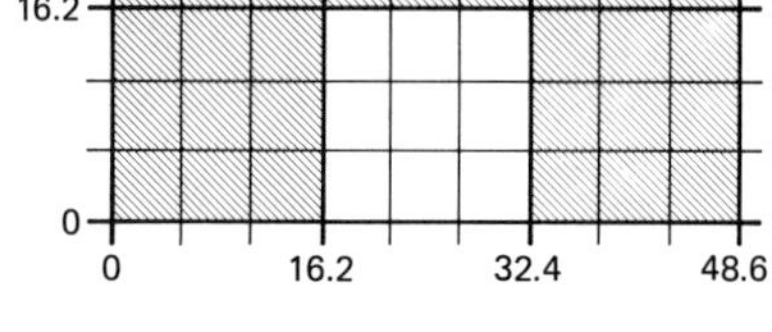

Figure 6.8
Harness hospital department laid out on a 5.4m planning grid located within 16.2m structural bays.

10,000 words of memory. To make matters worse, as we have seen, the number of modules required to describe a floor plan of given area grows exponentially as the dimensions of the module are decreased. Since many of the operations performed upon this type of representation involve iterating through the array and performing some operation upon each individual cell, growth in size of the array also tends to imply substantial increases in computation time.

To overcome the problem of excessive memory requirements, two variations of the simple two-dimensional array representation may be employed: *hierarchical arrays* and a form of *string* representation (Eastman 1970).

In a hierarchical array, grid cells are recursively subdivided into smaller cells as required to represent those portions of the plan in which fine detail occurs, as shown in *Figure 6.9.* Implementation of a hierarchical array representation is fairly straightforward in languages which have facilities which enable recursion, and construction of hierarchical arrays at execution time (*e.g.,* EULER). But this approach can become very unwieldy in languages like FORTRAN which do not have the necessary facilities. Use of hierarchical arrays often can result in substantial storage economies, but a price of increased complexity

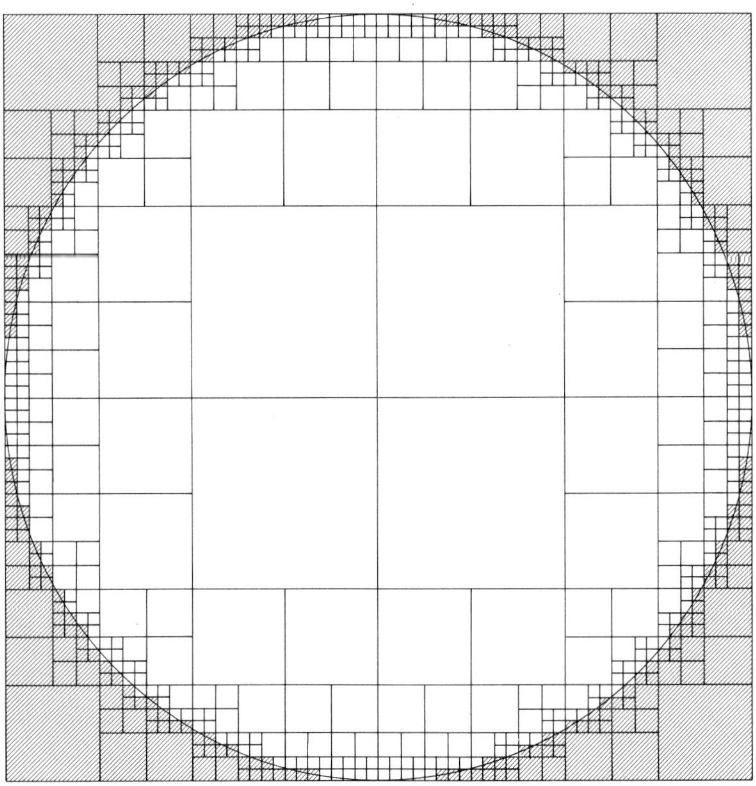

Figure 6.9
Representation of a plan form by a hierarchical array.

of procedures to extract information must be paid. There do not appear to be any reported instances of use of hierarchical arrays in architectural design programs, but they have been used for representation of floor plans in the memories of mobile automata (Nilsson and Raphael 1967, Nilsson 1969).

A number of variants of the string representation can be constructed (see *Figure 6.10*). The basic principle underlying all of them is that the two-dimensional array can be unfolded into a one-dimensional array, then compressed. *Figure 6.10(b)* illustrates the unfolding process. It can be seen that the resultant one-dimensional array consists of sequences of identical integers. The array can then be compressed by replacing each of these sequences by just two integers, the first giving the total number of identical integers in the sequence, and the second giving the integer from which the sequence is composed (*Figure 6.10(c)*). It is obvious that great compression can often be achieved by this means. But use of the compressed string representation necessitates use of a fairly laborious procedure to access a given grid location.

Rectangular grids

The concept of the square grid representation can easily be extended to allow for rectangular grid cells. This may be an advantage in situations where design of a floor plan is based upon use of a rectangular module, and it is desired to have the cells in the computer representation correspond to the module. It is merely necessary to store coefficients for the x-dimension and y-dimension of the module, and to apply these coefficients when calculating distances, areas, centroid locations, etc.

Cubic lattices

By utilizing three-dimensional instead of two-dimensional arrays, three-dimensional forms can be represented using the integer array technique (*Figure 6.11*). It should be noted, however, that the exponential growth in storage requirements with decreasing cell size is even more rapid in this case; every halving of the side-length results in an eight-fold increase in the number of cells. Hierarchical arrays and string representations may also be utilized in the three-dimensional case, and coefficients may be applied to produce a lattice composed of rectangular parallelepipeds. White (1972) and Cinar (1975) have published discussions of three-dimensional layout programs utilizing this type of data structure.

Non-rectilinear grids

In order to discuss representation of plan forms utilizing non-rectilinear grids, a brief excursion into the theory of symmetrical network patterns will be necessary. The following discussion is based

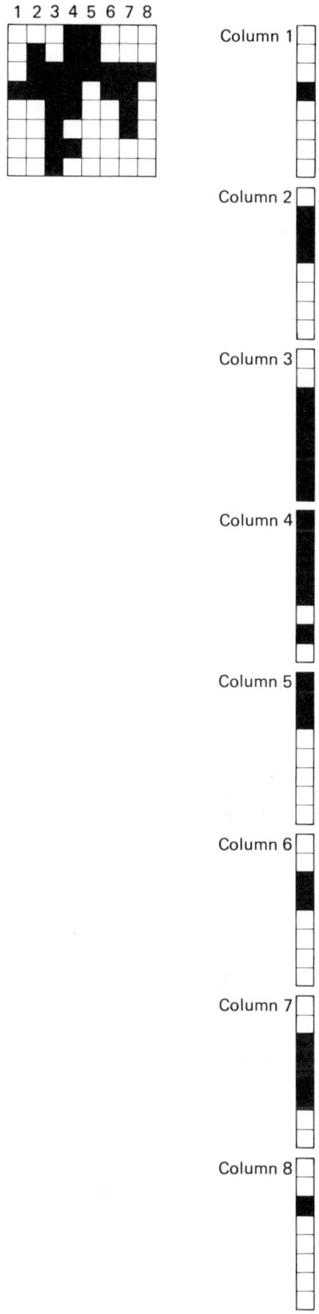

Number	Type
3	0
1	1
5	0
3	1
6	0
11	1
1	0
1	1
1	0
3	1
7	0
2	1
6	0
4	1
4	0
1	1
5	0

(c)

Figure 6.10
Compressed string representation. (a) Two-dimensional array representation of a form. (b) Two-dimensional array unfolded into a one-dimensional string. (c) Compressed format for storage of string.

upon A. V. Shubnikov's classic analysis, to which the reader is referred for a more detailed treatment (Shubnikov and Koptsik 1974).

Consider equally-spaced parallel rows of equidistant points, joined by straight lines, as illustrated in *Figure 6.12.* This may be

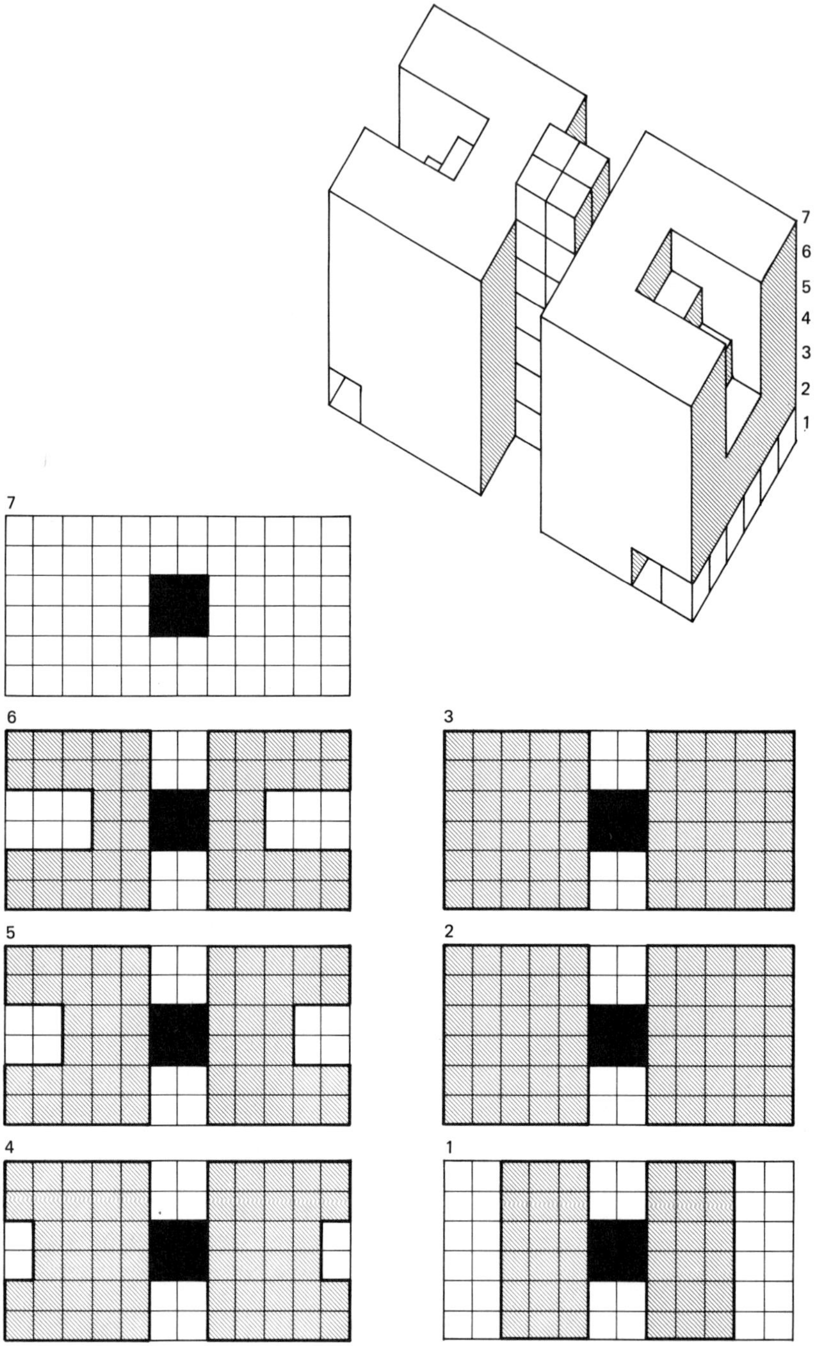

Figure 6.11
Representation of a built form as an assemblage of cubic modules.

termed a *parallelogram system of equivalent points.* A particular parallelogram system may be described by giving the side lengths x and y, and the angle θ between these sides. Forms represented as patterns of cells in a parallelogram system may be transformed by varying x, y

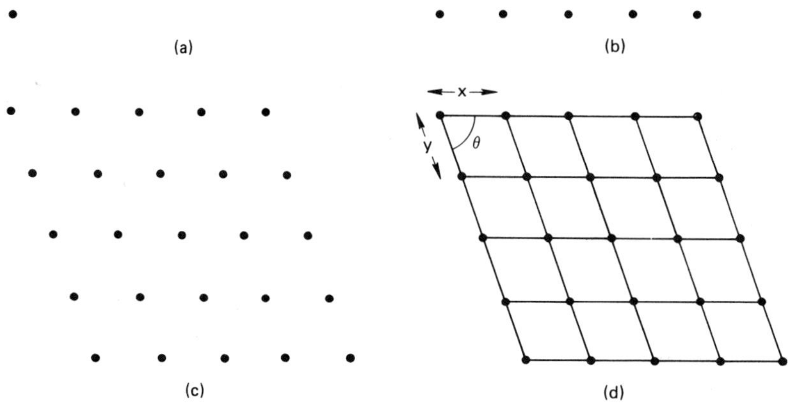

Figure 6.12
Generation of a parallelogram system of equivalent points. The particular system is described by the side lengths x and y and the angle θ. (a) Point. (b) Point translated along one axis to generate a row of equally spaced points. (c) Row translated along another axis to generate equally spaced rows. (d) Points connected by straight lines drawn parallel to the translation axes.

and θ, as shown in *Figure 6.13(a)*. This technique of transformation of form by varying the parameters of a parallelogram system was known to Dürer, who employed it to generate caricatures (*Figure 6.13(b)*). It can be shown that there are only five distinct types of parallelogram systems of equivalent points (*Figure 6.14*). Each particular cell in any of these systems may be uniquely identified by means of two or three coordinates.

A method for description of any floor plan constructed within a parallelogram system can now be shown. The steps are as follows:

1. Describe the parallelogram system by means of the parameters x, y, and θ, and assign coordinates to the cells.

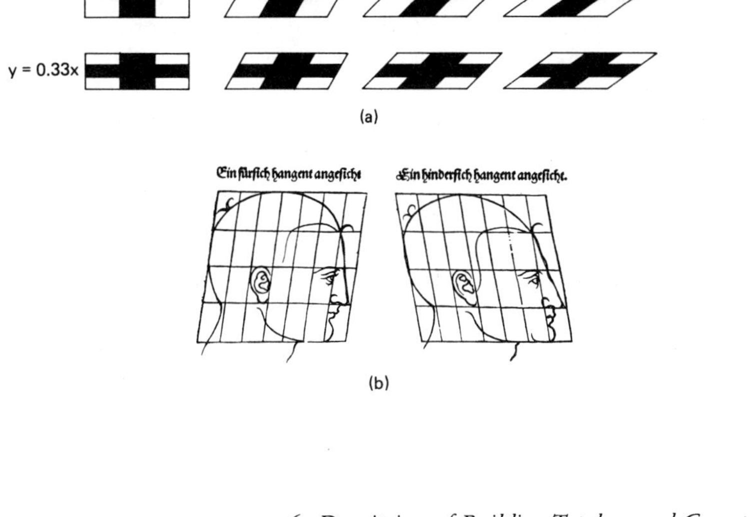

Figure 6.13
Transformation of forms by varying the parameters of parallelogram systems. (a) Tableau of plan forms produced by varying the parameters of y and θ. (b) Dürer's method of transforming faces by varying the parameters of a parallelogram system (illustration from the *Four Books of Human Proportions*).

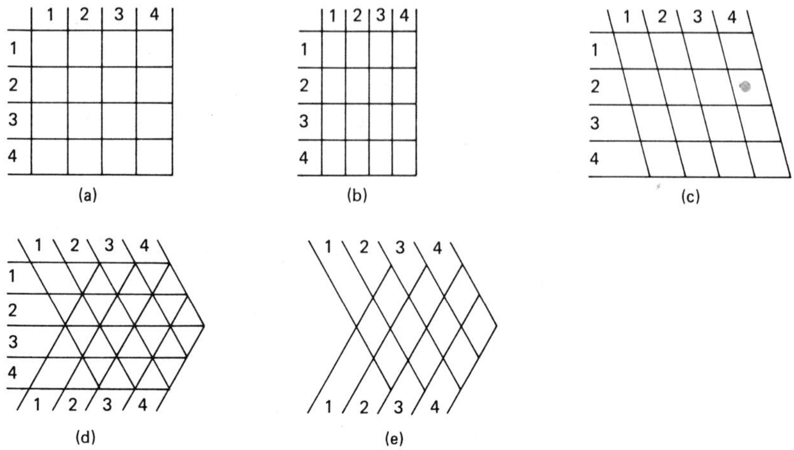

Figure 6.14
The five parallelogram systems of equivalent points. (a) Square. (b) Rectangle. (c) Oblique parallelogram. (d) Equilateral triangle. (e) Centered orthorhombic.

2. Assign integers to cells to represent different areas, as with the square grid representations discussed previously.
3. Store these integers in the corresponding locations of a two- or three-dimensional array.

An example is illustrated in *Figure 6.15*.

Further networks of equal figures can be obtained by means of additional operations. For example, a hexagonal network can be generated from the triangular network by grouping adjacent triangles, as shown in *Figure 6.16*.

Complex shapes formed by combination of equal figures

In the types of representations which we have been discussing, a complex shape is always represented as an aggregation of adjacent equal polygons or polyhedra. For example, a room in a floor plan might be described as an aggregation of squares, as shown in *Figure 6.17*. A question which immediately arises is, "How many different complex shapes can be formed from a specified number of elements?" Rather surprisingly, this question has no straightforward answer in most cases. The following paragraphs discuss some of the types of complex shapes which can be generated in this way, and their enumeration.

From an architectural point of view, one of the most interesting families of complex shapes formed from equal elements is the family of *polyominoes*. A polyomino is an edge-connected assemblage of squares (Golomb 1965). All the distinct polyominoes of up to six squares are shown in *Figure 6.18*. There is a very extensive mathematical literature on the enumeration of polyominoes (which is a difficult task) and on their properties. A comprehensive summary, together

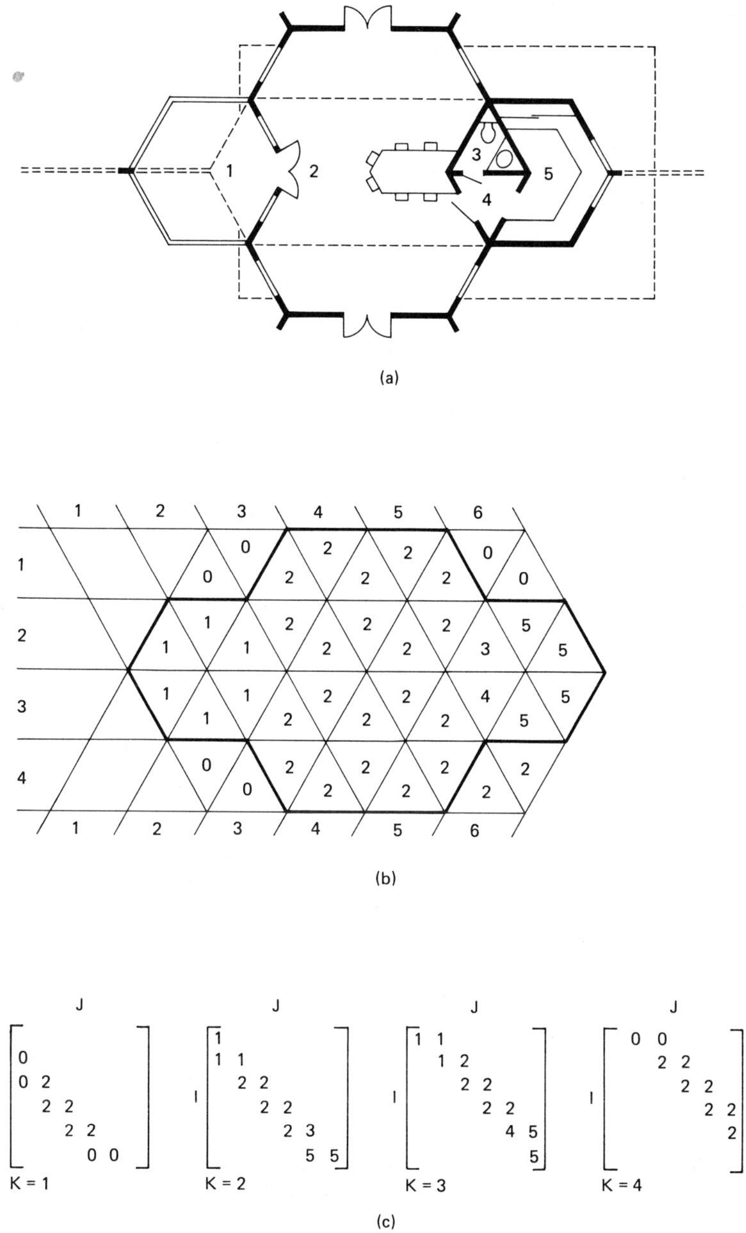

Figure 6.15
Encoding and storage of a plan which is based upon a triangular grid. (a) Project for a house-boat by Frank Lloyd Wright. (b) Representation of the plan by integers in a triangular grid. (c) Storage of the representation in a three-dimensional array.

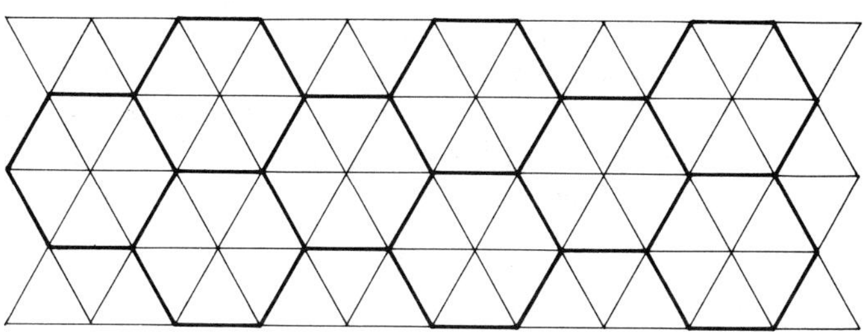

Figure 6.16
Generation of a hexagonal network from a triangular network.

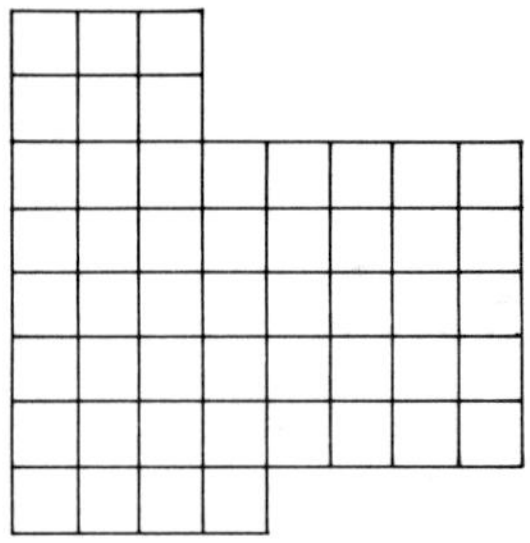

Figure 6.17
Representation of a complex form as an aggregation of squares.

with a discussion of architecturally important properties, has been published by Matela and March (1975).

By generalization of the concept of a polyomino, *polyiamonds* are edge-connected assemblages of equilateral triangles, *polyhexes* are edge-connected assemblages of regular hexagons, *polycubes* are edge-connected assemblages of cubes, and so on. The known numbers of all these various types of figures are shown in *Table 6.1*.

Table 6.1
Known numbers of polyominoes, polyiamonds, polyhexes, and polycubes (after Golomb (1965), and Lunnon (1971, 1972)).

Cells	Polyominoes	Polyiamonds	Polyhexes	Polycubes
1	1	1	1	1
2	1	1	1	1
3	2	1	3	2
4	5	3	7	7
5	12	4	22	23
6	35	12	82	112
7	108	24	333	
8	369	66	1,448	
9	1,285	160	6,572	
10	4,655	448	30,490	
11	17,073	1,186	143,552	
12	63,600	3,3334	683,101	
13	238,591	9,235		
14	901,971	26,166		
15	3,426,576	73,983		
16	13,079,255	211,297		
17	50,107,911			
18	192,622,052			

Enumeration of potential design solutions represented within grids and lattices

In the representations discussed in this section, particular design solutions are represented by the assignment of symbols to cells in a regular grid or lattice. The range of possible assignments constitutes a set U of potential designs. Where n integers are assigned to n cells, the number of possible assignments is n!. Where n integers are assigned to m cells, and $n < m$, the number of potential assignments is given by $m!/(m-n)!$. The growth in the number of potential solutions with increasing n thus takes place very rapidly, as shown in *Figure 6.19*.

Figure 6.18
The 56 polyominoes composed of 6 or fewer squares.

VARIABLY-DIMENSIONED GRIDS AND LATTICES

Another type of representation that is quite closely related to the square or cubic grid method of representation makes use of rectangles of varying dimension as the fundamental elements of the description.

n	n!	Log (n!)
1	1	0.0
2	2	0.69
3	6	1.79
4	24	3.18
5	120	4.79
6	720	6.58
7	5,040	8.53
8	40,320	10.60
9	362,880	12.80
10	3,628,800	15.10

(a)

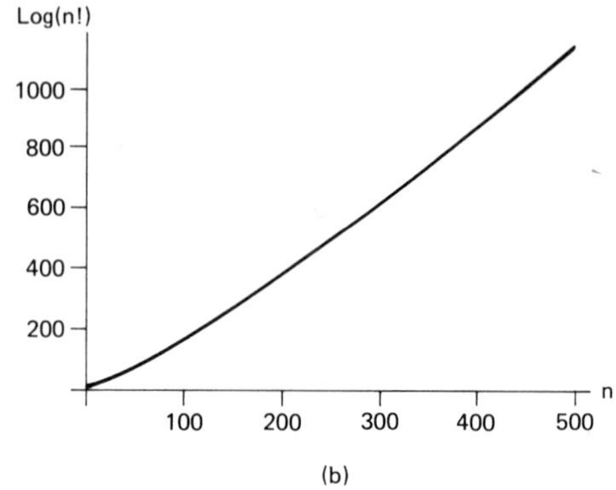

(b)

Figure 6.19
The exponential growth of n! (a) Small n. (b) Larger n.

Dimensionless representation of rectilinear shapes

Consider the three rectilinear objects shown in *Figure 6.20(a)*. Although their dimensions and proportions are quite different, they clearly have some shape properties in common: they are all "U-shaped" objects. The observation that dimensionally very different objects can be discerned to have common shape properties suggests

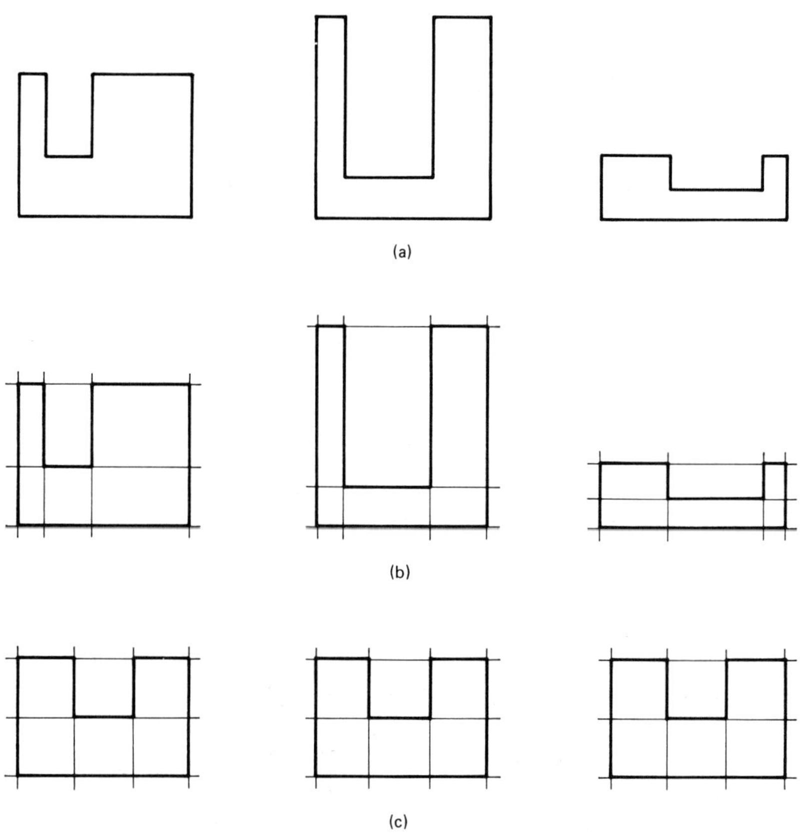

Figure 6.20
Dimensionless representations of similar rectilinear shapes. (a) Several U-shaped objects. (b) Imposition of minimum rectangular gratings. (c) Transformation to dimensionless representations.

that it may be possible to develop descriptive techniques in which shape and dimensions are specified separately. This can be accomplished by use of a *dimensionless representation* in conjunction with *dimensioning vectors.*

The concept of a dimensionless representation of a rectilinear shape is perhaps best explained by the following example. Consider again the series of apparently similar forms shown in *Figure 6.20(a)*. The reason for this apparent similarity becomes obvious if we surround each form by a rectangular frame, and superimpose a *minimum rectangular grating* (Newman 1954) as shown in *Figure 6.20(b)*. This minimum rectangular grating is formed by drawing horizontal and vertical lines across the frame in such a way that all vertices of the original form lie on an intersection, and each grating line intersects at least one vertex. It can be seen that the minimum grating for each form, in the example shown, consists of six rectangular cells. If we now adjust the dimensions of the minimum gratings so that each cell in the grating becomes square, as shown in *Figure 6.20(c)*, we find that each of the differently-dimensioned shapes reduces to the same U-shaped figure. Such a representation of a form within a uniform square grating may be termed its *dimensionless representation.*

The dimensionless representation of a rectilinear shape can be numerically encoded as a two-dimensional array of 1's and 0's. March (1976) has suggested that this array can then be unfolded to form a one-dimensional string of 1's and 0's, in other words a binary number. This binary number can then be re-expressed in octal, decimal or hexadecimal form. The encoding of the floor plan of one of Le Corbusier's Maison Minimum, using this scheme, is illustrated in *Figure 6.21.*

Dimensioning vectors

The dimensional properties of a particular rectilinear shape can be specified by defining X and Y dimensioning vectors, as shown in *Figure 6.22.* The elements of the X dimensioning vector describe the widths of the columns, and the elements of the Y dimensioning vector describe the widths of the rows. Given a dimensionless representation and dimensioning vectors, the dimensioned shape can be constructed. Applying different dimensioning vectors to a dimensionless representation will produce a family of shapes in which the constituent rectangles have different dimensions and areas, but the adjacency relations between these rectangles remain constant. Well-known examples of such families of shapes are the standard structural sections: rectangles, angles, I-sections, T-sections, and channels (*Figure 6.23*). Manufacturers' catalogues for structural sections often consist simply of tables of critical dimensions for the available section shapes.

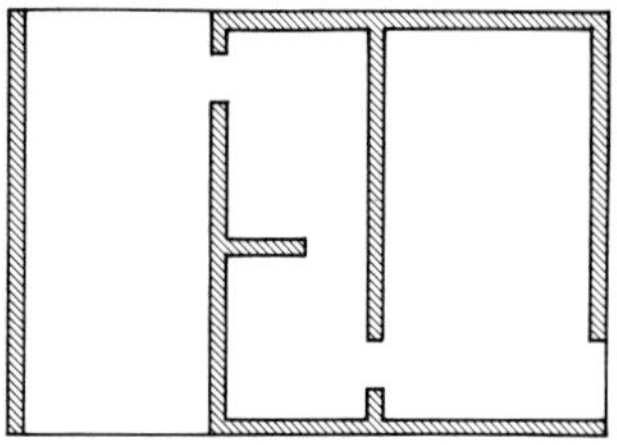

(a)

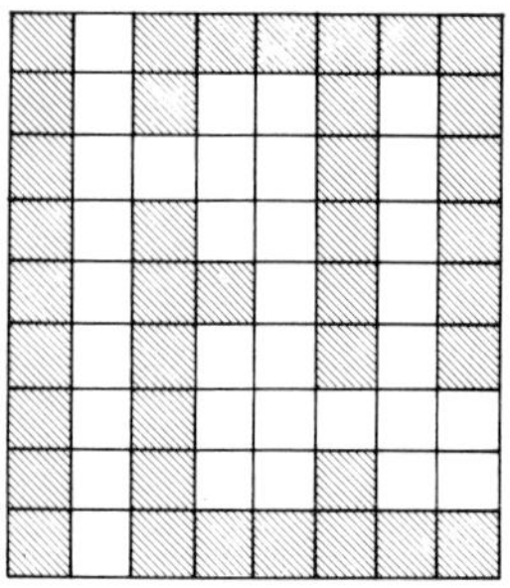

(b)

1011, 1111, 1010, 0101, 1000, 0101, 1010, 0101, 1011, 0101, 1010, 0101, 1010, 0000, 1010, 0100, 1011, 1111

(c)

BFA585A5B5A50A4BF

(d)

Figure 6.21 Encoding the dimensionless representation of the floor plan of a *Maison Minimum* (after March 1976). (a) Floor plan. (b) Dimensionless representation. (c) Binary code for unfolded dimensionless representation. (d) Corresponding hexadecimal code.

Rectilinear floor plans in dimensionless form

It is straightforward to extend the technique of dimensionless representation for use in description of floor plans. Instead of just using 1's and 0's to represent solids and voids, as in the examples discussed so far, we may use different integers to distinguish different rooms in a layout, as illustrated in *Figure 6.24.* This approach has two obvious advantages over the simple square grid representation which was introduced earlier: it can gain considerable storage economies, and it allows dimensions to vary continuously rather than in fixed modular increments. Of course, a price of increased complexity of manipulation operations must be paid.

A third, less obvious advantage of this method of representation is that the separation of shape-description from dimensional information allows the exhaustive enumeration of *generic solutions* to floor plan layout problems. Consider for example the class of floor plans generated by dissection of a rectangle into rectangles. For dissection into any given number of rectangles, the number of distinct

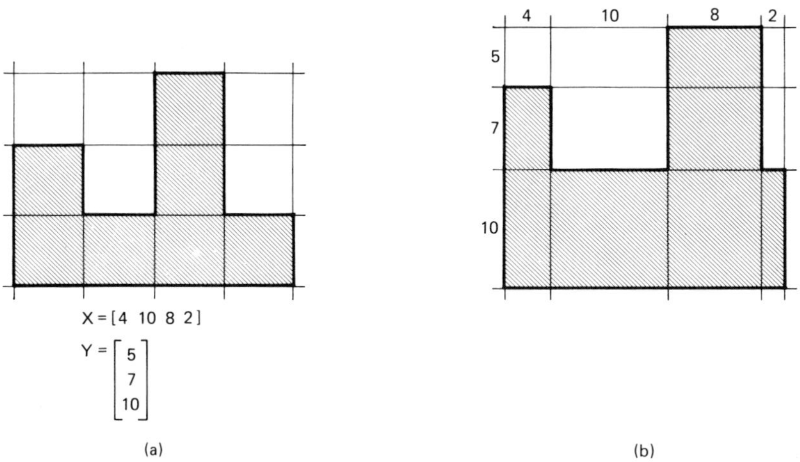

Figure 6.22
Description of a shape by a dimensionless representation plus dimensioning vectors. (a) Dimensionless representation plus dimensioning vectors. (b) Corresponding shape drawn to scale.

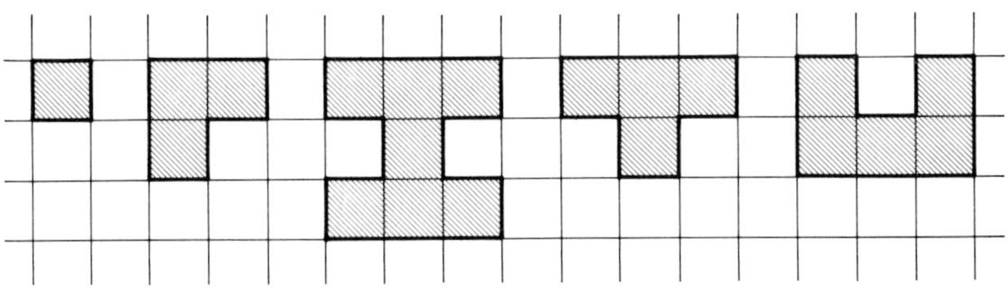

Figure 6.23
Dimensionless representations of standard structural sections.

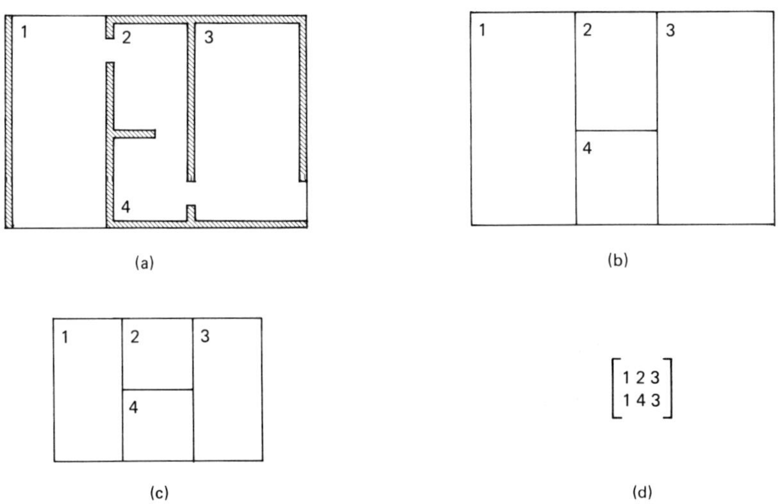

Figure 6.24
Use of an integer array to store a dimensionless representation of a floor plan. (a) Initial floor plan. (b) Outline floor plan. (c) Dimensionless representation of outline floor plan. (d) Integer array encoding dimensionless representation of outline floor plan.

dissections is limited, and there exists a simple algorithm for exhaustively enumerating these distinct dissections (Steadman 1976, Sauda 1975, Mitchell, Steadman and Liggett 1976). All the distinct dissections into up to six rectangles are illustrated, in dimensionless representation, in *Figure 6.25*. Ranges of specific floor plans can be pro-

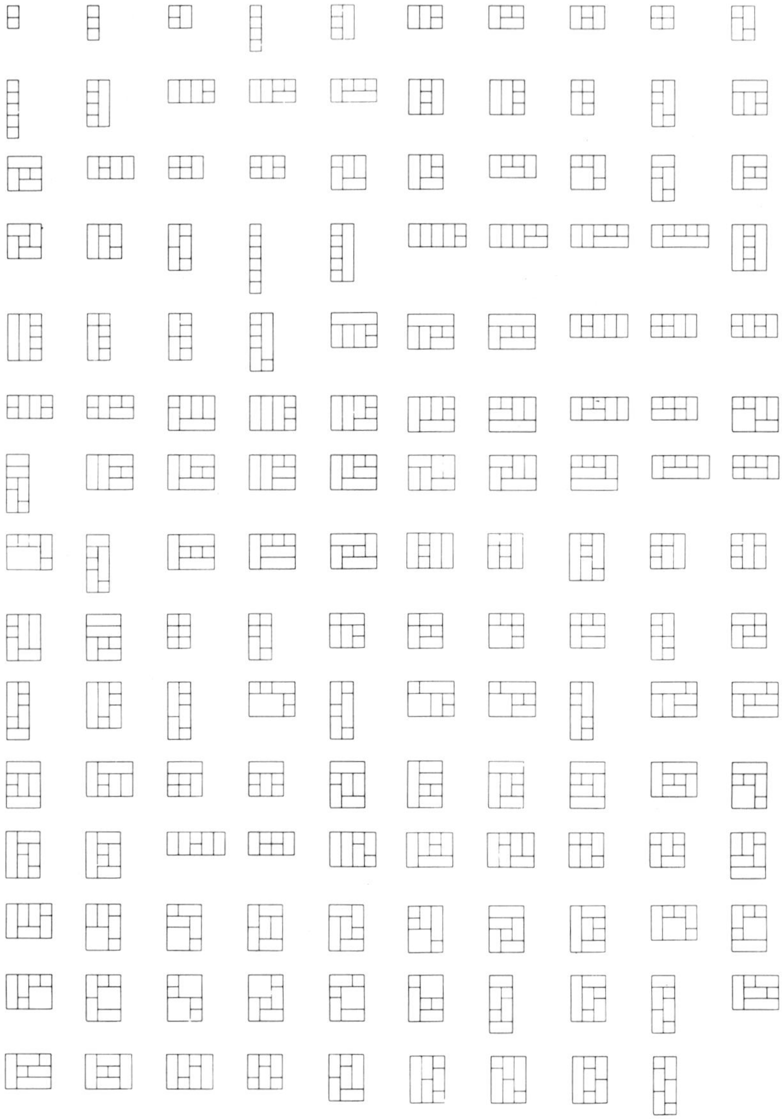

Figure 6.25
Dimensionless representations of all the dissections of a rectangle into six or fewer rectangles (from Mitchell, Steadman and Liggett, 1976).

duced by mapping activities into the cells of these dissections and applying dimensioning vectors.

Three-dimensional rectilinear forms

The technique of form description by means of dimensionless representation of shape plus dimensioning vectors may be extended to three-dimensional rectilinear forms. A three-dimensional minimum grating is employed, together with X, Y and Z dimensioning vectors. Several examples of dimensionless representations of buildings are illustrated in *Figure 6.26,* and the method for numerically encod-

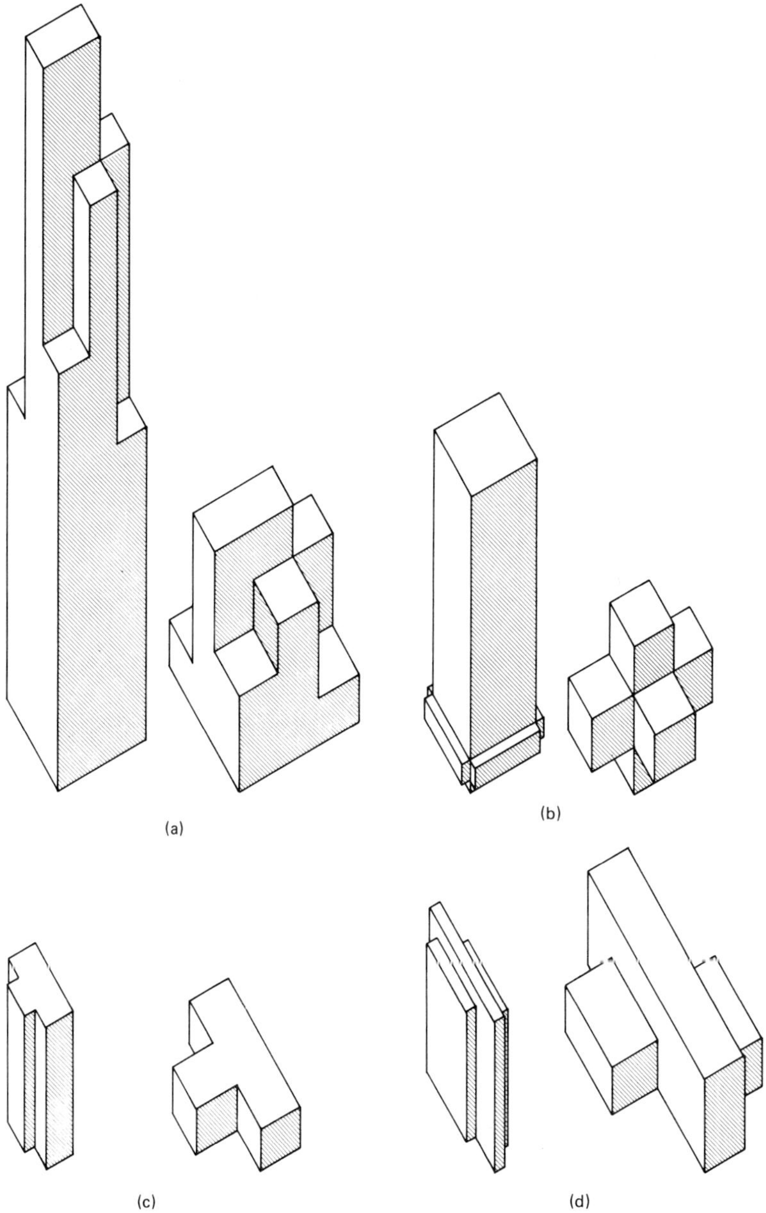

Figure 6.26
Examples of high rise office buildings and their dimensionless representations. (a) Sears Tower, Chicago (Skidmore, Owings, and Merrill). (b) Place Victoria, Montreal (Luigi Moretti and Pier Luigi Nervi). (c) One Charles Center, Baltimore (Ludwig Mies van der Rohe). (d) Thyssen-Rohrenwerke office, Dusseldorf (Hentrich and Perschnigg).

ing dimensionless representations of three-dimensional rectilinear forms is demonstrated in *Figure 6.27*.

Non-rectilinear forms

Non-rectilinear polygons and floor plans may also be reduced to dimensionless representations, as shown in *Figure 6.28*. Note, however, that in the non-rectilinear case a number of different orienta-

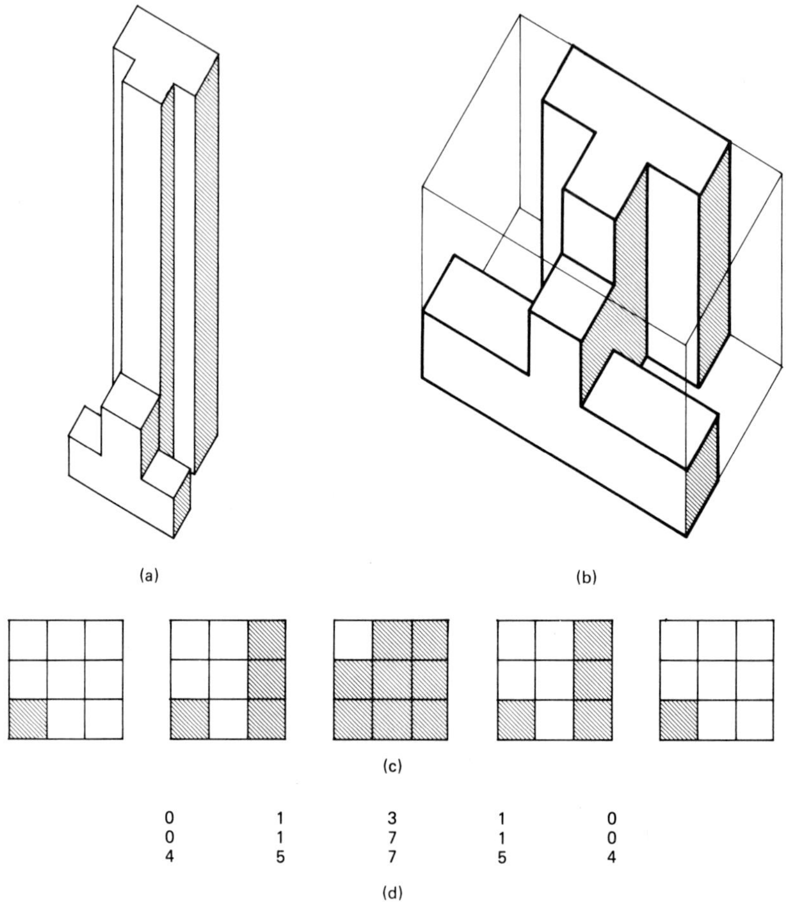

Figure 6.27 Numerically encoding the dimensionless representation of the Seagram Building, New York (after March 1976). (a) Scale drawing. (b) Dimensionless representation. (c) Representation of sections through the dimensionless representation as bit patterns. (d) Encoding of each row of each section as an octal digit.

tions of the frame with respect to the plan are possible, and that each different orientation will produce a different dimensionless representation. A further difference from the rectilinear case is that vertex angles do not necessarily remain constant as the dimensions of the grating are adjusted. Since walls need not necessarily lie along grating lines, the simple integer array form of representation cannot be employed.

Applications

Representations based upon variably-dimensioned grids and lattices appear to have found their widest application in automated floor plan layout programs. Eastman (1971, 1972, 1973) has developed a sophisticated program called General Space Planner which employs this representation. Eastman (1975) has also published a very useful library of FORTRAN subroutines for manipulation of plans represented in this way. Mitchell, Steadman and Liggett (1976) have

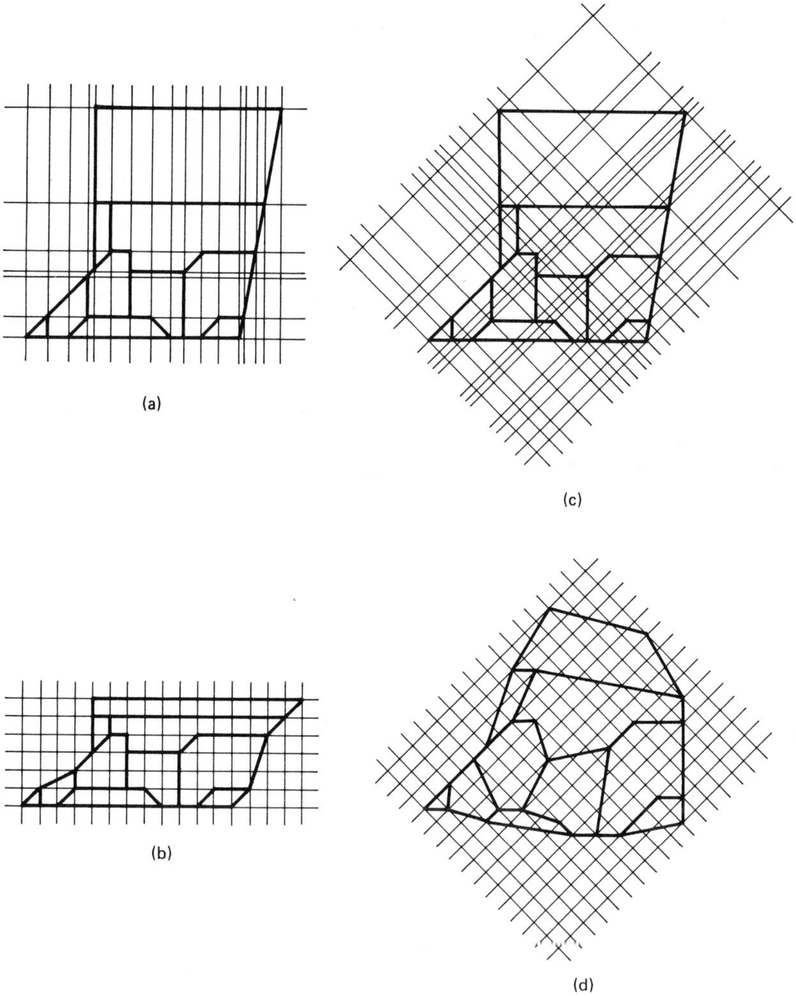

Figure 6.28
Dimensionless representation of a non-rectilinear plan (North Penn Visiting Nurse Association Headquarters, architects, Venturi and Short, 1960). (a) Grating aligned with north, south, and west walls. (b) Resultant dimensionless representation in a 6 X 16 grid. (c) Grating rotated 45° to align with northwest wall. (d) Resultant dimensionless representation in a 14 X 16 grid.

published a method for synthesis and optimization of small rectangular floor plans which also employs the representation.

POLYGON AND POLYHEDRON REPRESENTATIONS

The representational techniques discussed so far have all been based on *explicit* representation of spatial domains (by integers representing spatial elements). This approach differs from that followed in traditional architectural drawings, where spatial domains are *implicitly* represented by drawing edge-lines which define the *boundaries* of domains. Systems of representation based upon storing edge-lines of forms and spaces may also be utilized for describing buildings in computer memory. These may be classed as polygon and polyhedron representations.

Points, lines, polygons, and polyhedra

Figure 6.29
Representation of lines. (a) Representation of a straight line by the coordinates of its end points. (b) Representation of a line composed of straight segments by point-coordinates. (c) Approximation of a curved line by straight segments. (d) More accurate approximation by more segments.

Points are the basic building blocks of polygon and polyhedron representations. A point in space, relative to some given coordinate system, can be represented by its coordinates (x,y) in two-dimensional space or (x,y,z) in three-dimensional space. For reasons which will become clear as we proceed, it is convenient to think of these coordinate pairs or triples as *row vectors* [x y] or [x y z].

Since a *straight line* is defined by its end points (*Figure 6.29(a)*), it can be represented as a 2×2 matrix composed of the two coordinate pairs which specify the end points:

$$\begin{bmatrix} x_1 & y_1 \\ x_2 & y_2 \end{bmatrix}$$

Lines composed of n straight segments can be represented by $(n+1)$ points (*Figure 6.29(b)*). Similarly, curved lines can be

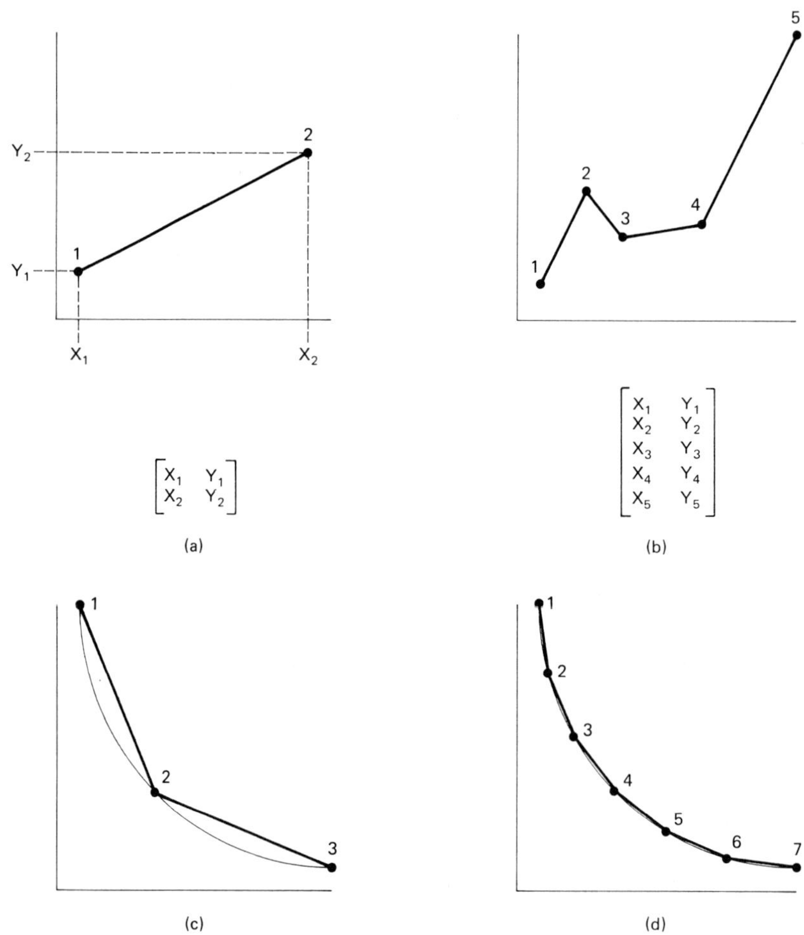

represented to any desired degree of accuracy by approximation with short straight segments, then encoding in this format.

Polygons are defined by lines which begin and end at the same point. Thus polygons (and closed curves) can also be represented in this format, as shown in *Figure 6.30.* Vertices are numbered cyclically. Either the first vertex is repeated at the end of the list (explicitly representing the last edge) or the last edge is implicitly represented by assuming that the last and first vertices are connected by an edge which closes the polygon.

The faces of *polyhedra* are polygons. A polyhedron can thus be represented by several point-matrices, each of which represents one of the faces (*Figure 6.31*). Some redundancy results, however. Each line is represented twice, since it divides two faces, and each point is represented at least twice. Just as two-dimensional curves can be approximated by straight line segments, three-dimensional curved sur-

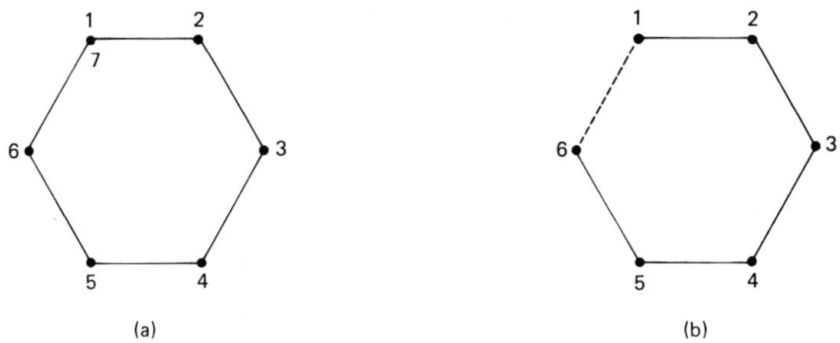

Figure 6.30
Representation of polygons. (a) Explicit closure. (b) Implicit closure.

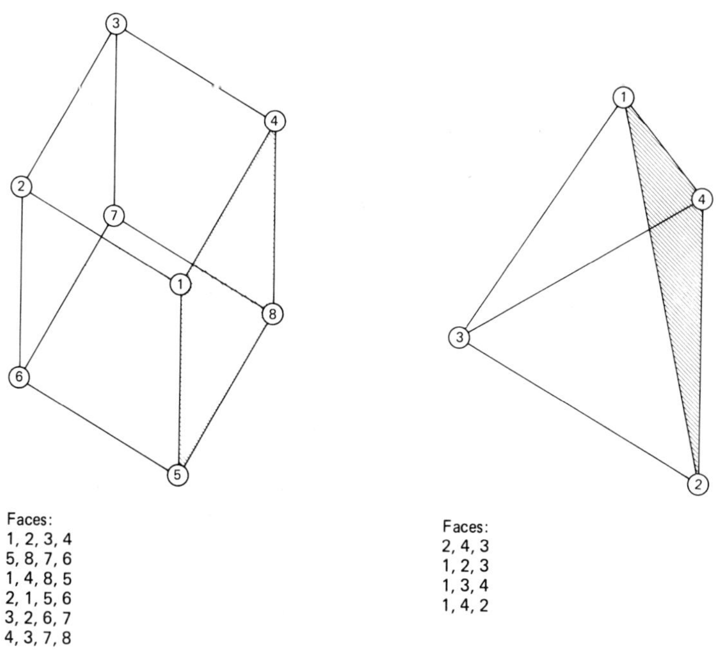

Figure 6.31
Representation of polyhedra.

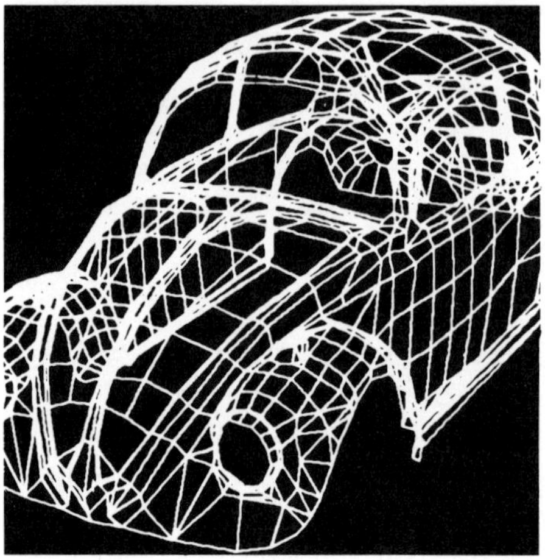

Figure 6.32
Representation of curved surfaces by polygonal faces.

faces can be approximated by polygonal faces (*Figure 6.32*). (Note, however, that unless the faces are triangles, they are not necessarily planar.)

Point-matrices can readily be stored in a computer by means of arrays or lists. This type of representation is very widely employed in computer graphics systems, since arrays or lists storing point-matrices are readily converted into instructions to a graphics output device to generate a picture. The following type of FORTRAN statement, for example, is often used to instruct a pen plotter to draw a line:

```
CALL LINE (X1,Y1,X2,Y2)
```

where X1,Y1, and X2,Y2, are coordinates describing the start-point and end-point, respectively, for the line on the plotting surface.

Explicit representation of topology

For many purposes, it is useful to treat a line figure as a *graph.* A graph may be defined as follows (Deo 1974):

> A *graph* $G=(V,E)$ consists of a set of objects $V=\{v_1, v_2, \ldots\}$ called *vertices,* and another set $E=\{e_1e_2, \ldots\}$, whose elements are *edges,* such that each edge e_k is identified with an unordered pair (v_i,v_j) of vertices.

Figure 6.33(a) is an example of a graph. More precisely, the figure represents one particular possible *geometric realization* of a graph composed of given sets of vertices and edges related in specified ways. An infinite number of alternative geometric realizations can be constructed for a given graph. Some examples are illustrated in *Figures 6.33(b) to (d).*

Incidence matrices and *adjacency matrices* can be used to numerically encode a graph for computer storage. An incidence matrix representing a given graph can be constructed as shown in *Figure 6.33(e).*

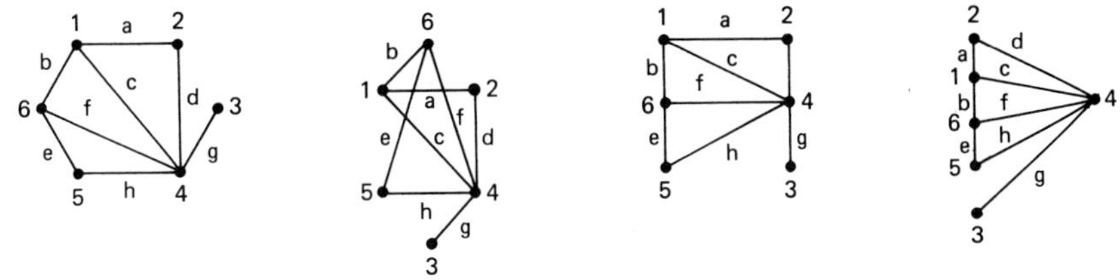

(a) (b) (c) (d)

	a	b	c	d	e	f	g	h
1	1	1	1	0	0	0	0	0
2	1	0	0	1	0	0	0	0
3	0	0	0	0	0	0	1	0
4	0	0	1	1	0	1	1	1
5	0	0	0	0	1	0	0	1
6	0	1	0	0	1	1	0	0

(e)

	1	2	3	4	5	6
1	0	1	0	1	0	1
2	1	0	0	1	0	0
3	0	0	0	1	0	0
4	1	1	1	0	1	1
5	0	0	0	1	0	1
6	1	0	0	1	1	0

(f)

Figure 6.33 (a-d) Several different geometric realizations of a graph. (e) Incidence matrix representation. (f) Adjacency matrix representation.

Rows represent vertices and columns represent edges. A matrix element a_{ij} is set equal to 1 if the jth edge is incident on the ith vertex, and to 0 if it is not. An adjacency matrix for a graph of n vertices is an $n \times n$ symmetrical matrix in which both rows and columns represent vertices. A matrix element a_{ij} is set equal to 1 if there is an edge between the ith and jth vertices, and to 0 if there is not (*Figure 6.33 (f)*). Both incidence matrices and adjacency matrices are readily stored as two-dimensional arrays.

Now a figure described by points and edge lines can be thought of as a graph, in which each vertex has associated coordinates. In other words, the coordinates describe how the graph is physically realized in two- or three-dimensional space. Thus a figure can be represented by means of a point-matrix, giving coordinates of all the vertices, plus an adjacency matrix giving *connections* between vertices, as shown in *Figure 6.34*. This representation technique eliminates redundancy in description of polyhedra and plane networks of polygons. Each point appears only once in the vertex list, and each line appears only once in the adjacency matrix. Lines will not be plotted twice when drawings are produced.

Sparse matrix techniques

A disadvantage with this point matrix/adjacency matrix technique is that it consumes excessive storage when the figure is large. For a figure composed of n points, an adjacency matrix of n^2 cells is required. Since the matrix is symmetrical, some economies can be achieved by storing only the entries on one side of the diagonal. But the number of cells still grows as $(n^2 - n)/2$. Much greater economies can be achieved by recognizing that the matrix will characteristically be very *sparse, i.e.,* it will consist mostly of 0's. The efficient storage of large sparse matrices is a common problem in computing, and numerous special techniques have been developed for this purpose (Bril-

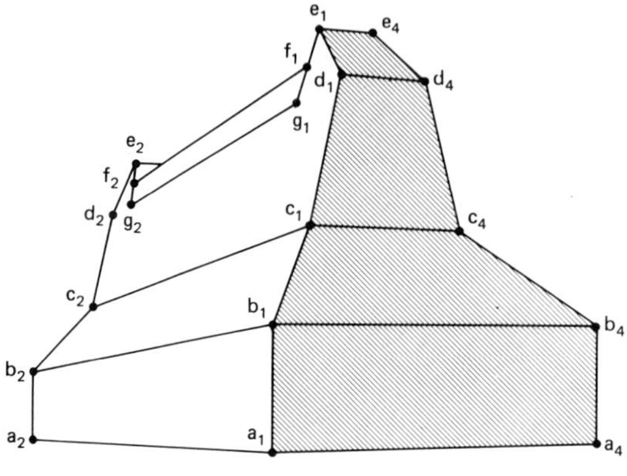

(a)

	x	y	z
a_1	−7.0	−25.0	0.0
a_2	−7.0	25.0	0.0
a_3	7.0	25.0	0.0
a_4	7.0	−25.0	0.0
b_1	−7.0	−25.0	5.0
b_2	−7.0	25.0	5.0
b_3	7.0	25.0	5.0
b_4	7.0	−25.0	5.0
c_1	−3.5	−20.0	8.75
c_2	−3.5	20.0	8.75
c_3	3.5	20.0	8.75
c_4	3.5	−20.0	8.75
d_1	−1.75	−20.0	15.0
d_2	−1.75	20.0	15.0
d_3	1.75	20.0	15.0
d_4	1.75	−20.0	15.0
e_1	−1.25	−15.0	17.5
e_2	−1.25	15.0	17.5
e_3	1.25	15.0	17.5
e_4	1.25	−15.0	17.5
f_1	−1.5	−14.0	16.25
f_2	−1.5	14.0	16.25
f_3	1.5	14.0	16.25
f_4	1.5	−14.0	16.25
g_1	−1.75	−13.0	15.0
g_2	−1.75	13.0	15.0
g_3	1.75	13.0	15.0
g_4	1.75	−13.0	15.0

(b)

	a_1	a_2	a_3	a_4	b_1	b_2	b_3	b_4	c_1	c_2	c_3	c_4	d_1	d_2	d_3	d_4	e_1	e_2	e_3	e_4	f_1	f_2	f_3	f_4	g_1	g_2	g_3	g_4
a_1		1		1	1																							
a_2	1		1			1																						
a_3		1		1			1																					
a_4	1		1					1																				
b_1	1					1		1	1																			
b_2		1			1		1			1																		
b_3			1			1		1			1																	
b_4				1	1		1					1																
c_1					1					1		1	1															
c_2						1			1		1			1														
c_3							1			1		1			1													
c_4								1	1		1					1												
d_1									1							1	1											
d_2										1					1			1										
d_3											1			1					1									
d_4												1	1							1								
e_1													1							1	1							
e_2														1					1			1						
e_3															1			1					1					
e_4																1	1							1				
f_1																	1					1		1	1			
f_2																		1			1		1			1		
f_3																			1			1		1			1	
f_4																				1	1		1					1
g_1																					1					1		
g_2																						1			1			
g_3																							1					1
g_4																								1			1	

(c)

Figure 6.34 Description of forms by vertex list and adjacency matrix. (a) Erich Mendelsohn's Luckenwalde Hat Factory (dye works), 1921–23. (b) Vertex list. (c) Adjacency matrix (zero entries omitted for clarity).

linger and Cohen 1972, Page and Wilson 1973). Some of these will be described.

One obvious approach is to exploit the property that, in principle, an entry can be represented by a single bit. A whole word is not needed. If individual bits of memory can be addressed, large savings result. For example, if the computer uses 32 bit words, storage of a 100×100 binary matrix in words requires $32 \times 100 \times 100 = 320{,}000$ bits. If stored as a bit pattern, only $100 \times 100 = 10{,}000$ bits are required. Storage requirements are cut by a factor of 32. Unfortunately, it is rarely possible to address individual bits.

Very great compression can be achieved by storing only *subscript pairs* identifying the non-zero entries. For example the binary matrix

$$\begin{bmatrix} 0 & 0 & 1 & 0 & 0 \\ 0 & 0 & 0 & 0 & 1 \\ 1 & 0 & 0 & 0 & 0 \\ 0 & 0 & 0 & 0 & 0 \\ 0 & 1 & 0 & 0 & 0 \end{bmatrix}$$

can be described by the following list of subscript pairs:

(1,3), (2,5), (3,1), (5,2)

The sparser the matrix, the greater the compression that can be produced by this means. The disadvantages of storage by subscript pairs is that entries can no longer be directly accessed by subscripts. To determine whether a given entry is 1 or 0, it is necessary to search the list for the corresponding subscript pair.

If the subscript pairs are stored in an array, the insertion and deletion of non-zero entries becomes difficult. For this reason, a list is normally utilized.

An alternative to a simple linearly-linked list for this purpose is a ring structure, in which each non-zero entry points to both the next non-zero entry to the right, and the next non-zero entry below, and the last non-zero entry in a row or column points back to the first. Alternative representations of a floor plan, using linearly-linked and ring-structures to store the adjacency matrix, are illustrated in *Figure 6.35*. The ring structure is more complex to implement than the

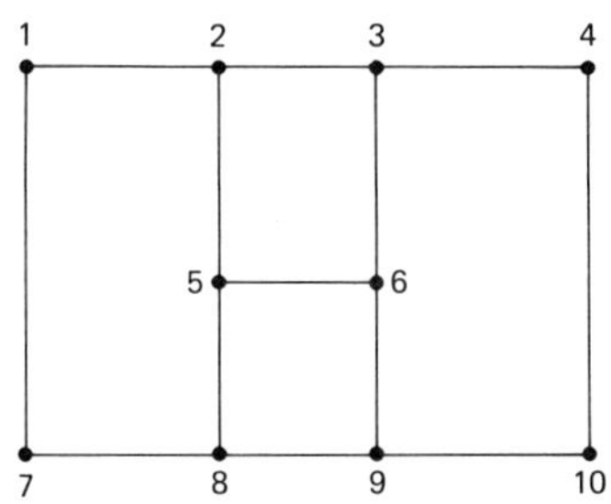

(a)

	1	2	3	4	5	6	7	8	9	10
1	0	1	0	0	0	0	1	0	0	0
2	1	0	1	0	1	0	0	0	0	0
3	0	1	0	1	0	1	0	0	0	0
4	0	0	1	0	0	0	0	0	0	1
5	0	1	0	0	0	1	0	1	0	0
6	0	0	1	0	1	0	0	0	1	0
7	1	0	0	0	0	0	0	1	0	0
8	0	0	0	0	1	0	1	0	1	0
9	0	0	0	0	0	1	0	1	0	1
10	0	0	0	1	0	0	0	0	1	0

(b)

Figure 6.35 Techniques for efficient storage of the adjacency matrix of a graph. (a) A floor plan represented as a graph. (b) Encoding of the graph as an adjacency matrix. (c) Storage of the adjacency matrix as a list of subscript pairs identifying non-zero entries. (d) Storage of the adjacency matrix in a ring structure. Non-zero entries in each row and each column of the matrix are represented by lists of subscript pairs. The last element of each row or column list points back to the head to complete a ring.

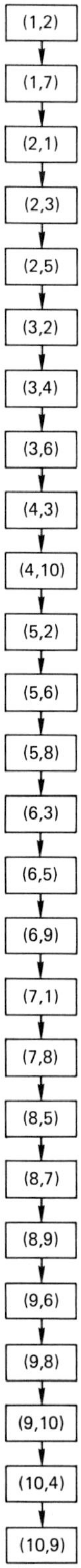

(c)

simple list, but it saves on the time taken to access an entry when the matrix is large.

Hierarchical representations

In the floor plan representation just described, *wall segments* and *corners* are the only elements that are explicitly identified. For many applications, it is necessary to also explicitly identify *rooms,* and to associate data (*e.g.,* name, floor area, use, internal temperature, etc.) with rooms. This can be accomplished by use of three cross-linked lists:

A *room-list,* containing data describing rooms, each element of which is cross-linked to three or more walls.

A *wall-list,* containing data describing wall segments, each element of which is cross-linked to two points.

A *point-list,* containing coordinates of vertices.

In effect, the floor plan is now represented as a *hierarchy* of spatial elements of different dimensionality. At the highest level are two-dimensional polygons. Each polygon is bounded by one-dimensional lines, and each line is bounded by two zero-dimensional points. Data can be associated with different levels of the hierarchy as required: details of corners at level 0, properties of wall-segments at level 1, and properties of rooms at level 2. The associations of elements of lower and higher dimensionality are recorded by the cross-linkages.

Pfefferkorn (1975) has developed a sophisticated heuristic floor plan layout program, known as DPS (Design Problem Solver), which employs a hierarchical polygonal representation of a similar type. DPS solves problems of arranging polygonal objects within polygonal spaces in accordance with specified constraints. Each polygon is represented as a set of edges, and each edge as a set of points. The language employed for implementation is LISP, which provides powerful facilities for construction and manipulation of the necessary list structures.

Geometric transformations upon point-matrices *

The geometric transformations of *scaling, translation, rotation,* and *reflection* in two- and three-dimensional space can very conveniently be performed upon objects represented by means of the techniques discussed in this section.

When a transformation is performed upon an object in two-dimensional space, each initial point (x,y) is transformed into a new point (x′,y′). The relations between x and x′, and between y and y′, may be expressed by means of equations.

* For more detailed discussions of this topic see Newman and Sproull (1973), Rogers and Adams (1976) and Forrest (1976).

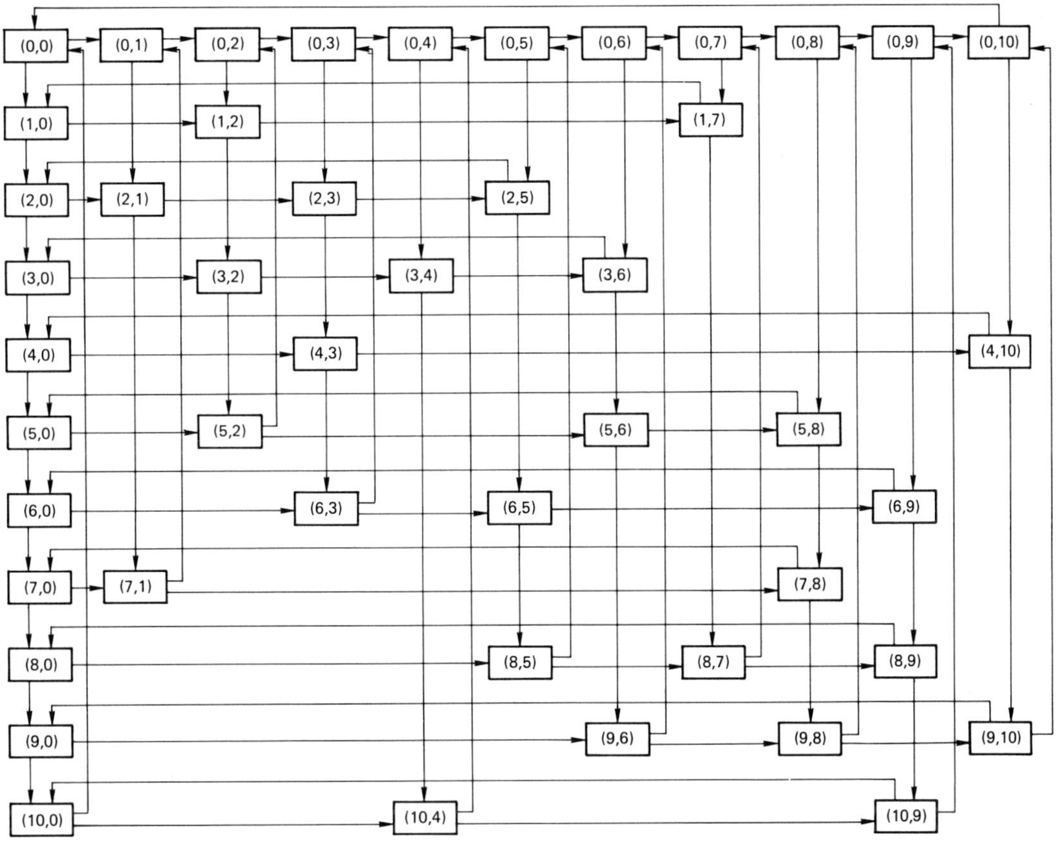

(d)

The translation of an object T_x units in the x direction and T_y units in the y direction is given by:

$$x' = x + T_x$$
$$y' = y + T_y$$

An example is shown in *Figure 6.36(a)*.

To rotate a picture through an angle θ about the origin of the coordinate system, the following equations are employed (see *Figure 6.36(b)*).:

$$x' = x \cos \theta + y \sin \theta$$
$$y' = -x \sin \theta + y \cos \theta$$

To scale a picture by a factor of S_x in the x direction and S_y in the y direction we use:

$$x' = xS_x$$
$$y' = yS_y$$

For undistorted enlargement or reduction, S_x and S_y must be set to the same value. If the scale factor is set at 0, the object reduces to a

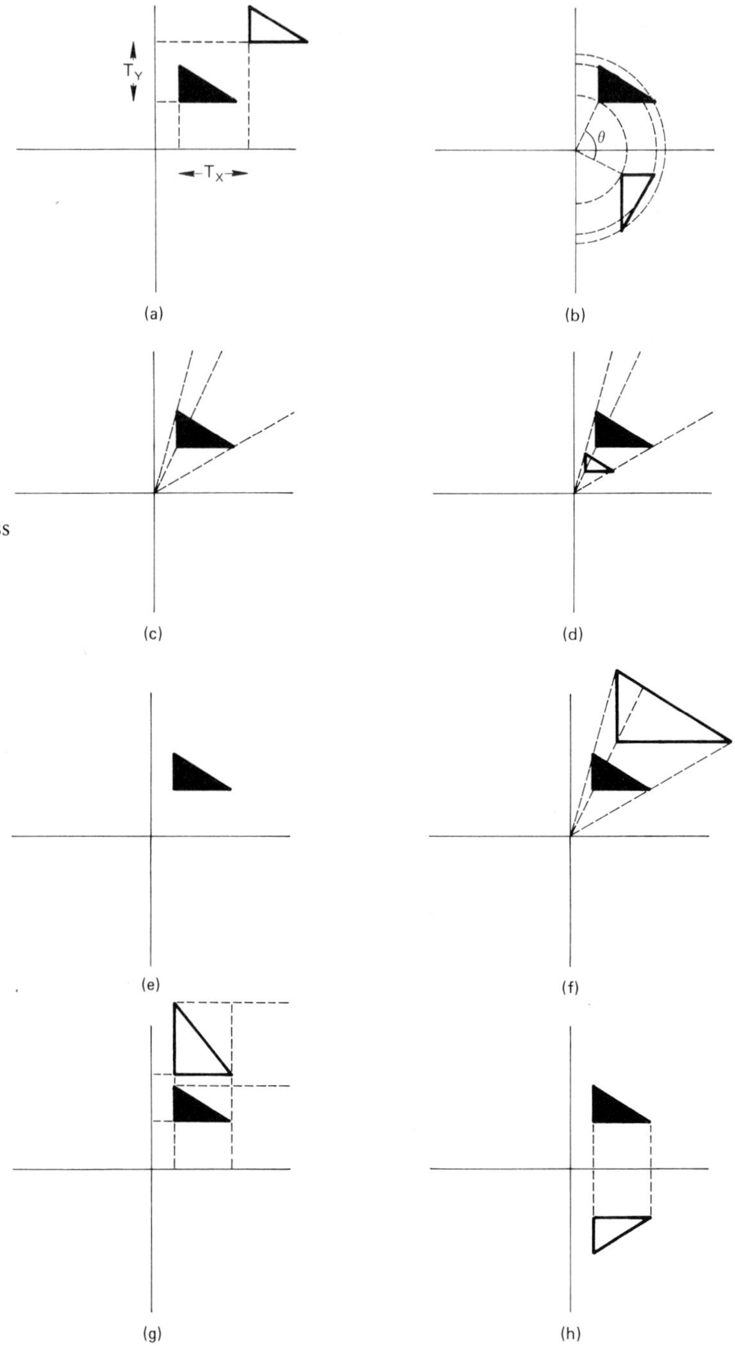

Figure 6.36
Some common two-dimensional geometric transformations. (a) Translation. (b) Rotation about the origin. (c) Scaling $S_x = S_y = 0$. (d) Scaling $S_x = S_y$ $0 < S_x < 1$. (e) Scaling $S_x = S_y = 1$. (f) Scaling $S_x = S_y$ $S_x > 1$. (g) Scaling $S_x = 1$ $S_y > 1$. (h) Reflection across X axis. (i) Reflection across Y axis. (j) Reflection across X and Y axis.

single point at the origin of the coordinate system (*Figure 6.36(c)*); if it is set between 0 and 1, the object is reduced in scale (*Figure 6.36(d)*); if it is set to 1, the object remains unchanged (*Figure 6.36(e)*); and if it is set to a value greater than 1, the object is

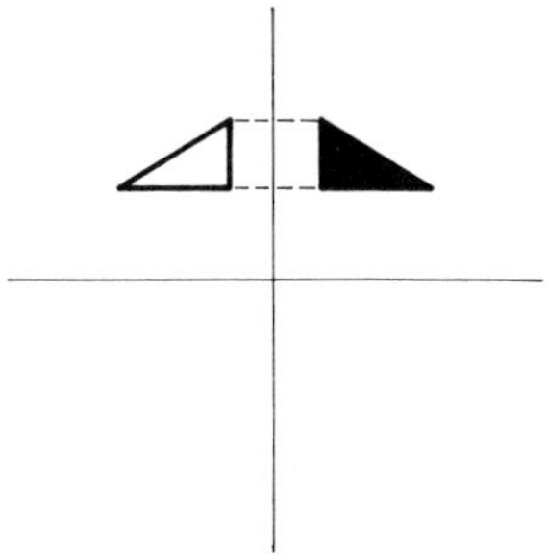

(i)

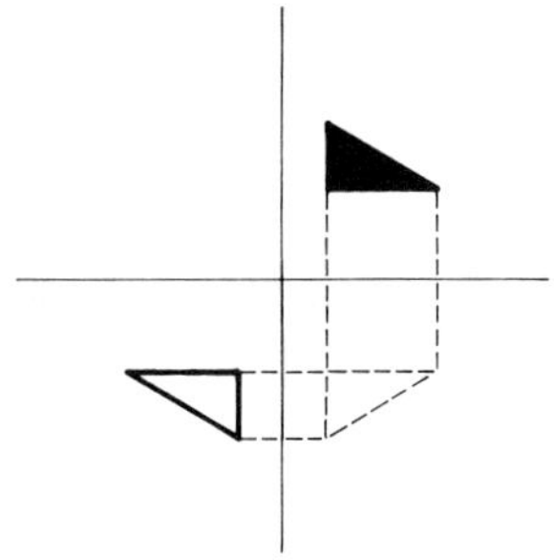

(j)

enlarged (*Figure* 6.36(*f*)). Where S_x and S_y are not set to the same value, elongations and shrinkages take place in directions parallel to the coordinate axes (*Figure* 6.36(*g*)).

To reflect a picture about the x-axis (*Figure* 6.36(*h*)) we employ:

$$x' = -x$$
$$y' = y$$

To reflect about the y-axis (*Figure* 6.36(*i*)) the equations are:

$$x' = x$$
$$y' = -y$$

Reflection about both axes (*Figure* 6.36(*j*)) results from:

$$x' = -x$$
$$y' = -y$$

It is rather cumbersome to actually perform transformations by means of these equations; and it has become common practice to employ transformation matrices instead. This has the advantage that *sequences* of transformations can always be represented by a single *concatenated* transformation matrix as follows:

$$[x' \; y' \; 1] = [x \; y \; 1] \begin{bmatrix} a_{11} & a_{12} & 0 \\ a_{21} & a_{22} & 0 \\ a_{31} & a_{32} & 1 \end{bmatrix}$$

Required transformations are specified by entering appropriate values for the terms a_{11}, a_{12}, etc. The third term, 1, added to the point-vector is necessary so that multiplication by a 3×3 matrix can take place.

The 3×3 concatenated transformation matrix is obtained by multiplying 3×3 matrices which represent the simple transformations of translation, rotation, reflection, and scaling. These matrices are as follows:

Translation: $\begin{bmatrix} 1 & 0 & 0 \\ 0 & 1 & 0 \\ T_x & T_y & 1 \end{bmatrix}$

Rotation: $\begin{bmatrix} \cos\theta & -\sin\theta & 0 \\ \sin\theta & \cos\theta & 0 \\ 0 & 0 & 1 \end{bmatrix}$

Scaling: $\begin{bmatrix} S_x & 0 & 0 \\ 0 & S_y & 0 \\ 0 & 0 & 1 \end{bmatrix}$

Reflection about x-axis $\begin{bmatrix} -1 & 0 & 0 \\ 0 & 1 & 0 \\ 0 & 0 & 1 \end{bmatrix}$

Reflection about y-axis $\begin{bmatrix} 1 & 0 & 0 \\ 0 & -1 & 0 \\ 0 & 0 & 1 \end{bmatrix}$

Reflection about both axes $\begin{bmatrix} -1 & 0 & 0 \\ 0 & -1 & 0 \\ 0 & 0 & 1 \end{bmatrix}$

For example, rotation 45° clockwise about the origin then enlargement in scale by a factor of 2 is given by:

$$\begin{bmatrix} \cos 45^\circ & -\sin 45^\circ & 0 \\ \sin 45^\circ & \cos 45^\circ & 0 \\ 0 & 0 & 1 \end{bmatrix} \begin{bmatrix} 2 & 0 & 0 \\ 0 & 2 & 0 \\ 0 & 0 & 1 \end{bmatrix}$$

Performing the multiplication produces the 3×3 transformation matrix:

$$\begin{bmatrix} 2\cos 45^\circ & -2\sin 45^\circ & 0 \\ 2\sin 45^\circ & 2\cos 45^\circ & 0 \\ 0 & 0 & 1 \end{bmatrix}$$

Substituting numerical values for sin 45° and cos 45° gives the final concatenated matrix:

$$\begin{bmatrix} 1.414 & -1.414 & 0 \\ 1.414 & 1.414 & 0 \\ 0 & 0 & 1 \end{bmatrix}$$

Figure 6.37 illustrates an application of this matrix to the transformation of a line, represented by the matrix

$$\begin{bmatrix} 1 & 1 \\ 2 & 2 \end{bmatrix}$$

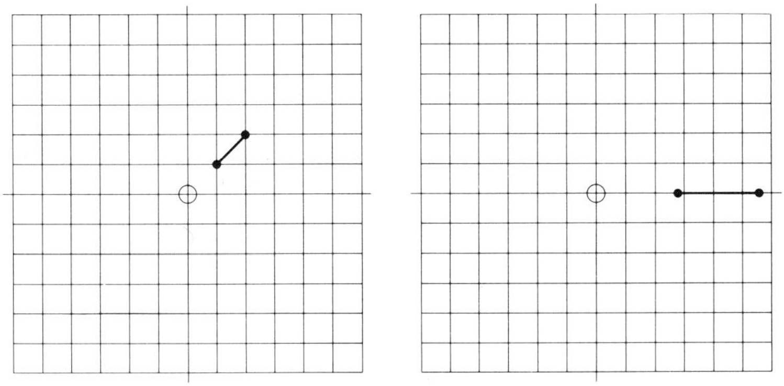

(a) (b)

Figure 6.37
Example of transformation of a line. (a) Initial line. (b) Transformed line.

The transformed line is given by

$$\begin{bmatrix} 1 & 1 & 1 \\ 2 & 2 & 1 \end{bmatrix} \begin{bmatrix} 1.414 & -1.414 & 0 \\ 1.414 & 1.414 & 0 \\ 0 & 0 & 1 \end{bmatrix} = \begin{bmatrix} 2.828 & 0 & 1 \\ 5.656 & 0 & 1 \end{bmatrix}$$

The use of transformation matrices to perform translation, rotation, scaling, and reflection in the plane can be extended to the three-dimensional case. Concatenated three-dimensional transformations can be represented by a 4×4 transformation matrix as follows:

$$[x' \ y' z' \ 1] = [x \ y \ z \ 1] \begin{bmatrix} a_{11} & a_{12} & a_{13} & 0 \\ a_{21} & a_{22} & a_{33} & 0 \\ a_{31} & a_{32} & a_{33} & 0 \\ a_{41} & a_{42} & a_{43} & 1 \end{bmatrix}$$

Matrices for the various individual transformations are:

Translation by distances T_x, T_y, and T_z

$$\begin{bmatrix} 1 & 0 & 0 & 0 \\ 0 & 1 & 0 & 0 \\ 0 & 0 & 1 & 0 \\ T_x & T_y & T_z & 1 \end{bmatrix}$$

Rotation through angle θ clockwise about the x axis (*Figure 6.38(a)*)

$$\begin{bmatrix} 1 & 0 & 0 & 0 \\ 0 & \cos\theta & -\sin\theta & 0 \\ 0 & \sin\theta & \cos\theta & 0 \\ 0 & 0 & 0 & 1 \end{bmatrix}$$

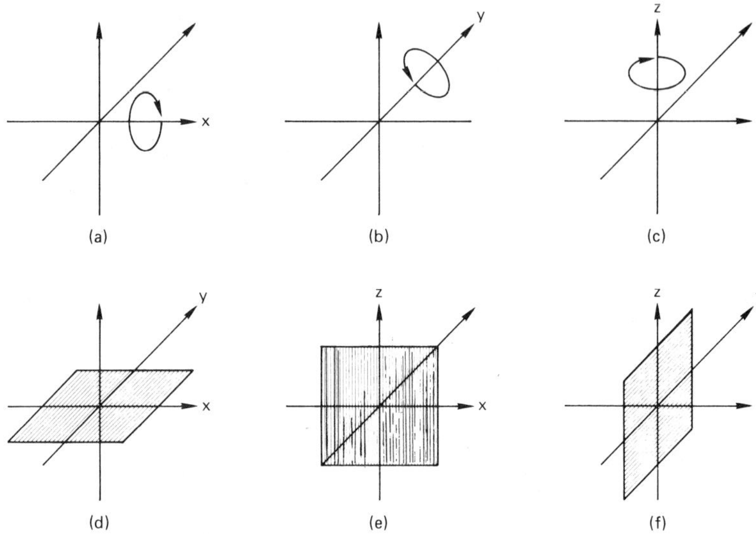

Figure 6.38
Conventions employed in three dimensional transformation matrices. (a) Rotation about x axis. (b) Rotation about y axis. (c) Rotation about z axis. (d) xy plane. (e) xz plane. (f) yz plane.

Rotation through angle θ clockwise about the y axis (*Figure 6.38(b)*)

$$\begin{bmatrix} \cos\theta & 0 & \sin\theta & 0 \\ 0 & 1 & 0 & 0 \\ -\sin\theta & 0 & \cos\theta & 0 \\ 0 & 0 & 0 & 1 \end{bmatrix}$$

Rotation through angle θ clockwise about the z axis (*Figure 6.38(c)*)

$$\begin{bmatrix} \cos\theta & -\sin\theta & 0 & 0 \\ \sin\theta & \cos\theta & 0 & 0 \\ 0 & 0 & 1 & 0 \\ 0 & 0 & 0 & 1 \end{bmatrix}$$

Scaling by factors S_x, S_y, and S_z

$$\begin{bmatrix} S_x & 0 & 0 & 0 \\ 0 & S_y & 0 & 0 \\ 0 & 0 & S_z & 0 \\ 0 & 0 & 0 & 1 \end{bmatrix}$$

Reflection across the xy plane (*Figure 6.38(d)*)

$$\begin{bmatrix} 1 & 0 & 0 & 0 \\ 0 & 1 & 0 & 0 \\ 0 & 0 & -1 & 0 \\ 0 & 0 & 0 & 1 \end{bmatrix}$$

Reflection across the xz plane (*Figure 6.38(e)*)

$$\begin{bmatrix} 1 & 0 & 0 & 0 \\ 0 & -1 & 0 & 0 \\ 0 & 0 & 1 & 0 \\ 0 & 0 & 0 & 1 \end{bmatrix}$$

Reflection across the yz plane (*Figure 6.38(f)*)

$$\begin{bmatrix} -1 & 0 & 0 & 0 \\ 0 & 1 & 0 & 0 \\ 0 & 0 & 1 & 0 \\ 0 & 0 & 0 & 1 \end{bmatrix}$$

A most interesting use of these transformation matrices occurs in the data structure employed to represent building geometry in the OXSYS integrated computer-aided design system, which is intended for use with the Oxford Method of construction (Richens 1975). The Oxford Method utilizes a strictly rectilinear geometry, as was illustrated in *Figure 3.14*. If each component is represented as an aggregation of rectangular parallelepipeds, then the whole building can be represented as an orthogonal assemblage of rectangular parallelepipeds, which can then very simply be described as follows:

Each parallelepiped is described by storing its three dimensions. The location of the parallelepiped is then given by storing coordinates for one corner. Finally, the orientation of each parallelepiped is given by storing the appropriate transformation matrix. Since all rotations must be 90°, the transformation matrix is binary, and can be stored in a special compressed format.

Topological operations *

In addition to the geometric operations which we have described, operations may also be performed to alter the topology of polygonal and polyhedral objects.

The addition or deletion of walls or rooms in a floor plan is a type of topological operation of particular interest here. The relationship between the numbers of corners (vertices), walls (edges), rooms and separate buildings is given by a slight restatement of a well-known formula due to Euler (*Figure 6.39(a)*):

$$(\text{corners}) - (\text{walls}) + (\text{rooms}) = (\text{separate buildings})$$

This relation continues to hold as operations of adding and deleting walls and rooms are performed. *Figure 6.39(b) to (h)* illustrates a sequence of such operations.

* For more detailed discussion of this topic see Baumgart (1972) and Eastman, Lividini and Stoker (1975).

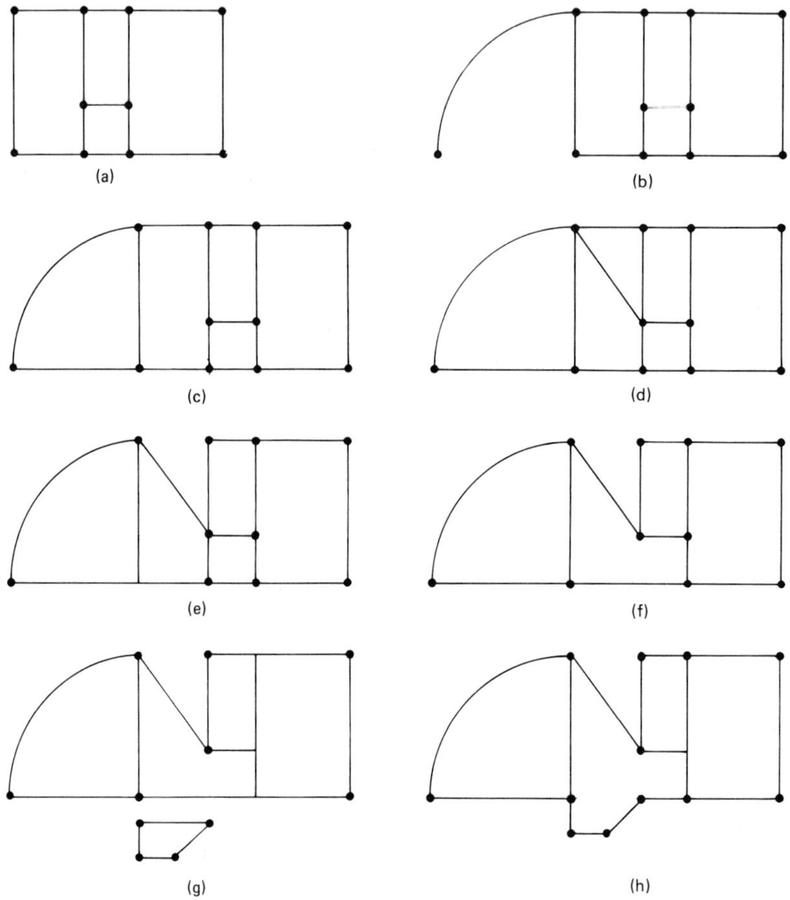

Figure 6.39
Euler's equation and floor plan topology. (a) (Corners) − (walls) + (rooms) = (buildings) 10 − 13 + 4 = 1. (b) Wall and corner added 11 − 14 + 4 = 1. (c) Wall added to enclose room 11 − 15 + 5 = 1. (d) Room subdivided by wall 11 − 16 + 6 = 1. (e) Wall and room deleted 11 − 15 + 5 = 1. (f) Wall removed to combine two rooms 11 − 14 + 4 = 1. (g) Separate building created 15 − 18 + 5 = 2. (h) Two buildings combined 13 − 16 + 4 = 1.

Table 6.2
The Euler operations for manipulating polyhedra (after Eastman, Lividini and Stoker 1975).

Operation	Equation (faces)	− (edges)	+ (vertices)	= (2* objects)	− (2* holes)
Construct edge and vertex		+1	+1		
Construct face and edge	+1	+1			
Construct object and face, destroy edge	+1	−1		+2*1	
Split an edge with a vertex		+1	+1		
Divide an object with a plane	+2			+2*1	
Fuse two objects and remove the common faces	−2			−2*1	
Remove two faces and construct a hole	−2				+2*1

Euler's formula also applies to three-dimensional configurations of polyhedra. For this case, it may be stated:

$$(\text{faces}) - (\text{edges}) + (\text{vertices}) = 2(\text{bodies}) - 2(\text{holes})$$

For example, a cube has 6 faces, 12 edges, and 8 vertices. Substituting in Euler's equation gives

$$6 - 12 + 8 = 2 \times 1 - 2 \times 0$$
$$2 = 2$$

It follows that any operation performed upon a polyhedral form to generate another polyhedral form must be consistent with Euler's equation, and that the basic operations needed to perform topological constructions or manipulations are as shown in *Table 6.2.* More complex operations can be expressed as combinations of these basic Euler operations.

Set operations

In addition to geometric transformations and Euler operations, it is often useful to perform *set* operations upon polygonal and polyhedral objects. *Figure 6.40,* for example, illustrates the operations of union, intersection, and difference of two polygons, while *Figure 6.41* shows the same operations performed upon polyhedra.

Software for manipulation

It can now be seen that at least three basic types of software are needed for manipulation of polygon and polyhedron representations: geometric transformation software; Euler operation software; and set operation software. All computer graphics systems incorporate geometric transformation software, and it is described in standard texts such as Newman and Sproull (1973). In many graphics systems now, the required matrix multiplications are carried out by special hard

Figure 6.40
Set operations on polygons.

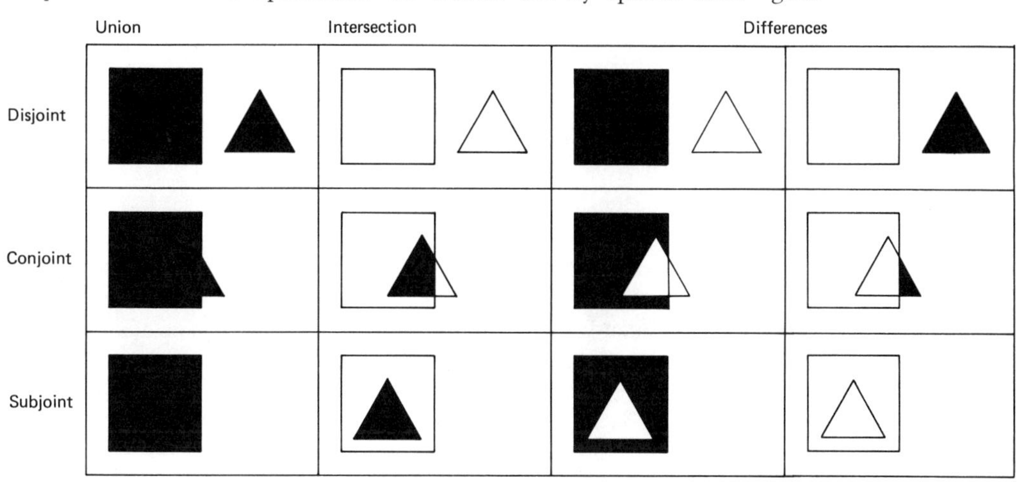

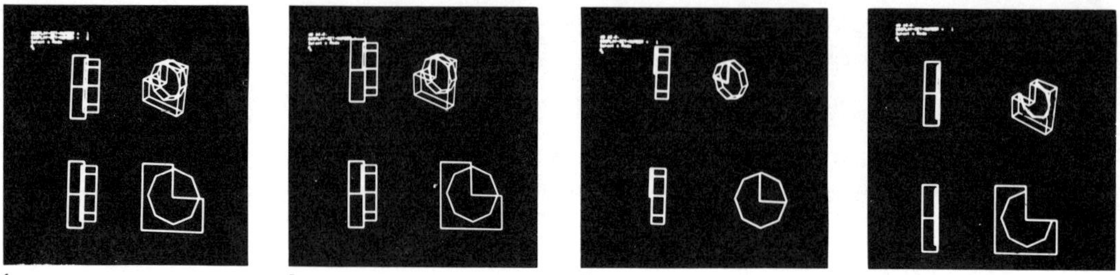

1 2 3 4

Figure 6.41
Set operations on polyhedra. Execution of set operations on polyhedra using the GLIDE language (Eastman and Henrion 1976). Frame 1 shows intersecting polyhedra in orthographic and perspective views. Frame 2 illustrates the result of the UNION operation. Frames 3 and 4 illustrate the two results of SUBTRACT. Not shown is INTERSECT.

wired or microprogrammed circuitry. Software for performing Euler and set operations has only more recently become available. Eastman and Yessios (1972) have published an efficient algorithm for performance of set operations on polygons, and a special purpose language called GLIDE (Eastman and Henrion 1976), which incorporates powerful facilities for performing geometric and topological operations upon polyhedra, has been developed at Carnegie-Mellon University.

Advantages and disadvantages

Polygon and polyhedron representations are very flexible and powerful representations. They can describe both spatial domains like rooms, and physical elements like walls, columns, and beams, to any desired level of accuracy. In principle, they are closely related to normal architectural drawings, and translation of these representations into graphic output can be easily accomplished. They may be employed for any purposes which require complete and accurate descriptions of building geometry.

There are some practical difficulties, however. For many types of architectural applications polygon and polyhedron representations tend to be difficult to implement and complex to manipulate. Certain types of information tend to be rather difficult to extract. In particular, the efficient detection of intersections, overlaps, and adjacencies of forms and spaces often presents a considerable problem (Comba 1968, Eastman 1970).

Polyhedron representations have been very widely employed in computer graphics and computer-aided design systems. Ivan E. Sutherland's early Sketchpad system (Sutherland 1963) is perhaps the most famous. Many commercially-marketed turnkey computer-aided design systems used in the manufacturing industry, for example, Computervision, Applicon, and AD 2000, employ polyhedron representations. Most of the integrated computer-aided architectural design systems that have been developed employ some form of polyhedron representation technique for comprehensive building description. Probably the most advanced application to building description is implemented in the Building Description System (BDS) developed at Carnegie-Mellon University (Eastman *et al* 1975).

DUAL-GRAPH REPRESENTATIONS

Where representations are regarded as graphs, as discussed in the previous section, it becomes possible to exploit some results from graph theory in order to develop further descriptive techniques which may be useful for particular purposes. This section introduces one such technique: the *dual-graph* representation of floor plans.

Concept of a dual-graph

Certain graphs possess the property of *planarity.* Deo (1974) defines planarity as follows:

> A graph G is said to be *planar* if there exists some geometric realization of G which can be drawn on a plane such that no two of its edges intersect. A graph that cannot be drawn on a plane without crossover between its edges is called *nonplanar.*

Conditions for planarity of graphs were first specified by the Polish mathematician Kuratowski (1930). He showed that a graph is planar if it does not contain as sub-graphs either of the two graphs (usually referred to as K_5 and $K_{3,3}$) shown in *Figure 6.42,* or any graph *homeomorphic* to either of them. (Two graphs are said to be homeomorphic if one graph can be obtained from the other by performance of operations of creation and merger of edges in series.) K_5 is the nonplanar graph with the smallest number of vertices, and $K_{3,3}$ is the nonplanar graph with the smallest number of edges.

A geometric realization of a planar graph divides the plane into *regions* as shown in *Figure 6.43.* Each region is bounded by a specific

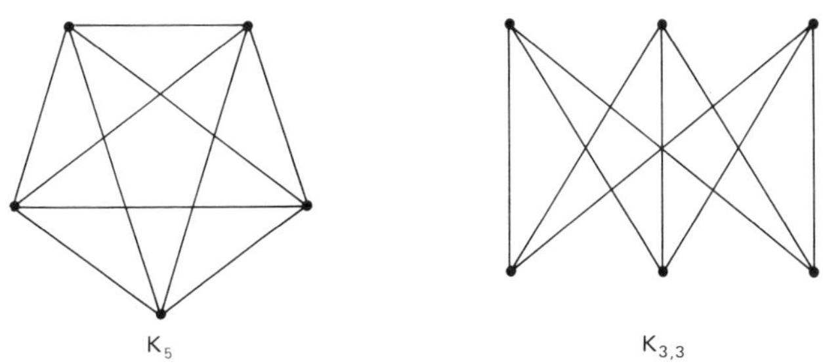

Figure 6.42
Kuratowski's nonplanar graphs.

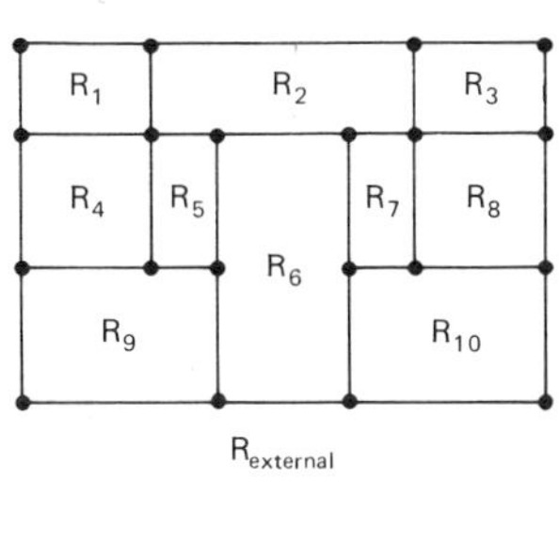

Figure 6.43
Floor plan represented as a planar graph, in which rooms correspond to internal regions, and the external region is of infinite extent.

set of edges. There exist both *internal regions* of finite area, and an *external region* of infinite extent. Thus we can now characterize a single-story floor plan as a geometric realization of a planar graph, in which edges represent wall segments, vertices represent intersections of wall segments, internal regions represent rooms, and the external region represents the exterior.

For any single-level floor plan there can be constructed a *planar dual* by the following procedure. Within each region (room) locate a vertex, as shown in *Figure 6.44* (*a*). Connect vertices in adjacent regions by an edge. The resultant figure is the dual of the original figure. Duals of floor plans are often referred to as *room adjacency graphs* because they represent the adjacency relations between rooms. It is often convenient to divide the external region into several different regions by the insertion of dummy walls of infinite length, as

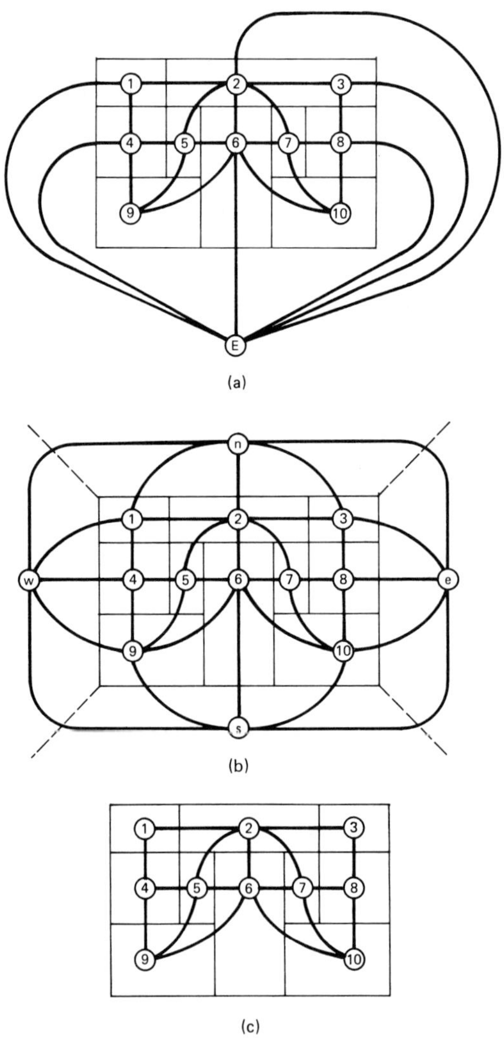

Figure 6.44
The dual of a planar floor plan. (a) Dual of the floor plan shown in Figure 6.43. (b) External region divided into "north," "east," "south," and "west" regions by insertion of dummy "walls." (c) External region ignored.

illustrated in *Figure 6.44 (b)*, so that orientations of rooms are indicated. Alternatively, the external region may be ignored altogether (*Figure 6.44 (c)*).

Floor plan topology

Room adjacency graphs can be encoded for computer storage by means of incidence and adjacency matrices (see *Figure 6.33*). Both incidence matrices and adjacency matrices may be readily stored in the computer as two-dimensional arrays. This provides a very convenient and economical way to represent and access data on floor plan topology. Whether or not two spaces are adjacent can be determined directly by accessing (by subscript) the appropriate entry in the adjacency matrix. The neighbors of a specified space may be determined by scanning along the appropriate row or column of the adjacency matrix. The wall segments bounding a given space may be determined by scanning across the corresponding row of the incidence matrix. The spaces divided by a given wall segment may be found by scanning down the appropriate column of the incidence matrix. Such topological data may be important in space-planning applications, and in certain types of structural, thermal, and acoustic analyses.

If the room adjacency graph becomes excessively large, then storage by means of one of the sparse matrix techniques discussed above may become necessary.

Shape and dimensional data

It is often convenient to associate shape and dimensional data about spaces with dual-graphs. For example:

> Areas, dimensions, and centroid locations of rooms might be associated with vertices (*i.e.,* the rows of incidence matrices, or the columns of adjacency matrices).
>
> Lengths, surface areas, orientations, etc., of wall segments might be associated with edges (*i.e.,* with columns of incidence matrices or with non-zero entries in adjacency matrices).

In this way, more complete geometric representations can be built up around a dual-graph. *Figure 6.45* shows a simple example. The floor plan is assumed to be composed of orthogonal rectangular rooms. Associated with each row of the incidence matrix for the dual-graph are the centroid coordinates, lengths, and widths of rooms. Associated with each column is the length of the corresponding wall segment.

Application to floor plan layout problems

The dual-graph representation of floor plans has suggested to many researchers a systematic, computer-implementable procedure for

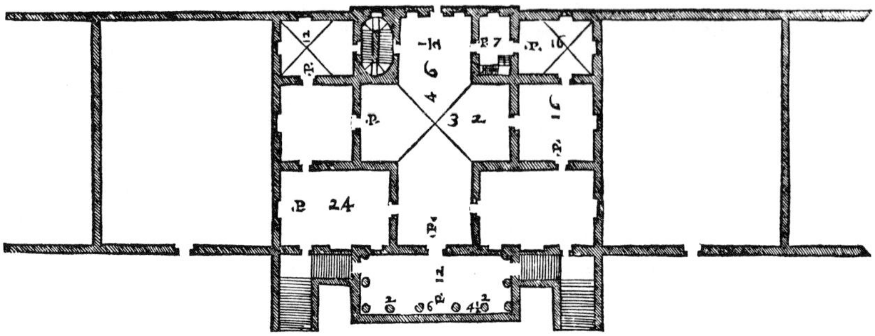

(a)

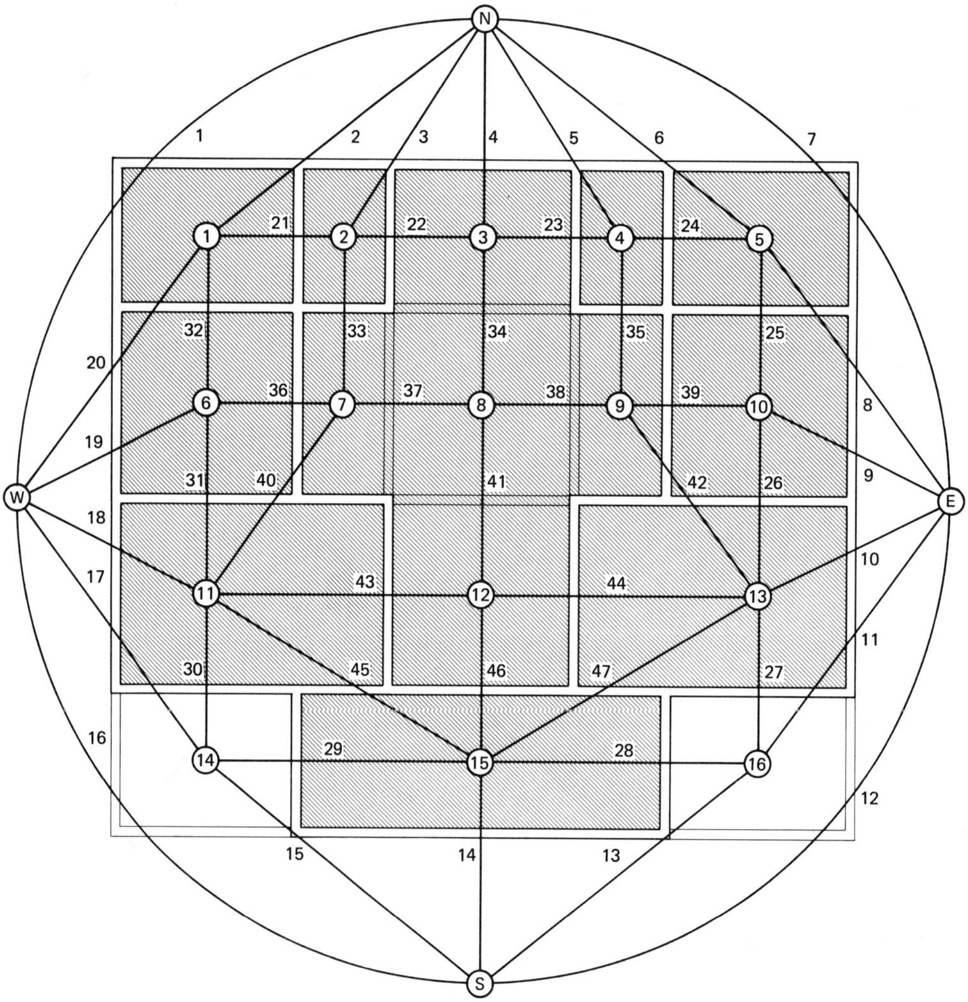

(b)

Figure 6.45
Representation of a floor plan by incidence matrix of dual graph plus room and wall segment data tables. (a) Plan of Palladio's Villa Malcontenta, 1560 (illustration from the *Quattro Libri.*). (b) Schematized plan represented as a dual graph. Note the insertion of "dummy" wall segments in order to make all spaces rectangular. (c) Incidence matrix of a dual graph (zero entries excluded for clarity). (d) Room data table. (e) Wall segment data table.

Wall segments

		1	2	3	4	5	6	7	8	9	10	11	12	13	14	15	16	17	18	19	20	21	22	23	24	25	26	27	28	29	30	31	32	33	34	35	36	37	38	39	40	41	42	43	44	45	46	47
Rooms	1		1																		1	1											1															
	2			1																		1	1											1														
	3				1																		1	1											1													
	4					1																		1	1											1												
	5						1	1																	1	1																						
	6																			1												1	1				1											
	7																																	1			1	1			1							
	8																																		1			1	1			1						
	9																																			1			1	1			1					
	10									1																1	1													1								
	11																		1												1	1									1			1		1		
	12																																									1		1	1		1	
	13										1																1	1															1		1			1
	14															1		1												1	1																	
	15														1														1	1																1	1	1
	16											1		1														1	1																			
External regions	N	1	1	1	1	1	1	1																																								
	E							1	1	1	1	1	1																																			
	S												1	1	1	1	1																															
	W	1															1	1	1	1	1																											

(c)

Room	Centroid coordinates x	y	Area
1	4	25	48
2	10	25	24
3	16	25	48
4	22	25	24
5	28	25	48
6	4	18	64
7	10	18	32
8	16	18	64
9	22	18	32
10	28	18	64
11	4	10	96
12	16	10	64
13	28	10	96
14	4	3	48
15	16	3	96
16	28	3	48

(d)

Segment	Length
1	Dummy
2	8
3	4
4	8
5	4
6	8
7	Dummy
8	6
9	8
10	8
11	6
12	Dummy
13	8
14	16
15	8

(e)

generation of floor plans which satisfy sets of adjacency requirements (Levin 1964, Krejcirik 1969, Seppanen and Moore 1970, Grason 1970, Steadman 1970, 1973, Cousin 1970, Mitchell 1975, and others). The basic steps of this procedure are as follows (see *Figure 6.46*):

1. Define an *adjacency requirements matrix,* specifying necessary adjacency relationships between spaces (*Figure 6.46 (a)*).
2. Test if the dual-graph corresponding to the adjacency requirements matrix is planar. If it is, go on to the next step. If it is not, the problem as defined has no solution.
3. Unfold the dual-graph so that no edges cross, *i.e.,* draw a planar realization (*Figure 6.46 (b)*).
4. Construct a corresponding floor plan by drawing in wall-segments as shown * (*Figure 6.46 (c)*).

* An astonishing proof due to Fary (1948) demonstrates that any planar graph can be realized without lines crossing using straight line segments only, and that a floor plan corresponding to the dual of such a graph can always be constructed using straight line segments only.

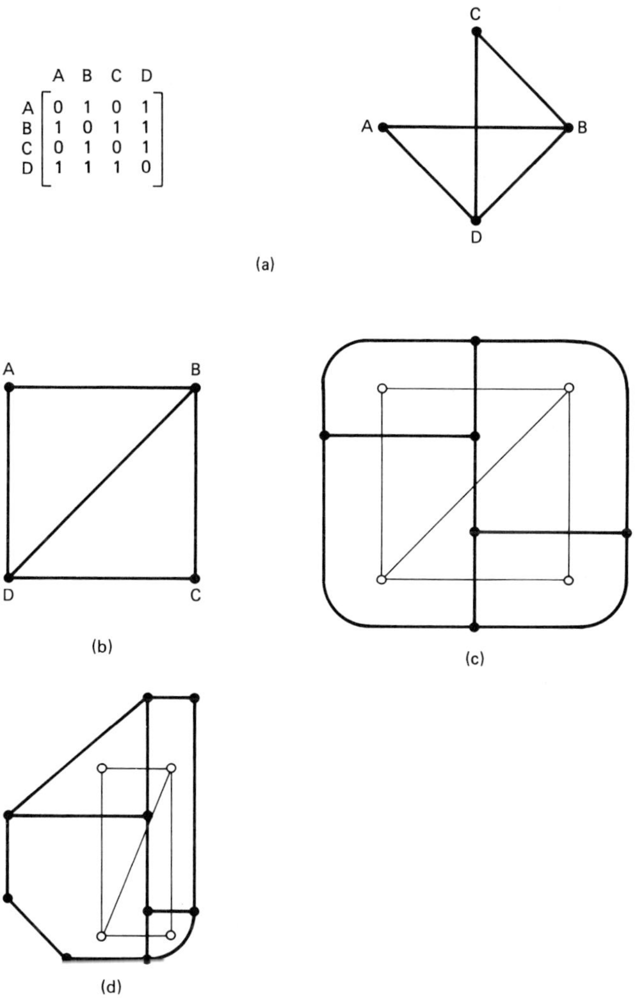

Figure 6.46 Procedure for constructing a floor plan corresponding to a specified adjacency requirements matrix. (a) Adjacency requirements matrix and its corresponding graph. (b) Graph unfolded in the plane. (c) Dual constructed (i.e. wall segments drawn in). (d) Shapes and dimensions of rooms adjusted.

5. Adjust the shapes, dimensions, and locations of rooms to comply with specified requirements (*Figure 6.46 (d)*).

Unfortunately, however, most of these steps involve quite difficult computational tasks. It might be thought, for example, that Kuratowski's theorem would yield a straightforward algorithm for planarity testing. This turns out not to be the case; and rather complex procedures, based upon alternative characterizations of planarity, are required for efficient planarity detection (Whitney 1932, 1933, MacLane 1937, Deo 1974). Algorithms for this purpose have been discussed by numerous authors, including Auslander and Trent (1961), Shirey (1969), and Bruno, Steiglitz and Weinberg (1970).

Unfolding of the dual-graph and construction of a corresponding floor plan can often be accomplished fairly readily using pencil and paper (as suggested by Levin 1964) or peg-board and elastic string (as suggested by Rittel 1970). However, computer programs for this purpose have proven to be complex and tedious to implement. Descriptions of typical approaches have been published by Krejcirik (1969), Seppanen and Moore (1969), and Grason (1970).

Due to the computational difficulties involved, this procedure has so far only been shown to be practical for small buildings, of the order of ten or fewer rooms.

Enumeration of potential solutions

By consideration of some relevant results from graph theory, it is possible to gain some understanding of the range of potential solutions implied by use of a dual-graph representation.

The number of simple *labeled* * graphs of n vertices is readily determined from the adjacency matrix. Each element of the matrix can take 2 states, 0 or 1, and up to $(n^2 - n)/2$ different linkages between pairs of vertices can be defined by entering 1's in the matrix. Thus the number of different simple graphs of n labeled vertices is given by

$$2(n^2 - n)/2$$

Determination of the numbers of simple *unlabeled* graphs is more difficult. The answer is given by a rather complex formula due to Polya (Deo 1974). Results from Polya's formula, for $n = 1$ to 8 are as follows:

n	1	2	3	4	5	6	7	8
number	1	2	4	11	34	156	1,044	12,344

Figure 6.47 illustrates all the connected planar graphs for $n \leq 5$, superimposed upon corresponding floor plans. There is only one non-planar graph where $n \leq 5$, the K_5.

A second interesting problem is the following. Given a set of activities, with adjacency requirements between those activities (*i.e.*, an adjacency requirements graph) and given a particular planar network of polygons, how many different ways (if any) can the activities be mapped onto polygons such that the adjacency requirements are met? In other words, how many different ways (if any) can the adjacency requirements graph be a sub-graph of the dual of the network? In practical terms, this is the problem of determining whether a given set of adjacency requirements between activities can be satisfied within a given floor plan arrangement.

Where there are n activities to be mapped, and n polygons, it is clear that there are n! potential mappings. For small n, it is feasible to solve the problem by running a simple computer program to enumerate all n! potential mappings. Various techniques can be em-

* Graphs in which each vertex is assigned a unique name or label.

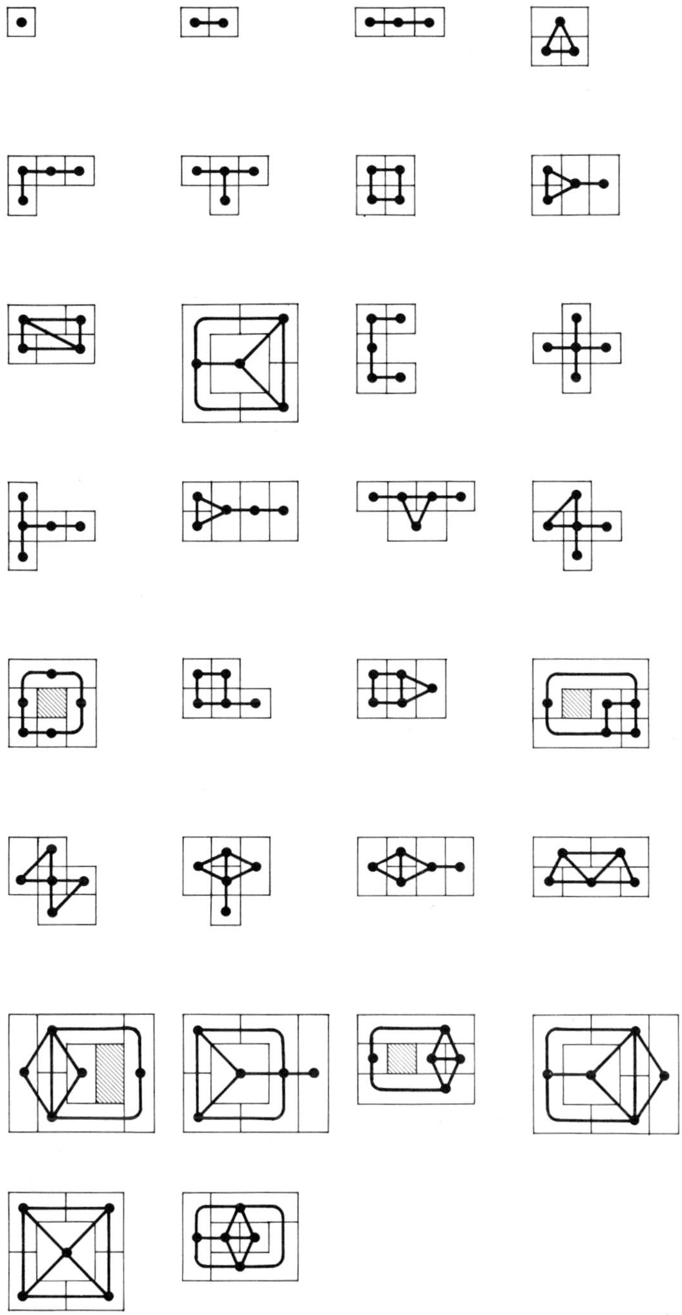

Figure 6.47
The simple connected planar graphs of five or fewer vertices, shown superimposed upon corresponding floor plans.

ployed to make the procedure more efficient by implicitly eliminating certain subsets of mappings from consideration at an early stage (Mitchell, Steadman and Liggett 1976). An example of mappings of an adjacency requirements graph onto a dissection of a rectangle is illustrated in *Figure 6.48*.

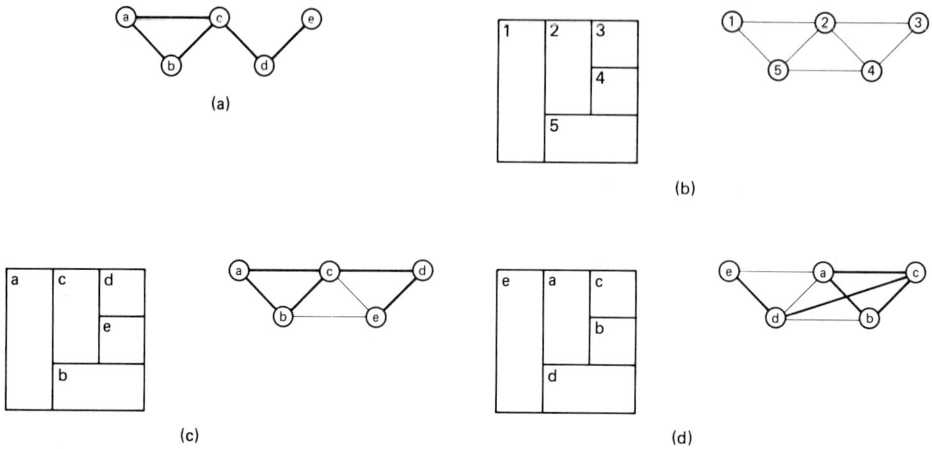

Figure 6.48
Mappings of an adjacency requirements graph onto a dissection of a rectangle. (a) Adjacency requirements graph. (b) Plan and its corresponding adjacency graph. (c) A mapping which meets the adjacency requirements. (d) A mapping which fails to meet the adjacency requirements.

Other applications of dual-graph representations of floor plans

In addition to their usefulness in floor plan layout applications, dual-graph representations have proven very useful in analyses involving considerations of flows between spaces, for example, heat flow, sound transmission, and circulation. Each vertex can be considered as a potential source or sink (of heat, sound, trips, etc.), and each edge as a channel (for thermal or sound transmission through a wall segment, circulation from one space to another, etc.).

Advantages and disadvantages

Dual-graph representations provide a means of describing floor plans purely at the topological level, without necessarily including any shape or dimensional data at all. They are thus useful for three basic purposes:

1) Representation of floor plans at a stage *before* shape and dimension decisions have been made.
2) Representation of floor plans as *flow systems.*
3) Utilization in conjunction with polygonal or other types of representations in order to provide more convenient access to topological data.

SMITH DIAGRAMS

The electrical network analogy

If a floor plan is known to consist of a dissection of a rectangle into rectangles, then an alternative though closely related graph theoretic representation known as a "Smith diagram" may be utilized

(Brooks *et al* 1940, Tutte 1966, March and Steadman 1974). A Smith diagram may be thought of as an "electrical network" as shown in *Figure 6.49*. Each east-west wall is represented by a "terminal." The "potential" at each "terminal" represents the distance from the south wall, and the "current" in each link represents the width of the space that it traverses. Similarly of course, a Smith diagram can be drawn from west to east.

The most important special property of the Smith diagram representation is that it facilitates checks for dimensional consistency and compliance with dimensional constraints in a floor plan, since it can be shown that Kirchoff's Laws for electrical networks must hold. We know from Kirchoff's first law that the current in a conductor is given by

$$\text{Current} = C\ (V_1 - V_2)$$

where

C = conductance
V_1 = larger voltage
V_2 = smaller voltage

Figure 6.49
Smith diagram representation of a rectangular floor plan. (a) East-west. (b) North-south. (c) Incidence matrix encoding.

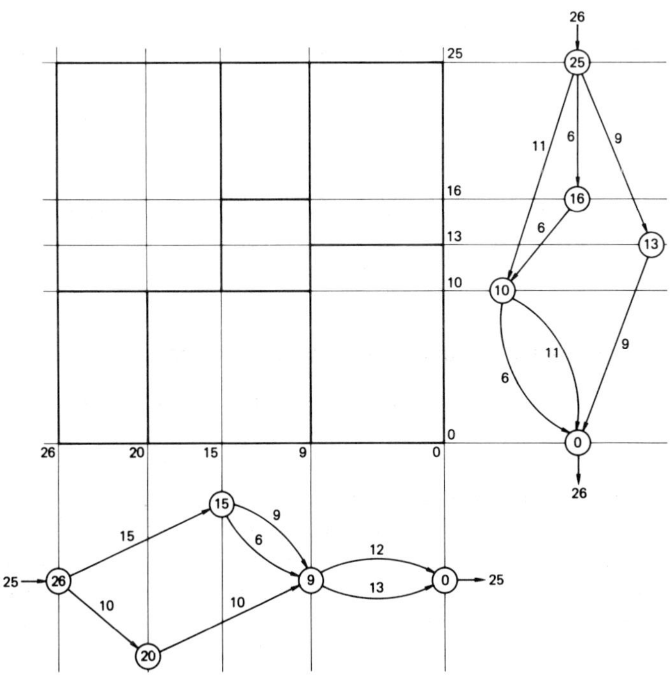

(a) (b)

	26	11	6	9	6	6	11	9	26
25	1	1	1	1					
16			1		1				
13				1				1	
10		1			1	1	1		
0						1	1	1	1

	25	10	15	10	6	9	13	12	25
26	1	1	1						
20		1		1					
15			1		1	1			
9				1	1	1	1	1	
0							1	1	1

(c)

Figure 6.50
Introduction of dummy walls into a floor plan in order to allow representation by a Smith diagram.

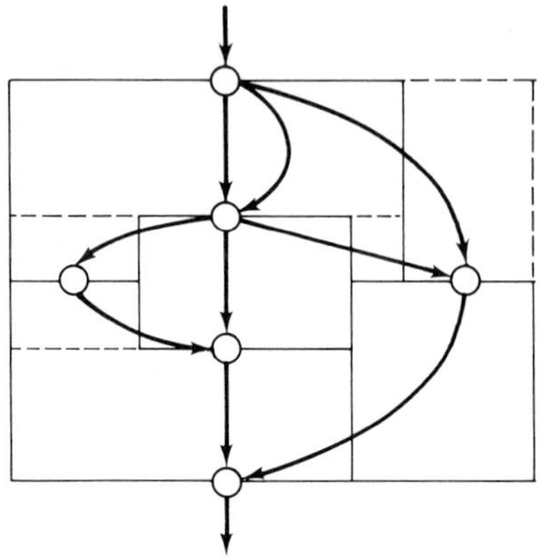

Interpreting this in terms of a rectangular floor plan, we see that $(V_1 - V_2)$ represents the length of the room, and C represents the proportion (ratio of length to width). The second law simply states that current entering a terminal must equal current leaving. In terms of the floor plan, this simply means that the sum of the widths of rooms on one side of a wall segment must equal the sum of the widths on the other.

A Smith diagram may be numerically encoded as an incidence matrix. Associated with each row (vertex) is a "potential," and associated with each column (edge) is a "current," as shown in *Figure 6.49.* This representation can then be stored in array form. The order in which the edges are arranged around a vertex in a Smith diagram indicates the order in which rooms occur, and this order must therefore be preserved in the incidence matrix. Using pencil and graph paper, the reader can soon convince himself that the complete plan can be reconstructed from this matrix.

Since any rectilinear plane shape may be dissected into rectangles, the Smith diagram representation can be generalized to deal with any rectilinear floor plan by the introduction of "dummy" walls and spaces, as illustrated in *Figure 6.50.*

Generation of floor plans using Smith diagrams

Smith diagrams have a rather interesting history. They were originally developed in 1937, by the self-styled "Important Members" of the Cambridge Trinity College Mathematical Society, in solving the classic mathematical problem of "squaring the square" (Brooks *et al* 1940). They are named after C. A. B. Smith, one of the "Important Members." The problem of squaring the square, which was long thought to have no solution, is to find some set of squares, no two the same size, which will fit together to form a larger square. By manipulation of Smith diagrams, the "Important Members" were able to construct many different such "perfect squares." An example is illustrated in *Figure 6.51.*

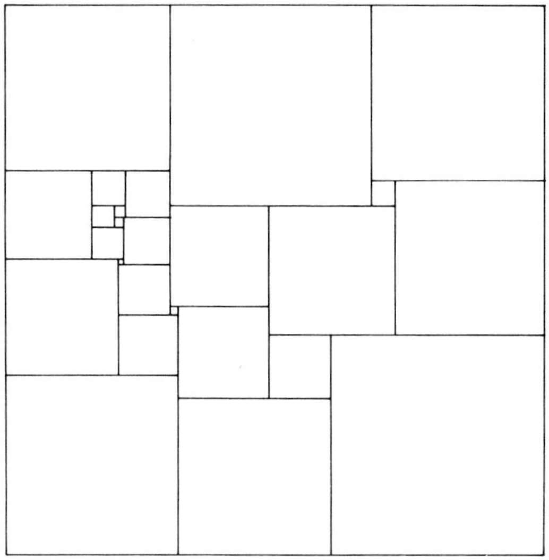

Figure 6.51
A perfect square.

The problem of synthesizing floor plans composed of rectangles packed within a rectangular envelope is closely analogous, and can also be solved with the aid of Smith diagrams. Essentially the procedure is one of systematic permutation of the orders of vertices around each node (*i.e.*, positions of rooms within the envelope), using Kirchoff's Laws and considerations of required adjacency between spaces to rapidly eliminate large classes of potential arrangements which cannot meet the specified requirements. The technique has been discussed in detail by Steadman (1970), and March and Steadman (1974). However, the combinatorial problem involved is a large one, and only small floor plans (of the order of 10 or fewer rooms) can be dealt with, even with efficient programming and a powerful computer.

GRAPH-THEORETIC REPRESENTATIONS IN THREE DIMENSIONS

Just as a floor plan may be treated as a planar graph, so may a section. (Note that a floor plan is really a horizontal section.) All the graph-theoretic representations that may be used for floor plans may also be employed for sections.

Figure 6.52(a) shows a building section regarded as a graph in which floor and wall segments are edges, and joints are vertices. The graph can then be encoded as an adjacency or incidence matrix, with associated dimensional and locational data, in the normal way. This is a particularly useful approach to describing the geometry of a building frame for purposes of structural analysis. The connectivity of members is explicitly recorded, data on the properties of members can

Figure 6.52
Graph representation of the section of the Yale School of Art and Architecture building (architect Paul Rudolph, 1958–64). (a) Section represented as a graph. (b) Dual of the section.

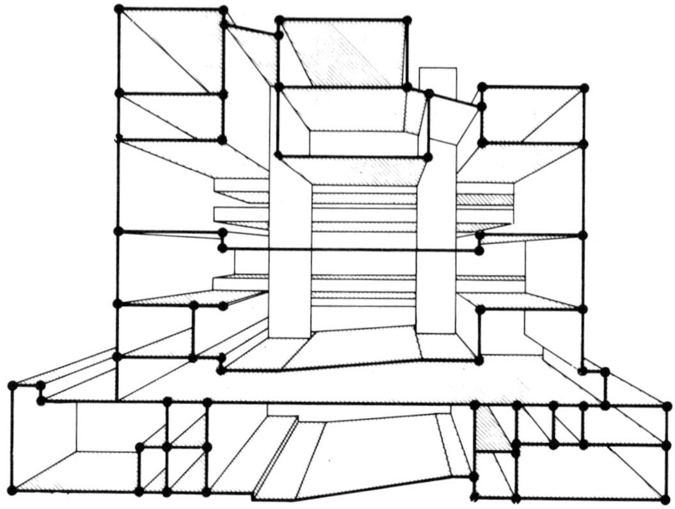

(a)

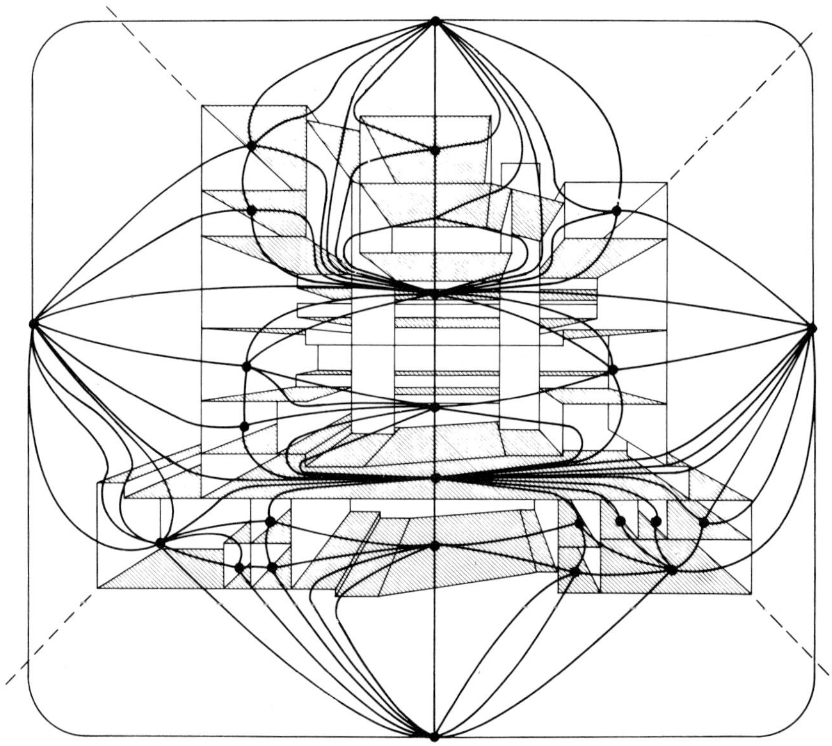

(b)

be associated with edges, and data on the properties of joints can be associated with vertices.

A dual-graph for the section can also be constructed, as shown in *Figure 6.52(b)*. In the same way that a dual-graph can be used to generate floor layouts that satisfy specified plan adjacency requirements, dual-graphs can also be employed to produce sections which satisfy specified adjacency requirements in a vertical plane.

In the Smith diagram representation of a section, "potentials" at vertices correspond to floor heights, and "currents" to the widths of spaces at the section plane. *Figure 6.53* illustrates a Smith diagram representation of the section of a unit in Le Corbusier's Marseilles block.

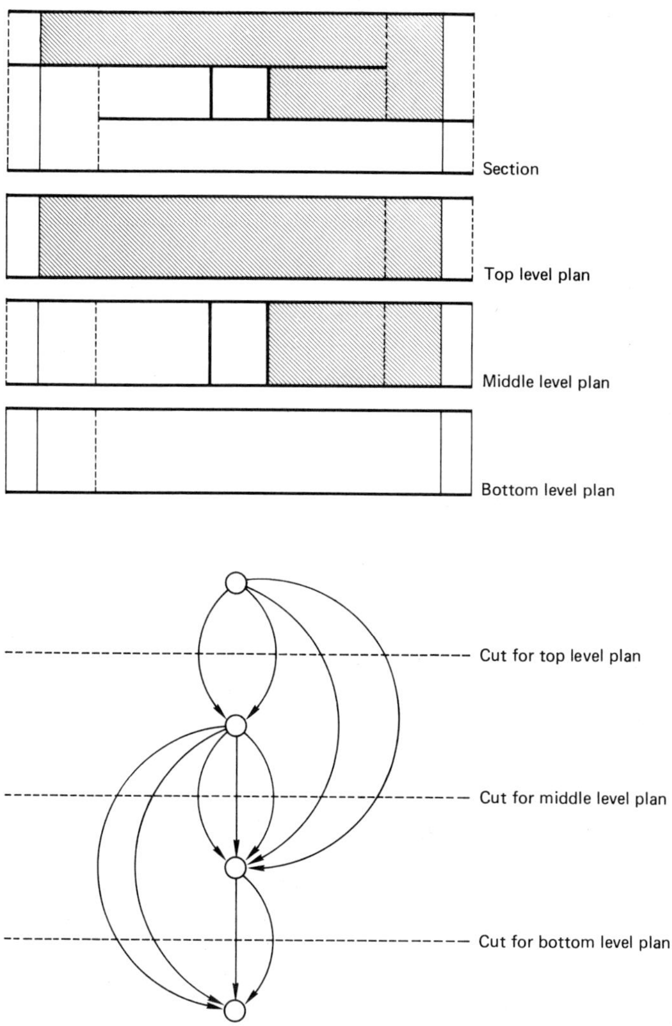

Figure 6.53
Vertical Smith diagram or Teague network representation of a unit in Le Corbusier's Marseilles block. Each vertex has associated with it a floor height, and each edge has associated with it the width of a room.

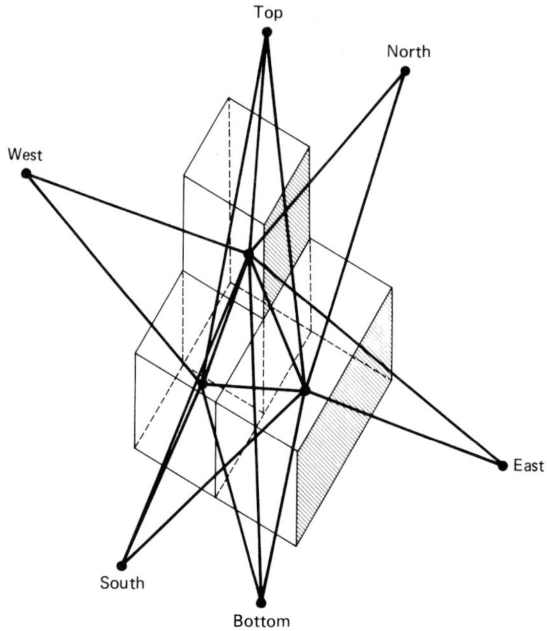

Figure 6.54
Three-dimensional adjacency graph for a simple three room building.

Adjacency graphs

Adjacency graphs can be constructed for three-dimensional built forms as well as for two-dimensional plans and sections. In the three-dimensional case, vertices represent polyhedral rather than polygonal regions, and edges represent two-dimensional wall, floor, or roof surfaces rather than projections of wall segments onto the floor plane (*Figure 6.54*). (However, such adjacency graphs, unlike adjacency graphs for planar networks of polygons, are not duals of the original figure.) Nonplanar adjacency requirements graphs can be satisfied in three dimensions (*Figure 6.55*).

Adjacency graph descriptions of three-dimensional built forms are primarily useful for representation of buildings as flow networks, for such purposes as heat flow or acoustic analysis. They may also be useful in preliminary cost estimation systems, where it may be necessary to infer the construction and properties of wall and floor surfaces from the usage of the spaces which they divide (Krauss and Myer 1968, Harmon 1973).

Teague networks

A second type of three-dimensional graph-theoretic representation, this time employing the Smith diagram principle, has been developed by Teague (1970). This representation is restricted to orthogonal assemblages of rectangular parallelepipeds. The dimensions and origin coordinates are listed for each parallelepiped, and vertical

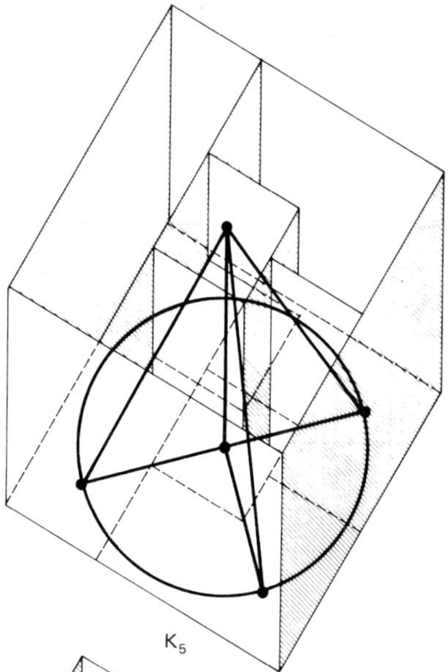

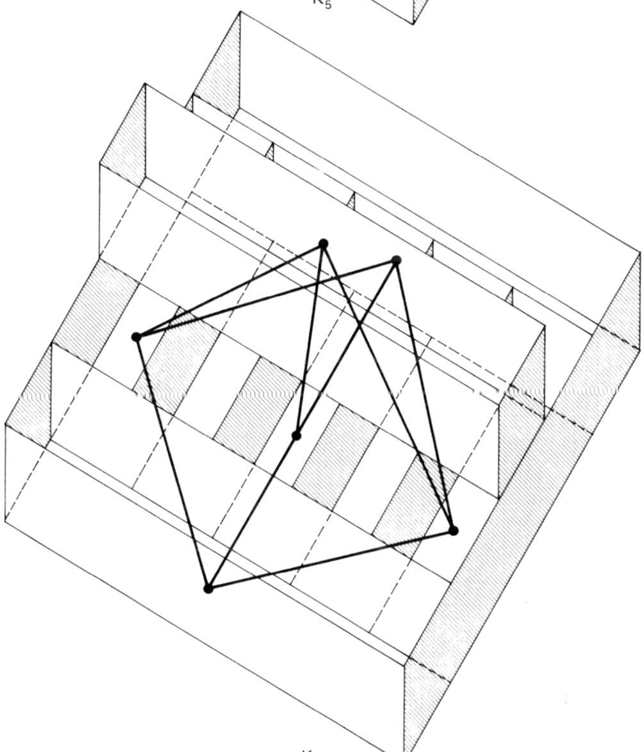

Figure 6.55
The nonplanar graphs K_5 and $K_{3,3}$ realized as three-dimensional adjacency graphs.

relations are described by means of a vertical Smith diagram (*Figure 6.53*). Forms are treated as assemblages of rectangular parallelepipeds. An important property of the Teague representation is that floor plans at any level can readily be produced by "cutting" the

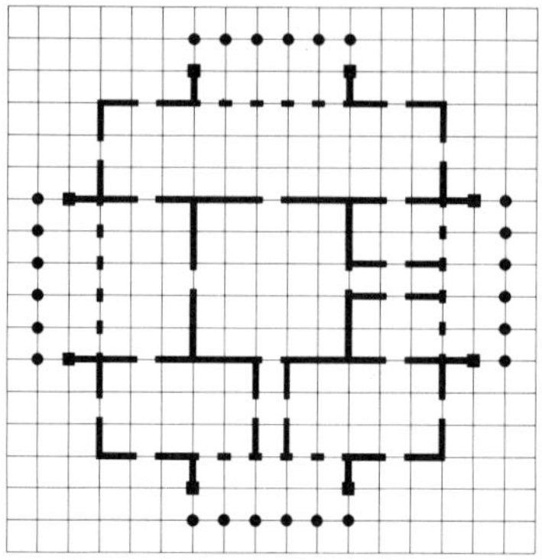

(a) Scheme for a villa from J. Gwilt's *Rudiments of Architecture* (1826)

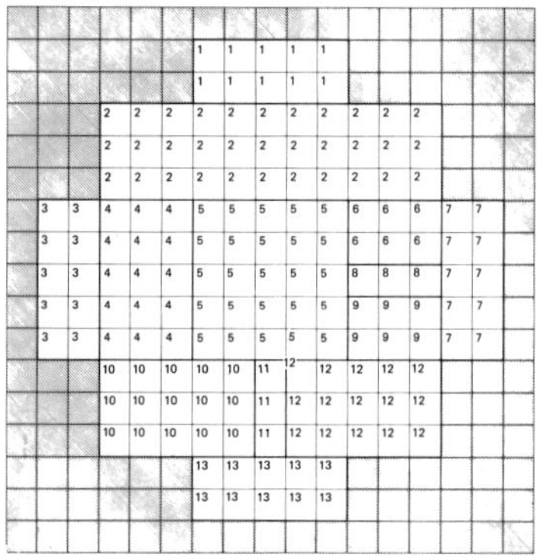

(b) Regular (square) grid representation

Advantages: Conceptual simplicity
Ease of implementation using array handling facilities of common programming languages
Spatial consistency is automatically maintained (since space is explicitly represented)
Many geometric computations, e.g. computing areas, testing for adjacency of spaces, are made simple

Disadvantages: Tends to consume excessive storage
Imposes a geometric discipline which may be inappropriate for many applications

Typical applications: Automated floor plan layout programs
Description of highly modular buildings

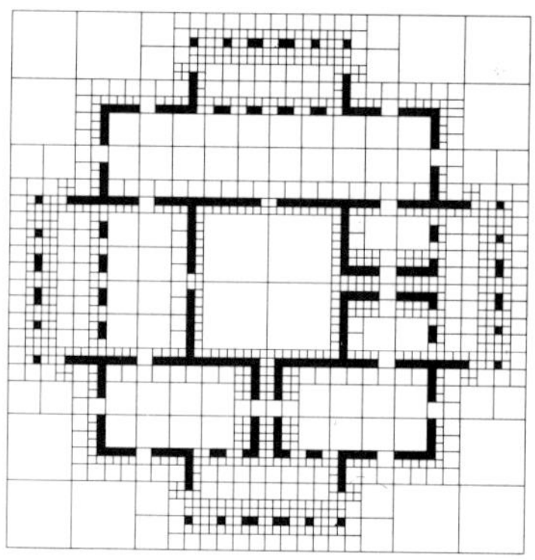

(c) Hierarchical array form of square grid representation

Advantages: Preserves many of the advantages of the simple square grid representation, while allowing relatively economical representation of fine detail

Disadvantages: Tends to be difficult to implement and manipulate, especially if the programming language employed does not incorporate the necessary facilities

Typical applications: No architectural applications reported
Mobile automata

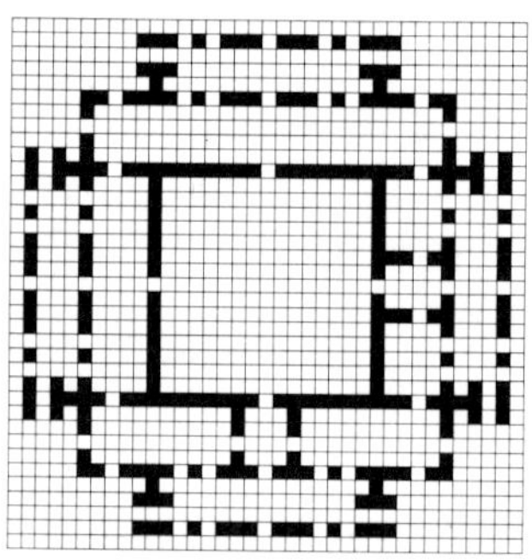

(d) Dimensionless representation (of solids and voids) in conjunction with dimensioning vectors

Advantages: Like the hierarchical array, preserves many of the advantages of the simple square grid representation, while allowing relatively economical representation of fine detail
Straightforward to implement and manipulate using array handling facilities of common programming languages

Disadvantages: Not well suited to description of non-rectilinear forms
Inefficient for description of very complex shapes

Typical applications: Comprehensive description of buildings of basically rectilinear geometry
Dimensional optimization programs

Figure 6.56 Comparison of different methods of geometric description.

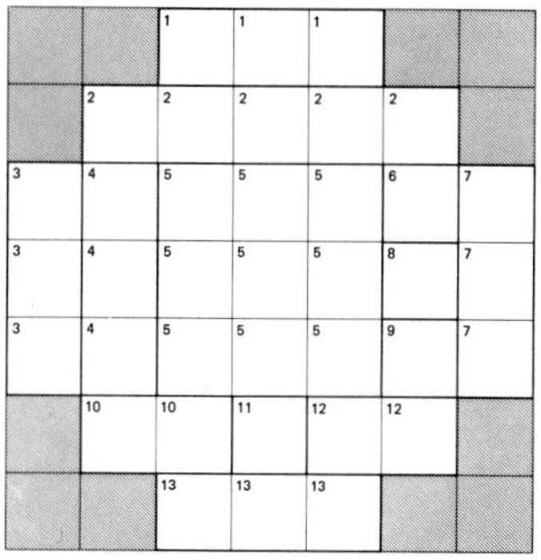

(e) Dimensionless representation (of spaces) in conjunction with dimensioning vectors

Advantages: Extremely efficient method for description of rectilinear forms

Preserves most of the advantages of the simple square grid representation

Separation of shape description from dimensional information facilitates efficient enumeration of generic plan forms

Disadvantages: Not well suited to description of non-rectilinear or complex shapes

Typical applications: Comprehensive description of buildings of basically rectilinear geometry

Automated floor plan layout programs

Dimensional optimization programs

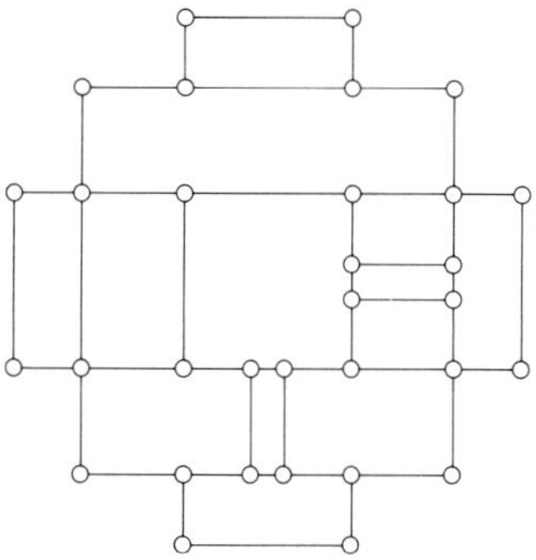

(f) Polygon (or polyhedron) representation

Advantages: Very general and flexible, imposes few restrictions on geometry

A large amount of research has been devoted to development of data structures and algorithms for handling this type of representation

Well suited to production of graphic output

Disadvantages: Sophisticated polygon or polyhedron representations tend to require the support of complex and extensive software

Implicit, rather than explicit representation of spaces causes serious difficulties in computing intersections, overlaps, adjacencies, etc.

Typical applications: Comprehensive building description

Graphics production applications

Spatial synthesis applications

Various engineering applications

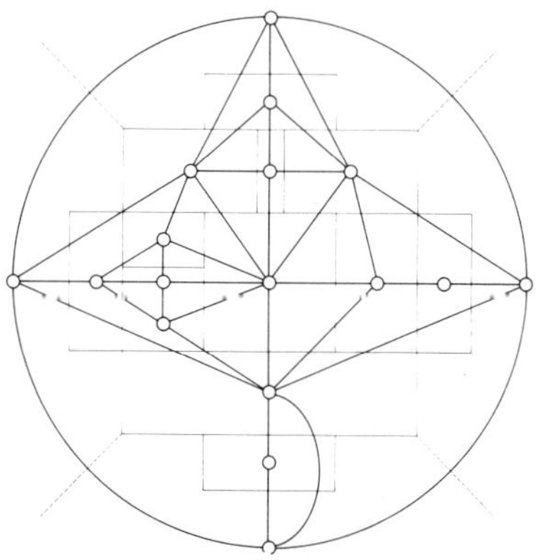

(g) Dual graph representation

Advantages: Directly and efficiently represents adjacencies between spaces

May be used as a basis for certain floor plan layout techniques

Can represent a floor plan concept before shape or dimension decisions have been made

Disadvantages: Essentially describes topology, and does not form a very convenient basis for developing a geometric description

Typical applications: Representation of very early layout concepts

Automated floor plan layout programs

Traffic or heat flow analysis

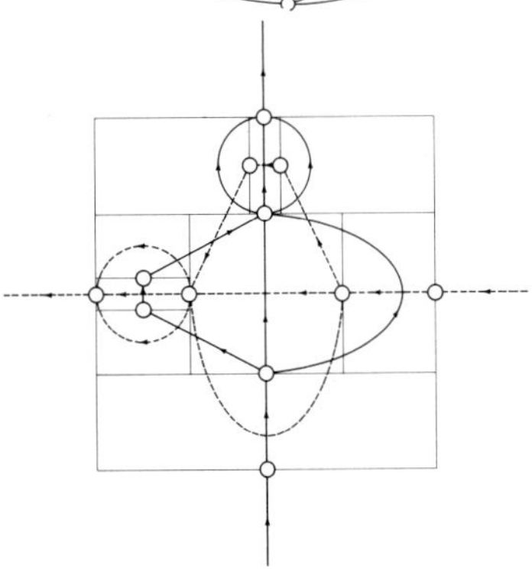

(h) Smith diagram (or Teague network) representation

Advantages: Very efficient for description of rectangular geometries

Allows exploitation of the "electrical network" analogy

Disadvantages: Restricted to rectangular geometries

Typical applications: Comprehensive description of buildings of basically rectangular geometry

Automated floor plan layout programs which exploit the "electrical network" analogy network as shown. With the addition of further networks, sections could also be produced in the same way.

An implementation of the Teague representation forms the basis of the BUILD subsystem of the ICES civil engineering system. Further extensions to this representation have more recently been developed at MIT. Jackson (1970) describes a data structure which combines the Teague representation with an adjacency graph. Additional modifications and extensions have been proposed by Harmon (1973).

COMPARATIVE SUMMARY

A wide variety of techniques for representation of building form have been discussed. The range of possibilities has by no means been exhausted, but the most important alternatives have been described. To gain an overall perspective, it is worth comparing the various representations in terms of the following characteristics:

Theoretical principle upon which the representation technique is based.

Typical operations performed upon the representation.

Characteristic applications.

Figure 6.56 illustrates equivalent descriptions of a simple floor plan, utilizing the different representation techniques that have been discussed, and summarizes their characteristics.

SUGGESTED READINGS

Chalmers, J.; Sampson, P.; and Webster, G. J. "Data Structure Used in Cedar: A Computer-Aided Building Design System," in *Programming Techniques in Computer-Aided Design,* edited by M. A. Sabin. London: NCC Publications, 1974.

Eastman, C. M. "Representations for Space Planning." *Communications of the ACM* 13, no. 4 (1970), pp. 242–250.

Eastman, C. M.; Lividini, J.; and Stoker, D. "A Database for Designing Large Physical Systems." *Proceedings of the 1975 National Computer Conference,* pp. 603–611. Montvale, New Jersey: AFIPS Press, 1975.

Forrest, A. R. "Computational Geometry: Achievements and Problems," in *Computer-Aided Geometric Design,* edited by R. E. Barnhill and R. F. Riesenfeld. New York: Academic Press, 1974.

Forrest, A. R. "Transformations and Matrices in Modern Descriptive Geometry," in *The Architecture of Form,* edited by L. March. Cambridge, England: Cambridge University Press, 1976.

Golomb, S. W. *Polyominoes.* New York: Scribner's, 1965.

Harary, F. *Graph Theory.* Reading, Mass.: Addison-Wesley, 1968.

March, L. "A Boolean Description of a Class of Built Forms," in *The Architecture of Form,* edited by L. March. Cambridge, England: Cambridge University Press, 1976.

March, L., and Steadman, P. *The Geometry of Environment.* Cambridge, Mass.: MIT Press, 1974.

Shubnikov, A. V., and Koptsik, V. A. *Symmetry in Science and Art.* New York: Plenum, 1975.

Steadman, P. "Graph-Theoretic Representation of Architectural Arrangement," in *The Architecture of Form,* edited by L. March. Cambridge, England: Cambridge University Press, 1976.

7 Standard Element and Detail Libraries

Instances of a particular element may often appear at many different points in a design. For example, a standard door or window might be employed throughout a building, a standard apartment or office layout might be used repeatedly, and so on. It is clearly redundant and uneconomical to store detailed information on the properties of a particular standard element with every instance which occurs. Instead, it is preferable to group this data in a single location and to provide cross-references to and from instances. Thus it is common practice to divide a building description into two parts: a *project data base* and an *element library data base* as illustrated in *Figure 7.1.*

Apart from the storage economies achieved, the structuring of building descriptions in this fashion has the great advantage that a standardized library data base, once developed, can be re-used for many different projects. This can result in very considerable savings of design effort, and can facilitate overall rationalization of the design process.

This chapter discusses the various types of element library data bases that are employed. They are classified under the following headings:

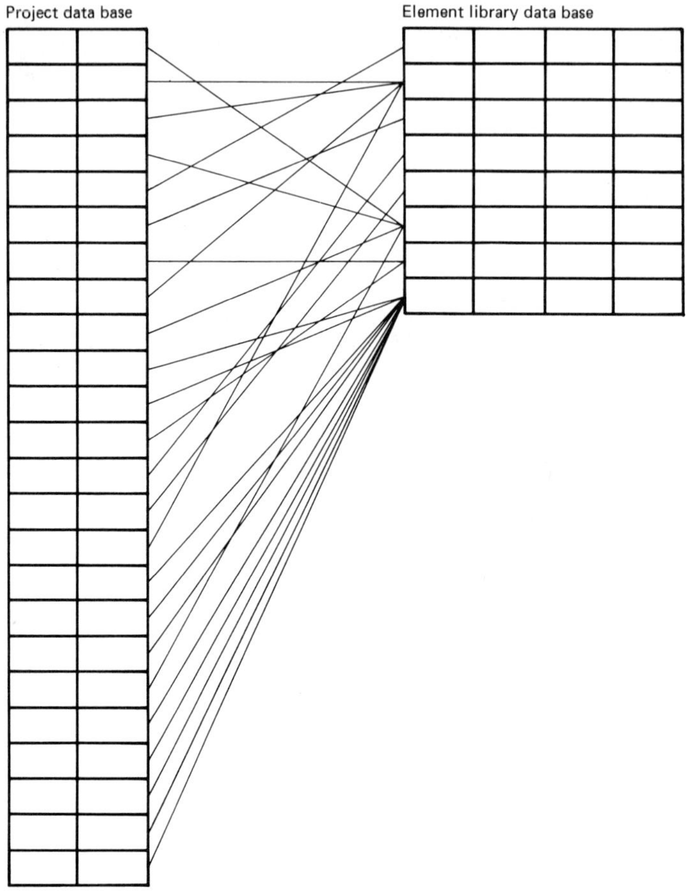

Figure 7.1
Cross-referenced project and element library data bases.

Standard plan element library data bases, e.g., standard office layouts, apartment units, hospital departments.

Building component and material library data bases, containing the type of data found in building products catalogues.

Master specification data bases, from which clauses pertaining to a particular project are selected.

Standard detail library data bases, recording details to be employed in commonly occurring situations.

These data bases may contain text, performance data, or geometric data, depending upon the particular type and application. For example, specification clause data bases typically contain strings of text, building materials data bases contain numerical data on such properties as cost, U-values, density, strength, etc., while plan element, detail, and component data bases often store geometric descriptions.

It is not necessary for both the element library and project data bases to be computer-based; combinations of traditional and computer-based techniques may be employed. It is quite common, for instance, to employ a standard specification clause data base and automated specification production system in conjunction with manually produced working drawings. Conversely, a computer-based project description might be cross-referenced to a catalogue of standard plan elements drawn on paper. However, the greatest advantages are potentially achievable if both data bases are computer-based.

An element library may be either *closed* or *open*. A typical closed element library is the catalogue of components of a closed component building system. Once created, a closed library alters little if at all. A general components and materials data base is a typical open element library. In this case, provision must be made for continual updating.

Element libraries also vary greatly in their *scope* of application. At one end of the spectrum are small, special element libraries created for use on one particular project. Libraries of somewhat wider scope might be utilized within a particular firm, or building program, for a number of projects. Most comprehensively, an element library might serve the entire building industry nation-wide. Typical libraries which are nation-wide in scope are national standard specifications, and industry-wide building products data bases.

The remainder of this chapter discusses examples of various types of element library data bases.

STANDARD PLAN ELEMENT LIBRARY DATA BASES

Several integrated systems make effective use of standard plan element library data bases. Harness and ARK-2 will be discussed.

Harness standard departments

The Harness hospital concept was introduced in Chapter 3 and illustrated in *Figures 3.13* and *6.8*. To recapitulate briefly, a Harness hospital is assembled by arranging standard, pre-designed departments along a circulation spine. A basic 16.2m square planning grid is employed throughout.

Each standard Harness department is planned complete with engineering services in one horizontal plane. The basic form of a department is thus a polyomino, composed of squares 16.2m on edge (Davis 1974). Since the number of possible polyominoes is finite (see *Figure 6.18* and *Table 6.1*), the range of potential department plan profiles is also limited. When considerations such as the requirement for natural lighting are introduced, further restrictions on potential profiles are imposed. It is thus possible to develop a library of standard department profiles, as illustrated in *Figure 7.2(a)*.

Within these profiles, detailed standard department plans are developed. *Figure 7.2(b)* shows a typical plan. These plans may be up-

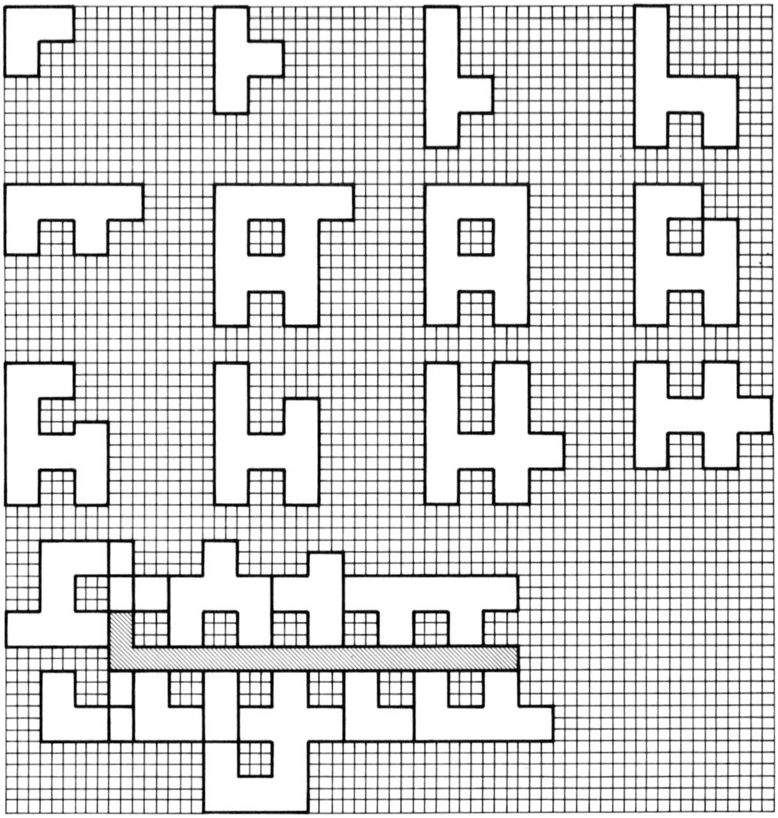

(a)

Figure 7.2
Harness hospital standard departments. (a) Standard department profiles, and their assembly along a circulation spine. (b) Plot of a standard department plan (adult day care).

dated and modified as technology develops and as feedback is received from buildings in use.

In the computer-aided design system developed for use in generating and evaluating Harness hospitals, a particular hospital configuration is economically described as an assemblage of standard departmental profiles along the circulation spine, and stored using a simple two-dimensional array data structure (see Square Grids in Chapter 6). Detailed information on the contents and internal layout of departments, on the other hand, is contained in a separate library of detailed standard department plans.

ARK-2 standard drawings

The ARK-2 system (see Integrated Systems in Chapter 3) takes a rather different approach. It provides facilities for creation of standard drawings, and storage of these drawings on magnetic tape. In addition, an interactive graphics interface is provided to allow the user to rapidly retrieve, scale, translate, rotate, and combine existing

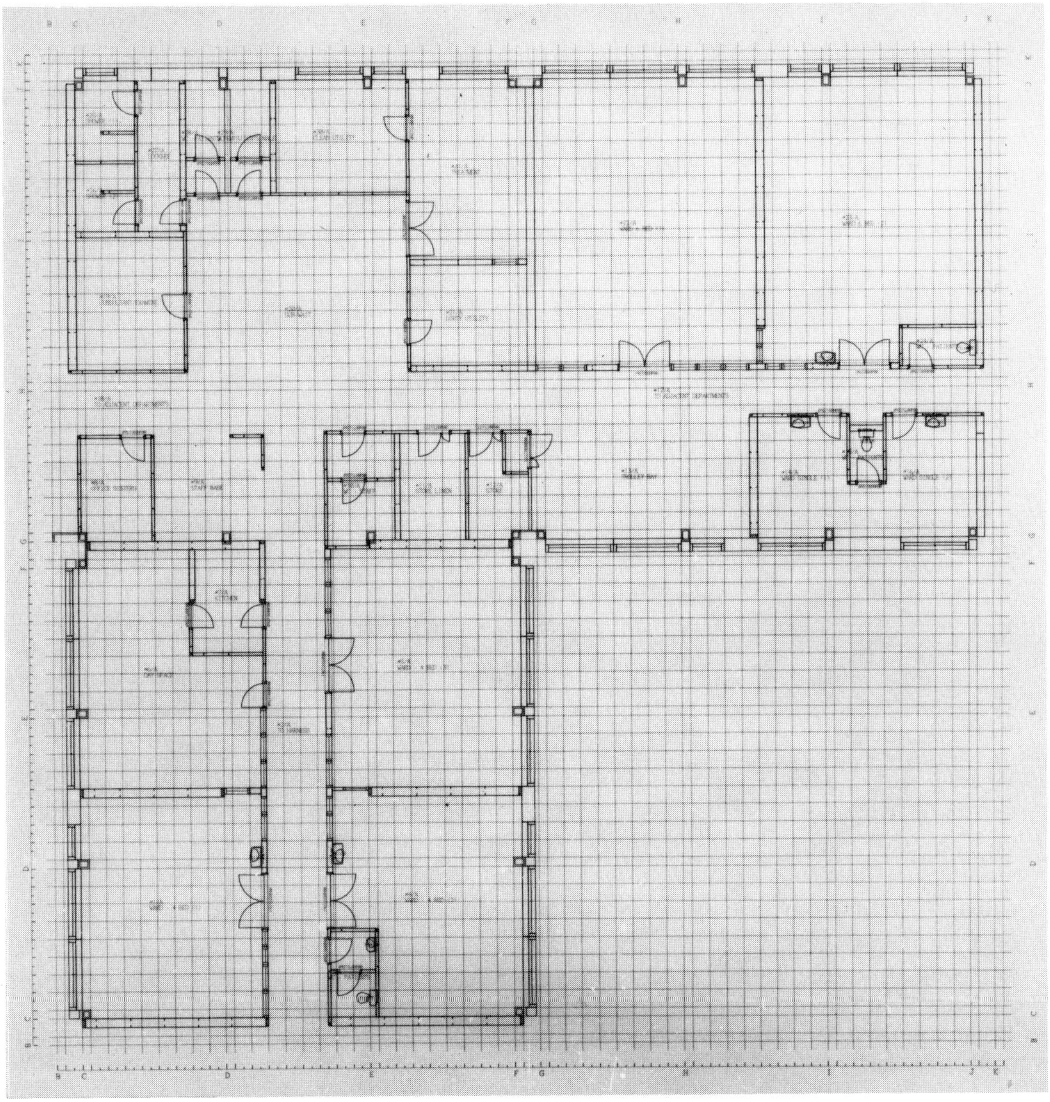

(b)

drawings to create new drawings. If a facility composed of repeated plan elements, such as a motel or apartment block, is to be designed, drawings of the standard elements are first created and stored. Then, the facilities of the graphics interface are employed to assemble combinations of these elements. An example of a drawing created in this way is illustrated in *Figure 7.3*.

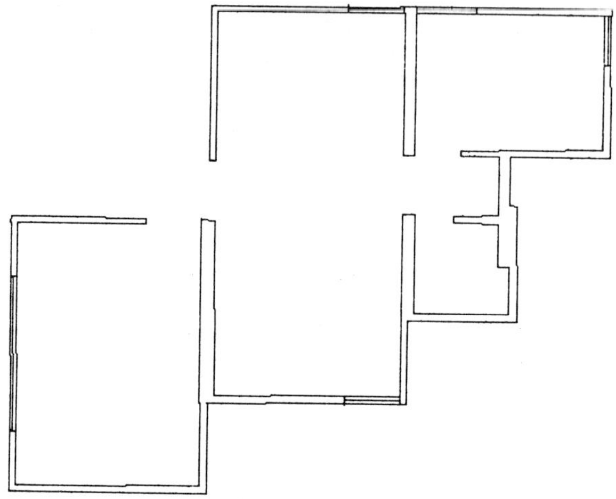

(a)

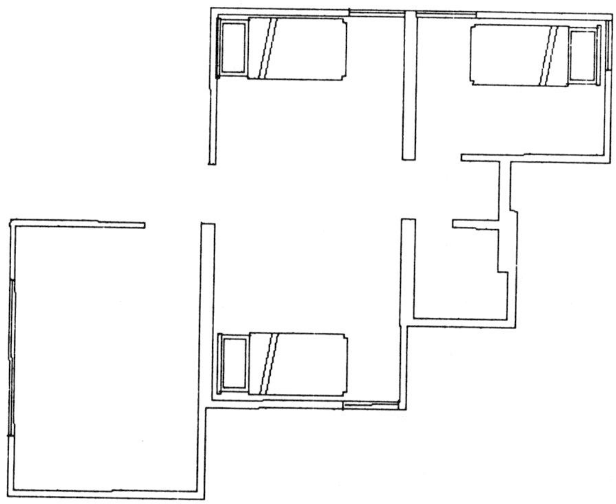

(b)

Figure 7.3
Creation of a drawing using the ARK-2 system. (a) Standard room outline. (b) Addition of beds. (c) Addition of further furniture. (d) Addition of further furniture, bathroom fixtures, and door swings.

BUILDING COMPONENT AND MATERIAL LIBRARY DATA BASES

Building component and material library data bases may be designed either for use with a particular closed building system, or to accept any component or material description that the user wishes to include.

Closed building system component library data bases

The OXSYS computer-aided design system is an excellent example of use of a building system component data base. OXSYS was originally developed for use in hospital design by the Oxford

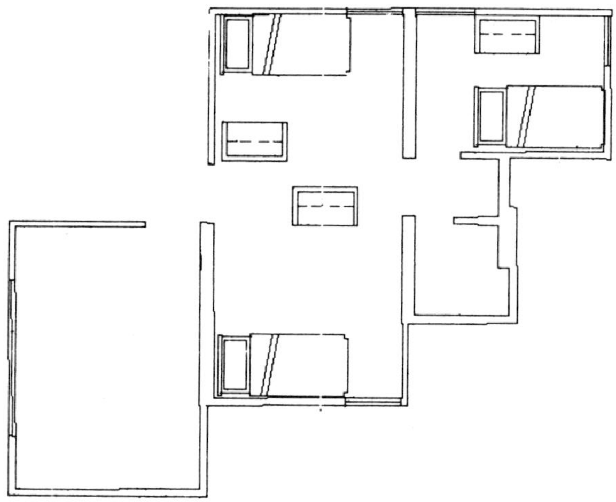

(c)

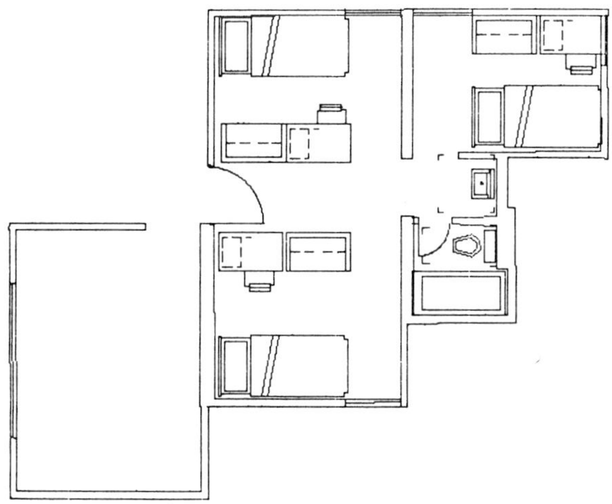

(d)

Regional Hospital Board in conjunction with the Oxford Method of Building, a component-based industrialized building system (Hoskins 1972).

The basic principles of the Oxford Method are as follows (CED Building Services 1974):

> Dimensional coordination based on a module of 100mm and a tartan planning grid of 600mm imposes a discipline on planning to enable standard components to be used.
>
> Use of a structural grid within the dimensional planning discipline.
>
> Rapid dry construction with maximum use of factory-made components.

Full integration of engineering services into the structure and design of the building.

Early enclosure of the building envelope to enable work to proceed despite bad weather.

Maximum and economic use of mechanical equipment on site and elimination of scaffolding.

Use of standard design data.

Use of carefully prepared performance specifications for individual components.

The construction technique is of the post, beam, and panel type illustrated in *Figure 3.14*. The major groups of industrialized components consist of substructure, steel framework, external cladding panels, external envelope, roof, concrete floor slabs, suspended ceilings, partitions, engineering services, finishes, furniture, and fittings. Coded and gridded drawings, together with standard sets of elemental details, are employed for constructional documentation.

The building description stored in computer memory by OXSYS consists of two major files, the component information file or CODEX, and the component location file or PROJECT FILE. The CODEX in turn is divided into the Master CODEX and the Project CODEX. The Master CODEX contains information about all standard Oxford Method components. This is set up and continually updated by the Oxford Regional Hospital Board research and development group responsible for the Oxford Method. Since the Master CODEX contains a large amount of data, much of which is superfluous for any particular project, the Master CODEX is edited to produce a subset of the information, a Project CODEX, for each project.

Components stored in the CODEX are classified into separate families and sub-families, and stored in a three-level hierarchically-indexed structure. The CODEX contains numerical and text data describing component properties like weight, U-value, etc., data for generating drawings of the elements, and codes describing permissible adjacency characteristics between components. An example of a drawing generated by OXSYS from the CODEX data is shown in *Figure 7.4*. The inclusion of permissible adjacency codes means that the CODEX defines not only the "vocabulary" of the Oxford Method, but also a good deal of its "syntax" as well. In addition, the file contains definitions and formats for property data, so that it is self-describing.

Although initially implemented for use with the Oxford Method, OXSYS is sufficiently general to allow substitution in the CODEX of any other component system which complies with the requirement that all components can be enclosed by orthogonal rectangular parallelepipeds. *Figure 7.5* shows some drawings of King's College Chapel, Cambridge, produced by OXSYS from a description stored in this way.

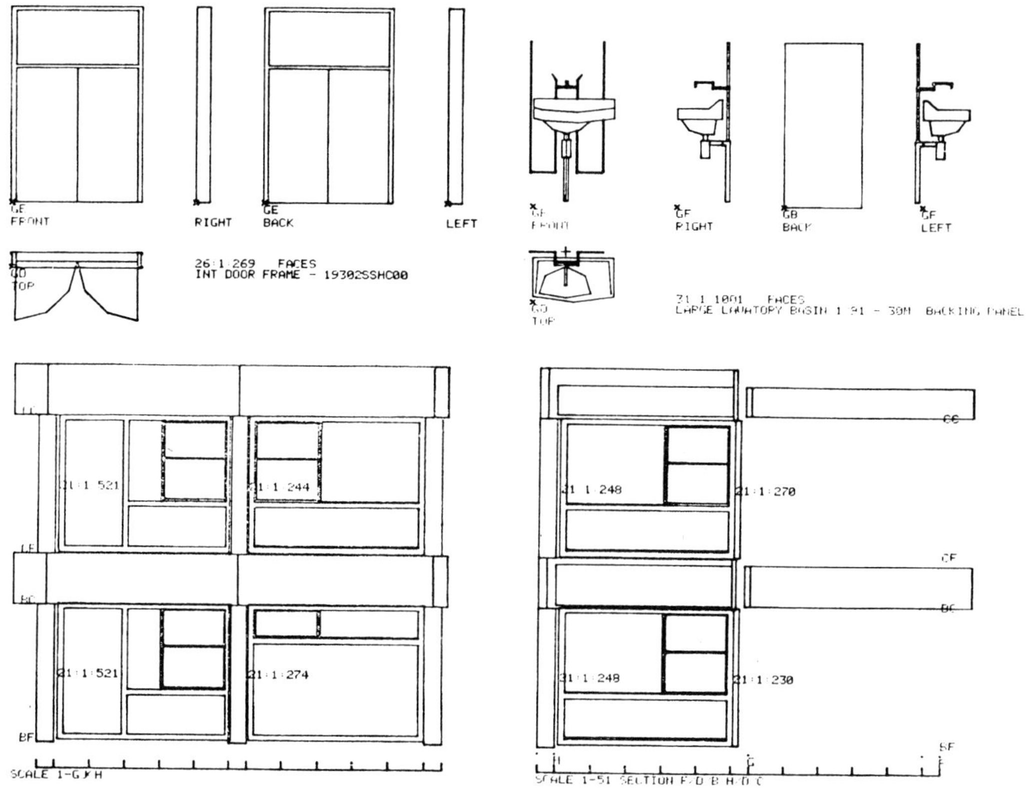

The BDS approach

Figure 7.4
Drawings produced by OXSYS from the CODEX of Oxford Method components.

It is not always possible or desirable to limit a computer-aided design system to use in conjunction with certain industrialized component systems. It may be necessary to employ an extensible, general component data base, capable of storing descriptions of almost any arbitrary components.

The most highly developed example of a general building component data base to date is incorporated in the Building Description System (BDS) developed at Carnegie-Mellon University (Eastman, Lividini, and Stoker 1975). The structure of the BDS data base is schematically shown in *Figure 7.6*. It employs a polyhedron representation, cleverly designed to minimize redundancy. The form of a component is initially represented by a *topology* (*Figure 7.6*(*a*)). Relations between locations of vertices are then defined by algebraic *expressions,* so that a *parametric model* representing a family of similar forms is produced (*Figure 7.6*(*b*)). By assigning particular values to variables in these expressions, a particular form from this family is defined (*Figure 7.6*(*c*)). Finally, *instances* of the form are produced by applying geometric transformations (*Figure 7.6*(*d*)).

The types of economies which are achieved by this hierarchical

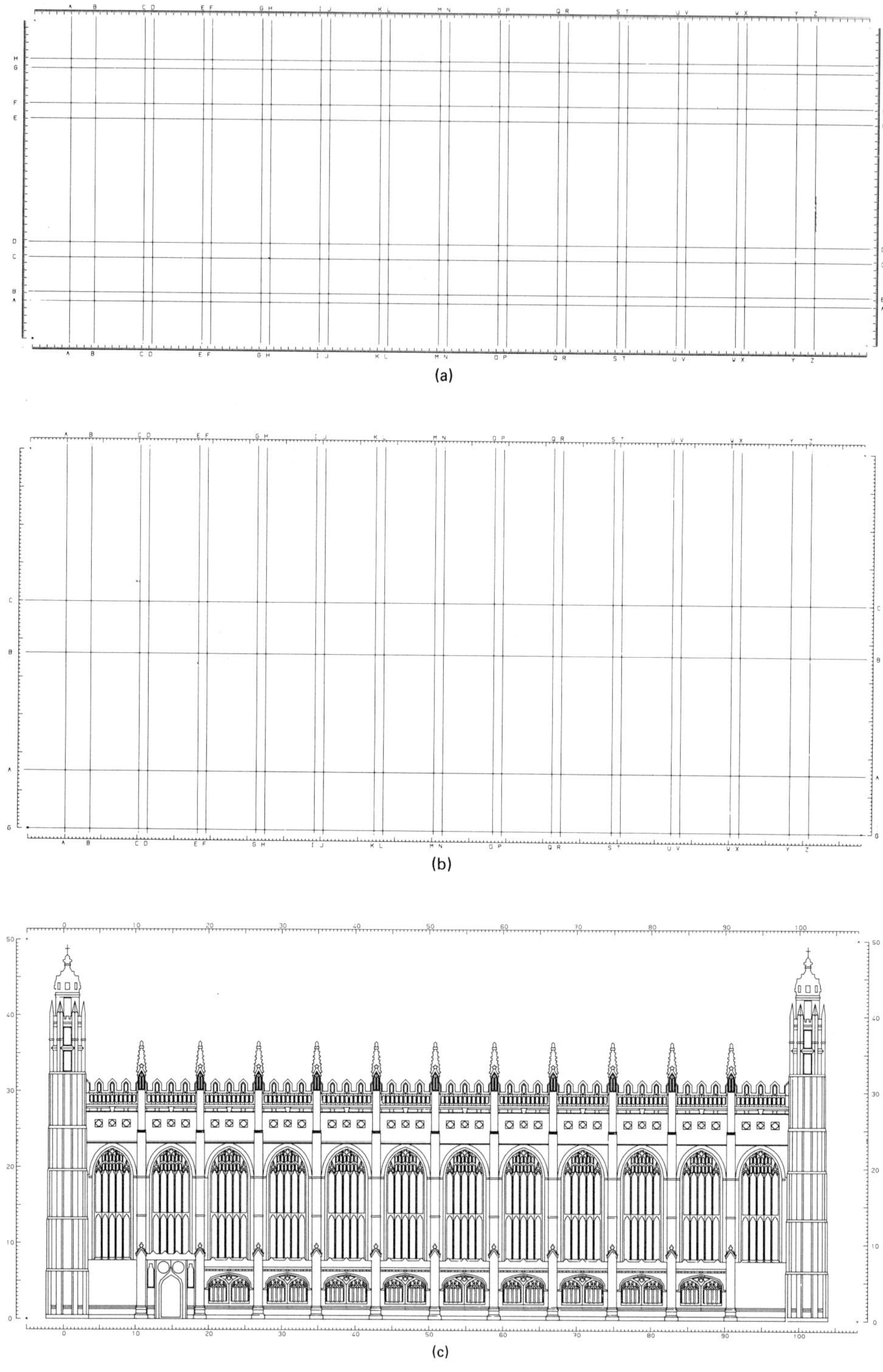

Figure 7.5
(a) Plan tartan grid. (b) Elevation tartan grid.
(c) Complete building description, with components located in tartan.

	a	b	c	d	e	f	g	h
a		1	0	1	0	0	0	1
b	1		1	0	1	0	0	0
c	0	1		1	0	1	0	0
d	1	0	1		0	0	1	0
e	0	1	0	0		1	0	1
f	0	0	1	0	1		1	0
g	0	0	0	1	0	1		1
h	1	0	0	0	1	0	1	

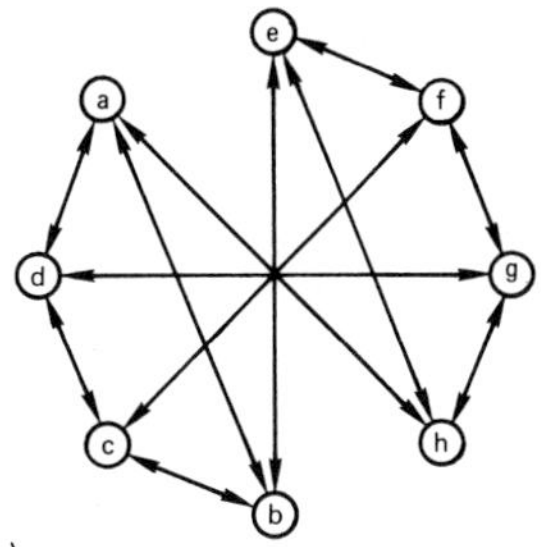

(a)

$$x_a = x_d = x_g = x_h = 0$$
$$x_b = x_c = x_f = x_e = x_1$$
$$y_d = y_c = y_f = y_g = 0$$
$$y_a = y_b = y_e = y_h = y_1$$
$$z_a = z_d = z_c = z_b = 0$$
$$z_h = z_g = z_f = z_e = z_1$$

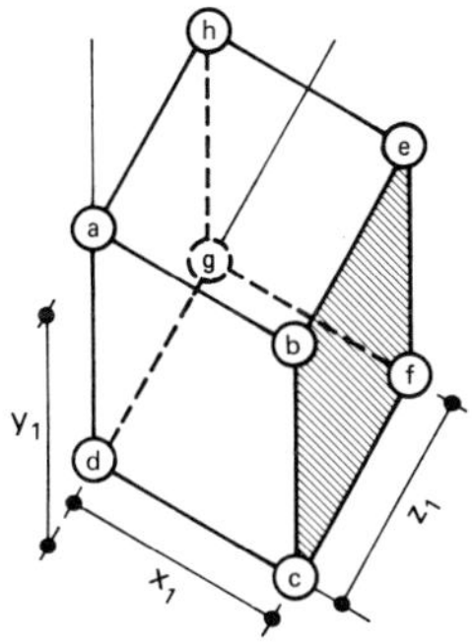

(b)

$$x_1 = 3.0$$
$$y_1 = 6.67$$
$$z_1 = 0.33$$

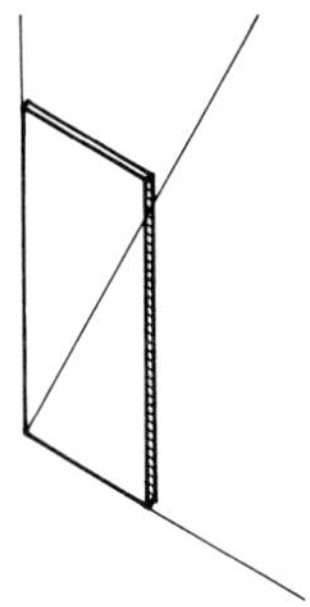

(c)

$$x_{org} = 16.0$$
$$y_{org} = 0$$
$$z_{org} = 24.0$$

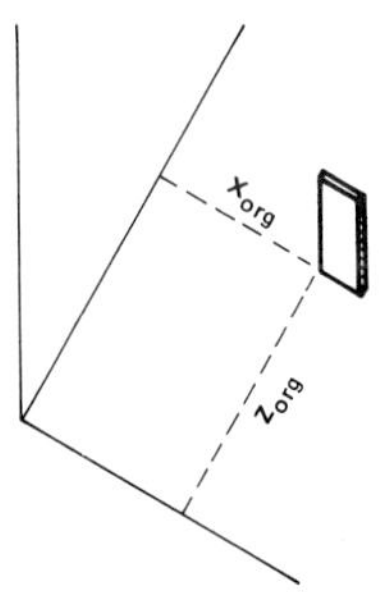

(d)

Figure 7.6
Representation of polyhedral components in the BDS system. (a) Topology. (b) Relations between locations of vertices described by algebraic expressions (relative to a local coordinate system). (c) Dimensions of the object fixed. (d) An instance of the object located within a global coordinate system.

approach to polyhedron description are illustrated in *Figure 7.7*. It can be seen that a number of parametric models may share a common topology, a number of forms may share a common parametric model, and a number of instances of a form may exist.

Attribute information which is stored in BDS in addition to

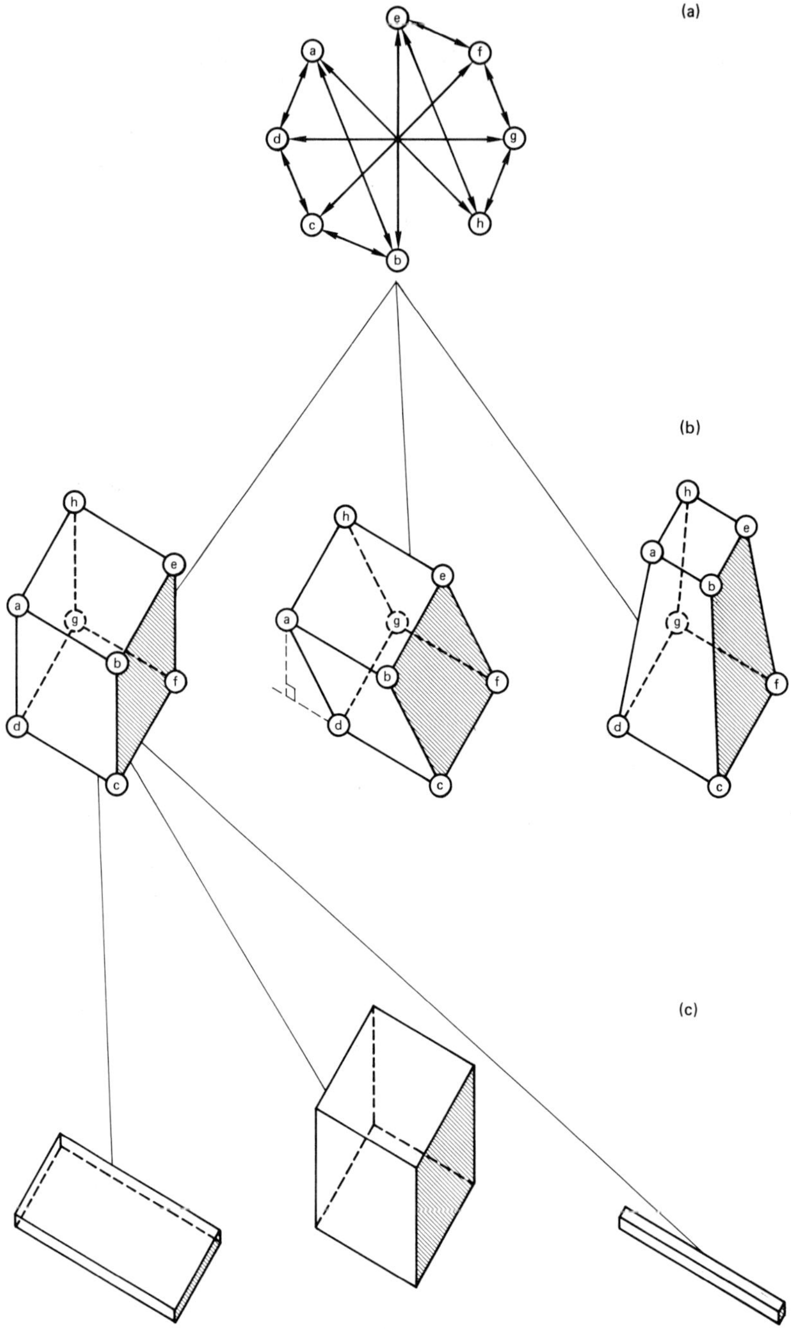

Figure 7.7
Reduction of redundancy by hierarchical description in the BDS system. (a) Topology. (b) Several parametric models sharing the same topology. (c) Several forms sharing the same parametric model.

topological and geometric data consists of such data as the component's manufacturer, cost, function, and performance properties. A particular attribute consists of three pieces of information: a name, a data type, and a value. Attributes may be stored (at appropriate levels in the hierarchy) with the topological and geometric descriptions of components. Alternatively, inverted file structures, grouping components with common attribute values, may be created.

BDS provides facilities for creating, deleting, and modifying component descriptions, assembling instances of components to create building designs, data base interrogation and generation of reports of various kinds, and running application programs.

Comprehensive, centralized building product library data bases

Comprehensive libraries of all the building components and materials potentially available for use by an architect tend to be very large. For example, a U.K. Department of the Environment study in 1971 estimated that there were about 300,000 to 400,000 different building products in use in Britain. Handling data bases of this magnitude, using existing data base management technology, is a fairly formidable and expensive, though technically feasible, undertaking. This suggests that comprehensive building product data bases should be maintained by centralized organizations, so that the considerable costs of collecting, verifying, storing, and updating information in the data base can be both minimized and spread over many users. Even so, it would probably be very difficult at present for a computer-based system to compete commercially with existing building product catalogues.

However, some work on the development of large scale, centralized commodity data bases has been undertaken in Britain, Canada, U.S.A., Sweden, Germany, Japan, France, and South Africa. Several prototype systems have been implemented (see Pennington 1967, Trout 1972). Other industries, for instance, electronics, production and control engineering, and metallurgy, have set up centralized data bases of comparable scale. Quite extensive feasibility studies for a national-scale, computerized product data base system for the construction industry have been undertaken in Britain (Bishop and Alsop 1969, Department of the Environment 1971).

Due to the magnitude of the data base management tasks involved, it seems likely that a centralized product data base would require a dedicated computer system equipped with extensive disk file facilities and data base management software, which could be remotely accessed via telephone lines. Implementation of such a system would require the development of a widely acceptable uniform classification scheme for building products, definition of properties to be included, and development of appropriate codes and formats for economical storage of data. Considerable research has been carried out on these problems. In 1971, for example, the Sweet's Division of the McGraw-Hill Information Systems Company began a research and development project aimed at development of a consistent and uniform system for organizing building product information, and in 1973 published a system known as the *Construction Matrix* with an associated *Master Grid* and *Guidelines Formats* for preparation of product data (Eldar 1973, Architectural Record 1973). In addition, a systematic product data verification method, such as the French *Agrément* system (Alsop and Day 1963), would also probably need to be instituted.

The task of encoding data for storage in a comprehensive building products data base would be a considerable one. The encoding might be carried out by a human operator, and the data input to the computer in coded form. Alternatively, the data might be input in a form closer to plain English, then automatically converted into a compressed coded form for storage. A prototype coding system for computer-stored construction products data has been published by Whiteside (1969). This system makes extensive use of short mnemonics in association with numerical data, and utilizes fixed format records wherever possible. It is based on the assumption that manufacturers would supply data in coded form, and it employs a format for data base records which closely corresponds with the format of the input code.

Associated with general building components and materials data bases would be search programs which allowed products to be retrieved by specified attributes and combinations of attributes. Availability of such a facility would result in considerable time savings in the product selection and specification phase of design. It would also help ensure that the most appropriate and economical choice was made for each situation.

Interrogation of the system could be carried out in a variety of ways. The architect might telephone a query to a trained operator, who would type in the data at a terminal and read back the results received, or mail a printout. This is the type of system now commonly employed for handling airline reservations. In the United States, Sweet's building products information service implemented in 1974 a telephone query system of this type called "Buyline." The Buyline data base contains names, addresses and telephone numbers of about 40,000 representatives of 1,400 building products manufacturers who appear in Sweet's Catalog Files. To locate a representative, the user calls a toll-free number and tells an operator the name of the manufacturer and his own location (by zip code). The operator types in this information, receives the answer on a CRT terminal screen, and reads it back. After about a year of operation, the service was receiving about 500 calls per day (Architectural Record, 1975). Alternatively, instead of using operators, a Touch-Tone® telephone might be employed to type in a query, and a voice-synthesis system utilized to read back the data over the telephone. Yet another alternative would be for the architect to employ an in-house computer terminal connected to the data base via the telephone system.

® Registered trademark of American Telephone and Telegraph Co.

MASTER SPECIFICATIONS

Traditional specification production procedures

Specification writers have always made extensive use of existing specification text when producing project specifications. Traditionally there have been two basic approaches. In the first, the specification for each job is written by hand. Specifications for prior jobs are invariably used as guides, and whole sections and paragraphs may be re-used by "cut-and-paste," but there is still a very considerable amount of labor involved. In the second, an attempt is made to make the process more efficient by taking advantage of the largely repetitive character of specifications, and utilizing pre-printed standard specification documents. These must usually be modified by striking out and inserting various sections and paragraphs to cover particular job conditions. A more recent variant of this latter approach is to use automatic tape-driven typewriters. The operation of the typewriter is monitored by an operator who can cause it to skip paragraphs as required, and who can insert paragraphs manually.

Automated specification production systems

Automated specification production systems have been in increasingly widespread use since the mid-1960's. The basic principles of operation of all such systems are essentially the same (Gero 1976). A library of standard specification elements (lines, clauses or paragraphs) is developed and stored on computer file. A text-editing system of some kind is then employed to assemble these elements of text as required, to make any necessary modifications, to insert any additional elements of text, and perhaps to automatically perform some simple indexing and numbering operations. A computer-controlled high-speed printer or typewriter is then used to produce a clean, properly set-out final copy. The final copy can either be made on paper and then reproduced, or put directly onto offset printing masters.

The principle can be illustrated by a simplified example. The following is a very short, line-based master specification:

```
0101   Breakfast shall consist of

0201   orange juice,
0202   tomato juice,
0203   grapefruit juice,

0301   boiled eggs,
0302   scrambled eggs,

0401   and coffee.
0402   and tea.
```

Selection of lines 0101, 0203, 0302, 0402, for example, would produce the clause:

> Breakfast shall consist of grapefruit juice, scrambled eggs, and tea.

It can be seen then, that a master specification constitutes a generative system for particular project specifications, not unlike the generative system proposed by Aristotle for producing descriptions of animals, which was discussed in Chapter 2.

Master specification files

There are two distinct types of tasks involved in the development of an automated specification production system. The first task is to develop a convenient and efficient system for performing the operations of manipulating and printing elements of text. The second is to develop, maintain, and update the master specification file.

Commercially-available automated specification systems are essentially either "empty" systems, which take care of editing, clerical, and production tasks but which require the user to develop his own master file, or "content-oriented" systems which provide a complete specification service. The SPECS system, developed by the APEC (Automated Procedures for Engineering Consultants) group, is an example of an "empty" system (Rosen 1971, Sussman, Logcher and Scotland 1971).

A distinct economic advantage of the "content-oriented" approach is that it allows the substantial cost of developing and maintaining the master file to be spread over a large number of users. This is particularly important for small design offices. Larger organizations may find it economical to develop and maintain master files tailored to their own specific needs. In the United States there now exist several computer-oriented master specifications which are used nationwide, for example, the PSAE (Production Systems for Architects and Engineers) system sponsored by the AIA, and the PIC (Pacific International Computing) system.

In Sweden, a comprehensive national master specification, oriented towards computer-generated building documentation, has been implemented (Birgerson 1967). For many years, a high degree of standardization in building communication has been normal in Sweden, largely due to use of the ByggAMA (National Standard Specification of Building Works), so the computer-based system represents an extension of a well-established tradition. The basis of the system is a code known as BDC, which is closely based on the earlier Danish CBC code. A central catalogue is published, which gives codes identifying standard specification clauses. In order to specify a material or component possessing certain required characteristics, it is merely necessary to give the appropriate identifying code. The codes are then key-punched, and the resultant data base can be automatically sorted in different ways and printed out in different formats not only to generate the job specification, but also to produce schedules, ordering lists, bills of quantities, etc.

Relational options

Some of the more recently developed automated specification systems incorporate quite sophisticated facilities for logically relating text elements and for automatic editing of the master specification, based upon the specification writer's answers to a few key questions. The use of a system developed by Syska and Hennessy (a New York consulting engineering firm), for example, is described as follows (Gilford 1972):

> Normally the project writer begins drafting his specification from the master copy, reviewing requirements and deleting from the master those parts not applicable to his project. Now, in place of the master copy, he receives a decision list which contains questions and statements about the project. Each question has two answers: yes or no, applies or does not, true or false. Examples of these are: Does the National Electric Code apply? Is this project in New York City? Is insulation required for primary chilled water piping?
>
> With answers to the decision list as complete as possible, they are presented to the computer program which interprets the requirements and decides which of the material in the master applies and which may be deleted. In cases where all answers have not been given, all possible related text concerning these questions is left in the master for the project writer's reference. The first draft is then printed and returned to the writer for further refinement.

Implementation in practice

The user may be provided with access to an automated specification system in a variety of ways. The simplest approach, which has apparently met with considerable commercial success, is to provide the user with a standard printed version of the master file. The items required are indicated by circling or some similar procedure, and any required modifications or additions are written directly on the printed form. This form is then submitted to a computer center where clerical staff prepare the necessary input data. Alternatively, a specification writer may interact directly with the system via a keyboard terminal.

Since specification writing is one of the most well-defined, standardized, and repetitive of architectural tasks, it has been one of the first to be successfully and widely automated. In many parts of the world specification services are widely available through commercial computer service bureaus, and large numbers of architectural offices successfully operate their own in-house systems.

STANDARD DETAIL LIBRARY DATA BASES

Libraries of standard construction details commonly form part of a building system. Most architectural design organizations develop libraries of standard details for use in their projects, whether or not particular systems or methods of building are employed.

Computer-based detail drawing files

The most straightforward approach to computer implementation of a standard detail library data base is to store standard detail drawings on tape, and to use the facilities of a computer graphic system to retrieve, modify, and plot them as required for a particular project. This is the approach followed in the ARK-2 system (Lee 1973). An example of a detail from an ARK-2 file is illustrated in *Figure 7.8*.

A more ambitious approach is to develop software which automatically generates appropriate details for particular situations. In other words, sketch designs are input and detailed working drawings are output. Automated detailing usually involves one or some combination of the following types of operations:

Component *location;*
Component *selection;*
Component *dimensioning.*

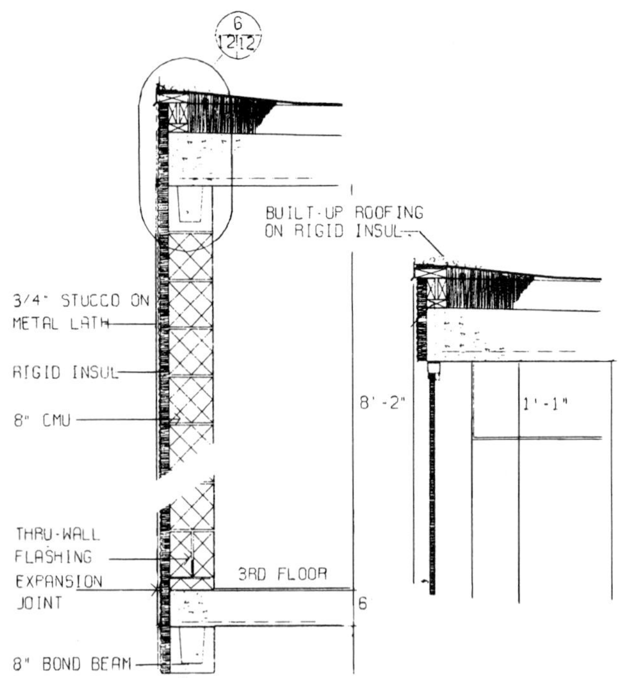

Figure 7.8
An example of a standard detail drawing created with the aid of the ARK-2 system.

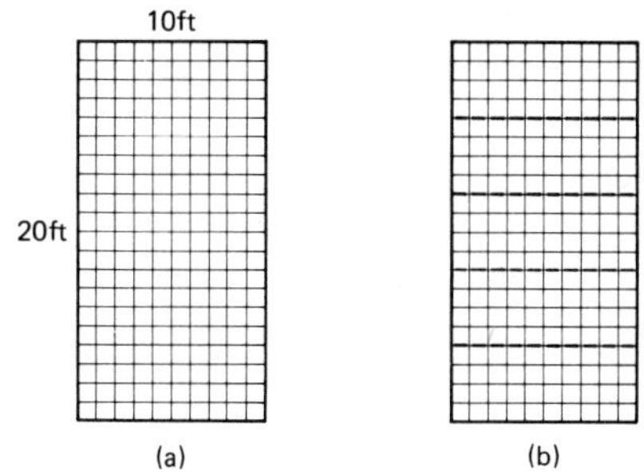

Figure 7.9
A simple example of component location according to well-defined rules. (a) Given plan. (b) Beams placed according to the rules: 1. Span across the short dimension. 2. Space beams at 4′0″ centers.

Automated component location

The locations of components in buildings are often determined according to quite simple and well-defined rules. For example, floor beams spanning a rectangular area might be located according to the following rules:

1. Span across the short dimension.
2. Space beams at 4′0″ centers.

The application of these rules is illustrated in *Figure 7.9*. It is fairly straightforward to develop computer programs which employ such rules to automatically "fill in" locations of beams, columns, cladding panels, etc. when given an outline design.

Automated component selection

Once a component location has been determined (either by the designer or by an automated detailing program) it is often possible to determine the particular *type* of component to be employed from the context. *Figure 7.10* illustrates the principle of this sort of operation. The conjectural system shown has a limited vocabulary of column

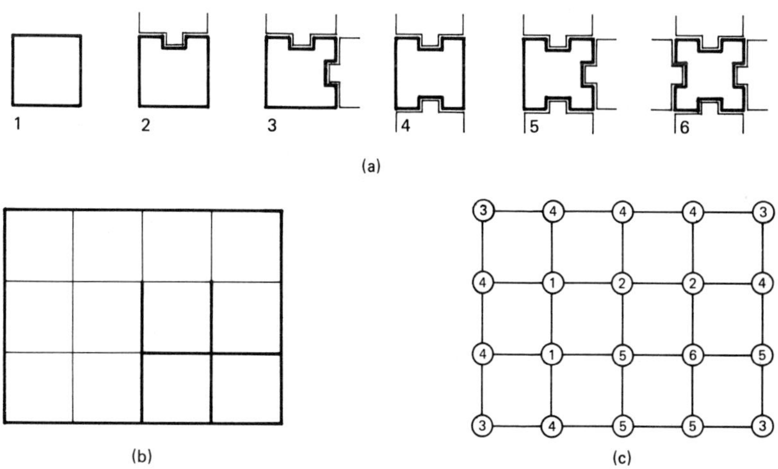

Figure 7.10
A simple example of component selection according to well-defined rules. (a) Range of standard column types. (b) Given plan. (c) Column types selected according to condition at each location.

types. When an outline floor plan is given, well-defined selection rules can be applied to choose column types according to the corner conditions which occur.

Automated component sizing

Sizing of members is a standard engineering task, and well-established text book algorithms are available for sizing beams, columns, slabs, footings, pipes, ducts, etc. Once component locations and types have been chosen, it is often possible to apply implementations of these algorithms to complete the detailing process.

Applications of automated detailing techniques

Very effective use is made of automated detailing techniques in the Harness hospital design system (Meager 1973, Jacobsberg 1975). The software incorporates a structural subsystem which automatically locates, chooses from a component file, counts, and totals the costs of structural components. These operations are performed very quickly and accurately on the basis of building layout data which is available at a very early stage in the design process. Thus the designer is able to rapidly explore the comparative structural costs of a wide range of alternative building forms, something that is impossible in conventional design processes.

The first step, in this structural design process, is to automatically locate beams and columns. This is a relatively straightforward task, since Harness hospitals employ a highly modular structural system, with beams and columns positioned according to simple, well-defined rules. Each located beam and column is then automatically assigned a "context" code. Beam context codes identify length, floor slab loading, internal or external position, and vertical relationship with other floors. Column context codes depend upon the beams supported and whether the column is at roof level. These context codes are essentially performance specifications, which may be utilized to select appropriate members from a component file. When the beams and columns have been selected, stub columns, foundations, eaves, floor slabs, roof-units, etc., are filled in according to their context in relation to the major structural components. Finally, the number of each type of component is totalled, and a total structure cost for the whole building is computed based upon known unit prices. A typical structural plan output by this system is illustrated in *Figure 7.11*.

Automated detailing capabilities are also incorporated in the OXSYS system (Applied Research of Cambridge 1975, Richens 1975). The automated detailing software here performs such tasks as "filling in" an appropriate beam layout once the basic plan geometry

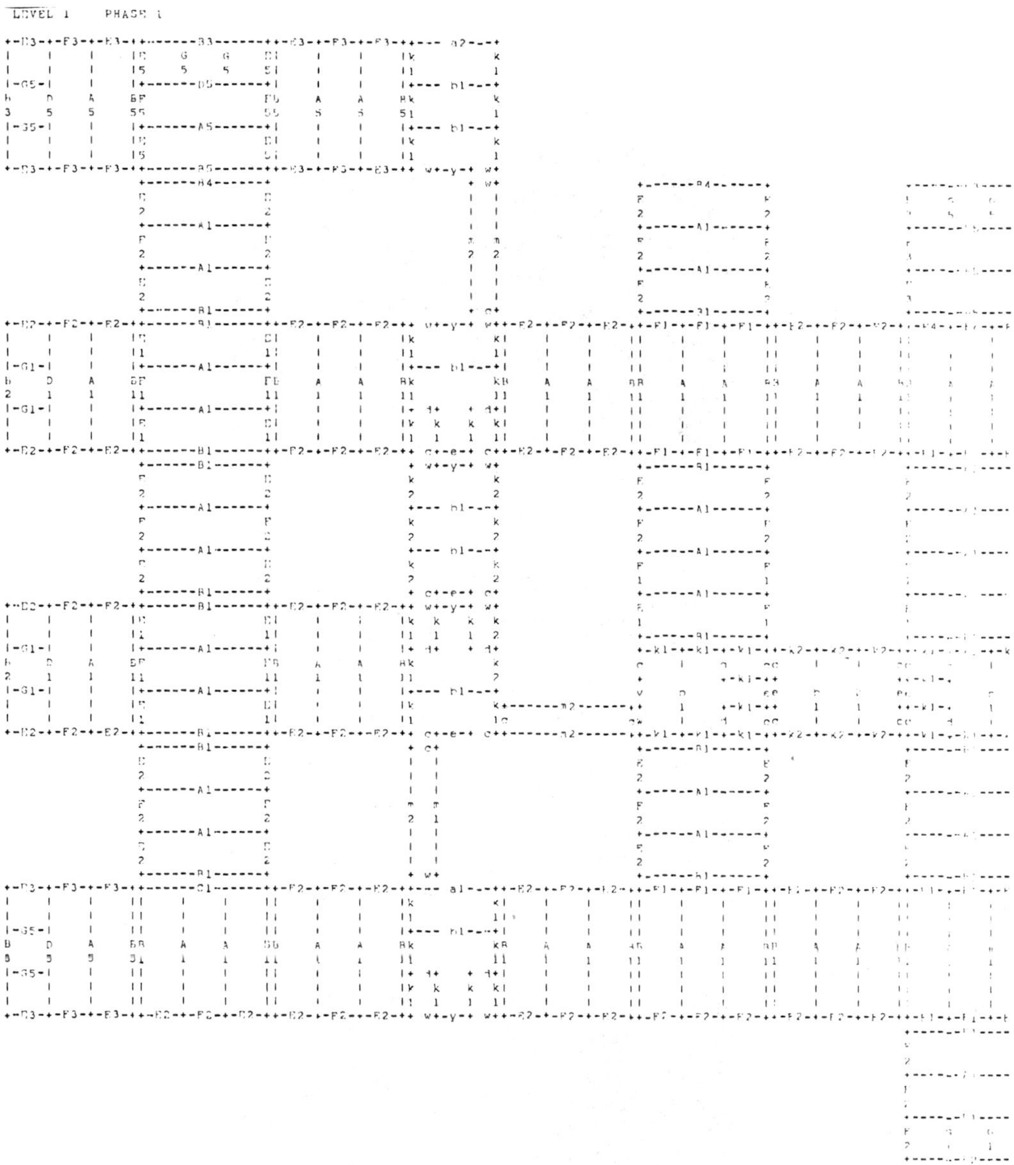

has been defined, designing framed openings for rooflights in specified locations, and selecting structural members and cladding elements. Examples of OXSYS-generated detailing are illustrated in *Figure 7.12* and *Figure 7.13*.

Figure 7.11
An example of a structural plan automatically generated by the Harness system.

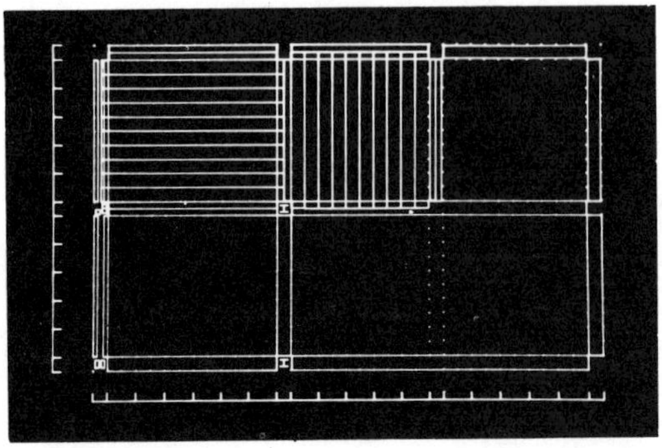

(a)

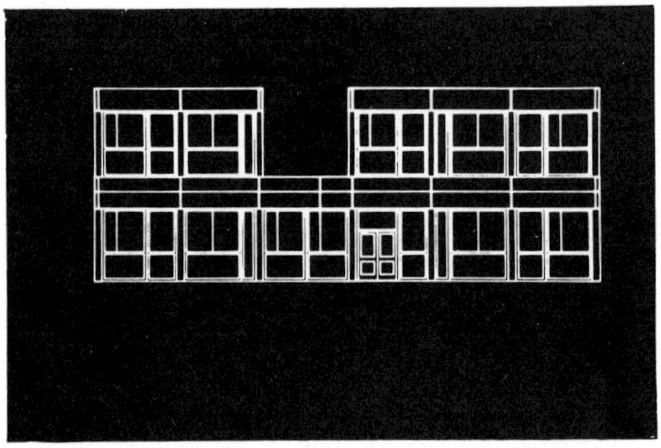

(b)

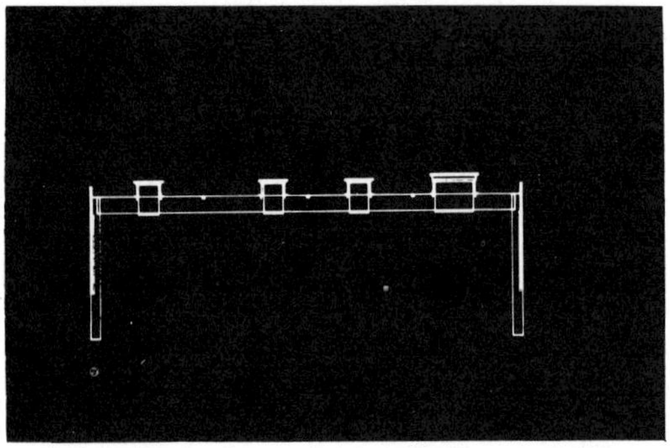

(c)

Figure 7.12 Automated floor slab, cladding, and rooflight detailing by OXSYS. (a) Automated location of floor slab elements (given beam and column locations). (b) Automated filling in of cladding panels on elevation (given plan and section). (c) Automated location and frame detailing of rooflights (given locations of main structural members).

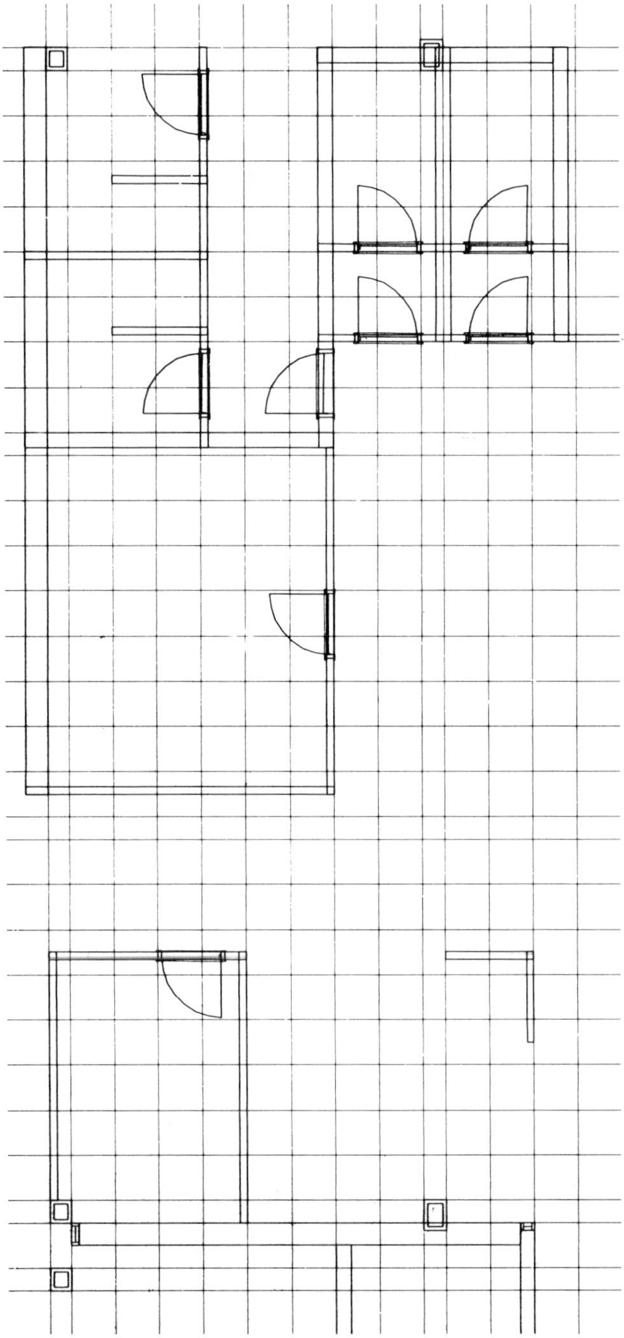

(a)

Figure 7.13
Automated partition corner detailing by the OXSYS system. (a) Plan without partition corner details. (b) Partition corner details automatically added by OXSYS.

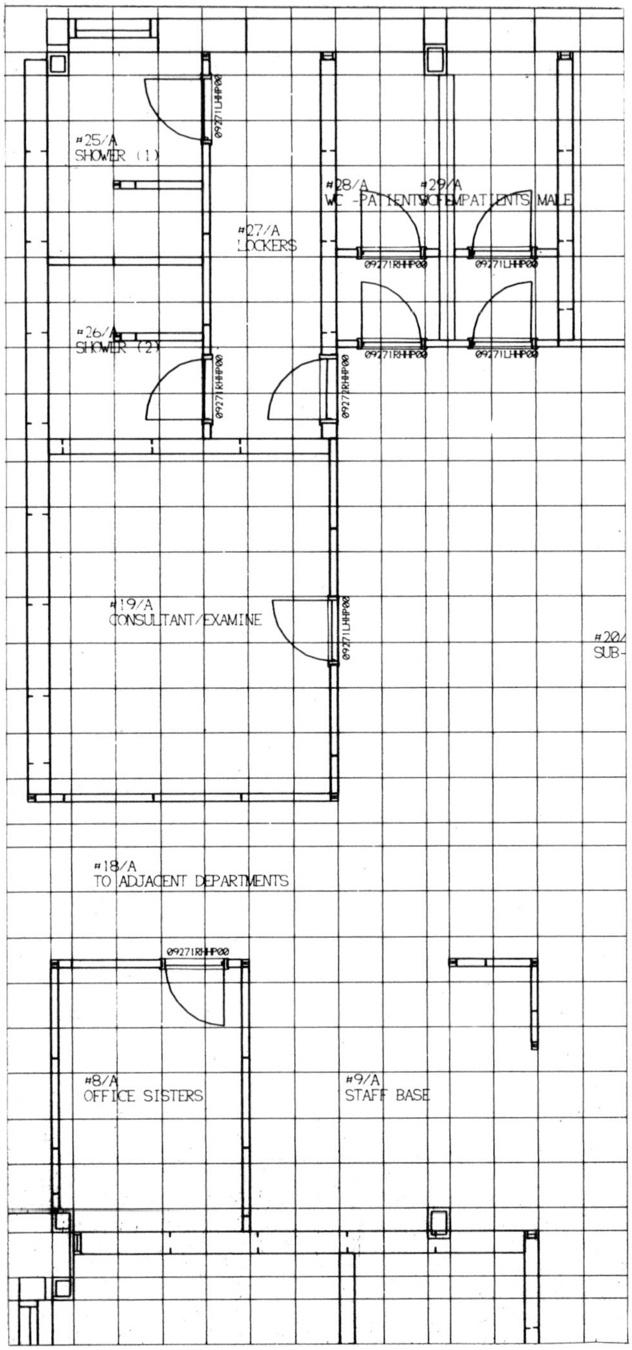

#25/A
SHOWER (1)
#26/A
SHOWER (2)
#27/A
LOCKERS
#28/A
#29/A
#19/A
CONSULTANT/EXAMINE
#18/A
TO ADJACENT DEPARTMENTS
#8/A
OFFICE SISTERS
#9/A
STAFF BASE

(b)

SUGGESTED READINGS

Department of the Environment. *Commodity Information for the Construction Industry: A Feasibility Study for a Commodity File.* London: Department of the Environment, 1971.

Eastman, C. M. "The Concise Structuring of Geometric Data for Computer Aided Design," in *Data Structures for Computer Graphics and Pattern Recognition,* edited by A. Klinger, T. Fu, and T. Kunii. New York: Academic Press, 1977.

Gero, J. S. "Specifications by Computer." *Architectural Science Review,* 19, no. 1 (1976), pp. 10–13.

Jacobsberg, J. "Computer Design Aids for Large Modular Buildings," in *Models and Systems in Architecture and Building,* edited by D. Hawkes. Hornby, Lancaster, England: The Construction Press, 1975.

Lee, K., ed. *Computer-Aided Architectural Design: 16 ARK-2 Articles.* Boston, Mass.: Center for Environmental Research, 1973.

Richens, P. "Geometry and Numbers in Building Systems," in *Models and Systems in Architecture and Building,* edited by D. Hawkes. Hornby, Lancaster, England: The Construction Press, 1975.

Rosen, H. J. "Computerized Specifications," chapter 18 of *Construction Specifications Writing: Principles and Procedures.* New York: Wiley, 1974.

Schruben, J. H. "National Master Specification System: A Technological Description." *Industrialization Forum* 4, no. 4, pp. 9–22.

Stanford Research Institute. *Automated Specifications: a Research Survey.* Washington, D. C.: Construction Specification Institute Publication No. STD-1, 1967.

8
Site Descriptions

So far we have discussed techniques for describing a building's fabric and geometry, but have not yet considered how to describe the site and the building's relation to it. As we shall see, many of the basic techniques that are used for building description can also be employed for site description.

The types of data which are normally recorded on site plans for architectural purposes may be classified according to their geometric character as follows:

Point data—locations of trees, bore-holes, service access points, spot levels, etc.

Line data—road networks, sewer networks, drainage networks, contours, boundaries, etc.

Surface data—topography, geology, soil conditions, ground cover, flood plains, etc.

Volume data—surrounding buildings, allowable building envelope, air-rights data, etc.

A computer-implemented site data base must also make provision for storage and manipulation of these categories of data. In this chapter, we consider in turn techniques for structuring descriptions of each particular type, then techniques for analysis and mapping.

POINT AND LINE DATA

Points

Point data arbitrarily distributed on a two-dimensional surface may, for most purposes, be stored in a simple sequential file as shown in *Figure 8.1*. Each record contains x and y coordinates, together with additional data fields as necessary. The file may be sorted by x or y coordinate, distance from any arbitrary point, or by any of the additional data fields as required.

Lines

Lines can readily be represented by coordinates of their end-points (see Section 6.4). However, the problem of numerically encoding lines for site description purposes differs somewhat from that of encoding lines for building description purposes. Buildings tend to be rectilinear, and lines occurring in building descriptions tend to be long and straight. On the other hand, boundaries of natural features, contours, etc., characteristically take on intricate curved shapes.

The encoding of curved lines is usually approached in two steps (Peucker 1972, Freeman 1974):

1. Approximate the line by a series of short, straight segments (vectors).
2. Encode the coordinates of the vectors in sequence.

Figure 8.1
A file of tree locations on a site, sorted on distances from entrance.

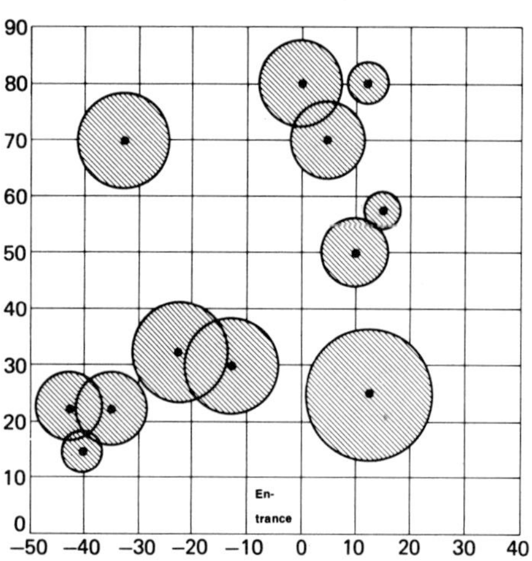

(a)

x	y	distance	diameter	height	condition
12.5	25	28	24	50	good
−11	30	32	17	42	good
−21	31	37	18	40	poor
−35	22	41	14	35	good
−40	14	42	8	18	poor
−42	22	47	12	25	good
10	50	51	12	20	good
15	58	60	7	10	good
5	70	70	14	27	poor
−32	70	77	17	22	good
0	80	80	16	30	poor
12	80	81	8	12	good

(b)

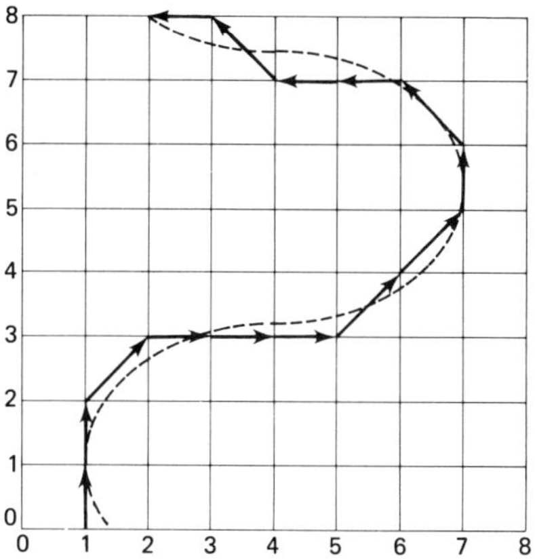

(a)

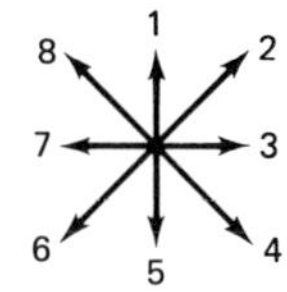

(b)

Absolute coordinates	Relative coordinates	Chain code
[1, 0]	Start	Start
[1, 1]	[0, 1]	[1]
[1, 2]	[0, 1]	[1]
[2, 3]	[1, 1]	[2]
[3, 3]	[1, 0]	[3]
[4, 3]	[1, 0]	[3]
[5, 3]	[1, 0]	[3]
[6, 4]	[1, 1]	[2]
[7, 5]	[1, 1]	[2]
[7, 6]	[0, 1]	[1]
[6, 7]	[−1, 1]	[8]
[5, 7]	[−1, 0]	[7]
[4, 7]	[−1, 0]	[7]
[3, 8]	[−1, −1]	[8]
[2, 8]	[−1, 0]	[7]

(c)

Figure 8.2
Methods for encoding curved lines. (a) Arbitrary curved line approximated by short straight segments with vertices at locations in a square grid. (b) The eight-chain code directions. (c) Alternative methods of encoding.

A variety of techniques may be employed for encoding the coordinates of the vectors (*Figure 8.2*). Some of the most widely utilized are:

Absolute coordinates. Each point is assigned x and y coordinates relative to a fixed origin.

Incremental encoding. Each point is assigned x and y coordinates relative to the previous point.

Chain encoding. The line is superimposed on a square grid, and approximated by vectors as illustrated. Each of the vectors can then be represented by a single digit between 1 and 8 by means of the coding scheme shown. Of course the position of the line in the grid must also be specified, for example, by specifying coordinates of the initium.

The choice of a coding technique depends upon the characteristics of the data and the types of operations and analyses to be performed. Absolute coordinates and incremental encoding are particularly suitable where lines are composed of relatively few, relatively long straight segments, and where operations of translation, rotation, and scaling are to be performed. Incremental encoding usually results in substantial storage savings over absolute coordinates. Chain encoding is relatively efficient for encoding of intricate, complex curved forms. Operations of computation of areas of closed curves, translation, and scaling are readily performed. Finding intersections of lines, and rotation, present more difficulties. The performance of various chain encoding schemes for various types of applications have been extensively studied, and are reported in detail in the literature (see Freeman 1961, 1974).

(a)

Figure 8.3
Representation of a path network. (a) The Labyrinth at Versailles (1673). (b) Representation as a network. (c) Incidence matrix format for encoding network.

Networks

Line data often represents flow networks on a site, for instance, roads or sewers. In this case it is usually necessary to explicitly represent the pattern of connectivity between vertices. *Incidence matrices* and *adjacency matrices* (see Explicit Representation of Topology in Chapter 6) are suitable for this purpose. The representation of a path network by means of an incidence matrix is shown in *Figure 8.3*. Associated with each row (vertex) are x and y coordinates, and associated with each column (edge) is a length.

SURFACE DATA

Data points

A surface such as a building site may be numerically represented by a set of *data points* distributed in some pattern across that surface. Values of data points might represent such data as the elevation or slope at the location of the data point, soil condition, type of ground cover, hydrological condition, etc. The data points might be distributed randomly, on a regular grid, on a grid of varying mesh size, along contour lines, or according to some special statistical design.

From a given set of data points representing a surface, a data value for any arbitrary point on the surface can be more or less accurately determined using one of the following assumptions (Peucker 1972):

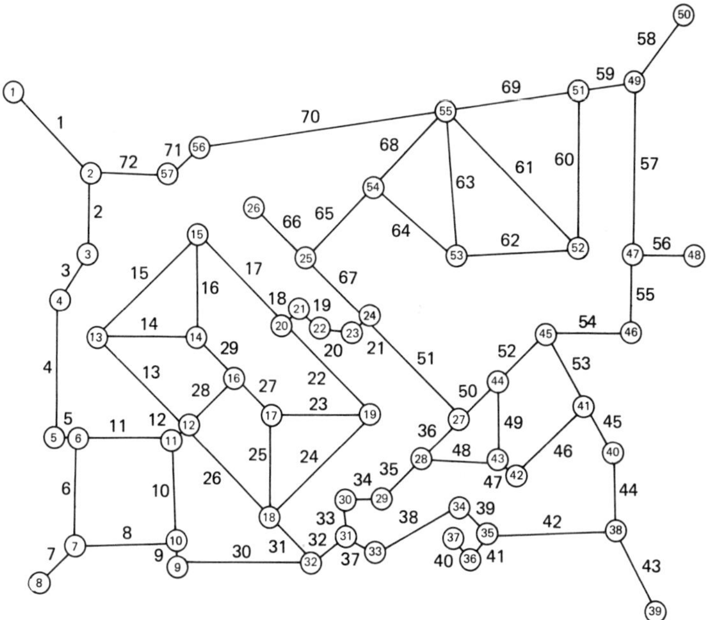

(b)

Edges	Length	Vertices 1	2	3	. . .	57
1		1	1	0	. . .	0
2		0	1	1	. . .	0
3		0	0	1	. . .	0
.	.	.	.	.	. . .	.
.	.	.	.	.	. . .	.
.	.	.	.	.	. . .	.
72		0	1	0	. . .	1

(c)

The surface varies discontinuously, and a data value represents the values of some specified polygon surrounding the data point. This is known as *choropleth* or *conformal* data. The polygons may be of arbitrary and irregular shapes and sizes, or may form a regular tesselation. Typical examples of choropleth site data are land use, zoning, geological, soil, and ground cover data.

The surface varies discontinuously, and a data value represents values for all points on the surface that are closer to the data point than to any other data point. This is known as *proximal* data.

The surface varies continuously, and each data point represents a *sample* taken at a particular point on the surface. The value may or may not contain error. Values for points elsewhere on the surface may be obtained by appropriate processes of *interpolation* and *smoothing*. Topographic and slope data are typically treated in this way.

Square grids

The simplest and most widely-employed technique for representation of area data for site description purposes is to utilize a square grid of data points, and to store the points in memory as a two-dimensional array, as discussed in Square Grids in Chapter 6. For storage on disk or tape, the two-dimensional array can be unfolded into a one-dimensional string.

The size of the grid to be employed is obviously an important consideration; if the grid-cells are too large then the representation is too approximate; if they are too small, excessive storage is required. Statistical considerations can be a useful guide in selecting a cell-size necessary to encode the data to a desired level of accuracy (Boehm 1967, Tobler 1969, Switzer 1974). One useful rule of thumb,

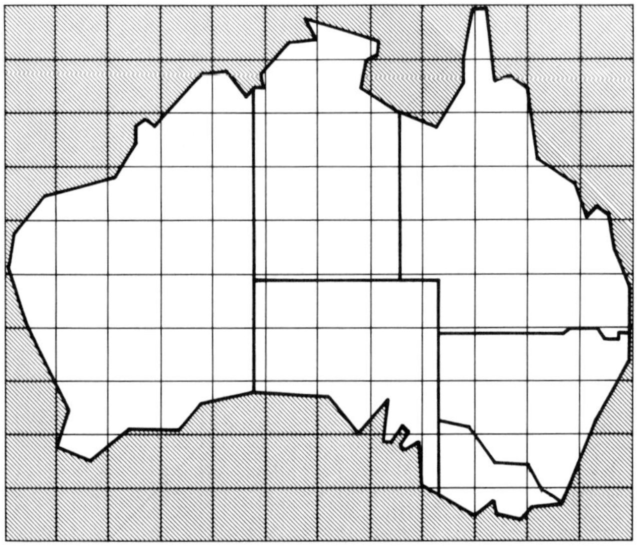

(a)

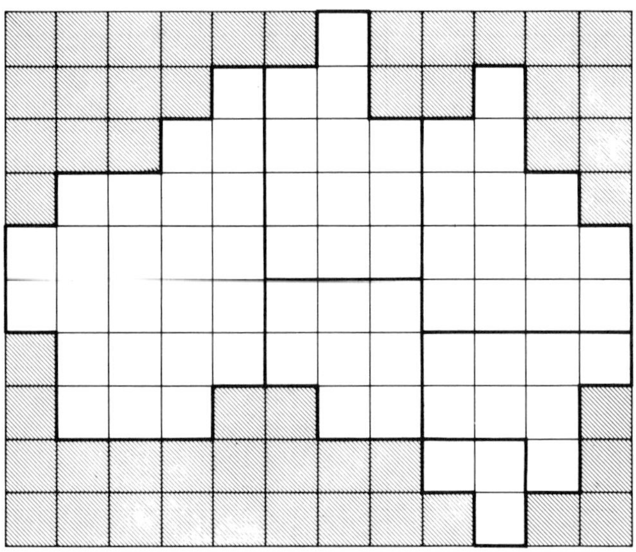

(b)

Figure 8.4
Conversion of data from choropleth map to square grid encoded form. (a) Choropleth map with superimposed grid. (b) Square grid representation.

derived from the sampling theorem, is that the cell dimension should be half the size of the smallest distinct features to be encoded.

Data which exists in other formats can be converted into square grid data by various means. For example, where data is obtained in choropleth map form, it may be encoded by superimposing the grid as shown in *Figure 8.4.* This process may either be carried out by hand or by computer. If executed by computer, the non-trivial operation of determining which polygon includes the given grid location must be performed. Each polygon must be tested against the grid location in turn. Several standard procedures exist for determining whether a point on a plane lies within an arbitrary polygon (Sutherland, Sproull and Schumacker 1974). The most widely used is based upon the well-known Jordan Curve Theorem. The principle is as follows: A straight line is drawn from the point in question to a point known to lie outside the boundary of the polygon, and the intersections between this line and the polygon boundary are counted (*Figure 8.5*). If the number of intersections is odd, the point must lie within the polygon; if the answer is zero or even, then the point must be outside. Care must be taken of the special case in which the test line runs through a vertex of the polygon. Baxter (1976) has published a FORTRAN subroutine which implements this algorithm.

Random proximal data points can be converted into square grid data by a simple process of assigning each grid point the value of the nearest data point.

A variety of interpolation procedures can be employed to convert arbitrarily arranged sample data points from a continuous surface into a square grid representation. Basically, interpolation procedures obtain interpolated values by taking some kind of inverse-distance-weighted average of some subset of data points (Shepard 1968). Variations occur in the subset of data points considered and in the inverse-distance-weighting function employed. For example, all data points might be considered, the n closest data points, or the data points within some specified radius. Inverse-distance-weighting might be

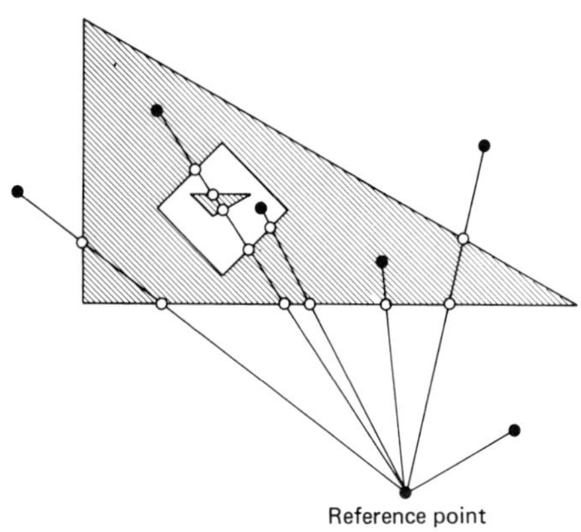

Figure 8.5
Construction used in testing whether or not a point lies within a polygon.

linear, *i.e.,* 1/d, or exponential, *i.e.,* 1/d, $1/d^2$, $1/d^3$, etc. One very common approach is to take the three closest data points and use an inverse distance squared function. This approach is intuitively appealing; it economizes on computation, and has been found to produce acceptable results for many applications. *Figure 8.6* graphically compares the results produced by several different interpolation procedures.

Once surface data has been converted into square grid format, it becomes relatively easy to manipulate, analyze, and display in various ways. Total areas of occurrence of particular conditions, for example, can be calculated by counting cells in which the specified condition occurs. Data of different types encoded within the same grid can be compared and combined very readily, since the data units are exactly comparable in extent and location, and can be accessed by the same subscripts. Very simple two-dimensional displays can be produced by expressing data values for cells as tones, colors, or symbols. For example the widely-used SYMAP mapping program (Fisher, Dougenik and Sheehan 1976) produces maps from square grid data on an ordinary line printer by overprinting symbols (*Figure 8.7*). An elegant

Figure 8.6
Comparison of interpolation procedures. (a) Data points. (b) Surface interpolated by the inverse distance weighting rule. (c) Surface interpolated by the inverse distance squared weighting rule. (d) Surface interpolated by the inverse distance cubed weighting rule.

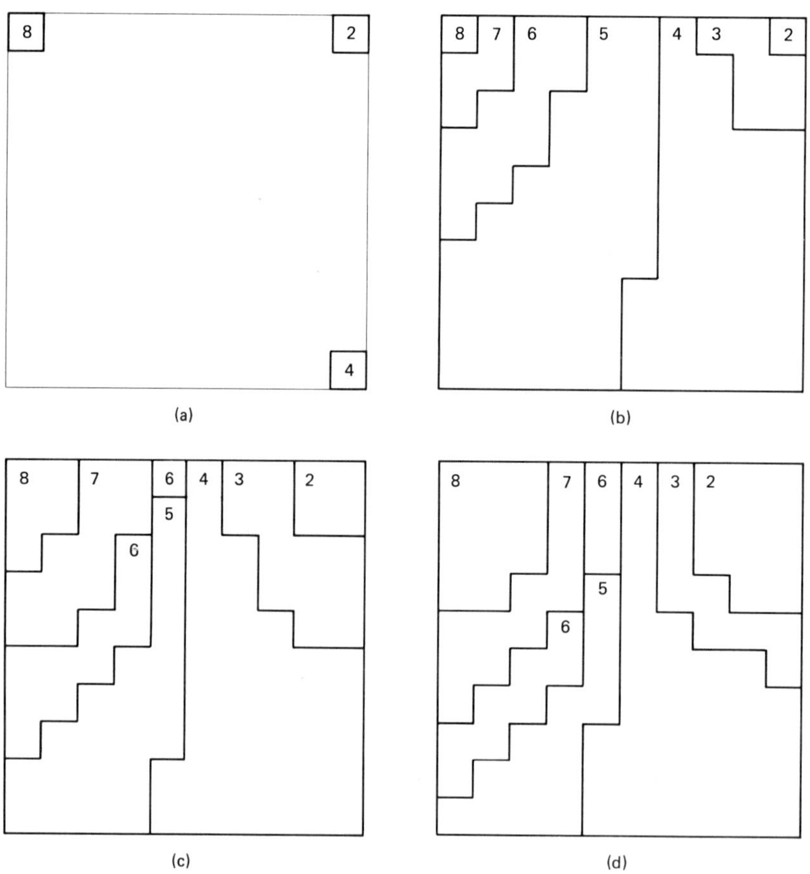

variation of this approach is to use a special "golf-ball" element on an electric typewriter output device to express data values as dots of varying sizes (*Figure 8.8*).

The use of a square grid format for encoding earth satellite reconnaissance data has encouraged development of some sophisticated pattern recognition and analysis procedures which operate upon square grid data (Rosenfeld 1969). Many of these may potentially be useful for architectural applications. There have been a few experimental applications to analysis of architectural and civil engineering site data (*e.g.*, see Wong and Au 1971), but as yet the potential has barely been explored.

Networks of triangles

Since the vertices of a triangle must always lie in a plane, and triangles uniquely have this property amongst all the polygons, an approximation of a three-dimensional surface by a network of triangles (rather than quadrilaterals or other polygons) possesses the unique property that all the polygonal faces are planar. Many potential computational advantages derive from this property, and this has suggested to some researchers that a topographic surface representation utilizing networks of triangles as a basis might have substantial advantages. Investigations in this direction have been described by Rhynsburger (1973), Peucker (1974), and Peucker and Chrisman (1974). As yet it does not appear that much practical use has been made of this type of representation in architectural applications, but it promises to be important in the future.

Mosaics of arbitrary polygons

Very often, choropleth data such as geological, soils, and ground cover data constitutes a mosaic of polygons of arbitrary size and shape. An alternative to conversion of this data into square grid format is to describe the polygonal boundaries, and to associate a data value with each polygon. The advantages over the square grid representation are that substantial storage economy and increased accuracy can be obtained. The disadvantage is that, for many purposes, computational complexity is greatly increased.

The simplest way to encode polygons is to treat each one as a separate entity. For example, one might begin with the first polygon, encode its boundary in clockwise sequence, then go on to the second polygon, and so on. The result is that most points and lines are encoded twice, and at corners where several polygons meet points may be encoded three or more times. This simple approach has severe disadvantages. A considerable amount of redundant data must be stored. Also, the process of digitizing coordinates of points is likely to introduce small discrepancies between coordinate values assigned to a point on the different occasions on which it is encoded. This causes

(a)

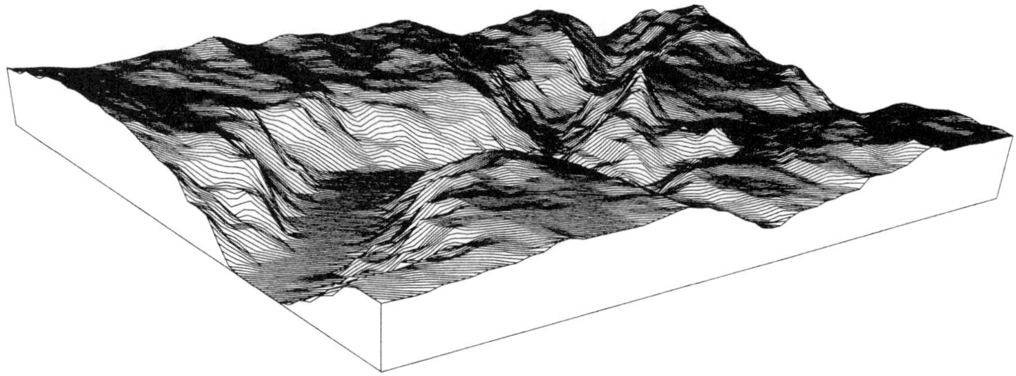

(b)

difficulties in performance of procedures which require matching of polygon boundaries, and generates "double" boundary lines and messy corners when plots are produced from the data base. To a certain extent these problems can be overcome by approximating all coordinates to locations in a coarse grid (*Figure 8.9*). Topological information, for example, adjacencies between polygons, lines intersecting at a given point, etc., is also difficult to extract from data structured in this way.

Figure 8.7
Output from the SYMAP and SYMVU programs (Harvard Laboratory for Computer Graphics and Spatial Analysis). (a) Contour map of Yosemite Valley, California, produced on a line printer by the SYMAP program. (b) Surface plot produced on a drum plotter from the same data by the compatible SYMVU program.

Figure 8.8
Grey scale map produced by an electric typewriter terminal equipped with a special "golf-ball" element (T. Sasada, Osaka University).

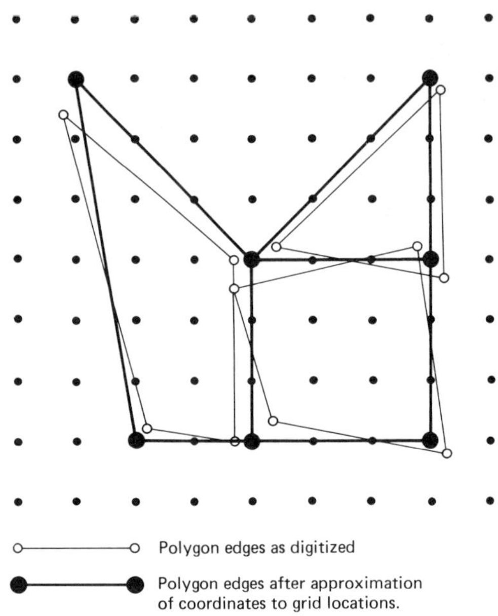

Figure 8.9
Approximation of digitized coordinates to locations in a coarse grid.

An obvious alternative, which overcomes many of these difficulties, is to digitize and store each point only once in a *point dictionary,* then to generate a *boundary list* for each polygon consisting of identifiers (*e.g.,* array subscripts) of the points in the dictionary from which it is composed. An example of the encoding of a mosaic of polygons in this way is illustrated in *Figure 8.10.* Many computer mapping programs utilize this type of data structure, for example, the CALFORM program developed by the Harvard Laboratory for Computer Graphics and Spatial Analysis.

Where extraction of topological information from the data base is an important consideration, it may be necessary to utilize more elaborate structures in which adjacencies and connections are explicitly represented (Peucker and Chrisman 1974). One approach to explicitly encoding topological data is illustrated by the Dual Independent Map Encoding (DIME) system developed by the U.S. Bureau of the Census for encoding street maps (Farnsworth 1970). In the DIME file, streets are encoded as straight line segments defined by coordinates of their end-points, and associated with each line segment is a code identifying the polygons on either side.

One of the most sophisticated schemes for encoding polygon data, based upon the DIME file principle, is the POLYVRT data structure developed at the Harvard Laboratory for Computer Graphics and Spatial Analysis (Peucker and Chrisman 1974). In a POLYVRT file, a point dictionary is stored on disk. The point dictionary is pointed to by a *chain list* stored in memory. Chains represent the boundaries between polygons. Each record in the chain list

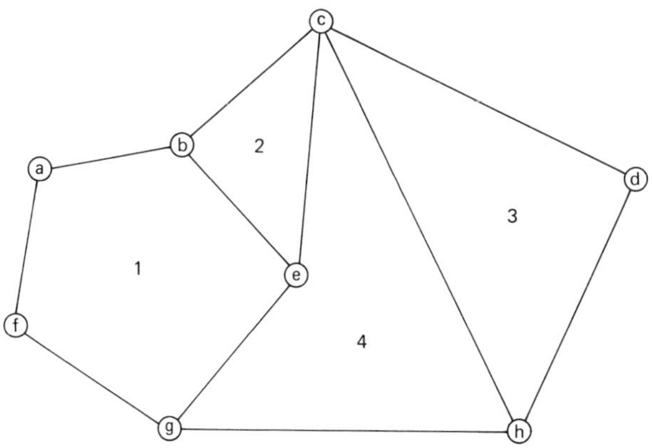

(a)

	X	Y
a	3	31
b	20	34
c	38	49
d	77	31
e	35	18
f	0	11
g	19	0
h	63	0

(b)

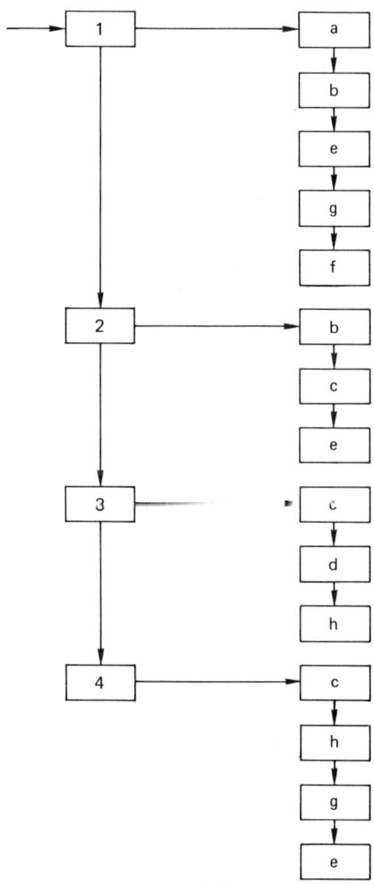

(c)

Figure 8.10 Representation of a mosaic of arbitrary polygons by a point dictionary and a boundary list. (a) Mosaic of arbitrary polygons. (b) Point dictionary. (c) Boundary list.

consists of the name of the chain, labels of the start and end vertices, and left and right polygons. A separate *vertex list* is pointed to from the chain list. Each polygon is represented by a record in a *polygon list,* which indicates its bounding chains.

Three-dimensional representation of topographic surfaces

Following conventional practice, we have so far assumed that topographic surfaces are adequately represented by planar maps, *i.e.*, by contour lines projected onto a plane or by a two-dimensional grid of levels. An alternative approach is to represent the surfaces as a three-dimensional mesh of lines (*Figure 8.11*).

Given a set of topographic data points describing the surface (*e.g.*, random spot levels, or a square grid of levels), the z (vertical) coordinate at any point x,y is given by

$$z = f(x,y)$$

where f is defined as an appropriate interpolation function (see Square Grids, above). If y is held constant and x is stepped in small increments, a line whose projection in the x,y plane is parallel to the x-axis is traced out. By incrementing y as well, a family of surface-defining lines can be traced out as shown in *Figure 8.11(c)*. By projecting the lines in perspective, a realistic picture of the three-dimensional surface is produced. Numerous programs which generate three-dimensional surface representations in this way are available.

Figure 8.11
Plots of a three-dimensional surface (Dynamic Graphics Inc., Berkeley, California). (a) Contour plot of a topographic surface. (b) Perspective projection of contours. (c) Surface represented as a mesh and plotted in perspective.

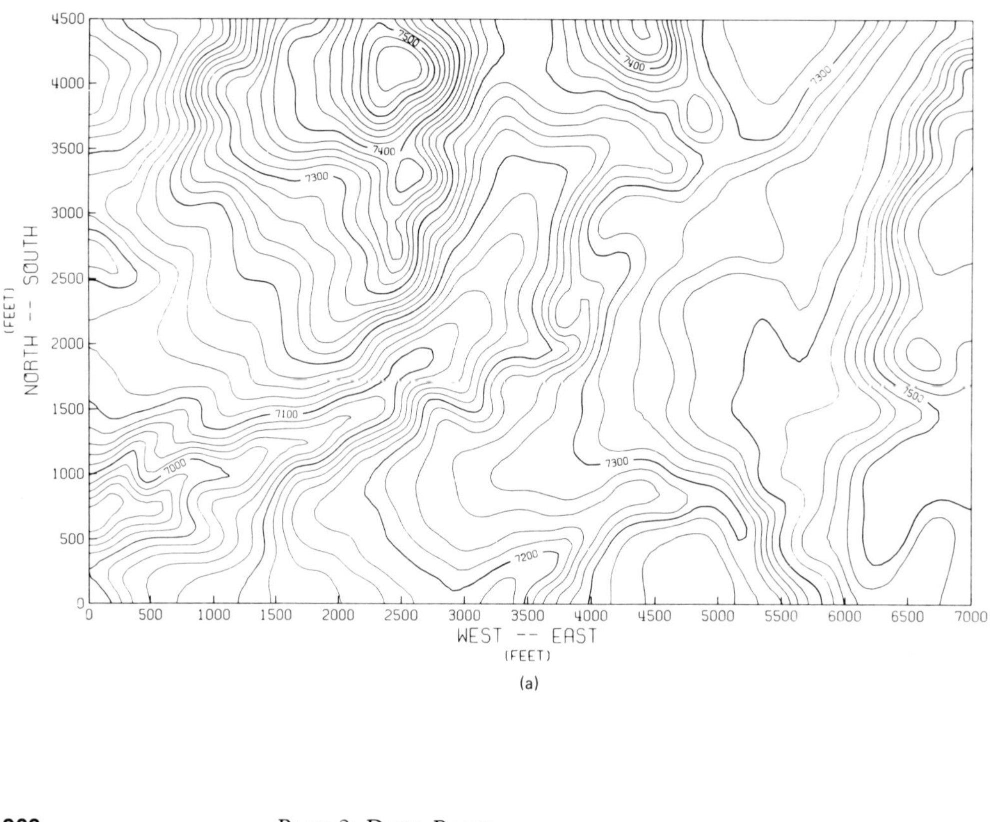

(a)

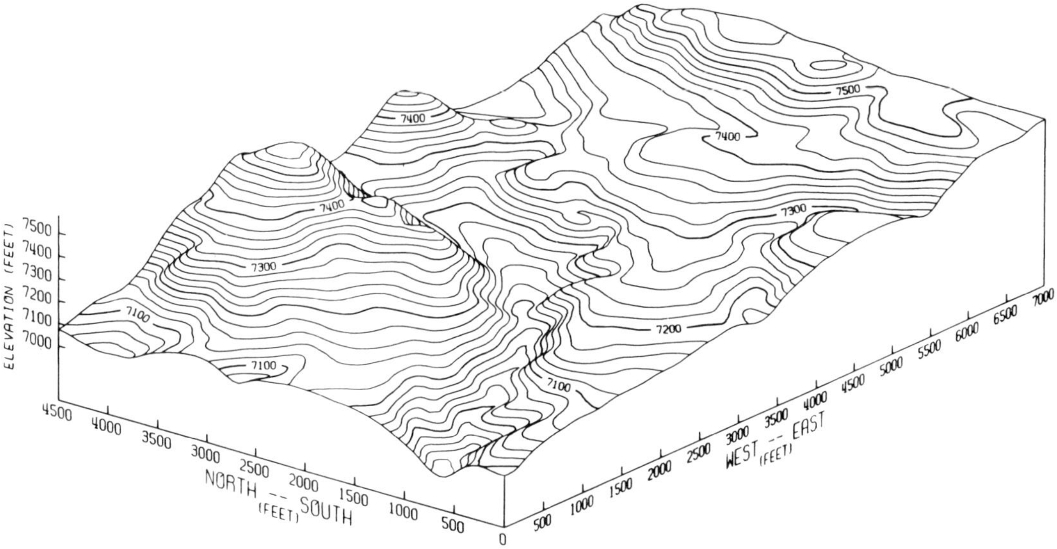

(b)

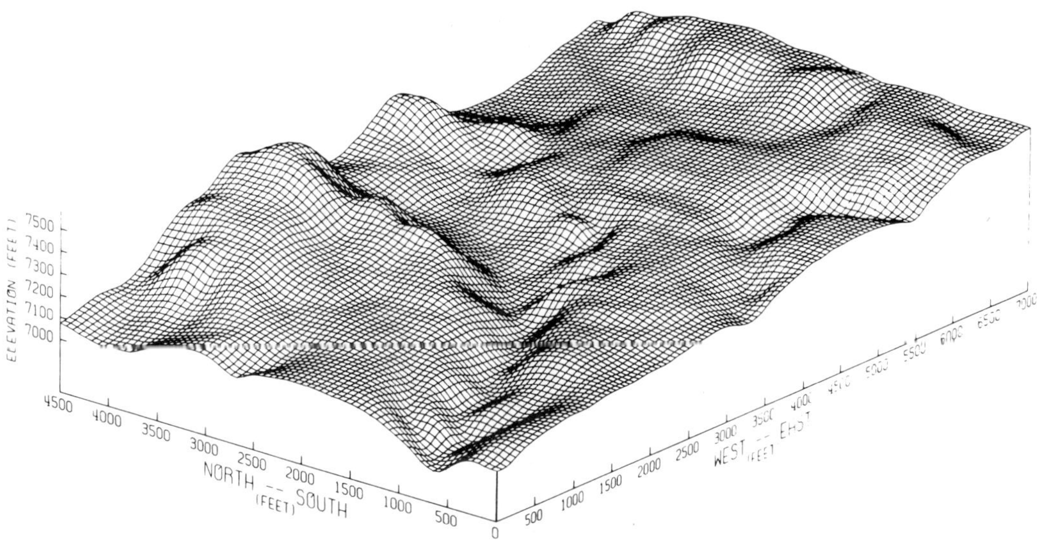

(c)

Building massing in urban areas

When describing urban sites, it is often necessary to record the massing of existing on-site and surrounding buildings. This can be done using the techniques of three-dimensional building description which were discussed in Chapter 6.

Data bases describing building massing in downtown areas of several large U.S. cities have been developed. *Figure 8.12,* for example, shows a plot from a data base describing downtown Chicago.

SITE DESCRIPTION SYSTEMS

Figure 8.12 *(opposite)* Plot from a data base, developed by Skidmore, Owings, and Merrill, showing built form in downtown Chicago. John Hancock building is at far right, Marina Towers near the center, and Sears Tower at the left.

A complete computer-based site description system consists of facilities for (1) inputting and storing site data; (2) transforming, operating upon, and generating maps from the data as required. The following paragraphs discuss some techniques that have been developed for these purposes.

Input and storage of site data

Traditionally, site data is stored in the form of maps and photographs. To numerically encode data in this format, and enter it into a computer, is usually a time-consuming and expensive process. However, there is now a strong trend towards storage of geographic data of all kinds in machine-readable form. For example, the U.S. Bureau of the Census now makes available magnetic tapes of geo-coded census data. Similarly, NASA makes available magnetic tapes of earth satellite reconnaissance data describing the surface of the earth at any specified location. Many cities and other agencies now have implemented or are developing detailed and comprehensive land use information systems. The LUMIS system (Paul and Landini, 1974) developed for the Santa Monica Mountains area in Southern California is a typical example. Most of these current systems are oriented towards urban and regional planning applications; they represent data at too coarse a level of resolution to be useful for most architectural site analysis and planning purposes. But it can be expected that the trend towards storage and dissemination of geographic data in machine-readable format will continue, and that it will become standard practice for architects to employ machine-readable site data.

Transformation and analysis of topographic data

It is often necessary to transform or to analyze topographic data in some way before such data can be used for a particular site analysis purpose. For example, it might be necessary to display contour lines, to compute slopes, aspects, and drainage directions, to take sections, to compute cut and fill to a specified datum, or to discover visible areas from a given viewpoint. Numerous programs have been developed for these purposes.

Automated contouring

Automated contouring from square gridded or random topographic data points has been the subject of extensive research, and there is a considerable body of technical literature on the subject. Discussions have been published by Bengtsson and Nordbeck (1964),

Morse (1968), and Peucker (1972), among others. Further references can be found in a bibliography by Taylor (1972).

To give some flavor of the operation of automated contouring programs, a very simple procedure for generating contour plots from random data points will be described. The surface is first divided into triangles by connecting adjacent points, as shown in *Figure 8.13*. Thus it may be regarded as a three-dimensional triangular network in which the x and y coordinates are given by the data values. Contours may be regarded as defined by horizontal planes which cut this network at specified levels. From elementary geometry we know that, if a particular contour plane cuts a triangular element, the intersect will be a straight line joining points on two of its sides. Thus a fairly simple procedure can be utilized to trace the path of a contour across a sequence of adjacent triangles, find the intersections on the sides of these triangles by linear interpolation, and hence generate a sequence of vectors describing the contour (*Figure 8.13(b)*).

This procedure is as follows. To find the starting point for a

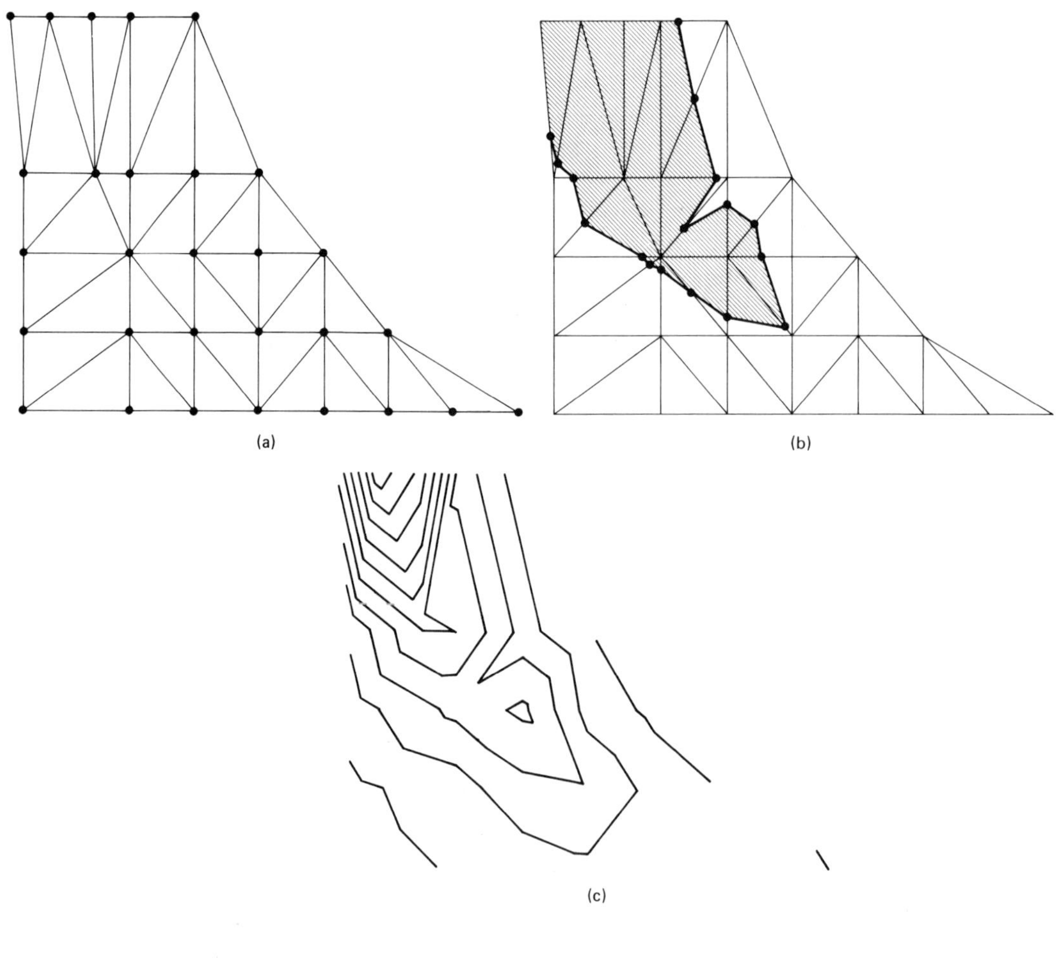

Figure 8.13
Steps in automated contouring. (a) Adjacent data points connected to produce a triangular network. (b) A contour plane cutting the network. (c) Complete contour map.

contour, the grid is first searched to discover a triangle edge whose vertices fall on opposite sides of the contour plane. The contour is then followed until it closes at the starting point or until it intersects a boundary of the grid. If a boundary is intersected, then the starting point is returned to, and the contour is followed in the opposite direction until a boundary is again reached. A complete contour map, produced using this technique, is shown in *Figure 8.13(c)*. If desired, a standard computer graphics technique known as *splining* (Rogers and Adams 1976) may be used to produce smoothly curved contours, as a final refinement.

Slope computations

The slope at a point on a surface can readily be computed using the type of construction shown in *Figure 8.14*. Note that the distance over which the slope is computed must be specified. Different distances may, in irregular terrain, give quite different slopes. The elevations of points needed for the slope computation may either be obtained by interpolation or directly from gridded topographic data points. If the slope at each point on a square grid is computed, then a complete slope map can be produced as shown in *Figure 8.15*. By

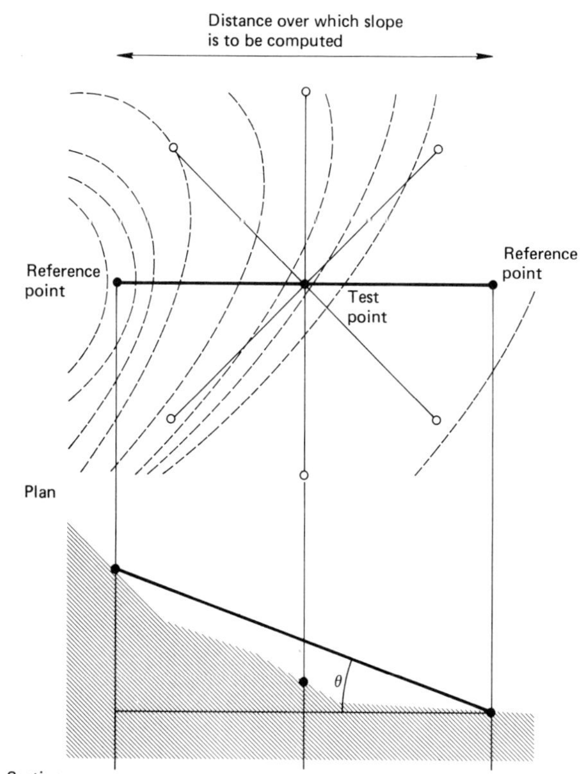

Figure 8.14
Construction for computing slope.

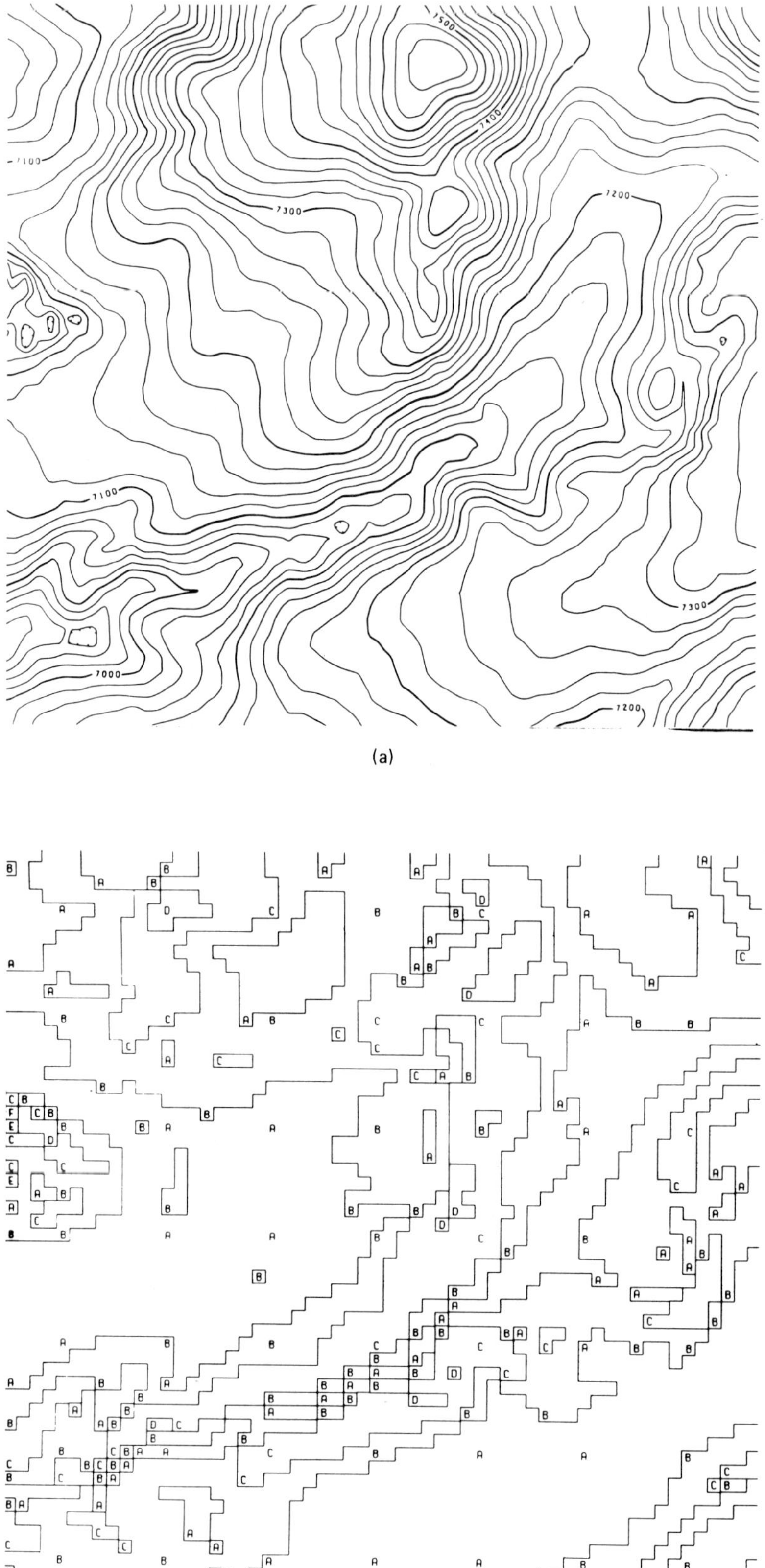

Figure 8.15
Computer generated and plotted slope map (Dynamic Graphics Inc., Berkeley California). (a) Contour map. (b) Corresponding slope class map. A = 0 – 10%, B = 10% – 20%, C = 20% – 30%, D = 30% – 40%, E = 40% – 50%, F = 50% +.

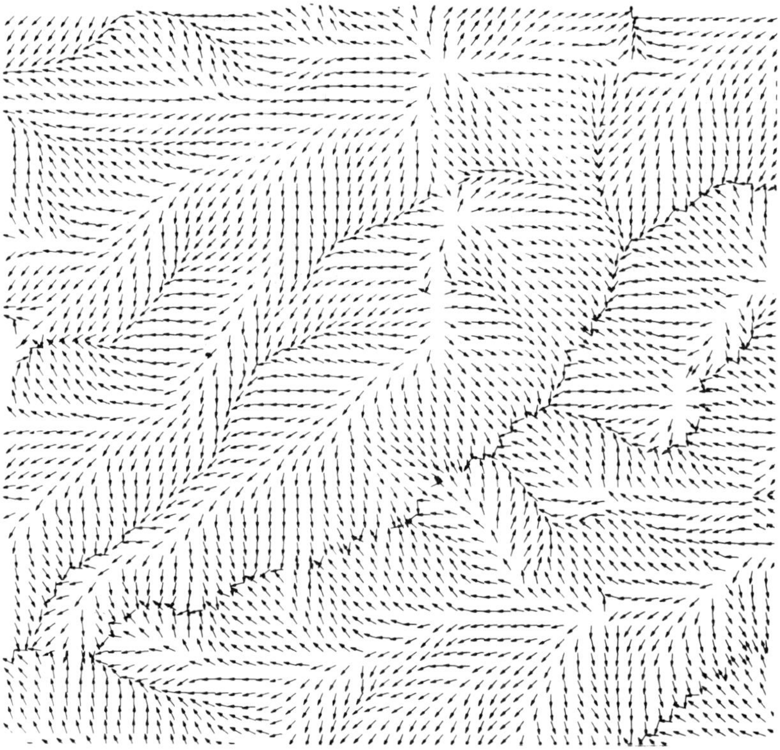

Figure 8.16
Aspect/drainage direction map, produced from the same data as Figure 8.15 (Dynamic Graphics Inc., Berkeley California).

recording, in addition, directions of greatest slope, aspect and drainage direction maps may also be produced (*Figure 8.15*).

Cut and fill computations

In analyzing potential building locations on a site, and in investigating potential grading requirements, an architect is often interested in volumes of cut and fill necessitated by setting grade at a given level, and in finding levels at which cut and fill are balanced. Cut and fill analysis is an interesting example of those tasks which, though straightforward in principle, often involve a great deal of repetitive computation. They are laborious to perform by hand, but are easily and rapidly accomplished by simple computer programs.

An elementary approach to automated cut and fill analysis is illustrated in *Figure 8.17*. Topographic information is encoded in the familiar square grid. This enables each cell of the grid to be treated as a square column of earth of known height. When the building datum and outline are known, it becomes a relatively trivial computational task to iterate through the array, subtract the datum from the elevation of each grid cell within the building outline, separately total positive (cut) and negative (fill) results, multiply totals by cell area, and thus compute total cut and fill volumes. Refinements to reflect the effects of compaction, banking, etc., can easily be introduced. To

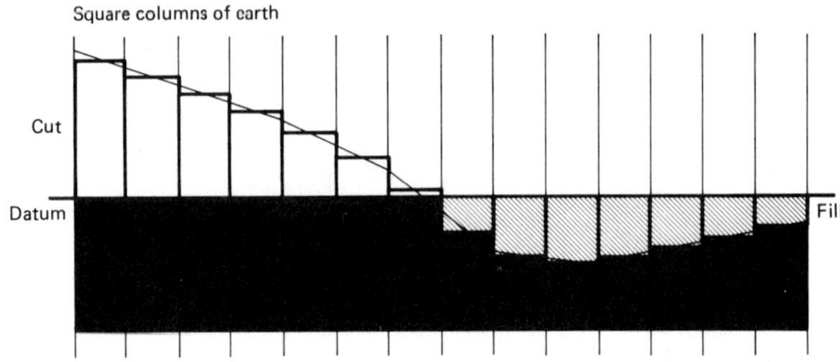

Figure 8.17 Construction used in computing cut and fill volumes from gridded topographic data.

find levels at which cut and fill are balanced, it is merely necessary to increment the building datum through a range of possible levels, repeating the cut and fill volume computation at each step.

View analysis computations *

Another example of a site analysis task that is laborious to perform by hand, yet readily accomplished by a simple computer program, is determination of the areas visible from a given station point on a topographic surface. A simple procedure which can be employed to determine whether a point p on the topographic surface is visible from an observer's station point s is shown in *Figure 8.18*. First, a straight line is drawn in plan from p to s. Elevations at closely spaced intervals along this line are then found by interpolation, and the tangents of the vertical angles subtended at the viewer's eye by these points are calculated. If the tangent at any intermediate point exceeds the tangent at p, then p is invisible. This procedure can readily be implemented as a computer program.

Overlaying site data

It is often useful to *overlay* different types of site data to produce some kind of a composite map. For example, given a topographic map, a ground cover map, and a hydrological map, it might be desired to overlay them to find areas suitable for building as defined by the criteria that slope should be less than 30%, existing stands of trees should not be disturbed, and buildings should not be located on a flood plain. If the maps are drawn to the same scale, and overlaid by a uniform square grid, this problem may be restated as follows. Find and display the set R of grid cells which is defined as the intersection of the set S of grid cells in which the slope is less than 30%, the set T of cells which do not contain trees, and the set F of cells which are not on the flood plain (*Figure 8.19*).

* See Amidon and Elsner (1968) for a more detailed discussion of this topic.

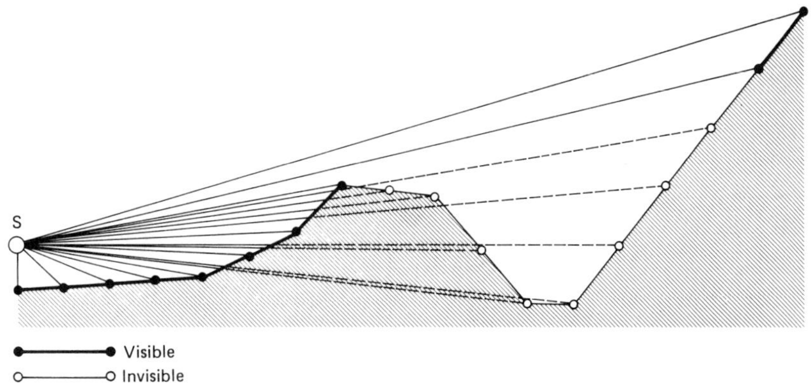

Figure 8.18
Construction employed in view analysis computations.

This selection rule can readily be stated as a Boolean expression in a programming language, for example the FORTRAN statement:

```
R(I,J) = S(I,J).LE.30.AND.T(I,J).EQ.FALSE.AND.F(I,J).EQ.FALSE.
```

where R is a logical array which stores values of .TRUE. when cell R(I,J) is the set R and .FALSE. when it is not, S is an integer array which stores slopes, and T and F are logical arrays which identify the cells included in sets T and F, respectively. Thus, the required composite map, stored in array R, could be generated by the FORTRAN statements

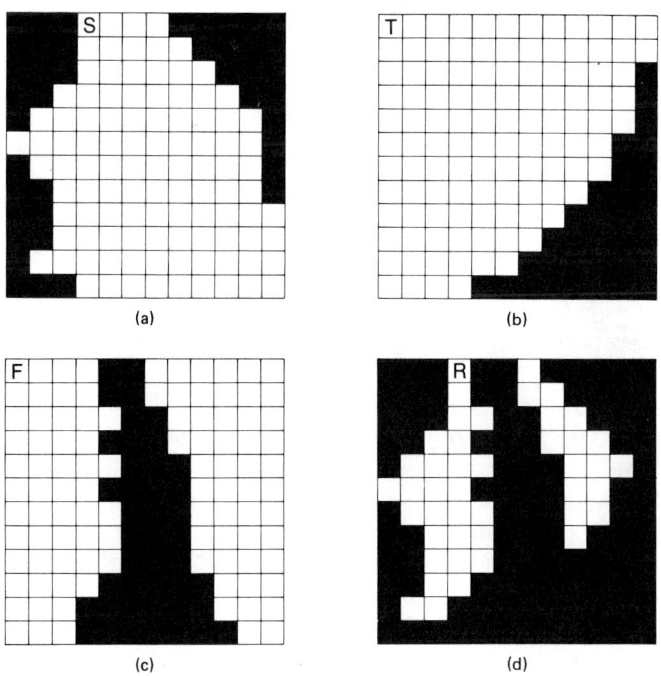

Figure 8.19
Overlaying site data. (a) Set S of cells in which slope is less than 30%. (b) Set T of cells which do not contain trees. (c) Set F of cells which do not lie on a flood plain. (d) Set $R \equiv S \cap T \cap F$ of cells suitable for development.

```
DO 1 I=1,MAXI
DO 1 J=K,MAXJ
1 R(I,J)=S(I,J).LE.30.AND.T(I,J).EQ.FALSE.AND.F(I,J).EQ.FALSE.
```

Instead of using a very simple Boolean selection rule, as in this example, more elaborate computations might be performed to generate the composite map. For example, different conditions recorded in the data arrays might be assigned values, say on a scale of 1 to 10, expressing "suitability for development." Thus slope conditions might be assigned values as follows:

Condition	*Suitability value*
0% – 5%	10
5% – 10%	9
10% – 15%	8
15% – 20%	7
20% – 25%	6
25% – 30%	5
>30%	0

The composite map (*i.e.*, values for the array R) could then be produced by summing their various suitability values as follows:

```
R(I,J)=S(I,J)+T(I,J)+F(I,J)
```

where R, S, T and F are now all integer arrays recording "suitability" values for cells. If desired, relative weights of importance WS, WT, and WF could be assigned to slope, ground cover, and hydrological conditions, respectively, and R(I,J) computed thus:

```
R(I,J)=WS*S(I,J)+WT*T(I,J)+WF*F(I,J)
```

The higher the value recorded in R(I,J), the more suitable for development is the corresponding square of land.

The alert reader may object that this type of procedure is mathematically suspect. First, it assumes that the effects of the various different factors on development suitability are independent and additive. This is clearly not the case in many situations: geological character, topography, vegetation, etc., tend to be interrelated and correlated in complex and subtle ways. Second, it is very difficult to find a satisfactory basis for assigning relative importance weightings to the various different factors involved. But experience has shown that, despite these theoretical objections, the method is in practice a very effective and reliable way of discovering and illustrating the pattern of developable land on a site.

The major advantage of automated overlay mapping over traditional hand techniques is that, once the basic data has been encoded in machine-readable form, a wide variety of maps can be produced very rapidly and cheaply. By varying parameters, the effect of varying costs, priorities, trade-off decisions, etc., on land use patterns can be illustrated and explored in a quick and easy way, especially if interactive graphics is employed. In addition, the possibility of utilizing a variety of different functions in generating "overlays" makes the technique much more flexible than hand techniques.

Numerous generalized overlay mapping programs have been developed. Two of the most widely used are CASAT (Ward, Grant and Chapman 1970) and OVERLAY (Dudnik 1971).

Computer mapping systems

A number of general purpose computer mapping programs, suitable for generating required site maps from machine-readable site data, are available (Dangermond 1972). Perhaps the best known and most widely used is the SYMAP program developed by the Harvard Laboratory for Computer Graphics and Spatial Analysis in the early 1960's (Dougenik and Sheehan 1976). SYMAP accepts as input a list of data points, and generates a grey-scale map consisting of overprinted line printer symbols (*Figure 8.7*). The program can produce conformant, contour, proximal, and dot maps, allows rescaling of raw data as required, and provides numerous graphic options. A related and compatible program, called CALFORM (Cartwright *et al* 1972) produces outline, conformant, or choropleth maps from data points using a plotter. Numerous examples of applications of the Harvard Laboratory for Computer Graphics and Spatial Analysis's mapping programs are shown in a manual known as the "Red Book," obtainable from the Laboratory.

A typical example of some output from a general-purpose mapping system, designed for use either with a plotter or graphics terminal, is shown in *Figure 8.20*.

For the particular application of site mapping and analysis, some special purpose programs have been developed. Several companies, for example McDonnell Douglas Automation of St. Louis, now offer sophisticated subdivision platting programs. Input typically consists of a preliminary layout, together with various dimensional constraints. The program then generates and plots a detailed and accurate plan, and produces reports as required on dimensions, areas, etc.

Integrated site description systems

A number of elaborate integrated systems have been developed for managing the analysis, reporting and mapping of land use data at an urban and regional scale (see for example Porter, Lloyd and Fleischer 1970, Kamnitzer and Hoffman 1972). Unfortunately though, most of the currently available software for handling site data at an

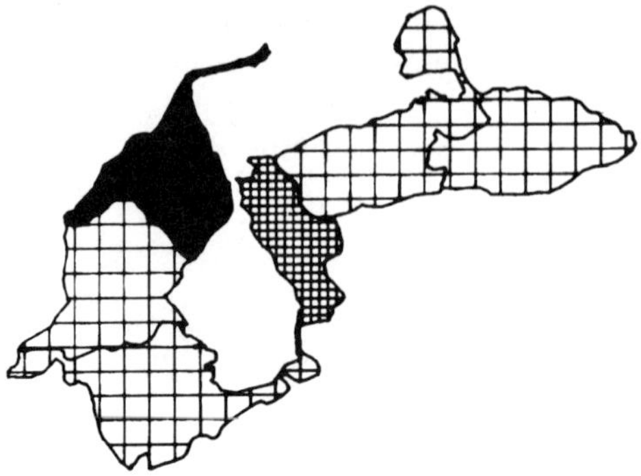

(a)

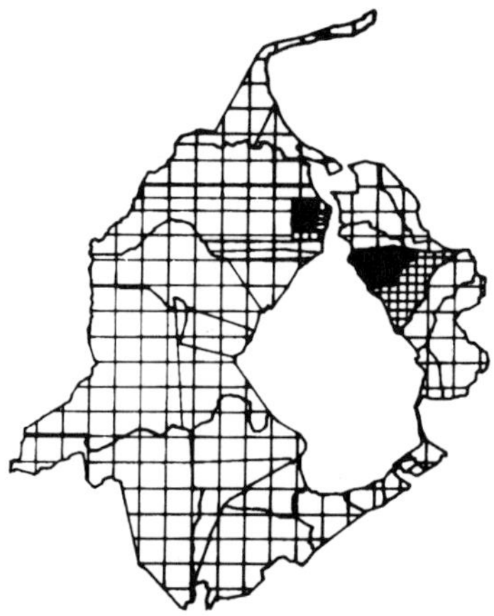

(b)

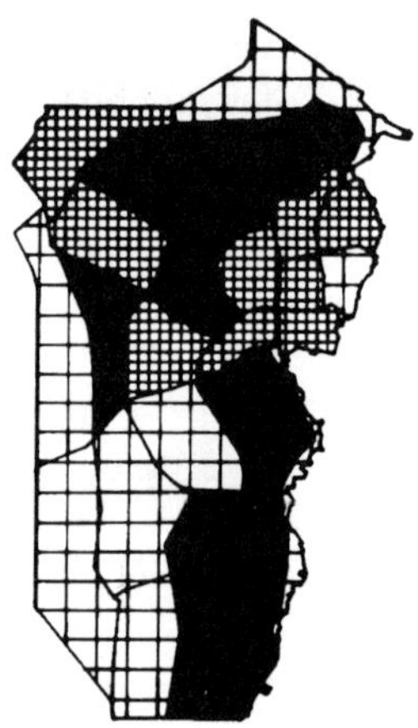

(c)

Figure 8.20
Computer-generated choropleth maps (POLYMAP, Applied Research of Cambridge, Cambridge, U.K.). (a) Percentage population distribution in the Zulia-Falcon region of Venezuela, by subregion divisions. (b) Percentage population distribution in the Zulia area of the Zulia-Falcon region, by municipal divisions. (c) Percentage population distribution in the city of Matacaibo in the Zulia area, by district divisions.

architectural scale is in the form of discrete application programs. This tends to limit its practical usefulness. An exception is the site layout system which forms part of the SSHA integrated system for housing design (Applied Research of Cambridge, 1975). This provides facilities for input of detailed descriptions of site plans, performing various area, volume and level computations, environmental evaluations and cost analyses, and generation of production drawings.

SUGGESTED READINGS

Baxter, R. S. "Data Processing," in *Computer and Statistical Techniques for Planners,* chapter 4. London: Methuen, 1976.

Bijl, A., and Shawcross, G. "Housing Site Layout System." *Computer-Aided Design* 7, no. 1 (January 1975), pp. 2–10.

Dougenik, J., and Sheehan, D. *SYMAP User's Reference Manual.* Cambridge, Mass.: Laboratory for Computer Graphics and Spatial Analysis, Graduate School of Design, Harvard University, 1976.

Peucker, T. K. "Computer Cartography." Resource Paper 17. Washington, D.C.: Association of College Geographers, Commission on College Geography, 1972.

Steinitz, C., ed. *Red Book.* Cambridge, Mass.: Harvard Graduate School of Design, Laboratory for Computer Graphics and Spatial Analysis, 1966 (with additions at intervals).

PART 3

INTERFACES

A user's "view" of data stored in computer memory is provided by input and output devices, controlled by appropriate software. These devices and software together constitute the person-machine *interface* of a computer system. The practical success of any application depends very directly upon the quality of this interface. Sophisticated data bases and clever programs are of little use in practice if data entry is cumbersome or expensive, if output is produced in inappropriate formats, or if the process of communicating with the computer is not sufficiently fluid and natural.

In this Part, the person-machine interface is studied in detail. Chapter 9: *Input and Output Devices,* broadly surveys the range of currently available types of input and output hardware, paying particular attention to devices which find extensive use in architectural applications. Chapter 10: *Alphanumeric Communication,* discusses ways of structuring the input and output of data in alphanumeric format, while Chapter 11: *Graphics,* discusses the input of data in graphic format, the production of plots and graphic displays, and techniques for computer generation of realistic visual simulations.

9
Input and Output Devices

With the utilization of computers in an increasingly broad variety of applications, a wide range of input and output devices have been developed, and new types of devices are continually appearing on the market. This chapter analyzes the input and output requirements of different types of architectural applications, surveys and compares the current range of available devices, and discusses their suitability for use for various different architectural tasks.

INPUT AND OUTPUT REQUIREMENTS OF ARCHITECTURAL APPLICATION PROGRAMS AND SYSTEMS

Numeric, text, and graphic data

The information that is processed in the performance of architectural design tasks may be in *numeric* form, in the form of English *text,* or in *graphic* format. Typically, for example, programs for performing structural and environmental computations require input of numerical data, and output numerical values for certain specified variables. Specification production is an example of an application involving the processing of English text. Programs for generating working drawings, perspectives, etc., produce output in graphic form, and often also require input of data which exists in the form of drawings. Depending upon whether numeric, text, or graphic data is to be processed, different types of input and output devices are appropriate.

Quantity of data

The quantities of data required by and output by architectural application programs vary enormously. At one extreme, simple architectural engineering and economic analysis programs typically require input of, and produce output consisting of values for a small number of variables. Conversely, programs for processing of programmatic data, schedules, bills of quantities, specifications, etc., typically require entry of large quantities of information, and produce voluminous output. Where large quantities of data must be handled, the speed with which input and output devices operate may become a critical consideration.

Quality requirements

In a traditional architectural design process, quick rough sketches are adequate for many purposes. Similarly, in computer-aided architectural design, it is often appropriate to employ cheap and simple graphic input and output devices and techniques where requirements for resolution, accuracy, and line quality are not too stringent. Conversely, where it is necessary to produce high quality artwork, for example, presentation perspectives, then it may be appropriate to utilize expensive and sophisticated digitizing and plotting equipment. It is generally an expensive mistake to employ input and output devices that produce higher quality results than an application warrants.

Batch versus interactive processing

One of the most important considerations in selecting input and output devices is whether *batch* or *interactive* processing is most appropriate for the task at hand. In batch processing, pre-defined data is operated upon by a pre-defined program. The user submits input data and initiates processing, then receives output data when processing is complete, but does not take part in the intervening steps. In interactive processing, user and machine carry on a continuous dialogue by means of an interactive terminal device such as an electric typewriter or cathode ray tube terminal.

For many well-defined, discrete architectural applications, such as production of a perspective from a digitized building description, or sorting a bill of quantities, batch processing may be both adequate and appropriate. Characteristically though, architectural design is an exploratory, incremental decision-making process which tends to be more effectively assisted by highly interactive systems. Almost all of the large-scale, integrated computer-aided architectural design systems that have been developed make provision for interactive performance of many design tasks.

Some typical tasks for which interactive processing is either highly advantageous or essential are:

Entry and checking of graphic data.

Manipulation, modification, and inspection of building descriptions.

Editing of data files.

Interrogation of data bases.

Automated data acquisition by computer.

Real-time moving graphics.

Interactive problem solving, in which computer and human operator act as a team.

Hard copy requirements

Many interactive terminals display text or pictures on the screen of a cathode ray tube, but do not produce any kind of output on paper. Teletype and typewriter terminals, printers, plotters, etc., on the other hand, permanently record data on paper or film. It is generally wasteful of time and money to produce permanent hard copy where a temporary screen display will suffice. Conversely, it is an absurdity for a user to manually copy needed information from a display screen.

Where discrete application programs are employed within the context of an essentially conventional design process, it is usually necessary to produce a good deal of hard copy output, which can be taken away for reference at the drawing board, for discussion with clients, etc. But where a comprehensive integrated system is employed, and much of the design work takes place at an interactive terminal, then much of the need to generate "working" hard copy is eliminated. Displays of any needed information can be generated from the system's data base as required.

Economic considerations

The selection of input and output devices that are appropriate and cost-effective for architectural applications requires consideration of many subtle trade-offs. In general, powerful devices such as sophisticated plotters, high speed printers, and advanced interactive graphic terminals, tend to be very expensive, and thus to require a very high volume of usage to justify acquisition. This tends to place them out of reach of all but the largest architectural design organizations, so programs which require their use must usually employ service bureau facilities. Fortunately however, numerous comparatively cheap alphanumeric and graphic terminal devices, which are adequate for many architectural tasks, have appeared on the market in recent years. These are being installed in increasing numbers in small- and medium-sized architectural offices.

The economic trade-offs between batch and interactive processing have been extensively studied.* Few studies have been specifically oriented towards design or similar tasks, however. Exceptions are a study by Shaffer (1965) of solutions to a queue-optimization problem, a well-known study of the travelling salesman problem by Michie, *et al* (1968), and a study of architectural spatial allocation problems by Cross (1974). It is difficult to generalize from the results of these studies, however, since they clearly depend on the particular types of tasks and the specific capabilities of the particular computer systems employed.

BATCH DATA ENTRY MEDIA AND DEVICES

Punch card systems

The traditional method of batch data entry is to prepare punch cards using an electromechanical *keypunch* device, and to read the cards into the computer via a *card reader.* Typical readers can process cards at the rate of about 800 per minute. The more expensive readers generally operate at faster rates than cheaper readers. Punch cards have the basic advantages that they are cheap and easy to handle (in small quantities), and punch card devices are widely available.

In addition to keypunches and readers, numerous other devices are available for processing punch cards. *Verifiers* are employed to check for keypunch errors, *interpreters* are used to print characters along the top of the card corresponding to the punched data, *sorters* sort cards into numerical or alphabetic sequences, and high speed card punches produce computer output in punch card form.

The use of punch cards in data processing dates back to the 19th century, and the modern electromechanical keypunch was largely developed in the 1920's and 1930's for use in preparing data for processing by accounting machines. When electronic computers began to

* Pioneering analyses of the potential advantages of man-machine problem-solving systems were published by Bush (1945), Licklider (1960), and Yntema and Torgerson (1961). Kaufman-Diamond (1972) has discussed system performance evaluation techniques. The effects of various factors affecting interactive system effectiveness have been investigated by Scherr (1966), Carbonell, Elkind and Nickerson (1968), Nickerson (1969), Sackman (1970, 1974), among others. Experimental studies of the comparative effectiveness of batch and interactive systems for performance of various types of tasks have been reported by Erikson (1966), Grant and Sackman (1967), Schatzoff, Tsao and Wing (1967), Smith (1967), and Adams and Cohen (1969).

become available in the 1950's, it was natural that the established punch card technology be adapted for computer data entry. The IBM Corporation has always held a dominant position in the keypunch market; by the mid-1960's it had installed over half a million machines, and held a 90% share of the market (Stender 1970). IBM's highly effective promotion of keypunch equipment has undoubtedly been a major factor in ensuring its continued widespread popularity.

Punched paper tape systems

The technique of recording data on punched paper tape was originally developed for use in recording and automatically transmitting telegraphic messages. Like punch card technology, it was subsequently adapted for use in data entry to computers. Modern paper tape processing equipment employs "5-channel" or "8-channel" paper tape, in which data is recorded in 5 or 8 parallel rows of round holes. The punched tape is commonly produced by tape punching devices which are attached to teletypes or to electric typewriters, and is read by special paper tape readers. Paper tape is very cheap, and paper tape handling devices are usually quite inexpensive. A disadvantage is that, once a paper tape has been generated, it is difficult to alter.

Magnetic tape drives

Since magnetic tapes are stored off line, and are mounted on a tape drive as required, a magnetic tape drive can be employed not only as a memory device, but also as a batch input and output device. Magnetic tapes have the advantages that they are compact, easily portable, quick to read and write, and can store the same amount of data as thousands of cards. Modern cassette tape drives are compact and inexpensive, and are finding increasingly wide application.

Tapes for input can either be computer generated or produced using a *key-to-tape* system.

Key-to-tape and key-to-disk systems

In key-to-tape systems, data is entered onto magnetic tape rather than punched cards or paper tape, and is then read into the computer via a magnetic tape reader. The first commercial key-to-tape devices were marketed in the United States by Mohawk Data Sciences in 1964, and by 1969 there were nearly 50,000 key-to-tape devices in operation (Cardenas 1973). These devices have a number of substantial advantages over keypunches and card readers: data can be keyed more rapidly; key-to-tape devices are almost silent (whereas keypunches are very noisy); magnetic tape is less bulky and more convenient to handle than cards; magnetic tape readers are an order of magnitude faster than card readers.

In *key-to-disk* systems, a number of keying stations are multiplexed to a minicomputer, and data is entered onto disk storage. This approach facilitates performance of sophisticated editing, formatting, verification, and validation operations.

It seems likely that key-to-tape and key-to-disk systems will eventually replace punch card systems in most applications requiring batch entry of data.

Special purpose alphanumeric data entry devices

Other types of data entry devices, which are used in specialized applications, include *optical character recognition, mark sense reading,* and *magnetic ink character reading* systems. Optical character recognition systems were first developed in the early 1960's. The simpler and less expensive systems read special optical typefonts only, while the more expensive systems accept ordinary printed text or even very carefully hand lettered material. Unfortunately, the cost of acceptably reliable optical character recognition equipment tends to be very high. Mark sense reading equipment is widely employed for processing multiple choice questionnaire and examination data. Magnetic ink character reading systems are most commonly utilized in the banking industry.

PRINTERS

Mechanical printers

Mechanical printers have traditionally been the standard means of outputing alphanumeric data. There are two basic types: *character* printers and *line* printers. Character printers print characters one at a time. Typical examples are electric typewriters and teletypes. They tend to be cheap, but relatively slow, and are rarely used for batch output. Line printers, which employ character chains or drums, can achieve very much higher printing speeds (in excess of 1000 lines per minute) by printing one complete line at a time on continuous rolls of paper, and are widely used for batch output of large volumes of data. Mechanical line printers are usually restricted to upper-case characters which is a disadvantage for a few applications such as production of specifications. Due to their speed and low cost, line-printers are quite often used to produce crude graphic output by positioning symbols on the page, and perhaps overprinting characters to produce tonal gradations.

Electrostatic printers

Since the early 1970's, *electrostatic printers* have become increasingly popular. Like a mechanical line printer, an electrostatic printer produces output on a continuous roll of paper. Styli positioned across the paper are employed to create electrostatic charges on special paper, which is then passed through a developer to produce a printed image. Characters are composed of patterns of small dots, usually within a 9 × 7 or 16 × 16 dot matrix. Electrostatic printers are relatively cheap, fast, and silent, and they can produce high quality results. Some models have the further advantage that they can double as high speed graphic output devices (see following section).

PLOTTERS

Pen plotters

Pen plotters are the most widely used devices for hard copy output of graphics, and have been extensively employed for automated production of architectural and engineering drawings. These devices operate by mechanically moving the plotting head over the surface of the paper under computer or computer-generated tape control. There are two basic types: drum plotters (*Figure 9.1*) and flat-bed plotters

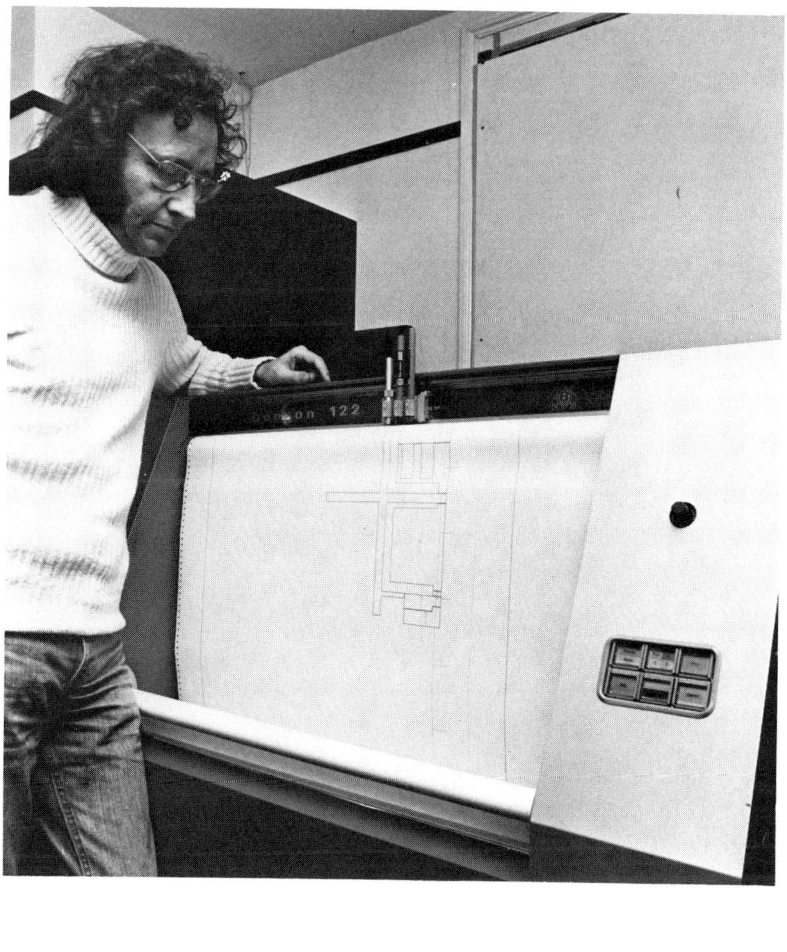

Figure 9.1
Drum plotter.

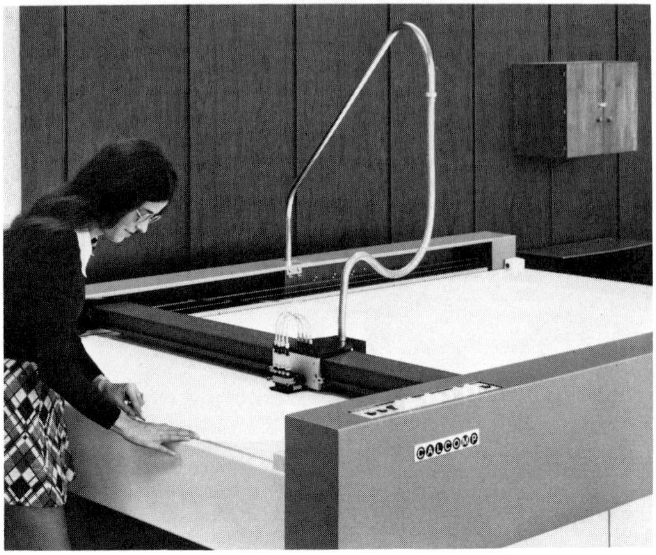

Figure 9.2
Flat-bed plotter.

(*Figure 9.2*). In a drum plotter, drawings are produced by combined longitudinal paper movements around the drum and lateral pen movements, whereas on a flat-bed plotter the plotting head moves over a flat surface in both x and y directions. Prices for pen plotters range from a few thousand dollars to hundreds of thousands of dollars.

The characteristics and levels of performance of different types of plotters vary enormously. Some of the more significant considerations which should be kept in mind when considering use of a pen plotter for architectural applications are discussed below.

The *size* of the drawing which can be produced is, of course, determined by the size of the plotter. Flat-bed plotters range in size from small units designed for plotting on 8½″ × 11″ sheets to huge units, sometimes over 20 ft. long, designed for producing full-scale engineering details. Since drum plotters draw on continuous rolls of paper, the maximum width of the drawing is determined by the width of the drum, but the length is essentially unlimited. Drums that are 30″ or more in width are not uncommon.

Most plotters will accept many different types of paper or plastic film as the *plotting medium*. The type of *pen* that is employed has a major effect on the quality of output. Ball-point and fiber-tip pens are very widely used, primarily for reasons of reliability and economy, but they produce results of inadequate quality for most architectural purposes. High quality results can be produced with liquid-ink-fed tubular pens, similar to standard drafting pens. However, these tend to suffer from problems in starting, clogging and drying up during plotting, and running out of ink during plotting of large drawings. Different line widths and colors can be achieved in a drawing by switching pens. More sophisticated and expensive systems allow for turret-mounted pens to be switched under program control. Less sophisticated systems simply pause to allow an operator to manually switch pens. In addition to pens, sophisticated flat-bed plotters can sometimes also be fitted with "light-heads" for plotting on photosensitive media, cutting heads of various types, and even laser heads for producing very high resolution artwork.

Many drum plotters utilize the *incremental* plotting method. The pen of an incremental drum plotter can move one small increment at a time to the left or right, while the paper can move a similar size increment up or down. This action produces a short line segment in any one of eight directions: up, down, left, right, or on a 45-degree diagonal. Curves and diagonals are approximated by sequences of short straight increments, and thus have a characteristic "stepped" appearance if the increment is not sufficiently fine. A trade-off must be made between increment size and plotting speed (the finer the increment, the slower the speed). Plots which have too coarse an increment are unacceptable for some architectural purposes, for example, presentation perspectives. The *line* plotting method, commonly employed with flat-bed plotters, produces straight lines between specified pairs of points. In this case, diagonals are smooth but curves must still be approximated by short straight segments.

The quality of a drawing that is produced by a pen plotter is also influenced by the *resolution, repeatability,* and *accuracy* of which the device is capable. Resolution is a measure of the number of separate points which can be distinguished on the plotting surface. This determines, for example, how close together points and lines can be drawn before they become indistinguishable. Repeatability describes the capability of the device to return to a previously plotted point. If repeatability is poor, polygons may not close, lines may not meet at vertices of figures, etc. Accuracy refers to the error in actual pen location as compared with specified pen location. Repeatability and accuracy to better than .001 inch are achievable with many plotters.

The *speed* of a plotter is often an important consideration. This is a function of three properties: the speed with which the plotting head can be moved to the starting point of a line, the speed at which a line can be drawn, and the acceleration that can be achieved in starting and stopping a line. Very high line drawing speeds, of the order of several thousand inches per minute, are available on some of the more expensive models. Acceleration is typically measured in milliseconds. The actual time taken to plot a drawing also depends, of course, on the order in which the lines are plotted, *i.e.,* on the amount of actual pen movement involved. For this reason, software is often utilized to sort lines to be drawn into an optimum sequence. Typically, on most available plotters, fairly simple drawings take several minutes to produce. Large and complex architectural drawings may take several hours. In general, pen plotters are rather slow by comparison with other available types of graphic output devices.

Microfilm plotters

Microfilm plotters produce images on 35mm photographic film by moving an electron beam very rapidly over the surface of a small cathode ray tube screen. Enlarged photographic prints are then produced as required. Microfilm plotters produce drawings much faster than pen plotters, and the 35mm negatives can be stored very compactly. Thus microfilm plotting has considerable advantages where a large number of drawings must be produced. It is commonly employed for such applications as producing logic drawings for computers.

Unfortunately though, microfilm plotters have limited resolution, and in addition, the small negative size makes it difficult to produce large architectural drawings satisfactorily. These problems have limited the use of microfilm plotters in architecture.

Precision cathode ray tube recording devices

Plots of grey scale or colored pictures may be produced using precision raster-scan * cathode ray tube recording devices. These produce much higher quality images than a normal TV monitor. Images are usually recorded on 35mm film. Successive exposures using three different colored filters are employed to generate colored pictures.

Laser beam diazo fiche plotters

A remarkable new type of plotter, analogous to microfilm plotters, has been developed by the U.K. firm of Laser-Scan Limited, and is finding application in production of architectural drawings. The Laser Scan plotter writes via a computer-controlled laser beam onto a 105 x 148mm diazo microfiche, which is then developed using a conventional diazo fiche processor. Diazo fiche has several advantages over 35mm microfilm. It is inexpensive, has excellent resolution, can be handled in daylight and developed in a few seconds using a fairly simple desk top machine. Fiches can be viewed using standard office viewer/printers, or can be enlarged onto acetate masters for production of blackline prints.

This approach to plotting combines the speed and economy usually associated with microfilm plotting with higher standards of resolution usually associated with pen plotting. The primary disadvantage is that the necessary equipment is bulky and extremely expensive (of the order of $100,000 in 1975). However, use for architectural applications via service bureau facilities seems feasible. The Laser-Scan Limited facilities in Cambridge, U.K., have been em-

* See Scan Display Systems, below.

ployed in this way for production of plotted output from the OXSYS integrated system.

Electrostatic plotting

The electrostatic printing devices, which were discussed earlier, may also be used as high speed plotters. Plots are generated by printing one horizontal row of dots at a time. The quality of the result depends very largely upon the resolution that is available. Models with resolutions of up to 200 points per inch are on the market. The major advantages of electrostatic printers are that they are relatively cheap devices (by comparison, for example, with good quality pen plotters), output is produced very fast, and they can double as printers. Major disadvantages are that resolution on many models is inadequate to produce good quality graphics, and that drum widths are usually very narrow (although some models have widths of up to 72″), severely limiting the sizes of drawings that can be produced. The ARK-2 integrated system (Stewart and Lee, 1971) relies upon an electrostatic printer for production of hard copy output.

In addition to plotting line drawings, electrostatic printers may also be employed to produce grey-scale output, as shown in *Figure 9.3*.

Figure 9.3
Grey scale plot produced by an electrostatic printer/plotter.

INTERACTIVE ALPHANUMERIC TERMINALS

Teletypes and electric typewriters

Teletypes and electric typewriters are very commonly employed as interactive alphanumeric terminals. They produce hard copy records of all input and output which takes place at the terminal. Typically they are employed for such purposes as entering, modifying, and debugging programs, editing data files, and conducting interactive design dialogues which involve exchange of relatively small amounts of alphanumeric data. To a limited extent (due to their relatively low speeds) they can be employed for production of printed output.

Many models provide a variety of character sets and type faces through use of interchangeable type balls or wheels. For example, a special type ball with the unusual character set of the APL language may be substituted for a standard ball when APL is in use.

Rudimentary graphics capabilities can be added in several ways. One approach that has been employed for architectural applications is to combine a small, inexpensive plotter with a teletype. An ingenious system developed by Wang Laboratories utilizes a special type ball on a standard electric typewriter terminal. This ball has dots at various locations within the area of a standard typed character. By typing different combinations of these dots, graphic output at a resolution of 100 points per inch can be produced.

Cathode ray tube alphanumeric terminals

A more recently developed type of alphanumeric terminal consists of a cathode ray tube screen for display of characters, plus a keyboard for character input. These devices are inexpensive, and have the advantages of speed and silence, but are unsuitable for use where hard-copy output from the terminal is desirable.

INTERACTIVE GRAPHICS TERMINALS

Refreshed cathode ray tube terminals

The refreshed cathode ray tube terminal was the first practical interactive graphics device to be developed and marketed. A typical refreshed cathode ray tube terminal looks very much like an ordinary television set equipped with a keyboard (*Figure 9.4*). The face of the tube is a phosphor-coated surface, which emits light when struck by an electron beam. Lines are generated by moving the electron beam over the face of the tube by means of electromagnetic fields set up across the path of the beam to deflect it as required. To produce

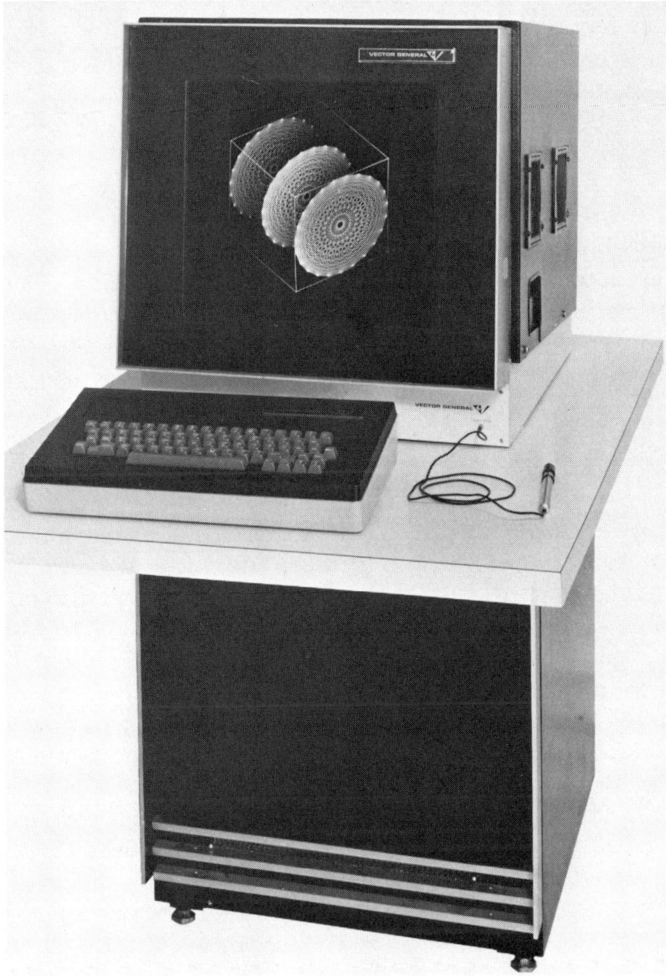

Figure 9.4
Refreshed cathode ray tube terminal (Vector General, Woodland Hills, California).

line-drawings, the terminal is normally provided with the origins and end points of lines, and it then moves the electron beam in a straight line between these points to display *vectors.*

Low-persistence phosphors are used in the screens of refreshed cathode ray tube terminals, with the result that an image only remains on the screen for a fraction of a second. This means that the picture must be constantly refreshed by the electron beam, driven by data stored in memory, if it is to remain visible. To avoid a flickering appearance, the image must be refreshed about 30 times per second. This property that the image must be refreshed has both advantages and disadvantages. The principal disadvantage is that computer resources (*i.e.,* CPU and memory) must continually be devoted to the refreshing process. The time taken to regenerate the picture is proportional to the number of vectors from which it is composed, and if too many vectors are displayed, the image will appear to flicker. Conversely, constant refreshing of the image has the advantage of allowing very rapid manipulation and modification of displays (*i.e.*, adding, deleting, and transforming graphic elements), and of making "moving" displays feasible. Thus graphic elements can be made to smoothly rotate and translate in relation to the frame, and continuous "pans" and "zooms" may be executed.

If the display is in close proximity to the computer, and is connected by a very high speed data link, it may be refreshed directly from memory. Where time-sharing is employed and where the terminal is remote from the central computer, this technique usually becomes impractical. In this case, the terminal is either provided with its own *buffer* core memory, or its own small, general purpose computer. Unfortunately, these arrangements usually add considerably to the cost of a terminal, and complexity to programming.

Some important limitations on refreshed tube displays for architectural applications are that the size of the screen is limited to about the size of a large television screen, the screen is usually slightly curved and loses resolution at the edges, and resolution, accuracy and line quality often tend to be marginally adequate on cheaper models. Furthermore, the display of a typical architectural drawing is invariably sufficient to make it flicker very perceptibly. In the past, the price of good refreshed display devices would run into tens or even hundreds of thousands of dollars, making them uneconomic for most architectural applications. More recently, the price of the smaller and less sophisticated refreshed tube displays has dropped to around the ten thousand dollar range.

Refreshed tube displays have been used in a few experimental architectural systems (Newman 1966, Negroponte 1970), but they have very rarely been employed in everyday practical architectural applications. An exception was in the West Sussex integrated system (see Computer-Aided Systems Building in Chapter 3), where a refreshed display terminal was employed for input of building descriptions by construction of drawings on the screen.

Storage tube terminals

During the 1960's, direct-view storage tubes (*Figure 9.5*) began to appear on the market. In these devices, a high-persistence rather than a low-persistence phosphor is employed in the cathode ray tube. Once a vector is written on the screen, it remains there essentially permanently. This eliminates the need for constant, rapid refreshing (and the devotion of computer resources to this task), and enables an image of any complexity to be displayed without flicker, but it also limits the possibilities for interactive manipulation of the display. Nothing on the screen can be deleted without completely erasing the screen and redrawing the modified picture. Screen erasure produces an unpleasant green flash, and redrawing the picture can take seconds or minutes. "Moving" displays, continuous pans, zooms, translations, rotations, etc., are of course impossible. However, many models allow

Figure 9.5
Storage tube terminal (Tektronix, Beaverton, Oregon).

faint "non-storing" cursors or cross-hairs to be displayed, and moved across the surface of the screen. On some models, the capability exists to scan the surface of the screen by an electron beam in order to sense the image that is displayed there, and to use this data to create a hard copy on paper.

Storage tube terminals are designed for remote use, and may be operated quite satisfactorily in a time sharing environment. They may be connected to the central computer via ordinary telephone lines, without the need for a local buffer or processor. Both text and vectors are transmitted through the line as standard character codes, so that the central computer can treat the storage tube terminal as an ordinary teletype or typewriter terminal. The use of ordinary telephone lines does make the transmission of complex pictures rather slow. This is particularly unsatisfactory when pictures must be redrawn after erasing.

Small, inexpensive, "desk-top" computer graphics systems, utilizing storage tube displays, have been available since 1975. Typically, these systems consist of a minicomputer, display, keyboard, and tape cartridge or floppy disk drive, integrated into a single compact unit. They usually may be used either as stand-alone systems or as remote terminals.

Important advantages of storage tube terminals for architectural applications include their comparatively low cost (often of the order of ten thousand dollars and sometimes much less), freedom from flicker, and reasonably high resolution and accuracy. Disadvantages include the limitations on interactive manipulation of displays, and generally small screen size (usually about 7″ × 10″, but larger displays are also available at a considerably higher price).

Storage tube terminals have been employed in several of the large scale integrated computer-aided architectural design systems that have been developed, notably CEDAR and ARK-2. They have also been acquired for teaching and research purposes by numerous schools of architecture.

A second type of storage tube terminal, operating on quite a different principle from the direct view type, is also now available. In this terminal, the image is initially displayed on a very small storage tube, and then read off using a scanning raster, and displayed on a standard black and white television screen. However, this type of terminal is much less widely used, and unless otherwise noted, references in this book to storage tube terminals are to the direct-view type.

Systems combining refresh and storage capabilities

In 1976, Tektronix Inc. introduced a new type of display system which combined refresh and storage capabilities. A limited number of refreshed vectors can be displayed on the screen simultaneously with an unlimited number of stored vectors. Thus a flicker-free display of a complex drawing can be maintained in storage mode, while the portion of the drawing that is actually being interactively manipulated is displayed in refreshed mode. Although currently more expensive than standard storage tube systems, this type of display appears to have considerable potential for use in architectural applications.

Scan display systems

Scan display systems employ TV monitors to produce grey scale or color pictures. The name arises from the way in which the electron beam is employed to generate images. Instead of *calligraphic* movement of the beam to draw vectors, as in refreshed and storage cathode ray tube devices, an electron beam of varying intensity is swept across the surface of the screen in a *raster-scan* pattern.

Scan display systems are not yet very common outside of research laboratories. Various existing systems are described by Noll (1971), Newman and Sproull (1973), and Denes (1975). The most important potential uses in architecture are for display of complex curved and folded forms, and for realistic visual simulation of proposed designs. Simulations are particularly effective if real time movement of the observer "through" the scene is possible. Experimental use of this type of architectural simulation was pioneered by Kamnitzer (1968) at UCLA.

Plasma panel terminals

Another type of interactive graphics device utilizing a *plasma panel* display (Newman and Sproull 1973), is potentially of considerable significance for architectural applications. Although still largely in the developmental stage, it may one day supersede refreshed and storage tubes for many applications. It can produce high-resolution images on a flat screen, does not require constant refreshing, yet allows selective erasure. Current models are limited to small screen size and slow write and erase rates, however.

The Laser-Scan terminal

The technique of laser beam plotting (see Laser Beam Diazo Fiche Plotters, above) may also be adapted for use in semi-interactive displays. The U.K. firm of Laser-Scan Limited manufactures a terminal (*Figure 9.6*) in which a laser beam writes a black line onto a sheet

Figure 9.6
Laser beam terminal/plotter (Laser-Scan, Cambridge, England).

of orange photochromic film. The image produced in this way is back projected onto a 1,000mm × 700mm screen. The photochromic film used to store the image is non-permanent, so the image gradually fades and eventually disappears. For prolonged viewing, the image must be redrawn at intervals. The machine contains a reel of film which can be wound on whenever a new drawing is to be started. The film eventually fatigues after repeated exposures, and must be replaced. A keyboard and tracker ball which moves a bright non-storing spot over the screen are provided at the console for interactive input.

The unique advantage of the Laser-Scan terminal is that it can display large, detailed drawings at a very high standard of resolution and accuracy. In this respect, its performance far surpasses other available types of terminals, and it would appear to be ideal for many architectural applications. However, current models are extremely expensive, and have not yet found widespread use.

INTERACTIVE GRAPHIC INPUT DEVICES

Graphical data is usually entered into a computer by specifying coordinates of points. Coordinates may be entered numerically, by punching them on cards or typing them in at a keyboard. But this process is slow, cumbersome, and error-prone. Consequently, numerous devices designed to allow more direct entry of graphic data have been developed. These may be broadly classified, according to their modes of operation, into the following groupings:

Tracing devices, with which the user traces or selects points on an existing drawing to enter their coordinates.

Positioning devices, which enable the user to move a small *cursor* or *tracking cross* across the surface of a display screen. At a signal, the current coordinates of the cursor are entered.

Selecting devices, which enable the user to indicate a particular point displayed on a screen.

Three-dimensional input devices, with which the user can enter three-dimensional coordinates of points.

Optical scanning devices, which are simply pointed at a drawing, photograph, or even a three-dimensional scene.

Tracing devices

Tracing devices are particularly appropriate for many computer-aided architectural design applications, since they can be used for input of existing drawings.

Several different types of tracing devices, based upon different physical principles, have been developed. One of the earliest, the

Rand tablet, consists of a ten-inch-square grid of 1,024 wires parallel to the x-axis and 1,024 wires parallel to the y-axis (fabricated using printed circuit methods). Electrical pulses are rapidly applied to the wires in sequence, in such a way that each grid point is uniquely identified. When a stylus (*Figure 9.8(a)*) is touched to the surface, it picks up pulses from the closest grid point, thus detecting coordinates on the tablet surface with an accuracy of about one-hundredth of an inch. Other types of tablets that are available employ voltage gradients within a resistive plate, or strip microphones arranged along two edges of the tablet combined with an ultrasonic sound-emitting stylus. Tablets the size of a normal drawing board are now commercially available (*Figure 9.7*).

Tablets may be employed either to digitize coordinates point-by-point, or to input sketched lines by returning a continuous stream of coordinates as the stylus is moved across the surface. Often the stylus incorporates a ball-point pen to produce records of sketches on paper taped to the tablet surface. By use of suitable software, the track of the stylus may also be instantaneously displayed on the screen of the terminal. Surprisingly enough, most people find it perfectly natural and satisfactory to sketch on a tablet beside the terminal without looking at the tablet at all, but receiving instantaneous visual

Figure 9.7
Tablet in use for digitizing site data (Tektronix, Beaverton, Oregon).

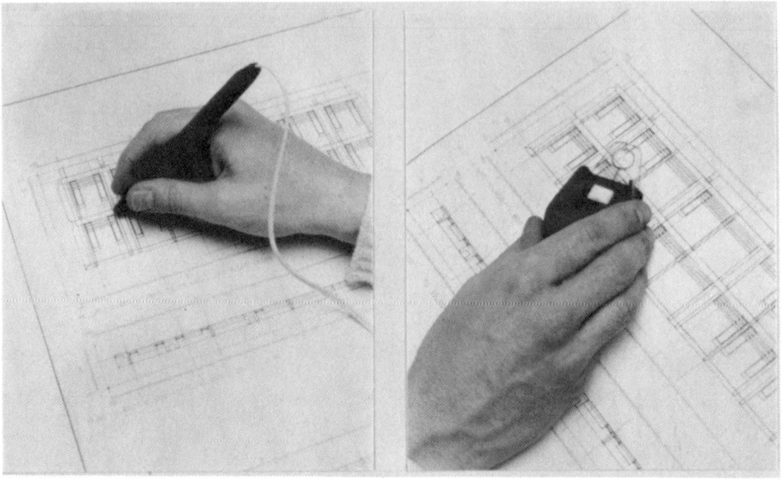

(a) (b)

Figure 9.8
Stylus and cross-hair devices employed to indicate points on tablet surface (Tektronix, Beaverton, Oregon). (a) Stylus. (b) Cross-hair.

feedback from the screen. This becomes rather more difficult, of course, if the sketch and the screen image are of greatly differing sizes.

Instead of using a stylus, a cross-hair device as illustrated in *Figure 9.8(b)* is sometimes employed. This allows points to be digitized to a very high level of accuracy.

Digitizing capabilities are often combined with a flat-bed plotter to make a *digitizer-plotter* work station. Numerous automated engineering drafting installations of this type are in operation (Jones 1973).

Positioning devices

Storage tube terminals often incorporate *x-y wheels* (*Figure 9.9*) for use as a positioning device. Movement of the small keyboard-mounted thumb-wheels causes non-stored x and y cross-hairs to be moved across the surface of the screen. When an appropriate command is given (by striking a key) the coordinates of the cross-hair intersection are entered. Architects usually find x-y wheels and cross-hairs rather natural to use to construct a drawing, since the cross-hairs are employed in similar fashion to the familiar parallel rule and triangle.

An interesting variant on the same principle is the *mouse.* This is a hand-held rolling device, containing two orthogonal wheels which contact the table surface. One wheel rotates for x-direction motion, and the other for y-direction motion. Potentiometers connected to the wheels generate voltages which position the cursor on the screen.

Yet another type of positioning device is the *joystick.* Up-down and left-right movements position the cursor. Some versions allow the stick to be rotated as well, for input of rotational information.

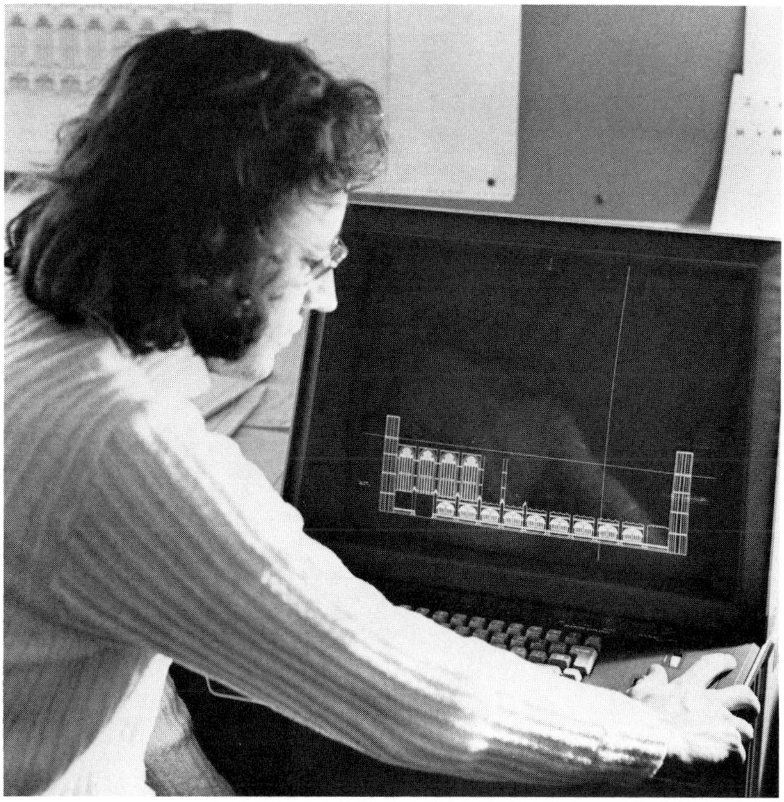

Figure 9.9
Storage tube terminal equipped with x-y wheels and cross-hairs for graphic input (Tektronix, Beaverton, Oregon).

Selecting devices

Light-pens (*Figures 9.10 and 9.11*) are employed, in conjunction with refreshed CRT displays, as selecting devices. A light-pen incorporates some kind of light sensing device, such as a photocell. When the pen is pointed at a dot or line displayed on the screen, the light sensing device generates an electrical pulse whenever that particular portion of the display is refreshed. Since the pulse occurs essentially simultaneously with the movement of the electron beam past the tip of the pen, the pulse can be used to identify the portion of the display currently being pointed to.

A light-pen can be used in two rather different ways, sometimes referred to as *pick-function* and *tracking cross* modes. In pick-function mode, the user employs the pen to select a figure displayed on the screen by pointing at it. In tracking cross mode, the pen is used to locate a small cross at any desired position on the screen. The pen does not, of course, actually move the cross. Instead, a feedback technique is used to reposition the cross at each refresh cycle, so that it remains centered under the field of view of the pen.

Figure 9.10
A light-pen and an experimental pressure-sensitive input device in use in an architectural space arrangement system developed by Masanori Nagashima at MIT in 1976.

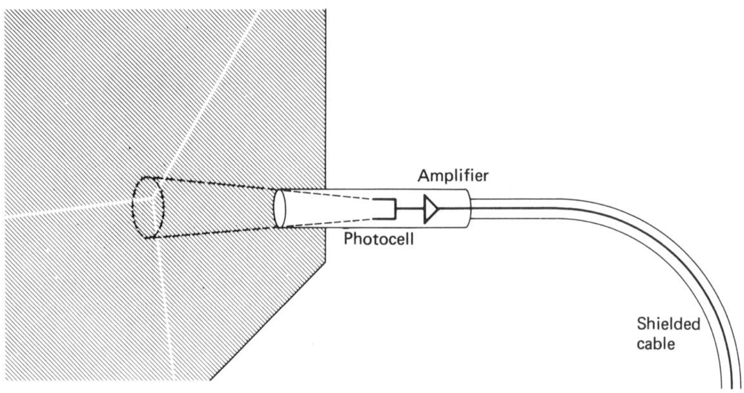

Figure 9.11
Principle of the light-pen.

Three-dimensional input devices

The devices which have been discussed so far all enter two-dimensional coordinates on a planar surface. Several devices have also been developed for the entry of three-dimensional coordinates.

One of the earliest of these was the *Lincoln wand,* developed at MIT's Lincoln Laboratories (Roberts 1966). This device utilizes four microphones to detect the location of a hand-held ultrasonic transmitter in three-dimensional space (*Figure 9.12*). Devices employing mechanical linkages can also be used for three-dimensional digitizing operations (*Figure 9.13*).

Quite a different approach to three-dimensional digitization is employed in a device developed by Sutherland (1974). This device is

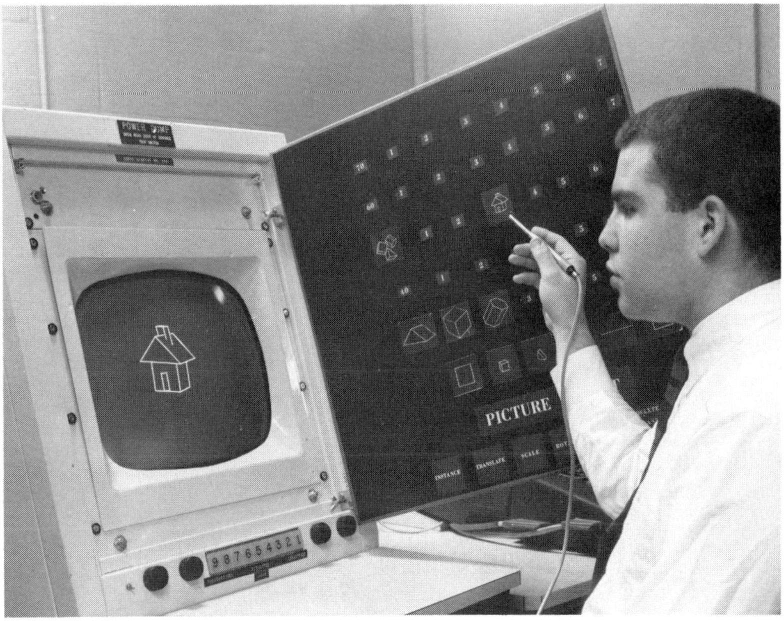

Figure 9.12
The Lincoln wand (Lincoln Laboratories, Lexington, Mass.)

Figure 9.13
Mechanical three-dimensional input device (University of Utah, Salt Lake City).

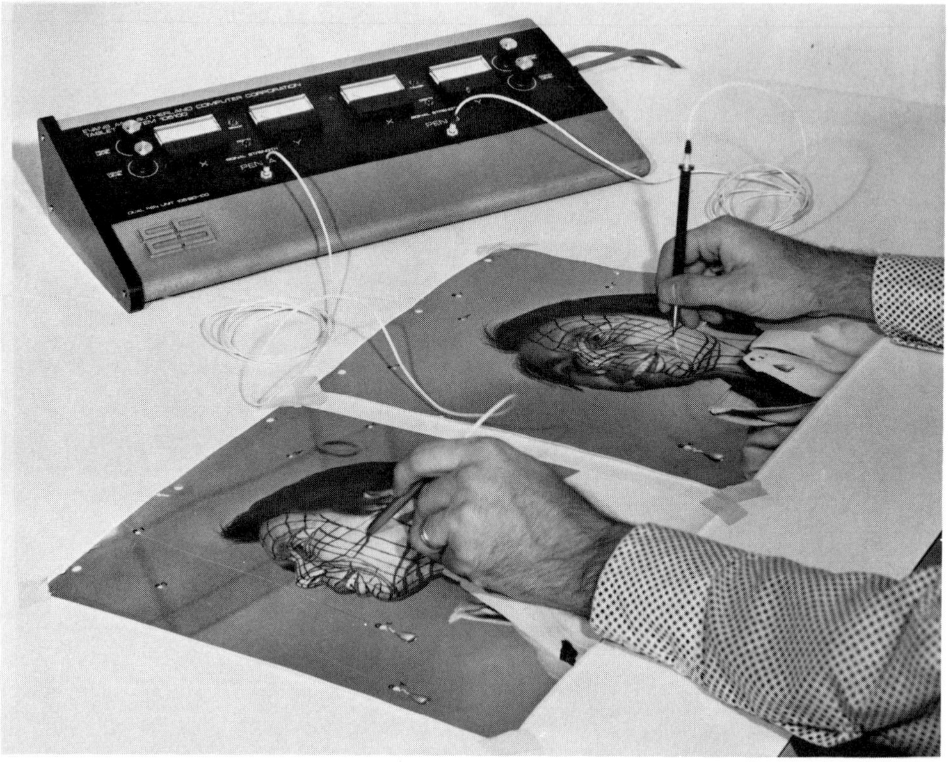

Figure 9.14
Dual-stylus tablet for three-dimensional input (Evans and Sutherland Computer Corporation, Salt Lake City, Utah).

essentially a large tablet, equipped with two styli (*Figure 9.14*). A pair of drawings or photographs, showing each point to be entered from two different angles, is taped to the tablet. One stylus is employed to digitize points on one representation, while the second stylus simultaneously indicates the corresponding points on the other. A special transformation is performed to convert the coordinates input in this way into the required x, y and z coordinates for each point.

Optical scanning devices

An ordinary television camera, or similar device, can be employed to input a grey-scale representation of a photograph, drawing, or three-dimensional scene to a computer. However, data entered in this manner usually requires very extensive and sophisticated processing in order to produce from it the types of useful geometric representations that were discussed in Chapter 6. For this reason, entry of graphic data via optical scanning devices is not yet feasible for most architectural applications.

DATA COMMUNICATIONS

Transmission codes

Data is transmitted between terminals and the computer, via some kind of communication channel, in the form of pulses representing *zero* and *one* bits. Several different methods are employed for encoding characters in binary format for transmission. Three of the most widely used codes are ASCII (American Standard Code for Information Interchange), BCD (Binary Coded Decimal), and EBCDIC (Extended Binary Coded Interchange Code). The ASCII code employs eight bits to represent a character, and can represent a total of 128 characters; BCD employs seven bits and represents 64 characters; while EBCDIC employs nine bits and represents 256 characters. In each case, one of the bits is used for error checking purposes. ASCII represents an attempt to standardize codes, and is now very widely used. EBCDIC is usually employed with IBM equipment. Because data transmission codes are not standardized, compatibility problems can arise if a terminal which uses one code is to be connected to a computer which uses another.

Communications channels

Data can be transmitted by cable, or via a microwave link. Special cables are often employed when transmitting data over short distances, but over longer distances the telephone network or some other utility is normally used.

Different types of links allow data to be transmitted at different rates. *Narrowband* links, for example, those employed in telegraph and Telex systems, allow data to be transmitted at rates ranging from a few dozen to a few hundred bits per second. Ordinary *voiceband* telephone lines allow transmission at rates of several hundred to several thousand bits per second. Special *wideband* links can transmit at rates up to several million bits per second.

Data transmission rate is often an important practical consideration. Many terminals can operate at rates much faster than voiceband telephone lines, and use in conjunction with telephone lines can result in very significant degradation of performance. In particular, graphics terminals of all kinds require high data transmission rates. Voiceband telephone lines, at best, are marginally satisfactory.

Modems and acoustic couplers

To prepare data for transmission over telephone lines, and to convert signals received via telephone lines into usable form, devices known as *modems* (*mod*ulator-*dem*odulators) are employed as illustrated in *Figure 9.15*. Speeds of operation of modems vary considerably, and

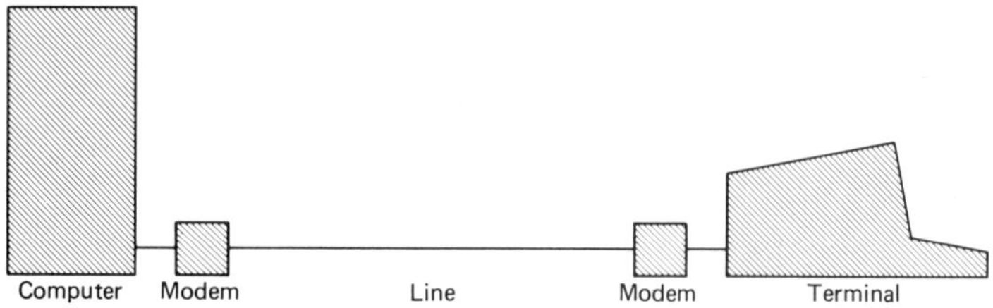

Figure 9.15
Use of modems in a data communications network.

high speed models tend to be more expensive than low speed models. Modems for use in conjunction with remote terminals are often designed to connect with normal telephone handsets via devices known as *acoustic couplers,* as shown in *Figure 9.16.*

ARCHITECTURAL WORK STATIONS

An *architectural work station* may be defined as a configuration of input and output and other devices intended for use by an architect in performing design tasks.

Although costs of processors, memory, and display devices are decreasing rapidly, hardware costs still tend to be quite a major concern in practical architectural applications, and architects must usually make do with the simplest and cheapest work station configurations possible.

Figure 9.16
Acoustic coupler connecting a terminal to a telephone handset.

Typewriter terminal stations

The most primitive kind of computer-aided architectural design work station is a teletype or typewriter terminal linked by telephone to a time-sharing system. This can be augmented by a small drum or flat-bed plotter to provide some graphic output capabilities. A very simple work station of this type can be employed for performing a wide range of structural, environmental, and economic analyses, and even (with ingenious programming) for some space planning tasks.

Storage tube stations

Storage tube terminals are rapidly growing in popularity for architectural applications. They are sufficiently cheap and reliable in many situations, and their capabilities are adequate for the vast majority of architectural tasks. A typical architectural work station today consists of one or more storage or storage/refresh tube terminals, equipped with x-y wheels or tablets, cassette tape or floppy disk drive, an electrostatic printer/plotter, and a 16K or 32K memory microcomputer or minicomputer. Such an installation might be linked remotely to a large time-sharing machine, equipped with additional peripheral devices such as high speed line printers and pen plotters.

A typical storage-tube-based architectural work station, representing an investment of around $50,000 to $75,000 at 1976 prices, is illustrated in *Figure 9.17.*

Other alternatives

The relatively high cost of refreshed cathode ray tube terminals, and the problem of flicker, result in these types of terminals finding

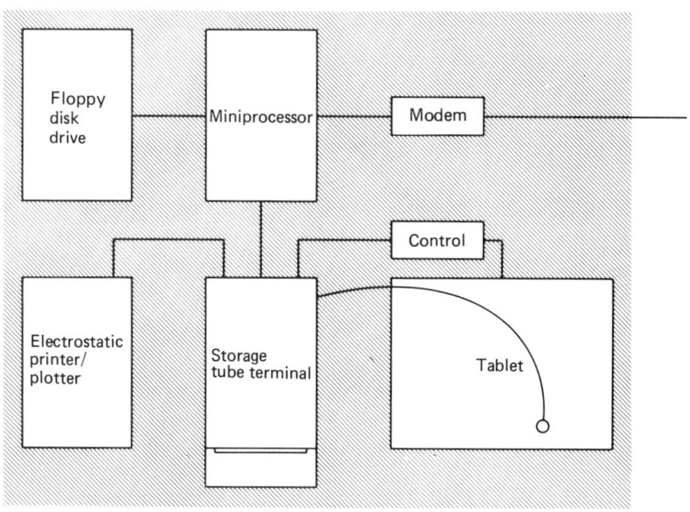

Figure 9.17
An architectural work station consisting of a storage/refreshed display, local processor, tape drive, tablet, and electrostatic printer/plotter.

little practical use in architecture (at least for the present). Plasma panel terminals seem a particularly attractive possibility for the future, but they have been little used as yet. Where the focus of application is high quality drafting, digitizer-plotter work stations are occasionally employed. But these seem better adapted to the production of large scale, very high precision engineering drawings than to most architectural applications.

SUGGESTED READINGS

Cardenas, A. F. "Data Entry: A Cost Giant." *Journal of Systems Management,* August 1973, pp. 35–42.

Jones, G. W., ed. *Computer-Aided Drafting Systems.* Buildford, Surrey: England, IPC Science and Technology Press, 1973.

Negroponte, N. "The Architecture Machine," in *Soft Architecture Machines,* appendix 1. Cambridge, Mass.: MIT Press, 1975.

Newman, W. M., and Sproull, R. F. *Principles of Interactive Computer Graphics.* New York: McGraw-Hill, 1973.

Webster, G. J., and Johnson, C. W. "The Evaluation and Selection of a Computer System for Interactive Design." *Computer Aided Design,* 8, no. 4 (October 1976), pp. 247–251.

The following trade journals carry frequent reviews and advertisements of new devices:

Computer Aided Design
Computer Decisions
Computerworld
Datamation

10
Alphanumeric Communications

A useful distinction can be drawn between alphanumeric communication with a computer which proceeds by the exchange of *formatted data,* and alphanumeric communication which is carried out through the medium of some kind of *language.* Data formats precisely describe the type and layout of the expected information. Typical examples of formats are:

> "An integer number right-justified in a 6-column field"
>
> "A floating point number with 5 decimal places"
>
> "A string of 25 characters."

A language, however, provides for construction of a wide range of expressions out of a specified vocabulary in accordance with specified rules of syntax. A language may either be "natural," like English, or highly formalized, like algebraic notation.

Most simple application programs employ predetermined input and output data formats which are specified by statements within the program itself. The user is required to input appropriate items of data in the specified sequence and format, and output is produced in a particular, fixed sequence and format. Input data items and formats for batch programs are typically described in written user documentation, while input data items and formats for simple interactive programs are often described in "prompts" which are typed out or displayed at the terminal.

Alternatively, provision may be made for the user to define formats which are convenient and appropriate for the task at hand. Data base management systems, for example, typically provide sophisticated facilities for user specification of the content and format of reports to be produced.

Although the exchange of formatted data is a perfectly adequate means of communicating with a computer for many practical purposes, it is often desirable to provide for more sophisticated and flexible communications via some appropriate language. In this case, the user must learn the vocabulary and syntax of the language to be employed, and a language processor must be written for the computer. The language processor accepts the user's input statements, interprets them, and selects the appropriate programs for execution in response. Languages employed for communications with a computer may, at one extreme, be close to a natural language like English, or at the other extreme, be highly abstract and formal.

The following sections discuss input and output of formatted data, and consider some types of languages which may find application in computer-aided architectural design.

FORMATTED DATA

Batch input and output

Input and output of formatted alphanumeric data is very commonly accomplished by use of the batch input and output facilities of general purpose programming languages like FORTRAN, ALGOL, and PL/1. For example, FORTRAN incorporates READ, WRITE, and FORMAT statements for this purpose. A typical FORTRAN READ statement might be:

READ (5,1)I,J,K

This may be interpreted as "Read from input device number 5 (by normal convention a punch-card reader), according to a format specified in FORMAT statement labelled 1, values for the variables I,J,K." The FORMAT statement specifies the type (*e.g.*, integer, real number, etc.) and location on the punch-card of the data to be read, for example:

1 FORMAT (10X,3I2)

This may be interpreted as "Expect 10 blank spaces, followed by 3 integers, each of which consists of 2 digits." WRITE statements are similar in form to READ statements. For example the values of I,J, and K might be written out again by the statement:

```
WRITE (6,2)I,J,K
```

The first number following the left parenthesis specifies the output device to be used. By normal convention, the number 6 specifies a line printer. The second number within the parentheses identifies the FORMAT to be used. An appropriate format here might be:

```
2 FORMAT (1X,3I2)
```

This specifies, "Advance the printer to a new line, and print 3 integers, each of which consists of 2 digits."

Interactive dialogues

Just as batch-oriented input and output devices like card readers and line printers may be addressed by FORTRAN READ and WRITE statements, so may interactive devices like typewriter terminals. For example, the convention might be adopted that the typewriter terminal is device number 8. Thus our example statements must be rewritten:

```
READ (8,1)I,J,K
```

and

```
WRITE (8,2)I,J,K
```

Using READ and WRITE statements addressed to an interactive terminal, an interactive dialogue between user and computer can be programmed. A typical interactive dialogue taking place during execution of a program has the following form:

1. The computer *prompts* the user by typing out a message requesting input of some information.
2. The user types some input.
3. The computer resumes execution of the program until further data are required.

This sequence of steps is then repeated from the beginning.

Prompts may be generated by use of WRITE and FORMAT statements, for example:

```
  WRITE (8,3)
3 FORMAT (' ENTER VALUES FOR I,J,K')
```

Although it is perfectly straightforward to program interactive dialogues using FORTRAN READ, WRITE and FORMAT statements (or their counterparts in comparable languages), this approach is not entirely satisfactory. FORTRAN was initially designed for use in batch rather than interactive environments, and the programming of interactive dialogues using its input/output facilities tends to prove rather tedious and clumsy. A number of more recently developed programming languages, most notably BASIC (Kemeny and Kurtz 1967) and APL (Katzan 1970), have been designed specifically for use in interactive environments, and provide input/output facilities which make programming of interactive dialogues much less cumbersome. For example, an APL * program to read in and print out the sum of values for I, J, and K might be written:

```
     ∇ ADD
[1]   'ENTER VALUE FOR I'
[2]   I←□
[3]   'ENTER VALUE FOR J'
[4]   J←□
[5]   'ENTER VALUE FOR K'
[6]   K←□
[7]   SUM←I+J+K
[8]   'SUM OF I,J,K='; SUM
     ∇
```

This generates dialogues like the following:

Computer	ENTER VALUE FOR I □:
User	287.853
Computer	ENTER VALUE FOR J □:
User	.4
Computer	ENTER VALUE FOR K □:
User	10000.0
Computer	SUM OF I,J,K = 10288.253

Using the full power of the language, which is barely hinted at in this very simple example, enables complex input and output operations to be specified very concisely and elegantly. Gero and Julian (1975) have published a detailed discussion of the use of the sophisticated facilities of APL to facilitate programming of a fairly complex interactive architectural design dialogue.

* The details of APL syntax need not concern us here. It is sufficient for our purpose to note that ∇ is employed to begin and end the program, enclosure of a text string in single quotes causes it to be printed out, ← signifies assignment, and □ signifies input.

NATURAL LANGUAGE DIALOGUE

It can be argued that use of a *natural language,* like English, is potentially the most powerful and flexible way of communicating with a computer. At present, it appears that natural language dialogue with computers is neither a wholly unrealistic fantasy nor a completely practical reality. The state of the art is advancing, and it can be expected that use of English (or at least fairly powerful subsets of English) will be increasingly important in the future.

Eliza-like systems

It has been shown by Weizenbaum (1966, 1967, 1976) that surprisingly simple programs can appear to "speak" and "understand" English well enough to engage a human in conversation. Weizenbaum implemented a program called *Eliza* which could very convincingly simulate a psychiatrist conducting an interview. A typical sample is as follows:

Patient	MEN ARE ALL ALIKE.
Eliza	IN WHAT WAY?
Patient	THEY'RE ALWAYS BUGGING US ABOUT SOMETHING OR OTHER.
Eliza	CAN YOU THINK OF A SPECIFIC EXAMPLE?
Patient	WELL, MY BOYFRIEND MADE ME COME HERE.
Eliza	YOUR BOYFRIEND MADE YOU COME HERE?
Patient	HE SAYS I'M DEPRESSED MUCH OF THE TIME.
Eliza	I AM SORRY TO HEAR THAT YOU ARE DEPRESSED.
Patient	IT'S TRUE, I AM UNHAPPY.
Eliza	DO YOU THINK COMING HERE WILL HELP YOU NOT TO BE UNHAPPY?
Patient	I NEED SOME HELP; THAT MUCH SEEMS CERTAIN.
Eliza	WHAT WOULD IT MEAN TO YOU IF YOU GOT SOME HELP?
Patient	PERHAPS I COULD LEARN TO GET ALONG WITH MY MOTHER.
Eliza	TELL ME MORE ABOUT YOUR FAMILY.
Patient	MY MOTHER TAKES CARE OF ME.
Eliza	WHO ELSE IN YOUR FAMILY TAKES CARE OF YOU?
Patient	MY FATHER.
Eliza	YOUR FATHER?
	etc.

Eliza simply recognizes certain key words, and uses a fairly simple logic to generate plausible-sounding responses. The impression that it "understands" is a complete illusion. As has been pointed out, it demonstrates not that computers possess intelligence, but that this type of conversation does not necessarily require intelligence.

Many Eliza-like programs have been implemented. Some of them talk about design. The following is an example of some dialogue with a program called IDEAS (Nevill and Crowe 1974). The subject is design of a clock.

Designer	LET'S TRY A CLOCK WITH COLOR OUTPUT.
IDEAS	DON'T CONSIDER FEASIBILITY FOR A WHILE.
Designer	A PERSON COULD LOOK AT THE CLOCK AND, SEEING THE COLOR, KNOW WHAT TIME IT IS.
IDEAS	THINK REALLY WILD.
Designer	A SPHERE OF COLOR THAT PULSES FOR SECONDS, AND CHANGES COLOR BANDS FOR MINUTES AND HOURS.
IDEAS	I MEAN REALLY WILD.
Designer	IT COULD BE SELF-CONTAINED AND INTERESTING TO LOOK AT.
IDEAS	THIS MIGHT LEAD SOMEWHERE.
Designer	THE CLOCK SHOULD BE PRETTY.
IDEAS	REVERSE THINGS, MAYBE PRETTY COULD BE THE CLOCK.
Designer	I AGREE, AND IT SHOULD BE CHEAP.
IDEAS	COULD I AGREE?
Designer	YES, BUT YOU HAVE AN INTERNAL CLOCK.
IDEAS	TRY INVERTING THINGS, REVERSE.
Designer	MAYBE PEOPLE COULD MAKE THEIR INTERNAL CLOCK WORK BETTER.
IDEAS	THINK OF THINGS RELATED TO MAKE.
Designer	BIO-FEEDBACK IS THE TECHNIQUE.

Natural language question-answering systems

More serious natural language dialogue systems are much more difficult to implement. The interpretation of natural language requires faciltities for parsing sentences, and for understanding the intended meaning of words. This is a more subtle task than it might at first appear, because sentences often contain ambiguities which can only be resolved by reference to context, general knowledge, etc. The sentence, "Time flies like an arrow" is a much-quoted example. Either "time" or "flies" or "like" could be the verb. If this is not clear, consider the following sentences:

"Catch flies like a trap."
"The plane flies like a bird."
"Fruit flies like a banana."

Because of the difficulty involved, successful natural language dialogue systems have usually utilized a somewhat restricted subset of English, and have been confined to answering questions about a specific data base. Well-known examples include BASEBALL (Green *et al,* 1961) which answers simple questions about baseball statistics, SAD SAM (Lindsay 1963) which discusses simple relations between people, STUDENT (Bobrow 1968) which understands and solves word algebra problems, and DEACON (Thompson 1966) which answers questions about military personnel. A discussion of systems developed during the 1960's is given by Bobrow (1968), and more recent work has been summarized by Winograd (1972).

Systems of this type could be developed for answering questions about some kind of architectural data base, for example, a building products file. At the time of writing no such systems were known to have been implemented.

Winograd's system

One of the most advanced natural language dialogue systems yet to be developed has been implemented by Winograd (1972) at MIT. This system is particularly interesting from an architectural viewpoint, because it discusses and executes spatial arrangement tasks. It simulates a toy robot operating in a world of simple three-dimensional geometric objects arranged on a flat surface (*Figure 10.1*). It can answer English questions about the properties of its world, understand and execute instructions given in English, and request clarification and additional information as necessary. An example of dialogue follows. (The system executes instructions as they are given, and reports "OK" on completion.)

Person	PICK UP A BIG RED BLOCK.
Robot	OK.
Person	GRASP THE PYRAMID.
Robot	I DON'T UNDERSTAND WHICH PYRAMID YOU MEAN. (Does nothing.)
Person	FIND A BLOCK WHICH IS TALLER THAN THE ONE YOU ARE HOLDING AND PUT IT INTO THE BOX.
Robot	BY "IT," I ASSUME YOU MEAN THE BLOCK WHICH IS TALLER THAN THE ONE I AM HOLDING.
	OK.
Person	WHAT DOES THE BOX CONTAIN?

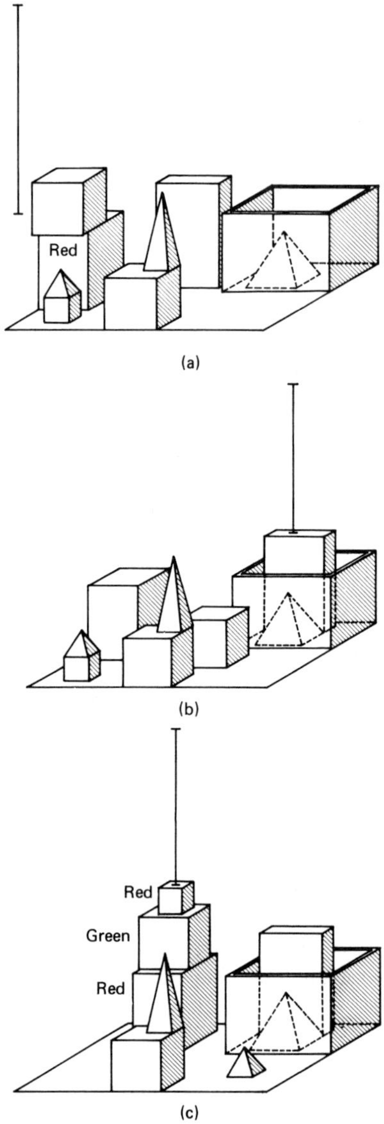

Figure 10.1
The world of Winograd's robot (after Winograd 1972). (a) "Pick up a big red block." (b) "Find a block which is bigger than the one you are holding and put it into the box." (c) "Would you please stack up both of the red blocks and either a green cube or a pyramid?"

Robot	THE BLUE PYRAMID AND THE BLUE BLOCK.
Person	WHAT IS THE PYRAMID SUPPORTED BY?
Robot	THE BOX.
Person	HOW MANY BLOCKS ARE NOT IN THE BOX?
Robot	FOUR OF THEM.
Person	IS AT LEAST ONE OF THEM NARROWER THAN THE ONE WHICH I TOLD YOU TO PICK UP?
Robot	YES, THE RED CUBE.
Person	IS IT SUPPORTED?

Robot	YES, BY THE TABLE.
Person	CAN THE TABLE PICK UP BLOCKS?
Robot	NO.
Person	CAN A PYRAMID BE SUPPORTED BY A BLOCK?
Robot	YES.
Person	CAN A PYRAMID SUPPORT A PYRAMID?
Robot	I DON'T KNOW.
Person	STACK UP TWO PYRAMIDS.
Robot	I CAN'T. (Tries and fails.)
Person	THE BLUE PYRAMID IS MINE.
Robot	I UNDERSTAND.
Person	I OWN BLOCKS WHICH ARE NOT RED, BUT I DON'T OWN ANYTHING WHICH SUPPORTS A PYRAMID.
Robot	I UNDERSTAND.
Person	DO I OWN THE BOX?
Robot	NO.
Person	DO I OWN ANYTHING IN THE BOX?
Robot	YES, TWO THINGS: THE BLUE BLOCK AND THE BLUE PYRAMID.
Person	WILL YOU PLEASE STACK UP BOTH OF THE RED BLOCKS AND EITHER A GREEN CUBE OR A PYRAMID?
Robot	OK.
	etc.

Although no system has yet been developed which can carry on this type of dialogue about non-trivial architectural problems, Nicholas Negroponte's prophetic little book, *The Architecture Machine* (1970) contains a brief scenario which illustrates the character that such a dialogue might take:

Machine	GEORGE, WHAT DO YOU THINK ABOUT THE CHILDREN'S ACTIVITIES IN THIS PROJECT?
Architect	HOW FAR MUST A CHILD WALK TO NURSERY SCHOOL?
Machine	THE AVERAGE DISTANCE IS 310 FEET.
Architect	EACH DWELLING UNIT MUST HAVE DIRECT OUTDOOR ACCESS AND AT LEAST THREE HOURS OF DIRECT SUNLIGHT.
Machine	OF THE CHILDREN WE WERE JUST DISCUSSING, 92 PERCENT MUST CROSS A ROAD TO GET TO SCHOOL.
Architect	WE WILL LOOK AT THAT LATER. WITH RESPECT TO DWELLING UNITS, WE MUST ASSUME AT LEAST TWO VEHICLES PER FAMILY.

Machine YOUR OZALIDS ARE READY. YOUR WIFE HAS JUST CALLED . . .

PROBLEM-ORIENTED LANGUAGES

A problem-oriented language (POL) is a special language designed for statement of a particular type of problem. An effort is made to utilize a vocabulary of familiar key words and syntax which is as "natural" and as easy as possible for the user. Problem-oriented languages have been extensively utilized in certain areas of engineering analysis and design, and there has been some application to architectural tasks.

Civil engineering languages

One of the best known problem-oriented languages is the Structural Design Languages (STRUDL) of the ICES integrated civil engineering system. The following is an example of a STRUDL program (from Walter 1967) which describes the tripod structure shown in *Figure 10.2,* specifies that it is made of 8WF31 rolled steel sections and bears a 10 kip load, requests an analysis, and indicates the type of results required:

```
'STRUDL 'TRIPOD' 'EXAMPLE PROBLEM'
TYPE SPACE FRAME
UNITS INCHES KIPS
JOINT COORDINATES
1 X 0.0 Z 0.0 Y 0.0 SUPPORT
2 Z −86.67 X 50.0 SUPPORT
3 X 100. SUPPORT
4 X 50. Y 86.67 Z −28.89
MEMBER INCIDENCES
1  1  4
2  2  4
3  3  4
MEMBERS 1, 2, 3 TABLE 'STEELWF' '8WF31'
LOADING 1
JOINT 4 LOAD FORCE Y− 10
LOADING LIST 1
STIFFNESS ANALYSIS
LIST FORCES DISPLACEMENTS ALL
FINISH
```

There are two elements of a problem-oriented language. The first is a set of programs which perform the specified problem-solving operations. The second is a language interpreter, which accepts the input problem statement and selects the appropriate programs for execution. The ICES civil engineering system provides special facilities

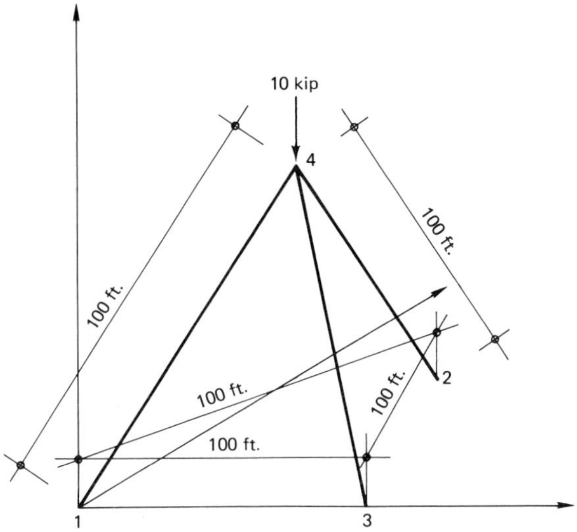

Figure 10.2
A steel tripod.

for building these two elements, and thus creating particular problem-oriented languages for various special civil engineering applications (Walter 1967). A FORTRAN-like programming language called ICETRAN is provided for creating problem-solving programs, and a special language called CDL (Command Definition Language) is provided for defining the external form of the problem-oriented language. Some examples of problem-oriented languages implemented within ICES using these facilities are COGO, ROADS, BRIDGE, TRANSIT, and PROJECT.

Query and reporting languages

Data base management systems typically incorporate special *query and reporting languages* which may be employed to request the output of information and to specify the required format. These languages are usually quite *non-procedural,* in the sense that they allow the user to request a report without describing the detailed sequence of operations needed to access the data base and extract the required information, sort it into the appropriate order, and print it out in the required format. For example, the following query might be employed to direct the GIS system (IBM 1970) to print out a report in standard format giving the identifying number, area, and floor of all offices in a space inventory that have an area greater than or equal to 100 square feet:

```
LOCATE OFFICE
WHEN AREA GE 100
LIST NUMBER, AREA, FLOOR
EXHAUST OFFICE
```

Architectural constraint description languages

Of special interest to architects are problem-oriented languages concerned with statement and solution of spatial arrangement problems. A simple example of this type of language has been implemented by Hamer (1973) for a Master's thesis project at UCLA. Hamer's system deals with arrangements in three dimensions of rectangular parallelepipeds. Each parallelepiped has a name (KITCHEN, BATHROOM, BEDROOM, etc.), and its dimensions may vary within defined limits. The arrangement problem to be solved is specified by means of a series of statements of the following form:

⟨relation name⟩ : ⟨parallelepipeds⟩

The required relations which may be specified between parallelepipeds are:

ACCESS	NOT ACCESS
ALIGNMENT	NOT ALIGNMENT
CONTIGUITY	NOT CONTIGUITY
PROXIMITY	NOT PROXIMITY
SAME CEILING	NOT SAME CEILING
SAME FLOOR	NOT SAME FLOOR
VISUAL ACCESS	NOT VISUAL ACCESS

Thus a typical arrangement problem might be stated as follows:

CONTIGUITY : CARPORT, KITCHEN
CONTIGUITY : KITCHEN, DINING
PROXIMITY : BEDROOM 1, BEDROOM 2, BATHROOM
PROXIMITY : LIVING, BATHROOM
NOT PROXIMITY : KITCHEN, BEDROOM 1
SAME FLOOR : ALL
VISUAL ACCESS : KITCHEN, PLAY AREA
NOT VISUAL ACCESS : LIVING, BATHROOM

The system then attempts to synthesize an arrangement which satisfies as many of these constraints as possible.

A conceptually similar, but more elaborate, language is employed in the IMAGE space planning system which was developed at MIT (Weinzapfel and Handel 1975). In this case, specification of a relationship to be achieved between two spaces is accomplished by typing the names of the two related spaces together with the name of the desired relationship. The following is an extract from a typical list of relations specified in this way:

NARTHEX			
	ADJACENT TO	4.00 FEET OF	NAVE
	ADJACENT TO	4.00 FEET OF	1 OF CIRCULATION
	NEARER THAN	25.00 FEET TO	BRIDES ROOM
	NEARER THAN	25.00 FEET TO	CHAPLIN
	NEARER THAN	25.00 FEET TO	ACTIVITY ROOM
	FARTHER THAN	25.00 FEET FROM	REF KITCHEN
	FARTHER THAN	25.00 FEET FROM	KITCHEN
	NEARER THAN	50.00 FEET TO	RESTROOMS
	MUST SEE	50.00 % OF	RECEPTION AREA
	MUST SEE	50.00 % OF	ADMINISTRATIVE
NAVE			
	ADJACENT TO	4.00 FEET OF	CHANCEL
	ADJACENT TO	4.00 FEET OF	CHOIR SEATING
	ADJACENT TO	4.00 FEET OF	NARTHEX
	ADJACENT TO	4.00 FEET OF	OUTDOOR WORSHIP
ACTIVITY ROOM			
	ADJACENT TO	4.00 FEET OF	KITCHEN
	ADJACENT TO	4.00 FEET OF	ASSEMBLY ROOM
	NEARER THAN	10.00 FEET TO	OUTDOOR WORSHIP
	NEARER THAN	25.00 FEET TO	NARTHEX

Space planning languages

Not only can special problem-oriented languages be developed for statement of spatial arrangement problems, but also for description of the operations to be performed in solution of those problems. For example, Yessios (1975) has implemented a language called SIPLAN for use in programming the solution of site planning problems. A typical SIPLAN program which generates the subdivision layout illustrated in *Figure 10.3(f)* is as follows:

```
1 – MODULE ADDA ↑ T@VVV $
2>VVV ↑ W#V#W :T:::Q $
3>V ↑ VV#W#W#VV :W:Q:W:Q $
4>VV ↑ TT*X :W:::Q $
5>TT = 4;6 :TT:Q:TT:Q $
6>T = 16;8 :VVV $
7>W = 1;R $
8>END $
9 OK: GRAMMAR IS SYNTACTICALLY PROPER.
10 – SPCC = :23,7;15,1;1,12;8,37;43,28;39,5 $
11 – CALL ADDA ; SPCC $
12 M.ADDA ↑ (T@(W#((TT*X)#W#W (TT*X))#W))
```

The program consists of four parts: a set of *productions* (lines 1 to 4), a set of *specifications* (lines 5 to 8), a description of a *global space* (line 10), and a command to execute the *pattern* defined by the productions with respect to the global space (line 11).

The specifications describe the primitive elements from which the site plan is to be composed (in this case lots and road segments). They are of two types: *domains* and *linkages*. A domain is "any properly delineated area and can be a lot, a garden, an existing use, the orthographic projection of a building, etc." A domain specification takes the following general form:

⟨domain name⟩ = d_h;d_v ⟨neighboring conditions⟩

The parameters d_h and d_v define dimensions, and the neighboring conditions are defined by a list of names of other elements that are acceptable as neighbors. Thus the following statement (line 5 of the program) defines a domain called TT, with dimensional parameters 4 and 6, and the 4 sides of which can take as neighbors elements named TT, Q, TT, Q, respectively, as shown in *Figure 10.3(a)*:

TT = 4;6:TT:Q:TT:Q$

A linkage is a "linearly structured element of constant width and of initially undefined length," forming a pedestrian pathway or a road. The general form of a linkage specification is:

⟨linkage name⟩ = W; ⟨color⟩

The parameter W defines the width, and color can take values R indicating a road or P indicating a pedestrian pathway. Thus the following statement (line 7 of the program) defines a linkage called W, which is a road of width 1, as shown in *Figure 10.3(b)*:

W = 1;R$

Productions define composition operations to be performed in order to combine elements into a pattern. The general form of a production is:

⟨composite name⟩ ↑ ⟨composition expression⟩ ⟨neighboring conditions⟩

The upward arrow is known as the *production symbol;* it divides the production into right-hand and left-hand sides. The left-hand side names the composite element formed as a result of the composition operation. Various different *composition operators* can be employed in the composition expression. For example, the *junction* operator # specifies the joining of two rectangular elements along matching sides. Following the composition expression, provision is made to specify new neighboring conditions for the composite element. For example, the following production (line 3 of the program) creates a composite element named V by joining elements named VV,W,W, and VV as shown in *Figure 10.3(c)*, and assigning the four sides of the composite the neighboring conditions W,Q,W and Q respectively:

V↑VV#W#W#VV:W:Q:W:Q$

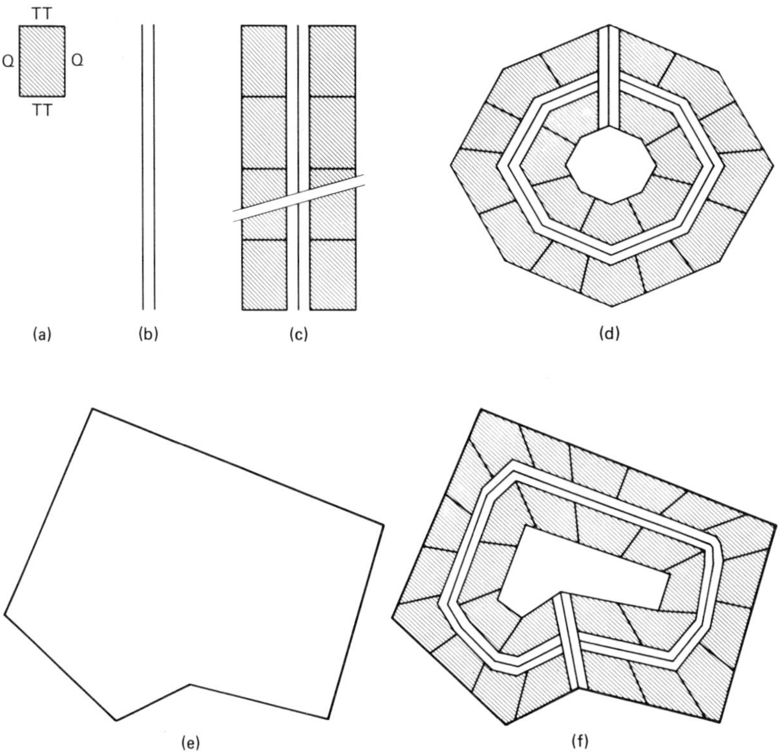

Figure 10.3
Solution of a site planning problem using SIPLAN. (a) Domain TT. (b) Linkage W. (c) Composite element V. (d) Pattern ADDA. (e) Global space SPCC. (f) Pattern ADDA executed with respect to the global space SPCC.

Execution of all the productions in the program creates a pattern called ADDA, as illustrated in *Figure 10.3(d)*.

The global space is a specific site with respect to which the pattern is to be executed. The expression which defines the global space (see line 10 of the program) consists of a name on the left-hand side and a list of coordinates defining its shape and dimensions on the right-hand side. *Figure 10.3(e)* illustrates the global space defined by line 10 of the program.

The CALL command has the general form

CALL ⟨module name⟩ ⟨space name⟩

and causes a specific pattern identified by the module name to be executed with respect to the global space identified by the space name. *Figure 10.3(f)* illustrates the effect of the following CALL (line 11 of the program):

CALL ADDA; SPCC$

The formal description of space planning operations in this way is certainly unfamiliar to architects, and may at first seem awkward and difficult. But the technique can be mastered with a little practice, and can then be a powerful aid. For example, a library of prototype patterns can be created and stored, then applied to various different sites as required by writing and executing simple programs of a few lines.

General architectural design languages

The development of increasingly sophisticated building description systems has led to interest in special languages for describing operations to be performed on building description data bases. Typical operations which a user might wish to specify include input and editing of building description data, generation of graphic displays and printed reports, automated detailing or solution of spatial arrangement problems, evaluation of spatial consistency of a design, and structural, thermal, or cost analysis. As yet, little work has been done on development of architectural design languages which would provide such broad capabilities. One pioneering effort is GLIDE (Eastman and Henrion 1976), a language with an Algol-like syntax, designed for use with Carnegie-Mellon University's BDS * building description system.

SUGGESTED READINGS

Eastman, C. M., and Henrion, M. *GLIDE: Language for a Design Information System.* Pittsburgh, Pennsylvania: Carnegie-Mellon University, Institute of Physical Planning, 1976.

Gero, J. S., and Julian, W. G. "Interaction in the Planning of Buildings," in *Spatial Synthesis in Computer-Aided Building Design,* edited by C. M. Eastman. New York: Wiley, 1975.

Martin, J. *Design of Man-Computer Dialogues.* Englewood Cliffs, New Jersey: Prentice-Hall, 1973.

Negroponte, N. "Languages for Architecture Machines," in *The Architecture Machine.* Cambridge, Mass.: MIT Press, 1970.

Nevill, G. E., and Crowe, R. A. "Computer Augmented Conceptual Design," in *Basic Questions of Design Theory,* edited by W. R. Spillers. Amsterdam, Holland: North-Holland, 1974.

Roos, D., ed. *ICES System: General Description.* Cambridge, Mass.: MIT Department of Civil Engineering Report R67-49, 1967.

Weizenbaum, J. "Eliza: A Computer Program for the Study of Natural Language Communication between Man and Machine." *Communications of the ACM,* 9, no. 1, (1966), pp. 36–45.

Winograd, T. *Understanding Natural Language.* New York: Academic Press, 1972.

Yessios, C. I. "Formal Languages for Site Planning," in *Spatial Synthesis in Computer-Aided Building Design,* edited by C. M. Eastman. New York: Wiley, 1975.

* See The BDS Approach in Chapter 7.

11 Graphics

Graphic communication between architect and computer is essential for most applications which involve description, manipulation, or analysis of building geometry. This chapter discusses fundamental computer graphic techniques and their application in computer-aided architectural design. Topics covered are graphic input, graphic output, three-dimensional graphics, realistic rendering of scenes by computer, graphic systems, and the potential for interfacing computer graphics systems with production machinery.

GRAPHIC INPUT

There are two basic operations involved in input of graphic data. First, points, lines, symbols, etc., are entered by inputting coordinates which describe their locations. Second, the data must usually be processed in some way to transform it from its original format into the type of structured representation that is required. Depending upon the type of input device used, and the type of internal representation desired, the graphic input process can be organized in numerous different ways. Some typical approaches are discussed below.

Digitization of two-dimensional line drawings

The crudest and simplest technique for entry of data describing a line drawing is to manually encode and type in or keypunch coordinates of points. Several different strategies can be followed in doing this. *Figure 11.1(a)* shows a simple line drawing which we will use to illustrate a variety of approaches.

The simplest technique is to input x and y coordinates for the two end points of each straight line segment. These coordinates can be entered in arbitrary order, and stored directly in a simple 4-column array, as shown in *Figure 11.1(b)*. However, this approach does not explicitly recognize that the picture is a more structured entity than a collection of line segments, *i.e.*, that line segments are associated into polygons.

If it is desirable for the application at hand to explicitly record the association of particular line segments with particular polygons, coordinates can be entered into a simple list structure as shown in *Figure 11.1(c)*. Each polygon is separately entered in turn, by starting at an arbitrary vertex, then inputting coordinates in clockwise order until a circuit back to the start vertex is completed.

Even more structure can be recognized in our example picture;

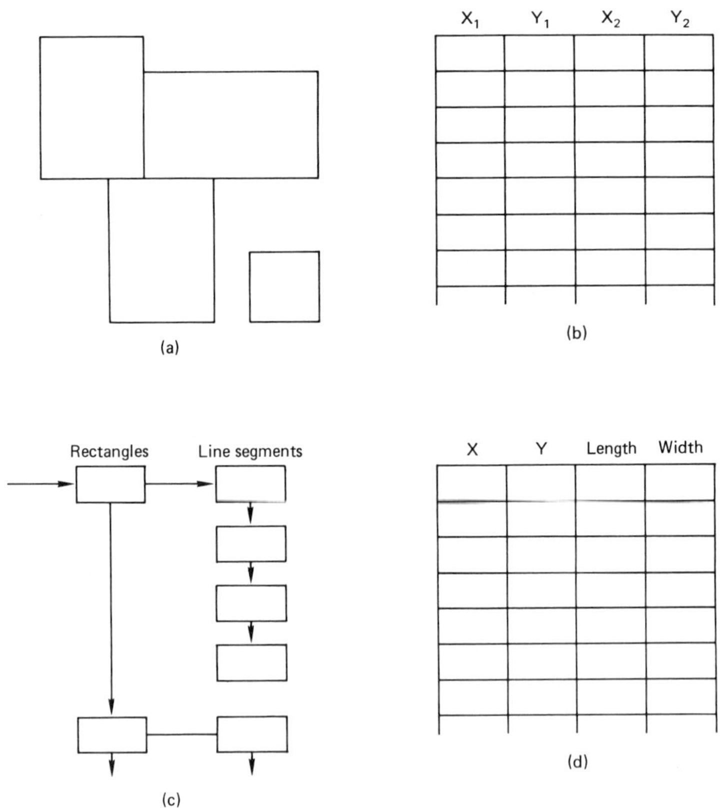

Figure 11.1 Techniques for input of a simple two-dimensional line drawing. (a) Simple line drawing. (b) Format for input and storage of lines by end points. (c) Simple list structure, associating line segments with rectangles. (d) Format for input and storage of rectangles by corner coordinates and dimensions.

it is composed entirely of orthogonal rectangles parallel to the coordinate system axes. Advantage can be taken of this fact to further simplify the digitization task. Each rectangle can be completely described by giving the coordinates of its bottom left corner, its length, and its width. The description can be stored in a simple array as shown in *Figure 11.1(d)*.

Architectural drawings are usually very highly structured in this sense. They typically consist of assemblages of standard graphic elements such as those shown in *Figure 11.2(a)*. Thus a drawing can be very concisely encoded for computer input by listing each occurrence of a standard graphic element, together with coordinates describing its location in the drawing.

Use of tablets or digitizers to enter coordinates

If a tablet or digitizer is available, coordinates of lines or standard graphic elements may automatically be digitized rather than taken off by hand. This approach is much faster, less cumbersome, and less prone to errors. Typically, when using a tablet or digitizer for input of architectural or engineering drawings, a menu of standard graphic symbols is shown on a printed sheet overlaid on part of the digitizing surface. A previously prepared layout sketch on gridded paper is taped to another part of the surface. A symbol is selected by pointing to it with the stylus, then positioned by using the stylus to indicate coordinates on the layout sketch. This approach is very widely employed in automated working drawing production systems.

One of the most ambitious systems of this type is the CADMAC system (Besant *et al* 1972) developed as a collaborative project between the Imperial College of Science and Technology in London and several private firms. The central feature of CADMAC is a reversible digitizing table, which is used as a digitizer for input and a plotter for output. The digitizing procedure makes use of a menu-card of standard graphic items mounted on the surface of the table, as described above. The system is designed for use by technicians with no knowledge of computing. It has been applied in a wide range of engineering fields, and a software system called BASYS (Building Aid System) has been developed to facilitate its application to architectural drafting (Auger 1972, Besant *et al* 1973, Computer Equipment Corporation, Ltd. 1972).

Use of selecting and positioning devices

Beginning with I. E. Sutherland's very important pioneering Sketchpad system (Sutherland 1963), an enormous amount of effort has been devoted to development of graphic input techniques which enable a user to "sketch" on the surface of a refreshed CRT using a light-pen. The effect of direct sketching is an illusion. What really happens with these systems is that coordinate data is taken from the

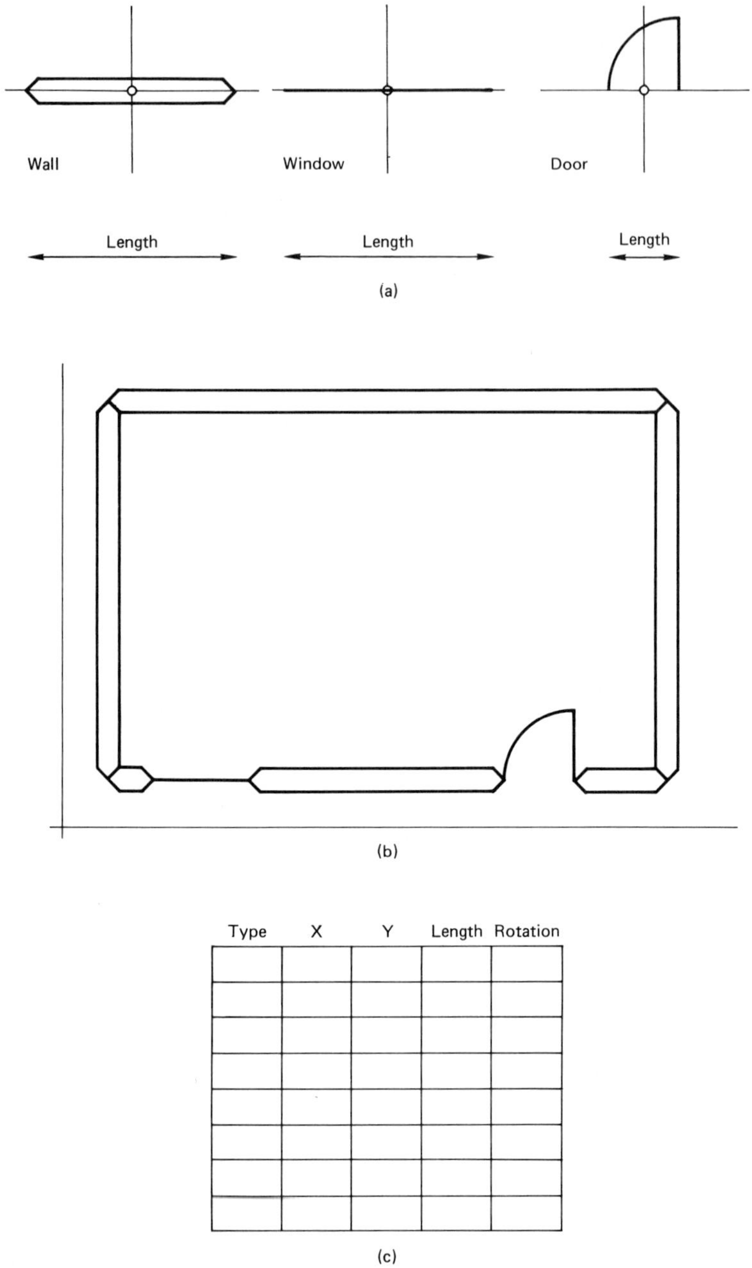

Figure 11.2
Input of a two-dimensional drawing composed of standard graphic elements. (a) Standard graphic elements shown superimposed on local coordinate axes. (b) Drawing composed of the standard graphic elements. (c) Data structure storing the drawing. (d) Input of the drawing using cross-hairs to identify coordinates and keyboard commands to identify elements. After each command, the element is displayed on the screen.

pen, and an appropriate graphic display is instantaneously produced as a result. Thus for example, an object can be made to appear as if "dragged" around the screen by a light-pen, by means of very rapid regeneration of the object at successive locations of the pen.

A great many clever techniques for facilitating on-line construction of drawings using the light-pen have been developed (see New-

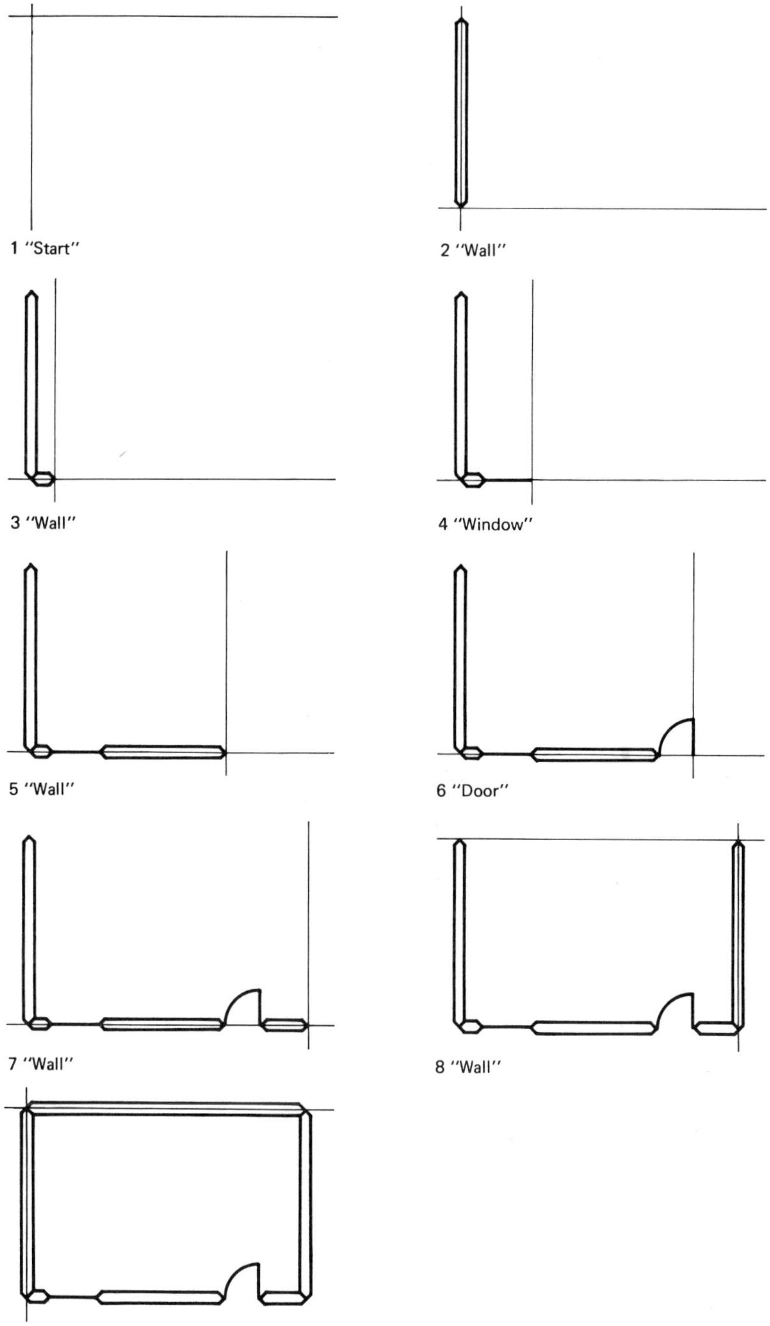

(d)

man and Sproull 1973 for an excellent summary). Perhaps the most widely used is positioning by means of a light-pen. Typically, a menu of standard graphic symbols is displayed, and the symbol to be positioned is indicated by pointing with the pen. Next, the pen is used to indicate the required location for the symbol, a key is depressed, and the symbol is instantaneously displayed at the specified location. Alternatively, the pen might be employed to "drag" the symbol across the screen to the required location. Straight lines may be positioned by indicating the two end-points with the pen, then depressing a key to connect the points by a vector. Some systems allow *rubber-band lines.* In this case, the location of one end of a line is fixed, and the other end is "dragged" around by the pen. Many systems provide facilities for constructing arcs, tangents, etc., and for fitting curves through specified points.

Unfortunately, these techniques require a refreshed type display, and devotion of considerable computational resources to maintain it. This has generally made their use for architectural design applications impractical, and they have been very little utilized for this purpose outside of university research settings. With the continued development of cheaper refreshed displays, and relatively cheap and powerful minicomputers, this situation may change.

A much more practical approach to on-line construction of architectural drawings, in most contexts, is to employ a low cost storage tube terminal equipped with x-y wheels and cross-hairs, or other positioning device. The advantages of highly dynamic interaction are lost, but implementation and operation become much less expensive.

Figure 11.2(d) illustrates the operation of a typical system for on-line construction of floor plans using a storage tube terminal equipped with x-y wheels. Coordinates are indicated by positioning the cross-hairs, with the aid of scales and grids displayed on the screen. Symbols to be displayed at the specified locations are indicated by typing in key words. With a little practice, this very simple system becomes surprisingly fast and natural to use.

Three-dimensional coordinates from two-dimensional drawings

For some applications it is necessary to input three-dimensional coordinates from two-dimensional drawings, for example, in order to generate a perspective from plans and elevations. Since a tablet, digitizer, or cross-hairs only returns two coordinates, this presents a problem. It would be possible to type in the additional coordinate at the keyboard, but this is a cumbersome and error-prone technique.

Fortunately, there exists an algorithm for reconstruction of (x,y,z) coordinates of a point given (x,y) coordinates from one drawing and (x,z) or (y,z) from another (Sutherland 1974). It can be employed with a pair of orthographic projections (e.g., plan and elevation), a pair of perspectives, or a pair of axonometrics, provided that each point to be input is shown on both drawings. Rogers and Adams (1976) have published BASIC subroutines which implement the algorithm.

Ambiguity may arise in three-dimensional input, however, due to coincident projections of vertices in the source drawings (*Figure 11.3*). These ambiguities may be resolved manually by the user, or automatically by a special heuristic program. Such programs operate by generating alternative interpretations of points for consideration, and testing each interpretation for consistency with various geometric theorems. A discussion of one program for this purpose has been published by Lafue (1976).

Sketch recognition

The most natural and general mode of graphic communication for an architect is the rapid and unconstrained freehand sketch. Thus it would be highly desirable to develop a graphic input system which enabled the computer to recognize what was intended by a designer's sketch. The sketch might be input by drawing it directly on a tablet, or by drawing it off-line and then placing it in front of a scanning device such as a television camera.

Sketch recognition is the graphic equivalent of natural language

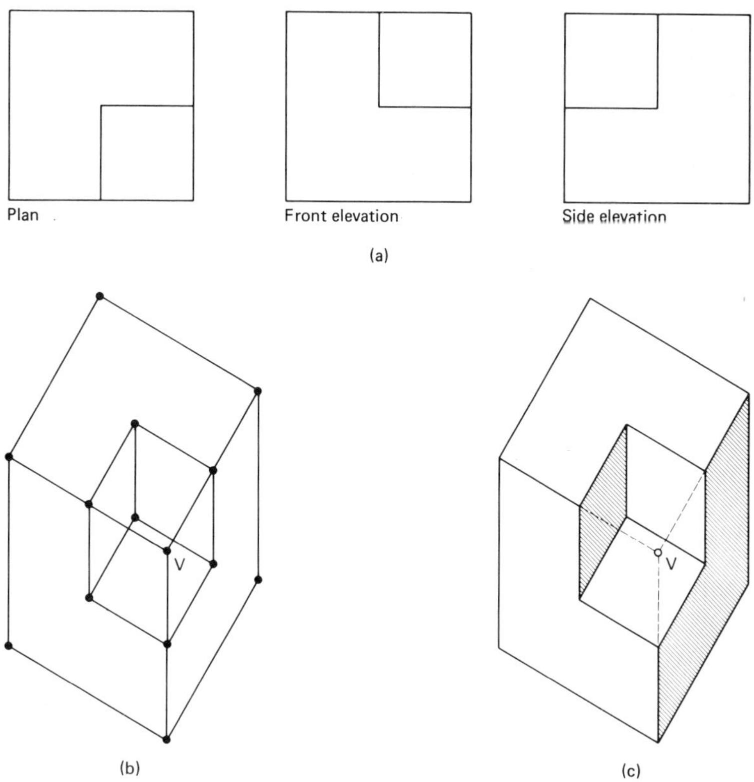

Figure 11.3 Ambiguity due to coincident projections of vertices. (a) Orthographic views of a polyhedral object. (b) Possible locations for vertices and edges. Note that there are too many vertices and edges to allow direct interpretation as a polyhedral object. (c) Geometric interpretation of (b) as a polyhedral object, made by assuming that vertex V and its incident edges are spurious.

interpretation. It involves quite directly analogous problems of parsing, resolution of ambiguities, etc. Theory and practical technology are developing quite rapidly. The earliest work was concerned with recognition of hand-lettered alphanumeric characters drawn with a stylus on a tablet (*e.g.*, see Teitelman 1964). It was shown that very simple algorithms could perform character recognition tasks reliably and efficiently. One of the most successful and widely used of these algorithms is the *Ledeen character recognizer* (Newman and Sproull 1973). Later, character recognition techniques were successfully extended to recognition of flow diagrams and other types of system diagrams in the GRAIL (Ellis, Heafner and Sibley 1969), BIOMOD (Groner, Clark, Berman and DeLand 1971), and other graphics systems.

A very simple demonstration program, illustrating some basic principles of input of architectural data using character recognition techniques, has been implemented by Sasada (1974). This program interprets floor-plan sketches on an element-by-element basis. The element to be recognized is first overlaid by a square grid, and the cells of the grid which are intersected by lines in the sketch are flagged (*Figures 11.4*(*a*) and *11.4*(*b*)). The computer system contains a file of *templates,* describing common graphic elements such as door-swings, against which this description mapped into the grid may be tested. The templates are described in probabilistic terms. They consist of square grids in which each cell contains a number expressing the probability that, for a sketch of the particular graphic element described, the cell will be intersected by a line. A template for a door-swing is illustrated in *Figure 11.4*(*c*). To recognize a graphic element, the program simply searches through the file of templates, and selects the one which most closely matches the gridded description under consideration. Like most character recognition systems, Sasada's program must be *trained;* each graphic element to be recognized is initially sketched several times on the tablet, and the entries in the template grid are derived from these training sketches. The program can be trained by different users to recognize sketches executed in different styles.

There exists an important difference between hand-printed characters and architectural sketches, however. Each character is clearly separated from its neighbors, and can be treated as a discrete entity, but the graphic elements of an architectural sketch are not so easily separable. Either the user must explicitly indicate where a particular symbol begins and ends, or else some kind of automatic segmentation into discrete elements must be attempted by the program. Effective automatic segmentation is not easy. This difficulty has limited the application of character recognition techniques to architectural sketch recognition.

Recent work on architectural sketch recognition has employed sophisticated image processing techniques. The most advanced work

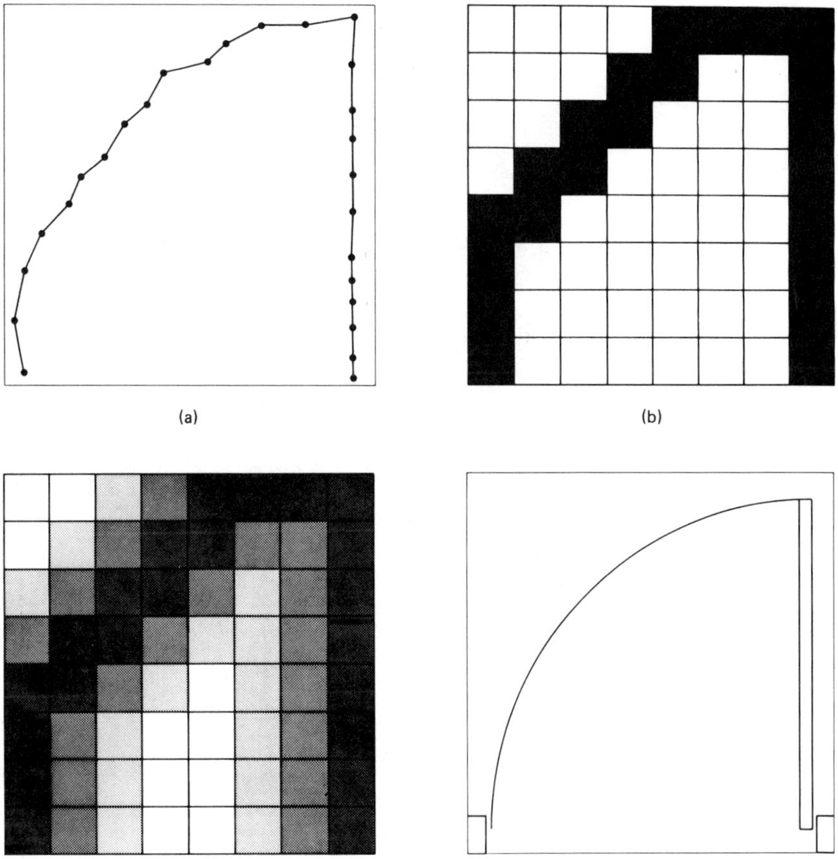

(a) (b) (c) (d)

has been carried out by the Architecture Machine Group at MIT, under the direction of Nicholas Negroponte. Their HUNCH program (Negroponte 1972, 1973, 1975, Taggart 1975) employs a wide variety of graphic clues to attempt to infer what is actually intended by a designer's rough, incomplete, and perhaps inherently ambiguous sketch. This involves such operations as recognizing when lines are "meant" to be straight, to be intersecting, to be parallel or perpendicular, etc. If the sketch is a perspective, a description in terms of plans and elevations can be derived. *Figure 11.5* gives some idea of the procedure followed: the sketch is first processed to find inferred straight lines and line intersections, lines are then made parallel and perpendicular, inferred "hidden" edge-lines are inserted, and a complete description is derived.

Figure 11.4
Character recognition. (a) Coordinate points input from tablet. (b) Points mapped into cells of a square grid. (c) Template. Tonal values express probability that a sketch of the object will have points in the particular cell. (d) Standard graphic symbol substituted for the recognized object.

Sketch recognition is certainly not yet an everyday practical reality in computer-aided architectural design; it is still restricted to research projects and "toy" demonstrations. But it appears to hold great potential for the future.

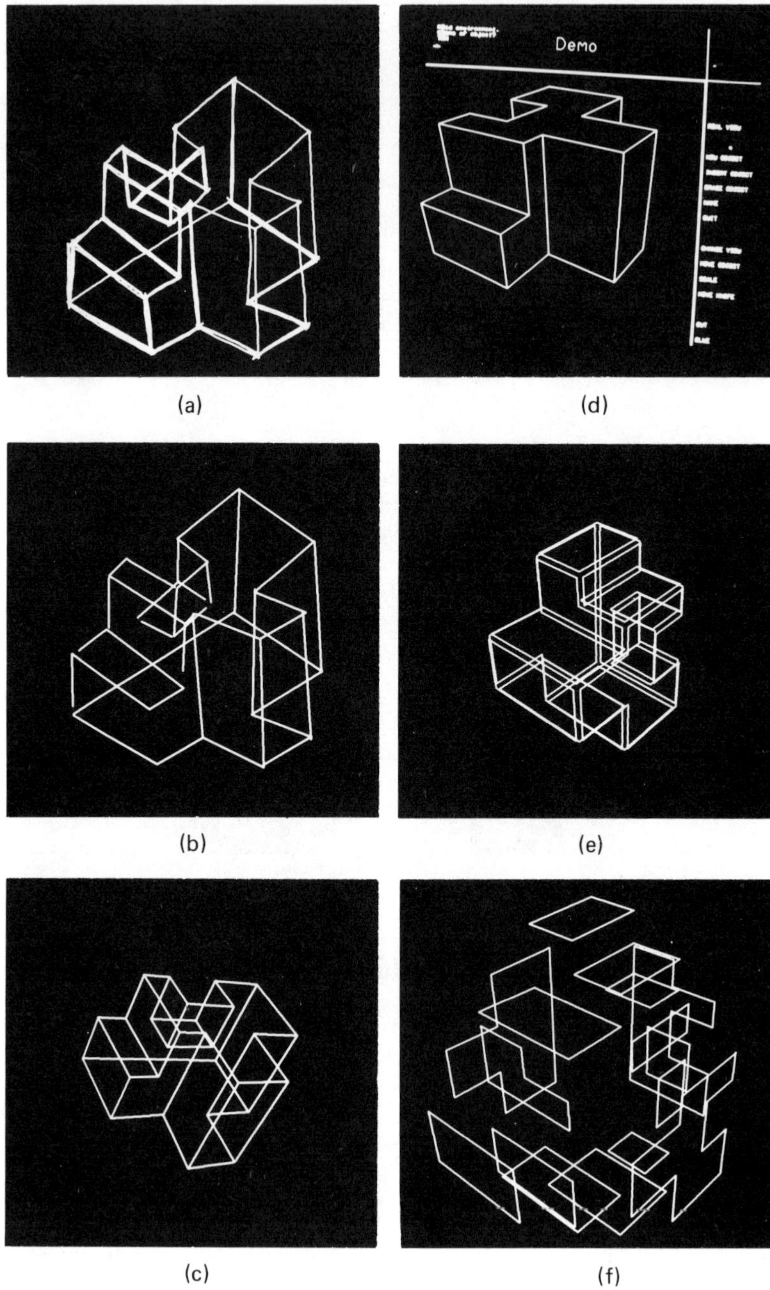

Figure 11.5
Architectural sketch recognition, by a system developed by Nicholas Negroponte and the Architecture Machine Group, MIT. (a) An input sketch drawn with a stylus on a tablet. (b) Straight lines found. (c) Object interpreted as a rectilinear polyhedral form. (d) Rotated perspective view of the object with hidden edge lines removed. (e) Exploded perspective from another viewpoint. (f) Further exploded perspective.

Scene analysis

Another potential approach to graphic input is to present a photograph of a three-dimensional model (or full-scale building) to a television camera. Alternatively, the camera might be pointed directly at the model or scene. To convert information input is this manner into a useful data structure, two operations must be performed. First, the television image must be processed to reduce it to a line diagram, *i.e.*, to a data structure encoding a description of a pattern of lines on a plane surface. Then, this line diagram must be processed to interpret it as a three-dimensional scene, *i.e.*, to generate a data structure consistently describing a configuration of three-dimensional objects. Both these operations are extremely difficult, but considerable research efforts have been devoted to scene analysis in recent years, and substantial progress is being made (Clowes 1972).

Roberts (1965) published the first account of a successful algorithm for extracting line diagrams from photographs. His method was to look for sharp changes in image intensity indicating edges of objects, then to execute a procedure for extracting successively larger line fragments in order to produce a line list. Further refinements have been introduced by Brice and Fennema (1970), Falk (1971) and others. *Figure 11.6* illustrates the operation of a typical line extraction algorithm.

Guzman (1969) introduced an efficient and quite reliable procedure for analyzing a line diagram into polyhedra. This approach was further developed by Huffman (1971) and Clowes (1971). The basis of the Guzman-Huffman-Clowes approach is the observation that only a small number of different types of vertices can occur in a line diagram describing a scene composed of polyhedra (see *Figure 11.7*). Each type of vertex might be interpreted in several ways, *e.g.*, as a convex corner, concave corner, two polyhedra touching at their corners, etc. But the number of potential interpretations is limited. From a knowledge of the geometry of polyhedra, rules governing the assignment of interpretations to vertices and lines, such that a spatially consistent interpretation of the complete scene is produced, can be determined. In other words, a kind of syntax for line drawings of polyhedra, can be described. To analyze a diagram, possible assignments of interpretations to edges and vertices are enumerated to find all those which comply with the rules, *i.e.*, which represent fully consistent interpretations of the entire scene as an assemblage of polyhedra. *Figure 11.8* illustrates an interpretation of a perspective of the Seagram Building, New York, which was generated in this way.

As yet the technology of scene analysis has not advanced to the point where it could have practical application in computer-aided architectural design. But it can be anticipated that it will at some point in the future.

GRAPHIC OUTPUT

The production of graphic output, for example, a plan, elevation, or perspective from a data structure storing a building or site description, requires three basic operations. First, the particular data needed to generate the picture must be extracted. This is a kind of report

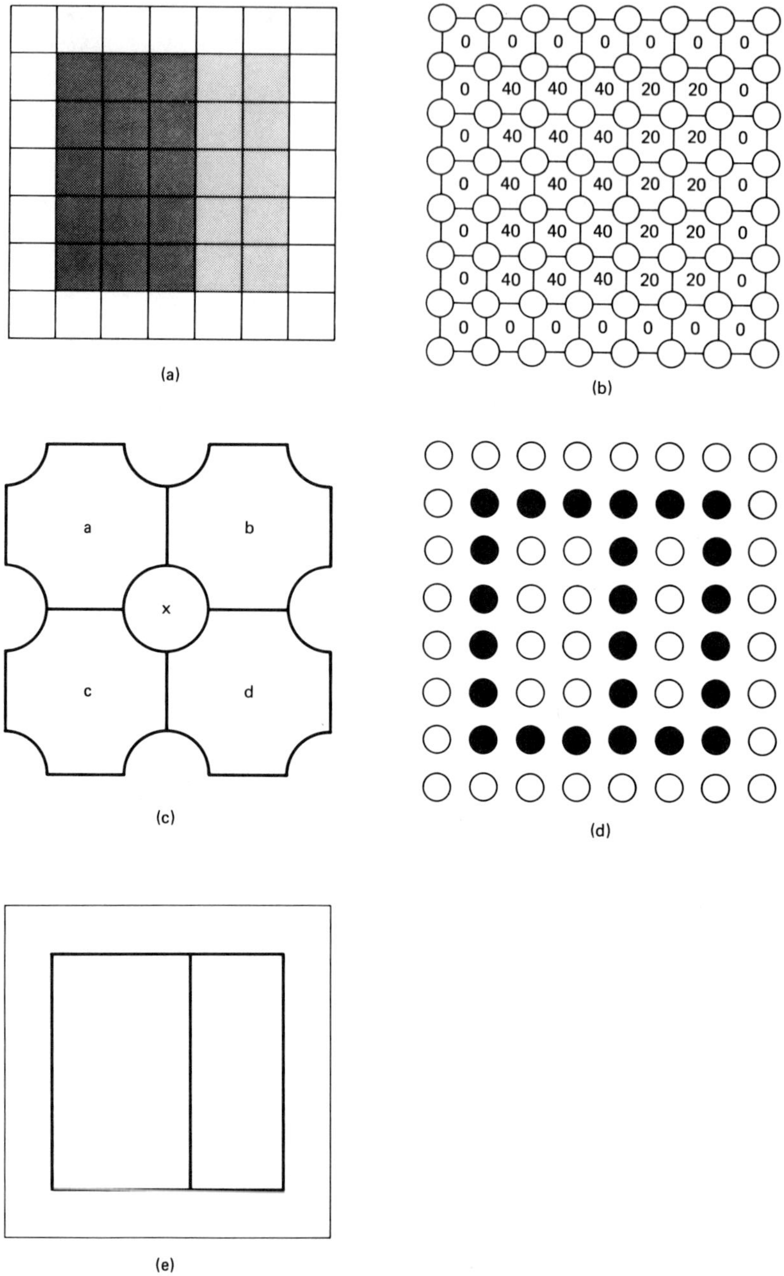

Figure 11.6
Line extraction. (a) Grey scale picture with superimposed grid. (b) Tonal values for each cell expressed numerically, and a second grid (whose points are shown by circles) is interlaced between the points of the first grid as illustrated. (c) Line extraction operator: $x = 1$ when $|a-d| + |b-c| \geq k$, else $x = 0$, where k is an adjustable value. (d) Result of applying the line extraction operator with k set at 20. (e) Line diagram generated by connecting adjacent points in (d) which have value 1.

generation operation, the precise details of which depend upon the representation technique and access procedures employed. Second, scale and other necessary transformations must be applied. Finally, actual display instructions for the display or plotting device must be generated. It will be convenient to consider these operations in reverse order.

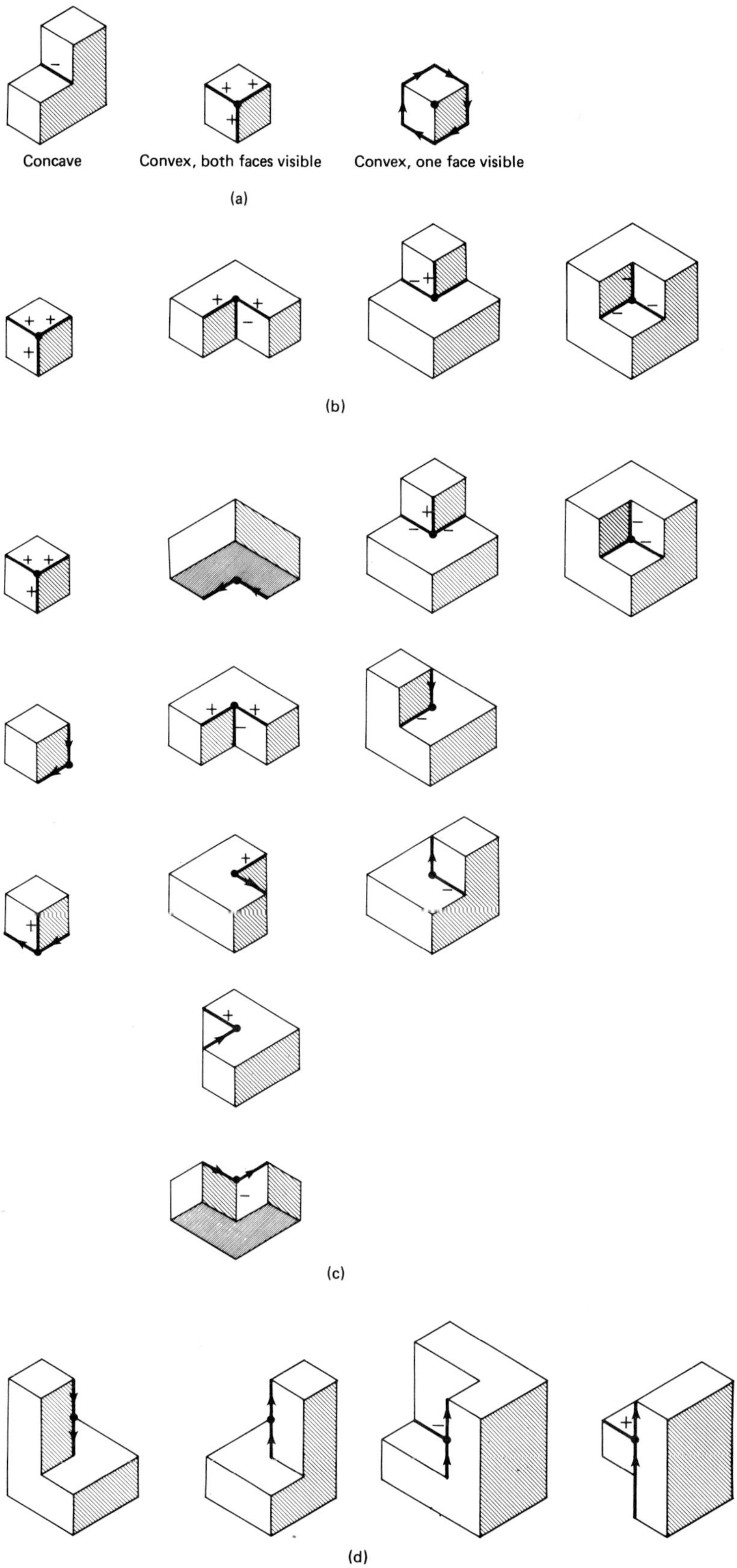

Figure 11.7
Analysis of a line diagram into polyhedra. (a) The three possible types of edges occurring in a scene, with their respective Huffman labels. (b) The four possible types of corners formed by the intersection of three orthogonal planes. (Note that there are more possibilities if we allow more than three planes to meet at the corner.) (c) The twelve different possible appearances of the four possible types of corners. (d) Types of vertices which do not represent corners.

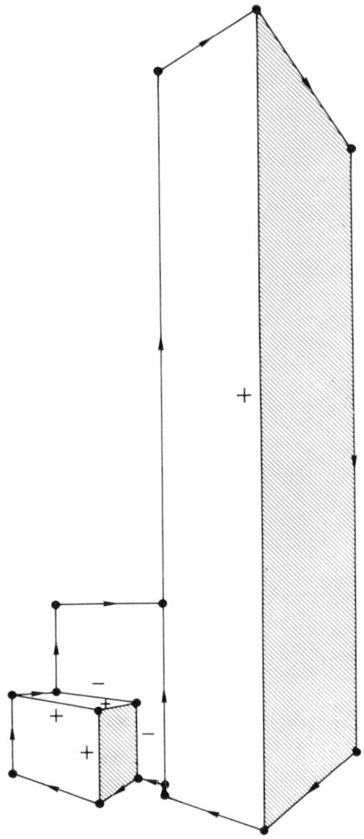

Figure 11.8
Perspective picture of the Seagram Building, New York, interpreted by the method illustrated in figure 11.7.

Primitive graphical functions

All graphic displays are constructed out of elementary graphic *primitives,* usually dots and/or vectors. Graphics display devices are driven by streams of instructions to display particular primitives at particular locations. These instructions are known as *display code,* and are generated by execution in a program of *primitive graphic functions.* Many programming languages incorporate such primitive graphical functions. For example, the SAIL language (Newman and Sproull 1973) utilizes the following for producing CRT displays:

MOVE (DX,DY);	move electron beam position (without drawing a line) from its current location a distance of DX in the x-direction and DY in the y-direction (*Figure 11.9*(*a*))
MOVE TO (X,Y)	move electron beam position (without drawing a line) from its current location to location (X,Y) (*Figure 11.9*(*b*))
LINE (DX,DY)	draw a line from the current location of the electron beam to a point DX units

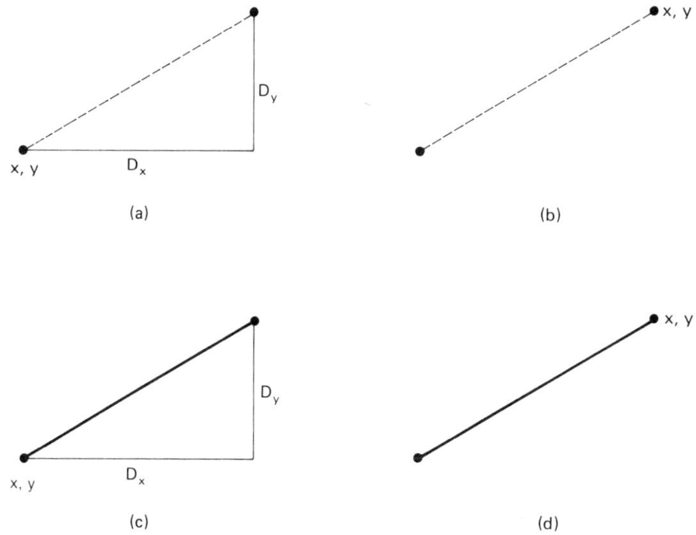

Figure 11.9 Primitive graphic functions provided by the SAIL language. (a) Move (D_x, D_y). (b) Move to (X,Y) (c) Line (D_x, D_y). (d) Line to (X, Y).

	distant in the x-direction and DY units distant in the y-direction (*Figure 11.9(c)*)
LINE TO (X,Y)	draw a line from the current location of the electron beam to location (X,Y) (*Figure 11.9(d)*)

The very popular FORTRAN programming language does not include a primitive graphical function. But it can be employed for writing graphics programs if special graphics subroutines are provided. For example, many implementations of FORTRAN allow the following type of subroutine call to be included in a program:

CALL MVBM (X,Y,IBEAM)

The parameters X and Y specify the coordinates to which the electron beam is to be moved, and IBEAM is given a value of 1 if the electron beam is to be switched on (*i.e.*, if a line is to be drawn) and 0 if it is to be switched off. When the user's program is loaded for execution, the system subroutine MVBM is automatically included.

Coordinate systems

Locations of points and lines to be generated by execution of primitive graphical functions are specified relative to some appropriate *coordinate system*. Various different coordinate systems may be defined. Firstly, there is an *absolute* coordinate system which is "built in" to the display hardware. For example, coordinates on a CRT display are commonly specified in terms of *raster-units*, measured from

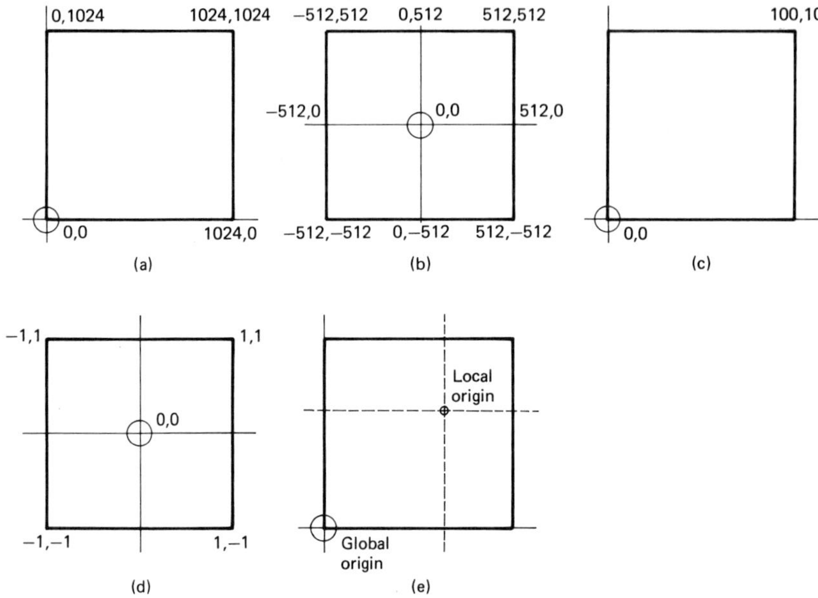

Figure 11.10
Coordinate systems. (a) Typical raster-unit coordinate system with origin at bottom left of display screen. (b) Origin shifted to center of display screen. (c) Site coordinate system defined by user. (d) Fractional coordinate system. (e) Relative coordinate system.

an origin at the bottom-left corner of the screen (*Figure 11.10(a)*). The size of a raster-unit depends upon the precision of the display, *i.e.*, the number of distinct addressable points on the screen. A typical display might be about 10 inches square, and have a precision of 1,024 × 1,024 addressable points. Thus a raster-unit would be about 0.01 inch.

Sometimes an alternative convention of locating the origin in the center of the display area is adopted (*Figure 11.10(b)*). Coordinates must then be *signed* either positive or negative.

For most applications, it is highly inconvenient for a user to work in raster-units or some other idiosyncratic, device-dependent measure. Thus it is common to express coordinates in terms of any system of measurement that is convenient for the particular purpose at hand, and to automatically perform the necessary conversions when required for display generation.

For example, the screen might be regarded by the user as representing a 100′ × 100′ building site, and coordinates describing a building plan on the site might be input in feet from the "bottom-left" corner (*Figure 11.10(c)*). To generate a display of the plan on a typical 1,024 × 1,024 point CRT, the user's coordinates would simply be converted into absolute screen coordinates by multiplication times 10.24.

One special type of coordinate system, which proves very convenient for use when performing transformations like scaling and rotation of pictures, is the *fractional* coordinate system with origin at the center (*Figure 11.10(d)*). Coordinates are expressed as signed real numbers between −1 and +1.

Rather than specifying absolute coordinates, it is sometimes much more convenient to work with a *relative* coordinate system (*Figure 11.10(e)*). When using relative coordinates, values are given with respect to a *local* origin, which in turn is located within a *global* coordinate system, as shown. The units employed in the local and global systems need not necessarily be the same. Local coordinate systems may be nested one within the other to any depth.

Generation of simple pictures

Coordinates needed for execution of primitive graphical functions can be defined in three basic ways: as *constants* within a program, as *data* stored in memory, or by means of a *procedure* which is executed to generate them as required.

Definition of coordinates by means of constants is illustrated by the following simple FORTRAN subroutine, which draws a square:

```
      SUBROUTINE SQUARE
1     CALL MVBM (500,500,0)
2     CALL MVBM (900,500,1)
3     CALL MVBM (900,900,1)
4     CALL MVBM (500,900,1)
5     CALL MVBM (500,500,1)
      RETURN
      END
```

Statement 1 moves the beam invisibly to location (500,500), and statements 2 through 5 draw a 400 × 400 square starting at the bottom left corner and progressing anti-clockwise (*Figure 11.11*).

This type of subroutine is not very flexible; it can only draw a square of a particular size at a particular location. Greater generality can be achieved by allowing for use of coordinate data retrieved from memory as follows:

```
      SUBROUTINE SQUARE
      COMMON POINTS (4,2)
      INTEGER POINTS
1     CALL MVBM (POINTS (1,1), POINTS (1,2), 0)
2     DO 3 I=2,4
```

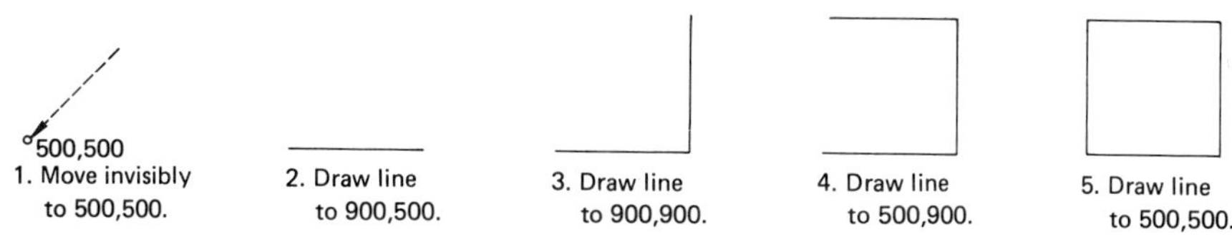

Figure 11.11 Steps in execution of a simple program to draw a square.

```
3    CALL MVBM (POINTS (I,1), POINTS (I,2), 1)
4    CALL MVBM (POINTS (1,1), POINTS (1,2), 1)
     RETURN
     END
```

The array POINTS stores coordinates of the vertices of the square to be drawn, statement 1 moves the beam invisibly to the start vertex, and statements 2 through 4 draw the square.

The square could also be generated procedurally as follows:

```
SUBROUTINE SQUARE (IX,IY,ISIDE)
CALL MVBM (IX,IY,0)
CALL MVBM ((IX+ISIDE),IY,1)
CALL MVBM ((IX+ISIDE), (IY+ISIDE),1)
CALL MVBM (IX,(IY + ISIDE),1)
CALL MVBM (IX,IY,1)
RETURN
END
```

The parameters IX,IY, and ISIDE represent respectively the x and y coordinates of the bottom-left corner of the square and the side-length. By calling the subroutine with different parameters, different square at different locations on the screen may be produced. For example,

```
CALL SQUARE (0,0,1000)
```

generates a square of side-length 1000 with its corner at the origin, while,

```
CALL SQUARE (138,223,65)
```

generates a square of side-length 65 with its corner at point (138,223).

The choice between description of a figure by data stored in memory or by a procedure involves a trade-off of memory versus computation requirements. Storage of data usually consumes more memory space, but procedural generation of data usually requires more computation.

Instances

In this example, each execution of the subroutine SQUARE generates a particular *instance* of a square, characterized by a particular location and particular dimension. Complex pictures can often be described as assemblages of instances of simple figures. For example, the following subroutine describes the grid pattern show in *Figure 11.12(a)* as a set of instances of a square:

```
      SUBROUTINE GRID
      DO 1 I=4,964,64
      DO 1 J=4,964,64
1     CALL SQUARE (I,J,60)
      RETURN
      END
```

The expanding pattern shown in *Figure 11.12(b)* is described by:

```
      SUBROUTINE EXPAND
      DO 1 I= 1,28
1     CALL SQUARE (I,I,(I*I) )
      RETURN
      END
```

An important aid, in writing graphics programs, is a library of appropriately parameterized subroutines which draw instances of standard graphic elements. A graphics subroutine library typically includes, at the lowest level, basic geometric figures like squares, rectangles, triangles, circles, arcs, ellipses, etc. Using these, subroutines to draw standard architectural symbols such as columns, door swings, windows, etc., can be developed very easily. From these, subroutines to generate even larger graphic entities, such as standard hotel room or work station plans, can be produced. Thus an understanding of the hierarchical structure of drawings, and the development of standard subroutines which effectively exploit this hierarchical structure, is the key to efficiently and elegantly writing programs to generate graphic output.

Euclidean transformations, clipping, and windowing

A description of a picture, or part of a picture, often requires some kind of Euclidean transformation (*i.e.*, scaling, translation, rotation, or reflection) before display. This can be accomplished by use of a two-dimensional transformation matrix to transform coordinate vectors, as discussed in Geometric Transformations upon Point Matrices in Chapter 6. For example, a FORTRAN sub-routine might be written to perform the required matrix multiplication, and called as follows:

```
      CALL TRANSF (CONCAT,COORD1,COORD2)
```

Where CONCAT is the concatenated 3×3 transformation matrix, COORD1 is an $n \times 3$ array of coordinates describing the initial figure, and COORD2 is an $n \times 3$ array of coordinates describing the transformed figure. (The third column of COORD1, necessary to make matrix multiplication possible, is simply filled with 1's. Simi-

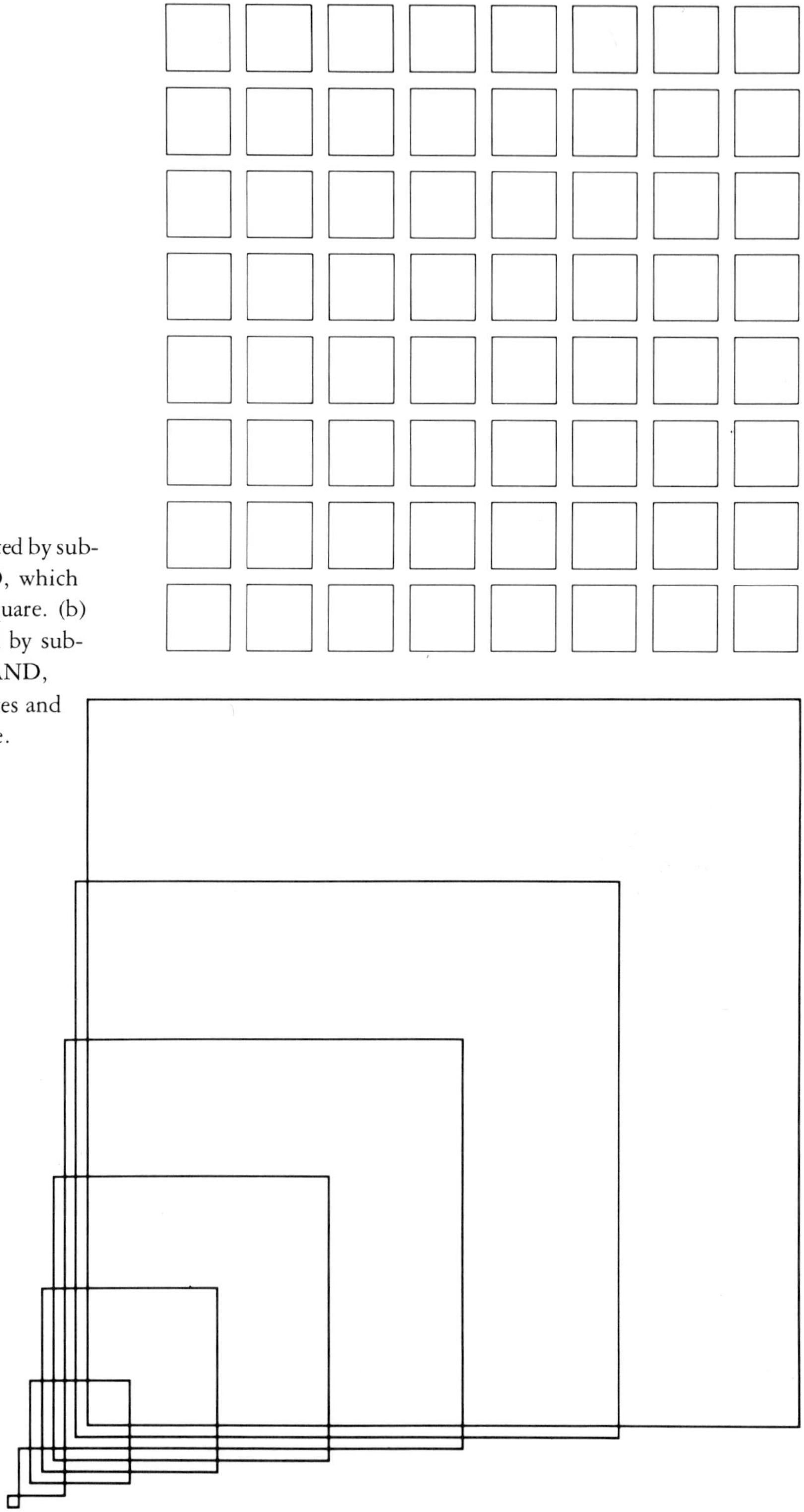

Figure 11.12
(a) Plot produced by subroutine GRID, which translates a square. (b) Plot produced by subroutine EXPAND, which translates and scales a square.

larly, the third column of COORD2 fills with 1's, which can be ignored.)

It is often convenient to write subroutines which draw standard graphic elements in such a way that they can be called with transformation parameters. In this case, the element is defined within the subroutine in terms of a local coordinate system, as illustrated in *Figure 11.13(a)*. When the subroutine is called, transformations are performed in order to locate an instance of that element as required within the global coordinate system of the larger picture. For example, a subroutine to display instances of a square might be called as follows:

CALL SQUARE (X,Y,ROT,WIDTH)

where X and Y give the location of the center of the square in terms of global coordinates, ROT specifies a rotation of the square around its center, and WIDTH gives the width in global coordinate units. Calls to a coordinate transformation subroutine are made from within SQUARE as required. Calling SQUARE with parameters X = 20, Y = 25, ROT = 45°, and WIDTH = 15 then produces a result within the global coordinate system as shown in *Figure 11.13(b)*.

Very often, it is desirable to display a picture which does not fit within the available screen area. To put it more precisely, some points in the picture have coordinates in the absolute screen-coordinate system which are not within the screen boundaries. If an attempt is made to display such a picture, on most display devices, unsatisfactory results will be produced. For example, a line which intersects one side of the screen may "wrap around" to reappear from the opposite side. To deal with this situation, it is common to utilize a *clipping* algorithm which determines which parts of the picture lie

Figure 11.13
Use of a subroutine with transformation parameters. (a) Square defined in a local coordinate system. (b) Instance of square displayed in global coordinate system.

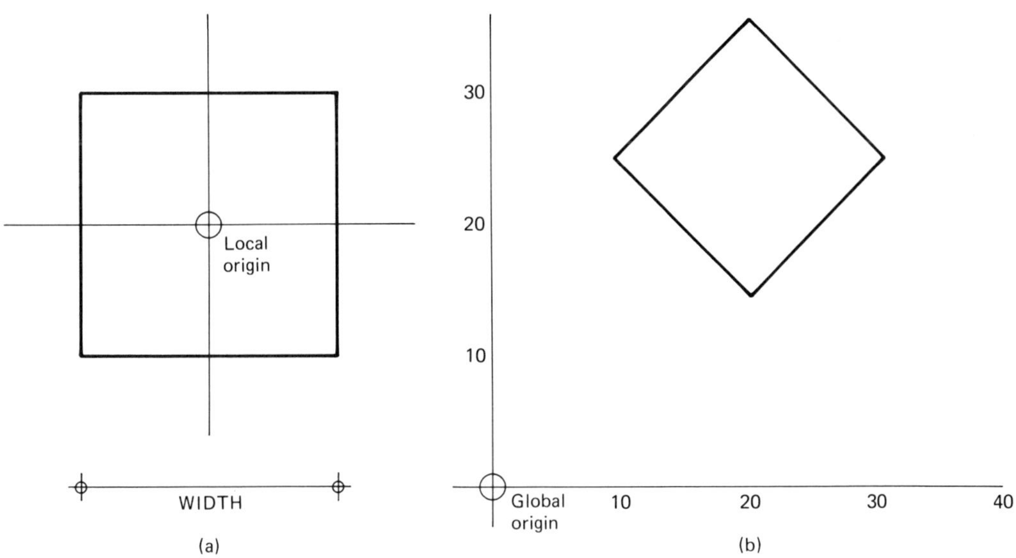

Figure 11.14
Clipping a picture to the edge of the display screen.

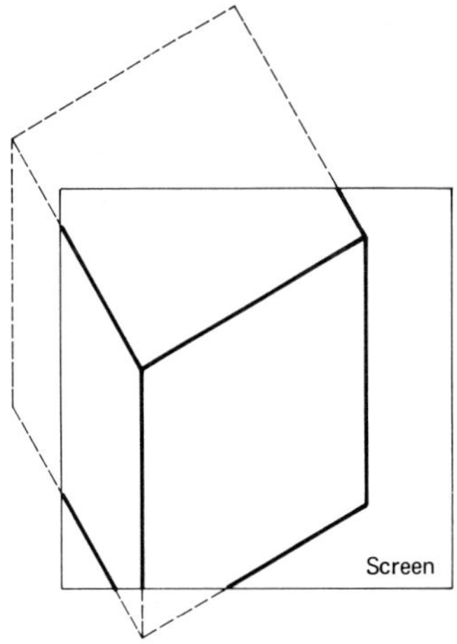

outside the screen boundary and eliminates them (*Figure 11.14*). A number of different clipping algorithms have been developed (see for example Newman and Sproull 1973), and implemented either as programs or as special-purpose hardware.

Although it is often convenient to clip to the edge of the screen, this is not mandatory. It may be desirable, for instance, to employ a rectangular portion of the screen for display of a picture as shown in *Figure 11.15,* and to use the remaining area for some other purpose such as display of text. Such a rectangular area, to which a picture is clipped, is known as a *viewport.* (Pictures can in fact be clipped to the boundaries of any arbitrary polygon (see Sutherland and Hodgman 1974), but rectangular viewports are most common.)

It is not necessary for pictures to be displayed through a viewport to be defined in terms of the screen coordinate system. They may initially be defined in terms of any arbitrary coordinate system, re-

Figure 11.15
Clipping a picture to an arbitrary viewport.

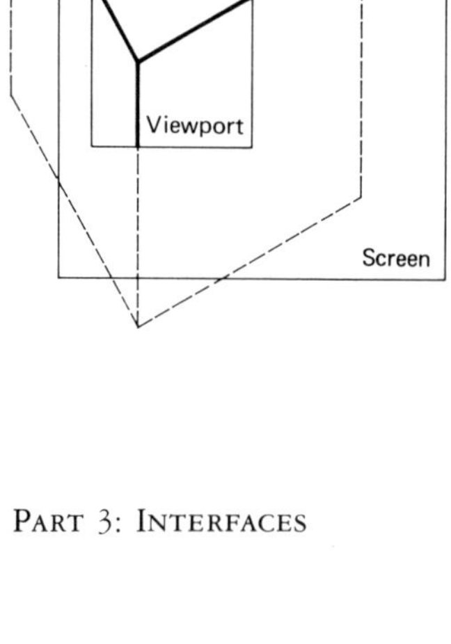

ferred to as the *page coordinate system,* then transformed into screen coordinates for display by use of a *windowing transformation.* To understand the windowing transformation, it is easiest to visualize the viewport as the viewfinder of a camera pointed at the drawing. By moving the camera left and right, up and down, and forward and back, different portions of the picture are projected onto the viewfinder screen. Newman and Sproull (1973) give full mathematical details of the windowing transformation.

The use of page coordinates and windowing transformation has several advantages. It allows pictures to be initially defined in terms of any units of measurement that are convenient, rather than units imposed by the display device. For example, an architectural drawing can be defined by giving coordinates in feet, and a large-scale map can be defined by giving the latitudes and longitudes of points. If clipping to the viewport is performed before applying the windowing transformation, then the computation involved in transforming points and lines outside the viewport is saved. It is easy to specify "pans" and "zooms" over the surface of the picture. To "pan" the sizes of the viewport and window are kept constant, but the location of the window is altered. To "zoom" the location of the window is kept constant, but its size is altered.

The transformations of pictures as discussed in this section can be performed either by means of special purpose hardware built into the display device, by software, or by some combination of the two. Transformation by software is most common. Programs which transform pictures for display are called *transformation systems.* Although it is certainly possible for a computer user to write his own transformation system in a language like FORTRAN, it usually makes little sense to do so, since numerous such systems are available. They either consist of a package of subroutines which the user loads in with his program, or they may be automatically loaded from the system library as required. Usually the transformation system forms part of a comprehensive *graphics package* or *graphics language,* designed to provide the programmer with a wide variety of useful graphics functions (see Graphics Systems, below).

Producing drawings and displays from stored building descriptions

Typically, the information needed to generate a picture of a building comes from two sources: from standard graphic detail embodied in subroutines which draw basic graphic elements; and from design decisions recorded in a building description stored as data in memory. Thus a program to produce the picture must both access the stored description and call standard subroutines. The following is a simple, illustrative example. It is a FORTRAN subroutine to plot a desk layout for an office floor. There are three types of desks, designated DESK1, DESK2, and DESK3. Locations and orientations of desks are stored in arrays DESK1(20,3), DESK2(20,3) and DESK3(20,3). Each row of each array contains an x-coordinate, a y-coordinate, and a rotation. The numbers of desks of each type are given by NDESK1, NDESK2, and NDESK3 respectively. Plan symbols for each desk type are drawn by subroutines named DDESK1, DDESK2, and DDESK3. These are called with three parameters: an x-coordinate, a y-coordinate, and a rotation.

```
      SUBROUTINE DESKS
      COMMON DESK1(20,3), DESK2(20,3), DESK3(20,3), NDESK1, NDESK2, NDESK3
      INTEGER DESK1, DESK2, DESK3
      DO1 I=1, NDESK1
1     CALL DDESK1(DESK1(I,1), DESK1(I,2), DESK1(I,3))
      DO 2 I=1, NDESK2
2     CALL DDESK2(DESK2(I, 1), DESK2(I, 2), DESK2(I,3))
      DO 3 I=1, NDESK3
3     CALL DDESK3(DESK3(I, 1), DESK3(I,2), DESK3(I,3))
      RETURN
      END
```

A result produced by execution of this program is illustrated in *Figure 11.16*.

Systems for automated drafting of working drawings can be developed, following the same principles illustrated by this simple example. The heart of such a system is a library of appropriately parameterized subroutines for drawing standard graphic symbols. Dimensions, locations, and orientations of elements can either be encoded by hand and keypunched or typed in, automatically digitized using a menu and tablet, cross-hairs, or light-pen, or extracted from a project data base that is already stored on disk or tape. A variety of output options can be provided, allowing the user to control scale, format, level and type of detail to be included, labelling and dimensioning, etc.

To date, the most successful applications of automated working drawing production systems that operate separately from an integrated project data base management system have been those involving a great deal of repetition of standard elements. For example, one early application in the United States was by William W. Bond and Associates of Memphis to produce drawings for motel buildings in the extensive Holiday Inn chain (Progressive Architecture 1968). Floor layouts for multi-story office buildings provide another particularly appropriate application, since there is a great deal of repetition from floor to floor, and the number of different graphic elements is fairly limited. A number of systems for this type of application are in

DESK1

X	Y	Rotation
5.0	21.0	90.0
11.0	21.0	180.0
11.0	15.0	270.0
5.0	15.0	0.0

DESK2

X	Y	Rotation
20.0	16.5	90.0
22.5	21.0	150.0
27.5	21.0	210.0
30.0	16.5	270.0
27.5	12.0	330.0
22.5	12.0	30.0

DESK3

X	Y	Rotation
4.5	4.5	270.0
11.0	4.5	270.0
17.5	4.5	270.0
24.0	4.5	270.0
30.5	4.5	270.0

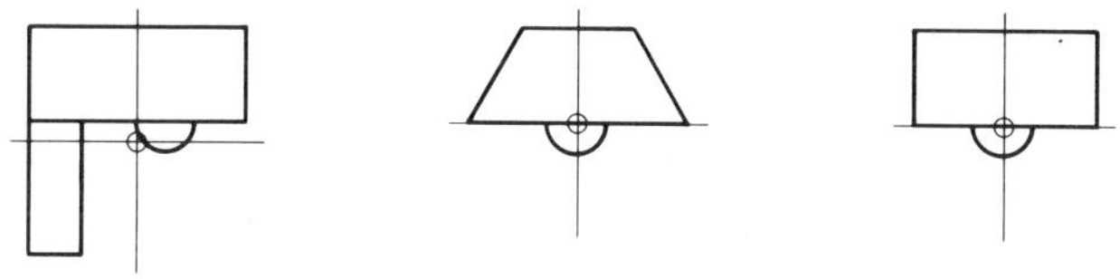

(a)

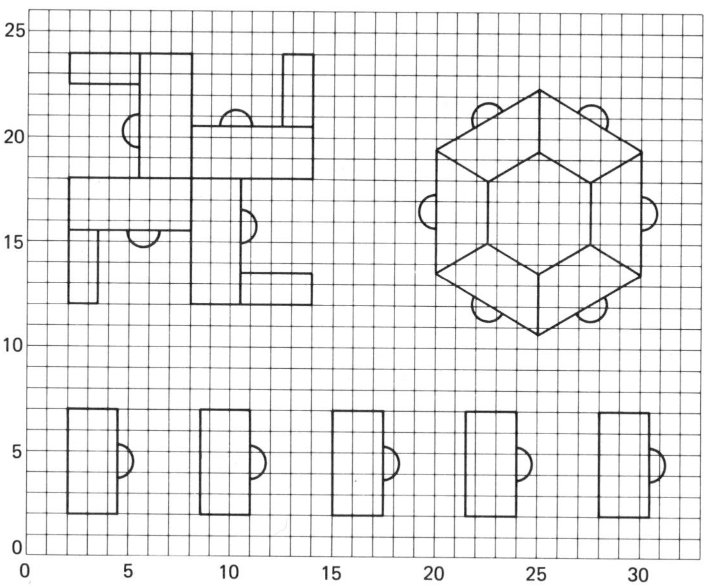

(b)

Figure 11.16 Typical plot generated by subroutine DESKS (building outline previously drawn). (a) Data. (b) Resultant plot.

commercial operation (Girardi 1972, Lee 1973, Greenberg 1974). Some typical output is illustrated in *Figure 11.17*.

Most building description systems and integrated computer-aided design systems provide facilities for plotting working drawings. The production of working drawings from a project data base may be regarded as a process of *report generation*, little different in principle from the familiar function of printed report generation performed by data base management systems. In each case, the user specifies the in-

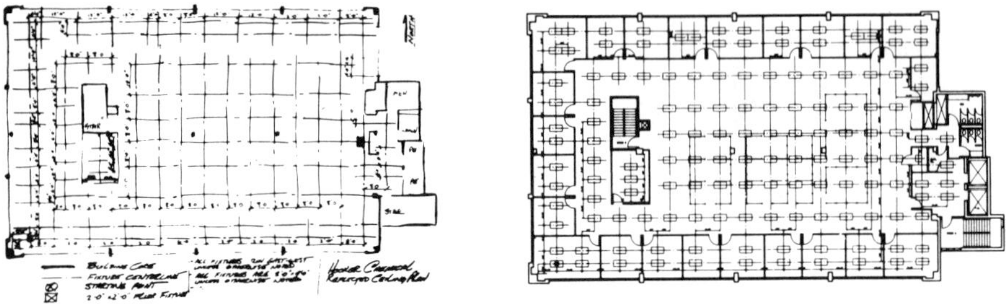

(a)

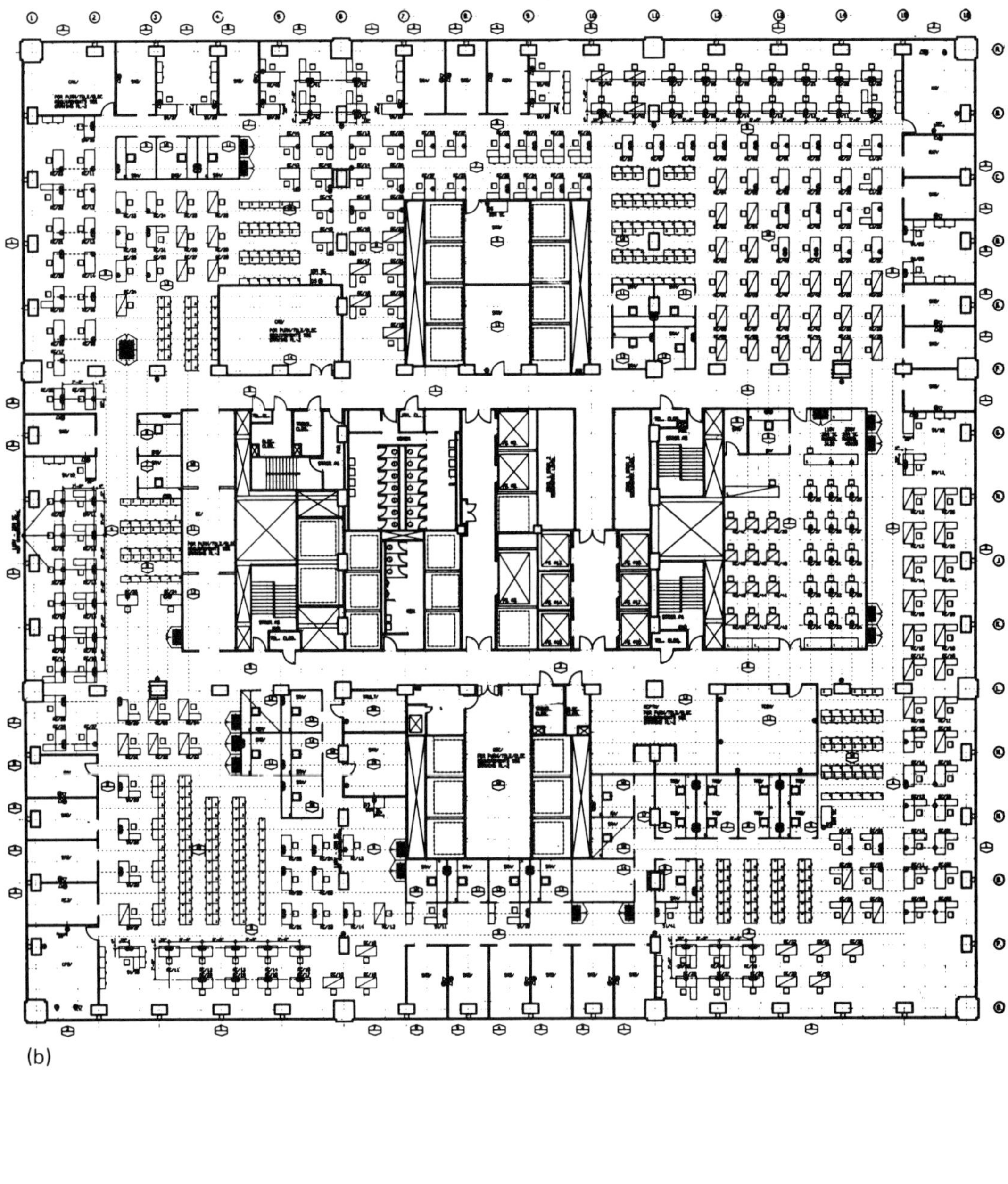

(b)

formation to be output, and the format requirements. If flexible formatting facilities are provided, then reports (either alphanumeric or graphic) organized in a wide variety of ways can be rapidly and cheaply generated as required for different bidding, contractual, management, and on-site working purposes.

Figure 11.17 *(opposite)* Working drawings produced by SLS Environetics Inc.'s MAN/MAC drafting system. (a) Designer's rough sketch for digitizing, and corresponding working drawing generated by plotting standard graphic elements at the indicated locations. (b) An example of a complex working drawing economically generated by plotting standard graphic elements: a furniture and partition layout for Sears Tower, Chicago.

THREE-DIMENSIONAL GRAPHICS

Although graphic output consists of pictures on two-dimensional surfaces, buildings are three-dimensional objects. Thus, in architectural computer graphics we are often concerned not only with the manipulation of two-dimensional pictures, but also with the transformation of objects in three-dimensional space, and the *projection* of three-dimensional scenes onto two-dimensional surfaces. The three-dimensional transformation matrices were given in Geometric Transformations upon Point Matrices in Chapter 6, and will not be further discussed here. Projection techniques are described below.

Traditional projection methods

Architects are familiar with many different types of projections. Most commonly used are *plans, elevations,* and other species of *orthographic* projection, *oblique* projections, *axonometrics, isometrics,* and *perspectives* of various kinds (see Dubery and Willats (1972) for a comprehensive discussion). A cube drawn in a number of different projections is illustrated in *Figure 11.18.*

Traditionally, projections have been produced by means of geometric constructions. The Renaissance architect and painter Leon Battista Alberti is generally credited with the invention of the first accurate perspective construction (although there is evidence that at least some elements of the theory of perspective were well understood much earlier). Alberti described his *construzioni legittima* in the treatise *Della Pittura,* written in 1436. Alberti's construction treats the picture plane as a "window" between the viewer and the object, and imagines visual rays from points on the object intersecting the picture plane as they converge to the viewer's eye. Its principle is nicely illustrated by a diagram from Andrea Pozzo's *Prospettiva de' Pittori ed Architetti* (*Figure 11.19*) which was published in the 18th century. Modern perspective constructions differ in detail from Alberti's, but employ the same basic principle.

Surprisingly, a practical general method for construction of orthographic views did not emerge until the beginning of the 18th century. Gaspard Monge, a French military engineer, developed a technique which at first was a French military secret, but later became the basis of modern engineering drawing. Standard texts on engineering

Figure 11.18
Various projections of a cube. (a) Orthographic. (b) Axonometric. (c) Isometric. (d) Oblique. (e) Perspective.

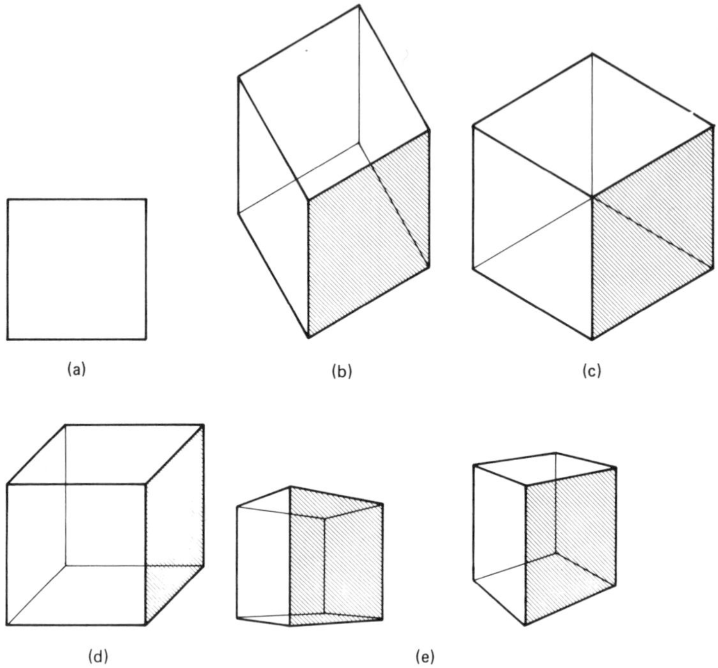

Figure 11.19
The principle of Alberti's perspective construction (from Andrea Pozzo's *Prospettiva de' Pittori ed Architetti,* 1723).

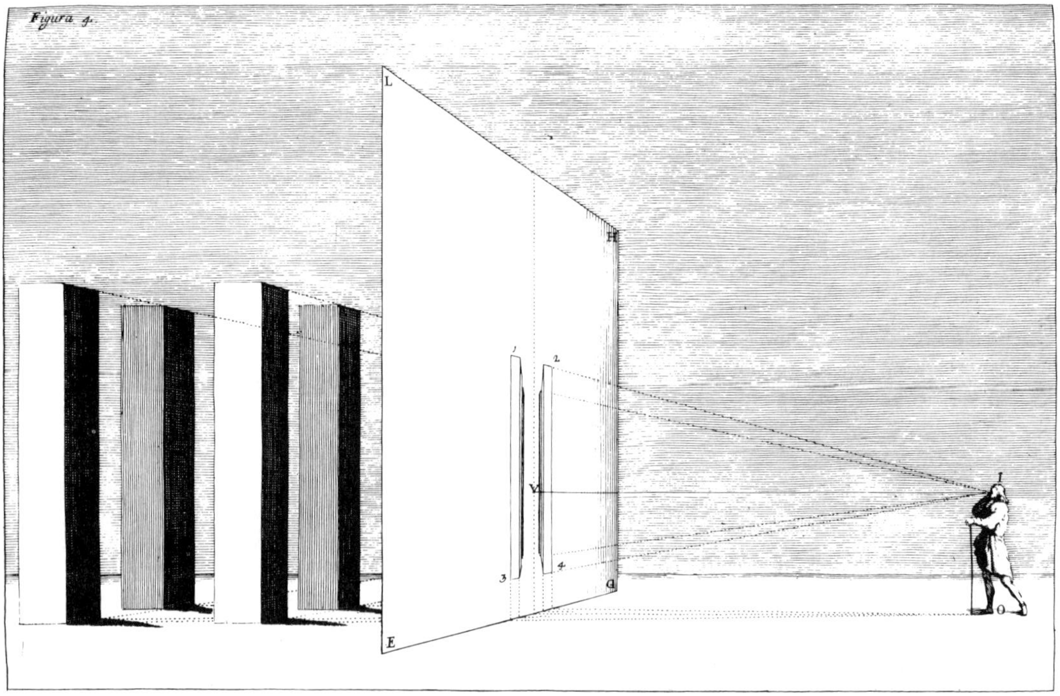

graphics (*e.g.*, Levens 1962) describe constructions for producing orthographic drawings in great detail. Constructions for isometric projection also go back to the early 18th century; their origin is usually credited to an Englishman, Sir William Farish.

These various well known geometric constructions are not employed in the production of projections by computer. Instead, coordinates are manipulated algebraically to produce equivalent results.

Orthographic projection

Orthographic projections are simplest to generate. An orthographic projection in the x,y plane can be produced merely by drawing the objects using x and y coordinates only, and ignoring the z values. Similarly, a projection in the y,z plane can be produced by ignoring x values, and in the x,z plane by ignoring y values. Thus an orthographic projection of an object can be displayed by (1) translating, rotating, and scaling the object so that it bears the required relation to the screen or viewport; then (2) drawing the object without regard to the values of the depth coordinates.

Perspective projection

Perspectives are slightly more complex. The object is first translated and rotated so that the viewer, the screen, and the object have the relation shown in *Figure 11.20,* and the object is described in terms of an *eye coordinate system* having its origin at the viewer's eye. (Note that the convention for labeling axes is that x_e and y_e axes align with the x_s and y_s screen axes.) The parameter a is the distance between the viewer and the screen, and b is the screen dimension. Screen coordinates x_s and y_s for any point of the object are then given by the following equations (Newman and Sproull 1973):

$$x_s = \frac{ax_e}{bz_e}$$

$$y_s = \frac{ay_e}{bz_e}$$

Two important properties of these equations should be noted. First, as z_e becomes very large, the ratio a/z_e tends to unity, so that the values of x_s and y_s vary little with depth. In other words, an orthographic projection corresponds to a perspective with the viewpoint at infinity. Second, the ratio a/b controls the values of x_s and y_s for a point at given depth z_e. In effect, this ratio controls the amount of foreshortening that will take place. If the ratio is high, the screen image will appear very foreshortened, as if taken with a telephoto lens. Conversely, if the ratio is low, a "wide-angle" view will be ob-

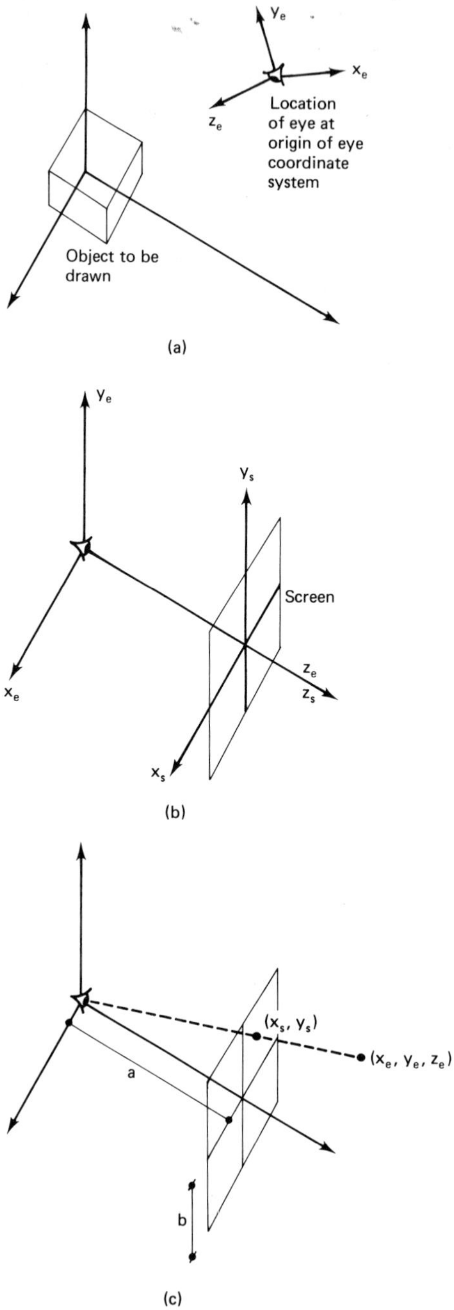

Figure 11.20
The perspective projection. (a) Relation of eye and object coordinate systems. (b) Relation of eye and screen coordinate systems. (c) The parameters a and b.

tained. "Zooms" can be executed simply by varying the ratio. The effect of greatest realism can be achieved if the *actual* viewer's eye really is at a distance *a* from the screen and the angle subtended at the eye by the edges of the screen does not exceed about 30°.

The perspective transformation described above may be expressed as a 4×4 transformation matrix. Full details of the derivation of the matrix are given by Newman and Sproull (1973), Rogers and Adams (1976), and Forrest (1976). BASIC subroutines for performing the transformation have been published by Rogers and Adams (1976).

By extension of the same general approach, programs can also be written to generate unusual types of perspectives such as the *cylindrical* and *spherical* perspective projections (Eichenberger 1970, Reggini 1974).

Three-dimensional clipping

Just as two-dimensional pictures need to be clipped to the boundaries of the viewport before display if unexpected and undesirable results are to be avoided, so perspectives must be clipped to the boundaries of the *viewing pyramid* (*Figure 11.21*). The generation of building *sections* may also be regarded as a three-dimensional clipping problem. A section is essentially an orthographic projection clipped to a specified plane passing through the building (*Figure 11.22*). Three-dimensional clipping is discussed in detail by Newman and Sproull (1973) and by Sutherland and Hodgman (1974).

HIDDEN LINE AND HIDDEN SURFACE ELIMINATION

The problem

When an orthographic or perspective transformation is applied to an opaque object, the result is a *wire frame* picture in which all edge-lines are displayed, whether or not they would be obscured by

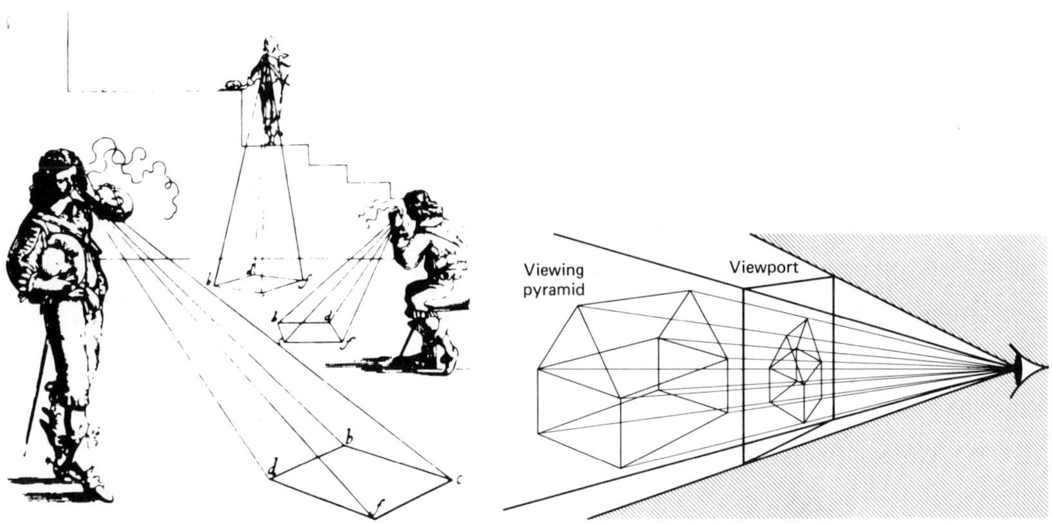

(a) (b)

Figure 11.21
Clipping to the boundaries of a viewing pyramid. (a) Viewing pyramids subtended by the viewer's eye. (b) Relation of viewport and viewing pyramid.

Figure 11.22
Sectioning a building. (a) Drawing of the church of Santa Sophia, Thessaloniki, from Auguste Choisy's *Histoire de l'Architecture.* (b) Views of a small house from various different angles, clipped to various different section planes (produced by BDS system, Institute of Physical Planning, Carnegie-Mellon University).

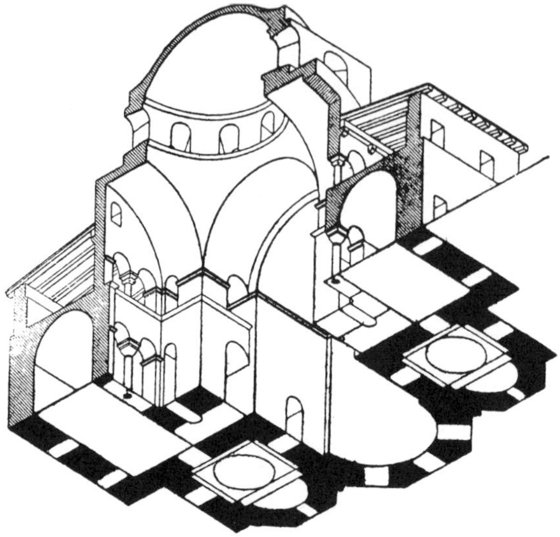

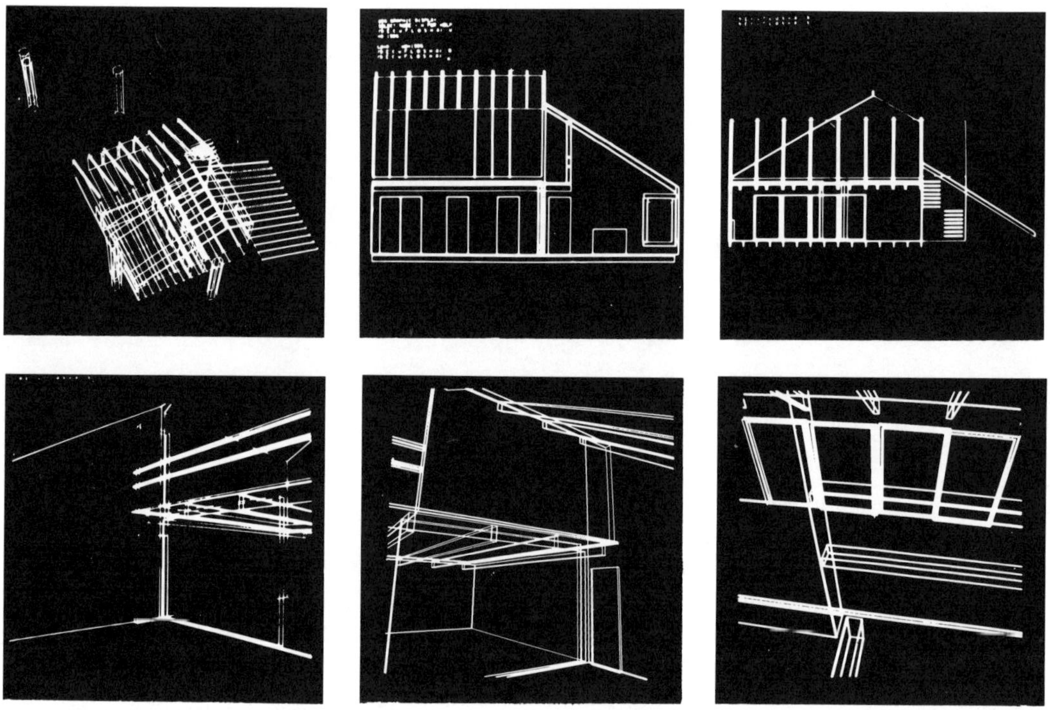

opaque surfaces and objects which lie closer to the viewer (*Figure 11.23(a)*). Wire frame pictures of complex objects are very confusing, and they are quite inadequate for most architectural applications. What is needed, for adequate display of complex opaque objects like buildings, is an algorithm for finding and eliminating all "hidden"

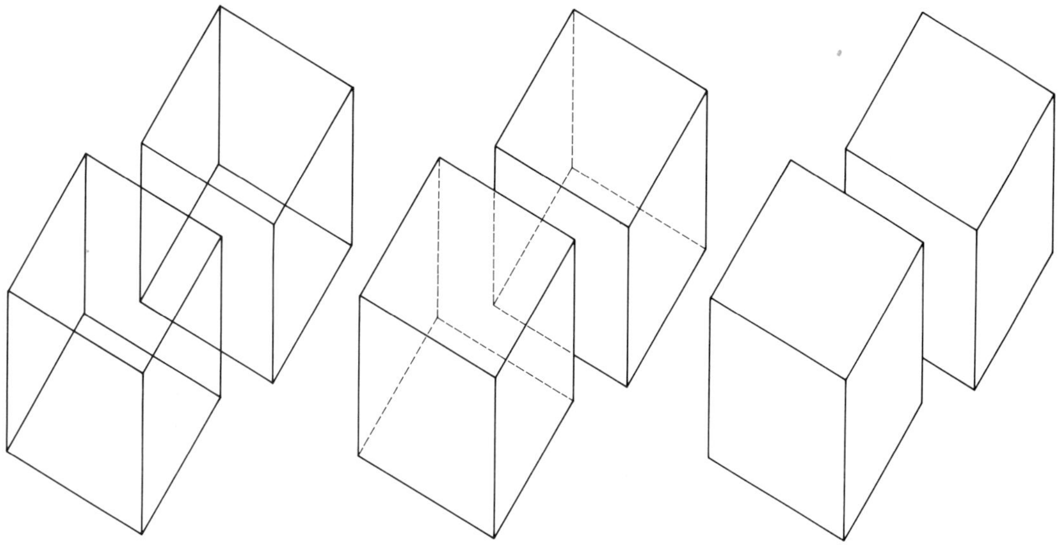

Figure 11.23
The hidden line problem. (a) Wire frame perspective. (b) "Hidden" edge-lines identified. (c) "Hidden" edge-lines removed.

edge-lines as shown in *Figures 11.23(b)* and *(c)*. Unfortunately, this is a difficult and time-consuming computational task, and the development of efficient hidden line removal algorithms has been one of the central research issues in computer graphics.

Where raster-scan displays producing shaded and/or colored perspectives are employed, the closely-analogous *hidden surface elimination* problem arises. In this case, obscured whole *surfaces* rather than just edge-lines must be discovered and eliminated. Because the hidden line and hidden surface problems are closely related, it is convenient to discuss them together.

Brute force solution

It is obvious that there exists a fairly straightforward "brute force" algorithm for hidden line removal; each polygon in the projected picture could simply be compared with every other polygon to determine whether any overlap existed. Clearly this approach would require $(n^2 - n)/2$ comparisons for a picture composed of n polygons. Thus the number of necessary comparisons grows quite rapidly with increasing n. A feeling for the rate of this growth can be gained by considering the numbers of comparisons necessary for "brute force" hidden line removal from a picture composed of arbitrarily arranged rectangular parallelepipeds, as shown in *Table 11.1.*

This exponential growth in the number of necessary comparisons of polygons makes "brute force" hidden line removal quite im-

Table 11.1
Numbers of comparisons required for brute force hidden line elimination in pictures composed of parallelepipeds.

Number of parallelepipeds	Total number of faces	Number of comparisons required
1	6	15
2	12	66
3	18	153
4	24	276
5	30	435
10	60	1,770
100	600	179,700
1,000	6,000	17,997,000
10,000	60,000	1,799,970,000

practical in pictures of realistic complexity. Thus a great deal of research effort has been devoted to searching for hidden line and surface elimination algorithms which are effective. Numerous such algorithms have been developed and implemented.

Use of coherence

In a definitive discussion of the subject, Sutherland, Sproull and Schumacker (1974) have demonstrated that all such algorithms capitalize upon some *coherence property* of the scene represented in order to achieve efficiencies. By "coherence" is meant the existence of some predictable pattern of relationships between elements of the picture. For example, some hidden surface algorithms oriented towards raster-scan displays capitalize upon *scan-line* coherence, *i.e.,* the fact that one TV scan line of output is likely to be nearly the same as the previous TV scan line. Algorithms oriented towards the production of animated displays often exploit *frame coherence, i.e.,* that the entire picture changes little between successive frames. Some algorithms suitable for architectural displays utilize *face coherence,* the property that individual polygons are generally small compared to the size of the display, and therefore relatively unlikely to conflict.

Example of a simple hidden line removal algorithm

To illustrate some of the basic principles of hidden line and surface elimination, one very simple and effective algorithm due to Paradis (1969) will be described. This particular algorithm removes hidden lines from a three-dimensional surface expressed as a square-gridded mesh (*Figure 11.24(a)*). It exploits the coherence property that portions of such a surface which are closer to the observation point cannot be covered by portions of the surface more distant. Thus it is possible to plot grid elements row by row in sequence, beginning from the nearest corner. The plotted area existing at any step can be treated as a polygonal *opaque region* bounded by upper and lower *horizons.* Subsequent lines to be plotted need only be compared with the outlines of the current opaque region, not with each individual grid element comprising the opaque region. The operation of the algo-

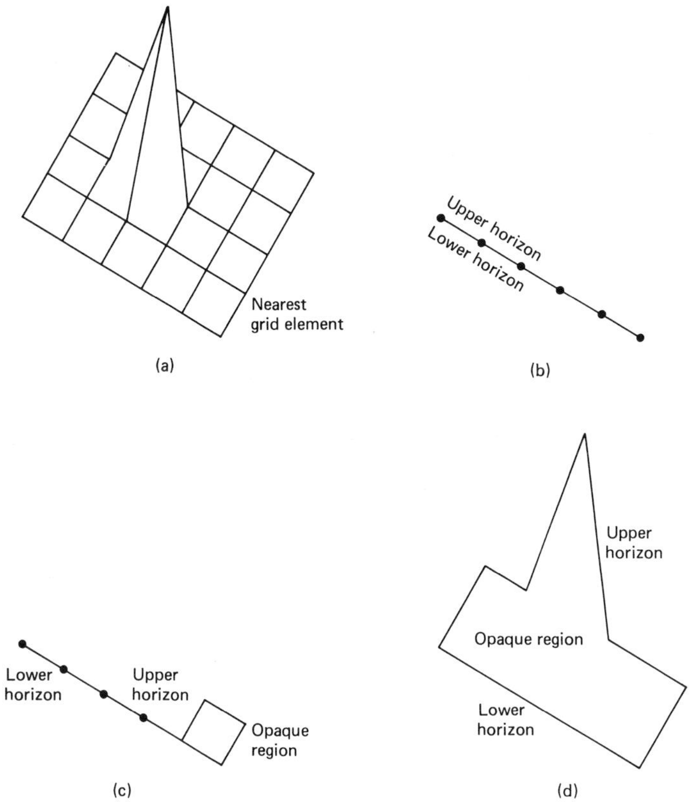

Figure 11.24 Operation of Paradis' hidden line removal algorithm (after Paradis (1969)). (a) Sample grid to be processed. (b) Coincident upper and lower horizons after the first row has been processed. (c) Upper and lower horizons after the first grid element of the second row has been processed. (d) Opaque region after two rows have been processed.

rithm is illustrated in *Figure 11.24(b)* to *(d)*. With this algorithm, processing time is close to a linear function of the number of polygons, rather than the rapidly growing exponential function characteristic of a simple "brute force" approach.

Comparison of available algorithms

The very high efficiency of the Paradis algorithm is made possible by the very high coherence of the type of scene to which it is applied; the polygons form a regular arrangement in plan, and an inherent ordering may be exploited. More complex and arbitrary scenes, like perspectives of buildings, are a good deal more difficult to handle. The first successful solution to the hidden line elimination problem for an arbitrary scene was developed by L. G. Roberts in the early 1960's (Roberts 1963). The Roberts algorithm is most effective for scenes composed of a collection of distinct objects (*e.g.,* aircraft), and is notable for its very effective use of linear programming techniques. Processing time grows approximately as the square of the number of objects in the scene. Subsequent hidden line elimination algorithms, introducing various new principles, were produced by Appel (1969), Galimberti and Montanari (1969), and Loutrel (1970).

All the algorithms discussed so far perform computations in *object space.* In other words, computations are performed to an arbitrary level of precision, independent of the size or resolution of the display to be generated. However, the level of precision achievable by carrying out calculations in object space is usually unnecessarily high, since the resolution of a typical display device such as a television monitor is quite limited. This suggests that substantial computational economies can potentially be achieved by carrying out calculations in *image space* instead, *i.e.,* calculating to the resolution of the particular display device to be employed.

Since the mid-1960's, a number of very efficient image space hidden surface elimination algorithms have been developed. A research group working for the General Electric Corporation produced a system, operational since 1968, which employs an image space algorithm in generation of real-time, moving, colored perspectives on a television monitor (Schumacker *et al,* 1969). This system was developed for NASA's Manned Spacecraft Center for use in visual simulation of such maneuvers as lunar landings. It has been experimentally utilized for the simulation of architectural environments (Kamnitzer 1968). Other effective image space algorithms have since been developed by researchers working at the University of Utah and at the Computer-Aided Design Centre, Cambridge, England (see Romney 1967, Warnock 1969, Bouknight 1969, Watkins 1971, and Newell 1972).

For the architect interested in practical production of perspectives of buildings, questions of relative efficiency of the algorithms, and of availability of implementations, become important.

No simple ranking of the efficiency of algorithms can be attempted, unfortunately, since relative effectiveness varies considerably with the type and complexity of the scene to be processed. A study by Sutherland *et al* (1974) has shown that all the algorithms referenced here are reasonably effective for use in relatively simple scenes, consisting of a few hundred polygons (*e.g.,* a simple rendering of a small building). Efficient image space algorithms (Schumacker, Romney, Warnock, Bouknight, Watkins, Newell) can practically handle images consisting of several thousand polygons (*e.g.,* a typical fairly detailed architectural rendering). However, the earlier object space algorithms (Roberts, Appel, Loutrel, Galimberti and Montanari) become impractically expensive. Only the Schumacker, Romney, and Warnock algorithms seem capable of dealing with very complex urban scenes consisting of 100,000+ polygons. Where real-time moving display generation is required, even the most efficient algorithms are severely limited, to at most a few hundred polygons.

Unfortunately, the publication of a new hidden line or hidden surface algorithm in the technical literature does not mean that it becomes available for practical use by architects. It must first be incorporated in some accessible implementation. There now exist numerous commercial architectural perspective services which utilize

Figure 11.25
An example of a plot produced by a commercial perspective program (Architect Frank Hope, graphics by Dynamic Graphics, Berkeley, California).

proprietary programs incorporating quite effective hidden line removal algorithms. *Figure 11.25* illustrates a typical result produced by such a service, at a cost competitive with hand drafting.* Most of the more sophisticated image space hidden surface elimination algorithms have been implemented for use with rather unusual and expensive types of display devices, and it is likely to be some time before these become commercially available at prices low enough to be of practical use to architects.

REALISTIC RENDERING OF THREE-DIMENSIONAL SCENES

In addition to removal of hidden lines and surfaces, a number of further techniques and effects can be employed to heighten the impression of reality reproduced by computer-generated displays of three-dimensional scenes. These include:

- Modulation of line intensity and focus with depth
- Realistic shadows, shading, highlights, etc.
- Color
- Movement
- Montage
- Stereoscopy

Modulation of line intensity and focus with depth

The creation of an impression of depth by modulation of line weight and quality is a technique very well known to architects and graphic artists (*Figure 11.26*). Although most types of displays are designed to draw lines of a single, fixed intensity, some have the capability to diminish line intensity or to make lines appear increasingly out-of-focus with increasing depth in the picture. Use of line

* Cost figures quoted by perspective services should be treated with extreme caution. A major component of total cost is the cost of preparing input data. If economies can be achieved in this step, *e.g.*, by composing the picture out of repeated similar elements, costs may be very low. Conversely, where such economies cannot be achieved, costs may be prohibitive.

intensity or quality as a depth cue is sometimes employed as a very much cheaper substitute for hidden line removal capability.

Pen plotters usually have interchangeable heads. By programming the plotting in appropriate sequence, and inclusion of instructions for switching heads, drawings with several different line weights can be generated.

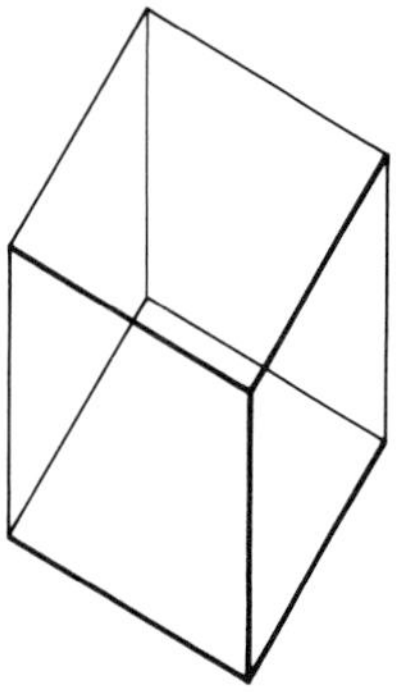

Figure 11.26
Variation of line weight to indicate depth.

Realistic shading, shadows, and rendering of surface

Rudimentary shaded pictures can be produced on a line- or dot-generating output device by means of cross-hatching or dot screens. However this approach is cumbersome, slow, and expensive. Furthermore, if attempted with a refreshed display, the large number of vec-

(a)

Figure 11.27
Shaded pictures (Henri Gouraud, University of Utah, Salt Lake City). (a) Faceted. (b) Smooth shaded.

tors will result in very severe flicker. Raster-scan display devices, such as television monitors and devices for generating photographic images, on the other hand, are very well adapted to the production of shaded pictures. Techniques of shaded picture production on raster-scan displays, combined with effective hidden surface elimination algorithms, have now advanced to the point where it is possible to produce shaded perspective renderings which are almost indistinguishable from photographs of a real scene.

The first task in generating a shaded picture is to calculate the *intensities* to be used in display of surfaces. Intensity is a function of very many physical and psychophysical variables, and accurate shading calculations tend to be complex and expensive. But quite acceptable results can be produced by use of simple rules like the following (Newman and Sproull 1973):

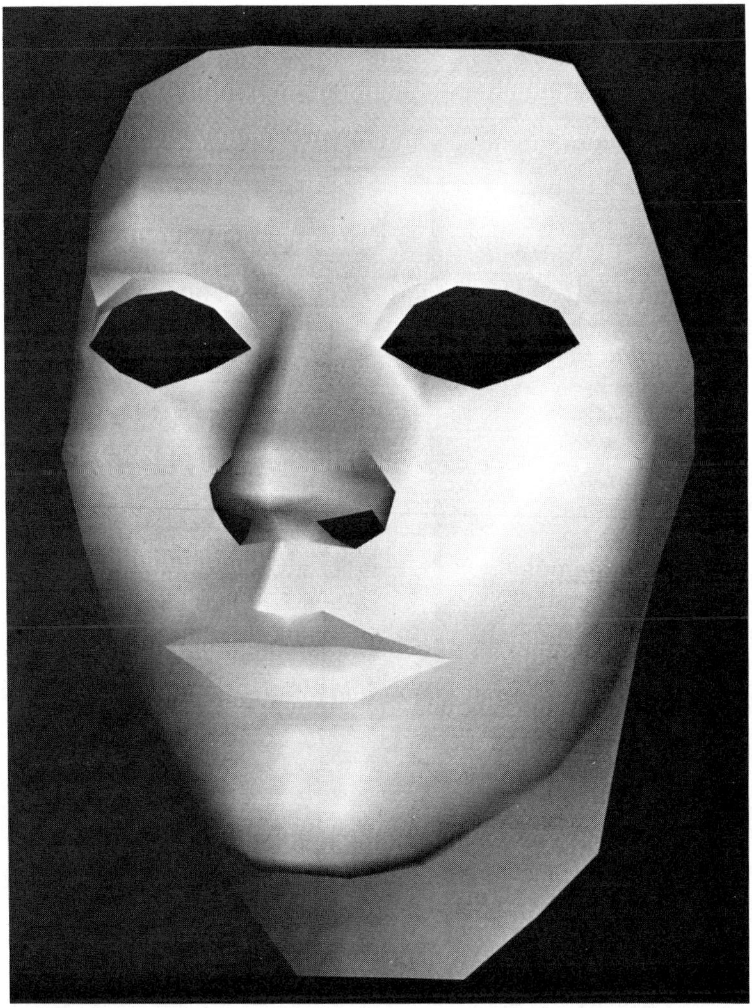

(b)

$$\text{Intensity} = a \cos \theta + b$$

where θ is the angle between a normal to the surface and the direction of the scattered light source, a is a parameter describing the reflectance properties of the surface, and b is a parameter controlling contrast.

Since curved surfaces must usually be approximated by polygons for computer representation and display, shaded pictures of curved surfaces present a faceted appearance (*Figure 11.27(a)*). However, by means of quite simple interpolation techniques (Gouraud 1971), the smooth appearance can be restored (*Figure 11.27(b)*). Further possible sophistications include rendering of highlights on reflective surfaces, and rendering of transparent and semi-transparent objects (*Figure 11.28*). All these have now been implemented by researchers at the University of Utah (Sutherland 1970, 1974, Resch 1974).

Realistic rendering of details of surface texture (brick patterns, wood grain, etc.) can in principle be accomplished, but in practice it presents severe computational difficulties. One reasonably effective

Figure 11.28
Curved transparent object, with highlights (University of Utah, Salt Lake City).

approach, developed by Catmull (1974), is to map photographs of texture patterns onto surfaces in computer-generated perspectives.

Cast shadows can be computed by performing a hidden surface computation relative to the location of the light source.

A special variant of the hidden surface problem, which is of particular interest in site-planning, is the generation of shaded representations of land form surfaces from topographical data (*Figure 11.29*). Practical algorithms for performing this task have been described by Yoeli (1967) and Brassel (1974).

Color

It is straightforward to include information indicating the colors of points, lines, or surfaces in a data structure describing an object. Some appropriate kind of "paint by the numbers" coding scheme can be employed. Through use of appropriate output devices, these codes can be converted into color output.

A plotter equipped with an interchangeable head loaded with different colored pens can be used as a very simple color output device. Some refreshed CRT terminals display drawings composed of colored lines. Raster-scan displays which produce colored output on a

Figure 11.29
A contour plot with hill shading added to render relief.

color television monitor or on photographic film have been in operation since the late 1960's. Used in conjuction with sophisticated hidden surface removal and surface shading algorithms, they are capable of producing spectacularly realistic displays.

A typical color code for a raster-scan display employs two bits to specify the intensity of each of the three components (red, green, and blue) of each point on the screen. Thus there are four possible intensities for each component, giving a range of $4 \times 4 \times 4 = 64$ different colors. This is sufficient for most practical purposes.

Movement

The dimension of simulated movement through an environment may be very simply introduced by generating an animated sequence of perspective views (by shifting the viewing point slightly for each frame). Simple line-drawing animations are quite cheap to produce in this way, and have been quite widely used in architecture and urban design. A more exciting possibility is to synthesize colored, half-tone perspectives, either for real-time display on a color TV screen or to produce animated videotapes or movies.

Real-time, half-tone, color display systems have been developed for simulation of aircraft and spacecraft landings, and ship-docking operations (Bunker 1975). They present a continuously moving "pilots-eye" view which alters in response to performance of various maneuvers. This requires generation of a new perspective about thirty times per second, a formidable computational task. Consequently, extensive use is made in these systems of special purpose hardware to achieve the required speed.

The pioneering system of this type was developed by General Electric, of Syracuse, New York, and delivered to NASA in 1967 (Elson 1967, Rougelot 1968, 1969, Nelson 1971). It was used for simulation of spacecraft maneuvers. Display capacity was limited to 240 polygons edges, and it did not incorporate smooth shading of curved surfaces. At UCLA, Peter Kamnitzer produced a film called *Cityscape* (1968), which demonstrated for the first time how this type of technology could be employed for simulation of movement through architectural environments. *Figure 11.30* illustrates a typical frame from this film.

In 1972, General Electric delivered a pilot training system to the U.S. Navy at Kingsville, Texas (Bunker 1975). This system incorporates three television screens, providing a 60° vertical and 180° horizontal field of view. The environment can contain up to 2,000 edges, of which up to 500 can be displayed at any one time. Smooth shading of curved surfaces is not incorporated.

In 1974, an even more advanced system was delivered to the U.S. Air Force for use in pilot training. A simulated cockpit is equipped with seven television screens, forming seven faces of a dodecahedron. The screens are 36″ in diameter, the largest ever built.

Figure 11.30
A frame from Peter Kamnitzer's 1968 film *Cityscape,* produced using General Electric's spacecraft landing simulator (School of Architecture and Urban Planning, UCLA).

The environment can contain up to 80,000 edges, of which 2,000 can be displayed at any one time. Smooth shading of curved surfaces is provided.

A number of firms now market half-tone, color image synthesis systems and services. General Electric of Syracuse produces computer-generated videotapes, which can be converted into film, from user-supplied data. Donald Greenberg (1974) of Cornell University has produced an animation of movement through the Cornell campus using this system. Some frames are illustrated in *Figure 11.31.* Evans and Sutherland Computer Corporation of Salt Lake City markets a real-time display system, which is driven by a PDP-10 computer. The MAGI group of Elmsford, New York has developed an extremely sophisticated system for production of animations. Currently these systems are all prohibitively expensive. Typical production costs range from hundreds to thousands of dollars per minute of animation. But it can be expected that costs will decrease in the future.

Montage

The techniques discussed so far have all required generation of the entire display by computer. Very realistic visual simulations of projects in their setting can be produced by using photo or video montage techniques to combine computer-generated perspective renderings with photographs of existing site conditions. A program for this purpose has been developed by the Cambridge Computer-Aided Design Center (Lever 1973). The system calculates the viewing parameters of the camera which produced the photographs to be used in

Figure 11.31
Some frames from a 1974 film by Donald Greenberg, which used a General Electric computer animation system to simulate movement through the Cornell University Campus (Program of Computer Graphics, Cornell University). (a), (b), (c) Observer "walks" across the Arts Quadrangle at Cornell University towards a new museum building by I. M. Pei. (d) Observer "looks back" from the museum.

the montage, using positional data of control points in the landscape. These derived viewing parameters are then used to plot a perspective. In this system, finished artwork must be manually produced from a line-drawing plotted by the computer. A more sophisticated system could utilize video montage techniques to superimpose a shaded raster-scan display on a video image.

Stereoscopic images and holograms

Computer-generated stereoscope images can be produced in a variety of ways. By slightly shifting the viewing point, right-eye and left-eye perspective images can be generated. These images can then be channelled to the appropriate eye by use of some kind of stereoscope arrangement, by an autostereo lenticular screen (Butterfield 1972), or by rapidly flashing right and left eye images alternately on the screen in synchrony with shutters in front of the eyes. Design applications of computer-generated stereograms have been discussed by Woolacott and Finney (1976), and Rogers and Adams (1976) have published BASIC subroutines for stereogram generation.

A particularly interesting possibility for architectural visual simulation is the head-mounted display (Sutherland 1968). This consists of a pair of head-mounted cathode-ray tubes channelling computer-generated perspectives to each eye, together with a system which enables the computer to sense the location and direction of gaze of the observer, and to adjust the display accordingly (*Figure 11.32*). Thus it becomes possible for the observer to walk around in a full-scale simulated three-dimensional environment. However head-mounted displays remain as yet in an early developmental stage; they are expensive in use of computer resources, and can only display crude and simple images.

It is often suggested that computer-generated holograms might be employed for three-dimensional display. But although holograms have in fact been successfully produced by computer (Jordan 1970), no feasible technique for generating holographic images of the size and complexity required for architectural applications has yet been developed or even seems likely in the foreseeable future.

GRAPHICS SYSTEMS

We have so far separately discussed the basic computer graphics operations: graphic input, production of graphic output, transformations, projections, and realistic rendering. In practice, it is useful to think in terms of *computer graphics systems* which integrate facilities for performing a number of these tasks.

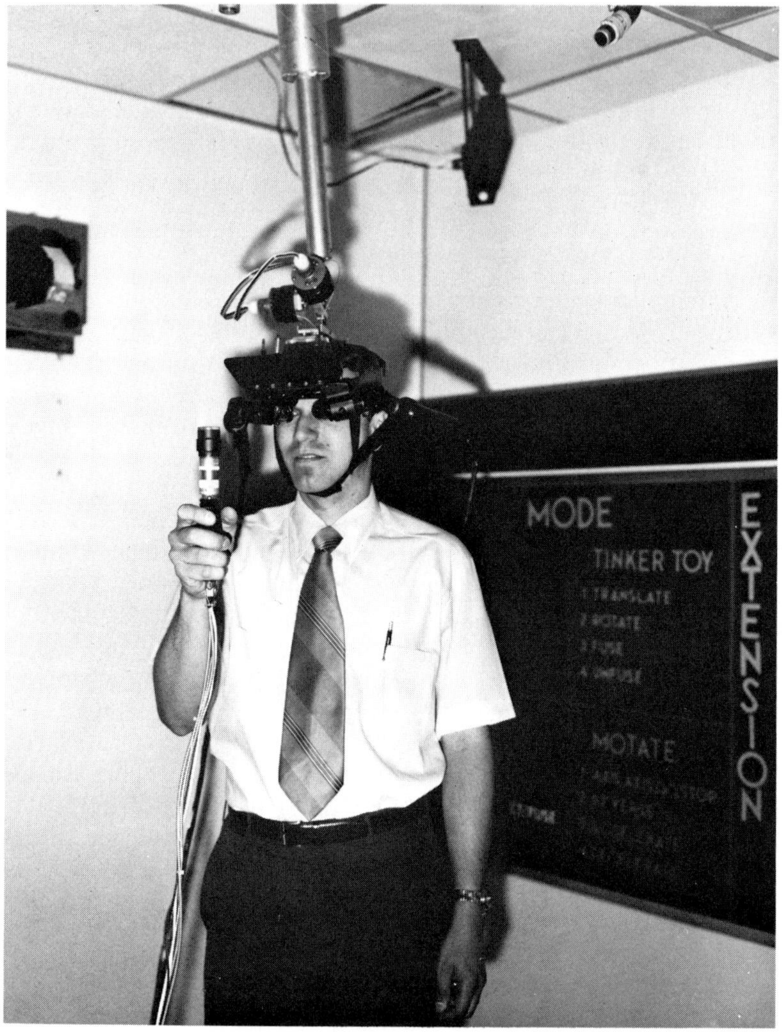

Figure 11.32
An experimental head-mounted display device at the University of Utah, Salt Lake City.

Elements of computer graphics systems

The basic elements of a comprehensive interactive computer graphics system are illustrated in *Figure 11.33*. They are the following (Newman and Sproull 1974):

Input devices used to provide data and control commands.

The *input handler* and *input routines,* software for dealing with signals received from input devices, making necessary adjustments to the application data structure, and passing control to other routines as specified by commands.

The *application data structure.* In architectural applications, this will normally consist of one of the types of building descriptions discussed in previous chapters.

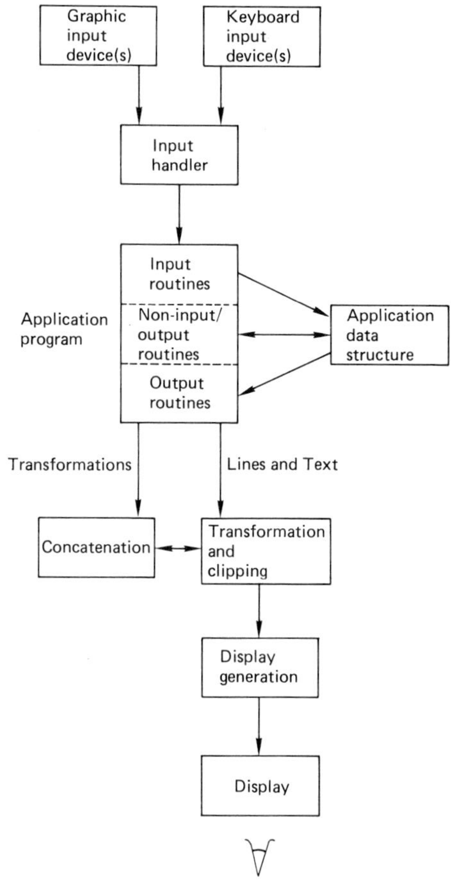

Figure 11.33
Elements of an interactive computer graphics system (after Newman and Sproull, 1974).

Application routines, which are employed to perform useful operations upon the application data structure, such as execution of structural and thermal analyses, performance of quantity take-offs, synthesis of floor plans, etc.

Output routines, which extract data necessary to generate a display from the application data structure, and define pictures to be displayed.

Transformation and clipping routines and the *concatenation routine* which combine to perform required transformations.

The *display generator* which converts the transformed and clipped information into signals to drive the display.

The *display* itself which physically generates the picture.

The input routines, application data structure, application routines, and output routines together constitute the *application program,* which is most often written by a user in a high level, general purpose programming language such as FORTRAN, ALGOL, or PL/1. The input devices and display together constitute the *graphics hardware.*

The input handler, transformation, clipping, and concatenation routines and the display generator together constitute the *graphics software system,* which is normally written by specialist systems programmers, and may be coded in assembly language or some unusual special purpose language.

Ideally, graphics systems should be designed so that application programs can be written in convenient, powerful, widely-used programming languages. The application program should be to a high degree independent of idiosyncrasies of the particular graphics hardware to be employed, and the application programmer should not need to have a detailed knowledge of the inner workings of the graphics software system. Unfortunately, these conditions are not met by many computer graphics systems, and this has proved to be a very major impediment to the development of effective architectural application programs.

Graphics software systems often appear in the form of either a *graphics package* (of subroutines which can be called from a user's program) or a special *graphics language.* Some examples are described below.

Graphics packages

A typical example of a graphics package is PLOT-10, developed for use with Tektronix storage tube graphics terminals. It consists of a set of subroutines which can be called from the user's FORTRAN program. Subroutines are provided for displaying points, solid and dashed lines, and text, for performing transformations, for clipping and windowing, and for accepting graphic input. The following is a typical example of a FORTRAN program which uses PLOT-10 subroutine calls. It draws an arbitrary figure whose coordinates are stored in the array XYLIST. Comments inserted in the program explain the various subroutine calls.

```
      SUBROUTINE FIGURE
      COMMON XYLIST (10,2)
      INTEGER XYLIST
C------ DEFINE SIZE AND LOCATION OF VIEWPORT ONTO
C------ SCREEN
      CALL SWINDO (512, 512, 512, 512)
C------ DEFINE SIZE AND LOCATION OF WINDOW ONTO
C------ FIGURE
      CALL VWINDO (67.,55.,200.,200.)
C------ INVISIBLY MOVE ELECTRON BEAM TO START POSI-
C------ TION
      CALL MOVEA (XYLIST(1,1),XYLIST(1,2))
```

```
C------ DRAW FIGURE
        DO 1 I=2,10
1       CALL DRAWA (XYLIST(I,1),XYLIST(I,2))
        RETURN
        END
```

The picture defined by this subroutine can be generated by execution of the call:

```
CALL FIGURE
```

Further examples of graphics subroutine packages are discussed by Gammill and Robertson (1973), Meads (1972), Rapkin and Abu-Gheida (1968), Sproull (1973), and Woodsford (1971). Some, like the OMNIGRAPH system described by Sproull, and the GINO system described by Woodsford, can be used with a number of different languages.

Graphics languages

An intrinsically more powerful and elegant approach (though more difficult to implement) than development of a subroutine package is to extend a high level general purpose programming language by adding graphics capabilities. An outstanding example of this approach is the EULER-G language (Newman, Gouraud and Oestreicher 1970), based upon Wirth and Weber's (1971) EULER. Using EULER-G, figures can be displayed by means of *display procedure calls,* for example,

```
FIGURE WITHIN [167,55,100,100] ONTO [0.5,0.5,0.25,0.25];
```

This draws a figure called FIGURE. The window onto FIGURE is specified by WITHIN [167,55,100,100], which means that the center of the window is at (167,55), and it has dimensions of 200×200. The viewport onto the screen is given by ONTO [0.5,0.5,0.25,0.25], *i.e.,* the center of the viewport is at (0.5,0.5) on the screen, and it has dimensions of 0.5×0.5. In this case the screen coordinate system has its origin at the center, and coordinates range from -1 to $+1$. Thus the viewport specified is in the upper right quadrant of the screen, as shown in *Figure 11.34.*

Other transformations and arguments may also be used. For example,

```
FIGURE WITHIN [167,55,100,100] AT [0,0] SIZE [1,1] ROT [3.14159];
```

displays the figure rotated π radians, at the center of the screen (0,0), onto a viewport of dimensions 1×1.

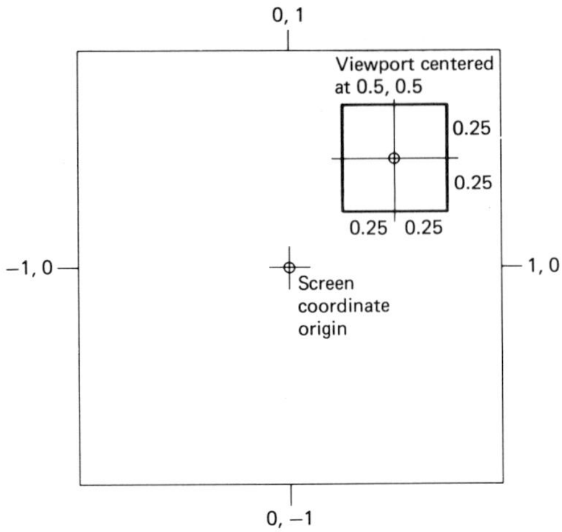

Figure 11.34
Viewport specified for FIGURE.

The procedure which defines FIGURE might be written as follows (where XYLIST is a list of coordinates):

```
FIGURE←*'BEGIN NEW I;
          MOVE TO XYLIST[1];
          FOR I←2 STEP 1 UNTIL LENGTH [XYLIST] DO
            LINETO XYLIST [I];
          END';
```

Further examples of languages extended to include graphics capabilities are described by Kulsrud (1968), Newman (1973), Sutherland, Forgie and Morello (1969), and Williams (1972).

INTERFACING PRODUCTION MACHINERY WITH COMPUTER GRAPHICS SYSTEMS

A logical extension of the idea that computer-controlled plotting or display devices can be used to generate drawings is the idea that computer-controlled machinery might also be used to produce three-dimensional scale models or even complete buildings. By combining both graphics and production devices with a computer in an integrated system, a very sophisticated design/production facility can be developed.

CAD-CAM

Automated industrial production machinery operating either under the direct control of computers or of computer-produced tapes is now widely employed in many fields of manufacturing. In some cases this production machinery is directly integrated with a computer-aided design system. In a computer-aided design system for designing computers as described by Adshead (1973), for instance, the output from the design system includes numerical control tapes for production of artwork and control of drilling and assembly operations. A number of systems, for example POLYSURF (Flutter and Rolph 1976) have been developed for interactive graphic design then generation of numerical control tapes for manufacture of curved-surface components. Integrated processes of this type are often referred to as CAD-CAM (Computer-Aided Design-Computer-Aided Manufacturing) processes. *Figure 11.35* illustrates a plastic foam model of a simple building, produced by a CAD-CAM system.

Applications to building component production

A very interesting system which illustrates some of the practical potentials of CAD-CAM in building design and construction has been implemented by the U.K. window manufacturing firm of Crittals, Ltd. (Hale 1968). It is designed to interface with production information for buildings in the SEAC (South Eastern Architects Collaboration) and SCOLA (Second Consortium of Local Authorities) industrialized building programs.

Operation is as follows. All windows included in a building are identified on architect's drawings by an 11-digit code, which describes type, size, construction, etc. Codes are taken off the drawings by a quantity surveyor, and a machine-readable file of codes is produced. This file is processed to produce collated priced lists, and other types of reports as required. The window units are produced on a special machine line. Shop instructions such as cutting, welding,

Figure 11.35
Plastic foam model of a simple building, produced by a CAD-CAM system.

and machine line instructions, itemized parts lists, etc. are generated by computer from the file of codes. To facilitate fixing on site, finished components are marked with codes, and are cross-referenced to computer-generated site instructions, such as bay location and sill layout documents.

The firm of Kellner Industries, in Fresno, California, has implemented a sophisticated, numerically controlled production line to produce timber wall frames. A computer system is used to generate control tapes, based upon architect's drawings. It is claimed that the production line runs at a nominal rate of 2,000 lineal feet of wall framing per eight-hour workday (enough for approximately 5 houses). Wall segments come off the line in reverse usage order, and wall segments for one house are bundled into a stack for trucking to the site.

At the University of Utah, Ronald Resch has combined an interactive computer graphics system for design and analysis of complex folded structural forms with a large flat-bed plotter equipped with cutting and scoring heads for production of components from sheet materials. *Figure 11.36* illustrates the steps in use of this system to design and produce a monument in the form of a huge Ukranian Easter egg for a small community in Canada.

Automated building assembly

It is easy to see, from these examples, the potential for integrating computer-aided architectural design systems with computer-controlled building component manufacturing processes. But the possibility for interfacing with complete automated building construction systems is rather remote. The process of actually putting the pieces of a building together, particularly that part of the process which must be carried out on site, requires the type of intelligent hand-eye coordination which at present can only be adequately provided by human operators (Simon 1966). No doubt current research and development efforts in the area of industrial robots which display hand-eye coordination (*e.g.*, Tenenbaum *et al* 1972) will eventually alter this situation, but it does not seem likely that fully automated construction of buildings will be a practical reality in the immediately foreseeable future. The first exceptions may be very special cases such as folded sheet or monolithic sprayed plastic foam structures, in which complex separate-component assembly procedures can be minimized or eliminated.

Plastic foam structures generated by computer-controlled placement machinery have been a popular topic of speculation among architects (Safdie 1970, Hilbertz 1971, Allen 1974). Moshe Safdie, for example, imagines a "magic housing machine," with which free-form curved plastic shapes are extruded from moving nozzles. A sketch by Edward Allen (*Figure 11.37*) illustrates a possible configuration for such a machine.

It is reported (Hilbertz 1973) that an attempt was made at a

Figure 11.36
Use of an interactive graphics system and flat-bed plotter to design and produce a complex polyhedral form (Ron Resch, University of Utah, Salt Lake City, photographs by Annette del Zoppo, Santa Monica, California). (a) Geometry of the object: an egg shape composed of triangular aluminum pieces whose size remains constant, and star-shaped pieces whose widths vary across the surface. (b) Use of interactive graphics system in design. (c) A display showing the surface geometry. (d) Manufacture of the pieces using a flat-bed plotter equipped with a cutting head. (e) Erection in Vegreville, Alberta.

(a)

(b)

(c)

(d)

(e)

design workshop held in Fargo, North Dakota in January 1973, to produce an ice building by use of a computer-controlled aqueous foam device. Three 65-foot telephone poles were arranged in an equilateral triangle 140 feet on the side. The poles were fitted with pulleys at the

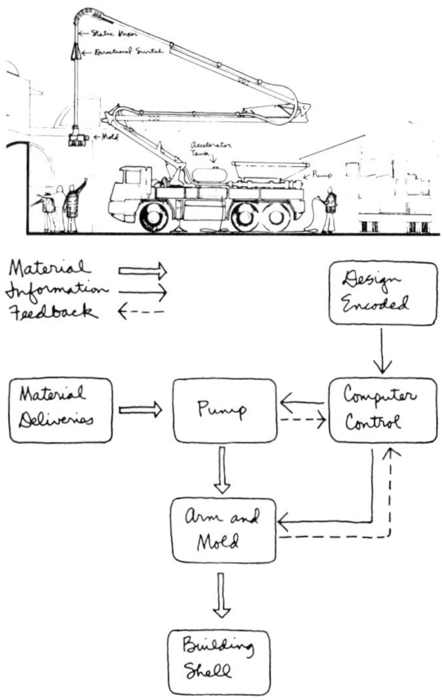

Figure 11.37
Sketch by Edward Allen for a computer-controlled continuous construction process.

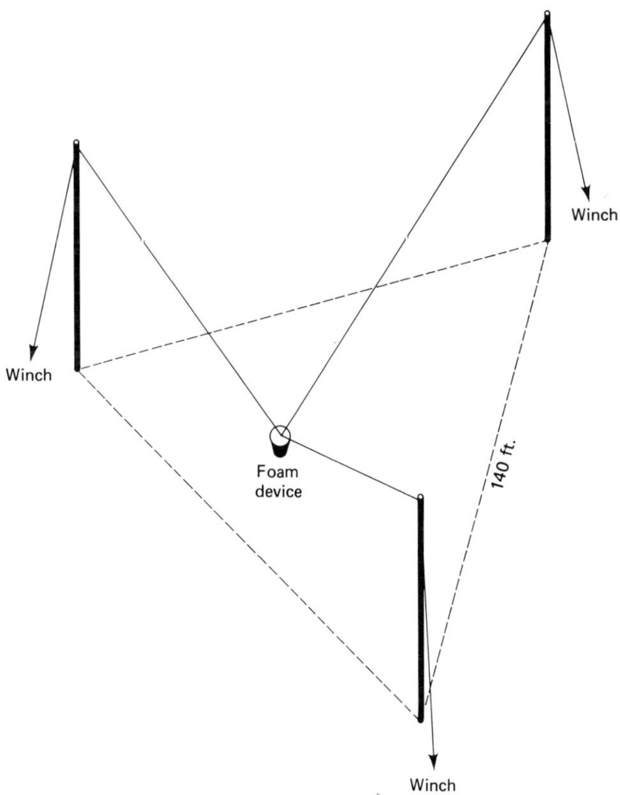

Figure 11.38
Configuration of a computer-controlled aqueous foam construction system designed by Wolf Hilbertz (1973).

top, and winches at the bottom, which actuated three cables running through the pulleys to support the foam generator (*Figure 11.38*). By manipulation of the winches, the foam generator could be moved to different locations and elevations within the triangle, and used to extrude a structural shape. The system was under the control of a Nova 800 computer, programmed to generate user-described forms. Apparently, "The system worked perfectly, and would have produced the first totally computer-built, manipulated and reclaimed structure, had it not been thwarted by the warm weather."

SUGGESTED READINGS

Greenberg, D. P. "Computer Graphics in Architecture." *Scientific American,* May 1974, pp. 98–105.

Guzman, A. "Decomposition of a Visual Scene into Three-Dimensional Bodies," in *Proceedings of the American Federation of Information Processing Societies.* Vol. 33. Washington, D. C.: Thompson Book Company, 1969.

Negroponte, N. "Recent Advances in Sketch Recognition," in *Proceedings of the 1973 National Computer Conference.* Montvale, New Jersey: AFIPS Press, 1973.

Newman, W. M. "Graphics Systems for Computer-Aided Design," in *Environmental Design: Research and Practice,* edited by W. J. Mitchell. Los Angeles, California: Proceedings of the EDRA3/AR8 Conference, School of Architecture and Urban Planning, UCLA, 1972.

Newman, W. M., and Sproull, R. F. *Principles of Interactive Computer Graphics.* New York: McGraw-Hill, 1973.

Newman, W. M., and Sproull, R. F. "An Approach to Graphics System Design." *Proceedings of the IEEE.* 62, no. 4 (April 1974), pp. 471–483.

Raphael, B. "Perception," in *The Thinking Computer,* chapter 7. San Francisco, California: W. H. Freeman, 1976.

Resch, R. D. "Portfolio of Shaded Computer Images." *Proceedings of the IEEE,* 62, no. 4 (April 1974), pp. 496–502.

Rogers, D. F., and Adams, J. A. *Mathematical Elements for Computer Graphics.* New York: McGraw-Hill, 1976.

Sedgewick, R. "Computer Graphics for Drafting." *Computer Graphics and Picture Processing* 3, no. 2 (June 1974), pp. 91–124.

Sutherland, I. E. "Computer Displays." *Scientific American,* June 1970, pp. 57–81.

Sutherland, I. E. "Structure in Drawings," in *Computer Aids to Design and Architecture,* edited by N. Negroponte. New York: Petrocelli/Charter, 1975.

Sutherland, I. E.; Sproull, R. F.; and Schumacker, R. A. "A Characterization of Ten Hidden Surface Algorithms." *Computing Surveys,* 6, no. 1 (March 1974), pp. 1–56.

PART 4

PROBLEM-SOLVING

Once the principles of encoding, storage, input, and output of architectural data are understood, the possibilities for development of programs to solve architectural problems of various types are virtually limitless. In this final Part, some of these possibilities are explored, and numerous examples of programs are critically analyzed. This cannot pretend to be a completely exhaustive survey, but it does attempt to cover the most central theoretical concepts and the most widespread and successful areas of practical application.

The sequence of topics roughly parallels the sequence of tasks and stages in a typical architectural project. Chapter 12: *Feasibility Analysis and Programming,* discusses computer-oriented techniques for problem structuring, feasibility analysis, and the space needs, interaction, and grouping analysis tasks which must be performed to generate and understand a program of requirements. Chapter 13: *Automated Spatial Synthesis,* focuses upon the generation of form in response to specified requirements. Chapter 14: *Performance and Cost Analysis,* deals with appraisal of the quality of proposed solutions.

12
Feasibility Analysis and Programming

The range of types of analyses that might be carried out at the feasibility study and programming stage of an architectural project is virtually unlimited. This chapter, therefore, does not attempt an exhaustive survey. Instead, some representative examples of successful applications of computer techniques to feasibility analysis and programming tasks are discussed, in order to develop a general understanding of the potentials for computer use in this area. Applications are grouped under four general headings: problem structuring, feasibility analysis, space needs analysis, and interaction and grouping analysis. Excluded are straightforward applications of the report generating facilities of data base management systems, which were discussed in Chapter 5; and standard statistical analyses, which are described in detail in any good basic statistics text.

PROBLEM STRUCTURING

The problem structuring task

The task of initial problem structuring in design has been described by Milne (1971) as follows:

The designer first tries to identify all the elements of his problem. These are the goals, requirements, constraints, or performance specifications which his final solution must satisfy. At this point, the situation seems to be in complete chaos. The designer's dilemma is not the lack of information; in fact, he is usually overwhelmed by more knowledge and more data than he can handle. Instead, his difficulty is the lack of structure. His task is to somehow organize all this information into a precise and consistent problem description, and then break it down into manageable sub-problems. By the process of articulating the problem elements and then establishing their relational structure, the designer begins to replace chaos and uncertainty with content and order.

Systematic problem structuring methods

In the early 1960's Christopher Alexander developed a systematic computer-based procedure for performing this initial problem structuring task, and published it in a highly influential book entitled *Notes on the Synthesis of Form* (1964). This was followed by an enthusiastic flurry of closely related research into the problem (Chermayeff and Alexander 1965, Bernholtz and Bierstone 1967, Miller 1969, Davis and Kennedy 1970, Milne 1970, Owen 1970). Since then, Milne (1971) has continued to improve and refine the technique, and has developed it into an efficient and reliable method that has been widely utilized not only in architecture, but also in planning and administrative science applications. The version of the technique which is described here is that developed by Milne.

The first step in the process is to write down a list of elementary problem statements. An example is illustrated in *Figure 12.1(a)*. According to Milne:

1 WILL NOT INCREASE CONGESTION ON ALREADY HEAVILY TRAVELED SURFACE STREETS

2 WILL NOT VISUALLY DIVIDE THE COMMUNITY

3 WILL NOT CREATE UNSIGHTLY STRUCTURES OF ANY KIND

4 WILL NOT CREATE NOISE POLLUTION

5 WILL NOT INTENSIFY AIR POLLUTION PROBLEM FOR LOCAL RESIDENTS

6 WILL NOT TRANSFORM THE CHARACTER OF THE PRESENT RESIDENTIAL STREETS

7 WILL NOT DIVIDE THE SOCIAL FABRIC OF THE COMMUNITY

8 WILL SIGNIFICANTLY REDUCE TRAVEL TIME FOR TRAFFIC THROUGH BEVERLY HILLS

9 WILL BE SAFE FOR PEDESTRIANS AND FOR SURFACE AND FREEWAY TRAFFIC

10 WILL NOT DISPLACE AN UNDUE NUMBER OF PEOPLE

11 WILL PROVIDE FOR RELOCATION WITHIN THE COMMUNITY

12 WILL NOT PUT FINANCIAL BURDEN ON ECONOMICALLY DEPRESSED CLASSES

13 WILL HAVE CONVENIENT ACCESS FOR LOCAL RESIDENTS

14 WILL ALLOW FOR FUTURE LOAD EXPANSION

15 WILL DISTRIBUTE INCREASE OR DECREASE IN LAND VALUES IN AN EQUITABLE MANNER WITHIN THE COMMUNITY

16 WILL PRESERVE NATURAL OR MAN-MADE AMENITIES

17 WILL PROVIDE FUNCTIONALLY DESIGNED FACILITIES FOR INTERCHANGE AMONG ALL THE VARIOUS VEHICULAR AND PEDESTRIAN SYSTEMS

18 WILL USE AIR RIGHTS

19 WILL INCLUDE LOCAL COMMUNITY PARTICIPATION IN THE PLANNING PROCESS

(a)

1	T																		
2	T	T																	
3	F	T	T																
4	T	F	F	T															
5	T	F	F	T	T														
6	F	T	T	T	T	T													
7	F	T	F	F	F	T	T												
8	T	F	T	T	T	T	T	T											
9	T	F	F	F	F	F	T	T	T										
10	F	F	F	T	T	T	T	T	F	T									
11	F	F	F	F	F	T	T	F	F	T	T								
12	F	F	F	F	F	F	F	F	F	T	T	T							
13	T	T	F	F	T	T	F	T	T	F	F	T	T						
14	T	F	F	F	F	F	F	T	T	T	F	F	F	T					
15	T	F	F	T	T	F	F	F	F	F	F	T	F	F	T				
16	F	T	T	T	T	T	F	T	F	F	F	F	F	F	F	T			
17	T	F	T	T	T	F	F	T	T	F	F	F	T	T	F	T	T		
18	F	F	T	T	T	F	T	F	F	F	T	F	F	T	T	F	T	T	
19	F	F	F	F	F	F	T	F	F	T	T	T	T	F	T	T	F	F	T

(b)

Figure 12.1
Steps in problem structuring using Murray Milne's CLUSTR program. (a) Elementary problem statements (for the design of a freeway to pass through Beverly Hills, California). (b) Interaction matrix (T signifies interaction, F non-interaction). (c) Some simplexes. (d) A portion of the final dendrogram.

```
THE SIMPLEX LIST

A SIMPLEX IS DEFINED AS A COMPLETELY CONNECTED SUBSET, THAT IS,
A CLUSTER IN WHICH EVERY ELEMENT INTERACTS WITH EVERY OTHER ELEMENT.
IN THEORY, A SIMPLEX IS THE SMALLEST "STRUCTURAL" COMPONENT OF THE PROBLEM.
IN PRACTICE, A SIMPLEX REPRESENTS A COHERENT FUNCTIONAL OR BEHAVIORAL
SUBSYSTEM.

THE NUMBER IN PARENTHESES IS THE NUMBER OF ELEMENTS IN THAT SIMPLEX


 1001 SIMPLEX ( 3) =     1   2  13

       1 WILL NOT INCREASE CONGESTION ON ALREADY HEAVILY TRAVELED SURFACE
         STREETS

       2 WILL NOT VISUALLY DIVIDE THE COMMUNITY

      13 WILL HAVE CONVENIENT ACCESS FOR LOCAL RESIDENTS


 1002 SIMPLEX ( 5) =     1   4   5   8  17

       1 WILL NOT INCREASE CONGESTION ON ALREADY HEAVILY TRAVELED SURFACE
         STREETS

       4 WILL NOT CREATE NOISE,POLLUTION

       5 WILL NOT INTENSIFY AIR POLLUTION PROBLEM FOR LOCAL RESIDENTS

       8 WILL SIGNIFICANTLY REDUCE TRAVEL TIME FOR TRAFFIC THROUGH
         BEVERLY HILLS

      17 WILL PROVIDE FUNCTIONALLY DESIGNED FACILITIES FOR INTERCHANGE
         AMONG ALL THE VARIOUS VEHICULAR AND PEDESTRIAN SYSTEMS


 1003 SIMPLEX ( 4) =     1   4   5  15

       1 WILL NOT INCREASE CONGESTION ON ALREADY HEAVILY TRAVELED SURFACE
         STREETS

       4 WILL NOT CREATE NOISE POLLUTION

       5 WILL NOT INTENSIFY AIR POLLUTION PROBLEM FOR LOCAL RESIDENTS

      15 WILL DISTRIBUTE INCREASE OR DECREASE IN LAND VALUES IN AN
         EQUITABLE MANNER WITHIN THE COMMUNITY


 1004 SIMPLEX ( 5) =     1   5   8  13  17

       1 WILL NOT INCREASE CONGESTION ON ALREADY HEAVILY TRAVELED SURFACE
         STREETS

       5 WILL NOT INTENSIFY AIR POLLUTION PROBLEM FOR LOCAL RESIDENTS

       8 WILL SIGNIFICANTLY REDUCE TRAVEL TIME FOR TRAFFIC THROUGH
         BEVERLY HILLS

      13 WILL HAVE CONVENIENT ACCESS FOR LOCAL RESIDENTS

      17 WILL PROVIDE FUNCTIONALLY DESIGNED FACILITIES FOR INTERCHANGE
         AMONG ALL THE VARIOUS VEHICULAR AND PEDESTRIAN SYSTEMS


 1005 SIMPLEX ( 5) =     1   8   9  13  17

       1 WILL NOT INCREASE CONGESTION ON ALREADY HEAVILY TRAVELED SURFACE
         STREETS

       8 WILL SIGNIFICANTLY REDUCE TRAVEL TIME FOR TRAFFIC THROUGH
         BEVERLY HILLS

       9 WILL BE SAFE FOR PEDESTRIANS AND FOR SURFACE AND FREEWAY TRAFFIC

      13 WILL HAVE CONVENIENT ACCESS FOR LOCAL RESIDENTS

      17 WILL PROVIDE FUNCTIONALLY DESIGNED FACILITIES FOR INTERCHANGE
         AMONG ALL THE VARIOUS VEHICULAR AND PEDESTRIAN SYSTEMS


 1006 SIMPLEX ( 5) =     1   8   9  14  17

       1 WILL NOT INCREASE CONGESTION ON ALREADY HEAVILY TRAVELED SURFACE
         STREETS

       8 WILL SIGNIFICANTLY REDUCE TRAVEL TIME FOR TRAFFIC THROUGH
         BEVERLY HILLS

       9 WILL BE SAFE FOR PEDESTRIANS AND FOR SURFACE AND FREEWAY TRAFFIC

      14 WILL ALLOW FOR FUTURE LOAD EXPANSION

      17 WILL PROVIDE FUNCTIONALLY DESIGNED FACILITIES FOR INTERCHANGE
         AMONG ALL THE VARIOUS VEHICULAR AND PEDESTRIAN SYSTEMS


 1007 SIMPLEX ( 4) =     2   3   6  16

       2 WILL NOT VISUALLY DIVIDE THE COMMUNITY

       3 WILL NOT CREATE UNSIGHTLY STRUCTURES OF ANY KIND

       6 WILL NOT TRANSFORM THE CHARACTER OF THE PRESENT RESIDENTIAL
         STREETS

      16 WILL PRESERVE NATURAL OR MAN-MADE AMENITIES


 1008 SIMPLEX ( 3) =     2   6   7

       2 WILL NOT VISUALLY DIVIDE THE COMMUNITY

       6 WILL NOT TRANSFORM THE CHARACTER OF THE PRESENT RESIDENTIAL
         STREETS

       7 WILL NOT DIVIDE THE SOCIAL FABRIC OF THE COMMUNITY


 1009 SIMPLEX ( 3) =     2   6  13
```

(c)

```
PROBLEM STRUCTURE


THIS SEMI-LATTICE STRUCTURE PRINTOUT SHOWS THE ELEMENTS THAT
"DROP OUT" AT EACH LEVEL, BUT WHICH ARE
CONTAINED IN THAT CLUSTER  AND ALL CLUSTERS BELOW THAT LEVEL


            +-+ 1010
            |    8 WILL SIGNIFICANTLY REDUCE TRAVEL TIME FOR TRAFFIC THROUGH
            |        BEVERLY HILLS
            |
          +-+   2004
          | |    3 WILL NOT CREATE UNSIGHTLY STRUCTURES OF ANY KIND
          | |   16 WILL PRESERVE NATURAL OR MAN-MADE AMENITIES
          | |
          | +-+ 1007
          |      2 WILL NOT VISUALLY DIVIDE THE COMMUNITY
          |
        +-+     3003
        | |      6 WILL NOT TRANSFORM THE CHARACTER OF THE PRESENT RESIDENTIAL
        | |          STREETS
        | |
        | +---+ 1008
        |        2 WILL NOT VISUALLY CIVIDE THE COMMUNITY
        |        7 WILL NOT DIVIDE THE SOCIAL FABRIC OF THE COMMUNITY
        |
      +-+       4004
      | |
      | +-----+ 1029
      |         16 WILL PRESERVE NATURAL OR MAN-MADE AMENITIES
      |         19 WILL INCLUDE LOCAL COMMUNITY PARTICIPATION IN THE PLANNING
      |              PROCESS
      |
    +-+         5003
    | |
    | |     +-+ 1020
    | |     |   11 WILL PROVIDE FOR RELOCATION WITHIN THE COMMUNITY
    | |     |
    | |   +-+   2006
    | |   | |    6 WILL NOT TRANSFORM THE CHARACTER OF THE PRESENT RESIDENTIAL
    | |   | |        STREETS
    | |   | |   10 WILL NOT DISPLACE AN UNDUE NUMBER OF PEOPLE
    | |   | |
    | |   | +-+ 1019
    | |   |      8 WILL SIGNIFICANTLY REDUCE TRAVEL TIME FOR TRAFFIC THROUGH
    | |   |          BEVERLY HILLS
    | |   |
    | +---+     3006
    |     |      7 WILL NOT DIVIDE THE SOCIAL FABRIC OF THE COMMUNITY
    |     |
    |     +---+ 1023
    |           11 WILL PROVIDE FOR RELOCATION WITHIN THE COMMUNITY
    |           18 WILL USE AIR RIGHTS
    |
  +-+           6002
  | |
  | |       +-+ 1027
  | |       |   15 WILL DISTRIBUTE INCREASE OR DECREASE IN LAND VALUES IN AN
  | |       |        EQUITABLE MANNER WITHIN THE COMMUNITY
  | |       |
  | |     +-+   2010
  | |     | |   12 WILL NOT PUT FINANCIAL BURDEN ON ECONOMICALLY DEPRESSED CLASSES
  | |     | |
  | |     | +-+ 1026
  | |     |     13 WILL HAVE CONVENIENT ACCESS FOR LOCAL RESIDENTS
  | |     |
  | +-----+     3007
  |       |     19 WILL INCLUDE LOCAL COMMUNITY PARTICIPATION IN THE PLANNING
  |       |          PROCESS
  |       |
  |       | +-+ 1025
  |       | |   12 WILL NOT PUT FINANCIAL BURDEN ON ECONOMICALLY DEPRESSED CLASSES
  |       | |
  |       +-+   2007
  |         |   10 WILL NOT DISPLACE AN UNDUE NUMBER OF PEOPLE
  |         |   11 WILL PROVIDE FOR RELOCATION WITHIN THE COMMUNITY
  |         |
  |         +-+ 1022
  |              7 WILL NOT DIVIDE THE SOCIAL FABRIC OF THE COMMUNITY
  |
+-+             7001
  |
  |         +-+ 1015
```

(d)

> All elements should be written at the same level of generality, should deal unambiguously with only one issue, should not overlap with other elements, and all the elements taken together should completely describe the problem, leaving no issues uncovered.

It is usually found that a satisfactory list of elements can be developed, especially if a group "brainstorming" session among members of the project team is conducted.

The next step is to define an interaction matrix, which shows interrelations between elements. Milne describes the process as follows:

> The designer establishes the relational structure of his problem by deciding which pairs of problem elements interact with each other. This decision is usually facilitated if the designer asks the question, "Will my solution of element 'A' either conflict or concur with my solution of element 'B'?" If the answer is "yes," an interaction exists. If the solution to element "A" is indifferent to the solution to element "B," then no interaction exists. The designer proceeds in this manner to test every pair of elements.

An example of an interaction matrix, for the list of elements shown in *Figure 12.1(a)*, is illustrated in *Figure 12.1(b)*.

The element list and the interaction matrix are then input to a computer program which employs an algorithm based upon graph theory to sort the elements into *clusters.* Each cluster consists of a subset of elements that are tightly interrelated by many links between themselves, but which have relatively few links to elements outside the cluster. Thus each cluster defines a relatively discrete subproblem. In the algorithm employed by Milne, the clusters may overlap to a certain extent. Some other algorithms produce completely non-overlapping clusters. Some clusters output by Milne's algorithm are illustrated in *Figure 12.1(c)*.

The algorithm next proceeds to hierarchically recombine small clusters to form successively larger clusters, printing out each new cluster generated, and eventually produces one large cluster which consists of all elements and represents the total problem.

In effect, the algorithm structures the set of initial elementary problem statements into a hierarchy of increasingly larger subproblems. To show the hierarchial pattern of interrelations between sub-problems, it is convenient to produce a *dendrogram,* as illustrated in *Figure 12.1(d)*.

The principles of Milne's structure finding algorithm, known as CLUSTR, are most easily understood if the interaction matrix is represented in terms of its equivalent graph, as shown in *Figure 12.2.* The clustering problem may then be understood as one of partitioning the graph into subgraphs, such that as few edges as possible are cut in the process. The initial partitioning into subgraphs is made by finding all *maximally-connected subgraphs,* or *simplexes.* A simplex is a graph in which every vertex is directly connected to every other vertex

	a	b	c	d	e	f	g	h	i	j	k
a	0	1	0	0	0	0	0	0	0	0	0
b	1	0	1	1	0	0	0	0	0	0	0
c	0	1	0	1	0	1	0	0	0	0	0
d	0	1	1	0	1	0	1	1	0	0	0
e	0	0	0	1	0	0	0	1	0	0	0
f	0	0	1	0	0	0	1	0	0	0	0
g	0	0	0	1	0	1	0	1	1	0	0
h	0	0	0	1	1	0	1	0	1	1	0
i	0	0	0	0	0	0	1	1	0	1	0
j	0	0	0	0	0	0	0	1	1	0	1
k	0	0	0	0	0	0	0	0	0	1	0

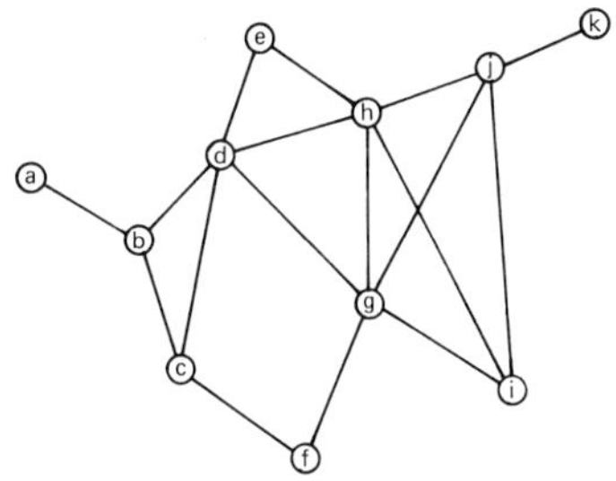

Figure 12.2
An interaction matrix and its equivalent graph.

(*Figure 12.3(a)*). Thus it represents the densest possible pattern of connections between a set of vertices. A large simplex of course contains smaller simplexes, but these lower order simplexes are ignored; the largest possible simplex which can be formed is taken in each case. Simplexes are not disjoint, but tend to overlap (*Figure 12.3(b)*), hence the overlapping character of the clusters that are produced.

To recombine simplexes to form large subgraphs, the following strategy is employed. Every simplex is compared with every other simplex, and in each case the ratio of existing number of edges to theoretical maximum number of edges in the resultant (not necessarily connected) subgraph is computed. For example, the graph shown in *Figure 12.3(b)* has 9 edges connecting the 5 vertices, compared with a theoretical maximum of $(5^2 - 5)/2 = 10$ edges for a 5 vertex graph. Thus the ratio is 0.9. The pair with the highest ratio is then combined. Successive applications of this procedure to the set of

Figure 12.3
Simplexes and their combination. (a) Simplexes of order 1 to 6. (b) Overlap of simplexes.

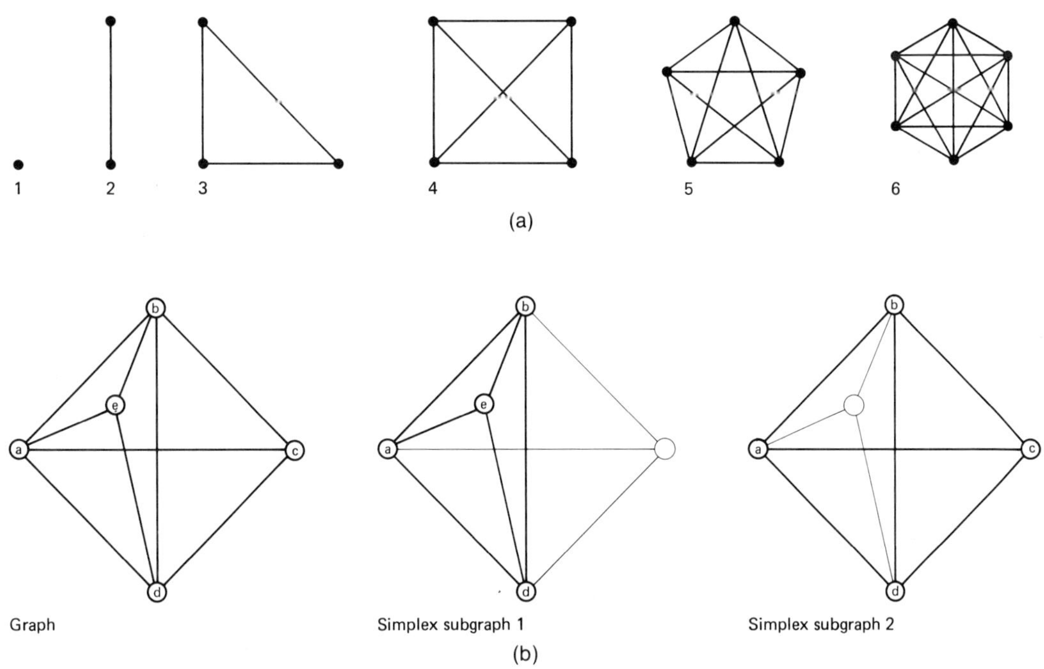

subgraphs generates a hierarchy of successively larger and more sparsely connected subgraphs. Combinatorial strategies of the type followed by CLUSTR are notoriously difficult computationally, but the procedures employed are quite efficient, and the program can handle problems of up to about 100 elements without difficulty.

Limitations of systematic problem structuring methods

In common with other techniques for revealing structure in data, for example, factor analysis and multi-dimensional scaling, the theoretical foundations for this type of analysis are more obscure and controversial than one would like. But there seems to be little doubt that, carefully applied, it can produce very useful results in practical situations. The principal disadvantage is that it is a very laborious and somewhat error-prone technique. It usually takes quite a lot of effort to develop an initial list of elements. Even worse, the number of potential interactions between elements grows as an exponent of the number of elements, and filling out the interaction matrix can take an excessive amount of time. For example, in a problem of 100 elements, very conservatively allowing 30 seconds to make each interaction decision, it takes over 40 hours to complete the matrix. A further criticism that can be made is that it takes an unrealistically static view of the design process. It is assumed that criteria can be fairly completely stated at the very beginning of the design process. But as we saw in Chapter 2, many important criteria may only be revealed by actually engaging in the search for a solution. Because of these restrictions, problem structuring methods are most appropriate for use in the initial stages of new and complex problems, where previous experience and existing prototype solutions provide little guidance.

FEASIBILITY ANALYSIS

Feasibility analysis problems

Feasibility analysis is becoming an increasingly crucial step in design and construction processes. It is at the feasibility analysis stage that the basic parameters of a project are set, and critical design constraints and objectives are established. Traditionally, feasibility analysis for building construction projects has relied primarily upon experience and informed professional judgment. Today, some very powerful computer-based mathematical techniques are available to assist. They do not reduce or eliminate the need for accurate basic information and sound judgment as the basis for decision making, but they do enable the implications of available information to be rigorously and exhaustively explored.

The first step in the mathematical formulation of a feasibility analysis problem for computer solution is to list the key decision variables, parameters and constraints. For example, key decision variables in a simple feasibility analysis for a high rise office building might be plan area, number of floors, and general standard of construction. Parameters might include land cost, construction cost, interest rates, etc. Constraints on height, total floor area, etc., might be set by building codes. Next, a mathematical model which interrelates the key decision variables, parameters, and constraints is constructed. The model is then manipulated for the purposes of *enumeration* of ranges of feasible solutions, *evaluation* of options against various criteria, *optimization* of an objective, or *sensitivity analysis* to explore the effects of variations in the values of key variables, parameters, and constraints.

Although some simple feasibility analysis calculations can be carried out by hand or with the aid of an electronic calculator, larger and more complex analyses necessitate use of a computer. The following subsections describe some important computer-based mathematical feasibility analysis techniques, and discuss examples of their use.

Morphological analysis

Undoubtedly the simplest and most general of all useful feasibility analysis techniques is *morphological analysis.* To perform a morphological analysis, the design variables to be considered are first listed, together with the range of potential alternatives for each one. For example, the variables and alternatives for a house might be:

Variable	*Alternatives*
Wall construction	1. Brick
	2. Concrete block
	3. Precast concrete panels
	4. Timber stud framing
Floor construction	1. Concrete slab
	2. Timber
Roofing	1. Bituminous
	2. Metal
	3. Terra-cotta

An exhaustive catalogue of potential solutions (not all of which are necessarily feasible) can then be generated by systematically enumerating and listing combinations of alternatives, as shown in *Figure 12.4.* Of course in this simple example, the enumeration could easily be performed by hand. But where there are more variables and alternatives, it becomes worthwhile to use a computer to generate and print out the catalogue.

The purpose of morphological analysis is to insure that the

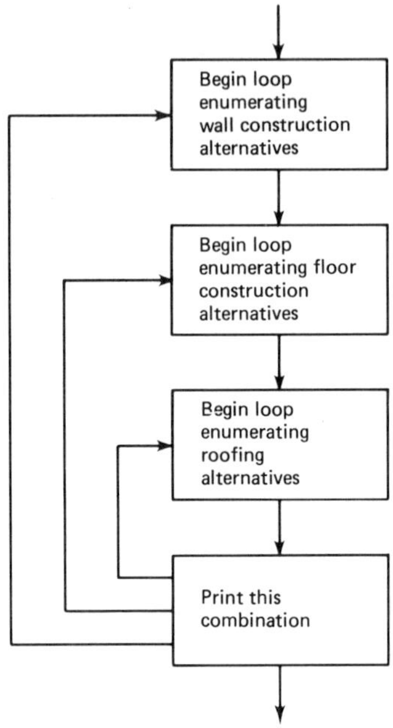

Figure 12.4
A procedure for exhaustive enumeration of potential house types.

complete range of potential solutions is brought explicitly to the decision maker's attention, and to suggest possibilities that might otherwise be overlooked. Although it may appear rather simple-minded, and it is obviously very limited by the rapid growth in combinatorial possibilities as the numbers of variables and alternatives increase, it has been widely and successfully employed in a number of fields. For example, Zwicky (1962) has discussed its use in the design of rocket propulsion system, Norris (1963) employed it in the design of racing cars and boats, Bridgwater (1968) and Gregory (1969) have described applications in chemical process plant design, Jantsch (1967), Ayres (1969), and others have advocated its use in technological forecasting, and Turley, Richardson and Hanse (1975) have reported an application to health care systems planning.

Method of incompatibility matrices

A great disadvantage of the morphological analysis technique is that it often generates large numbers of nonsensical or infeasible combinations. It would be a considerable improvement if these could be automatically eliminated. The *method of incompatibility matrices* provides a powerful and efficient way of doing this.

The basic assumption underlying the method of incompatibility matrices is that most nonsensical or infeasible solutions arise because of the existence of *pairwise incompatibilities* between alternatives. A pairwise incompatibility exists if an alternative *a* of variable A cannot be combined with an alternative *b* of variable B.

Pairwise incompatibilities between alternatives are most conveniently described by means of binary *incompatibility matrices.* The rows of an incompatibility matrix represent the alternatives for one variable, and the columns the alternatives for another. An entry of 1 in the matrix indicates that the corresponding alternatives are compatible, and an entry of 0 indicates that they are not. Where there are n variables, then $(n^2 - n)/2$ matrices are required to define all compatibilities and incompatibilities.

The following simple example, taken from an actual project, illustrates the use of incompatibility matrices. The task was to investigate stereoscopic simulation systems which might be employed for museum displays. The fundamental principle of stereoscopy is that slightly differing perspective images must be separately channelled to the viewer's right and left eyes. The basic variables which characterize different stereoscopic display systems are (1) image production method; (2) image separation method, and (3) image viewing method.

Investigation revealed the following ranges of alternatives for each variable:

1. *Image production method*
   1. Printed (drawings, photographs, etc.)
   2. Projected (slides and films)
   3. Electronic (television, CRT displays, etc.)
2. *Image separation method*
   1. Side-by-side images
   2. Cross-polarized or complementary-colored superimposed images
   3. Alternate narrow vertical strips of right and left eye images
   4. Time sequence of rapidly alternating right and left eye images
3. *Image viewing method*
   1. Viewing hoods (*e.g.*, stereoscopes)
   2. Cross-polarized or complementary-colored spectacles
   3. Lenticular screens (as used in 3D postcards)

Incompatibilities between alternatives arise because of the physical principles involved, and out of technological considerations. The following incompatibility matrices were defined.

Matrix 1

		Separation			
		1	2	3	4
Production	1	1	1	1	0
	2	1	1	1	1
	3	1	1	1	1

Matrix 2

		Viewing 1	2	3
Production	1	1	1	1
	2	1	1	1
	3	1	1	1

Matrix 3

		Viewing 1	2	3
Separation	1	1	0	0
	2	1	1	0
	3	0	1	1
	4	1	1	0

When incompatibility matrices have been defined, the total *number* of feasible solutions can be found by a simple matrix manipulation procedure (Harary *et al* 1965). Of more interest in this context, however, is the possibility of using incompatibility matrices to implicitly eliminate subsets of potential solutions from consideration. The type of procedure shown in *Figure 12.5(a)* can be used.

The state-action graph for this problem, with the portion of the graph actually searched by the procedure, is shown in *Figure 12.5(b)*. It can be seen that search along any branch is terminated as soon as a vertex representing an incompatible combination of alternatives is encountered, since all combinations springing from that vertex must contain the same incompatible pair. Thus feasible solutions are exhaustively enumerated without searching the entire tree. Where the tree is large, the amount of searching that can be eliminated in this way may be very significant.

Luckman (1969) has published a detailed discussion of use of the method of incompatibility matrices in architectural design. Friend and Jessop (1969) have discussed applications to urban design and planning. Ehrenkrantz (1975) has discussed use of incompatibility matrices in large scale system building projects.

Figure 12.5 (*opposite*) An exhaustive enumeration procedure (for the display system design problem) which makes use of incompatibility matrices to implicitly eliminate subsets of potential solutions from consideration. (a) Flow diagram of the enumeration procedure. (b) State-action tree explored by the procedure shown in (a). White vertices indicate combinations of alternatives containing incompatabilities. Heavy edges show the portion of the tree which is actually traversed.

Optimization by enumeration

Morphological analysis makes explicit the complete range of potential solutions. The method of incompatibility matrices introduces feasibility considerations. Further refinements are to incorporate *resource constraints,* and to utilize a measure of *performance,* which is a function of the design variables and the parameters of the problem, and which can be employed to rank feasible solutions in order of desirability.

A variety of different measures of the "cost" of a project may be

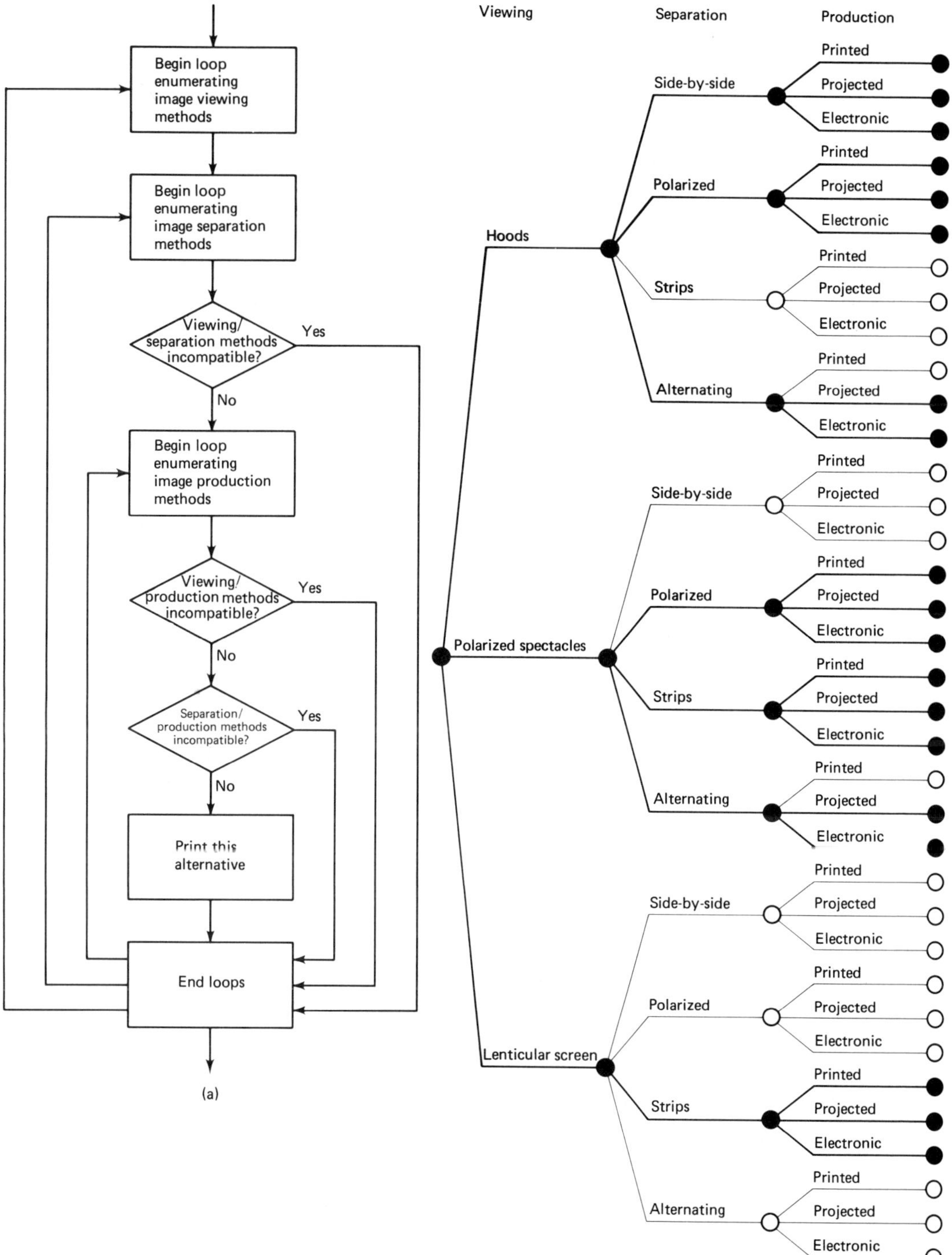

Begin loop enumerating image viewing methods
Begin loop enumerating image separation methods
Viewing/ separation methods incompatible?
Yes
No
Begin loop enumerating image production methods
Viewing/ production methods incompatible?
Yes
No
Separation/ production methods incompatible?
Yes
No
Print this alternative
End loops
Viewing
Separation
Production
Hoods
Polarized spectacles
Lenticular screen
Side-by-side
Polarized
Strips
Alternating
Printed
Projected
Electronic

(a) (b)

employed in stating resource constraints and in defining the objective to be optimized. The most common is simply *initial construction cost.* Its limitations are obvious, and there have consequently been many attempts to overcome them by performing economic analyses over the lifetime of the building in various ways, taking into account such factors as expected building life, maintenance costs, interest rate, taxation, and risks involved. These result in measures of *cost-in-use* which bring to the present all future costs in such a way that comparisons can be made on an equal basis. Further widely-used measures include *cost-effectiveness* and *cost-benefit* measures of various types. Detailed discussions and comparisons of these different measures are given by Stone (1966, 1975), Markus, *et al* (1971), and Harmon (1973).

The particular forms of the cost equations employed in defining constraints and objectives, and the values of the constants in the equations, must be determined by study of the known costs of previously constructed buildings. Several interesting case studies in the development of such cost models have been reported. Nadel (1967) discusses development of a cost model for apartment buildings, to be used by the New York City Housing Authority. Tumarkin (1968) shows how regression analysis can be employed to determine constants in the cost equations, and analyzes several hundred hospital, educational, and dormitory buildings. Steyert (1972) has published curves expressing construction costs of high rise apartment buildings as functions of various different design variables.

The purpose of formulating a model of this type is to find an optimum solution, and perhaps to determine the sensitivity of the optimum to variations in design decisions, parameters, and constraints. The simplest way to do this is to utilize a computer program which systematically increments values of design variables through allowable ranges in order to exhaustively enumerate potential solutions. At each step, a check is made for compliance with constraints; if the alternative is feasible, the value of the objective is computed and the results are printed out. For example, the procedure shown in *Figure 12.6(a)* might be employed to perform a simple analysis of a high rise office building. The building is assumed to be rectangular in plan, and the design variables are plan length, plan width, and number of stories. The permissible ranges of variation are:

Figure 12.6 (*opposite*) Flow diagram of a simple program for computing the optimum size of an office building by exhaustive enumeration. (a) Procedure for enumerating all feasible solutions. (b) Procedure for producing only the optimum solution.

LENGTH	$80' - 100'$
WIDTH	$80' - 120'$
STORIES	$15 - 50$

A four-foot square plan module is to be employed. Thus there are $5 \times 10 \times 35 = 1{,}750$ potential solutions. There is a constraint on total floor area, and the objective is to maximize percentage return on investment, computed as a function of floor area. The procedure essentially consists of three nested loops. If desired, it can be modified to produce only the optimum solution as shown in *Figure 12.6(b)*.

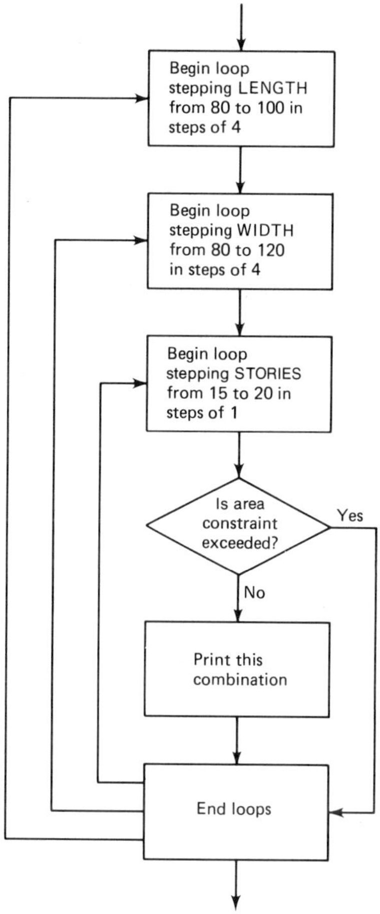
Begin loop stepping LENGTH from 80 to 100 in steps of 4
Begin loop stepping WIDTH from 80 to 120 in steps of 4
Begin loop stepping STORIES from 15 to 20 in steps of 1
Is area constraint exceeded?
Yes
No
Print this combination
End loops

(a)

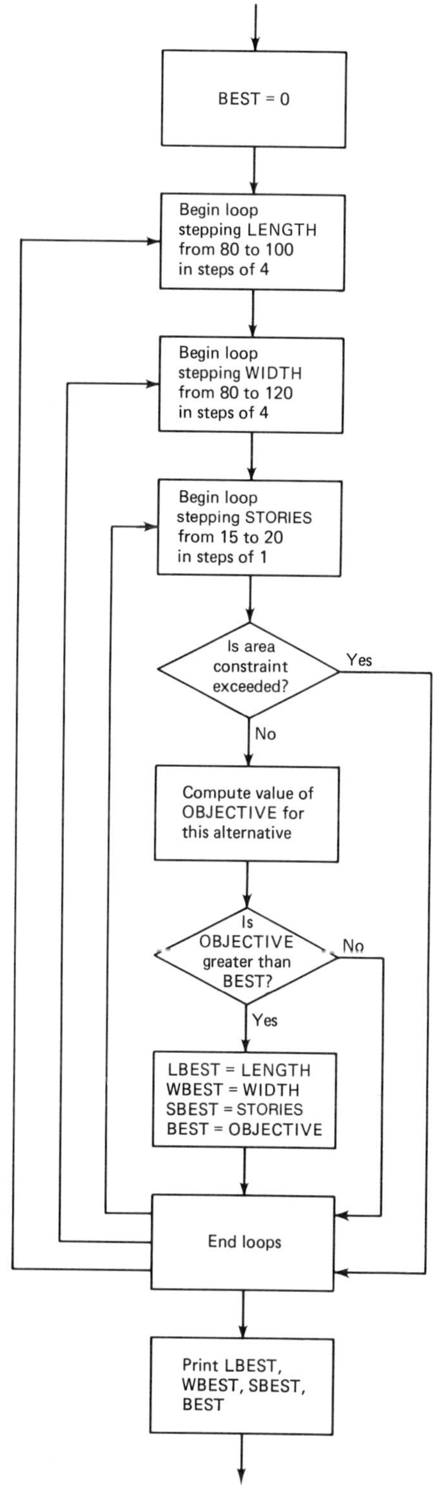
BEST = 0
Begin loop stepping LENGTH from 80 to 100 in steps of 4
Begin loop stepping WIDTH from 80 to 120 in steps of 4
Begin loop stepping STORIES from 15 to 20 in steps of 1
Is area constraint exceeded?
Yes
No
Compute value of OBJECTIVE for this alternative
Is OBJECTIVE greater than BEST?
No
Yes
LBEST = LENGTH
WBEST = WIDTH
SBEST = STORIES
BEST = OBJECTIVE
End loops
Print LBEST, WBEST, SBEST, BEST

(b)

Quite a few feasibility analysis programs of this type have been implemented and put into use. One of the earliest was a program developed by Thomsen (1965) for the firm of Caudill Rowlett and Scott. This program is oriented towards high rise office buildings, and produces analyses of construction cost, cost per square foot of floor area, net income from the project, percentage return, etc., as functions of the number of floors in the building. Perhaps the best-known program of this type is the Building Optimization Program (BOP) developed and employed by the firm of Skidmore, Owings and Merrill (Harper 1968). The BOP model assumes that the design for an urban high-rise office building can be reasonably well described in terms of values for a small number of key design variables: building width, length, floor area per story, number of floors, and service-core dimensions. Permissible ranges of values and increments for these variables are specified (either by the user, or by means of default values based upon the firm's experience with earlier projects), and the program enumerates all possible combinations of values, computes estimated construction cost and other measures for each combination, and prints out the results. Similar approaches to feasibility analysis for apartment buildings have been described by Mogel (1969), and Gero and James (1972), and Hartkopf (1973) has discussed the analysis of a warehouse building.

Optimization by linear programming

Although the enumeration technique for finding an optimum solution is very general and flexible in its application, and produces excellent results, it obviously becomes impractical where the number of potential solutions is very large. In this case, more powerful optimization techniques must be employed. One of the best known and most widely employed such techniques is *linear programming.*

The basic theory and techniques of linear programming are extensively discussed in numerous available texts (see Grawoig 1967 for an elementary introduction, and Luenberger 1973 for a more advanced treatment) and will not be covered here. Instead, the general form of linear programming problems will be characterized, and a typical architectural example will be illustrated.

A linear programming problem is characterized by real-number variables, constraints defined by means of linear inequalities (and perhaps equalities as well), and an objective which is a linear function of the design variables. The following is a trivial example. The width W of a rectangular room can vary from 4.5 ft. to 12.3 ft., and the length L can vary from 6.8 ft. to 14.9 ft. It is decided that the proportion ratio L/W must be in the range 0.67 to 1.0. Furthermore, it is desired to minimize the total perimeter 2 (L + W) of the room. This problem can be stated as an elementary linear program thus:

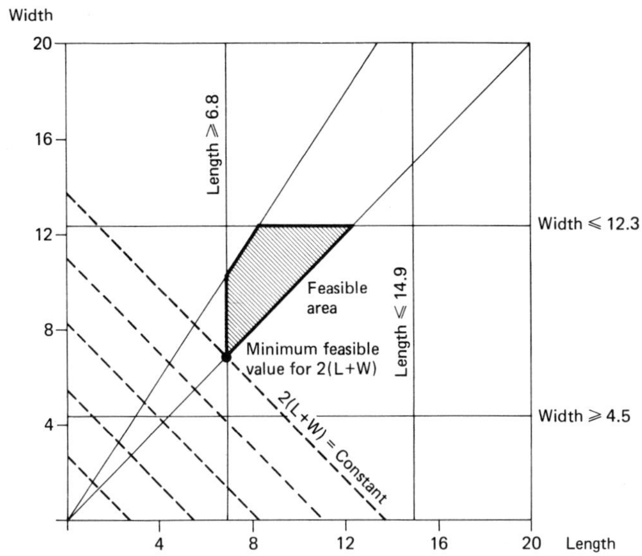

Figure 12.7
The principle of linear programming.

minimize	$2L + 2W$
subject to	$L \geqslant 4.5$
	$L \leqslant 12.3$
	$W \geqslant 6.8$
	$W \leqslant 14.9$
	$L \geqslant 0.67W$
	$L \leqslant W$

The constraints, together with the feasible solution area which they define, are illustrated in *Figure 12.7.* The objective function can be represented by a series of parallel lines as shown. We can see immediately that the optimum solution is found at one of the vertices of the convex polygon formed by the constraints.

Where the number of variables exceeds three, direct graphical solution in this way is of course no longer possible. But the property that the optimum solution will be found at a vertex of a convex region (of multi-dimensional space) continues to hold, and this can be exploited as the basis for very powerful and efficient solution procedures. Computer programs now exist which can solve linear programming problems consisting of thousands of variables and constraints with comparative ease.

The following is a typical example of a non-trivial architectural feasibility analysis problem formulated as a linear program. An extensive development site is found to break down into areas as follows:

Land type category	*Area (acres)*
A. Prime buildable land	100
B. Buildable	875
C. Marginally buildable	3,814
D. Poor	2,003

Residential development, consisting of some mix of the following unit types, is proposed:

Unit types	*Units/acre*
1. Houses on large lots	1
2. Small detached houses	5
3. Clustered units	10
4. Multi-story apartments	20

It is generally more expensive to construct units on the less suitable land. Average construction costs (thousands of dollars per unit) for different types of units on land of different suitability are as follows:

Unit types	*Land type category*			
	A. Prime	B. Buildable	C. Marginal	D. Poor
1. Large lots	50	55	75	100
2. Detached	25	30	40	50
3. Cluster	22	24	30	36
4. Multi-story	20	21	22	23

Expected average sale prices for the different types of units are as follows:

Unit types	*Unit prices (thousands of dollars)*
1. Large lots	125
2. Detached	45
3. Cluster	40
4. Multi-story	35

The objective is to maximize total profit on the development, defined as total sales less total construction cost. The numbers of units of specific type to be built in a given land type category may be designated as follows:

Unit type	*Land type category*			
	A. Prime	B. Buildable	C. Marginal	D. Poor
1. Large lots	A1	B1	C1	D1
2. Detached	A2	B2	C2	D2
3. Cluster	A3	B3	C3	D3
4. Multi-story	A4	B4	C4	D4

Thus total sales =

$$
\begin{aligned}
&125\,(A1+B1+C1+D1)\\
+\;&45\,(A2+B2+C2+D2)\\
+\;&40\,(A3+B3+C3+D3)\\
+\;&35\,(A4+B4+C4+D4)
\end{aligned}
$$

And total costs =

$$
\begin{aligned}
&50A1+55B1+75C1+100D1\\
&+25A2+30B2+40C2+50D2\\
&+22A3+24B3+30C3+36D3\\
&+20A4+21B4+22C4+22D4
\end{aligned}
$$

Subtracting total costs from total sales, *objective to be maximized* =

$$
\begin{aligned}
&75A1+70B1+50C1+25D1\\
&+20A2+15B2+5C2+5D2\\
&+18A3+16B3+10C3+4D3\\
&+15A4+14B4+13C4+12D4
\end{aligned}
$$

Since the total capacity of the site cannot be exceeded, the following constraints must apply:

(a) *Land capacity constraints*

$$
\begin{aligned}
A1+0.2A2+0.1A3+0.05A4 &\leq 100 \text{ acres}\\
B1+0.2B2+0.1B3+0.05B4 &\leq 875 \text{ acres}\\
C1+0.2C2+0.1C3+0.05C4 &\leq 3814 \text{ acres}\\
D1+0.2D2+0.1D3+0.05D4 &\leq 2003 \text{ acres}
\end{aligned}
$$

In addition, market analysis discloses the following limits on potential sales:

(b) *Market constraints*

$$
\begin{aligned}
A1+B1+C1+D1 &\leq 950 \text{ units}\\
A2+B2+C2+D2 &\leq 3873 \text{ units}\\
A3+B3+C3+D3 &\leq 2500 \text{ units}\\
A4+B4+C4+D4 &\leq 1800 \text{ units}
\end{aligned}
$$

Planning regulations limit the percentage area of the site that can be developed, the total number of families to be located on the site, and require a minimum provision for low cost housing to be made, as follows:

(c) *Area constraints*

$$
\begin{aligned}
&(A1+B1+C1+D1)\\
&+(0.2A2+0.2B2+0.2C2+0.2D2)\\
&+(0.1A3+0.1B3+0.1C3+0.1D3)\\
&+(0.05A4+0.05B4+0.05C4+0.05D4) \leq 3000 \text{ acres}
\end{aligned}
$$

(d) *Population constraints (assuming one family per unit)*

$$(A1+B1+C1+D1)$$
$$+(A2+B2+C2+D2)$$
$$+(A3+B3+C3+D3)$$
$$+(A4+B4+C4+D4)\leq 5000 \text{ units}$$

(e) *Minimum provision for low cost housing*

$$A4+B4+C4+D4\geq 1000 \text{ units}$$

As formulated, the problem has 16 variables and 11 constraints. IBM's well-known MPS linear programming system was employed to generate a solution in a few seconds of computation. The optimum values were found to be (*Figure 12.8*):

A1 = 0	B1 = 647.5	C1 = 302.5	D1 = 0
A2 = 0	B2 = 0	C2 = 0	D2 = 0
A3 = 225.0	B3 = 2275.0	C3 = 0	D3 = 0
A4 = 1550.0	B4 = 0	C4 = 0	D4 = 0

The corresponding value of the objective was $124,150,000.

In interpreting the results of this type of analysis, the inherent limitations of the formulation must be kept clearly in mind. In this case, the following limitations should be particularly noted. First, it does not say anything about the specific *location* of housing on the site. The "average construction cost" parameters distribute site preparation costs evenly over all units without considering location, but some lots (*e.g.*, those requiring long service lines and access roads) will obviously be more expensive to develop than others. The formulation also ignores various potential interactive effects. For example, it as-

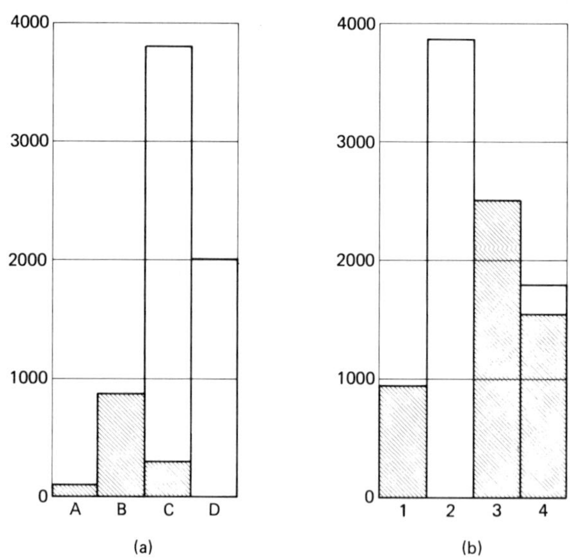

Figure 12.8 Linear programming solution to site development optimization problem. (a) Acres of land in each category developed in optimum solution (hatched) compared with land capacity constraints. (b) Numbers of units of each type developed in optimum solution (hatched) compared with market constraints.

sumes that the markets for different types of units are independent, that locating high cost housing with a large volume of low cost housing will not affect its price, and so on. Issues of sequencing, staging, and levels of cash flow are not dealt with. The objective function is highly oversimplified.

General purpose linear programming software packages suitable for performing this type of analysis are widely available, and some such packages are implemented at most university and commercial computer centers. In addition to linear programming packages, many other types of optimization programs are also available. A very useful survey, complete with FORTRAN listings of important algorithms, has been published by Kuester and Mize (1973). Gero (1973, 1975) has discussed architectural applications.

SPACE NEEDS ANALYSIS

Problems

Space needs analysis basically involves taking data about people, activities, and equipment to be accommodated in a project, and translating it into a set of precise spatial requirements. The initial data might consist of the results of interviews with clients and users, questionnaire survey data, observational studies, standard guidelines, or investigations of previous similar projects.

Computer-based techniques are beginning to revolutionize this phase of design, since they make possible the efficient manipulation of large volumes of data, and the performance of much more extensive and sophisticated analyses than had been possible in the past. In the following subsections, some typical examples are described.

Simple empirical models

The traditional approach to estimation of accommodation requirements for a facility is to utilize simple empirical formulae, based upon previous experience. For example, a typical formula for a number of university lecture room seats which should be provided per head of enrollment is

$$\frac{h \times f \times \sigma}{\lambda}$$

where

h = average number of hours of teaching per student per week

f = frequency factor

σ = occupancy factor

λ = length of teaching week (hours)

The *frequency factor* is an empirically derived estimate of the average percentage of the teaching week that a lecture room will be in use, and the *occupancy factor* is an estimate of the average percentage of available seats actually occupied when a lecture room is in use. It is very straightforward to write simple computer programs which project space needs based upon this type of formula, and numerous such programs have been implemented (see Volpel 1969 and Hoover 1972 for excellent examples).

Not only may required areas be projected by use of simple empirical models, but lists of spaces to be provided in a particular type of facility can also be generated. For example, Skidmore, Owings and Merrill of New York have implemented a system called HPIS (Hospital Planning Information System) which, when given the number of beds in the proposed facility, and several additional parameters, generates a listing of required spaces, together with cost and area summary data. To do this, it draws upon an historical data base of nationwide hospital operating statistics, a library of building costs, and a library of space sizes.

Although simple empirical models can be very useful, they have certain limitations. Projection from prior experience carries with it the risk that mistakes of the past will be perpetuated. Furthermore, there is a possibility that new conditions and policies may, unknown to the analyst, invalidate some of the basic assumptions underlying the projection. Perhaps most important of all, this type of model provides no firm basis for optimization of space usage, or for examining the sensitivity of space and facility needs to variations in activity patterns and space use policy.

Timetable models

An alternative approach, which can potentially overcome many of these difficulties, is to develop a detailed computer-based model of the activity system that the facility must accommodate. The parameters of the model can then be varied to examine the effects of different assumptions and policies.

A typical application of this latter approach is in school design. If a proposed weekly timetable for a given subject area is known, then a diagram plotting class size against number of periods taught per week can be plotted as shown in *Figure 12.9.* A second stepped line, representing a proposed distribution of classrooms of different sizes, can then be plotted on the same axes as illustrated. The difference between the two lines represents unused capacity, so the better the match of the two lines the closer the fit between accommodation need and accommodation provision. This graphical method is readily translated into a computer algorithm (Markus 1972, Th'ng and Davies 1975), which can be employed to explore the effects of different enrollment patterns and timetabling and classroom size policies, and to

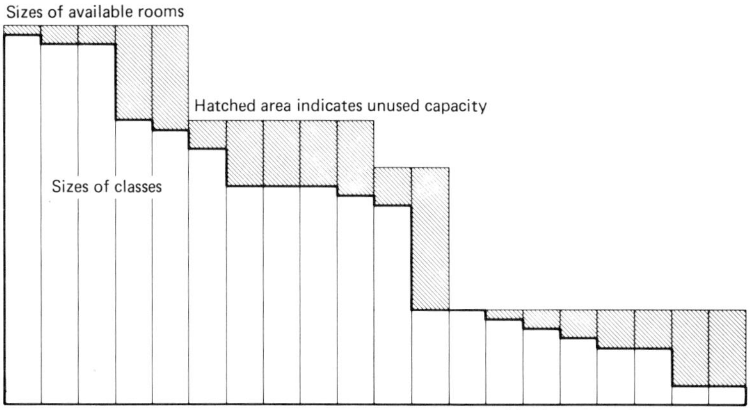

Figure 12.9
Graphic method for determining optimum mix of classroom sizes in a school (after Th'ng and Davis, 1974).

find optimum distribution of classroom sizes implied by particular activity patterns.

Another approach to modeling this type of problem (Bullock 1974) makes interesting use of graph theory. In this case, the starting point for analysis is data on a school or university's total range of course offerings, together with data on classes which cannot be scheduled in simultaneous or overlapping time slots. It can be shown that the problem of constructing a timetable which complies with these scheduling constraints is isomorphic with the well-known and widely studied graph theoretic problem of assigning colors to the vertices of a graph such that no two adjacent vertices share the same color. For a given graph, the minimum number of colors necessary to accomplish such a coloring is known as its *chromatic number.* Returning to the analogy with timetabling, it can be shown that the chromatic number of a graph representing a given timetabling problem corresponds to the maximum number of classrooms which may be in use at any one time without violating scheduling constraints. Finding the chromatic number of a large graph is not easy, but efficient computer programs have been developed which produce good estimates, and such programs may be employed for finding an upper bound on the number of classrooms needed to accommodate a given schedule of classes. The structure of a teaching space needs model based upon this theory, developed by Applied Research of Cambridge (1975) is illustrated in *Figure 12.10.*

Queuing models

In facilities such as supermarkets, department stores, cafeterias, etc., use of simple *queuing models* may be an appropriate way to project space needs. A study by Desai and Yanouzas (1970) of an Athens department store is a good example. Data was collected on customer service times at cashier and wrapping stations, and a regression analy-

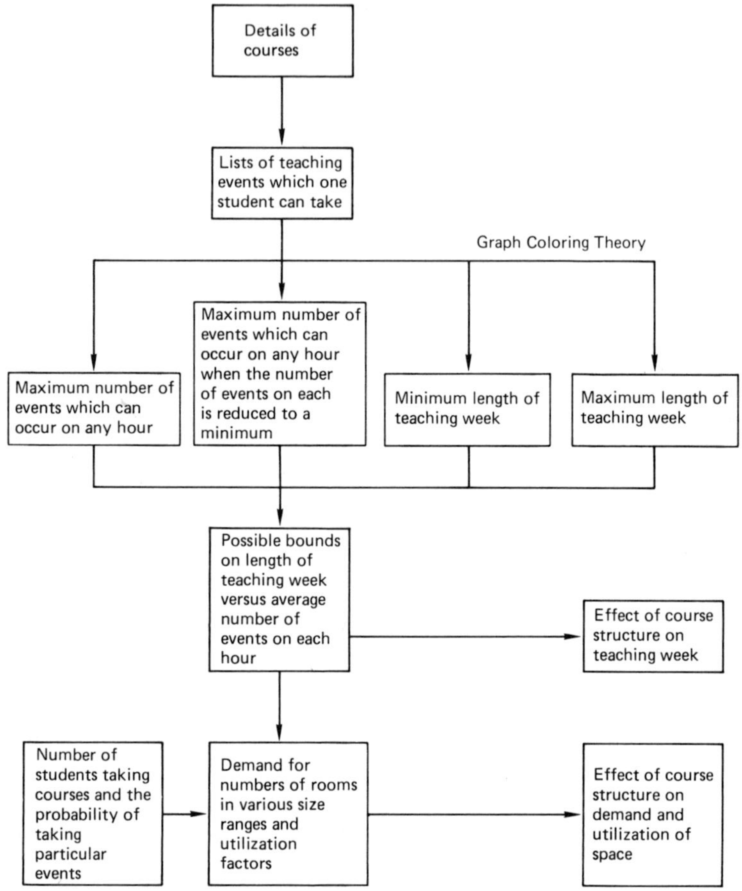

Figure 12.10 Structure of a teaching space needs model, developed by Bullock (1974), based upon graph coloring theory.

sis was conducted to find the relation between number of active cashiers or wrappers and service time. The resultant model could be employed to find the number of stations necessitated by setting a waiting time criterion at any particular level. Bolling (1972) has described an analogous use of a queuing model for analysis of hospital emergency room facilities requirements.

Discrete event digital simulation models

In more complex service facilities, such as air terminals, clinics, etc., it may not be possible to employ simple analytical queuing models. In this case, *discrete event digital simulation models* (Fishman 1973) may be utilized. A discrete event digital simulation model describes processes in terms of *states* and *events*. For example, the states and events experienced by a customer approaching a service window might be as follows:

Enter queue	(Event)
Wait in queue	(State)
Begin business at service window	(Event)
Conduct business	(State)
Depart	(Event)

It can be seen that the occurrence of an event results in a change of state. A discrete event simulation model is a computer program whose execution simulates the occurrence of events (and hence changes of states) in a system over time, and which prints out statistical data on states of the system that are of interest, for example, queue lengths. Normally, the facility to be simulated is represented as a flow network, for example, as shown in *Figure 12.11*.

Discrete event digital simulation models can be written using general purpose programming languages, but it is generally much easier to employ one of the many special *simulation languages* that have been developed. Among the best known and most widely used are GPSS (Schriber 1972), SIMSCRIPT (Kiviat, Villaneuva, and Markowitz 1969), and SIMULA (Dahl and Nygaard 1966).

An excellent example of a discrete event digital simulation model which can be used to investigate accommodation needs is a multi-story industrial parking structure model developed by Broad (1969). The model is programmed in GPSS, and its scope includes movement of people to the structure, vertical transportation within the structure, exit of cars from the structure, and entry of cars to the surrounding street system. The primary output is a graph (*Figure 12.12*) showing the frequency distribution of the times taken by entering and exiting individuals to pass through the system. Design features such as total capacity of the parking structure, numbers and locations of exit ramps, stairs, elevators, etc., can be varied, and the effects on transit times studied. In this way, a configuration which adequately meets transit time performance standards can be determined.

Extensive studies of the design and utilization of hospital facilities, conducted using SIMSCRIPT discrete event digital simulation models, have been carried out at Yale University (Fetter and Thompson 1965, Thompson and Goldin 1975). A maternity suite model, for example, allows exploration of relations between the capacity of the suite, patterns of demand, operating policies, and levels of service provided. A model of a surgical pavillion allows experimentation with different configurations of special and general purpose operating rooms, and with different scheduling policies for their use. A model of an outpatient clinic focuses primarily on patient waiting time, and a ward model is defined for analysis of the economics of different mixes of private and multibed rooms under various conditions.

Broad's parking structure model and the Yale hospital models,

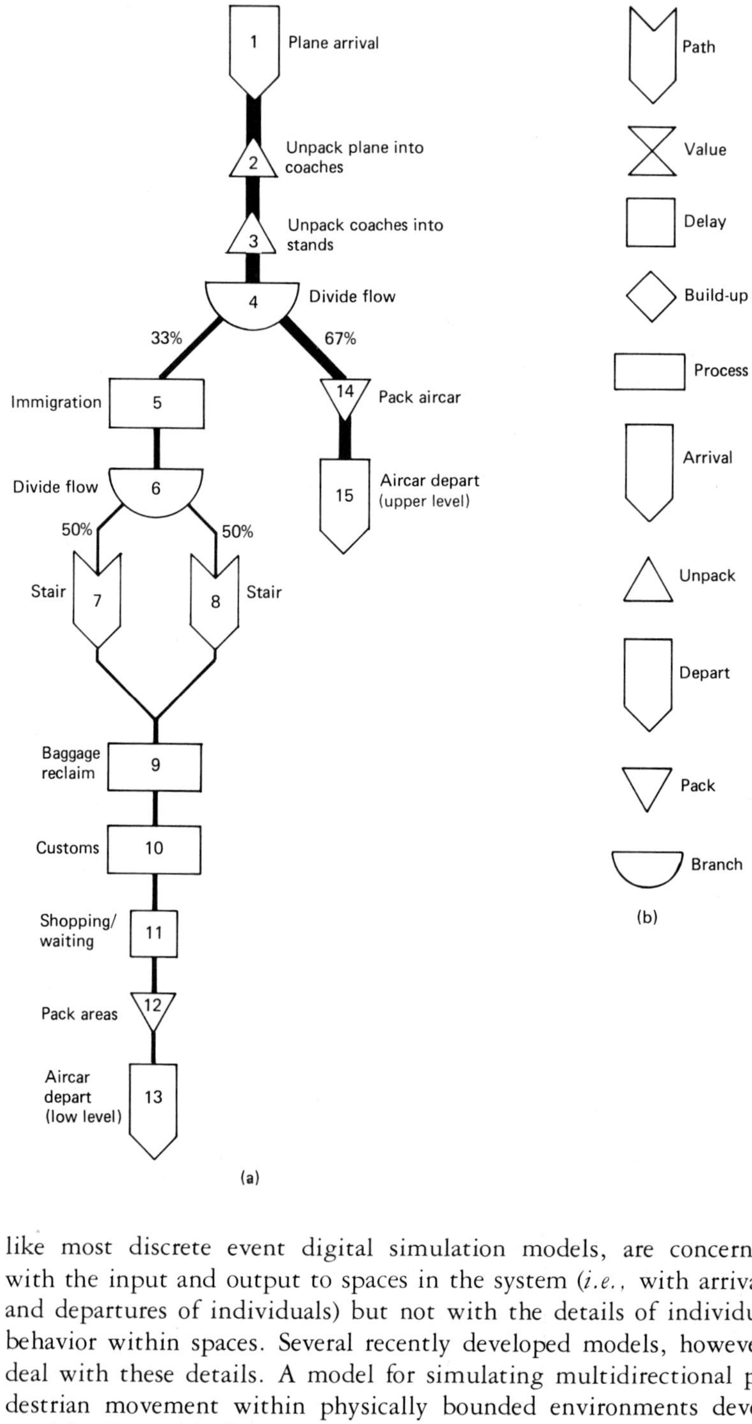

Figure 12.11
An airport arrivals building represented as a network for simulation (after Applied Research of Cambridge (1973)). (a) Flow diagram. (b) Key to flow diagram symbols.

like most discrete event digital simulation models, are concerned with the input and output to spaces in the system (*i.e.*, with arrivals and departures of individuals) but not with the details of individual behavior within spaces. Several recently developed models, however, deal with these details. A model for simulating multidirectional pedestrian movement within physically bounded environments developed by Baer (1974) is typical. His purpose is to develop rules for dimensioning and controlling the safety of pedestrian circulation spaces. The model is programmed in SIMULA. Input consists of a

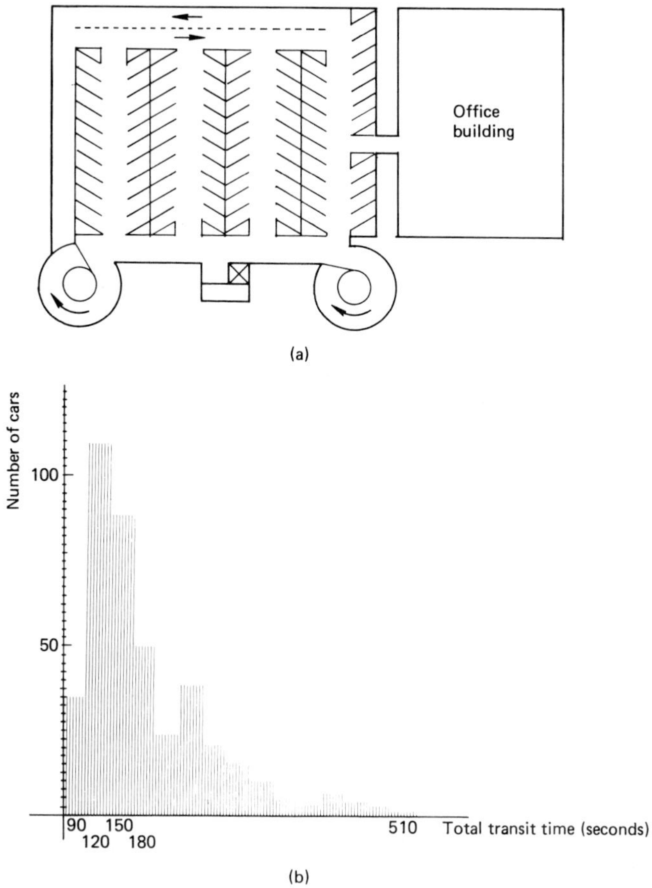

Figure 12.12
Broad's (1969) parking structure simulation: typical results. (a) Typical configuration of a simulated parking structure. (b) Result of simulation: plot of total transit times against different numbers of cars passing through a 448-car structure.

description of the shape of the space, locations of entry and exit points, and descriptions of individual pedestrians within the system. The described physical properties of each pedestrian are volume (approximated by a circle), velocity of movement, and direction of movement. In addition, further parameters describe each individual's physical goal and subgoals, capability to evaluate obstacles, and purpose. Output consists of a sequence of "snapshots" of the space, showing the locations of pedestrians at successive increments of time (*Figure 12.13*).

A wide variety of applications of discrete event digital simulation modeling to accommodation requirements analysis for different types of facilities have been reported in the literature. For example, Campion (1968) describes a simple simulation of customer flow through a cafeteria/dining room complex, programmed in ALGOL, Evensmo (1969) discusses simulations of warehouse operations using SIMULA, Kenney and Murray (1971) analyze hospital facilities, Calderbank and Kirke (1972) describe use of a program for simulation of traffic flow in air terminals, and Lozar (1974) simulates user move-

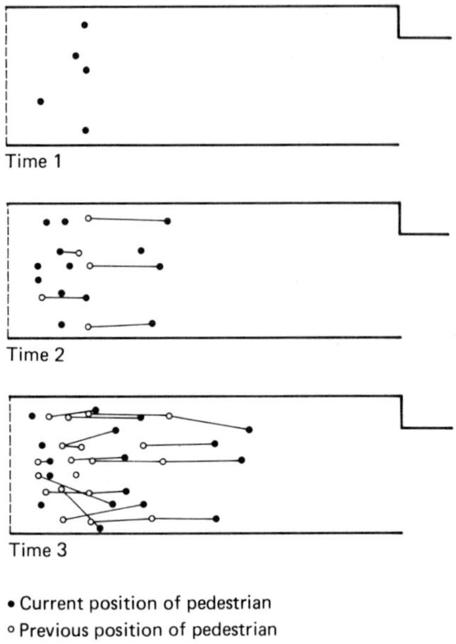

Figure 12.13
Baer's (1974) pedestrian flow simulation: "snapshots" of pedestrian location at successive increments of time.

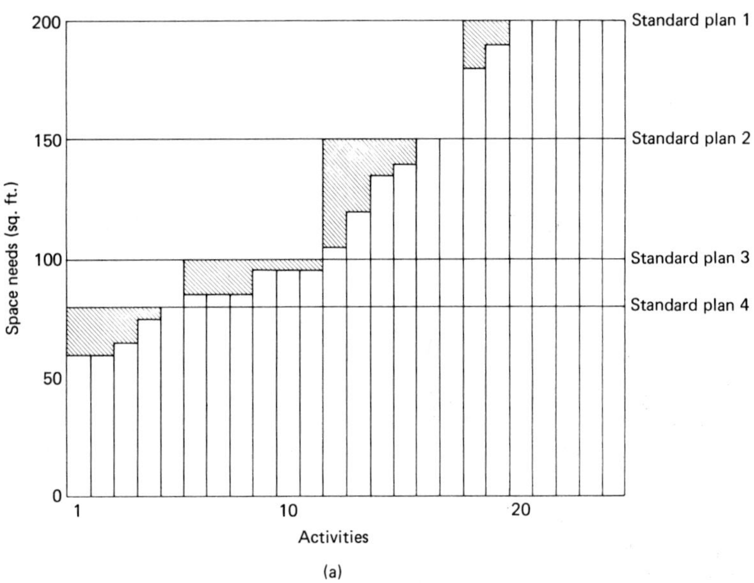

Unit type	Number 0 - 3	4 - 8	9 - 24
200	2000	1500	1400
150	1600	1400	1300
100	1250	1150	1100
80	1100	1100	1100

(b)

Figure 12.14
Dynamic programming solution of a room-size normalization problem. (a) Graph of space requirements compared with capacities of standard plans. Shaded area indicates difference between space requirements and minimum area solution. (b) Cost table. (c) Principle of dynamic programming solution.

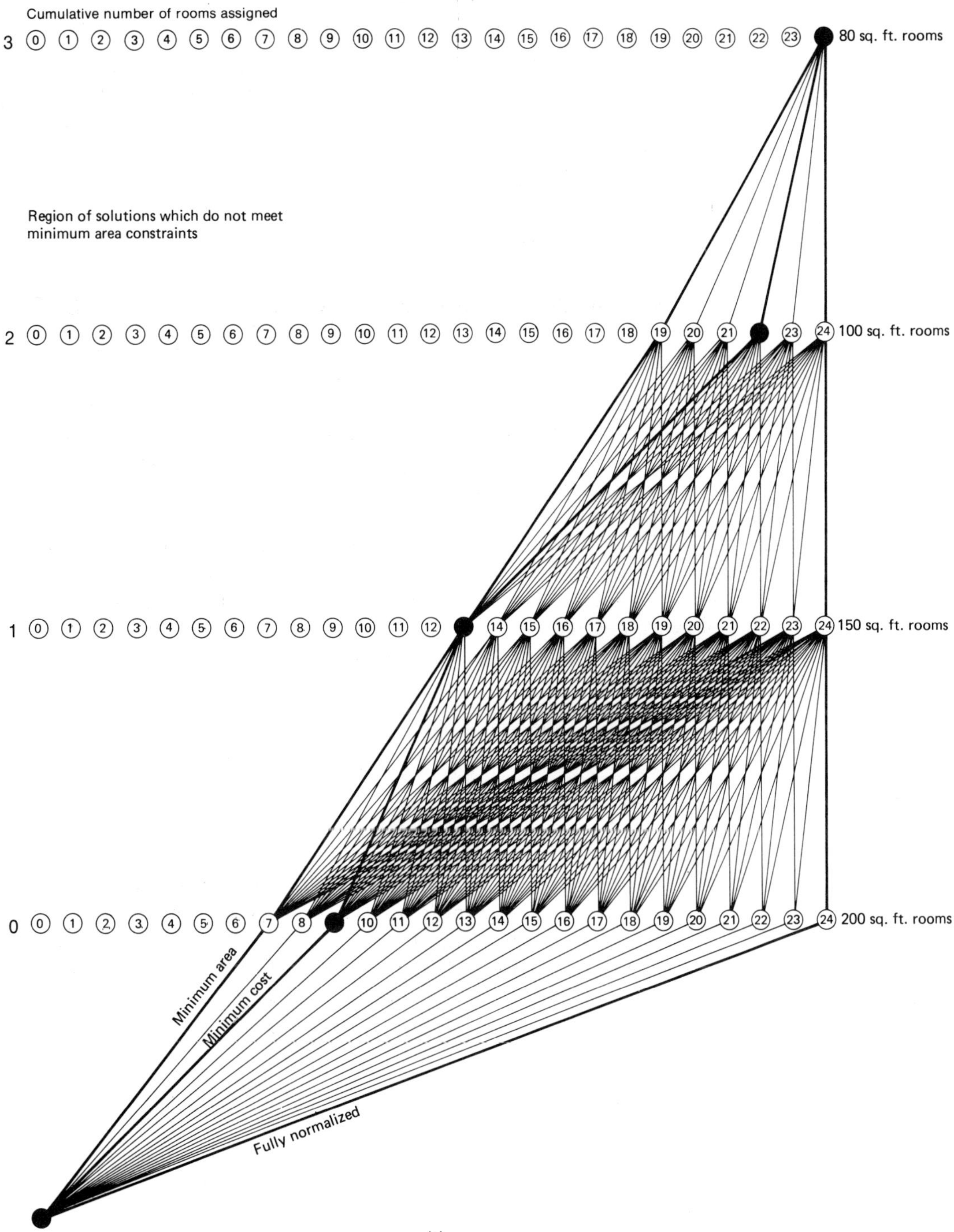

Cumulative number of rooms assigned
3
2
1
0
80 sq. ft. rooms
100 sq. ft. rooms
150 sq. ft. rooms
200 sq. ft. rooms
Region of solutions which do not meet
minimum area constraints
Minimum area
Minimum cost
Fully normalized

(c)

ment and location within dining halls. Perhaps the most widespread application has been simulation of elevator system performance in high rise office buildings (Parlow 1966, McGuinness 1967, Forwood 1971, Penz 1971, Fleming 1973, Frederking and Penz 1973). Applied Research of Cambridge (1973) has developed a general purpose "movement in building" simulator, which can be used to simulate a wide variety of facilities. General discussions of a range of applications have been published by Burberry (1970), Ridyard (1970), Bazjanac (1971), and Kahan (1972).

Normalization in space needs analysis

Often a space needs analysis will reveal that numerous activities require similar but not exactly the same sized spaces, as shown, for example, in *Figure 12.14(a)*. In this case, it is usually considered desirable to define a number of standard sized spaces, and to allocate each activity to a sufficiently large standard space. In our example, we assume that standard spaces of 80 sq. ft., 100 sq. ft., 150 sq. ft. and 200 sq. ft. are chosen.

Where mass-produced components, such as wall and ceiling panels, are employed in construction of spaces, there is often a potential to reduce costs by repetition of exactly similar components. In our example, let us assume that costs of producing different numbers of the various standard sized spaces are as follows:

Area	*0–3*	*4–8*	*9–24*
200	$2000	$1500	$1400
150	$1600	$1400	$1300
100	$1250	$1150	$1100
80	$1100	$1100	$1100

The problem now is to assign activities to standard sized spaces in such a way as to minimize total cost, while meeting all the area requirements. By exhaustive enumeration it can be shown that there are 650 feasible solutions to this assignment problem, and that the minimum cost is $30,300 for the following assignment:

2 activities to 80 sq. ft. spaces
9 activities to 100 sq. ft. spaces
4 activities to 150 sq. ft. spaces
9 activities to 200 sq. ft. spaces

The operation of determining this optimum assignment is known as *normalization* (Distefano and Nagy 1972, Gero 1976).

It is easy to solve small scale normalization problems of this type by means of exhaustive enumeration, but where hundreds or thousands of activities are involved the resultant combinatorial explosion renders this simple approach infeasible. In this case, the more sophisticated technique of *dynamic programming* (Denardo 1975) may be employed most effectively.

Figure 12.14(c) illustrates the principles of the dynamic programming approach. The vertical axis represents successively smaller space sizes, and the horizontal axis represents the *cumulative* number of activities assigned at each stage in the process of successive assignment of the 15 activities to the 4 standard sized spaces. The available choices at each stage in this process are represented by directed edges of a network. Each of these edges (decisions) has an associated cost, so the problem now is to find a minimum cost path from the source vertex to the terminal. An upper bounding path is defined by the size constraints, and a lower bounding path by a "fully normalized" design, *i.e.*, one in which all activities are assigned to spaces of the largest standard size.

For this type of network, the following *principle of optimality* may be stated: A minimum cost path must have the property that, regardless of the path taken to reach a particular vertex, the remaining decisions must constitute a minimum cost path from that vertex to the terminal. Thus, the following simple procedure of "working backwards" through the graph in successive stages provides a systematic means of discovering the minimum cost path from the source to the terminal:

1 List costs of all edges pointing to the vertex in row 3 of the diagram (*i.e.*, the terminal).

2 List costs of all edges pointing to the vertices in row 2.

3 Using information available from steps 1 and 2, find and record the minimum cost path from each vertex in row 1 to the terminal.

4 List costs of all edges pointing to the vertices in row 1.

5 Using information available from steps 3 and 4, find and record the minimum cost path from the vertex in row 0 (*i.e.*, the source) to the terminal.

Generalizing the principle embodied in this procedure to problems involving m standard spaces, we may state it concisely as the following *dynamic recursive relationship:*

$$f_n(s) = \text{minimum } [c_{sj} + f_{n-1}(j)] \text{ for } n = 1 \text{ to } m$$

where

s = current vertex

n = number of edges which must be traversed to go from s to the terminal

$f_n(s)$ = cost of cheapest path from s to the terminal

j = any vertex which is pointed to directly from s

c_{sj} = cost of the edge connecting s and j

$f_{n-1}(j)$ = known cost of cheapest path from j to terminal

The general procedure, then, is to step the value of n from 1 to m (*i.e.*, to "back" through the network), at each step computing $f_n(s)$ for each vertex s in the current column, and recording the path from s to the terminal which yields $f_n(s)$. The cost of the cheapest path from the source v_0 to the terminal is eventually given by $f_m(v_0)$. For large networks, the computational savings resulting from use of this procedure rather than exhaustive enumeration are usually very substantial, since it implicitly eliminates many branches from consideration.

Analogous dynamic programming techniques have been applied to other aspects of space needs analysis, feasibility study, and design. Gero (1976) discusses applications to site development feasibility studies, elevator zoning, campus planning, and structural design. Palmer (1968), Distefano and Nagy (1972) and Gero and Sharma (1976) describe diverse applications to structural design.

Limitations of computer models for space needs analysis

The principal limitation on the use of computer models in the analysis of space needs is that they tend to require a great deal of accurate and detailed input data, which is rarely readily available, and which may be difficult and expensive to collect. Furthermore, the modeling effort itself is often quite a lengthy and expensive process.

INTERACTION AND GROUPING ANALYSIS

Interaction matrices

The most convenient format for representation of data describing interactions and interrelations between activities or spaces in a proposed or existing building is an *interaction matrix*. This subsection discusses the types and methods of construction of interaction matrices, and the following subsections will then introduce some techniques for computer analysis of interaction matrices.

An interaction matrix is a square matrix in which rows and columns represent spaces or activities, and each entry describes a relation between the corresponding pair of spaces or activities. For example, relations between spaces in a five room house might be represented by means of a square matrix *R*:

$$
\begin{array}{c c} & \begin{array}{ccccc} 1 & 2 & 3 & 4 & 5 \end{array} \\
R = \begin{array}{c} 1 \\ 2 \\ 3 \\ 4 \\ 5 \end{array} & \left[\begin{array}{ccccc} 0 & r_{12} & r_{13} & r_{14} & r_{15} \\ r_{21} & 0 & r_{23} & r_{24} & r_{25} \\ r_{31} & r_{32} & 0 & r_{34} & r_{35} \\ r_{41} & r_{42} & r_{43} & 0 & r_{45} \\ r_{51} & r_{52} & r_{53} & r_{54} & 0 \end{array} \right] \end{array}
$$

where each element r specifies some kind of relation between the corresponding pair of rooms. The diagonal is undefined, since it represents the relation of each space to itself. Interaction matrices are commonly symmetrical, but they need not necessarily be so.

Relations given in an interaction matrix may either be *normative* (a requirement to be met) or *descriptive* (a situation which exists), and may refer to a *topological* relation (adjacency or non-adjacency), a *geometric* relation (*e.g.*, distance) or an *activity* relation (*e.g.*, traffic flow). Thus we can list six different basic types of interaction matrices:

Normative matrix of topological requirements. For example, specifying which spaces should and should not be adjacent.

Normative matrix of geometric requirements. For example, specifying maximum permissible separations.

Normative matrix of activity requirements. For example, specifying required levels of traffic flow capacity.

Descriptive matrix of topological data. For example, the room adjacency matrix for an existing building.

Descriptive matrix of geometric data. For example, walking distances between rooms in an existing building.

Descriptive matrix of activity data. For example, pedestrian traffic flow volumes between activities in an existing building.

The data in an interaction matrix may be expressed using any one of a number of different *measurement scales*, as follows:

Binary scale, which has only two points, 1 or 0, signifying that a property either exists or does not;

Nominal scale, which has a number of points signifying a number of categories, for example, "yes," "maybe," "no," expressed as 1, 0, −1;

Ordinal scale, in which the points representing categories are rank-ordered according to some criterion, for example, "small," "medium," "large," expressed as 1, 2, 3;

Interval scale, in which magnitudes are expressed in distances from an arbitrary starting point, as in a coordinate system;

Ratio scale, in which magnitudes are expressed relative to some standard, without reference to an origin, as in distances expressed as ratios of the standard foot or meter.

Normative data

Normative matrices of topological requirements are often expressed in binary form, for example:

1 = adjacency required

0 = indifferent

It is also common to express topological and geometric requirements data on ordinal *preference scales*, for example:

3 = close proximity essential
2 = proximity very important
1 = proximity desirable
0 = indifferent
−1 = proximity undesirable
−2 = separation very important
−3 = wide separation essential

Where more precise preference information is available, an interval scale may be employed. For example, "importance of proximity" might be expressed on a scale of 0 to 10. A value of 4 in this case expresses twice the importance of a value of 2, or half the importance of a value of 8.

For developing matrices of normative data, various systematic procedures are available. For example, the technique of paired comparisons (David 1963) may be employed to generate rank orderings. Where numerical weights must be assigned, Churchman, Ackoff, and Arnoff's (1957) method for weighting objectives may be utilized.

Descriptive data

Where descriptive data is to be tabulated, a decision must be made on the particular measure to be employed. For example, there are a variety of ways to measure room to room distances. First, the measurements might be taken from points interior to the rooms, for example, their centroids, or alternatively from the doorways. Second, actual measured distance along circulation routes might be taken (*Figure 12.15(a)*) or a simpler surrogate utilized. Two common surrogates are *straight line* distance (*Figure 12.15(b)*) and *city block* distance (*Figure 12.15(c)*). Straight line distance, perhaps modified slightly by a "detour coefficient," may be an excellent approximation in situations such as an open office landscape, where distances between work stations must be measured. City block distance usually provides a very good approximation where circulation takes place through a rectilinear corridor system. Tabor (1976) has carried out a detailed study of the properties of various different measures of circulation distance in buildings.

Where various different modes of circulation are employed in a building, for example, corridors, stairs, escalators, elevators, etc., some measure of circulation time or "cost" is likely to be a better indicator of proximity than distance. For example, a study by Archer (1963) suggests (arbitrarily) that a foot traveled vertically in a building might be assumed to take about twice as long as a foot traveled horizontally. Cinar (1968) proposes to take unit horizontal distance as one

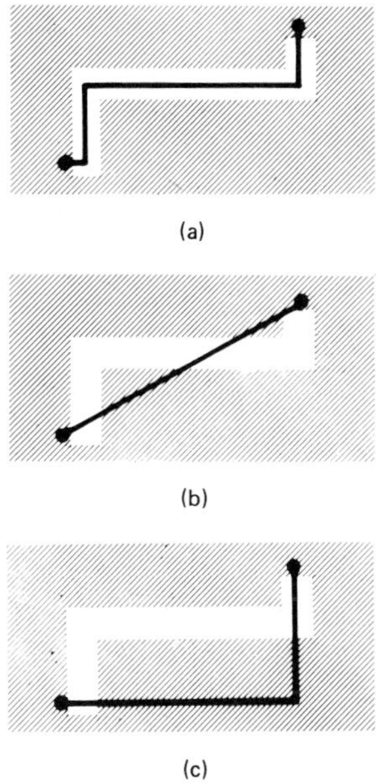

Figure 12.15
Alternative ways of measuring circulation distance in a building. (a) Actual circulation distance. (b) Straight line distance. (c) City block distance.

tenth of its vertical equivalent to express either "the time and energy consumed in movement between two floors, or the capital and operating cost of transportation equipment." Moseley (1963) has published curves, based upon observational data, showing relations between travel-time-equivalent horizontal and vertical distances.

Volume of traffic or materials flow of various kinds has been very widely employed as an empirical measure of functional interaction between activity centers in a system. For example, many studies of pedestrian traffic flow in hospitals have been conducted (Nuffield Provincial Hospitals Trust 1955, Whitehead and Eldars 1964, Souder, *et al* 1964). For offices, measures like volumes of file folder flow have been employed as empirical measures of interaction (Brooks 1970). Whitehead (1966, 1970) has reported use of circulation flow data in optimization of the layout of warehouses and schools. In plant layout, flow of materials between work centers has been very extensively employed as a measure of interaction (Hillier 1963, Hillier and Connors 1966, Anderson 1973, Muther 1974). One of the difficulties with use of these types of traffic flow data to measure interaction, of course, is that volumes of flow may very well be sensitive to changes in building layout and operational policies. In order to overcome this difficulty, there have been a few attempts to develop traffic flow models which can be employed to generate matrices in response to these considerations (Ray 1975).

It is obvious that different types of circulation in an activity system may have different costs or weightings attached to them, which may modify the measures of interaction given by a simple circulation volume matrix. It costs more in terms of salaried time for a senior surgeon to walk a certain distance than it does for an orderly, for instance. Thus a study by Cinar (1968) assigns a salary-dependent circulation cost weighting of 12 to medical staff, 3 to nurses, 3 to patients, and 1 to visitors. Of course the weights for patients and visitors represent judgments of the relative "value" of patient and visitor time.

Cluster analysis

Interaction matrices containing either normative or descriptive data represent patterns of spatial or functional association between activities or spaces. Unfortunately, these patterns are not directly discernible from inspection of the matrices in any but the very simplest cases. Large arrays of numbers are simply not comprehensible. Some appropriate technique must be employed to reveal and clarify the design implications of the data. One approach, which will be discussed in the next chapter, is to use the matrices as input to an automated floor plan layout program. A second alternative, which will be considered here, is to use one of the available computer-based *data analysis* techniques that have been developed for revealing structure in data matrices. The two most appropriate are *cluster analysis* and *multidimensional scaling.*

Cluster analysis is essentially a technique for sorting or classifying a set of entities into subsets, such that the members of each subset are closely interrelated to each other, and relatively weakly related to other entities outside the subset. If the entities to be clustered are activities or spaces in a building, and interrelations are defined by means of an interaction matrix, then the subsets produced by cluster analysis is represent relatively discrete *functional groupings* of activities or spaces.

An enormous variety of cluster analysis techniques have been developed, and different techniques generally produce somewhat (though not completely) different results. It is not possible to say in general that any particular technique is "best"; different techniques are suitable for different types of classification tasks. The basic concept was initially proposed in the eighteenth century by M. Adanson, a biologist faced with the task of classifying a large number of shellfish specimens collected on a voyage to Senegal. During the 1930's R. C. Tryon introduced a form of cluster analysis for classification tasks in the social and behavioral sciences. But it was not until the early 1960's, with the general availability of modern high speed computers, that cluster analysis in its modern form began to be developed and widely applied. Important areas of application have been biological classification, aggregation problems in economics, analysis of psychological data, and pattern recognition. Excellent comparative discussions of principles, techniques and applications have been published by Ball (1970), Jardine and Sibson (1971), Sneath and

Sokal (1973), Duran and Odell (1974), Everitt (1974) and Hartigan (1975).

The type of clustering technique most suitable for use in analysis of interaction matrices depends upon the particular type of data which the matrix contains. If the data is in binary form, then one of the algorithms developed for use in problem structuring is appropriate. Where data is in interval or ratio form, for example, in a weighted circulation flow matrix, the techniques known as *single linkage clustering* and *average linkage clustering* are likely to prove most effective.

The principle of single linkage clustering is most easily understood if the matrix is represented by its equivalent graph, in which vertices represent spaces or activities, and edge weights represent circulation flow levels (*Figure 12.16(b)*). Zero-valued edges are not shown. If the graph is redrawn with only the heaviest links shown (*Figure 12.16(c)*), then it is partitioned into subgraphs. By repeating the process with successively lighter links (*Figures 12.16(d), (e)*), successively larger subgraphs are generated, until one large graph is

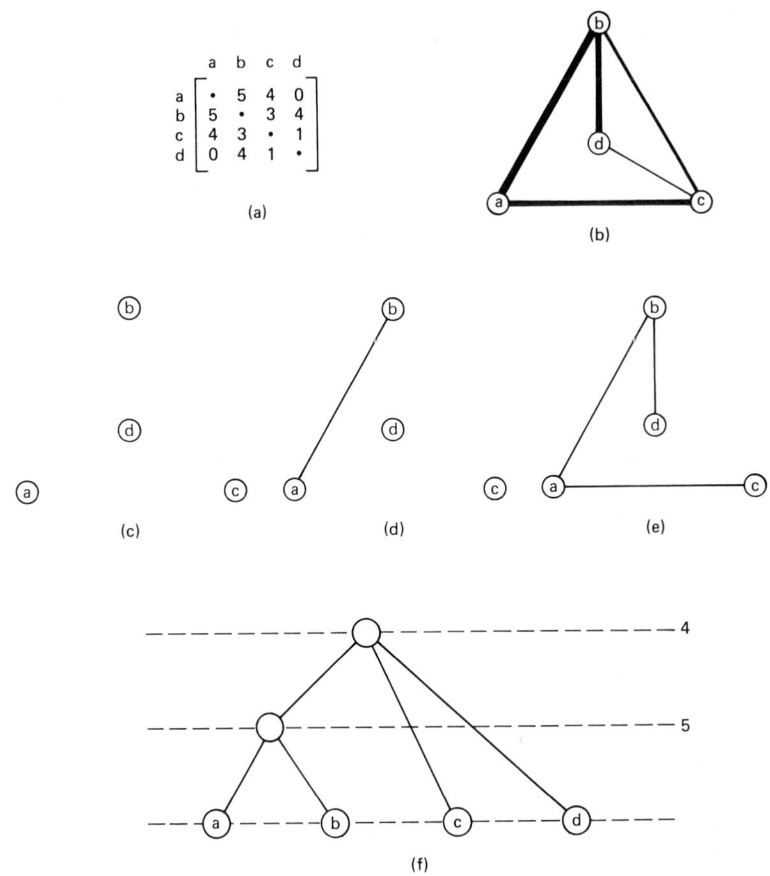

Figure 12.16
Single linkage cluster analysis. (a) Interaction matrix. (b) Equivalent graph. (c) Links of weight >5. (d) Links of weight >4. (e) Links of weight >3. (f) Dendrogram.

eventually formed. The dendrogram for clusters thus generated is shown in *Figure 12.16(f)*. Computer programs have been written which efficiently perform single linkage cluster analysis on hundreds or even thousands of entities.

A characteristic of single linkage analysis is that it ignores the possibility that a number of weak links may together be more important than one strong link. Further, it often tends to "chain" together rather long, linear clusters. Not only are such clusters relatively weakly interconnected, this "chaining" also produces a tendency to form very large (and hence useless) clusters very fast. To overcome these potential disadvantages, average linkage methods have been developed.

One straightforward version of average linkage clustering, known as the *unweighted pair-group* technique (*Figure 12.17*), proceeds as follows. The first step is to link the most strongly associated pairs, as in single linkage clustering. The interaction matrix is then recalculated, as shown. In the new matrix, clustered entities are grouped together, and in each row and column representing a cluster, the interaction values are recalculated as the *average* interaction value for members of that cluster. The process is repeated to generate a hierarchy of clusters. The resultant dendrogram is shown in *Figure 12.17(b)*.

An experimental comparison by Tabor (1970) of single and average linkage cluster analyses of circulation flow data for a large office has shown that both produce very useful results. Single linkage clustering identifies large fundamental functional groupings very efficiently and reliably. Average linkage clustering gives a rather more fine-grained representation, but it may in fact generate many minute differentiations which have little real meaning. Tabor's conclusion is that, "Simultaneous use of average and single linkage, since virtues and defects of both are opposed, combine the former and nullify the latter."

Multidimensional scaling

If the inverse of each entry in the interaction matrix is calculated, then the resultant values may be thought of as representing *dis-association* rather than *association* between spaces or activities. The lower the disassociation value, the closer or more important the interrelation. Thus matrix entries may be thought of as representing *distances* in a multidimensional space between points representing spaces or activities. Closely associated spaces or activities are close together, and weakly associated spaces or activities are far apart. If the points in multidimensional space could be projected into two dimensions such that the distance relation between points were preserved as closely as possible, then a two-dimensional diagram representing spatial relations in a rather similar way to a standard architectural bubble diagram would be produced.

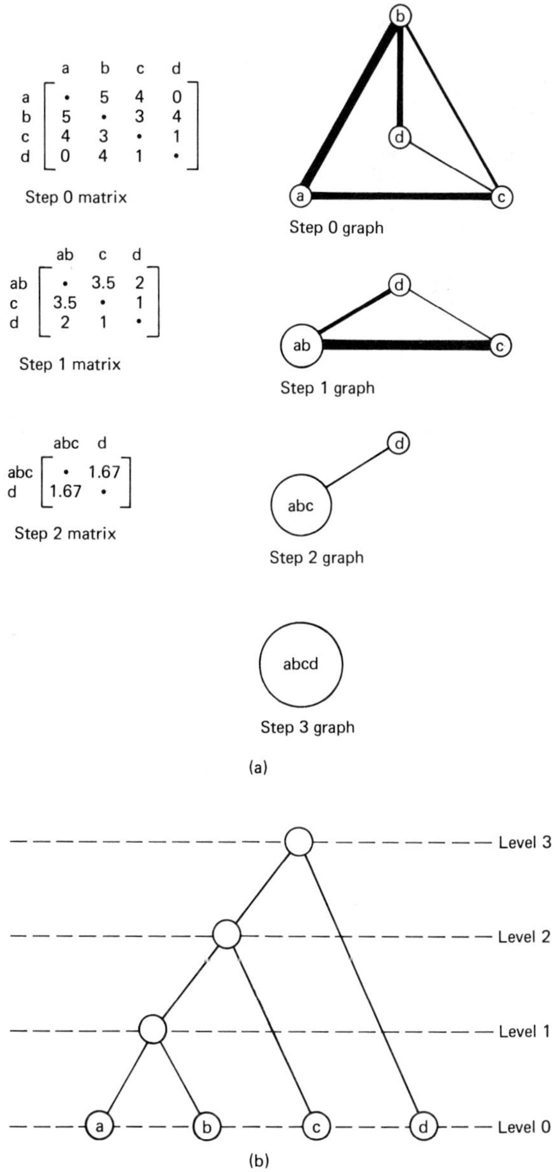

Figure 12.17
Unweighted pair-group clustering. (a) Steps in unweighted pair-group clustering. (b) Resultant dendrogram.

The techniques of multidimensional scaling may be employed for this purpose. The algorithms employed are complex, and are atill under development, so they will not be described here. (For discussions of various approaches and techniques see Shepard 1962, Kruskal 1964, Shepard, Rommey and Nerlove 1972.) The type of result which can be produced is shown in *Figure 12.18(b)*. Distances between points represent strengths of association, as do line weights. For comparison, a single linkage dendrogram for the same data is shown in *Figure 12.18(c)*.

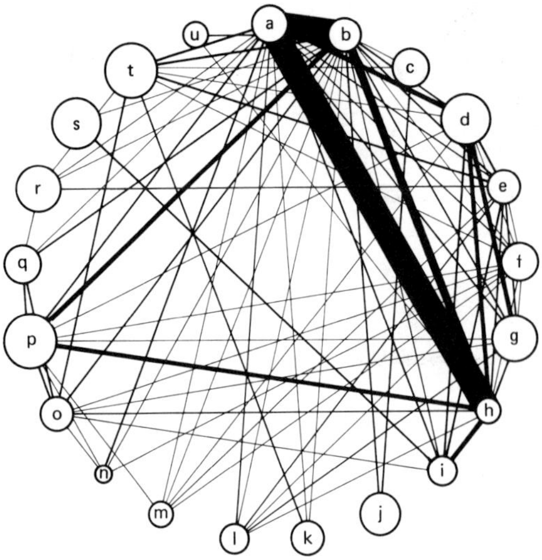

(a)

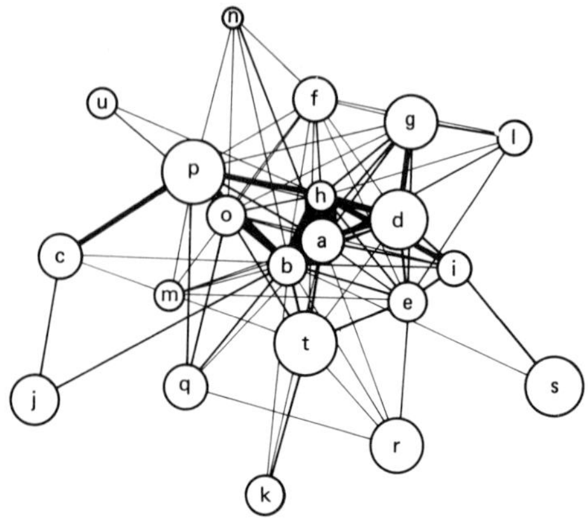

(b)

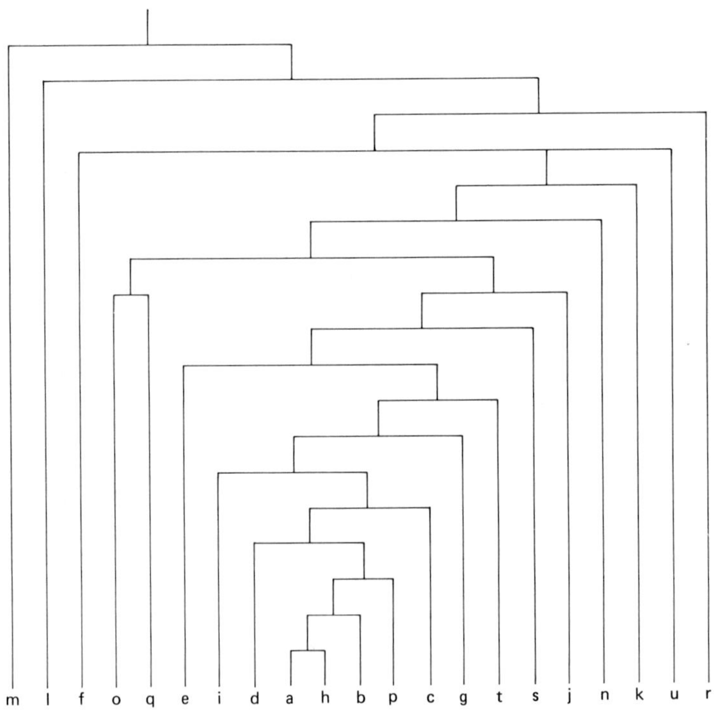

(c)

Stacking plans

In multi-story office building planning, a common early step is to produce a *stacking plan* showing the assignment of particular spaces to particular floors. Since intra-floor communication is much easier than inter-floor communication, the general objective is to group sets of closely related spaces together on each level, and to avoid splitting closely related spaces apart on separate levels. In addition, an attempt is made to place closely interrelated groupings of spaces on closely adjacent floors. The production of a stacking plan can be regarded as the performance of a special type of cluster analysis, in which the additional constraints are introduced that each cluster's total area shall lie within some specified limits. Numerous computer programs have been written to produce stacking plans, and are in widespread use. *Figure 12.19* illustrates some typical output from a program employed by Morganelli-Heumann of Los Angeles.

Algorithms employed in stacking plan programs have mostly been of an *ad hoc* character, imitating traditional hand methods. A typical approach is as follows. First, spaces are assigned to floors by hand to give some reasonable initial arrangement, and some appropriate formula is used to compute a measure of circulation cost for this arrangement. A reasonable cost formula might be

$$\sum_{i=1}^{n} \sum_{j=1}^{n} F_{ij} I_{ij}$$

where

F_{ij} = number of floors separating spaces i and j

I_{ij} = entry in interaction matrix indicating strength of relation between spaces i and j.

Next, the computer is employed to attempt to improve this arrangement by execution of the following simple permutational procedure:

1 Randomly select a space on any floor

Randomly select a second space, of approximately the same size, on any other floor

Transpose these spaces

Compute new circulation cost

If new circulation cost is lower than old circulation cost go to 2, else

Transpose spaces back to their previous locations

2 If specified number of trial transpositions not yet completed go to 1, else

End

Figure 12.18 (*opposite*) Use of multidimensional scaling to analyze an interaction matrix for an office layout problem. (a) Input data. Sizes of circles represent areas of spaces and line weights represent strengths of interaction. (b) Bubble diagram generated by multidimensional scaling. (c) Single linkage cluster dendrogram generated from the same data.

```
**********************************************
*                                            *
*   MORGANELLI - HEUMANN & ASSOCIATES        *
*            STACKING PLAN                   *
*    OWENS-ILLINOIS BLDG. DEC. 1977          *
*            APR 9,1976                      *
*                                            *
**********************************************

+-----+------------------------------+-------+
!FLOOR!        DIVISION OR           ! SQUARE!
! NO. !      DEPARTMENT NAME         !FOOTAGE!
+-----+------------------------------+-------+
   23 !SPARE AREA    EXECUTIVE       !  1356     1000.
      !CONFERENCE AREA               !   409   420006.
      !EXEC.     LANIGAN, CANTER, ADAMS!  1525 600000.
      !                         TOTAL!  3290*       AND THERE ARE  3290 SQ. FT. AVAILIABLE ON THE FLOOR.

+-----+------------------------------+-------+
   22 !PLANNING & ANALYSIS  BECK, R. R.!  3474 530000.
      !MARKET & ECON. RES.   LOTSHAW, E!  1505 550000.
      !                         TOTAL!  4979*       THERE ARE  3660 SQ. FT. AVAILIABLE ON FLOOR 22,
                                                 THE ASSIGNED AREAS MUST BE COMPRESSED BY 1319 SQ.FT.
+-----+------------------------------+-------+
   21 !SPECIAL OPERATIONS     ULLOM ,J.!   379 310000.
      !CORP. REAL ESTATE    GRAHAM, J.!  1650 320000.
      !O-I DEV. CORP.       HALEY, J. W.!  1143 321000.
      !CORP FACILITIES     RUDOWSKY, W.!  1016 330000.
      !PROPERTY MGMT        MOFFET,   J.!   514 331000.
      !                         TOTAL!  4702*       THERE ARE  4057 SQ. FT. AVAILIABLE ON FLOOR 21.
                                                 THE ASSIGNED AREAS MUST BE COMPRESSED BY  645 SQ.FT.
+-----+------------------------------+-------+
   20 !SYS. & DATA PROCESS DAVIS,  W.L.!  3751 360000.
      !                         TOTAL!  3751*       THERE ARE  4057 SQ. FT. AVAILIABLE ON FLOOR 20,
                                                 THE ASSIGNED AREAS MAY BE EXPANDED BY  306 SQ.FT.
+-----+------------------------------+-------+
   19 !I.R.S. AUDITORS               !   647 226100.
      !CREDIT & ADJUSTMENT LEVEY,  L.C.!  3172 615400.
      !                         TOTAL!  3819*       THERE ARE  4057 SQ. FT. AVAILIABLE ON FLOOR 19,
                                                 THE ASSIGNED AREAS MAY BE EXPANDED BY  238 SQ.FT.
+-----+------------------------------+-------+
   18 !COPY CENTER                   !   249 330006.
      !PERSONNEL          HORNEY,  W.G.!  2877 614000.
      !                         TOTAL!  3126*       THERE ARE  4057 SQ. FT. AVAILIABLE ON FLOOR 18,
                                                 THE ASSIGNED AREAS MAY BE EXPANDED BY  931 SQ.FT.
+-----+------------------------------+-------+
+-----+------------------------------+-------+
   16 !PURCHASING       FARMER, L H JR.!  5972 340000.
      !TRANSPORTATION        OLSEN, L.!  5121 350000.
      !                         TOTAL! 11093*       THERE ARE  9032 SQ. FT. AVAILIABLE ON FLOOR 16,
                                                 THE ASSIGNED AREAS MUST BE COMPRESSED BY 2061 SQ.FT.
+-----+------------------------------+-------+
   15 !MANUFACTURING       LEMIEUX,  J.!  4692 612000.
      !PROD PLAN & DISTRM MORGAN   J.M.!  3288 613000.
      !PLANNING          THREADGILL,T.!  1360 615200.
      !                         TOTAL!  9340*       THERE ARE  9032 SQ. FT. AVAILIABLE ON FLOOR 15,
                                                 THE ASSIGNED AREAS MUST BE COMPRESSED BY  308 SQ.FT.
+-----+------------------------------+-------+
   14 !RJE TERMINAL ROOM             !   604 360001.
      !ADV PACKAGE DEV.     WILLIAMS,P.!   531 520000.
      !GLASS CONTAINER      JONES,B.B.!  1480 610000.
      !SALES & MARKETING GROWTH AREA  !  1595 611001.
      !PLAN'G & CONTROL  WESSELMAN, L.!   379 615000.
      !COMPTROLLER          KELLER, R.A.!  4408 615100.
      !                         TOTAL!  8997*       THERE ARE  9032 SQ. FT. AVAILIABLE ON FLOOR 14,
                                                 THE ASSIGNED AREAS MAY BE EXPANDED BY   35 SQ.FT.
+-----+------------------------------+-------+
   13 !SALES & MARKETING   COOPER, C.M.!  9032 611000.
      !                         TOTAL!  9032*       AND THERE ARE  9032 SQ. FT. AVAILIABLE ON THE FLOOR.

+-----+------------------------------+-------+
   12 !KOHRING, CARTER, AND GUERITEY !  8945 223000.
      !                         TOTAL!  8945*       THERE ARE  9032 SQ. FT. AVAILIABLE ON FLOOR 12.
                                                 THE ASSIGNED AREAS MAY BE EXPANDED BY   87 SQ.FT.
+-----+------------------------------+-------+
   11 !COMPTROLLER         TIGGES  K.E.!  1166 220000.
      !CORP. STAFF COMP.   PALLANTE, T.!  1864 221000.
      !ARTHUR YOUNG AUDITORS         !  1495 223001.
      !TAXATION            HICKEY, C.J.!  4466 226000.
      !                         TOTAL!  8991*       THERE ARE  9032 SQ. FT. AVAILIABLE ON FLOOR 11,
                                                 THE ASSIGNED AREAS MAY BE EXPANDED BY   41 SQ.FT.
+-----+------------------------------+-------+
   10 !SALARY PAYROLL         FLACK, R.!  2131 223110.
      !CONFERENCE AREA               !   516 420005.
      !CONSUM/TECH PRODUCT MILLER, R.F.!  1000 800000.
      !LILY-LIBBEY        ACHENBACH,W.!  1251 810000.
      !                         TOTAL!  4898*       THERE ARE  9032 SQ. FT. AVAILIABLE ON FLOOR 10,
                                                 THE ASSIGNED AREAS MAY BE EXPANDED BY 4134 SQ.FT.
+-----+------------------------------+-------+
    9 !INTEL PROPERTY        CLICK,   M.!  9466 120000.
      !                         TOTAL!  9466*       AND THERE ARE  9466 SQ. FT. AVAILIABLE ON THE FLOOR.

+-----+------------------------------+-------+
    8 !GENERAL LEGAL      MOREHEAD, D.!  8834 110000.
      !                         TOTAL!  8834*       AND THERE ARE  8834 SQ. FT. AVAILIABLE ON THE FLOOR.

+-----+------------------------------+-------+
    7 !WAR ROOM                      !  1500      12.
      !GENERAL LEGAL GROWTH          !  4470 110001.
      !INTEL PROPERTY GROWTH         !  1956 120001.
      !FOOD SERVICE, CAFETERIA       !   970 420003.
      !                         TOTAL!  8896*       THERE ARE  9542 SQ. FT. AVAILIABLE ON FLOOR  7,
                                                 THE ASSIGNED AREAS MAY BE EXPANDED BY  646 SQ.FT.
+-----+------------------------------+-------+
    6 !EXECUTIVE FLOOR               ! 11249     100.
      !                         TOTAL! 11249*       AND THERE ARE 11249 SQ. FT. AVAILIABLE ON THE FLOOR.

+-----+------------------------------+-------+
    5 !GRP.INS./CREDIT UNION         !   993 330004.
      !DISPENSERY                    !  1495 330005.
      !G.O.P.  TIPPEN                !   602 330007.
      !COMMUNICATIONS        HUMMEL, R.!  5663 333000.
      !                         TOTAL!  8753*       THERE ARE  8618 SQ. FT. AVAILIABLE ON FLOOR  5.
                                                 THE ASSIGNED AREAS MUST BE COMPRESSED BY  135 SQ.FT.
+-----+------------------------------+-------+
    4 !CONFERENCE AREA               !  1072 420001.
      !INTERNATIONAL      SPENGLER, W.! 14120 700000.
      !                         TOTAL! 15192*       AND THERE ARE 15192 SQ. FT. AVAILIABLE ON THE FLOOR.

+-----+------------------------------+-------+
+-----+------------------------------+-------+
   31 !CREDIT                CROSS,   A.J.!  2480 214000.
      !INTERNATIONAL GROWTH          !  3981 700001.
      !                         TOTAL!  6461*       THERE ARE  5637 SQ. FT. AVAILIABLE ON FLOOR 31,
                                                 THE ASSIGNED AREAS MUST BE COMPRESSED BY  824 SQ.FT.
+-----+------------------------------+-------+
+-----+------------------------------+-------+
      !SYSTEMS PLANNING    KENNEDY,   J.!  3644 224000.
      !LIBRARY                       !  1200 550001.
      !                         TOTAL!  8326*       THERE ARE  8160 SQ. FT. AVAILIABLE ON FLOOR  3,
                                                 THE ASSIGNED AREAS MUST BE COMPRESSED BY  166 SQ.FT.
+-----+------------------------------+-------+
+-----+------------------------------+-------+
   32 !TREASURER              LOCK, R.W.!  1542 210000.
      !FUNDS & FIN. SERV.    WEYRAUCH,D!   771 211000.
      !FINANCE             HALMRAST, D.!  2566 213000.
      !                         TOTAL!  4879*       THERE ARE  5656 SQ. FT. AVAILIABLE ON FLOOR 32,
                                                 THE ASSIGNED AREAS MAY BE EXPANDED BY  777 SQ.FT.
+-----+------------------------------+-------+
+-----+------------------------------+-------+
    2 !TOTAL COMPENSATION     MCCORMACK!  5402 511000.
      !LABOR RELATIONS     O'SHEA, J.L.!  2119 512000.
      !HUMAN RESOURCES    CHADWELL, J.!  3053 513000.
      !PERSONNEL RELATIONS    MARKS,E.!  1039 513100.
      !SAFETY & HEALTH    ROGERS, C.E.!  2663 514000.
      !CORP. PERSONNEL          MCHUGH!  1757 511000.
      !                         TOTAL! 16233*       THERE ARE 16482 SQ. FT. AVAILIABLE ON FLOOR  2,
                                                 THE ASSIGNED AREAS MAY BE EXPANDED BY  249 SQ.FT.
+-----+------------------------------+-------+
    1 !LOBBY AREA                    !  7247      10.
      !RECEIVING DOCK                !   862 330003.
      !CORP. RELATIONS    PAQUETTE, J.!  9608 400000.
      !                         TOTAL! 17717*       THERE ARE 17501 SQ. FT. AVAILIABLE ON FLOOR  1,
                                                 THE ASSIGNED AREAS MUST BE COMPRESSED BY  216 SQ.FT.
+-----+------------------------------+-------+
      +------------------------------+-------+
```

Figure 12.19 Typical output from a stacking plan program (Morganelli-Heumann and Associates, Los Angeles).

Obviously, numerous refinements could be introduced to make this procedure more effective. In general, quite good results can be produced by execution of permutational procedures of this type.

Standardization analysis

Another type of grouping analysis that is important in office design is *standardization analysis.* Typically, data on work station requirements for office employees is generated by means of a questionnaire survey. The object of standardization analysis is to group employees with similar work station requirements together, so that a standard work station type can be developed for each grouping. Cluster analysis programs can very effectively be employed to perform this task.

The basic approach is as follows. First, the questionnaire responses are expressed as an $n \times t$ data matrix, where the n rows represent the n employees and the t columns represent questions, for example, as follows:

		Questions 1	2	3	4	5
Employees	1	r_{11}	r_{12}	r_{13}	r_{14}	r_{15}
	2	r_{21}	r_{22}	r_{23}	r_{24}	r_{25}
	3	r_{31}	r_{32}	r_{33}	r_{34}	r_{35}
	4	r_{41}	r_{42}	r_{43}	r_{44}	r_{45}
	5	r_{51}	r_{52}	r_{53}	r_{54}	r_{55}
	6	r_{61}	r_{62}	r_{63}	r_{64}	r_{65}

The responses r 'might be expressed on any kind of measurement scale, binary, nominal, ordinal, interval, or ratio. For example, need or lack of need, for an item of equipment might be expressed as 1 or 0, or requirement for storage space might be given in square feet. For purposes of providing a simple worked example, we will assume a binary matrix as follows:

		Questions 1	2	3	4	5
	1	0	1	1	1	1
Employees	2	0	1	0	0	1
	3	1	1	1	0	0
	4	1	1	1	1	1
	5	1	1	0	0	0
	6	0	0	0	0	0

Next, an $n \times n$ matrix of *coefficients of similarity* is computed by comparing rows. In our example, the similarity matrix will be dimensioned 6×6. A great many different formulae may be employed for computing the similarity coefficients, depending upon the type of data collected (Sneath and Sokal 1973). Where data is binary, the following *simple matching coefficient* is often used as a measure of similarity S_{ab} between rows *a* and *b:*

$$S_{ab} = m/n$$

where m = number of matching column entries
n = total number of columns.
The value varies from 0 indicating maximum dissimilarity, to 1 indicating a perfect match. In our example, the similarity matrix computed in this way would be:

	1	2	3	4	5	6
1	1.0	0.6	0.4	0.8	0.2	0.2
2	0.6	1.0	0.2	0.4	0.6	0.6
3	0.4	0.2	1.0	0.6	0.8	0.4
4	0.8	0.4	0.6	1.0	0.4	0.0
5	0.2	0.6	0.8	0.4	1.0	0.6
6	0.2	0.6	0.4	0.0	0.6	1.0

Single or average linkage clustering is next performed upon the similarity matrix to sort employees into subsets having similar work station needs. *Figure 12.20* shows the result of performing single-linkage clustering on our example matrix. Further statistical analysis of the properties of each cluster can be conducted if necessary. Standard work stations can then be designed for particular clusters.

SUGGESTED READINGS

Aguilar, R. J., and Hand, J. E. "A Generalized Linear Model for Optimization of Architectural Planning," in *Proceedings of the 1968 Spring Joint Computer Conference.* Washington, D. C.: Thompson Books, 1968.

Alexander, C. *Notes on the Synthesis of Form.* Cambridge, Mass.: Harvard University Press, 1967.

Broad, E. "Planning a Multilevel Car Park." *Industrial Engineering,* September 1969, pp. 17–23.

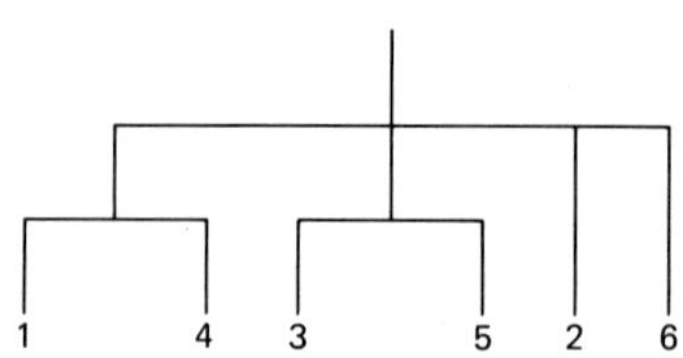

Figure 12.20
Dendrogram for standardization analysis problem.

Browne, J. J., and Kelly, J. J. "Simulation of Elevator for World's Tallest Building." *Transportation Science* 2, no. 1 (1968), pp. 35–56.

Bullock, N. O. A. "Modeling the Demand for Teaching Space." *Environment and Planning B* 1, no. 1 (1974), pp. 69–104.

Bullock, N. O. A.; Dickens, P.; and Steadman, P. "A Theoretical Model for University Planning," in *Urban Space and Structures,* edited by L. Martin and L. March. Cambridge, England: Cambridge University Press, 1972.

Evensmo, J. "The Use of Computer Simulation in Planning the Layout and Operation of a Warehouse." *Computer-Aided Design,* Autumn 1969, pp. 32–36.

Fetter, R. B., and Thompson, J. D. "The Simulation of Hospital Systems." *Operations Research,* September–October 1965, pp. 689–711.

Friend, J. K., and Jessop, W. N. "Towards a Technology of Strategic Choice," in *Local Government and Strategic Choice,* pt 3. Beverly Hills, California: Sage Publications, 1969.

Gero, J. S. "Dynamic Programming in the CAD of Buildings," in *Proceedings of the Second International Conference on Computers in Engineering and Building Design.* Guildford, Surrey, England: IPC Science and Technology Press, 1976.

Gregory, S. A. "Morphological Analysis: Some Simple Explorations," in *Design Methods in Architecture,* edited by G. Broadbent and A. Ward. New York: Wittenborn 1969.

Harper, G. N. "BOP: An Approach to Building Optimization," in *Proceedings of the 1968 ACM National Conference.* Washington, D. C.: Thompson Books, 1968.

Milne, M.A. "CLUSTR: A Program for Structuring Design Problems," in *Proceedings of the 8th Design Automation Workshop.* New York: Association for Computing Machinery, 1971.

Tabor, P. "Analyzing Communication Patterns," in *The Architecture of Form,* edited by L. March. Cambridge, England: Cambridge University Press, 1976.

Tabor, P. "Analyzing Route Patterns," in *The Architecture of Form,* edited by L. March. Cambridge, England: Cambridge University Press, 1976.

13
Automated Spatial Synthesis

Automated spatial synthesis is one of the most interesting, difficult, and controversial areas of computer-aided architectural design. In general terms, the problem may be stated as follows. *Given* a data structure capable of representing a range of building designs *find* a state of the data structure (*i.e.*, a particular design solution) such that specified *objectives* and/or *constraints* are complied with. From this formulation, it can be seen that the quality or usefulness of a solution generated depends upon three things:

1. The capability of the data structure to represent an appropriate range or potential solutions at an appropriate level of detail.
2. The capability of the constraints and/or objectives to accurately and comprehensively reflect important design criteria.
3. The capability of the solution generation procedure to efficiently find solutions which best fit the criteria.

Data structures for building description were extensively discussed in Chapter 6, and it will be assumed here that that chapter has been read and understood. The following section describes alternative formulations (in terms of objectives and constraints) of automated spatial synthesis problems, and this is followed by a discussion of alternative solution generation procedures.

FORMULATION OF ARCHITECTURAL SPATIAL SYNTHESIS PROBLEMS

Quadratic assignment formulation

The earliest, and perhaps still the most popular, formulation of the architectural spatial synthesis problem is as a *quadratic assignment* problem. This formulation is very general, and may be employed for a wide variety of spatial arrangement problems in which circulation cost or some directly analogous objective is to be minimized. In addition to architectural applications, it has been used in such tasks as location of warehouses or other facilities within transportation networks (Koopmans and Beckmann 1957), regional land use planning (Brotchie 1969), and the backboard wiring problem in electronics (Hanan and Kurtzberg 1972).

The quadratic assignment problem was initially formulated in a classic paper by Koopmans and Beckmann (1957). The basic task is to allocate a set of indivisible facilities to a set of locations in such a way that the following objective is minimized

$$\text{Total circulation cost} = \sum_{i=1}^{n} \sum_{j=1}^{n} G_{ij}C_{ij}$$

where

n = number of facilities to be assigned ($\leqq$ number of locations)

G_{ij} = a measure of distance between pairs of located facilities i and j

C_{ij} = a measure of circulation cost per unit distance between i and j

In architectural floor planning applications, the set of locations is commonly taken as the set of cells in a square grid, as shown in *Figure 13.1(a)*. This grid is, of course, readily represented by a two-dimensional array of appropriate dimensions. The entire grid might be employed, or a polygon representing a building outline, lot limits, etc., might be defined within the grid as shown in *Figure 13.1(b)*.

Each space to be located in the plan is then considered to be composed of an appropriate number of square modules, according to required floor area, as shown in *Figure 13.1(c)*. Each square module is represented by an integer defining the space to which it belongs, so that the floor plan layout problem is represented as a problem of assigning integers to locations in a two-dimensional array.

Values for G_{ij} may be computed directly from array subscripts. Either straight line or city block distance may be employed as appro-

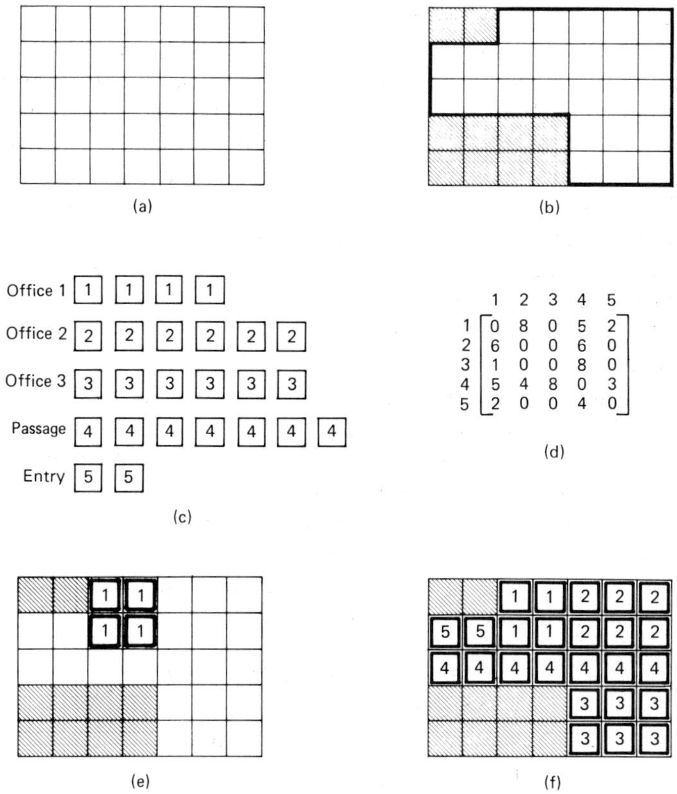

Figure 13.1
Floor plan layout as a quadratic assignment problem. (a) Grid of locations. (b) Building boundary within the grid. (c) Modules to be assigned. (d) Interaction matrix. (e) Preassigned space. (f) One of the many possible assignments of modules to locations.

priate (see *Figure 12.15*). Values for C_{ij} may be taken from an interaction matrix of circulation data. (In addition, an arbitrary high interaction value between modules of the same space is often introduced to prevent "splitting" of spaces.) For example, if the circulation data matrix gives number of trips per week, the objective minimized is total distance traveled by building users. If values are given in terms of travel time or cost per unit distance, then either time spent in circulation or the total cost of that time respectively is minimized.

Numerous variations of this basic formulation are possible. The objective is often modified, for instance, to reflect the assumption that some locations may be regarded as more valuable for particular purposes than others. The modified objective is

$$\sum_{i=1}^{n} \sum_{j=1}^{n} G_{ij}C_{ij} + F_{ij}$$

where F_{ij} is the fixed cost of assigning module i to location j. This term might be employed, for example, to reflect a preference of high status employees for corner locations in an office floor layout.

Very often some spaces may be *preassigned,* to reflect prior design decisions, as shown in *Figure 13.1(e)*. In the case of no defined building perimeter, and no preassigned spaces, an arbitrarily chosen space may be assigned to a central location in the grid to form a nucleus around which an appropriately shaped plan can be "grown."

Of course, there is no restriction to a two-dimension square modular grid. Rectangular, triangular and hexagonal grids, and even irregular grids of polygons of roughly equal area may be employed just as well. Three-dimensional cubic and other lattices may also be utilized to define three-dimensional spatial synthesis problems in quadratic assignment terms.

A quadratic assignment formulation is appropriate *only* in situations where circulation efficiency or some directly analogous objective is regarded as *the* primary determinant of the plan. This might conceivably be more or less the case in facilities such as industrial plants, warehouses, offices, parts of hospitals, educational facilities, libraries, and department stores. Some statistics can be displayed which suggest the importance of circulation cost considerations in these cases. A case study of a U.K. hospital operating theater conducted by Whitehead and Eldars (1964), for example, concluded that the annual operating cost of the theater broke down as follows:

- 7% for buildings and equipment (amortized at 5% of initial cost per annum);
- 22% for maintenance, cleaning, heating, lighting and materials;
- 71% for staff salaries and wages.

Of total staff time in the operating theater, it was estimated that 38% was spent just walking between rooms, so pedestrian movement represented about 23% of annual operating cost.

Some further important theoretical limitations of the quadratic assignment formulation should be noted. It takes no account of shape constraints on spaces. The effects of wall locations and other obstructions are not directly considered. It does not recognize any difference between circulation space and other types of space. It may produce "splitting" of spaces in the plan. The objective function incorporates some assumptions which may be doubtful. Prest and Turvey (1965) point out that to accept it "it is necessary to assume that one time-saving of sixty minutes is worth the same as sixty time-savings of one minute" although "it is clear that some time-savings are valueless." Another possibly doubtful assumption is that circulation flow volumes are independent of the actual configuration of the plan.

A practical limitation is that the collection of necessary circulation and cost data may in many cases be difficult and expensive, if not impossible. In response to this problem, data developed on the basis of experience and subjective professional judgment is very commonly employed in place of actual circulation and cost data. While this practice often produces very plausible looking results, it is difficult to say exactly what these results may mean.

There is no known analytical solution or efficient algorithm for quadratic assignment problems, and very little prospect of discovering one; nor is there a direct way of computing the optimum value of the objective. Enumeration and search procedures of various kinds must be employed. (Some of these are described in the next section.) Even the most powerful currently available procedures can only deal with at most a few hundred modules. No known procedure, with the trivial exception of exhaustive enumeration, guarantees to produce the optimum solution, although most of the better procedures are known to reliably produce solutions of excellent quality.

Because of the limitations of the quadratic assignment formulation, it is most appropriately and effectively employed for certain fairly restricted and specialized floor plan layout problems, most notably layout of work stations on an open office landscape floor, industrial plant layout, and warehouse layout.

Adjacency requirements graph formulation

An alternative approach to formulation of floor plan layout problems is to define a set of adjacency requirements between spaces which must be met, in other words, to specify an *adjacency requirements graph* which must be a subgraph of the dual-graph * of the plan. This graph may be encoded in matrix format. *Figure 13.2* illustrates a typical example of a layout problem formulated in this way.

An adjacency requirements graph formulation may be employed in conjunction with almost any technique for representation of built form. Integer array representations, dimensionless representations,

* See Dual-Graph Representations in Chapter 6.

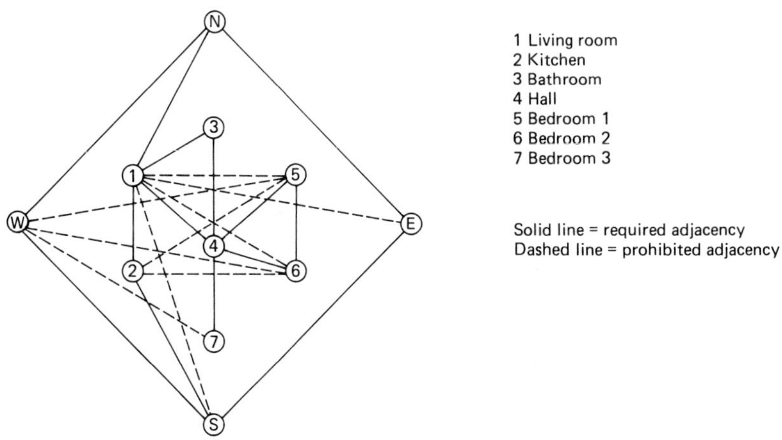

Figure 13.2
An adjacency requirements graph for a floor plan layout problem.

and polygon representations have all been utilized. The graph theoretic representations are, of course, especially closely related to this particular formulation.

The adjacency requirements graph formulation contrasts with the quadratic assignment formulation in two important ways. First, it explicitly specifies in detail the *structure* of the spatial system, rather than requiring optimization of an aggregated measure of the system's *performance.* This makes it much more natural and appropriate for general use in architectural design. Second, it relies upon constraints rather than an objective to identify acceptable solutions. This means that, depending upon the properties of the constraints, there may be multiple acceptable solutions, a unique solution, or no solutions. Thus the design task might be to exhaustively enumerate acceptable solutions, to find any acceptable solution, or to demonstrate whether or not solutions exist.

Dimensional constraints and objectives

An adjacency requirements graph, by itself, usually provides insufficient definition of the characteristics of acceptable solutions. It is normally necessary to give information on dimensional, proportion, and shape constraints as well, if a useful result is to be generated.

Dimensional constraints may be stated by means of *equalities,* for example,

$$\text{length} = x$$

or in terms of *inequalities,* for example,

$$\text{length} > x_1$$

$$\text{length} < x_2$$

Typically, dimensional constraints are applied to the following properties either of a particular object or space or of the building as a whole:

length
width
perimeter
floor area
surface area
volume

In addition, constraints on maximum and minimum allowable distances between objects or spaces may be specified.

Various dimensional properties may also be utilized as objectives to be minimized or maximized in a design. Minimization of a particular dimension, or of total floor area, volume, or surface area are all common objectives. By use of appropriate coefficients, estimated cost can be expressed as a function of floor area or volume, and expected heat losses and gains can be expressed as functions of surface area. These may be appropriate objectives to minimize in some circumstances.

The forms of the functions which describe these various dimensional constraints and objectives have a major effect in determining the ease or difficulty of mathematical solution of spatial synthesis problems. Objectives and constraints involving length, width, perimeter, and distance are usually describable by means of linear functions, but objectives and constraints involving areas and volumes must contain multiplicative terms, and are thus nonlinear. Functional form is also determined in part by the building representation technique employed. For example, where a square grid representation is employed, dimensions must be integer multiples of the module size, so objectives and constraints are defined by integer-valued functions. Where a polygon representation is used, or where dimensioning vectors are employed in conjunction with a dimensionless representation, functions describing dimensional constraints may take on real values. In general, it is a great advantage if nonlinear and integer-valued functions can be avoided. Unfortunately, this is rarely possible in practice.

Ratio constraints and objectives

In some cases, important properties of built forms may be described by means of *ratios* of dimensions or areas. For example, the plan *proportion* of a rectangular room is defined as the ratio of length:width, and it may be desired to impose proportion constraints in order to prevent the room either from becoming too long and narrow or too square. For non-rectangular objects, proportion constraints may be applied to the *bounding rectangle,* as shown in *Figure 13.3*.

Since compactness of built form clearly relates in a general way to construction cost and operating efficiency of a building, attempts are sometimes made to optimize some kind of *compactness ratio,* such as perimeter:floor area, or surface:volume ratio (*Figure 13.4*).

Most ratio constraints and objectives of practical importance are described by linear functions, so they tend to introduce few additional computational problems.

Figure 13.3
Bounding rectangle of a non-rectilinear shape.

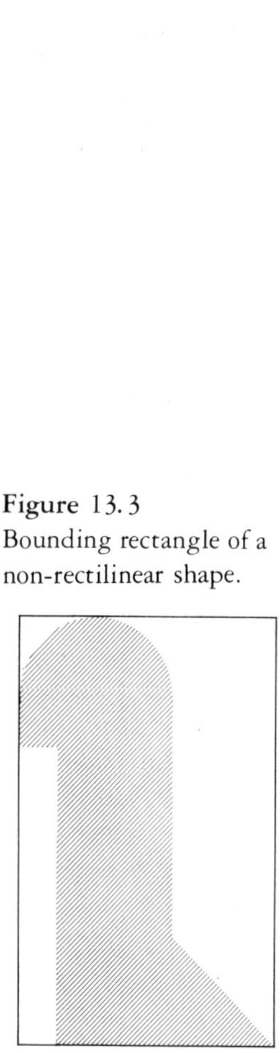

Shape constraints

Shape constraints have been given relatively little attention by developers of spatial synthesis programs, although they are obviously of considerable importance. The usual approach to constraining the shape of a two-dimensional object, such as the plan of a room, is to employ some measure of similarity to a reference shape such as a rectangle. A typical example, applicable to rectilinear plan forms, is illustrated in *Figure 13.5*. A minimum bounding rectangle is drawn around the shape as shown, and the shape's percentage coverage of its

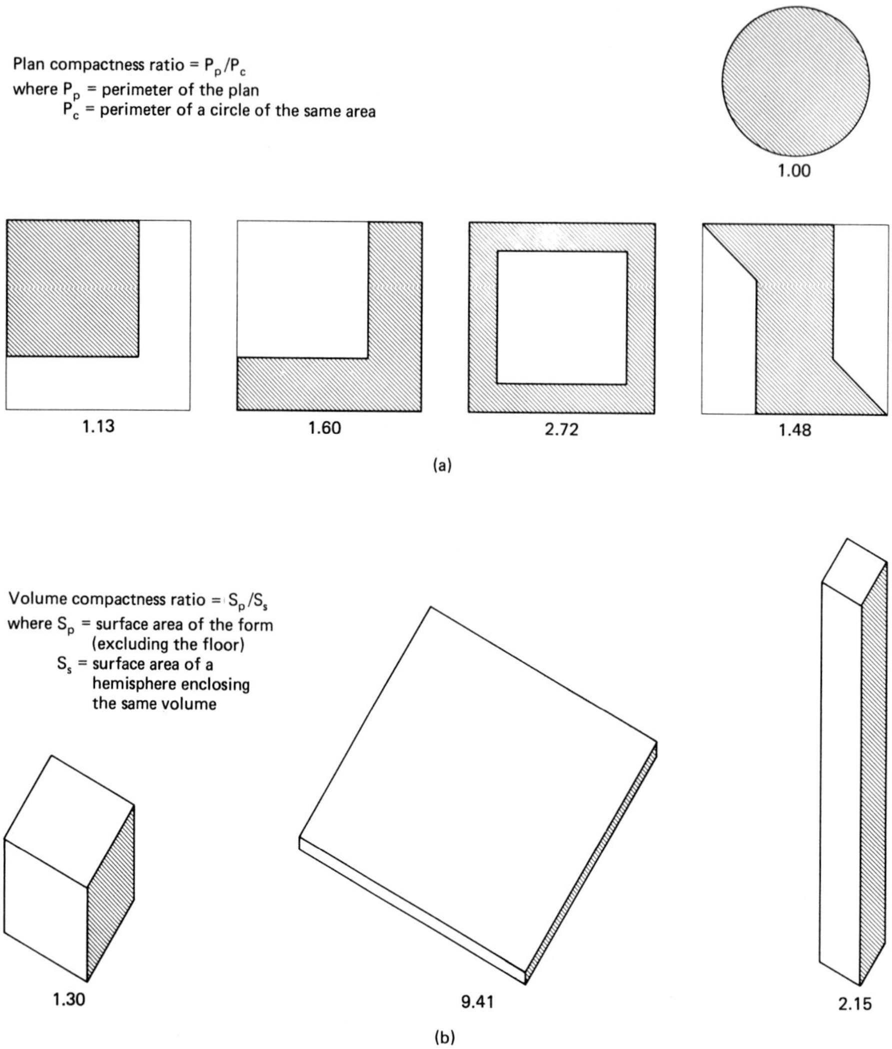

Figure 13.4
Compactness ratios. (a) Plan compactness ratios for several shapes enclosing the same areas. (b) Volume compactness ratios for several forms enclosing the same volumes.

minimum bounding rectangle is calculated. The value is low if the shape is very irregular, and 100% if the shape is in fact rectangular. Thus a plan shape can be constrained to be reasonably "rectangular" by setting a minimum allowable value for rectangle coverage. Similar measures based on coverage of other polygons, circles, ellipses, etc., can be developed. For three-dimensional forms, bounding rectangular parallelepipeds and other polyhedra, spheres, etc., may be similarly employed.

Numerical description of arbitrary closed figures has become an important topic for geographers interested in classifying and comparing shapes of territories, biologists concerned with the shapes of organisms, psychologists measuring visual preferences, and computer scientists working on pattern recognition. Numerous different measures of shape have been developed by researchers in these fields in recent years. Typical examples are described by Attneave and Arnault (1956), Bunge (1966), Haggett and Chorley (1969) and March and Steadman (1974). Some examples are illustrated in *Figure 13.6.* They may be useful for specification of shape constraints on built form in some situations.

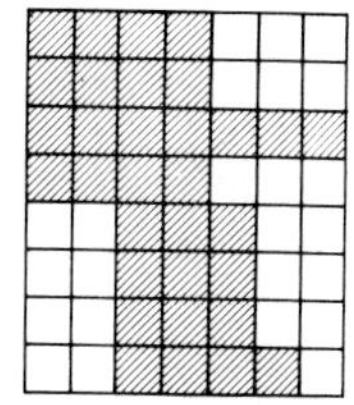

Figure 13.5
Bounding rectangle coverage of a rectilinear plan shape.

Constraint graphs

Some appropriate combination of adjacency, dimensional, ratio, and shape objectives and constraints is very often sufficient to appropriately describe the criteria for a spatial synthesis problem. But in many problems, it may be important to consider a variety of types of relations between objects in addition to adjacency/non-adjacency. This is particularly the case in site planning, and furniture and equipment layout problems, in which discrete objects are relatively sparsely distributed within a spatial domain. Typical examples of further relations which might be important are that an object should or should not be visible from another object, that two or more objects should be aligned, that two objects should be symmetrical about some axis, and so on.

Where a variety of different types of relations between objects must be dealt with, a *constraint graph* is an appropriate technique to employ. An example is shown in *Figure 13.7.* A constraint graph closely resembles an adjacency graph, except that each edge is now

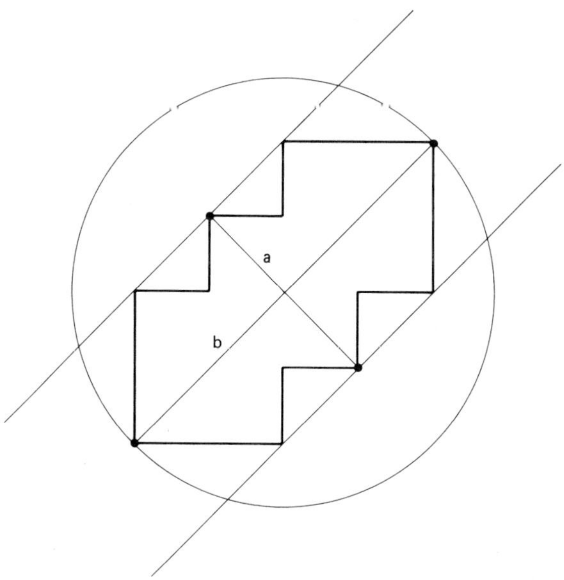

Figure 13.6
Some measures of shape (after Haggett and Chorley (1969)). (a) Variables employed in shape measures.

	Form ratio $4a/\pi a^2$	Circularity ratio $4\pi a/p^2$	Elongation ratio $2/a\sqrt{\frac{a}{\pi}}$	Ellipticity ratio $4a/\pi ab$
 Garvey house, Urbana, Illinois	1.00	1.00	1.00	1.00
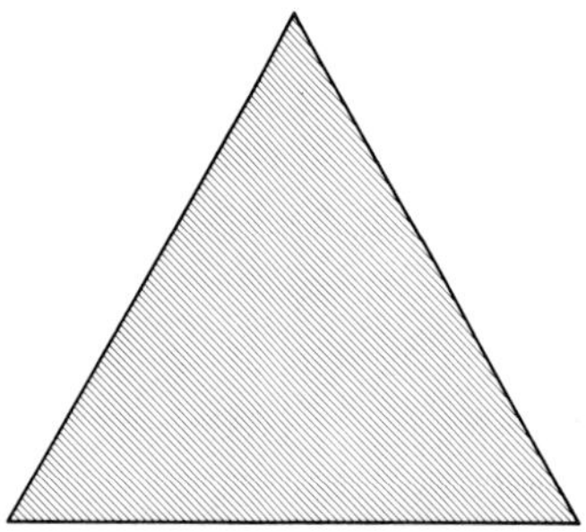 Adams house, Vinita, Oklahoma	0.74	0.60	0.86	0.74
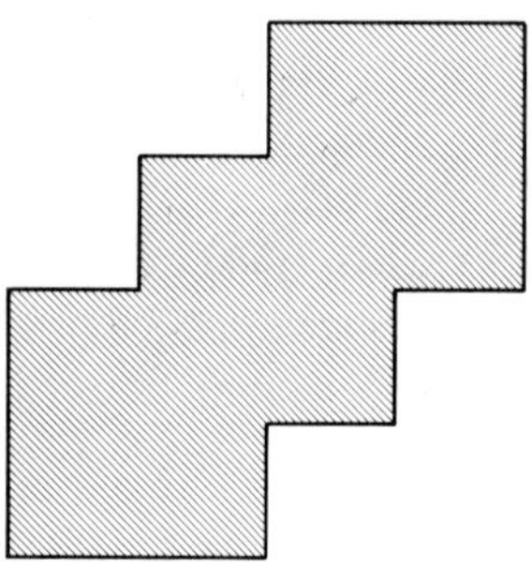 Wilson house, Pensacola Bay, Florida	1.59	0.49	1.26	0.80
 Trinity Baptist Church, Duncan, Oklahoma	0.91	0.91	0.95	0.91

Figure 13.6
(b) Plan shapes of some projects by Bruce Goff (no common scale).

Plan	Form ratio $4a/\pi a^2$	Circularity ratio $4\pi a/p^2$	Elongation ratio $2/a\sqrt{\frac{a}{\pi}}$	Ellipticity ratio $4a/\pi ab$
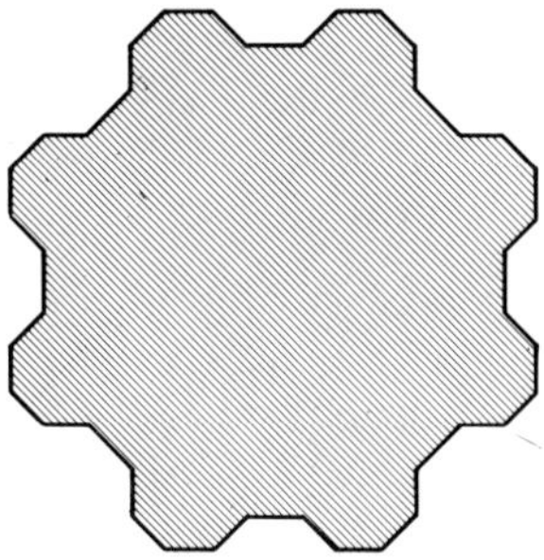 Nicol house, Kansas City, Missouri	1.00	0.70	1.00	1.00
 Gutman house, Gulfport, Mississippi	0.67	0.39	0.82	0.67
 Pollock house, Oklahoma City	0.85	0.52	0.92	0.85
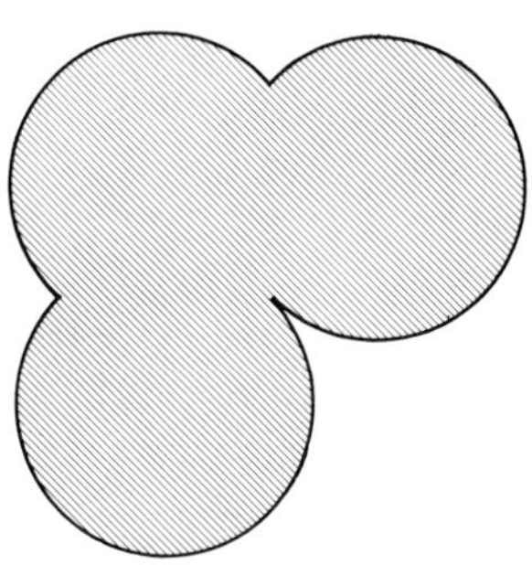 Mc Cullough house, Wichita Falls, Texas	1.62	0.91	1.27	1.21

Figure 13.6
(c) Plan shapes of some projects by Bruce Goff (no common scale).

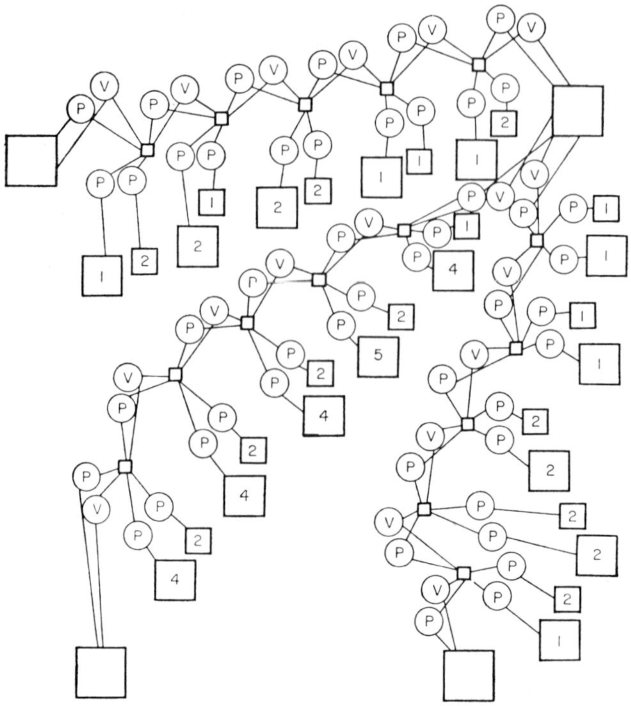

Figure 13.7
A constraint graph for a site layout problem (from Weizapfel and Handel (1975)). Squares represent housing units and other buildings, and the characters in the small circles are constraint labels. A label P indicates that the buildings linked by the constraint should be near to each other, and a label V that there should be visual access.

labeled to represent the type (and perhaps value) of the relation that is indicated. Eastman (1975) and Pfefferkorn (1975) have employed constraint graphs in the formulation of furniture and equipment layout problems, and Weinzapfel and Handel *et al* (1975) have used constraint graphs to formulate site planning and three-dimensional building design problems.

Where a constraint graph formulation is utilized, the task may either be to find a solution which is feasible in the sense that it meets all constraints, or else to find a solution which meets as many of the defined constraints as possible, and as closely as possible (assuming that the problem is over-constrained). In the latter case, the optimization of some measure of "closeness of fit" may be taken as the objective. For example, Weinzapfel and Handel (1975) employ an error function such that when a constraint is satisfied the error is 0, and any dissatisfaction results in a non-zero value for the error function.

Syntactic formulations

Another approach to describing complex patterns of relational requirements is to formally define a *shape grammar* which incorporates an appropriate set of relational rules. A *shape* may be defined, for present purposes, as a finite arrangement of lines on a planar surface. One shape is a *subshape* of a second shape if and only if every part of the first shape is a part of the second shape. Using these concepts of shape and subshape, a shape grammar may now be defined as follows (Stiny 1976):

A *shape grammar* SG has four parts:

1. V_T is a finite set of shapes.
2. V_M is a finite set of shapes.
3. R is a finite set of *shape rules* of the form u→v where u and v are shapes made up of shapes in V_T or of shapes in V_M. The shape u must have a subshape made of shapes in V_M.
4. I is a shape made up of shapes in V_T or shapes in V_M. The shape I must have a subshape made up of shapes in V_M.

A shape grammar SG is given by the 4-tuple: $SG = \langle V_T, V_M, R, I \rangle$. Shapes made up of shapes in V_T are called *terminals*. Shapes made up of shapes in V_M are called *markers*. No subshape of a terminal is a subshape of a marker. This condition insures that terminals and markers in shapes can be distinguished uniquely. For a shape rule u→v in the set R, u is called the *left side* of the shape rule; v is called the *right side* of the shape rule. The shape I is called the *initial shape*.

A shape is generated by a shape grammar $SG = \langle V_T, V_M, R, I \rangle$ by beginning with the initial shape I and recursively applying shape rules in the set R until no shape rule can be applied. A shape rule u→v applies to a shape s if and only if there is a Euclidean transformation G such that G (u) is a subshape of s. The result of applying the shape rule u→v to the shape s under the Euclidean transformation G is the shape produced by replacing the occurrence of G(u) in s with G(v). The shape generation process terminates when no shape rule in the set R can be applied. The *language* defined by a shape grammar is the set of shapes generated by the shape grammar that are made up of terminals or parts of terminals only.

Figure 13.8(a) illustrates how a simple shape grammar can be employed to define rules for combining half-hexagon tables into groupings. The terminal vocabulary VT consists of one element, a half-hexagon. There is also only one marker, the black circle, in VM. The shape rules R define allowable ways of combining tables edge-to-edge. In addition, provision is made for removing the marker, so that the generation process can terminate. The initial shape I consists of a table and a superimposed marker. *Figure 13.8(b)* shows various shapes in the language defined by SG. These were all generated by beginning with I, applying shape rules in some particular sequence and finally applying the marker-removal rule. The reader can easily generate many more possibilities.

Shape grammars have been discussed in detail by Stiny (1975) and Gips (1975). Architectural applications are dealt with in a paper by Stiny (1976). The types of architecturally important grammars that can be defined include floor plan layout grammars, furniture arrangement grammars, and site layout grammars. Once a grammar has been defined, a computer can be employed to generate forms in the corresponding language. The task may either be to enumerate forms

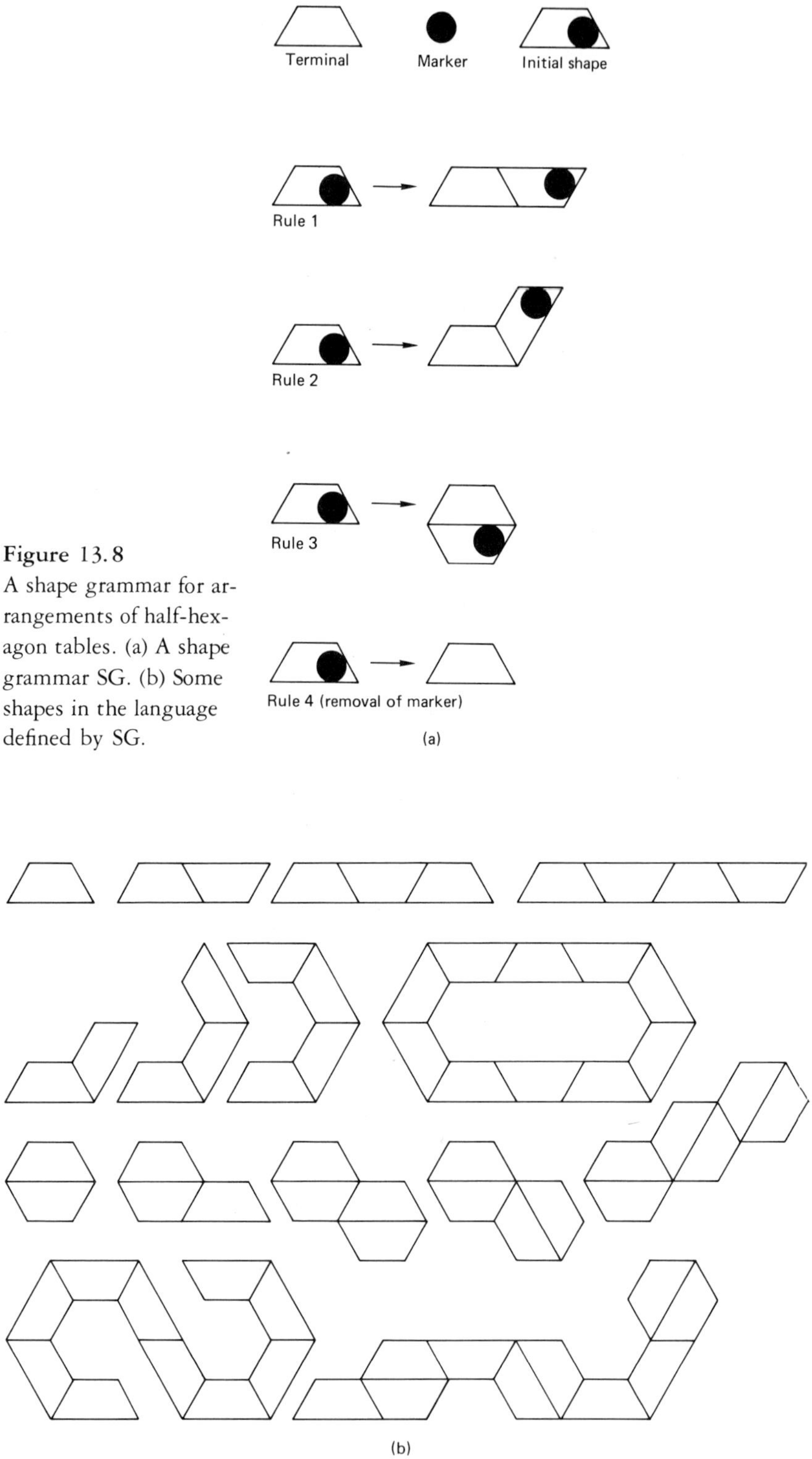

Figure 13.8
A shape grammar for arrangements of half-hexagon tables. (a) A shape grammar SG. (b) Some shapes in the language defined by SG.

in the language, or to produce particular forms in the language that have some particularly desirable properties.

TYPES OF SOLUTION SYNTHESIS PROCEDURES

Strong and weak solution synthesis procedures

We now turn from considering the task of problem formulation to a discussion of solution synthesis procedures. According to the model of design processes which was introduced in Chapter 2, a solution synthesis procedure is a procedure for producing or making explicit for consideration members of the set U of potential solutions to a problem. Hopefully, these potential solutions are members of the goal set G. A useful distinction between *strong* and *weak* methods for this purpose has been introduced by Newell (1973):

> A method has two sides. On the one hand, it demands certain information about any task to which it is to be applied. This shows up in the "givens" of the problem statement. These demands for information may be stringent or liberal. On the other hand, the method delivers certain things in the way of results—or at least chances of results—for various expenditures of effort. Again, it may deliver a lot or a little, and it may do so with certainty or with plausibility, and cheaply or dearly. In general, the more information available the better the results that can be obtained. Conversely, strong results imply strong information demands, and weak demands can yield only weak results.

A typical example of a strong problem-solving method is the simplex method for solving linear programming problems in economics. This method is easily implemented as a computer program which produces the required results very quickly and cheaply. But it imposes some extremely stringent requirements. To use it, we must find a way to model the problem as one of finding appropriate values for a set of real variables. Furthermore, we must know how to express the solution criteria in terms of an appropriate linear objective function and linear constraints. Thus its applicability is restricted to a very narrow and specific domain of problems.

A typical example of a weak method is the random-search method for finding a path through a maze. It is extremely inefficient, and will normally result in exploration of numerous dead-ends before a satisfactory solution is found. But it requires absolutely no knowledge of the structure of the maze, and it can be applied equally appropriately to any maze with any structure. Indeed some form of general random search procedure can be employed for solution of any reasonably well-defined problem that one can imagine.

Procedures applicable to architectural spatial synthesis problems

Architectural spatial synthesis involves a spectrum of problem types, ranging from those to which very strong methods are applicable, to those for which only very weak and general methods may be employed. Strong methods tend to be applicable only to those tasks which are usually thought of as being rather narrow and technical, while many broad central problems respond only to very weak methods. For this reason, important automated architectural spatial synthesis techniques often relate rather less closely to typical engineering and operations research methods than might be expected, and rather more to the "weak and general" methods characteristic of artificial intelligence systems.

The following sections discuss a range of synthesis procedures, arranged roughly in order from the weakest and most general to the strongest and most specific. The completely general, but usually inefficient *generate-and-test* procedure is introduced first. Next, somewhat less general but more powerful *improvement* procedures are considered. *Heuristic search* techniques, which are mostly borrowed from the field of artificial intelligence, are considered next, then *linear and nonlinear programming* techniques borrowed from operations research. Finally, the application of *analytical* procedures is discussed.

GENERATE-AND-TEST PROCEDURES

The weakest and most general of all problem-solving methods follows directly from the formulation of problems in terms of a set U of potential solutions and a goal set G. It is usually called *generate-and-test.* Members of the set U of potential solutions are simply produced in some sequence until a member of G is discovered (*Figure 13.9*). Perhaps the most famous example of successful use of a generate-and-test procedure occurred in Thomas Edison's development of the incandescent lamp. It is reported that he systematically tested some 1,600 potential filament materials before finding one which possessed the desired characteristics.

Figure 13.9
The generate-and-test procedure.

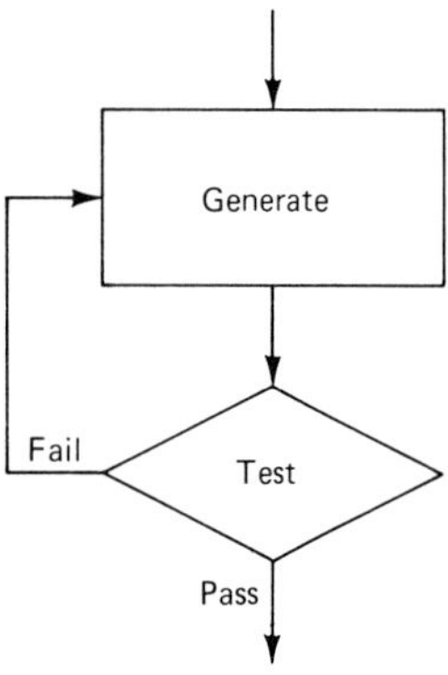

The sequence of production may constitute either a systematic or a random sampling of the elements of U. If satisfactory solutions do in fact exist, then the generate-and-test procedure is guaranteed to find one, provided that the procedure is allowed to cycle long enough, since eventually all the elements of U will be produced. The difficulty is that, in real design problems of any magnitude or complexity, astronomically long sequences of trials would need to be cycled through before a satisfactory solution was discovered.

Exhaustive generate-and-test

Nonetheless, simple "brute force" enumeration of the elements of U has occasionally been used as a procedure for automated generation of solutions to certain strictly limited classes of floor plan layout problems. Mitchell, Steadman and Liggett (1976), for example, have enumerated (up to the case of eight rectangles) all topologically distinct mosaics of rectangles packing together to completely fill a larger containing rectangle, and suggest that this can be a useful basis for an approach to the design of small houses. They point out that when a complete enumeration is once made, the enumerated possibilities may be stored on computer file, and appropriate solutions to particular problems retrieved as required; thus the potentially high computation cost of the initial enumeration might be spread over a large number of subsequent applications.

Utilizing a graph-theoretical approach analogous to that of Mitchell, Steadman and Liggett, Grason (1970) had earlier developed a program which exhaustively enumerated mosaics of rectangles in order to find floor plans satisfying adjacency and dimensional requirements. However, run times of the order of several hours on a large and powerful computer were reported for problems involving six or more rectangles.

Random generate-and-test

Rather more frequently than exhaustive enumeration, random or constrained-random sampling of the elements of U has been employed in automated solution of floor-plan and site-plan layout problems by generate-and-test. The ALDEP floor plan layout program described by Seehof and Evans (1967) uses a simple square grid representation of floor plans, and attempts to assign modules to grid locations such that adjacency requirements between spaces are met. Each adjacency requirement has associated with it a numerical importance weighting. A random sampling strategy, in conjunction with some very simple assembly rules, is employed to very rapidly and cheaply generate plans for consideration. Each plan that is produced is scored by summing the importance weightings of the adjacency requirements that are met. The plans for which the score exceeds a specified minimum value are printed out. A typical result is shown in *Figure 13.10.* The program does very well at cheaply producing a large number of layouts which meet the adjacency requirements with an acceptable level of success. But the formulation is too simplistic for the results to be very useful for most practical architectural purposes.

A particularly interesting application of random sampling techniques to investigation of site plans has been reported in a thesis by Laios (1974). Laios' program sequentially places housing units on a site by attaching new units to the edges of units already placed in position (*Figure 13.11*). Restrictions on permissible attachments are

Number	Area (sq. ft.)	Area (10ft. × 10 ft. modules)
1	610	6
2	1537	15
3	2532	25
4	2417	24
5	1721	17
6	3321	33
7	1630	16
8	3239	32
9	2014	20
10	2024	20
11	2210	22

(a)

	1	2	3	4	5	6	7	8	9	10	11
1	X	A	D	B	D	D	D	C	C	D	F
2	A	X	D	C	D	D	D	D	D	D	D
3	D	D	X	D	D	C	C	D	D	B	C
4	D	D	D	D	B	D	D	D	D	D	D
5	C	D	D	A	X	D	D	B	D	D	B
6	D	D	B	D	D	X	A	D	D	D	D
7	B	C	D	D	B	D	X	D	C	D	D
8	D	C	D	D	C	D	D	X	D	D	D
9	B	D	D	C	D	D	D	D	X	C	D
10	D	D	D	D	D	D	D	D	D	X	C
11	F	D	D	D	D	D	D	D	D	C	X

Code	Interpretation
A	Absolutely essential to be located near department.
B	Essential to be located near department.
C	Important to be located near department.
D	Optional to be located near department.
F	Undesirable to be located near department.
X	No preference of department to itself.

(b)

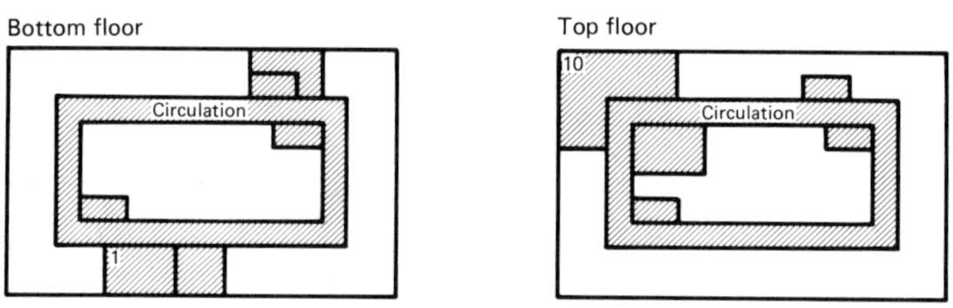

(c)

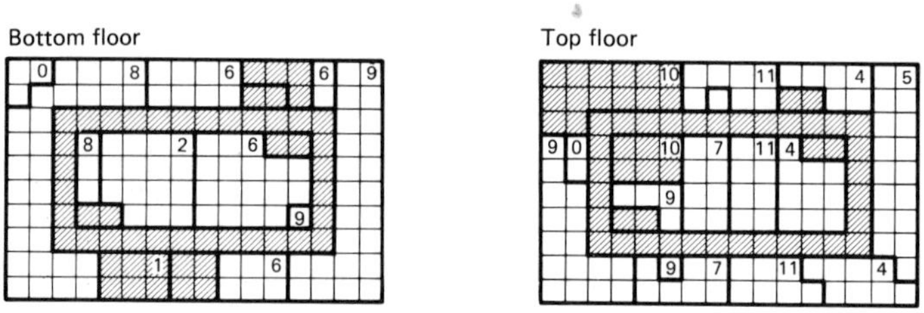

(d)

Figure 13.10
Typical result produced by the ALDEP floor plan layout program (after Seehof and Evans (1967)). (a) Department areas. (b) Interaction matrix. (c) Building outline and preassigned departments (hatched). (d) Layout generated by a run of ALDEP.

specified; for example, a window in a located unit may not be closed off by attachment of a new unit. At each step, the program is faced with a range of choices about which type of unit to place next, and where amongst the range of permissible positions to locate it. A random number generator is used to make these choices. The purpose of the program is not to generate specific design alternatives, but rather to investigate the characteristic, generic properties of patterns which

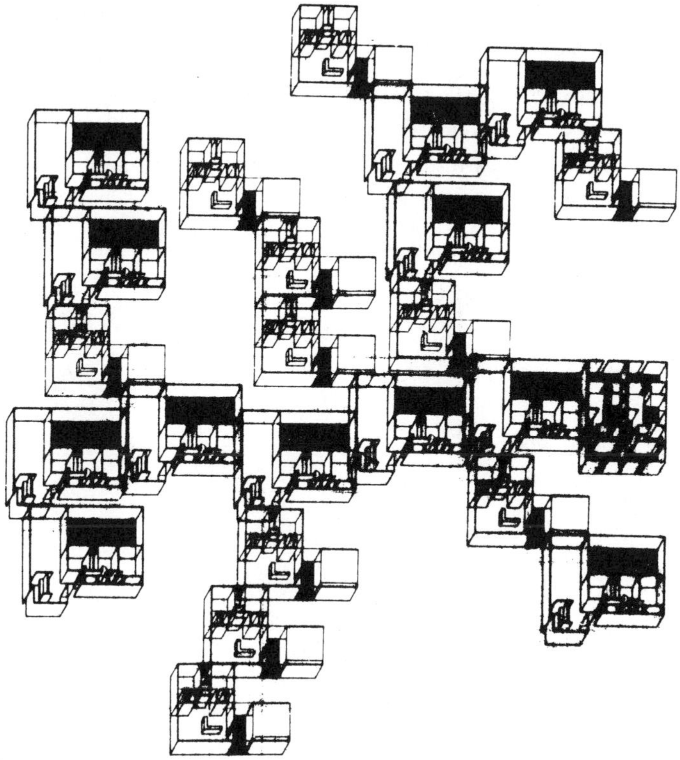

Figure 13.11
Site plan produced by a constrained random generation process (Dimitrious Laios, School of Architecture and Urban Planning, UCLA).

evolve as a result of particular mixes of unit types and attachment restrictions.

Teicholz (1969), Fromboluti (1971), and Velez-Jahn (1972) also describe programs which produce floor and site-plan arrangements by use of random number generators in conjunction with some simple assembly rules.

IMPROVEMENT PROCEDURES

Blind variation and selective retention

A straightforward extension of the generate-and-test approach is to utilize an *evolutionary* or *improvement* strategy, in which an initially given design is incrementally improved by means of some sequence of small modifications. The concept of an improvement strategy is perhaps best introduced by means of an analogy. Imagine that you are lost on a hillside on a very dark night, and that you can only see a few feet in any direction. Your objective is to reach the highest peak in the neighborhood. A simple (though not very clever) strategy would be the following:

1. Walk a few feet in any randomly chosen direction from your present position P to a new position P_1
2. Stop, and assess whether P_1 is higher than P
3. If so, call P_1, P and repeat the process from step 1, else
4. Retrace steps to P, choose a new direction, and try again.

As stated above, this strategy does not incorporate a termination rule. A reasonable rule to include might be:

> After 10 unsuccessful attempts to move from P, stop and assume that you are now located at the peak.

Figure 13.12
A simple improvement procedure for finding the peak of a hill. (a) Typical path generated by a simple improvement procedure for finding a peak. (b) Where more than one peak exists in the neighborhood the procedure may only find a local peak.

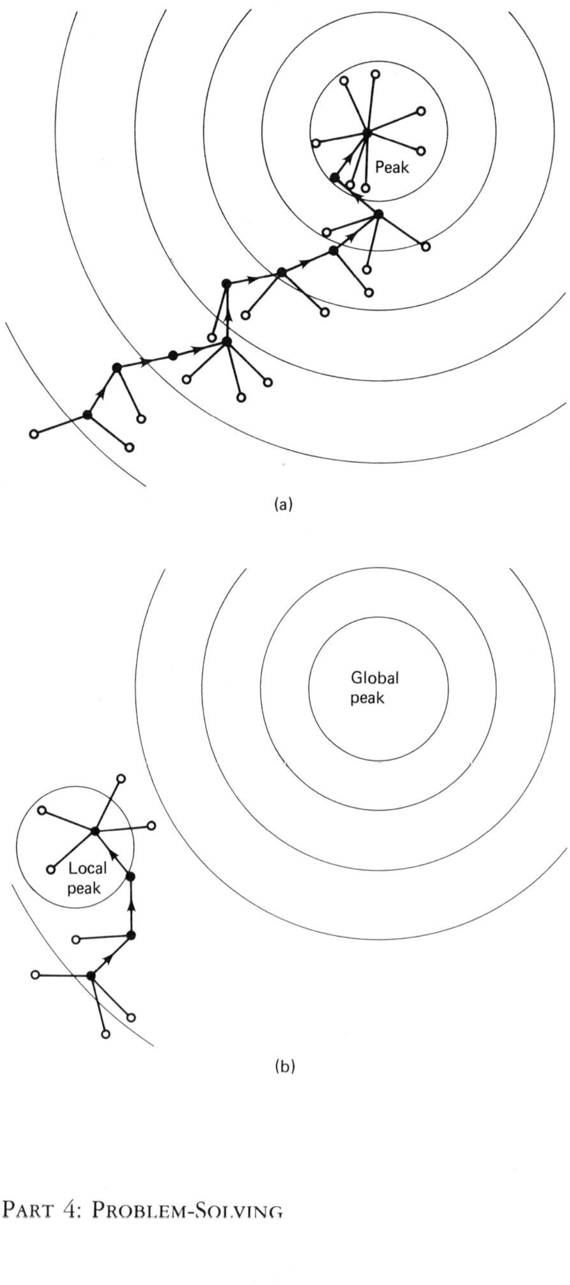

Assuming that only one peak exists in the neighborhood, as shown in *Figure 13.12(a)*, this strategy will necessarily guide you to it. You know to terminate the search when you reach the peak, since movement in any direction from that point results in a descent. The strategy is not so reliable in more complex topography (*Figure 13.12(b)*) however, since it has no way of distinguishing between purely "local" peaks and the highest peak.

This is essentially the Darwinian model of evolution, in which mutations are randomly generated, but only those which are in some sense "better" survive. It has been suggested by numerous authors, notably Popper (1961) and Campbell (1960), that this is a very general and fundamental type of problem-solving process.

Evolutionary strategies of this type can be applied to the solution of spatial arrangement problems in which it is possible to start with some initial configuration, make incremental changes, and test the effect of each change on the value of an objective function. An illustrative application to a trivial spatial arrangement problem is shown in *Figure 13.13*. The starting configuration is a random field of 30% black and 70% white squares (*Figure 13.13(a)*), and the objective is to rearrange the squares so that there are as few direct adjacencies of black squares with white squares as possible. It is obvious that the optimum solution must be a tight cluster of black squares. To

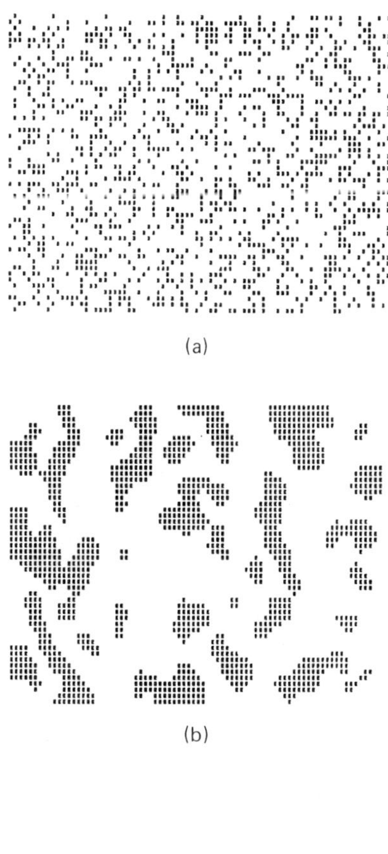

(a)

(b)

Figure 13.13
Application of an improvement procedure to a spatial arrangement problem. (a) Initial random field. (b) Result produced by transposition procedure. The system had reached effective stability after approximately 200,000 attempted transpositions for approximately 900 successes.

solve this problem by computer, we might employ the following blind variation and selective retention procedure:

1. Randomly select a black square and a white square
2. Transpose
3. If number of direct adjacencies of black squares with white squares is reduced go to 1, else
4. Transpose back to original locations

   Go to 1

For a termination rule, we can specify that the procedure should stop after some large number (say 10,000) of successive unsuccessful transpositions.

The result produced by application of this strategy (*Figure 13.13(b)*) illustrates two important properties of improvement strategies. First, it is obvious that a "local" rather than "global" optimum is normally reached, *i.e.*, (in this case) a configuration of numerous small black clusters rather than one large black cluster. The exact form of the result produced depends on the starting configuration and the sequence of attempted transpositions.

Figure 13.14
A "greatest improvement" procedure for finding the peak of a hill. (a) Flow diagram of procedure. (b) Typical path traced out in moving to a peak. Dots represent reference points and shaded circles represent search radii.

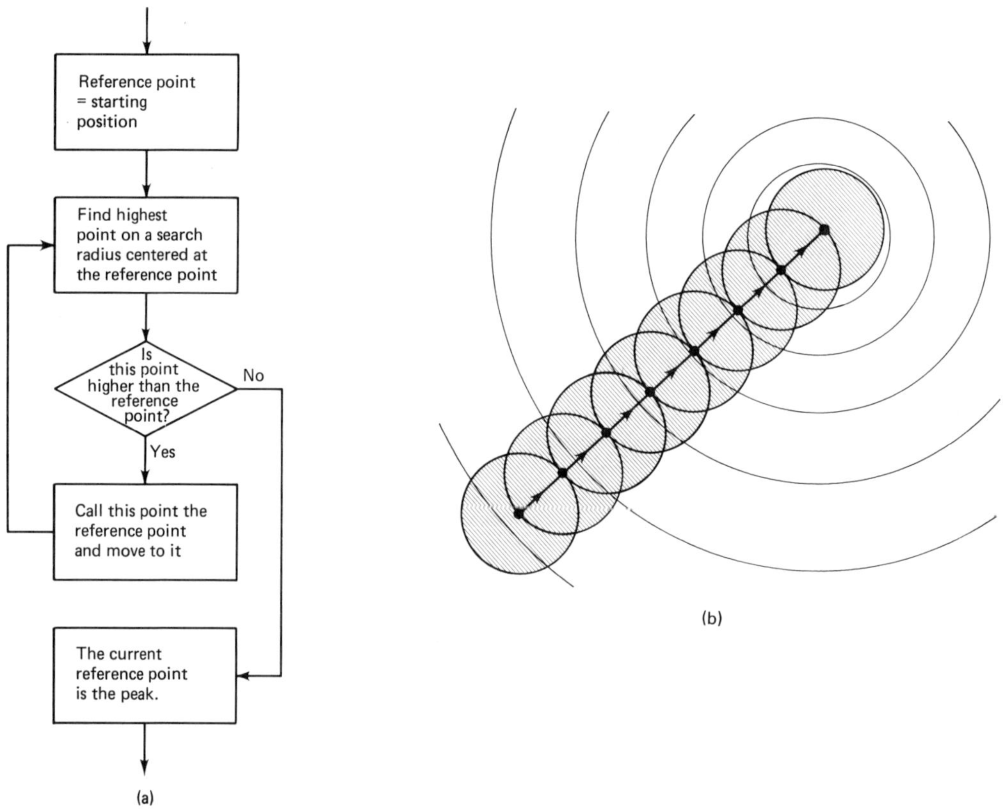

"Greatest improvement" procedures

An obvious improvement over blind variation and selective retention, which it is often possible to make, is to head in the direction of "greatest improvement" rather than in a randomly chosen direction. The application of this strategy to the problem of finding the highest peak in the neighborhood is shown in *Figure 13.14*.

"Greatest improvement" procedures have been quite widely used in floor plan layout programs. One of the earliest and best known of these programs is CRAFT (Armour and Buffa 1963). CRAFT utilizes a square grid representation of a floor plan, and employs the quadratic assignment formulation of the floor plan layout problem. It begins with an initial layout input by the user, and computes the value of the quadratic objective function for that layout. Subject to certain simple restrictions, which insure, for instance, that rooms will not be split up, all possible transpositions of pairs of square modules are then considered. The transposition which results in the greatest improvement in the objective function is executed. This cycle is repeated until no further significant improvements in the value of the objective function can be made. An example is shown in *Figure 13.15*.

This strategy is fairly expensive computationally, and unfortunately, the amount of computation required grows as the square of the number of modules in the plan. It is feasible to deal with problems involving 40 or fewer spaces, but computation cost would grow very steeply for larger problems. Very significant improvements over the initial value of the objective function can be made, but often at the expense of twisting spaces into unacceptable shapes.

Department	Area (Hundreds of Square Feet)
A	27
B	18
C	27
D	18
E	18
F	18
G	9
H	9
J	9
K	24
L	60
M	42
N	18
P	24
R	27
S	75
T	64
U	41
V	27
W	45

(a)

Figure 13.15
Typical results produced by the CRAFT program (from Armour and Buffa, 1963). (a) Required departmental areas for a plant layout problem. (b) Interdepartment interaction matrix. (Figures represent material handling costs expressed in dollars per annum per one-hundred feet moved.) (c) Initial layout generated by hand. Total annual material handling cost = $10,164. (d) Local optimum solution generated by CRAFT. Total annual material handling costs are reduced by 23% to $7,862.09. Departments with dark outlines have not been altered.

	A	B	C	D	E	F	G	H	J	K	L	M	N	P	R	S	T	U	V	W
A	0.	1.800	1.200	0.	0.	0.	0.	0.	0.	1.040	1.120	0.	0.	1.200	0.	0.	0.	0.	0.	0.
B	1.800	0.	0.960	24.450	0.780	0.	13.950	0.	1.200	1.350	0.	0.	0.	0.	0.	0.	0.	0.	6.900	0.
C	1.200	0.960	0.	0.	0.	2.210	0.	0.	3.150	3.900	0.	0.	0.	13.050	0.	0.	0.	0.	13.650	0.
D	0.	24.450	0.	0.	1.C80	5.700	7.500	0.	2.340	0.	0.	1.400	0.	0.	0.	0.	0.	1.500	15.750	0.
E	0.	0.780	0.	1.080	0.	0.	2.250	1.350	0.	1.560	0.	0.	0.	0.	1.350	0.	0.	0.	0.	0.
F	0.	0.	2.210	5.700	0.	0.	6.150	0.	0.	0.	0.	0.450	0.	0.	0.	0.	0.	1.050	0.	0.
G	0.	13.950	0.	7.500	2.250	6.150	0.	24.000	0.	1.870	0.	0.	0.	0.960	0.	0.	0.	1.650	0.	3.750
H	0.	0.	0.	0.	1.350	0.	24.000	0.	0.	0.	0.	0.	0.600	0.	0.	0.	0.	0.	7.500	33.450
J	0.	1.200	3.150	2.340	0.	0.	0.	0.	0.	0.	0.	0.	0.	7.500	0.	0.	7.500	0.	0.	0.
K	1.040	1.350	3.900	0.	1.560	0.	1.870	0.	0.	0.	0.360	12.000	0.	18.600	1.920	0.	0.	0.	5.250	0.
L	1.120	0.	0.	0.	0.	0.	0.	0.	0.	0.360	0.	2.250	0.	3.000	0.960	22.500	–0.	–0.	–0.	0.
M	0.	0.	0.	1.400	0.	0.450	0.	0.	0.	12.000	2.250	0.	0.	0.	1.650	0.	15.000	0.	8.400	0.
N	0.	0.	0.	0.	0.	0.	0.	0.600	0.	0.	0.	0.	0.	8.000	1.040	6.000	0.	0.	0.	0.
P	1.200	0.	13.050	0.	0.	0.	0.960	0.	7.500	18.600	3.000	0.	8.000	0.	9.750	0.	0.	0.900	0.	0.
R	0.	0.	0.	0.	1.350	0.	0.	0.	0.	1.920	0.960	1.650	1.040	9.750	0.	0.	5.250	0.	0.	0.
S	0.	0.	0.	0.	0.	0.	0.	0.	0.	0.	–0.	0.	6.000	0.	0.	0.	12.000	0.	0.	0.
T	0.	0.	0.	0.	0.	0.	0.	0.	7.500	0.	–0.	15.000	0.	0.	5.250	12.000	0.	0.	7.500	0.
U	0.	0.	0.	1.500	0.	1.050	1.650	0.	0.	0.	–0.	0.	0.	0.900	0.	0.	0.	0.	4.650	0.
V	0.	6.900	13.650	15.750	0.	0.	0.	7.500	0.	5.250	–0.	8.400	0.	0.	0.	0.	7.500	4.650	0.	0.
W	0.	0.	0.	0.	0.	0.	3.750	33.450	0.	0.	0.	0.	0.	0.	0.	0.	0.	0.	0.	0.

(b)

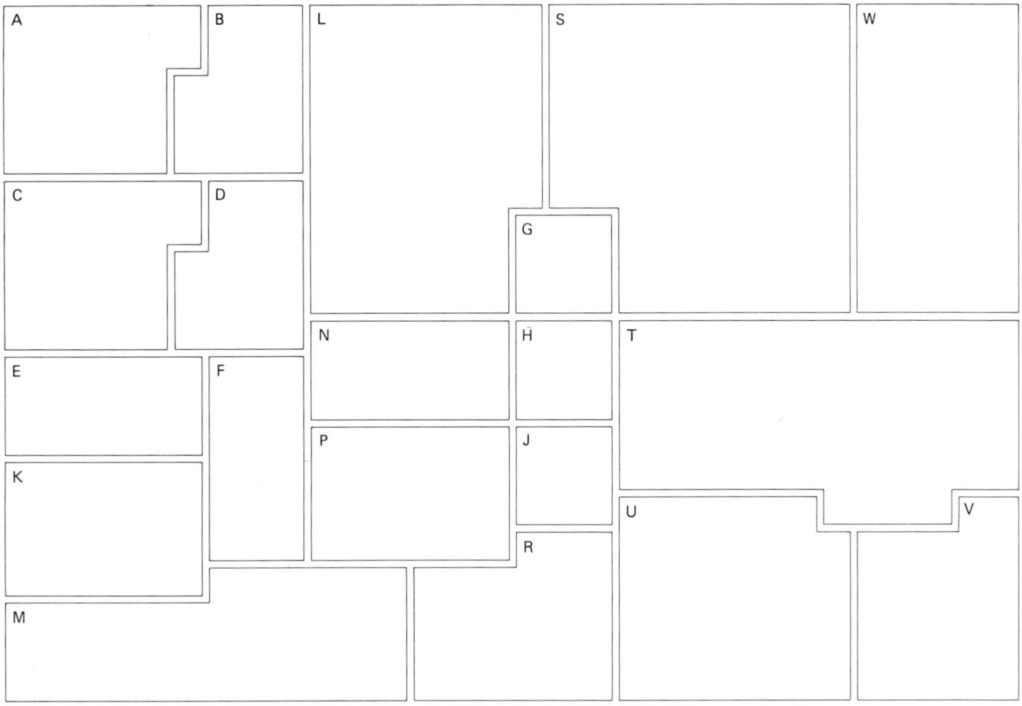

(c)

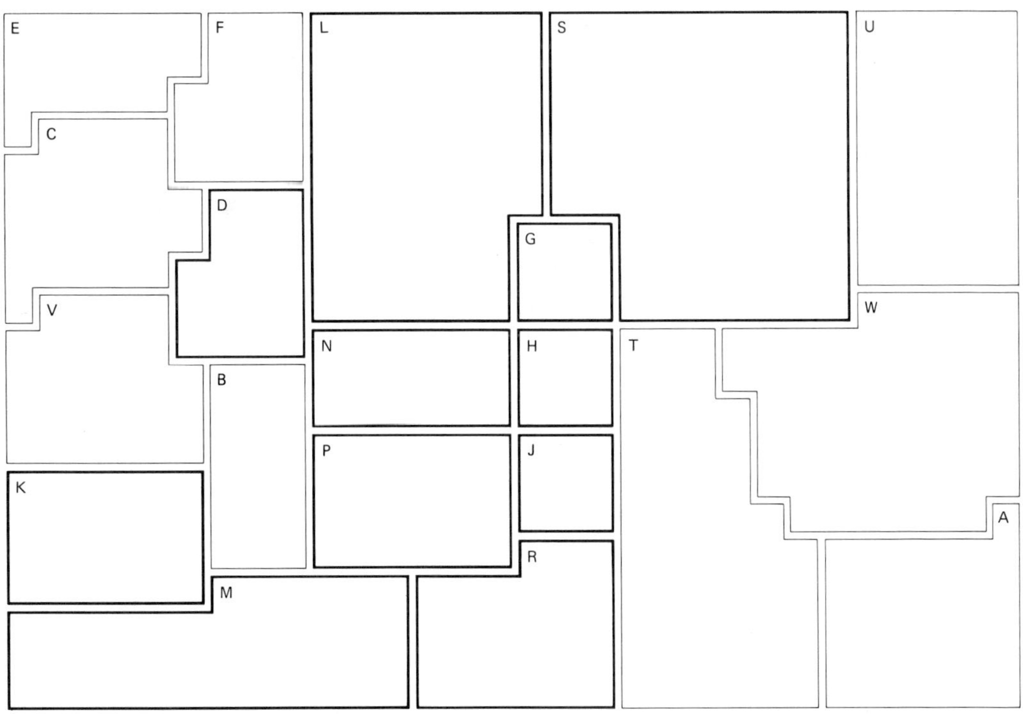

(d)

Numerous variations on the basic CRAFT principle have been developed. Cinar (1968, 1975) has implemented a version which deals with multi-story layouts. Lew and Brown (1970) describe a version which allows the areas of spaces to vary between specified limits. Vollmann, Nugent and Zartler (1968) have developed a version for assigning people to offices in an existing building layout. In this case, there is no need to geometrically represent the floor plan other than by a matrix of office-to-office trip distances. Pairwise switches of office assignments which result in cost reductions are made until no further improvement can be produced. *Figure 13.16* shows a typical result. Willoughby (1975) has published a discussion of further applications to practical problems.

Quite a different "best improvement" strategy is employed by the IMAGE system (Weinzapfel and Handel 1975). IMAGE represents spaces as rectangular parallelepipeds, each given dimensions and a location and rotation within a coordinate system. As in CRAFT, an initial configuration is input by the user. A constraint graph defines

Figure 13.16
Some typical arrangements generated by Vollmann, Nugent and Zartler's (1968) pairwise switching program.

An oil company building

1 Geologist A
2 Geologist B
3 Geologist C
4 Landman
5 Geologist D
6 Geologist E
7 Land secretary
8 Geologist F
9 Geology secretary
10 Files A
11 Files B
12 Files C
13 Regional manager secretary
14 Production clerk A
15 Production clerk B
16 Legal secretary
17 Assistant division manager
18 Engineer A
19 Engineer B
20 Division manager
21 Engineer C
22 Engineer D
23 Production clerk C
24 Attorney
25 Receptionist
26 Production supervisor
27 Production clerk D
28 Accounting clerk
29 Office manager
30 Production secretary
31 Xerox
32 Storage area
33 Files D
34 Files E

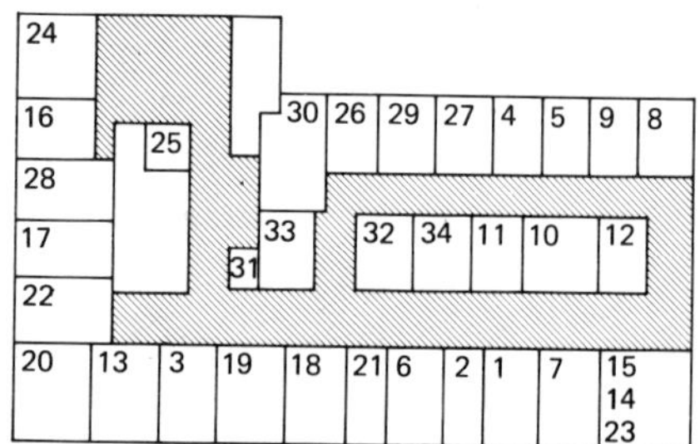

Solution a: produced by hand. Circulation cost = $172.78

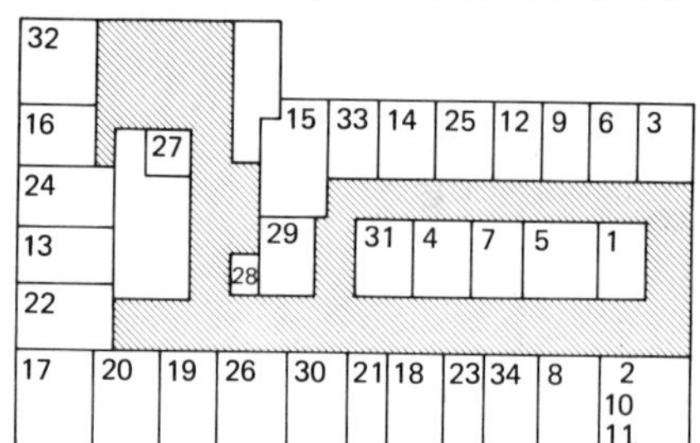

Solution b: improved solution generated by program. Circulation cost = $98.30

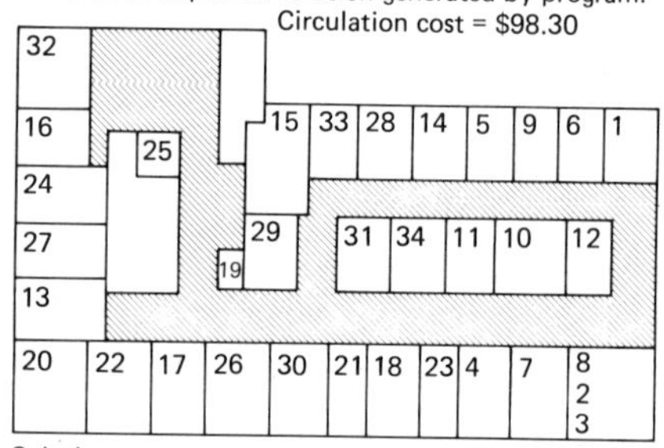

Solution c: generated by program after
10, 11, 12, 13, 16, 20, 24, 25, 31, 32, 33, 34
fixed in position in response to various functional constraints. Cost = $103.82

solution criteria in terms of such properties as proximity, alignment, visual access, circulation, etc., between parallelepipeds. Dimensional constraints are also employed. Constraints can be differentially weighted to indicate relative importance.

The IMAGE synthesis procedure makes incremental changes to each parallelepiped in succession, temporarily holding all others constant. Properties which may be altered are dimensions, location, and rotation. An error function indicates how closely the current state of the parallelepiped matches each constraint, and the classical *least-mean-squares-fit* * method is employed to generate a new state which best reduces the total error. Successive applications of this procedure generate arrangements which improve incrementally towards the objective of zero error. *Figure 13.17* illustrates some typical results.

All these programs suffer from the difficulty inherent in improvement procedures in that they tend to get "stuck" on local optima. The problem can be overcome to a certain extent by choosing a variety of different starting points, by introducing random perturbations when the system appears to be "stuck," and so on; but nonetheless it remains a serious inherent weakness. Unfortunately, experience with CRAFT-like procedures has shown that the quadratic objective function tends to display very complex behavior; there are a great many local optima, and these local optima often appear to be rather "flat," *i.e.,* large numbers of different arrangements have roughly the same value for the objective. Thus it seems reasonable to assume that these types of programs rarely do in fact produce globally optimum solutions.

Willoughby (1975, 1976) has pointed out that the strategy of starting CRAFT-like programs at a variety of places in order to deal

* See Weinzapfel and Handel (1975) for details.

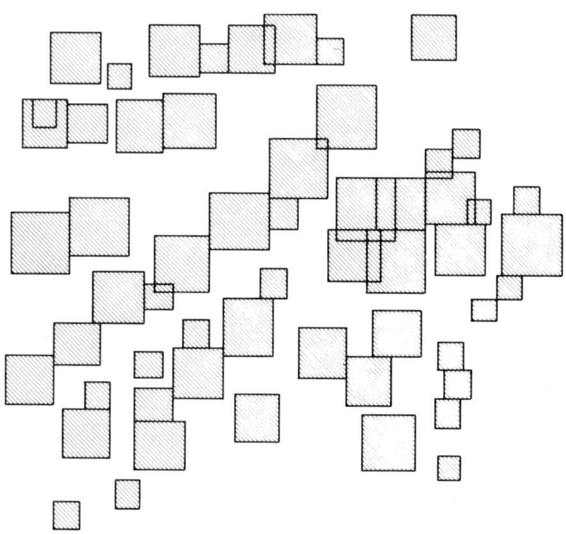

Figure 13.17
A typical result produced by the IMAGE system: a site layout generated in response to the constraint graph shown in figure 13.7 (after Weinzapfel and Handel (1975)).

with the problem of local optima amounts to sampling from a distribution of starting points to find one that leads to a good solution. Statistical methods can be employed to determine an appropriate sample size. A reasonable approach, for example, is to cease sampling when the expected cost of continuing to sample would be greater than the expected benefit from taking more samples. Willoughby derives the following approximate formula for computing the optimum sample size according to this criterion

$$n = \sqrt{(R/C)}$$

where

n = the optimum sample size,

R = difference in circulation cost between the best and worst plans generated,

C = cost of one run of the program.

The value of R is initially unknown, but a reasonable estimate can be made. After a few runs of the program on the problem, real values can be substituted.

The following numerical example illustrates the operation of this formula. In a study of office layout for an organization located in the Economist building in London, it was found that after 20 runs of a layout program, the difference in circulation cost between the best and worst plans generated was 12.80 Pounds per week (approximately $22 per week). Assuming that the suite of offices is to be occupied by the client organization for 100 weeks, this represents a total cost difference of 1,280 Pounds. The cost of a single run of the program was 0.75 pounds, so the optimum sample size was $\sqrt{(1280/0.75)}$ = approximately 41. A lower cost per run, or a greater difference between the best and worst plans, would justify a larger sample. Conversely, a higher cost per run or a lesser difference between the best and worst runs would imply a smaller sample.

Improvement procedures compared with generate-and-test

So far we have seen that a generate-and-test procedure is applicable to virtually any type of problem, and is guaranteed to find a solution if one exists, but is likely to be very inefficient. It is a general but weak method. Conversely, an improvement strategy can often converge on a good solution quite quickly, but the domain of problem-types to which it can be applied is much more limited. It is stronger, but less general. Specifically, the use of improvement strategies is limited to situations in which we can devise some satisfactory means of comparatively evaluating proposals to determine which is "closer" to the desired result. Furthermore, unless we are willing to accept local optima, or have some technique for getting away from local optima, it must be known that the objective function is unimodal. Improvement procedures are likely to be most useful in situations where a fairly good initial arrangement can be specified as the starting point.

HEURISTIC SEARCH PROCEDURES

Principle of heuristic search

Both the generate-and-test and improvement procedures that we have so far described require the state of the data structure to be fully-specified before any evaluation of a potential solution takes place. Another important class of methods, known as *heuristic search procedures,* is characterized by solution-generation in a sequence of stages, with evaluations based on the partially-specified state of the data structure being made at each step.

This type of serial decision making process is conveniently represented by a state-action tree in which the root vertex represents the initial state of the data structure, branches represent alternative operations which may be performed, internal vertices represent partially-specified states (*i.e.,* incomplete proposed solutions), and terminal vertices represent full-specified states.* Any permissible sequence of operations which may be performed to generate a proposed solution (*i.e.,* a fully-specified state of the data structure) may be represented as a path through the tree. A heuristic search procedure works by utilizing *a-priori* knowledge about the structure of the problem, combined with knowledge gained from evaluations performed upon partially-specified states of the data structure, in order to select an appropriate sequence of operations to execute (*i.e.,* an appropriate path through the tree).

The details of different heuristic search procedures vary, depending upon the types of knowledge which they utilize. In the extreme case, no evaluations are performed at internal vertices and no special knowledge at all is utilized to select operations; the tree is simply explored in systematic or random fashion. (This becomes equivalent to generate-and-test.) In the most powerful, sophisticated procedures (exploiting specific knowledge about the structure of the particular problem) are employed to perform evaluations at internal vertices and thus guide the search. The following subsections discuss some examples of techniques for organizing the overall search strategy, for evaluating alternative branches in the tree, for recognizing when to backtrack, and for planning the search process.

* Strictly speaking, the diagram need not necessarily be a tree, but may be a graph of more complex structure. But the process of search through a tree is more clearly and simply described, so our discussion will be limited to trees. The generalization to graphs can readily be made (see Nilsson 1971).

Breadth-first and depth-first search methods

Exploration of a tree can either be conducted in a *breadth-first* or *depth-first* fashion, or by some combination of the two. In pure breadth-first search, all the vertices at one level in the tree are generated before any vertices at the next level are considered (*Figure 13.18(a)*). A simple exhaustive breadth-first search procedure may be stated as follows (Nilsson 1971):

1 Put the start vertex on a list called OPEN.

2 If OPEN is empty go to 8, else

3 Remove the first vertex on OPEN and put it on the end of a list called CLOSED. Call this vertex V.

4 Generate all immediate successors of vertex V.

5 If vertex V has one or more immediate successors, put these successors at the *end* of OPEN and provide pointers from them back to V, else

6 Vertex V is a terminal vertex. Trace back pointers and output this potential solution.

7 Go to 2

8 End

The steps in execution of this algorithm on the simple tree shown in *Figure 13.19* are as follows:

		OPEN	CLOSED
Step 1	Put vertex 1 on OPEN.	1	
Step 2	Put 1 on CLOSED		1
Step 3	Put successors of 1 at end of OPEN, with pointers to 1	2(1) 3(1)	1
Step 4	Put 2 at end of CLOSED	3(1)	1 2(1)
Step 5	Put successors of 2 at end of OPEN, with pointers to 2	3(1) 4(2) 5(2)	1 2(1)
Step 6	Put 3 at end of CLOSED	4(2) 5(2)	1 2(1) 3(1)
Step 7	Put successors of 3 at end of OPEN, with pointers to 3	4(2) 5(2) 6(3) 7(3)	1 2(1) 3(1)
Step 8	Put 4 at end of CLOSED	5(2) 6(3)	1 2(1)

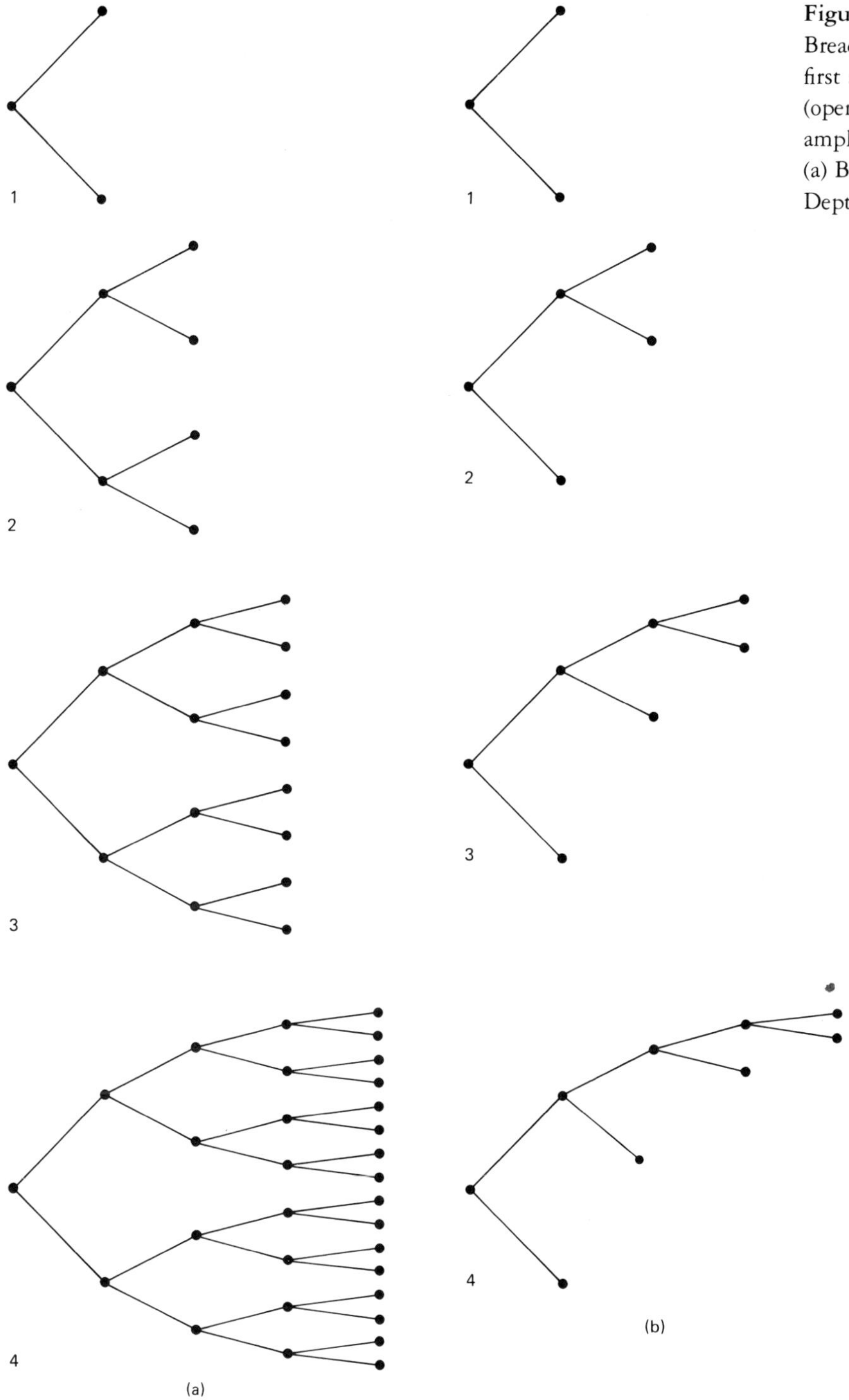

Figure 13.18. Breadth-first and depth-first search procedures (operating in this example on a binary tree). (a) Breadth-first. (b) Depth-first.

		OPEN	CLOSED
		7(3)	3(1) 4(1)
Step 9	Output solution 4, 2, 1	5(2) 6(3) 7(3)	1 2(1) 3(1) 4(2)
Step 10	Put 5 at end of CLOSED	6(3) 7(3)	1 2(1) 3(1) 4(2) 5(2)
Step 11	Output solution 5, 2, 1	6(3) 7(3)	1 2(1) 3(1) 4(2) 5(2)
Step 12	Put 6 at end of CLOSED	7(3)	1 2(1) 3(1) 4(2) 5(2) 6(3)
Step 13	Output solution 6, 3, 1	7(3)	1 2(1) 3(1) 4(2) 5(2) 6(3)
Step 14	Put 7 at end of CLOSED		1 2(1) 3(1) 4(2) 5(2) 6(3) 7(3)
Step 15	Output solution 7, 3, 1		1 2(1) 3(1) 4(2) 5(2) 6(3) 7(3)
Step 16	End		

In pure depth-first search, a path through the tree is first explored to the end, then further alternatives are generated by a systematic backtracking procedure (*Figure 13.18(b)*). A simple exhaustive depth-first search procedure is (Nilsson 1971):

1 Put the start vertex on a list called OPEN.

2 If OPEN is empty go to 8, else

3 Remove the first vertex on OPEN and put it on the end of a list called CLOSED. Call this vertex V.

4 Generate all immediate successors of vertex V.

5 If vertex V has one or more immediate successors, put these successors at the *beginning* of OPEN, and provide pointers from them back to V, else

6 Vertex V is a terminal vertex. Trace back pointers and output this potential solution

7 Go to 2

8 End

Steps in execution on the tree shown in *Figure 13.19* are as follows:

		OPEN	CLOSED
Step 1	Put vertex 1 on OPEN	1	
Step 2	Put 1 on CLOSED		1
Step 3	Put successors of 1 at beginning of OPEN, with pointers to 1	2(1) 3(1)	1
Step 4	Put 2 at end of CLOSED	3(1)	1 2(1)
Step 5	Put successors of 2 at beginning of OPEN, with pointers to 2	4(2) 5(2) 3(1)	1 2(1)
Step 6	Put 4 at end of CLOSED	5(2) 3(1)	1 2(1) 4(2)
Step 7	Output solution 4, 2, 1	5(2) 3(1)	1 2(1) 4(2)
Step 8	Put 5 at end of CLOSED	3(1)	1 2(1) 4(2) 5(2)
Step 9	Output solution 5, 2, 1	3(1)	1 2(1)

Figure 13.19
Tree used in search procedure examples.

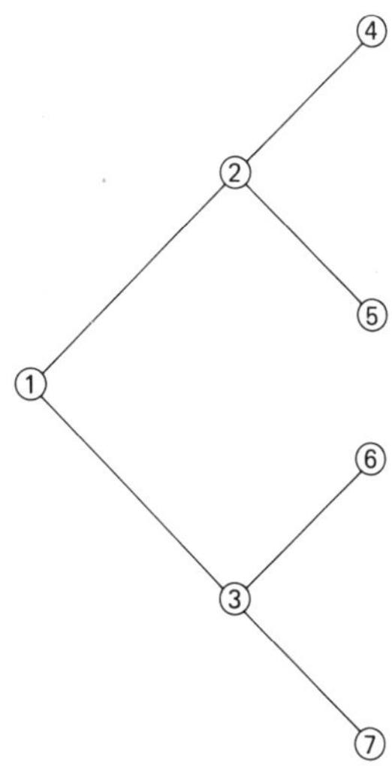

		OPEN	CLOSED
			4(2) 5(2)
Step 10	Put 3 at end of CLOSED		1 2(1) 4(2) 5(2) 3(1)
Step 11	Put successors of 3 at beginning of OPEN, with pointers to 3	6(3) 7(3)	1 2(1) 4(2) 5(2) 3(1)
Step 12	Put 6 at end of CLOSED	7(3)	1 2(1) 4(2) 5(2) 3(1) 6(3)
Step 13	Output solution 6, 3, 1	7(3)	1 2(1) 4(2) 5(2) 3(1) 6(3)
Step 14	Put 7 at end of CLOSED		1 2(1) 4(2) 5(2) 3(1) 6(3) 7(3)
Step 15	Output solution 7, 3, 1		1 2(1) 4(2) 5(2) 3(1) 6(3) 7(3)
Step 16	End		

Heuristic information and branch selection

In principle, both breadth-first and depth-first search will exhaustively enumerate potential solutions. In practice, the enormous extent of the tree usually makes exhaustive search infeasible. It is necessary to make use of some strategy for rapidly eliminating large portions of the tree from consideration. In other words, step 4 of the search procedures described above must be replaced by a step like the following:

4 Generate a *subset* of the successors of vertex V, according to some specified selection rule.

A typical example of the types of selection rules that can be used in architectural applications is the following. Let us assume that we wish to create a floor plan layout within a 25 × 25 square modular grid, as shown in *Figure 13.20(a)*, such that specified adjacency requirements between spaces are met.

The first decision to be made is which space should be placed first. A reasonable decision rule would be:

Rule 1 Select the space which has the highest number of adjacency relations with other spaces.

The next question is where to locate it in the grid. The following rule could be utilized:

Rule 2 Place the first module in the center of the grid.

For placement of subsequent modules of this space, the following is a reasonable rule:

Rule 3 1 List all empty grid locations which are directly adjacent to located modules.

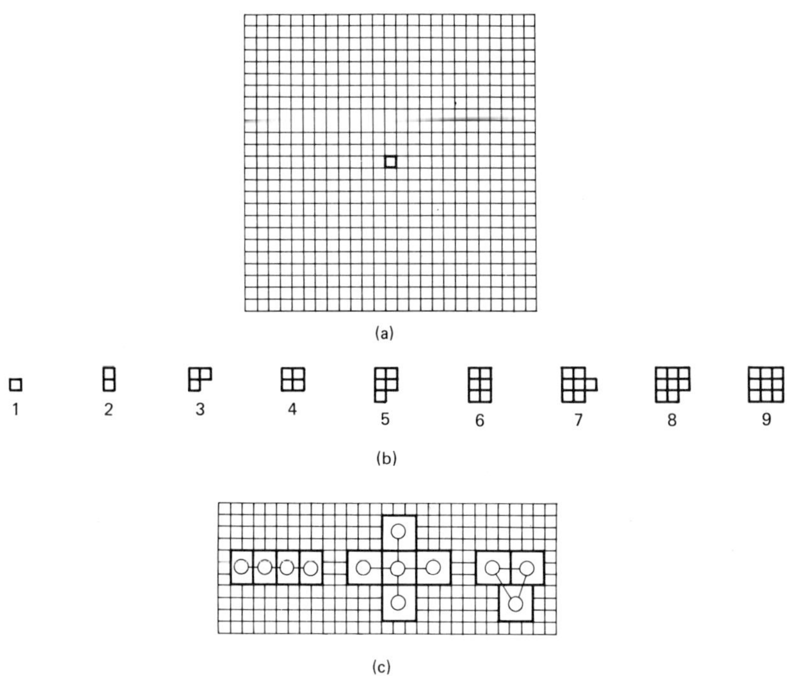

Figure 13.20
Empirical heuristic rules for floor plan layout. (a) First module placed in the center of the grid. (b) Growth of a room shape in response to rule 3. (c) Arrangements of related rooms generated by application of rules 4 and 5.

2 If there is only one location, select it, else

3 For each such empty grid location, count the number (between 1 and 8) of adjacent located modules.

4 Select the grid location which has the highest number.

5 If more than one possibility remains after step 4, make a random choice from among them.

The effect of application of this rule is shown in *Figure 13.20(b)*. It "grows" a shape which always approximates a square as closely as possible.

To select subsequent spaces for placement, the rule might be:

Rule 4 Select the unlocated space which has the highest total number of adjacency relations with spaces which have already been located.

To "grow" these subsequent spaces, an extended version of Rule 3 might be used:

Rule 5 1 List all empty grid locations which are directly adjacent to located modules.

2 If there is only one location, select it, else

3 For each remaining potential location, count the number (between 1 and 8) of adjacent located modules of the *current* space, and eliminate all locations which have a lower number of adjacencies than the maximum which occurs.

4 If there is now only one location, select it, else

5 For each remaining potential location, count the number (between 0 and 8) of adjacent located modules of *any other adjacency-related* spaces to the current space, and eliminate all locations which have a lower number of adjacencies than the maximum which occurs.

6 If there is now only one location, select it, else

7 Make a random choice.

The effect of this rule is shown in *Figure 13.20(c)*. It "grows" spaces which fairly closely approximate a square in shape, and which are located so as to simultaneously satisfy as many adjacency requirements as possible.

Numerous floor plan layout programs which employ plausible selection rules of this type to locate modules within a square grid have been developed. The best of them are computationally very efficient, capable of locating thousands of modules in a few seconds, and produce results of excellent quality. Some of the best known are programs by Whitehead and Eldars (1964), Lee and Moore (1967), Spillers (1970), Willoughby (1970), and Mitchell and Dillon (1972).

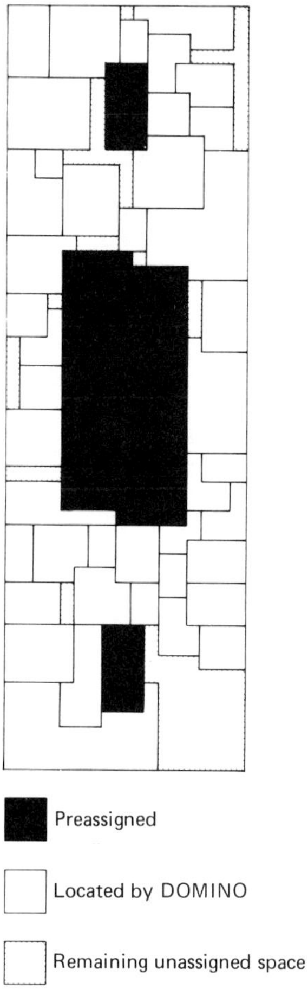

(a)

(b)

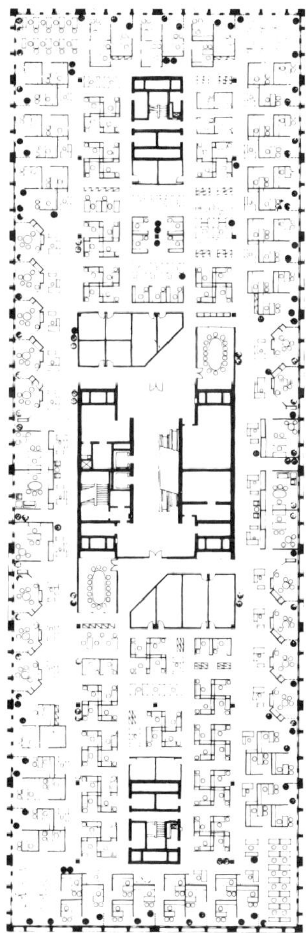

(c)

Figure 13.21 Application of DOMINO, an empirical heuristic floor plan layout program, to planning an office floor (Morganelli-Heumann and Associates, Los Angeles). (a) Block layout generated by DOMINO. (b) Block layout used as a basis for detailed layout. (c) Final plan.

A typical result, produced by the DOMINO program of Mitchell and Dillon, is shown in *Figure 13.21*.

For solution of floor plan layout problems formulated in quadratic assignment terms, various heuristic strategies using selection rules based upon mathematical analysis of the properties of the state-action tree have been developed. The *implicit enumeration* procedure of Graves and Whinston (1969) is an excellent example. For each potential solution there exists a corresponding value of the quadratic objective function, and for each internal vertex in the tree there exists a mean value for the objective for all potential solutions which spring from that vertex. It is possible to efficiently compute these mean values *without* enumeration of the corresponding potential solutions. This makes possible a strategy of computing mean expected values of the objective function for available branches at each decision point, and then selecting the branch which has the lowest value.

Figure 13.22 uses a trivial problem to illustrate this strategy graphically. The task is to arrange four shaded squares in a row. Interactions are specified as follows:

		1	2	3	4
1	Black	3	2	1	0
2	Dark	2	3	2	1
3	Light	1	2	3	2
4	White	0	1	2	3

Adjacent locations are assumed to be unit distance apart. The optimum solution occurs when the squares are arranged to form a greyscale, *i.e.*, "black, dark, light, white" or "white, light, dark, black." In either of these cases, the value of the objective is given by

$$(2 \times 1) + (1 \times 2) + (2 \times 1) + (0 \times 3) + (1 \times 2) + (2 \times 1) = 10$$

The diagram shows mean values for the objective at each branch in the state-action tree for the problem, and illustrates that, in this case, a strategy of selecting branches with the lowest values does, in fact, generate one of the optimum solutions.

This strategy does not rigorously guarantee generation of an optimum solution, but experience has shown that it consistently generates excellent quality solutions to quadratic assignment floor plan layout problems. Unfortunately, computation grows as the square of the number of modules to be located, and it is thus limited to problems having a maximum of about 100 modules. An application to office landscape layout has been described by Liggett (1972), and Fullenwider (1972) has discussed an application to department store planning.

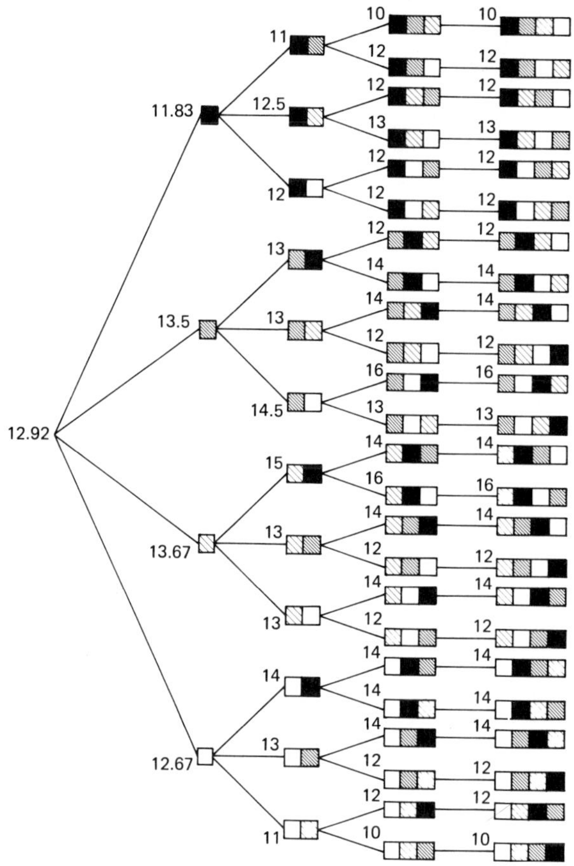

Figure 13.22
State-action tree for a quadratic assignment problem, with the mean expected value for the objective function at each branch shown.

Backtracking

None of the programs discussed so far engage in any backtracking through the state-action tree; a decision is never reconsidered once it is made. It is often desirable, in heuristic search programs, to incorporate a capability to recognize that a particular sequence of decisions has led to a "dead end" from which no satisfactory solution can result, and to backtrack to a previous vertex and restart the search along an alternative branch.

This procedure of backtracking is characteristic of human problem-solving processes. *Figure 13.23* illustrates two examples of sequences of moves made by human subjects solving a simple problem of packing shapes within a rectangle. It can be seen that the basic pattern is as follows:

1. A sequence of decisions is made until it becomes obvious that a dead-end has been reached;
2. The configuration produced is partially destroyed by removal of pieces;

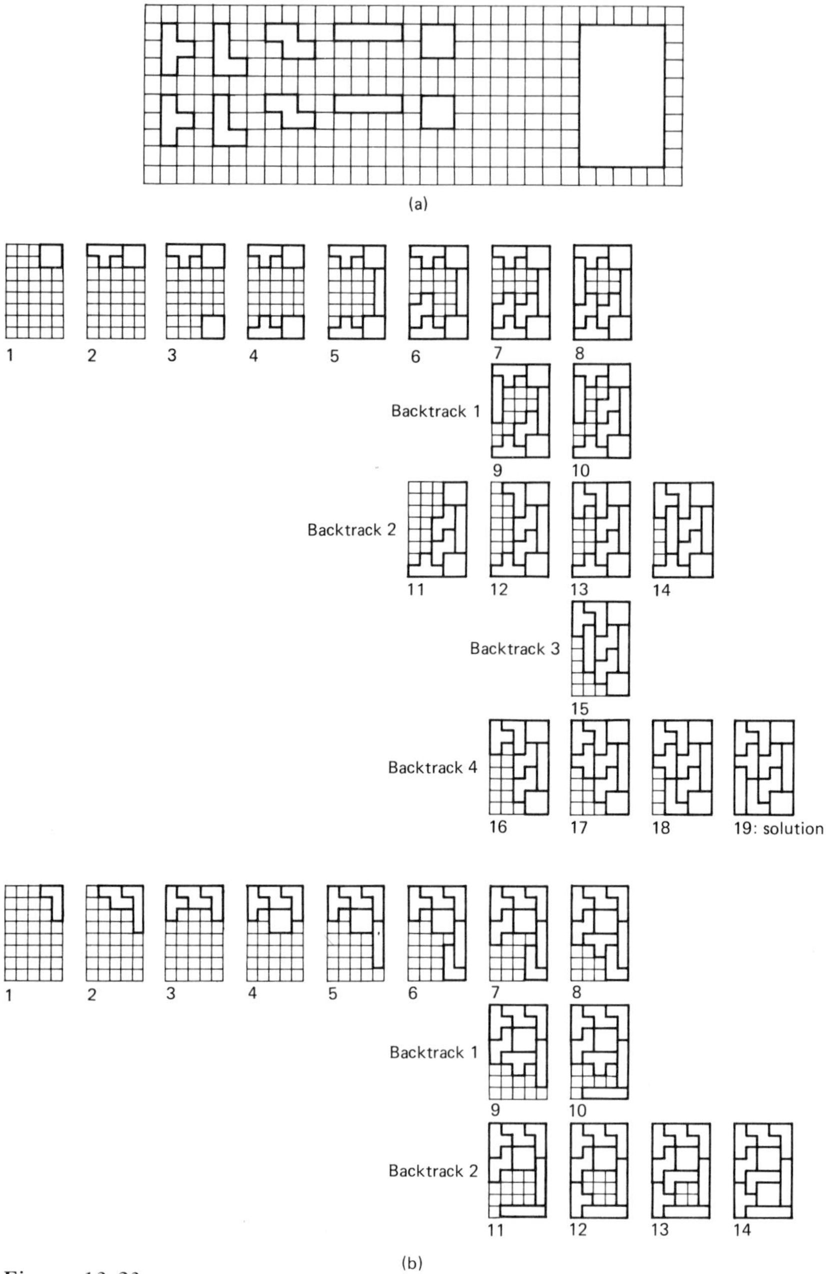

Figure 13.23
Backtracking in human problem solving. (a) Problem: pack polyominoes on the left into the rectangle on the right. (b) Two solution protocols.

3. Another sequence of decisions is made until either a solution is found or it again becomes obvious that a dead-end has been reached.

The pattern is repeated until a satisfactory solution results.

Typical backtracking moves made by a floor plan layout pro-

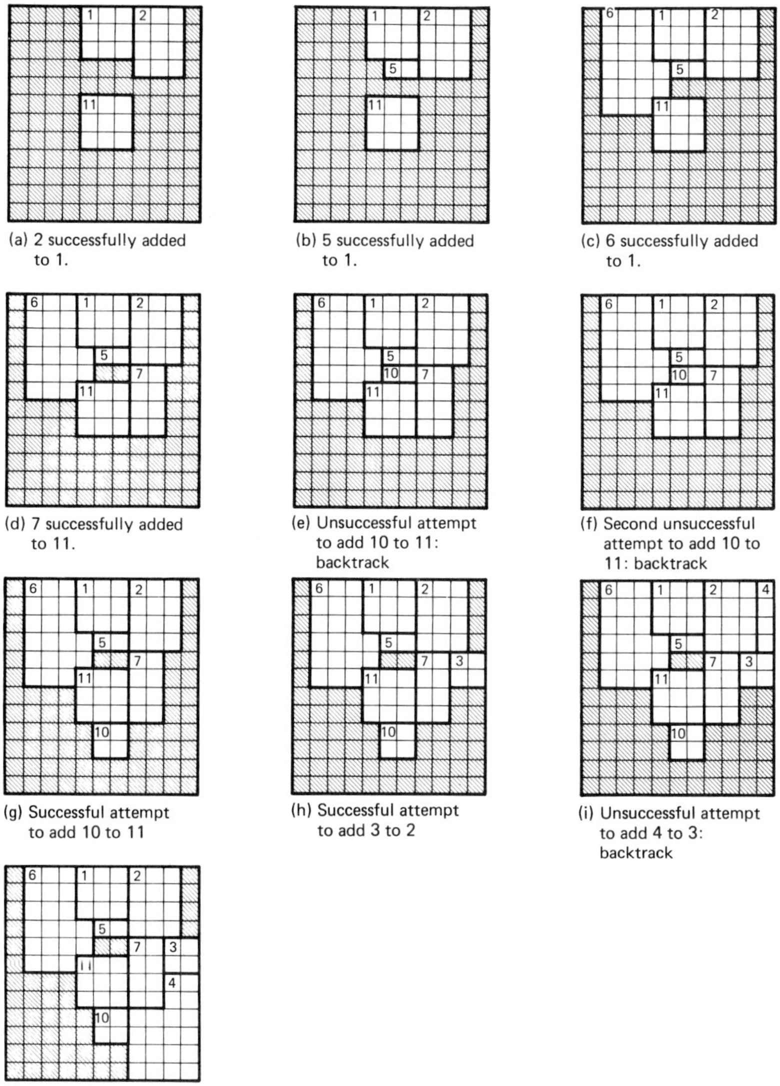

(a) 2 successfully added to 1.

(b) 5 successfully added to 1.

(c) 6 successfully added to 1.

(d) 7 successfully added to 11.

(e) Unsuccessful attempt to add 10 to 11: backtrack

(f) Second unsuccessful attempt to add 10 to 11: backtrack

(g) Successful attempt to add 10 to 11

(h) Successful attempt to add 3 to 2

(i) Unsuccessful attempt to add 4 to 3: backtrack

(j) Successful attempt to add 4 to 3

Figure 13.24 Backtracking by the DOMINO floor plan layout program (Mitchell and Dillon 1972). The program attempts to add new spaces to the perimeters of located spaces to which there are high interactions. Backtracking is necessary if there is insufficient room for the added space at the chosen perimeter location. A new perimeter location is then selected and tried.

gram working within a square grid are illustrated in *Figure 13.24*. Modules of a space are located until a situation is reached in which further modules must still be placed but no space remains. The located modules are then removed, and the process is restarted at another, hopefully more satisfactory, point.

Planning

One characteristic shared by all the heuristic search programs discussed so far is they make one decision at a time, without "planning ahead," by breaking the total problem down into sub-problems. This greatly exacerbates the difficulty of the combinatorial task. For example, a problem of assigning 8 modules to 8 locations has $8! = 40{,}320$ potential solutions. If it can be tackled as 2 discrete sub-problems of assigning 4 modules to 4 locations, then the number of potential solutions is reduced to $2(4!) = 48$, a reduction by a factor of roughly 1,000. This calculation is a little misleading, since it does not consider mutual compatibility of sub-problem solutions, but it does indicate the enormous potential savings.

One of the first heuristic search spatial synthesis programs to incorporate partitioning of the problem into sub-problems was developed by Beaumont (1967). From analysis of a circulation flow matrix (see Interaction and Grouping Analysis in Chapter 12), Beaumont's program first breaks down the list of spaces to be located into a binary tree of spatial subgroups (*Figure 13.25(a)*). An amoeba-like process is then employed to generate a layout. The first pair of spatial subgroups is laid out by successively locating one square module of one, then a module of the other, and so on (*Figure 13.25(b)*). Each of these subgroups is then redivided and so on until all spaces are laid out.

A sophisticated use of planning is contained in a more recent program called DPS (Design Problem Solver) developed by Pfefferkorn (1975). DPS arranges furniture or equipment in a room in accordance with a constraint graph specifying proximity, separation, and other requirements. At each step of the solution generation procedure, an attempt is made to insert a new element into the design such that no constraints are violated. The design is complete and satisfactory when all elements have been successfully inserted in this way.

If serious difficulty is encountered in satisfactorily inserting a new element, a diagnostic procedure is entered. The elements involved in the violated constraints are treated, in the diagnostic procedure, as a separate sub-problem, and an attempt is made to create a "macro-element" from them which satisfies all their mutual constraints. When this has been achieved, an attempt is then made to reinsert the macro-element into the design.

Capabilities and applications of heuristic search programs

Heuristic search procedures can be quite "strong" in the sense discussed earlier. They can often deliver very good solutions for most problems to which they are applied, and can do so reasonably economically. But in general, the stronger heuristic search procedures are fairly limited in the types of problems to which they are applicable. This is because they often gain their strength by exploiting very specific knowledge about a particular type of problem. Graves and Whinston's implicit enumeration procedure, for example, exploits

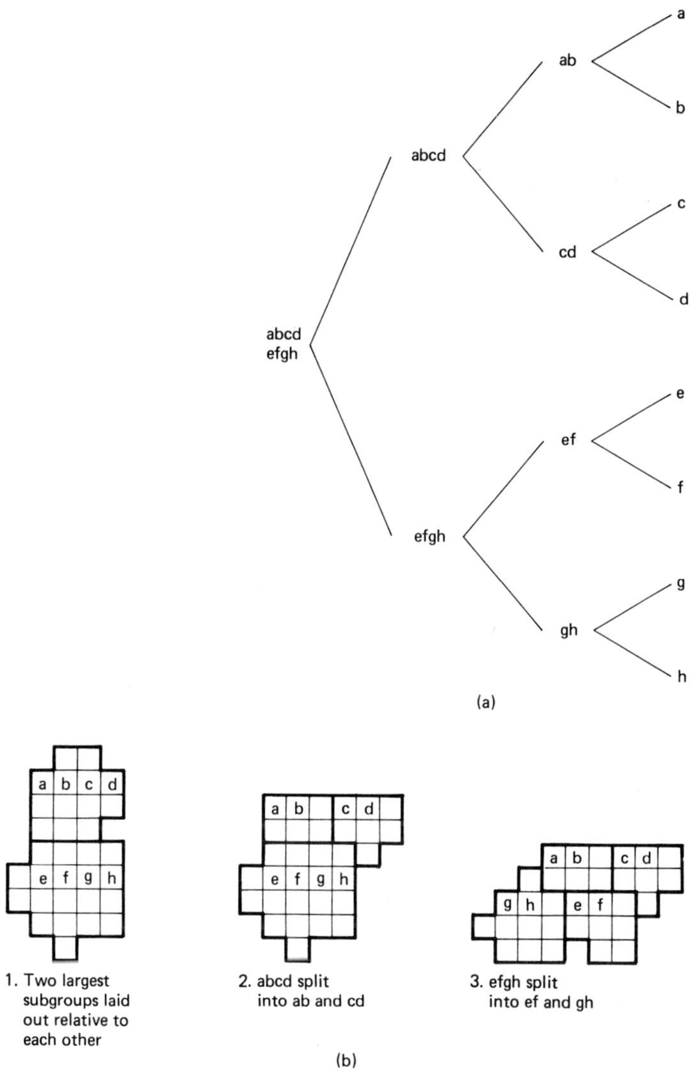

Figure 13.25
Use of planning in Beaumont's (1967) floor plan layout program. (a) Breakdown into spatial subgroups. (b) Layout and subdivision of subgroups.

specific properties of a specific type of objective function. Other programs utilize extensive architectural knowledge.

The brief discussion which has been given cannot begin to do full justice to the range of ingenious concepts and techniques that have been incorporated in heuristic search programs. For more detailed discussions of basic principles, with numerous examples, see Nilsson (1971), Slagle (1971), Newell and Simon (1972), Uhr (1973), Jackson (1974) and Raphael (1976). Excellent discussions of architectural applications are given in papers by Eastman (1971, 1973), and in a recent book edited by Eastman (1975). Comparative analyses of the performance of various programs have been published by Gilmore (1961), Hillier and Connors (1966), Nugent, Vollmann and Ruml (1968), Roberts (1969), Muther and McPherson (1970), Tabor (1970), Broadbent and O'Keefe (1972), Ritzman (1972), Dudnik and Krawczyk (1973), Moore (1973) and Bleck and Lewis (1975). Extensive bibliographies, giving references to numerous heuristic spatial synthesis programs, are given in these publications, and in a bibliography by Bunselmeier (1973).

Most of the early applications of heuristic search programs in architecture were to floor plan layout problems involving arrangement of square modules. At Carnegie-Mellon University, two very successful heuristic search programs for laying out furniture or equipment within spaces have been developed. These are GSP (Eastman 1971, 1972, 1973) and DPS (Pfefferkorn 1975). The Harness hospital integrated computer-aided design system incorporates a heuristic search automated layout program called HAPA, which locates standard departments around a circulation route defined by the user to produce complete, multi-story hospital layouts (Gray 1975).

NONLINEAR AND LINEAR PROGRAMMING

Even stronger, but correspondingly less general techniques than heuristic search are *nonlinear programming* and *linear programming* methods. These methods were initially developed for solution of economic, operations research, and engineering problems, but they have found some interesting applications to floor plan synthesis problems.

Nonlinear programming

Nonlinear programming has been used in conjunction with dimensionless representations of floor plans to generate optimum dimensioned layouts with respect to some cost criterion and subject to certain functional constraints (Mitchell 1974, 1975, Sauda 1975, Mitchell, Steadman and Liggett 1976, McGovern 1976). The following is a typical example.

Figure 13.26(a) shows, in dimensionless representation, a proposed layout for a small house. Dimensional constraints are specified as follows:

Room	Minimum length (ft)	Maximum length (ft)	Minimum width (ft)	Maximum width (ft)	Minimum area (ft^2)	Maximum area (ft^2)	Maximum proportion ratio
1 living room	8·0	20·0	8·0	20·0	150·0	300·0	1·5:1
2 kitchen	6·0	18·0	6·0	18·0	50·0	120·0	
3 bathroom	5·5	5·5	8·5	8·5			
4 hall	0	15·0	3·5	6·0	0	72·0	

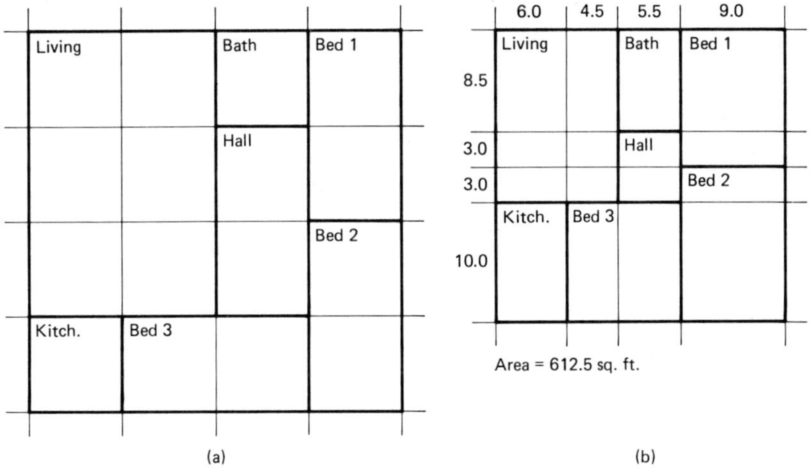

Figure 13.26
An example of application of nonlinear programming to a floor plan layout problem. (a) Dimensionless representation of layout. (b) Optimum dimensions found by nonlinear programming.

Room	Minimum length (ft)	Maximum length (ft)	Minimum width (ft)	Maximum width (ft)	Minimum area (ft^2)	Maximum area (ft^2)	Maximum proportion ratio
5 bedroom 1	9·0	20·0	9·0	20·0	100·0	180·0	1·5:1
6 bedroom 2	8·0	18·0	8·0	18·0	100·0	180·0	1·5:1
7 bedroom 3	10·0	17·0	10·0	17·0	100·0	180·0	1·5:1

The problem is to choose values for the dimensioning vectors such that these constraints are met, and the following objective is minimized:

$$\sum_{r=1}^{7} a_r c_r$$

where

a_r is the total floor area of room r, and
c_r is the construction cost per square foot for room r.

This is a very simple construction-cost formula. A more elaborate objective function could obviously be formulated if desired. Values for the coefficient c_r are as follows:

Room	1 living	2 kitchen	3 bath	4 hall	5 bedroom	6 bedroom	7 bedroom
c_r	1·0	2·0	2·0	1·0	1·0	1·0	1·0

The problem is nonlinear, due to the presence of multiplicative terms representing areas in the constraints and objectives. Powerful nonlinear programming algorithms now exist for finding solutions to problems of this form. They cannot absolutely guarantee to generate the optimum solution, but experience has shown them to be extremely reliable and efficient. In this case, a program developed by Clasen, Graves and Lu (1974) was employed to find the solution shown in *Figure 13.26(b)* in about two seconds of computation on a 360/91 computer. It would be quite feasible to handle much larger problems, consisting of hundreds of variables and constraints.

Linear programming

Standard linear programming techniques are applicable and will very efficiently generate a solution or report infeasibility where this type of dimensioning problem can be formulated in terms of the optimization of a *linear* objective function subject to *linear* constraints. Typical linear objectives are maximization or minimization of overall plan length, width, perimeter, or proportion ratio. Typical linear constraints are upper and lower bounds on allowable lengths, widths, perimeters, and proportion ratios of individual rooms and of the overall plan envelope.

An immediately obvious limitation of the linear programming approach is that area constraints are nonlinear, and thus cannot be incorporated in a linear programming formulation. Furthermore, objectives representing such important properties as construction cost, heat loss, etc., are also functions of floor area.

However, problems involving terms representing floor area can be formulated for linear programming solution if values for one of the dimensioning vectors are known at the outset. Consider the plan (in dimensionless representation) of a mobile trailer unit illustrated in *Figure 13.27(a)*. Severe restrictions on allowable width constrain the y dimensioning vector to the values shown. Constraints on lengths, widths, areas, and proportions of the various rooms are defined as follows:

Room	*Minimum area* (ft^2)	*Maximum area* (ft^2)
1 bath 1	75.0	80.0
2 bed 2	160.0	180.0
3 utility	50.0	80.0
4 kitchen	150.0	200.0
5 dining	100.0	125.0
6 bed 1	180.0	200.0
7 hall	—	60.0
8 living	180.0	200.0
9 bath	60.0	80.0
10 family room	100.0	125.0

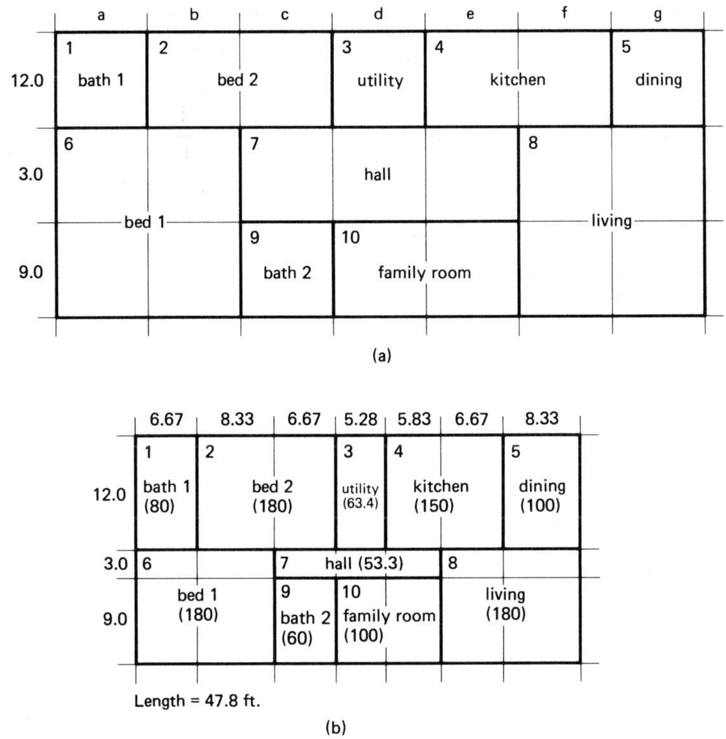

Figure 13.27 An example of application of linear programming to a floor plan layout problem. (a) Dimensionless representation of a "double wide" (24 ft.) mobile home unit, with dimensioning vector along short side fixed. (b) Optimum solution drawn to scale.

The objective is to minimize overall length of the trailer subject to these constraints. Thus the problem can be formulated as:

$$\text{Minimize } (a+b+c+d+e+f+g)$$

subject to:

	$g \leq 10\cdot42$
$a \geq 6\cdot25$	$(a+b) \geq 15\cdot0$
$a \leq 6\cdot67$	$(a+b) \leq 16\cdot67$
$(b+c) \geq 13\cdot33$	$(c+d+e) \leq 20\cdot0$
$(b+c) \leq 15\cdot0$	$(f+g) \geq 15\cdot0$
$d \geq 4\cdot17$	$(f+g) \leq 16\cdot67$
$d \leq 6\cdot67$	$c \geq 6\cdot67$
$(e+f) \geq 12\cdot5$	$c \leq 8\cdot89$
$(e+f) \leq 16\cdot67$	$(d+e) \geq 11\cdot11$
$g \geq 8\cdot33$	$(d+e) \leq 13\cdot89$

Figure 13.27(b) illustrates the optimum solution, found in a fraction of a second of computation, by a standard linear programming system.

Linear programming procedures are much more powerful than any of the techniques discussed previously. They guarantee to produce the optimum solution, and they do so with great efficiency. The price which must be paid, however, is that their application is restricted to a relatively narrow range of problem types.

ANALYTICAL PROCEDURES

Analytical procedures are the most powerful of all. Non-trivial architectural spatial synthesis problems which can be solved analytically are rare, but contrary to general opinion, they do exist.

One of the most interesting such tasks might be termed the *Palladio Problem*. Consider a floor plan in dimensionless representation, such as that shown in *Figure 13.28(a)*. Let us assume that we wish all the rooms to be squares. This requirement can be expressed by the following set of simultaneous linear equations:

$$x_1 = y_1, \quad x_2 = y_1, \quad x_1 + x_2 = y_2, \quad x_1 = 1$$

By substitution

$$y_2 = 2$$

The resultant plan is shown in *Figure 13.28(b)*.

If we expand the problem to allow proportioning requirements other than 1 : 1 (that is, 2 : 1, 3 : 2, etc.), there is no longer a single solution. If, for example, we take the proportion 2 : 1, there are now two different ways a proportioning requirement can be met by each room. Room length could be twice room width or vice versa. Two proportioning equations for each room, therefore, can be formulated. To proportion a plan, a system of equations composed of one equation for each room must be selected.

There is not, then, a unique set of simultaneous equations for proportioning a plan. In general, there are 2^n sets of equations where n is the number of rooms in the plan. *Figure 13.29(b)* shows a portion of a tree diagram which represents exhaustive enumeration of all possible combinations of simultaneous equations for the particular proportioning problem illustrated in *Figure 13.29(a)*.

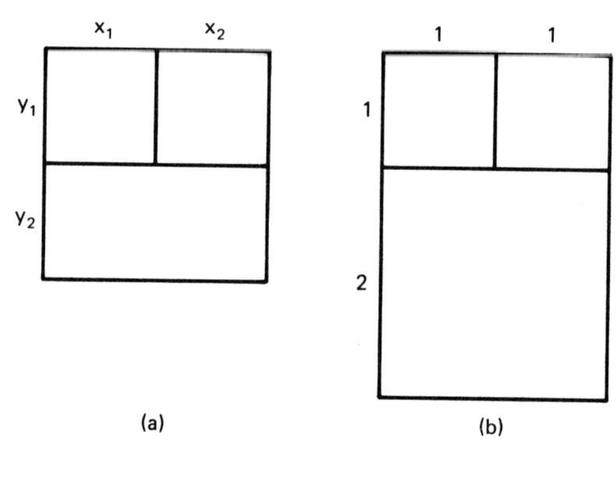

Figure 13.28 Algebraic solution of a simple proportioning problem.

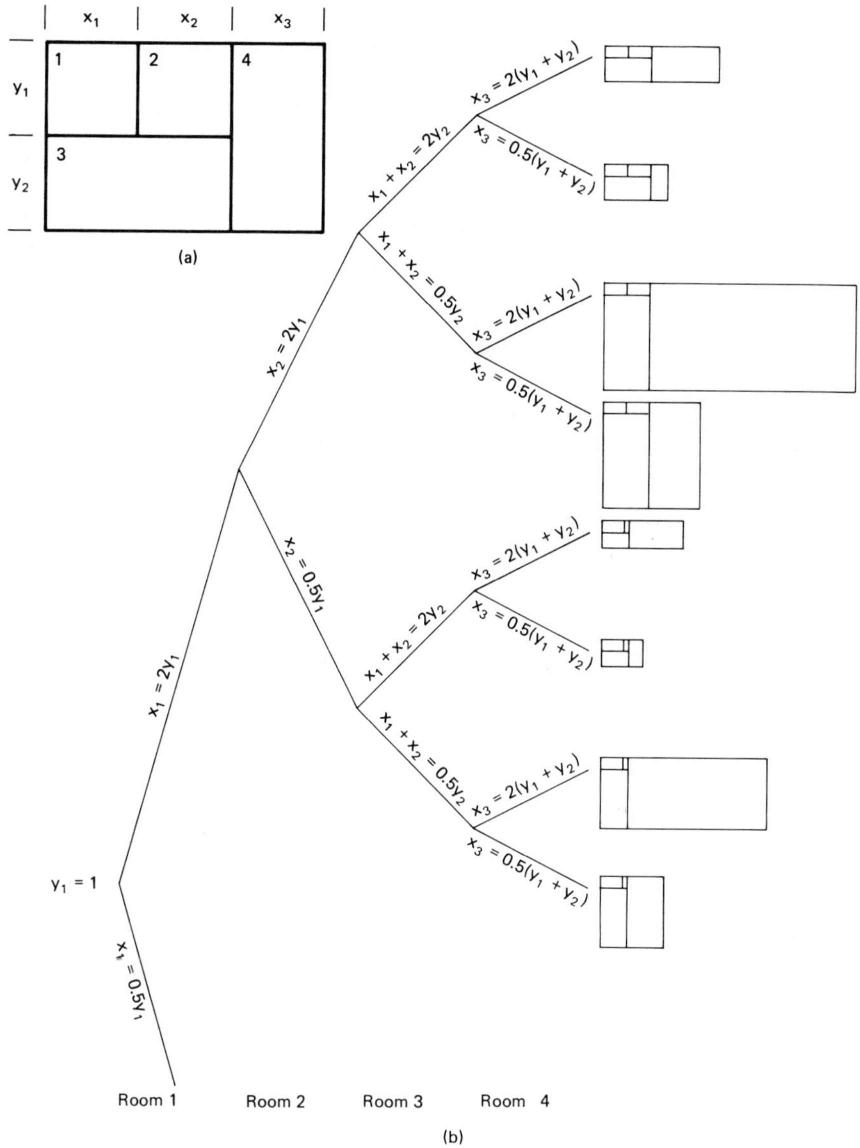

Figure 13.29 Proportioning problem for a plan (a) where all rooms are to be 2:1. (a) Dimensionless plan. (b) Systematic generation of correctly proportioned plans by solution of simultaneous linear equations.

It is, of course, possible to specify proportion requirements which are unrealizable within a given plan. In this case it will be found that the simultaneous equations have no meaningful solution.

The dimensioning problem as formulated in this way may be solved either by hand or by computer, with any of the standard methods * for solving systems of simultaneous linear equations, for example, substitution, elimination, the Gaussian method, or the Cramer method. Where the number of rooms is greater than about

* See Grawoig (1967) for an elementary introduction.

three or four, the number 2^n of different systems of equations which must be considered becomes quite large:

n	2	3	4	5	6	7	8
2^n	4	8	16	32	64	128	256

SUGGESTED READINGS

Eastman, C. M. ed. *Spatial Synthesis in Computer-Aided Building Design.* New York: Wiley, 1975.

Grason, J. "An Approach to Computerized Space Planning Using Graph Theory," in *Proceedings of the 8th Design Automation Workshop.* New York: Association for Computing Machinery, 1971.

Mitchell, W. J.; Steadman, J. P.; and Liggett, R. S. "Synthesis and Optimization of Small Rectangular Floor Plans." *Environment and Planning B* 3, no. 1 (1976), pp. 37–70.

Mohr, M. *A Computer Model of the Design Process that Uses a Concept of an Apartment Floorplan to Solve Layout Problems.* Cambridge, Mass.: MIT Department of Civil Engineering Report R71-36, 1971.

Newell, A. "Heuristic Programming," in *Progress in Operations Research,* edited by J. Aronofsky. Vol. 3. New York: Wiley, 1969.

Scott, A. J. *Combinatorial Programming, Spatial Analysis and Planning.* London: Methuen, 1971.

Stiny, G. "Two Exercises in Formal Composition." *Environment and Planning B* 3, no. 2 (1976), pp. 187–210.

Willoughby, T. "Searching for a Good Design Solution," in *The Architecture of Form,* edited by L. March. Cambridge, England: Cambridge University Press, 1976.

14
Performance and Cost Analysis of Solutions

Techniques for performance and cost analysis of solutions are considered in this chapter. Following an introductory discussion of the role of performance and cost analysis in architectural design, different types of analyses are considered in turn: analysis of the plan, structural analysis, environmental analysis, cost analysis, and analysis for compliance with regulatory codes.

PERFORMANCE AND COST ANALYSIS IN ARCHITECTURAL DESIGN

Appraisal of proposed solutions

Like most decision making and design processes, architectural design proceeds through general stages of pre-design analysis, solution synthesis, and solution appraisal. Appraisal has been characterized (Markus 1972) as "a retrospective act by which the designer establishes the quality of his solution." If appraisal of a solution reveals unacceptable deficiencies, then it becomes necessary to redesign, or even to develop the analysis further. As has been noted by many authors (*e.g.*, Asimow 1962), this establishes a basic iterative structure for design processes.

Early iterations are often quick, they utilize incomplete and imprecise data, and represent potential solutions in a rough and abstract way. With further iteration, the project data base develops in detail and refinement, and correspondingly more precise and sophisticated analysis, synthesis, and appraisal procedures are employed.

The three basic steps necessary in the appraisal of proposed solutions have been described by Markus (1972) as follows:

1. *Representation*
   The solution is modeled in any suitable way. The model might be verbal, mathematical, visual or even "full scale" (in this sense a building-in-use is a full and complete "model" of the design).
2. *Measurement*
   This is a neutral activity in which the performance of the model is obtained on as wide a variety of counts as necessary. Costs, environmental conditions, flexibility, space utilization and ergonomic effects are among those that suggest themselves easily. Aspects of performance whose measure is a human response, *e.g.*, value judgments of the qualities of an object, can sometimes be obtained from simulations.
3. *Evaluation*
   The measured results are now evaluated: cost-benefit analysis; aesthetic and value judgment; comparison with ideal, average or statutory performance standards found in the analysis, conformity with constraints recorded in the analysis (these presuppose a process by which normative data is carried through the process from analysis to appraisal)—all these and other techniques are appropriate.

Role of specialized consultants

In all but the simplest architectural design projects, most of the work of *measurement* of cost or performance (step 2 above) is carried out by specialist consultants. These typically include the quantity surveyor (or cost consultant), structural engineer, and mechanical engineer. In recent years, it has become increasingly common to include social and behavioral scientists as well.

In general, consultants must employ different types of representations than architectural drawings in order to execute their cost or performance measurement tasks. Quantity surveyors must "take off" quantities from drawings before they can produce cost estimates, and structural and mechanical engineers must translate graphic data into appropriate numerical formats. These processes of translation between representations consume considerable time and resources, introduce possibilities for error, and reduce the number of design iterations that can be made.

Role of the computer

Computer-based techniques may assist the appraisal process in two distinct ways. First, and most obvious, programs may be written to automatically execute cost or performance measurement procedures. Quantity surveyors, structural, and mechanical engineers have developed a great many programs for these purposes, and they have been in extensive everyday use for some time.

Second, in the context of integrated systems, the computer may be employed to overcome problems of representation. For example, cost, structural, and environmental analysis programs might all be designed to operate upon a central, computer-stored project data base. Alternatively, a computer-based building description system employed by the architect might be given the capability to automatically generate data sets formatted as required by the consultants' analysis programs. In either case the step of manual preparation of data for analysis, with attendant delays and probability of error, is eliminated.

The combination of analysis programs with an integrated project data base and interactive graphics interface is potentially exceedingly powerful, since it can reduce the time needed to perform an analysis from days or weeks to seconds or minutes. This makes possible very rapid iteration through the type of process illustrated in *Figure 14.1* and the efficient exploration of a much wider range of alternatives than would otherwise be feasible. It also provides the designer with an opportunity to learn a great deal about the consequences of design decisions, and to develop a very sophisticated understanding of his problem. Most integrated systems are designed to exploit these potentials.

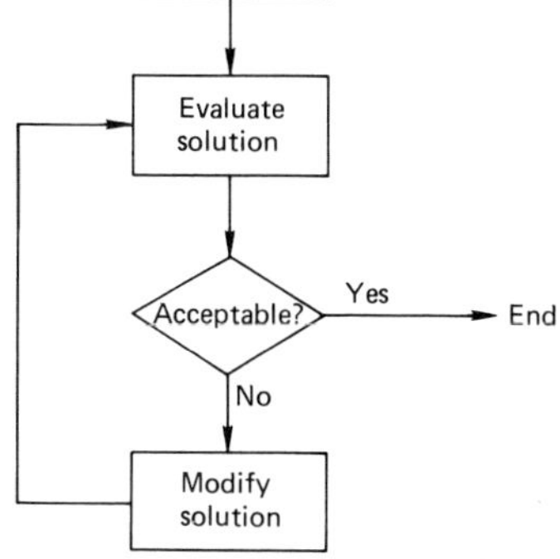

Figure 14.1
Simplified flow diagram, illustrating the iterative structure of a typical design process.

The remainder of this chapter will discuss specific computer-based cost and performance analysis techniques. The emphasis is upon the architect's needs, and the integration of these techniques into his design process. With few exceptions, the details of particular analysis algorithms are omitted, since this would take us into specialized fields of engineering that are beyond the scope of this book.

ANALYSIS OF THE PLAN

Compliance with the brief

The automated checking of a plan for compliance with the basic provisions of the brief is a fairly straightforward computational task. The U.S. Army Corps of Engineers Construction Engineering Research Laboratory at Champaign, Illinois has developed a system called SEARCH for this purpose (Bryant, Dains and Spoonamore 1975) which clearly illustrates the principles involved.

SEARCH is designed for use in the Corps of Engineers' military construction program. Within this program, dimensional and relational criteria for the design of such facilities as barracks, mess halls, recreation centers, etc., are documented in detailed design guides. SEARCH provides facilities for entering and storing design criteria from these guides, digitizing and storing floor plans, checking the plans for compliance with the criteria, and printing out evaluative reports. Criteria are entered interactively, via a keyboard, and plans are digitized using a graphic tablet and storage tube terminal. An evaluative report consists of several parts: a listing of all spaces with their actual and required floor areas, and floor area errors; a ranked list of the most unsatisfactory spaces; a list of unsatisfied required relationships between spaces. A typical digitized plan is illustrated in *Figure 14.2(a)*, and an evaluative report produced by SEARCH is shown in *Figure 14.2(b)*.

Circulation system efficiency

Quantitative analysis of circulation system performance has been rare in the past, since although the principles are fairly simple, the computations required are extensive. But in the context of a computer-aided design process, sophisticated circulation system performance analysis is quite feasible.

One common approach is to use the quadratic assignment objective as a formula for measuring overall circulation system efficiency in a proposed design. In this context, it may be stated

$$\text{Total circulation cost} = \sum_{i=1}^{n} \sum_{j=1}^{n} G_{ij} \quad C_{ij}$$

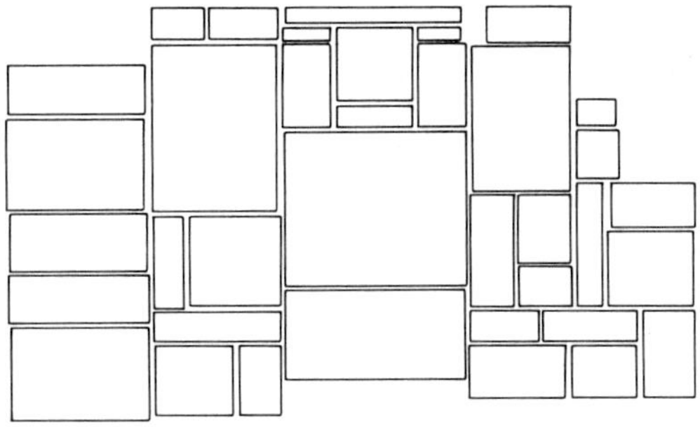

(a)

(b)

---SPACE---	---REQUIRED AREA-- MAX	---- MIN	--ACTUAL---- AREA	ERROR---- OVER	UNDER	PAGE--
Restrooms	195	175	557	362		9
Mechanical	0		326	326		0
Mchc		0	(326)		0	
Choir Seating	150	100	397	247		9
Storage	75	50	276	201		9
Ref Circulation	580	385	322		63	9
Chancel	500	400	344		56	9
Post Chaplin	260	240	215		25	9

(c) *** Chancel connected ***** ERROR POINTS * 148

---RELATIONSHIP--------			--GROUP:SPACE--	ERROR--	PAGE
nearer than	25′	to	1 of Choir Room	17	5
nearer than	25′	to	1 of Post Chaplin	40	5
nearer than	25′	to	1 of Chaplin	35	5
enclosed in	0′		1 of Nave	16	11
views	100%	of	1 of Activity Room	40	12

*** Activity Room connected ***** ERROR POINTS * 97

---RELATIONSHIP			GROUP:SPACE	ERROR	PAGE
adjacency by	4′	to	1 of Kitchen	56	8
adjacency by	4′	to	1 of Assembly Room	41	41 8
nearer than	10′	to	1 of Outdoor Worship	*******	******* 8

Figure 14.2
Use of SEARCH to analyze a plan for compliance with the requirements of the brief. (a) Floor plan as input to SEARCH. (b) Part of area analysis. (c) Part of relational analysis.

where

n = total number of activity centers between which circulation takes place

G_{ij} = distance between activity centers i and j

C_{ij} = a measure of circulation cost per unit distance between i and j.

As before, value for C_{ij} must be obtained from a matrix of circulation flow data. But since a design is now defined, values for G_{ij} may be measured directly and accurately by tracing appropriate routes through the plan. A map meter might be employed on drawings, and the values obtained entered numerically. Alternatively, routes might be traced out using light-pen or tablet. An even more highly automated approach is to employ a "shortest path" algorithm to find routes.

A pioneering comparative study of the efficiency of alternative hospital ward designs employing this quadratic formula was carried out at Yale–New Haven Hospital in 1958 (Thompson and Pelletier 1962, Thompson and Goldin 1975). An extensive survey of traffic flow in wards was conducted, and the resultant data employed to compute circulation costs for a variety of alternative ward designs (single corridor, double corridor, circular, etc.). To provide a basis for comparison of wards containing different numbers of beds, circulation costs were standardized as follows:

$$\text{Circulation cost per bed} = t/b$$

where

t = total circulation cost as computed by the quadratic formula

b = number of beds in the ward

It was found that circular and square designs were generally most efficient, and (surprisingly) that circulation cost per bed was not directly related to the number of beds in the ward.

A difficulty with use of the quadratic circulation cost formula in this way is that it gives an absolute value for circulation cost, rather than a value relative to some standard scale. Thus it is difficult to tell whether a particular layout is better or worse than might normally be expected. This can be overcome by first summing the circulation cost over all possible arrangements as follows:

$$S = \sum_{i'=1}^{n} \sum_{j'=1}^{n} \sum_{i=1}^{n} \sum_{j=1}^{n} G_{ij} \quad C_{ij}$$

then dividing by n!, the number of possible arrangements, to produce a mean expected value:

$$\text{mean expected value} = S/n!$$

This provides a standard for comparison.

Another difficulty with the quadratic formula is that it gives no indication of which activity centers are most severely "mislocated" in the plan, thus contributing most to circulation cost. An indication of this can be obtained by assuming that, since in general the greater the value of C_{ij} the closer together spatial elements i and j should be; relationships of the following form should hold in a well-constructed layout

$$G_{ij}\, C_{ij} = K$$

where K is a constant determined by the size of the building and the magnitude of the different values for C_{ij}. Thus a measure of the "appropriateness" of the distance between a pair of elements in a layout may be derived as follows:

$$\text{Appropriateness} = \frac{G_{ij}\,C_{ij} - G_m\,C_m}{G_m\,C_m}$$

where

G_m is the mean value for G

C_m is the mean value for C

A value of 0 indicates that i and j are probably appropriately located in relation to each other, a high positive value indicates that they are probably too far apart, and a high negative value indicates that they are probably too close together. This type of evaluation is performed by programs described by Willoughby, *et al* (1970) and Maver (1970).

A good example of a current circulation system performance evaluation program is incorporated in the Harness integrated computer-aided hospital design system (Shirley 1974). This system employs the quadratic circulation cost formula to give a basic measure of circulation efficiency for a proposed layout. Since Harness hospitals are part of an extensive ongoing hospital building program, this can be compared with corresponding values for other hospitals designed to the same brief. The following additional indices are also computed:

Individual department pair circulation costs $= G_{ij}\,C_{ij}$

Average circulation cost $= T/N$

where

$T =$ total circulation cost

$N =$ number of department pairs

Average distance walked per trip $= T/C$

where

$C =$ total traffic (unweighted)

Coefficient of variation $= \sqrt{\sum_{i<j} (C_{ij} - C_A)^2 / (N-1)C_A^2}$

where

$C_A =$ average circulation cost.

Department pair circulation costs are displayed by means of a histogram (*Figure 14.3(a)*). In a satisfactory layout, the histogram should have a peak at the left hand side and no tail, while the coeffi-

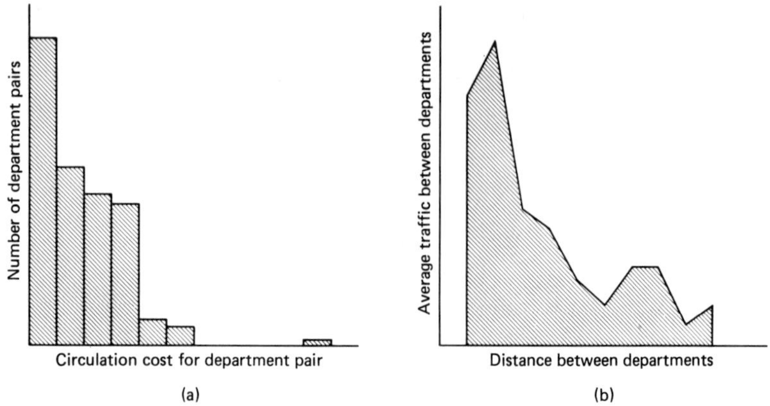

Figure 14.3
Some typical output from the Harness hospital circulation cost analysis program. (a) Department pair circulation cost histogram. (b) Interdepartmental traffic flow graph.

cient of variation should be low. Values for C_{ij} are plotted against G_{ij}, as shown in *Figure 14.3(b)*. In a good layout, the curve should slope downwards indicating a general inverse relation between interdepartmental weighted traffic flow and distance. In addition to their uses in general evaluation of layouts, the results of these analyses are also employed as input to an automated elevator placement algorithm.

Shortest path calculations

In analyzing the efficiency of circulation systems, it is often desirable to compute shortest circulation distances from a point in the plan to other points, rather than to measure these distances by hand. If the circulation system is represented as a network, then this can be accomplished by application of a *shortest path* algorithm. Numerous different shortest path algorithms have been developed (Pollack and Wiebenson 1960, and Dreyfus 1969), and many of them are suitable for this application. As an example, an efficient algorithm developed by Dijkstra (1959) will be described.

Figure 14.4(a) illustrates a simple circulation network, and *Figure 14.4(b)* its description by means of an adjacency matrix in which the non-zero entries represent the distances between adjacent vertices. The vertex from which we wish to compute distances is denoted *s*. For purposes of this example, we will take vertex 1 as *s*.

The Dijkstra algorithm, which we can use to find distances from *s*, employs three lists, called *A*, *B*, and *C* respectively. Each entry in *A*, *B*, or *C* consists of the name of a vertex, together with an associated label giving the minimum distance through the network from *s* to that vertex. The algorithm is as follows:

1. Place all vertices on list *C*.
2. Transfer vertex *s* to list *A*, call it *n*, and set its label to 0.
3. Set labels of all other vertices to ∞.

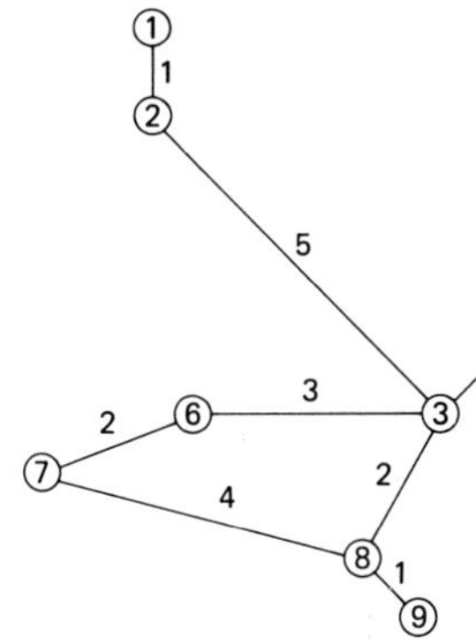

(a)

	1	2	3	4	5	6	7	8	9
1		1							
2	1		5						
3		5		4		3		2	
4			4		3				
5				3					
6			3				2		
7						2		4	
8			2				4		.1
9								1	

(b)

Figure 14.4 Dijkstra shortest path algorithm example. (a) Example network. (b) Corresponding adjacency matrix, in which non-zero entries indicate distances between vertices (zero-entries omitted for clarity).

4. Consider all vertices *R* connected to vertex *n* just transferred to list *A*. If a particular vertex *r* is on list *B*, check if the sum of the label on *n* plus the length of the edge connecting *n* and *r* is less than the label of *r*. If so, replace the label on *r* with the shorter distance. If a particular vertex *r* is on list *C*, transfer it to list *B* and change the label to the sum of the label on *n* plus the length of the edge connecting *n* and *r*.
5. Transfer the vertex on list *B* which has the minimum label to list *A*, and call it *n*.
6. Unless all vertices are on list *A*, return to step 4.

The algorithm terminates with all vertices on list *A*, and with the label of each vertex indicating the minimum distance through the network from *s*.

The steps in execution are as follows:

		A	B	C
Step 1	Put all vertices on *C* and set all labels to ∞			1[∞] 2[∞] 3[∞] 4[∞] 5[∞]

		A	B	C
				6[∞] 7[∞] 8[∞] 9[∞]
Step 2	Put 1 on *A* and set its label to 0	1[0]		2[∞] 3[∞] 4[∞] 5[∞] 6[∞] 7[∞] 8[∞] 9[∞]
Step 3	Put 2 on *B* and set its label to 0 + 1	1[0]	2[1]	3[∞] 4[∞] 5[∞] 6[∞] 7[∞] 8[∞] 9[∞]
Step 4	Put 2 on *A*	1[0] 2[1]		3[∞] 4[∞] 5[∞] 6[∞] 7[∞] 8[∞] 9[∞]
Step 5	Put 3 on *B* and set its label to 1 + 5	1[0] 2[1]	3[6]	4[∞] 5[∞] 6[∞] 7[∞] 8[∞] 9[∞]
Step 6	Put 3 on *A*	1[0] 2[1] 2[6]		4[∞] 5[∞] 6[∞] 7[∞] 8[∞] 9[∞]
Step 7	Put 4, 6, and 8 on *B*, and adjust labels	1[0] 2[1] 3[6]	4[10] 6[9] 8[8]	5[∞] 7[∞] 9[∞]
Step 8	Put 8 on *B*	1[0] 2[1] 3[6] 8[8]	4[10] 6[9]	5[∞] 7[∞] 9[∞]

		A	B	C
Step 9	Put 7 and 9 on *B* and adjust labels	1[0] 2[1] 3[6] 8[8]	4[10] 6[9] 7[12] 9[9]	5[∞]
Step 10	Put 6 on *A*	1[0] 2[1] 3[6] 8[8] 6[9]	4[10] 6[9] 7[9] 9[9]	5[∞]
Step 11	Reset label on 7 to 9 + 2	1[0] 2[1] 2[6] 8[8] 6[9]	4[10] 7[11] 9[9]	5[∞]
Step 12	Put 9 on *A*	1[0] 2[1] 3[6] 8[8] 6[9] 9[9]	4[10] 7[11]	5[∞]
Step 13	Put 4 on *A*	1[0] 2[1] 3[6] 8[8] 6[9] 9[9] 4[10]	7[11]	5[∞]
Step 14	Put 5 on *B* and set its label to 10 + 3	1[0] 2[1] 3[6] 8[8] 6[9] 9[9] 4[10]	7[11] 5[13]	
Step 15	Put 7 on *A*	1[0] 2[1] 3[6] 8[8] 6[9] 9[9] 4[10] 7[11]	5[13]	
Step 16	Put 5 on *A*	1[0] 2[1] 3[6]		

A	B	C
8[8]		
6[9]		
9[9]		
4[10]		
7[11]		

Circulation system simulation

The circulation flow simulation techniques which were discussed earlier for use in space and facilities needs estimation may also be employed in circulation system performance evaluation. In this case, the purpose is to check the adequacy of a specific design proposal rather than to estimate the characteristics which any design should have.

One of the most ambitious circulation simulation systems yet to be proposed for this purpose was also one of the earliest: the COPLANNER system for evaluation of circulation systems in hospitals (Souder, *et al* 1964). COPLANNER was an interactive graphics system which allowed the designer to vary proposed building layout by using a light-pen to manipulate a cathode ray tube display. The system had access to an extensive and detailed data base of traffic flow information for hospitals. Layout proposals were evaluated by a sophisticated simulation of the operation of the circulation system over a period of time. In many ways COPLANNER was ahead of its time, and it was difficult to justify use of such an elaborate system solely for the purpose of conducting layout evaluations. However, it illustrated the way in which circulation evaluation facilities can be combined with an interactive graphics interface, and it seems likely that COPLANNER-like capabilities will eventually be incorporated as a standard feature in integrated computer-aided design systems.

STRUCTURAL ANALYSIS

Structural analysis and optimization algorithms

Since the first modern structural analysis formulae were developed in the 16th and 17th centuries by Galileo and Simon Stevin, structural analysis and design have relied heavily upon mathematical procedures (Hamilton 1952). It is not surprising then, that structural analyses for buildings and building elements were among the first reported applications of newly emergent computer technology in the 1950's. By 1958 the Structural Division of the American Society of Civil Engineers was able to hold its first Conference on Electronic Calculation, at which numerous different programs were reported. Most of the early programs merely implemented well-established algorithms which had originally been developed for hand computation, such as the moment-distribution method for analysis of stresses in frames and continuous beams, which had been introduced by Hardy Cross in the 1930's.

But it was soon realized that computer-implementation of procedures now made practical very sophisticated algorithms requiring massive amounts of computation. This led to the programming of algorithms which could only be practically executed by computer. Examples include an extensive class of programs employing matrix methods in the solution of large systems of simultaneous equations, and programs for simulating the complex behavior of a multi-story building frame under earthquake loading. In addition, it became practical not only to implement analysis algorithms, but also to develop programs for optimization of structural member layout and sizes. Many of the standard structural analysis algorithms now in use are described, with examples of FORTRAN code, in a text by Harrison (1973). Structural optimization algorithms and their computer implementation are extensively discussed in a volume edited by Gallagher and Zienkiewicz (1973).

An elementary example of an implementation of a simple structural analysis algorithm is illustrated in *Figure 14.5*. This algorithm computes internal forces in a thin shell hemispherical dome. According to the membrane theory of shells (Cowan 1971), two types of forces must be considered, the *hoop forces* and the *meridianal forces*. The hoop forces act along horizontal circles around the dome, and the meridianal forces act along vertical circles passing through the crown (*Figure 14.5(a)*). The formulae for these forces are:

$$\text{Hoop force} = wR(1/(1+\cos\theta) - \cos\theta)$$

$$\text{Meridianal force} = wR(1/(1+\cos\Theta))$$

where

w = load per unit area of the shell surface

R = radius of curvature of the dome

θ = the angle subtended by the element under consideration at the crown.

A positive value indicates a tensile force, and a negative value a compressive force.

Figure 14.5(b) illustrates some output from a simple APL program written to plot these hoop and meridianal forces against the angle subtended at the crown for a dome spanning 120 ft. carrying a load of 50 lb./sq. ft. The results show that meridianal compressive forces increase from the crown to the springing, while hoop forces are compressive at the crown, decrease to zero at an intermediate point, and are tensile at the springing. (For convenience, both compressive and tensile forces have been plotted in the same quadrant.)

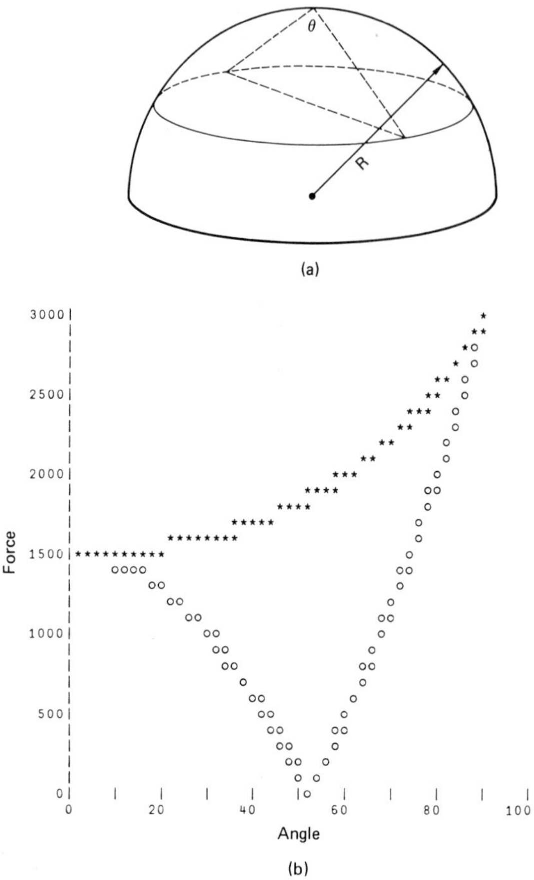

Figure 14.5
Analysis of the hoop and meridianal forces acting in a hemispherical dome. (a) A hemispherical dome. (b) Graph of hoop forces (o) and meridianal forces (*) plotted against angle Θ subtended at the crown, where R = 120 ft. and load = 50 lb./sq. ft.. The plot was produced at a typewriter terminal using the graphing facilities of the APL language.

Structural computation languages

In the early 1960's, a further significant development in the computerization of structural computations was the emergence of large scale, comprehensive structural computation systems based upon the *problem-oriented language* concept. The pioneering system of this type, STRESS (Structural Engineering Systems Solver), was developed at MIT in the early 1960's (Fenves 1965). A direct successor to STRESS was STRUDL (Structural Design Language), developed as a subsystem of the very large ICES (Integrated Civil Engineering System) (Logcher 1970). STRUDL employs a very flexible problem-oriented language, which makes the system cheap and speedy for use in practice. A version utilizing an interactive graphics interface has also been implemented (Biggs *et al* 1973). STRESS and STRUDL have been very widely accepted and put into everyday use, particularly in the United States.

A similar sequence of development of large-scale integrated structural systems has taken place in Europe. Early examples include the SPAN and CLEAT systems. The very ambitious GENESYS (General Engineering System) system, developed in the U.K., is a descendant both of ICES on one side and SPAN and CLEAT on the other (Alcock and Shearing 1970, GENESYS Center 1973).

Structural analysis in integrated systems

Most integrated computer-aided design systems incorporate a structural analysis subsystem, which enables the user to perform many routine structural computations. *Figure 14.6,* for example, illustrates some typical output from the steel beam analysis and design subsystem of the OXSYS integrated system (Hoskins 1972). *Figure*

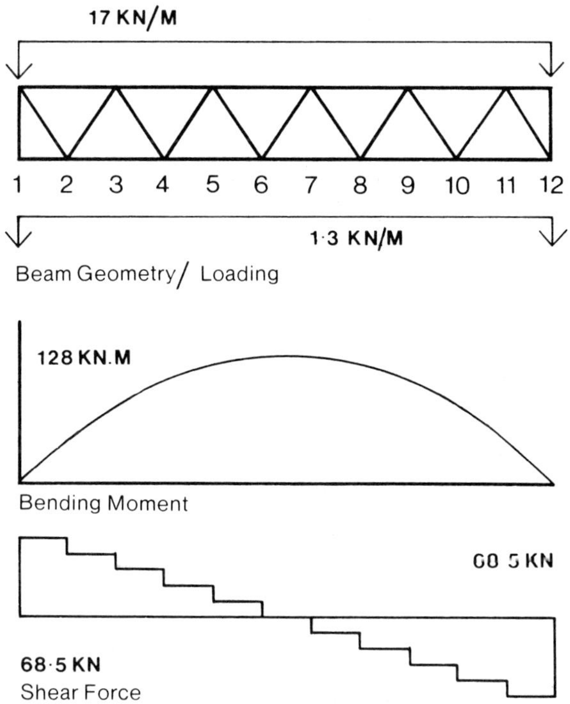

(a)

BEAM MEMBERS

		OXSYS CODE		STEEL SECTIONS
TOPCHORDS	LEFT	11:1:16	ANGLE	80.0X60.0X8.0
	RIGHT	11:1:16	ANGLE	80.0X60.0X8.0
BOTCHORDS	LEFT	11:1:10	ANGLE	50.0X50.0X6.0
	RIGHT	11:1:10	ANGLE	50.0X50.0X6.0
LACINGS BAY 1	LEFT	11:1:10	ANGLE	50.0X50.0X6.0
	RIGHT	11:1:10	ANGLE	50.0X50.0X6.0
BAY 2	LEFT	11:1:10	ANGLE	50.0X50.0X6.0
	RIGHT	11:1:10	ANGLE	50.0X50.0X6.0
BAY 3	LEFT	11:1:10	ANGLE	50.0X50.0X6.0
	RIGHT	11:1:10	ANGLE	50.0X50.0X6.0

LIVE DEFL. 2 MM. TOTAL DEFL.6 MM. TOTAL BEAM WEIGHT 446KG

(b)

Figure 14.6
Type of structural analysis automatically performed by OXSYS.

14.6(a) shows bending movement and shear diagrams as displayed in response to a loading pattern, which is either calculated automatically from the building description or specified by the user. *Figure 14.6(b)* shows a table of sections required to fabricate the beam, as automatically selected by OXSYS.

ENVIRONMENTAL ANALYSES

Environmental comfort criteria play a critical role in almost all architectural design problems. Numerous different quantitative measures of environmental performance are employed, but the following are among the most common:

Climatic	Air temperature
	Relative humidity
	Rate of air movement
	Period of insolation
Illumination	Daylight factor
	Artificial lighting illumination level
	Glare index
Acoustic	Noise level
	Reverberation time
	Speech privacy

Analyses with respect to these criteria may be performed for two purposes, either to predict capital and operating costs of keeping criteria within specified limits of acceptability, or to determine whether a specific proposed design can meet criteria of environmental acceptability. In general, well-known existing models may be employed in performing most of these analyses (Hawkes 1975).

The following paragraphs briefly discuss some typical examples of automated environmental analysis techniques.

Thermal analysis

The types of analyses of thermal performance which might be carried out in a building design process vary somewhat according to building type, design objectives, and the sequence of decision making that is followed. Gupta, Spencer and Muncey (1971) have categorized the main types of analyses into four groups as follows:

Calculation of indoor air temperature in the absence of artificial cooling or heating.

Calculation of indoor air temperature when some heat is being removed or added but the indoor temperature is still variable.

Calculation of heat gains or losses and cooling or heating loads when the indoor air temperature is kept constant at a known value.

Calculation of heat gains or losses and cooling or heating loads when the indoor air temperature is variable and specified . . . the case of 'temperature swing'.

Figure 14.7 illustrates an example of output from a simple thermal analysis program. The program is written in the interactive APL language, and computes the heat loss through the external shell of a building according to the well-known simplified formula:

$$\text{Heat loss} = \sum_{i=1}^{n} u_i a_i \quad \text{(Btu/hour/degree temperature difference)}$$

where

n = number of surfaces

u_i = average thermal transmittance of surface i

a_i = area of surface i (sq. ft.)

In the example shown, heat loss through a pyramidal roof spanning a 40 ft. square building is calculated for roof pitches varying from 0° to 60°, and the results are plotted using the graphing facilities of the APL language.

Since the patterns of heat flow in a building are exceedingly complex, it has in the past been standard practice to employ simplified, approximate formulae like that above in performing thermal analyses (see the *ASHRAE Handbook of Fundamentals* (1974) and Maver (1971) for discussions of numerous standard formulae and procedures). But the widespread availability of computers has now made it feasible to go beyond these simple methods, and to utilize more sophisticated procedures that do not rely upon such restrictive assumptions (Fitzgerald 1971, Feinberg 1974). In addition, the availability of very detailed, machine-readable meteorological record tapes has made it practical to utilize more detailed and accurate weather data. Concurrently, the increasing concern with minimizing energy cost in buildings has made more accurate and reliable thermal evaluation procedures a pressing necessity. In the late 1960's, ASHRAE developed a set of algorithms for accurate calculation of energy requirements of buildings, and these were implemented in the form of a very large and complex FORTRAN program for use in design of U. S. postal buildings (Lokmanhekim 1971). In addition, a number of consulting firms and research groups have developed comparable proprietary programs. Among these are AXCESS (Edison Electric Institute, New York), E-CUBE (GATE, San Antonio, Texas), ESA (Ross F. Meriwether and Associates, San Antonio, Texas), MACE (McDonnell Douglas Automation Company, St. Louis, Missouri), and TRACE (Trane Company, La Crosse, Wisconsin).

Integrated computer-aided design systems quite often incorpo-

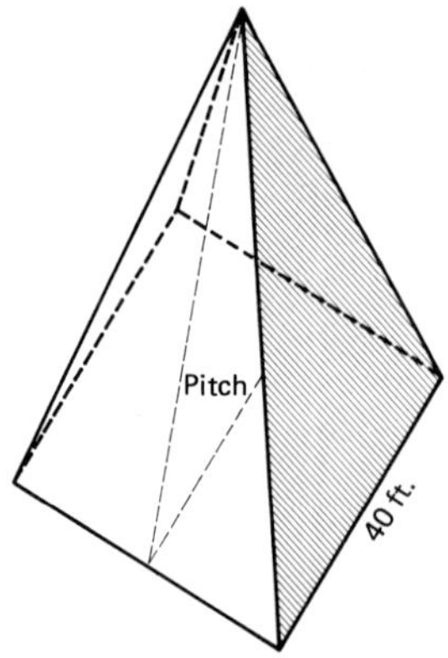

(a)

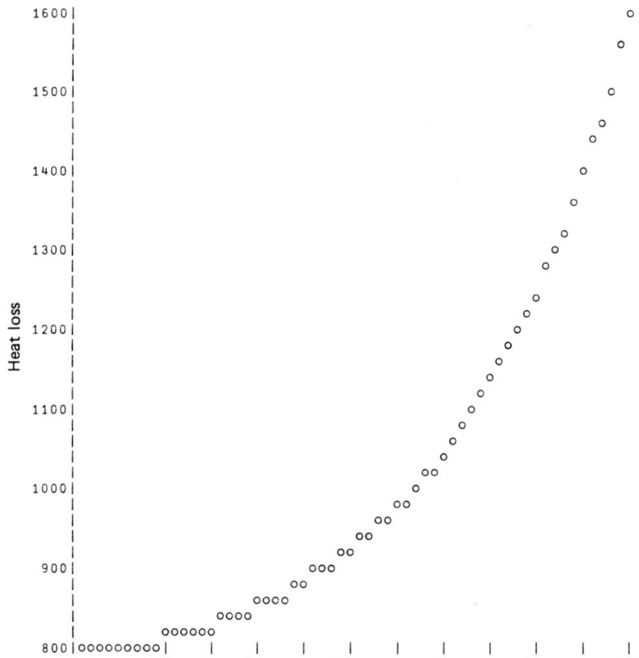

(b)

Figure 14.7
Simple thermal analysis performed by an APL program, with results plotted at a typewriter terminal using the graphing facilities of APL. (a) A pyramidal roof. (b) Heat loss (Btu/hour/degree) plotted against roof pitch, where $u_i = 0.5$

rate thermal analysis facilities. For example, the OXSYS system (Hoskins 1972) performs the type of analysis shown in *Figure 14.8*, allowing the user to rapidly evaluate the thermal characteristics of alternative envelope configurations at any early stage in the design process.

SUMMARY OF THERMAL EVALUATION LEVEL //B 4 DEPARTMENTS ANALYSED

HEAT LOSS THROUGH EXTERNAL FABRIC				
EXPOSED FLOOR	0.0 SQ.M.			
UNDERCROFT FLOOR	271.2 SQ.M.	@ 6.60 W/M2.	=	1789.7
EXT. EDGE SOLID SLAB	0.0 M.			
BASEMENT WALL	0.0 SQ.M.			
UNDERCROFT WALL	0.0 SQ.M.			
SOLID PANELS	121.9 SQ.M.	@ 21.78 W/M2.	=	2654.9
GLAZED PANELS(SOLID)	30.5 SQ.M.	@ 21.78 W/M2.	=	663.7
GLAZING	50.8 SQ.M.	@123.20 W/M2.	=	6257.3
COLUMN COVERS	23.3 SQ.M.	@ 22.97 W/M2.	=	535.4
FASCIA	79.4 SQ.M.	@ 35.49 W/M2.	=	2816.9
CLERESTORY SOLID	0.3 SQ.M.	@ 18.26 W/M2.	=	5.1
CLERESTORY GLAZED	1.6 SQ.M.	@123.20 W/M2.	=	194.8
ROOF	79.0 SQ.M.	@ 17.38 W/M2.	=	1373.1
ROOFLIGHTS	4.2 SQ.M.	@132.00 W/M2.	=	548.9
VENTILATION LOSS	854.1 CU.M.		=	15501.9
		TOTAL LOSS	=	32341.6
OCCUPANCY GAIN				
LYING DOWN	58.4 PEOPLE	@ 90.00 W/PERSON	=	5255.2
SITTING	14.6 PEOPLE	@115.00 W/PERSON	=	1678.8
WALKING	14.6 PEOPLE	@160.00 W/PERSON	=	2335.7
RUNNING	0.0 PEOPLE			
CASUAL GAIN			=	0.0
LIGHTING GAIN	292.0 SQ.M.		=	2433.0
		TOTAL GAIN	=	11702.7
HEAT BALANCE =	20638.9 WATTS	= 70.69 WATTS/SQ.M.		LOSS

Figure 14.8
Typical output from the OXSYS thermal analysis program.

Insolation and shadow pattern analysis

The calculation of sunlight and shadow patterns on, in, and around buildings is a straightforward but very laborious task if performed by hand. The following trigonometric formulae can be used to compute the sun's azimuth and altitude as functions of location on the face of the earth, time of year, and time of day (see *Figure 14.9(a)*):

$$\sin Z = \sin t . \cos d . \sec H$$

$$\sin H = \sin L . \sin d . + \cos L . \cos d . \cos t$$

where

Z = sun's azimuth

H = sun's altitude

L = latitude

d = declination of the sun (*i.e.*, the angle formed between a line connecting the center of the earth with the center of the sun and the plane of the earth's equator)

t = time of day (expressed in degrees)

The sun's declination varies with the time of year. Weekly values are given in *Table 14.1*, and additional intermediate values may be found

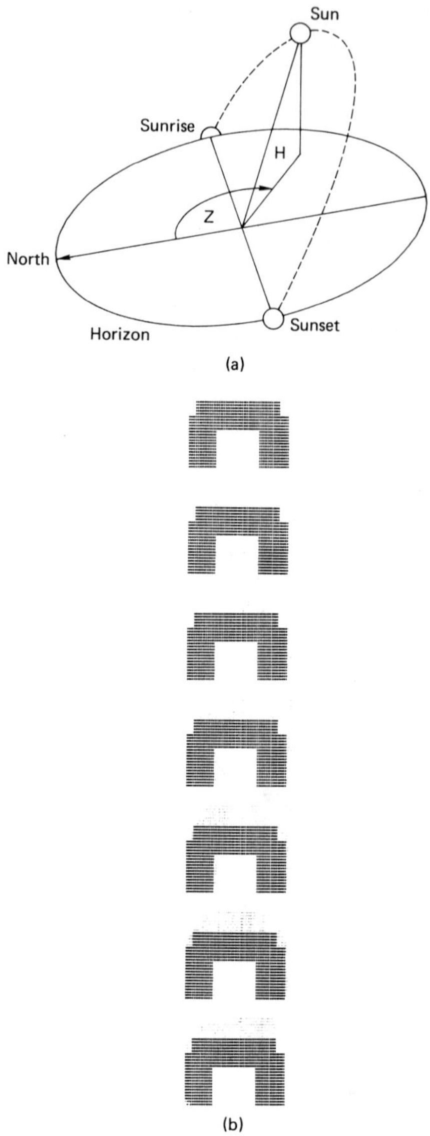

Figure 14.9
Shadow pattern computations. (a) Sun position diagram. (b) Typical output from a simple shadow computation program showing cast shadows around a building at successive time increments.

by interpolation. The value of t is measured from the noon position of the sun, and is given by

$$t = 15h$$

where

h = number of hours before or after noon.

From a knowledge of sun location, the position of the shadow projected by any point onto any planar surface can be calculated by means of elementary trigonometry. The outline of the shadow cast by

Date		Declination	Date	
June	22	+23°–30′	———	
	15	+23°–15′	June	29
	8	+22°–45′	July	6
	1	+21°–55′		13
May	25	+20°–50′		20
	18	+19°–25′		27
	11	+17°–40′	Aug.	3
	4	+15°–45′		10
Apr.	26	+13°–20′		18
	19	+11°– 0′		25
	12	+ 8°–30′	Sept.	1
	5	+ 5°–55′		8
Mar.	28	+ 2°–50′		16
	21	0°– 0′		23
	14	− 2°–50′	Oct.	1
	7	− 5°–35′		8
Feb.	28	− 8°–15′		15
	21	−10°–50′		22
	14	−13°–15′		29
	7	−15°–30′	Nov.	5
Jan.	31	−17°–30′		12
	24	−19°–20′		19
	17	−20°–50′		26
	10	−22°– 0′	Dec.	3
	3	−22°–50′		10
Dec.	27	−23°–20′		17
———		−23°–30′		22

Table 14.1
Declinations of the sun.

a polygonal object onto a planar surface can be generated by connecting the projected locations of its vertices. (See Givoni 1976 for a concise and complete summary of the principles of sun path and shadow plotting.) Since most high level, general purpose programming languages incorporate trigonometric functions, it is a simple matter to write a computer program to perform these calculations for purposes of computing the shadow cast by a building onto the ground plane, or shadows cast on simple elevations. *Figure 14.9(b)* shows some typical output from such a program.

A more complicated shadow-casting problem, of considerable architectural importance, is to compute the outline of the patch of sunlight cast through a window into a room. The difficulty arises out of the quite complex conditions generated by overlapping of shadows cast by the wall surface, window reveals, and horizontal and vertical sunshading devices. *Figure 14.10(a)* illustrates the variety of different conditions which can result from overlapping of shadows cast on a rectangular window by overhangs and side fins, and *Figure 14.10(b)* shows a computer-generated plot of the trajectory of a patch of sunlight cast through a rectangular window onto a floor plane. Tseng-Yao Sun (1968) has published formulae which may be employed to compute window insolation.

The general problem of computing cast shadows in three-dimensional built environments is quite complex and difficult. It is

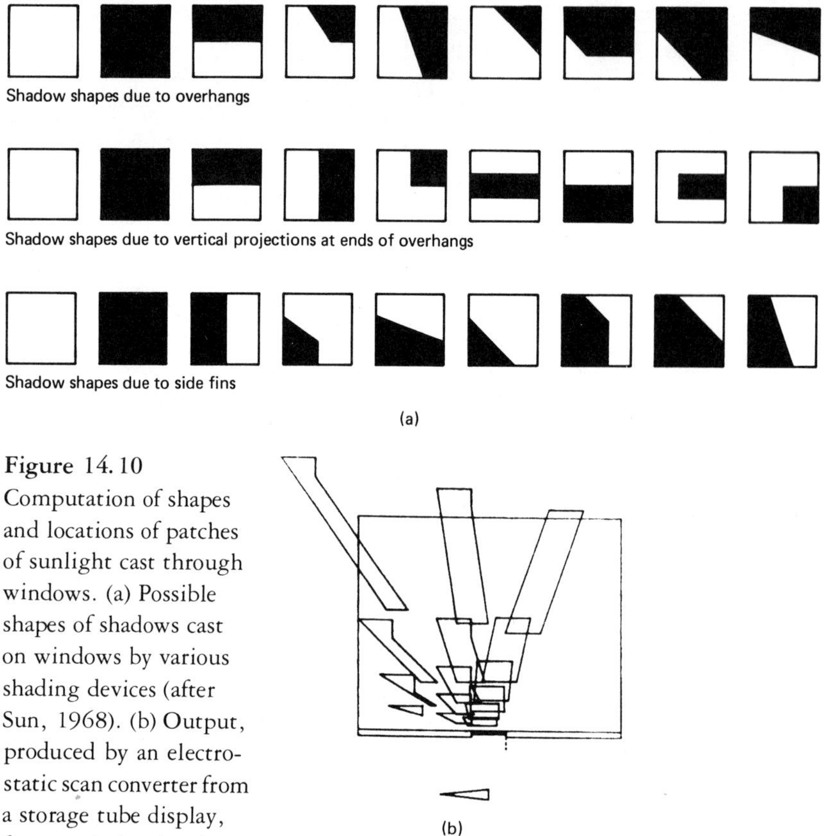

Figure 14.10
Computation of shapes and locations of patches of sunlight cast through windows. (a) Possible shapes of shadows cast on windows by various shading devices (after Sun, 1968). (b) Output, produced by an electrostatic scan converter from a storage tube display, from a window insolation program written by Murray Milne, School of Architecture and Urban Planning, UCLA. The window shown is in a building located in Los Angeles, faces west, and has 1.5 ft. wide scan fin along its southern edge. Sunlight patches are shown at successive in tervals through the day for midwinter (left), the equinoxes (center), and midsummer (right).

essentially identical with the problem of producing a perspective projection of a complex scene with hidden surfaces removed. The approach is to first compute a perspective projection, taken from a viewpoint determined by the sun's altitude and azimuth and at a distance of infinity, then to use a hidden surface removal algorithm to determine the surfaces "seen" by the sun. Those not "seen" are in shadow.

For any shadow pattern computations, whether of the simplest or the most complex type, a full description of relevant building and site geometry is necessary. If this description must be specially input, then the time and cost spent in data preparation and input may well not be justified by the results obtained. But if the information can be automatically extracted from a project data base, then the analysis can be produced very rapidly and cheaply.

Natural and artificial lighting analysis

Quantitative techniques for predicting the level of natural lighting within a building as a function of its physical properties first began to emerge in the 19th century. But since the formulae describing the relations between natural lighting conditions and physical properties of a building in terms of "first principles" of physics are rather complex and difficult to manipulate, they are rarely used directly in practice. Instead, simplified techniques which yield approximate results are employed, for example, the *Waldram diagram* method, daylight factor tables, daylight factor protractors, and simplified formulae. Even these simplified methods, though, are quite time consuming. Furthermore, they generally yield acceptably accurate results only for simple, standard situations, and are unable to cope with non-standard and highly obstructed cases.

For automated computation of daylight factors, the basic formulae developed by Hopkinson and others may be employed directly (Hopkinson, Petherbridge and Longmore 1966, Hawkes and Stibbs 1969, McKay 1972).

The principles upon which these formulas are based are illustrated in *Figure 14.11*. In the first instance, the natural illumination at a point in a room will depend upon the area of the sky vault that is subtended at the point by the window (*Figure 14.11*(*a*)). Obviously this will vary with the location of the reference point. Furthermore, the illumination contributed by each small element of a large light source, such as a window, varies with the position of the element, in a pattern as shown in *Figure 14.11*(*b*). Additional complications are that the luminance of a patch of sky varies with its altitude, and that the light transmitted through glazing varies with the angle of incidence. Adjustment for these factors yields the type of pattern shown in *Figure 14.11*(*c*). To evaluate the sky component of illumination at a point we must, in effect, sum the contributions of the patches of sky which lie within the area subtended by the window at that point. Finally, the sky component must be adjusted by addition of reflected components. The result may be expressed either in some units of illumination or as a daylight factor. The computations involved are straightforward, but extremely tedious to perform by hand.

Figure 14.11(*d*) shows a computer-generated daylight factor contour diagram for a rectangular room lit by windows in one wall. This diagram was generated by running a program to evaluate a daylight factor formula for a grid of locations within the room, then plotting the resultant data points using a standard contouring algorithm.

A similar technique can be employed to plot levels of artificial illumination. The illumination due to a point source at a specified location (see *Figure 14.12*(*a*)) is given by:

$$\text{illumination} = \frac{I\cos\theta}{D^2}$$

where

I = itensity of the light source in candelas in the direction of the point

Figure 14.11
Daylight factor computations. (a) Solid angle of sky vault subtended at a point in a room by the window. (b) Typical pattern of contributions to illumination at a point on a horizontal working plane by elements of a window (uncorrected for variations in sky luminance and effects of glazing). (c) Pattern corrected for variations in luminance of an overcast sky and effects of clear transparent glazing. (d) Daylight factor contours for a room, produced by the DOC DAYLIGHT program (Design Office Consortium, Cambridge, England).

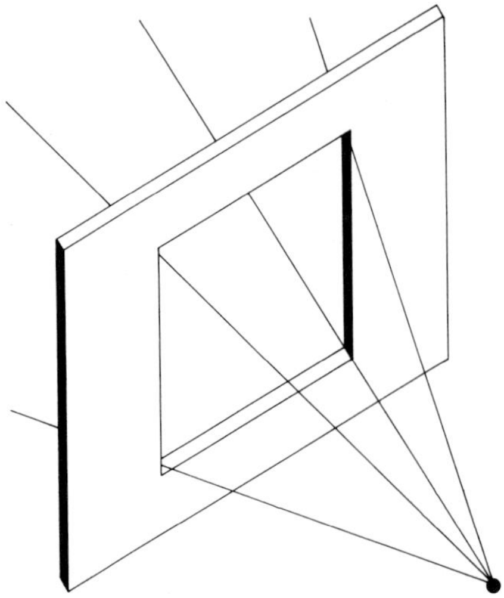

(a)

4	4	5	6	6	7	7	8	8	8	8	8	8	7	7	6	6	5	4	4
4	5	5	6	7	7	8	8	9	9	9	9	8	8	7	7	6	5	5	4
4	5	5	6	7	8	8	9	10	10	10	10	9	8	8	7	6	5	5	4
4	5	5	6	7	8	9	9	10	10	10	10	9	9	8	7	6	5	5	4
4	4	5	6	7	8	9	9	10	10	10	10	9	9	8	7	6	5	4	4
3	4	5	5	6	7	8	9	10	10	10	10	9	8	7	6	5	5	4	3
3	3	4	5	5	6	7	8	9	9	9	9	8	7	6	5	5	4	3	3
2	3	3	4	4	5	6	6	7	7	7	7	6	6	5	4	4	3	3	2
1	2	2	2	3	3	4	4	4	5	5	4	4	4	3	3	2	2	2	1
0	1	1	1	1	1	1	1	2	2	2	2	1	1	1	1	1	1	1	0

Horizon

(b)

3	3	4	5	5	6	6	7	7	7	7	7	7	6	6	5	5	4	3	3
3	3	4	5	5	6	7	7	8	8	8	8	7	7	6	5	5	4	3	3
3	3	4	5	5	6	7	7	8	8	8	8	7	7	6	5	5	4	3	3
3	3	4	4	5	6	7	7	8	8	8	8	7	7	6	5	4	4	3	3
2	3	3	4	5	5	6	7	7	8	8	7	7	6	5	5	4	3	3	2
2	2	3	3	4	5	5	6	7	7	7	7	6	5	5	4	3	3	2	2
1	2	2	3	3	4	4	5	5	6	6	5	5	4	4	3	3	2	2	1
1	1	2	2	2	3	3	3	4	4	4	4	3	3	3	2	2	2	1	1
1	1	1	1	1	2	2	2	2	2	2	2	2	2	2	1	1	1	1	1
0	0	0	0	0	0	1	1	1	1	1	1	1	1	0	0	0	0	0	0

Horizon

(c)

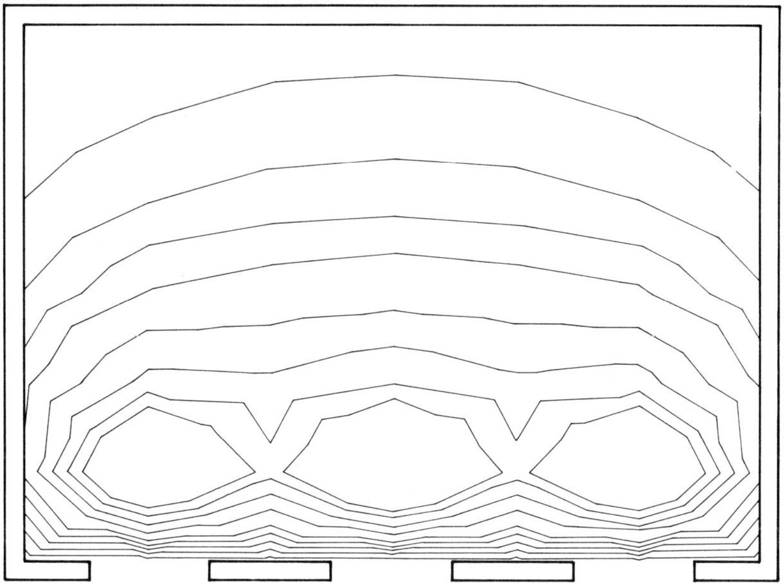

(d)

θ = angle between the normal at the point and the direction of the light source

D = distance of the point from the source

Figure 14.12(b) is an example of a computer-generated illumination contour diagram for a rectangular room illuminated by two unequal point sources. It was produced by employing a simple FORTRAN program to generate a file of data points by evaluation of the formula, then using these points as input to a standard computer mapping program.

Typical examples of lighting analysis programs, based upon these types of formulae, are described by Elliott and Fitzgerald (1965), Hankins (1969), Illuminating Engineering Society (1972), Simpson and Carter (1973), and Design Office Consortium (1976).

The formulae described above can be elaborated in various ways. In particular, they can be modified to take into account light reflected off surfaces, and the effects of various types of obstructions. Recently, some very sophisticated programs, which can be employed to analyze

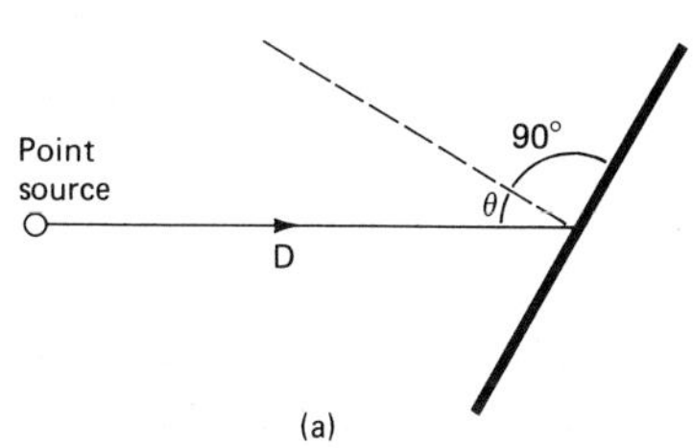

(a)

Figure 14.12
Artificial lighting computations. (a) Illumination from a point source. (b) Illumination contour plot for two unequal point sources in a rectangular room.

(b)

illumination conditions with great precision in highly critical contexts, have been developed (Plant and Archer 1972, Stibbs 1976). But because of their expense, application in design (as opposed to research) situations could only be justified in extraordinary circumstances.

Acoustical analysis

Basic formulae, suitable for performing elementary acoustic analyses of proposed designs, are given in any standard text on architectural acoustics (*e.g.*, Parkin and Humphries 1958, Lawrence 1970). These are readily implemented as quite simple computer programs (see Atal *et al* 1966, Boyer and Degelman 1966, Degelman 1968, Simon and Rien 1968, Campion 1970, Hawkes and Stibbs 1971, Powell 1973).

Figure 14.13 illustrates some output from an elementary acoustical analysis program. Reverberation time for a rectangular room is computed according to the following formula:

$$\text{Reverberation time} = \frac{0.49V}{a}$$

where

V = volume of room in cubic feet

a = total number of absorbtion units (Sabins)

The total number of absorbtion units is given by:

$$\text{Sabins} = \sum_{i=1}^{n} S_i C_i$$

where

n = number of different surface materials used in the room

S_i = total surface area (square feet) of material i

C_i = absorbtion coefficient of material i at the specified frequency

In this example, absorbtion coefficients are assumed as follows:

	Floor	*Walls*	*Ceiling*
125 hertz	0.05	0.02	0.2
500 hertz	0.05	0.02	0.65
2,000 hertz	0.1	0.04	0.75

The room under consideration is assumed to be square, with a ceiling height of 10 ft., and the output is a plot of reverberation times against side dimensions. The graphing facilities of the APL language were employed to produce the results shown.

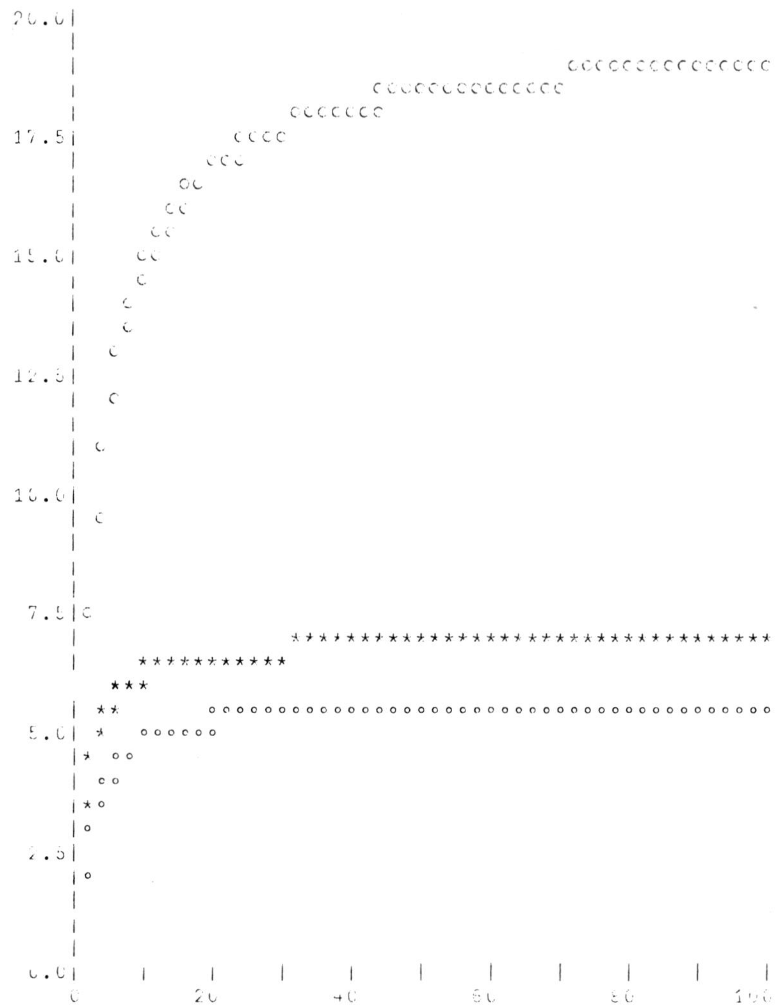

Figure 14.13
APL plot of reverberation time (seconds) against side length (feet) of a square room, at 125 hertz (top), 500 hertz (middle) and 2000 hertz (bottom).

Integration of environmental analyses

Relations between the geometric and physical properties of a building and its environmental performance are quite complex, as shown in *Figure 14.14*. It is clear then, that it is highly desirable for an architect to have an *integrated* view of the environmental consequences of design decisions. It should be possible to simultaneously see the effects of a design decision on the full range of important environmental criteria, so that trade-offs can be explored. The environmental model developed at the Cambridge University Martin Center for Architecture and Urban Studies (Hawkes and Stibbs 1969, Hawkes 1976) is an excellent example of a program which can be used for this purpose. From one set of input data, describing the

Geometric and physical properties of building

Environmental performance criteria	Room dimensions	Size and location of adjacent buildings	Location of room within building mass	Orientation of building	Dimension and location of window openings	U-values	Reflectances	Sound reduction indices	Loudness reduction coefficients	Thickness of surfaces	Density of surfaces
Air temperature	■	■	■	■	■	■	□	□	□	■	■
Relative humidity	□	□	□	□	□	□	□	□	□	□	□
Rate of air movement	■	□	■	□	■	□	□	□	□	□	□
Daylight factor	■	■	■	□	■	□	■	□	□	■	□
Sunlight period	□	■	■	■	■	□	□	□	□	■	□
Illumination level	■	□	□	□	□	□	■	□	□	□	□
Glare index	■	□	□	□	□	□	■	□	□	□	□
Color temperature	□	□	□	□	□	□	□	□	□	□	□
Interior visual privacy	■	□	■	□	□	□	□	□	□	□	□
Exterior visual privacy	■	■	■	□	■	□	□	□	□	□	□
Blackout	■	■	□	□	■	□	□	□	□	□	□
Interior view	■	□	□	□	□	□	□	□	□	□	□
Exterior view	■	■	■	■	■	□	□	□	□	□	□
Maximum noise level	■	□	■	□	■	□	□	■	■	□	□
Reverberation	■	□	□	□	□	□	□	■	□	□	□
Aural privacy	■	□	■	□	■	□	□	■	■	□	□

Figure 14.14
Relations between the geometric and physical properties of a building and its environmental performance (after Hawkes 1971).

design and specifying necessary parameters, a comprehensive environmental analysis is produced. For each individual room, daylight factors at specified reference points, artificial lighting requirements, the various components of heat gain and loss, and total heating and cooling load curves are generated.

Taking an integrated view of environmental performance also suggests that it should be possible to optimize some criterion such as total yearly energy cost of a building, subject to appropriate thermal, lighting, and acoustical performance constraints. An optimization model of this type, suitable for use at the sketch design stage, has been formulated by Gupta (1970). An iterative procedure, which converges to at least a local optimum solution, is employed to find values for 15 independent design variables specifying insulation, thermal inertia, glazing, shading, siting, and surface treatments.

COST ESTIMATION

Three basic steps are involved in producing a cost estimate for a building:

1. *Collection and tabulation of cost data* for the types of materials and components to be used in the building.
2. *Enumeration and tabulation of quantities* of components and materials to be used in the building.
3. *Application of costs to quantities* in order to obtain an estimate of total construction cost.

Automated techniques have been developed to assist at each of these steps. They will be considered in turn. (The reader should keep in mind that construction cost estimation is a complex task, which cannot be discussed in detail here. We will deal only with some of the more important computational aspects.)

Cost data

The familiar architect's building costing manuals (*e.g.*, Dodge 1975) are essentially unit price data files, which are updated at regular intervals. Standard data base management facilities may be employed for maintaining, updating, interrogating, and generating reports from these files as required.

The different types of materials, labor, and equipment employed in building are extremely numerous, their costs are likely to change quite rapidly, and future costs are likely to be difficult to predict. Thus the construction and updating of an accurate cost information file can be a formidable undertaking. A very interesting solution to this problem was employed in the West Sussex County Council's integrated computer-aided design system (Paterson 1974). West Sussex employs a *serial tendering* procedure, under which the County Council architects prepare a schedule of unit items of construction work covering every item likely to be used in the County Council building program over a given period (*e.g.*, two years). Contractors are then invited to price these items on the basis that they would be given a guaranteed quantity of work over the specified period, and the lowest tender (bid) is accepted based on a theoretical bill of quantities which proportions anticipated types of work. Different contractors are appointed in this way for different areas of the County and for different sized contracts. Files of established contractors' prices were held in the computer, ready to be applied to particular building design descriptions at any time. In principle, the West Sussex system allowed very effective cost control at the design stage, and allowed the time spent at the pre-contract phase of a project to be very substantially reduced.

If a traditional bidding procedure is employed, however, files of costs cannot be stabilized in this way. One approach to development of a cost file in the context of traditional bidding procedures is simply to abandon the attempt to predict *actual* construction costs, and to focus on comparison of the *relative* costs of different design alternatives. The cost file contains approximate values, which fairly accurately reflect comparative costs of different materials and techniques. This was the approach followed in the IBIS system (North Carolina Fund 1967) which was primarily oriented towards comparative cost evaluations for low-cost housing projects.

Some attempts have been made to develop large-scale computer-based information systems which would begin to allow actual costs to be predicted more accurately in the context of a traditional bidding process. An example is the BIDS system (Winslow 1972) which collects and analyzes information about the construction market in a region. An initial version of BIDS was put into operation for the Binghamton region of New York State early in 1971.

Quantities

Traditionally, quantities of components and materials in a building are taken off drawings by specialist measurers or cost estimators, and recorded in standardized format for later sorting and summarization. Handling this information, once it has been taken off, is a very straightforward data processing task. It is merely necessary to keypunch the data, enter it into the computer, and employ the computer to sort and summarize it in any required way. Computer systems have been widely and successfully employed by quantity surveyors and cost estimators for this purpose since the early 1960's (Britch 1963, Dent 1964, Smart 1966, Royal Institution of Chartered Surveyors 1967, Monk and Dunstone 1968, Department of the Environment 1972). Some non-trivial issues of standardization and coordination must be dealt with if this type of application is to be successful, but the computer processing aspect presents little difficulty.

To assist in counting and measuring items from drawings, the Swedish company Samdata AB has developed a special hardware device known as a *quantity calculator* (Collier 1974). This consists of a paper tape punch, an electronic desk calculator, and two special electronic pencils. One of these pencils incorporates a small serrated wheel in the tip, and is employed to take off linear distances. The other incorporates a ballpoint pen with a built-in switch and is employed to count and mark off items. Items taken off are entered directly onto paper tape, and the keypunching step is thus eliminated.

In integrated systems, the same building description that is stored in the central project data base, and which is used for production of working drawings and for other purposes, may be directly scanned to take off and summarize quantities. The task of manual taking off is eliminated.

Once a file of quantities has been produced, it may be processed directly to generate a cost estimate, or it may be used to produce printed documents (bills of quantities, schedules and materials lists, materials orders, etc.), sorted and summarized in different ways, according to the needs of various different members of the building team.

Production of estimates

Production of an estimate is a straightforward arithmetic process once satisfactory cost and quantity files have been established. The basic equation is

$$\text{Estimated total cost} = \sum_{i=1}^{n} Q_i(M_i + L_i + E_i)$$

where

n = number of materials

Q_i = total quantity of material i

M_i = unit price for material i

L_i = unit price for labor used in placing material i

E_i = unit price for equipment used in placing material i

Numerous refinements can of course be introduced.

In the early stages of a project, sufficiently detailed quantity data needed for use of this equation may not be available. In this case, various approximate surrogates may be employed (Collier 1974). These will be discussed in roughly decreasing order of precision.

The *cost per element* equation analyzes buildings into unit-priced basic elements such as exterior walls, interior walls, floor slabs, roof decks, etc. Material, labor, and equipment unit prices are added together. The equation thus becomes

$$\text{Estimated total cost} = \sum_{i=1}^{n} Q_i \, El_i$$

where

El_i = unit price for element i.

This equation, which is suitable for use at the sketch design stage, can approach in accuracy an estimate based upon quantities.

A closely analogous approach, the *cost per story-enclosure* method, employs the following basic equation:

$$\text{Estimated total cost} = A_f P_f + A_r P_r + A_w P_w$$

where

A_f = total floor area

P_f = unit price for floors

A_r = total roof deck area

P_r = unit price for roof decks

A_w = total surface area of enclosing walls

P_w = unit price for enclosing walls

Weighting factors may be introduced to allow for the effects of different building heights.

At the early sketch design stage, or even at the briefing stage, the very approximate *cost per square foot* approach may be used. In this case, the equation reduces to

$$\text{Estimated total cost} = A_f P_a$$

where

A_f = total floor area

P_a = average cost/unit floor area.

Sometimes a unit of enclosed volume is employed, rather than a unit of floor area, in this type of calculation.

At the very earliest stage of a project, before even approximate floor areas are known, the *cost per place* method is the only alternative. A "place" in a facility might be a pupil, a bed, a seat, etc. The equation is

$$\text{Estimated total cost} = N_p P_p$$

where

N_p = number of places to be provided for

P_p = average cost per place

Naturally it produces only a very approximate result.

Automation of these calculations is a very straightforward data processing application. The obvious advantage of automation is that a great deal of slow and costly clerical work is eliminated, and a source of human error is removed. A less obvious advantage is that cost analyses can very readily be broken down and reported in a wide variety of different ways as required.

Predictive estimating

A fundamental difficulty with cost estimating techniques which are based upon detailed enumeration of quantities of materials and components is that they can usually be employed only at a very late stage in the design process, when a sufficiently detailed building description finally becomes available. The deficiencies of alternative, highly simplified methods are notorious. In an integrated computer-aided design system, this difficulty can potentially be overcome by use of a technique which has become known as *predictive estimating.* The concept of predictive estimating has been described by Krauss and Myer (1968) as follows:

> Predictive estimating would be done by using a computer-stored body of general information about buildings, together with a program system for generating from this information a detailed "predicted" image of a specific building on the basis of statements from the designer concerning the type, size, and location of the project to be designed. This predicted image would be complete and would contain the same order of detail found in a final, prebid estimate. As design decisions were made, the architect would modify the stored image to reflect his evolving design by entering specific information into the computer. This information would specify the materials and equipment comprising the building, the building geometry, and, by means of various indexes, the degrees of construction quality or difficulty.

The structure of a predicting/costing model which might be used in this process is illustrated in *Figure 14.15.* A predictive cost estimating program of this type known as PCE, primarily oriented towards high-rise apartment buildings, has been implemented at MIT by Harmon (1973).

An integrated approach to estimating and cost accounting

The problem of cost estimation has so far been looked at strictly from the viewpoint of an architect engaged in design of a building. Taking a broader view, cost estimation can be viewed as part of a cyclical management process, as illustrated in *Figure 14.16.* Each of the parts of the process is interdependent with the others. The estimate provides data necessary for planning the construction process, cost accounting and project control take place within the framework set by the plan, and cost accounting data from past jobs is used as the basis for production of estimates. Taking such an integrated view, a comprehensive software system for construction estimation, planning, and control can be developed. For example, Samdata AB of Sweden have developed a system based upon the concept illustrated in *Figure 14.16.* Each of the boxes represents one of the basic programs. The output from each program may be used directly as input to the next. This type of integrated construction management system will undoubtedly find increasingly widespread application. The potential for interfacing with computer-aided design and documentation systems is obvious.

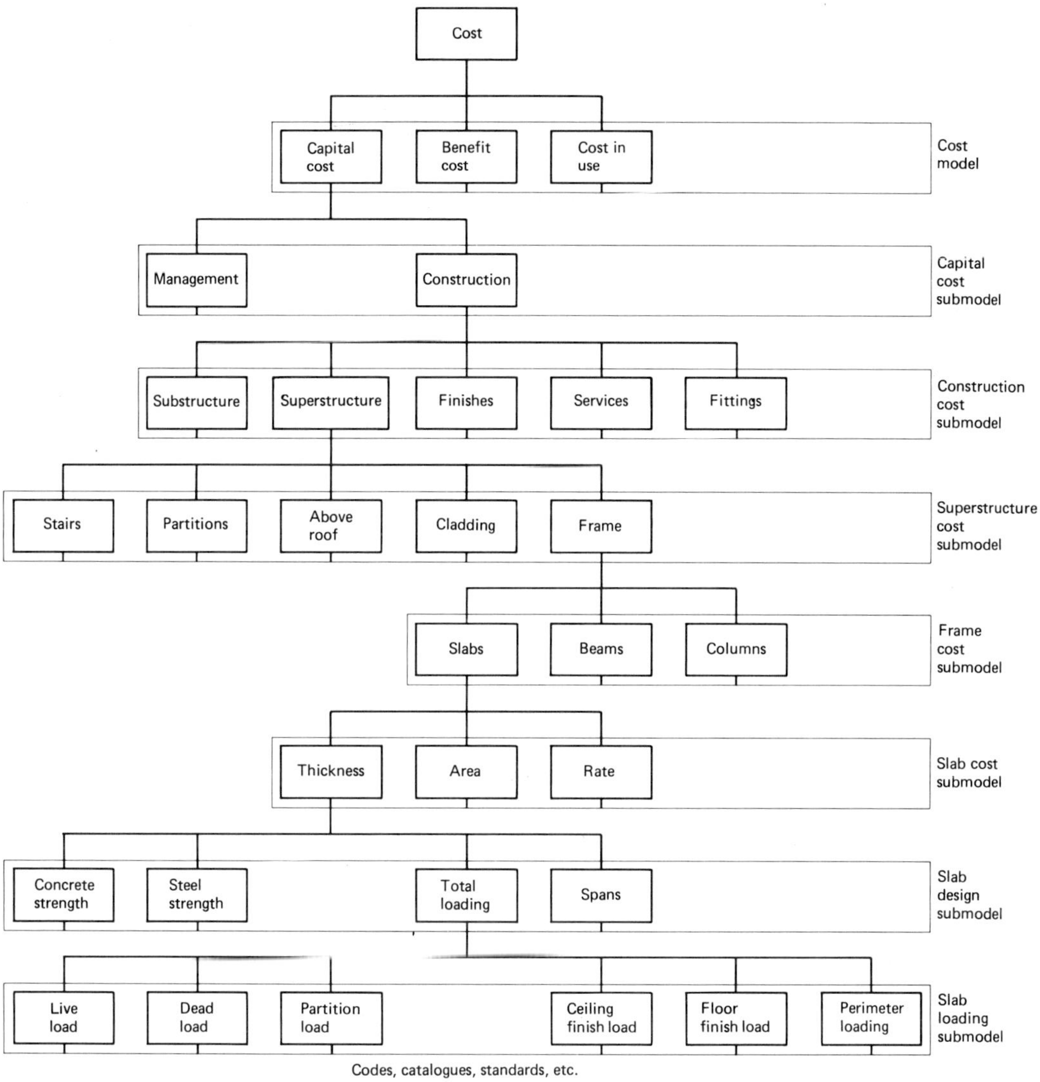

Figure 14.15
Structure of a predicting/costing model (after Krauss (1972)).

CHECKING FOR COMPLIANCE WITH REGULATORY CODES

Facilities for automated checking for compliance with regulatory codes are potentially useful at several levels. First, they might be employed by the architect during the design process, to ensure that code constraints are appropriately met. Second, they might be employed by reviewing agencies to automate the very time-consuming review process. Automated review can also provide an opportunity for the reviewing agency to automate compilation of data bases, which are needed for various planning and administrative purposes, describing construction in its area of jurisdiction.

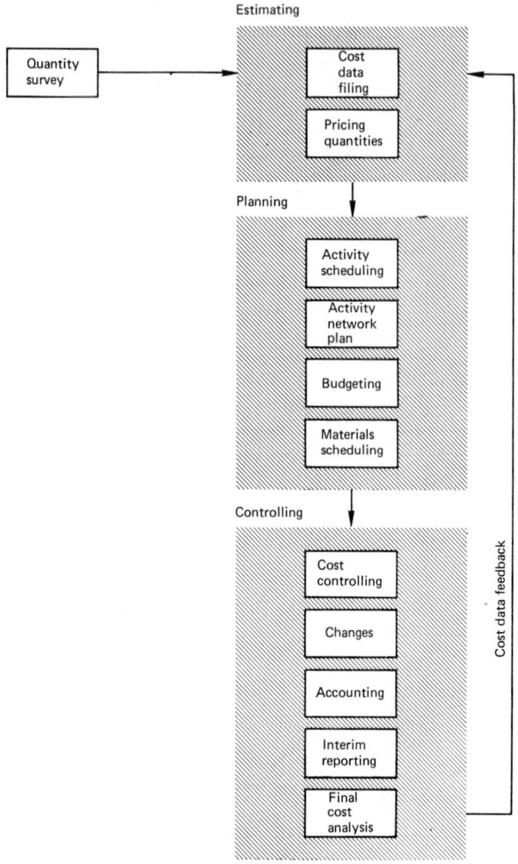

Figure 14.16 Structure of an integrated software system for construction estimation, planning, and cost control.

Types of code requirements

A feasibility study for automated code checking (Bolt Beranek and Newman 1965) carried out for the U.S. National Bureau of Standards has pointed out that building code requirement statements can broadly be classified as:

Statements about spaces and functions;

Statements about materials and construction methods;

Statements about equipment.

Along another dimension, a distinction can be drawn between:

Statements which specify required levels of performance;

Statements which prescribe particular products, dimensions, arrangements, etc.

Yet another distinction can be made between:

Statements which provide for quantitative measures;

Statements which provide for judgmental determination of compliance.

Some of these types of statements pose particular difficulty if automated code checking is to be implemented. In particular, although performance specifications are often highly desirable, they complicate the checking process, since they allow for a requirement to be satisfied in a wide variety of ways. The system must either make provision for all of these, or else make provision for the intervention of expert human judgment.

A further potential difficulty with performance specifications, especially those relating to structural and environmental properties, is that there often exist a number of alternative computational procedures for analyzing the expected performance of a design. Codes often specify the particular procedure to be employed. However, the specified procedures often pre-date widespread use of "computer" methods, and either are not well adapted to computer implementation, or give rather more conservative results than more sophisticated computer-implemented procedures that are now available.

Automated compliance checking procedures can be developed where criteria are explicit and quantitative, but not where reliance is placed upon judgmental determination.

Organization of the automated code checking process

The simplest approach to automated code checking would be to employ clerical staff to take off required data from design documents and code it for batch processing. Alternatively, some kind of interactive system might be employed for data entry. In either case, the data entry step is likely to be a bottleneck in the process. Where an integrated computer-aided design system is employed, however, the potential exists to eliminate this step by extracting data directly from the computer-stored project data base.

The primary output from an automated code checking process would consist of a report of violations and of situations where insufficient data were available to allow checking. A useful by-product might be the addition of a description of the building to the checking agencies' files.

Examples

A description of a simple prototype system, intended to review designs for compliance with the New York building code, has been published by Slutzah (1971). Input to this system is in the form of answers to a series of questions about critical properties of the design. These answers are either entered on a questionnaire form for keypunching and batch entry, or input interactively in response to prompts at a teletype terminal. The program consists of a set of FORTRAN subroutines which check these answers, and sometimes further data which have been computed from them, against provisions of the code. For example, the code section regulating the location and design of building marquees reads in part as follows:

> (4) MARQUEES—Marquees may be erected on public buildings, theaters, hotels, terminals, large department stores, supermarkets, multifamily dwellings, and similar buildings of an essentially public nature, or upon a warehouse or market in an Established Market Area as designated by reference standard RS4-3, so as to project beyond the street line, but not nearer than 2 ft. to the curb line, provided that no parts of such marquees are less than 10 ft. above the ground or sidewalk level. Marquees must not be more than 2 ft. to curb lines hereafter established or changed. When measured from top to bottom, marquees shall not be thicker nor shall the fascia be higher than 3 ft. This dimension shall include all decorations, but shall exclude any tension supports suspending the marquee from the wall . . .

The subroutine which checks for compliance with these provisions requires data identifying building type, and giving the projection height above the ground, and depth of each marquee, etc. Execution of the subroutine results in generation of condition codes which identify whether a marquee is permitted, and whether the projection, height, and depth requirements are met. Based upon tables of such condition codes, the system finally produces a printed report giving the results of the review, as shown in *Figure 14.17*.

A discussion of further research on automated code checking, carried out under National Bureau of Standards sponsorship at the State University of New York at Buffalo, has been published by Masterson (1972).

At the time of writing, no full-scale, practical automated code checking system has been implemented. It appears though, that computational difficulties present less of an obstacle to the implementation of automated code checking systems than the nature of typical

C. PERMISSIBLE PROJECTIONS

1. MARQUEE ON THE FRONT OF THE BUILDING AT COORDINATES 100.0, 40.0 IS NOT SPECIFICALLY PERMITTED ON THIS CLASS BUILDING. BUILDING DEPARTMENT APPROVAL REQUIRED.

   APPROVED BY: ______________________

   DATE: ______________________

2. MARQUEE ON THE FRONT OF THE BUILDING AT COORDINATES 100.0, 40.0 MEETS ALL CODE REQUIREMENTS

3. ENTRANCE ON THE FRONT OF THE BUILDING AT COORDINATES 100.0, 40.0 MEETS ALL CODE REQUIREMENTS

4. MARQUEE ON THE SIDE OF THE BUILDING AT COORDINATES 200.0, 200.0 DOES NOT MEET THE CODE MINIMUM OF 10 FEET OF CLEARANCE OVER SIDEWALK

5. ENTRANCE ON THE SIDE OF THE BUILDING AT COORDINATES 200.0, 200.0 MEETS ALL CODE REQUIREMENTS

Figure 14.17
Part of a building code compliance report (from Slutzah (1971)).

current building codes and review processes themselves. In the United States at least, it is difficult to imagine much progress in the direction of automated code checking until problems of lack of standardization and coordination, imprecision and logical inconsistency in codes are dealt with.

SUGGESTED READINGS

Forwood, B. "Computers and Building Services: A Review." *Architectural Science Review* 19, no. 1 (1976), pp. 17–21.

Harrison, H. B. *Computer Methods in Structural Analysis.* Englewood Cliffs, New Jersey: Prentice-Hall, 1973.

Hawkes, D. *The Development of an Environmental Model.* Working Paper 55. Cambridge, England: Cambridge University Center for Land Use and Built Form Studies, 1971.

Hawkes, D. "Modeling the Environmental Performance of Built Forms," in *The Architecture of Form,* edited by L. March. Cambridge, England: Cambridge University Press, 1976.

Krauss, R. I., and Myer, T. H. "Computer-Aided Cost-Estimating Techniques," in *Computer Applications in Architecture and Engineering,* edited by G. N. Harper. New York: McGraw-Hill, 1968.

Kusuda, T. ed. *Use of Computers for Environmental Engineering Related to Buildings.* Washington, D. C.: National Bureau of Standards, 1971.

March, L. "Elementary Models of Built Forms," in *Urban Space and Structures,* edited by L. Martin, and L. March. Cambridge, England: Cambridge University Press, 1972.

Markus, T. A. ed. *Building Performance.* New York: Halsted Press, 1972.

Masterson, C. "A Computer-Based Code System," *Industrialization Forum* 3, no. 3, (1972), pp. 13–21.

Monk, K. W., and Dunstone, P. H. "Quantity-Surveying by Computer: 1961–68." *Building,* May 31, 1968, pp. 67–68.

Shirley, E. "Circulation Analysis and Lift Placement in Hospitals." *Computer-Aided Design* 6, no. 4 (1974), pp. 206–210.

Steadman, P., and Archer, D. "Models to Predict and Control Energy Use in Buildings." *The Heating and Ventilating Engineer,* August 1975, pp. 12–16.

Stibbs, R. "Prediction of Surface Luminances in Architectural Space," in *The Architecture of Form,* edited by L. March. Cambridge, England: Cambridge University Press, 1976.

Teague, L. C., and Stoker, D. F. "Use of Computer in Preliminary Structural Design of Buildings." *Comput. Struct.* 3, no. 1 (January 1973), pp. 3–16.

Bibliography

This is not an exhaustive bibliography on computer-aided architectural design; it lists only those references cited in the text. In many cases there exist alternative, sometimes equally good, references by other authors. These were eliminated in order to conserve space. Where an author has published essentially the same material in several different forms, only the most widely available version has been included. Except where historically important, outdated material has been eliminated. With a few necessary exceptions, references in languages other than English have not been included. Published sources have been preferred to unpublished research reports, but in many cases citation of unpublished material has been unavoidable. Fortunately, it is often possible to obtain unpublished reports either by writing to the source organization, or via the National Technical Information Service, Washington, D.C.

Aben, H. (1975)
"Computer-Aided Architecture in the Soviet Union," in N. Negroponte (ed.), *Computer Aids to Design and Architecture.* New York: Petrocelli/Charter.

Adams, J., and Cohen, L. (1969)
"Time-Sharing Versus Instant Batch Processing: An Experiment in Programmer Training." *Computers and Automation,* vol. 18, no. 3.

Adshead, H.G. (1973)
"Total Technology: Integrating Design with Production," in J. Vlietstra and R.F. Weilinga (eds.), *Computer-Aided Design.* Amsterdam, Holland: North-Holland Publishing Company.

Agabadian, R., and Tshigogidze, G. (1971)
"Applications of Computer Technology to Architectural Design." *Industrialization Forum,* vol. 3, no. 1 (Oct. 1971), pp. 45–48.

Aguilar, R.G. (1971)
"Architectural Optimization Under Conditions of Uncertainty," in M. Kennedy (ed.), *Proceedings of the Kentucky Workshop on Computer Applications to Environmental Design.* Lexington, Kentucky: University of Kentucky.

Aguilar, R.J., and Hand, J.E. (1968)
"A Generalized Linear Model for Optimization of Architectural Planning." *Proceedings of the Spring Joint Computer Conference.* Washington, D.C.: Thompson Books.

Alberti, L.B. (1485)
De re aedificatoria (facsimile edition of Leoni's English translation of 1726 edited by J. Rykwert, London, Tiranti, 1955).

Alcock, D.G., and Shearing, B.H. (1970)
"GENESYS: An Attempt to Rationalize the Use of Computers in Structural Engineering." *The Structural Engineer,* vol. 48, no. 4 (April 1970), pp. 143–152.

Alexander, C. (1964)
Notes on the Synthesis of Form. Cambridge, Mass.: Harvard University Press.

Allen, E. (1970)
Continuous Construction–A Research Report. Cambridge, Mass.: MIT Department of Architecture.

Allen, E. (ed.) (1974)
The Responsive House. Cambridge, Mass.: MIT Press.

Alsop, K., and Day, A.G. (1963)
"The French Agrément System." *The Builder,* 26 July 1963.

Amidon, E.L., and Elsner, G.H. (1968)
Delineating Landscape View Areas: A Computer Approach. Berkeley, California: U.S. Department of Agriculture, Forest Research Note PSW-180.

Anderson, D.M. (1973)
"New Plant Layout Information System." *Industrial Engineering,* April 1973, pp. 32–36.

APEC (1972)
Abstracts of Computer Programs. Dayton, Ohio: APEC.

Appel, A. (1969)
"The Notion of Quantitative Invisibility and the Machine Rendering of Solids." *Proceedings of the 22nd National Conference of the ACM.* Washington, D.C.: Thompson Books.

Applied Research of Cambridge (1973)
Movement in Building Simulator. Cambridge, England: Applied Research of Cambridge.

——— (1974)
Integrated Building and Equipment Scheduling. Cambridge, England: Applied Research of Cambridge.

——— (1975)
Higher Education Planning. Cambridge, England: Applied Research of Cambridge.

——— (1975)
SSHA System. Cambridge, England: Applied Research of Cambridge.

——— (1975)
Software Infrastructures for Integrated System Development. Cambridge, England: Applied Research of Cambridge.

——— (1976)
OXSYS-BOS: Short Technical Description. Cambridge, England: Applied Research of Cambridge.

Archer, L.B. (1963)
"Planning Accommodation for Hospitals and the Transportation Problem Technique." *Architects' Journal,* July 1963, pp. 139–142.

Architects' Journal (1964)
"CBC: Coordinated Building Communication." *Architects' Journal,* 25 March 1964, pp. 670–672.

Architectural and Engineering News (1963)
"Automation in Architecture." *Architectural and Engineering News,* special issue, March 1963.

Architectural Record (1973)
"Sweet's Refines Logic of the Product Search." *Architectural Record,* August 1973, pp. 65–66.

——— (1975)
"Sweet's 'Buyline' Service to Specifiers Reports 500 Calls Per Day." *Architectural Record,* October 1975, p. 37.

Armour, G.C., and Buffa, E.S. (1963)
"A Heuristic Algorithm and Simulation Approach to Relative Location of Facilities." *Management Science,* vol. 9, no. 2, pp. 294–309.

Ashby, W.R. (1968)
"Some Consequences of Bremermann's Limit for Information Processing Systems," in H.L. Oestreicher and D.R. Moore (eds.), *Cybernetic Problems in Bionics.* New York: Gordon and Breach.

ASHRAE (1974)
Handbook of Fundamentals. New York: ASHRAE.

ASHRAE Task Group on Energy Requirements for Heating and Cooling of Buildings (1975)
Subroutine Algorithms for Heating and Cooling Loads to Determine Building Energy Requirements. New York: ASHRAE.

Asimow, M. (1962)
Introduction to Design. Englewood Cliffs, New Jersey: Prentice-Hall.

Atal, B.S., et al. (1966)
"Evaluation of Acoustic Properties of Enclosures by Means of Digital Computers." *Journal of the Acoustical Society of America,* vol. 40, no. 2, pp. 428–433.

Attneave, F., and Arnoult, M.D. (1956)
"The Quantitative Study of Shape and Pattern Perception." *Psychological Bulletin,* vol. 53, no. 6, pp. 452–471.

Auger, B. (1972)
The Architect and the Computer. New York: Praeger.

Auslander, L., and Trent, H.M. (1966)
"On the Realization of a Linear Graph Given Its Algebraic Specification." *Journal of the Acoustical Society of Australia,* vol. 33, no. 9 (Sept. 1966), pp. 1163–1192.

Ayres, R.U. (1969)
Technological Forecasting and Long Range Planning. New York: McGraw-Hill.

Baer, A. (1974)
"A Simulation Model of Multidirectional Pedestrian Movement Within Physically Bounded Environments," in D. Carson (ed.), *Proceedings of the EDRA 5 Conference.* Stroudsberg, Pennsylvania: Dowden, Hutchinson, and Ross.

Baer, A., and Eastman, C.M. (1976)
The Consistency of Integrated Databases for Computer Aided Design. Pittsburgh, Pennsylvania: Carnegie-Mellon University, Institute for Physical Planning.

Ball, G.H. (1970)
Classification Analysis. Palo Alto, California: Stanford Research Institute.

Banham, R. (1960)
Theory and Design in the First Machine Age. 2d ed. New York: Praeger.

Bannister, T.C. (ed.) (1954)
The Architect at Mid-Century: Evolution and Achievement. New York: Reinhold.

Baumgart, B. (1972)
Winged Edge Polyhedron Representation. Palo Alto, California: Stanford University Artificial Intelligence Project Report AIM-179.

Baxter, R.S. (1976)
Computer and Statistical Techniques for Planners. London: Methuen.

Bazjanac, V. (1971)
"Computer Simulation: A Realistic Assessment." *Progressive Architecture,* July 1971, pp. 80–83.

——— (1974)
"Another Way Out?" *Progressive Architecture,* April 1974, pp. 88–89.

Beaumont, M.J.S. (1967)
Computer-Aided Technique for the Synthesis of Layout and Form with Respect to Circulation. Unpublished Ph.D. thesis, Department of Engineering, University of Bristol, England.

Bellman, R.E., and Zadeh, L.A. (1970)
"Decision Making in a Fuzzy Environment." *Management Science,* vol. 17, no. 4, pp. B141–B164.

Bemis, A.F. (1936)
The Evolving House. Cambridge, Mass.: MIT Press.

Bengtsson, B., and Nordbeck, S. (1964)
Construction of Isarithms and Isarithmic Maps by Computers. Lund, Sweden: University of Lund, BIT 4 87–105.

Bernholtz, A., and Bierstone, E. (1966)
"Computer-Augmented Design." *Design Quarterly,* 1966/1967, pp. 41–52.

Berry, P.C. (1969)
APL/360 Primer. White Plains, New York: IBM Manual No. C20-1702.

Besant, C.B., Hamlyn, A., Jebb, A., and McClintock, P. (1973)
"The Use of CADMAC Systems in General Drafting," in G.W. Jones (ed.), *Computer-Aided Drafting Systems.* Guildford, Surrey, England: IPC Science and Technology Press.

Besant, C.B., Jebb, A., Eagles, A.J., and Saunders, P.W. (1972)
"CADMAC: A Fully Interactive Computer-Aided Design System." *Computer-Aided Design,* January 1972, pp. 67–70.

Biggs, J.M., Logcher, R.D., Schumacher, B., and Sowards, R.D. (1973)
Interactive STRUDL Graphics. Cambridge, Mass.: Department of Civil Engineering, MIT.

Bijl, A. (1971)
"Computer-Aided Architectural Design," in R.D. Parlow and R.E. Green (eds.), *Advanced Computer Graphics.* New York: Plenum.

——— (1972)
"Application of CAAD Research in Practice: A System for House Design." *Proceedings of the International Conference on Computers in Architecture.* London: British Computer Society.

Bijl, A., Renshaw, T., and Barnard, D.F. (1971)
"The Use of Graphics in the Development of Computer-Aided Environmental Design for Two-Story Houses," in T. Kusuda (ed.), *Use of Computers for Environmental Engineering Related to Buildings.* Washington, D.C.: National Bureau of Standards.

Bindslev, B. (1964)
Series of articles on CBC in the weekly *Architects' Journal,* 25 March 1964 to 24 Feb. 1965, and 24 Jan. 1968 to 7 Feb. 1968.

Birgerson, B. (1967)
"CBC/BCD as a National System." *RIBA Journal,* September 1967, pp. 394–399.

Bishop, D., and Alsop, K. (1969)
A Study of Coding and Data Coordination for the Construction Industry. London: Ministry of Public Building and Works.

Bledsoe, W.W. (1961)
"A Basic Limitation on the Speed of Digital Computers." *IRE Transactions on Electronic Computation,* ED-10, 530.

Block, T.E., and Lewis, W.P. (1975)
A Review of Plant Layout: Problems and Methods. Melbourne, Australia: University of Melbourne, Department of Mechanical Engineering.

Blue, H. (1974)
"Contract Documentation of Dimensionally Coordinated Buildings Using a Computer with Peripheral Graphic Display and Reproduction Units." *DMG-DRS Journal,* vol. 8, no. 4, pp. 218–221.

Bobrow, D.G. (1968)
"Natural Language Input for a Computer Problem-Solving System," in M.L. Minsky (ed.), *Semantic Information Processing.* Cambridge, Mass.: MIT Press.

Boehm, B.M. (1967)
"Tabular Representation of Multivariate Functions." *Proceedings of the 22nd National Conference of the Association for Computing Machinary.* New York: Association for Computing Machinery.

Bolling, W.B. (1972)
"Queuing Model of a Hospital Emergency Room." *Industrial Engineering,* September 1972, pp. 26–31.

Bolt, Beranek and Newman Inc. (1965)
Computer-Aided Checking of Design Documents for Compliance with Regulatory Codes. Washington, D.C.: National Bureau of Standards, Institute of Applied Technology, Report No. 1260.

Borges, J.L. (1964)
"The Library of Babel," in *Labyrinths: Selected Stories and Other Writings.* New York: New Directions Publishing Corp.

Boroff, M. (1971)
"Creativity, Poetic Language, and the Computer." *Yale Review,* vol. 60, no. 4, pp. 481–512.

Boston Architectural Center (1964)
Architecture and the Computer. Proceedings of the First Boston Architectural Center Conference. Boston, Mass.: Boston Architectural Center.

Bouknight, J. (1969)
Improved Procedure for Generation of Half-Tone Computer Graphics Presentations. Urbana, Illinois: University of Illinois, Coordinated Science Laboratory Report R-432.

Bouknight, J., and Kelley, K. (1970)
"Algorithm for Producing Half-Tone Computer Graphics Presentations with Shadows and Movable Light Sources." *Proceedings of the Spring Joint Computer Conference.* Montvale, New Jersey: AFIPS Press.

Boyer, L.L., and Degelman, L.O. (1966)
Acoustical Design for Optimum Reverberation Time. University Park, Pennsylvania: Pennsylvania State University, Department of Architectural Engineering.

Brassel, K. (1974)
"Developments in Automated Hill Shading." *Context* (Newsletter of the Harvard Laboratory for Computer Graphics and Spatial Analysis), April 1974, p. 4.

Bremermann, H.J. (1967)
"Quantum Noise and Information." *Proceedings of the 5th Berkeley Symposium on Mathematical Statistics and Probability,* vol. 4. Berkeley, California: University of California Press.

Brice, C.R., and Fennema, C.L. (1970)
"Scene Analysis Using Regions." *Artificial Intelligence,* vol. 1, no. 3, pp. 205–226.

Bridgwater, A.V. (1968)
"Long Range Process Design and Morphological Analysis." *The Chemical Engineer,* April 1968, pp. 75–81.

Brillinger, P.C., and Cohen, D.J. (1972)
Introduction to Data Structures and Non-Numeric Computations. Englewood Cliffs, New Jersey: Prentice-Hall.

Britch, A.L. (1963)
"Quantity Surveying by Electronic Computers." *Architects' Journal,* 27 (March 1963), pp. 669–674.

Broad, E. (1969)
"Planning a Multilevel Car Park." *Industrial Engineering,* September 1969, pp. 17–23.

Broadbent, G.H., and O'Keefe, J. (1972)
"An Appraisal of the Role of Space Planning Techniques Within the Design Process." *Proceedings of the International Conference on Computers in Architecture.* London: British Computer Society.

Broers, A.N., and Hatzakis, M. (1972)
"Microcircuits by Electron Beam." *Scientific American,* November 1972, pp. 34–44.

Brooks, G.H. (1970)
Project Themis: Information Processing. Industrial Engineering Department, Auburn University.

Brooks, R.L., Smith, C.A.B., Stone, A.H., and Tutte, W.T. (1940)
"The Dissection of Rectangles into Squares." *Duke Mathematical Journal,* vol. 7, pp. 312–341.

Brotchie, J.F. (1969)
"A General Planning Model." *Management Science,* vol. 16, no. 3 (Nov. 1969), pp. 265–266.

Browne, J.J., and Kelly, J.J. (1968)
"Simulation of Elevator for World's Tallest Building." *Transportation Science,* vol. 2, no. 1, pp. 35–56.

Bruno, J., Steiglitz, K., and Weinberg, L. (1970)
"A New Planarity Test Based on 3-Connectivity." *IEEE Transactions on Circuit Theory,* vol. CT-17, no. 2 (May 1970), pp. 197–206.

Bryant, D.A., Dains, B., and Spoonamore, J.H. (1975)
SEARCH: Systematic Evaluation and Review of Criteria for Habitability. Champaign, Illinois: U.S. Army Corps of Engineers, Construction Engineering Research Laboratory.

Bullock, N.O.A. (1974)
"Modeling the Demand for Teaching Space." *Environment and Planning B,* vol. 1, no. 1 (June 1974), pp. 69–104.

Bunge, W. (1966)
Theoretical Geography. Lund, Sweden: C.W.K. Gleerup.

Bunker, W.M. (1975)
"Computer Generation of Images: The Multi-Purpose Tool." *S.P.I.E. Proceedings,* vol. 59, pp. 25–39.

Bunselmeier, E. (1973)
Computerized Location-Allocation. Monticello, Illinois: Council of Planning Librarians, Exchange Bibliography no. 414.

Burberry, P. (1970)
"Analytical Techniques: Simulation." *Architects' Journal,* February 1970, pp. 521–524.

Burgess, D., and Leather, G. (1968)
"Information Scheduling by Computer." *RIBA Journal,* vol. 75, no. 1 (Jan. 1968), pp. 36–38.

Bush, V. (1945)
"As We May Think." *Atlantic Monthly,* July 1945, pp. 101–108.

Butterfield, J.F. (1972)
"Autostereoscopic Screens." Sherman Oaks, California: Stereotronics Television Co.

Cagan, C. (1973)
Data Management Systems. Los Angeles, California: Melville.

Calderbank, G., and Kirke, A.G. (1971)
"An End to Terminal Guesses." *Design,* October 1971, pp. 62–63.

Campbell, D.T. (1960)
"Blind Variation and Selective Retention in Creative Thought as in Other Knowledge Processes." *Psychological Review,* vol. 67, no. 6, pp. 380–400.

Campion, D. (1968)
Computers in Architectural Design. New York: Elsevier.

——— (1970)
"Computer-Aided Acoustical Analysis." *Building,* 8 May 1970, pp. 111–116.

Campion, D., and Reynolds, T. (1974)
"Computers in Architecture in the U.K." *DMG-DRS Journal,* vol. 8, no. 4, pp. 182–199.

Carbonell, J.R., Elkind, J., and Nickerson, R. (1968)
"On the Psychological Importance of Time in a Time-Sharing System." *Human Factors,* vol. 10, no. 9 (April 1968), pp. 135–142.

Cardenas, A.F. (1973)
"Data Entry: A Cost Giant." *Journal of Systems Management,* August 1973, pp. 35–42.

——— (1974)
Analysis and Performance of Inverted Data Base Structures. San Jose, California: IBM Research Technical Report RJ1375.

Carr-Saunders, A.M., and Wilsón, P.A. (1933)
The Professions. Oxford, England: Clarendon Press.

Catmull, E. (1974)
A Subdivision Algorithm for Computer Display of Curved Surfaces. Salt Lake City, Utah: University of Utah, Department of Computer Science, Report UTEC-CS.-74-133.

Caudill, W.W. (1971)
Architecture by Team. New York: Van Nostrand Reinhold.

CED Building Services (1974)
Build for Health. London: CED Building Services.

Chalmers, J.R. (1972)
"The Development of CEDAR: A Computer-Aided Design System with Graphics Using a Central Computer Operating through Terminals." *Proceedings of the International Conference on Computers in Architecture.* London: British Computer Society.

Chermayeff, S., and Alexander, C. (1965)
Community and Privacy. New York: Doubleday.

Churchman, C.W., Ackoff, R.L., and Arnoff, L. (1957)
Introduction to Operations Research. New York: Wiley.

CIB (1968)
Information Flow in the Building Process: Classification and Coding for Computer Use. Oslo, Norway: Norwegian Building Research Institute. CIB Report 13B.

Cinar, U. (1968)
The Planning of Multi-Story Buildings: A Systems Analysis and Simulation Approach. Lancaster, England: University of Lancaster, Department of Operational Research.

——— (1975)
"Facilities Planning: A Systems Analysis and Space Allocation Approach," in C.M. Eastman (ed.), *Spatial Synthesis in Computer-Aided Building Design.* New York: Wiley.

Clark, W.E. (1967)
Development of a Notation and Data Structure for Computer Applications to Building Problems. Los Angeles, California: Bolt, Beranek and Newman Inc., Report 1398.

Clasen, R.J., Graves, G.W., and Lu, J.Y. (1974)
Sortie Allocation by a Non-Linear Programming Model for Determining a Munitions Mix. Santa Monica, California: Rand Corporation.

Clowes, M.B. (1971)
"On Seeing Things." *Artificial Intelligence,* vol. 2, pp. 79–116.

——— (1972)
"Scene Analysis and Picture Grammars," in F. Nake and A. Rosenfeld (eds.), *Graphic Languages.* Amsterdam, Holland: North-Holland Publishing Co.

CODASYL (1974)
CODASYL Data Description Language. Washington, D.C.: National Bureau of Standards, Handbook 113.

CODASYL Systems Committee (1971)
Feature Analysis of Generalized Data Base Management Systems. New York: Association for Computing Machinery.

Codd, E.F. (1970)
"A Relational Model of Data for Large Shared Data Banks." *Communications of the ACM,* vol. 13, no. 6, pp. 377–387.

Cogswell, A.R. (1969)
"Programming and a Computer-Based Cost Analysis System." *Building Research,* vol. 6, no. 2 (April/June 1969), pp. 33–35.

Cole, A. (1972)
The Design System: Its Development and Evaluation. Lund, Sweden: University of Lund.

Collier, K. (1974)
Fundamentals of Construction Estimating and Cost Accounting. Englewood Cliffs, New Jersey: Prentice-Hall.

Comba, P.G. (1968)
"A Procedure for Detecting Intersections of Three-Dimensional Objects." *Journal of the ACM,* vol. 15, no. 3 (July 1968), pp. 354–356.

Computer Equipment Corp. Ltd. (1972)
BASYS: A Fully Interactive Computer-Aided Design System for the Building Industry. London: Computer Equipment Corp. Ltd.

Construction Specifications Institute (1972)
Uniform Construction Index. Washington, D.C.: Construction Specifications Institute.

Cooley, M.J.E. (1972)
Computer-Aided Design: Its Nature and Implications. Richmond, Surrey, England: Amalgamated Union of Engineering Workers.

Cousin, J. (1970)
Topological Organization of Architectural Space. Montreal, Canada: University of Montreal Press.

Cowan, H.J. (1971)
Architectural Structures. New York: American Elsevier.

Cowan, H.J., Gero, J.S., Ding, G.D., and Muncey, R.W. (1968)
Models in Architecture. New York: Elsevier.

Craik, K.J.W. (1943)
The Nature of Explanation. Cambridge, England: Cambridge University Press.

Crook, M.J. (1969)
"The Pre-Victorian Architect: Professionalism and Patronage." *Architectural History,* vol. 12, pp. 62–78.

Cross, N. (1974)
Human and Machine Roles in Computer-Aided Design. Milton Keynes, England: The Open University.

Culver, W.H., and Mehran, F. (1971)
Coherent Optical Logic. Yorktown Heights, New York: IBM Watson Research Center Report RC-3533.

Dahl, O., and Nygaard, K. (1966)
"SIMULA: An Algol-Based Simulation Language." *Communications of the ACM,* vol. 9, no. 9 (Sept. 1966), pp. 671–678.

Daniel, P.T. (1973)
"A Plant and Buildings Draughting and Scheduling System," in J. Vlietstra and R.F. Wielinga (eds.), *Computer-Aided Design.* Amsterdam, Holland: North-Holland Publishing Co.

David, H.A. (1963)
The Method of Paired Comparisons. New York: Hafner.

Davis, C. (1974)
"The Harness System." *Hospital Engineering,* vol. 28 (January 1974).

Davis, C.F., and Kennedy, M.D. (1970)
"EPS: A Computer Program for the Evaluation of Problem Structure," in

G.T. Moore (ed.), *Emerging Methods in Environmental Design and Planning.* Cambridge, Mass.: MIT Press.

Dawson, J.W. (1961)
"The Computer in Building Design." *Architectural and Engineering News,* vol. 3, no. 12 (December 1961), pp. 14–19.

Degelman, L.O. (1968)
Acoustical Design for Optimum Reverberation Time Including Air Absorbtion. University Park, Pennsylvania: Pennsylvania State University, Department of Architectural Engineering.

——— (1969)
MODCON: A Tool for Computer-Aided Design of Buildings. University Park, Pennsylvania: Pennsylvania State University, Department of Architectural Engineering, Report 69-1.

Denardo, E.V. (1975)
Dynamic Programming: Theory and Application. Englewood Cliffs, New Jersey: Prentice-Hall.

Denes, P.B. (1975)
"A Scan-Type Graphics System for Interactive Computing." *Proceedings of the Conference on Computer Graphics, Pattern Recognition, and Data Structure.* Los Angeles, California: UCLA Extension.

Dent, C. (1964)
Quantity Surveying by Computer. Oxford, England: Oxford University Press.

Deo, N. (1974)
Graph Theory with Applications to Engineering and Computer Science. Englewood Cliffs, New Jersey: Prentice-Hall.

Department of Commerce (1968)
The DIME Geocoding System. Washington, D.C.: U.S. Bureau of Census.

Department of the Environment (1971)
Commodity Information for the Construction Industry: A Feasibility Study for a Commodity File. London: Department of the Environment.

——— (1972)
ENVIRO: The DOE Computer System for Bills of Quantities. London: Department of the Environment.

Desai, H., and Yanouzas, J. (1970)
"Where Simple Queuing Models Work." *Industrial Engineering,* July 1970, pp. 15–19.

Design Office Consortium (1976)
DOC Daylight. Cambridge, England: Design Office Consortium.

Dijkstra, E.W. (1959)
"A Note on Two Problems in Connection with Graphs." *Numerische Mathematik,* vol. 1, 1959, pp. 269–271.

Dineen, G.P. (1955)
"Programming Pattern Recognition." *Proceedings of the 1955 Joint Computer Conference.* Montvale, New Jersey: AFIPS Press.

Distefano, N., and Nagy, D. (1972)
"A Normalization Procedure in Building Methodology," in W.J. Mitchell (ed.), *Environmental Design: Research and Practice,* Proceedings of the

EDRA3/AR8 Conference. Los Angeles, California: School of Architecture and Urban Planning, UCLA.

Dodd, G.C. (1969)
"Elements of Data Management Systems." *Computing Surveys,* vol. 1, no. 2 (June 1969), pp. 118–132.

Dodge Building Cost Services (1975)
1976 Dodge Construction Systems Costs. New York: McGraw-Hill Information Systems Co.

Dougenik, J., and Sheehan, D. (1976)
SYMAP User's Reference Manual. Cambridge, Mass.: Laboratory for Computer Graphics and Spatial Analysis, Harvard Graduate School of Design.

Dreyfus, S.E. (1969)
"An Appraisal of Some Shortest Path Algorithms." *Operations Research,* vol. 17, no. 3 (May–June 1969), pp. 395–412.

Dubery, F., and Willats, J. (1972)
Drawing Systems. London: Studio Vista.

Dudnik, E.E. (1971)
"Overlay," in C. Steinitz (ed.), *Red Book.* Cambridge, Mass.: Laboratory for Computer Graphics and Spatial Analysis, Harvard Graduate School of Design.

Dudnik, E.E., and Krawczyk, R. (1973)
"An Evaluation of Space Planning Methodologies," in W.F.E. Preiser (ed.), *Environmental Design Research,* Proceedings of the EDRA 4 Conference. Stroudsberg, Pennsylvania: Dowden, Hutchinson, and Ross.

Duncker, K. (1945)
"On Problem Solving." *Psychological Monographs,* vol. 58, no. 5, whole issue.

Duran, B.S., and Odell, P.L. (1974)
Cluster Analysis: A Survey. Berlin: Springer-Verlag.

Durand, J.N.L. (1802)
Précis des Leçons d'Architecture. Paris: École Polytechnique.

Eastman, C.M. (1969)
"Cognitive Processes and Ill-Defined Problems: A Case Study from Design," in D.E. Walker and L.M. Norton (eds.), *Proceedings of the International Joint Conference on Artificial Intelligence.* Washington, D.C.: Mitre Corporation.

——— (1970)
"On the Analysis of Intuitive Design Processes," in G.T. Moore (ed.), *Emerging Methods in Environmental Design and Planning.* Cambridge, Mass.: MIT Press.

——— (1970)
"Representations for Space Planning." *Communications of the ACM,* vol. 13, no. 4 (April 1970), pp. 242–250.

——— (1971)
"GSP: A System for Computer-Assisted Space Planning." *Proceedings of the 1971 Design Automation Workshop.* New York: Association for Computing Machinery.

——— (1971)
Heuristic Algorithms for Automated Space Planning. Pittsburgh, Pennsylvania: Carnegie-Mellon University, Institute for Physical Planning, Report no. 17.

——— (1972)
"Preliminary Report on a System for General Space Planning." *Communications of the ACM,* vol. 15, no. 2 (Feb. 1972), pp. 76–87.

——— (1973)
"Automated Space Planning." Artificial Intelligence, vol. 4 (1973), pp. 41–64.

——— (1975)
Spatial Synthesis in Computer-Aided Building Design. New York: Wiley.

——— (1975)
A Building Description System. Pittsburgh, Pennsylvania: Carnegie-Mellon University, Institute for Physical Planning, Research Report.

——— (1975)
"Mini Space Planner: A Set of Fortran Routines for Building Space Planning Programs," in C.M. Eastman (ed.), *Spatial Synthesis in Computer-Aided Building Design.* New York: Wiley.

——— (1976)
"Databases for Physical System Design: A Survey of U.S. Efforts." *Proceedings of the CAD76 Conference.* London: ICP Press.

Eastman, C.M., Fisher, D., Lafue, G., Lividini, J., Stoker, D., and Yessios, C. (1974)
An Outline of the Building Description System. Pittsburgh, Pennsylvania: Carnegie-Mellon University, Institute for Physical Planning, Research Report No. 50.

Eastman, C.M., and Henrion, M. (1976)
GLIDE: Language for a Design Information System. Pittsburgh, Pennsylvania: Carnegie-Mellon University, Institute for Physical Planning.

Eastman, C.M., and Lividini, J. (1976)
Spatial Search. Pittsburgh, Pennsylvania: Carnegie-Mellon University, Institute for Physical Planning, Research Report.

Eastman, C.M., Lividini, J., and Stoker, D. (1975)
"A Database for Designing Large Physical Systems." *Proceedings of the 1975 National Computer Conference.* Montvale, New Jersey: AFIPS Press.

Eastman, C.M., and Yessios, C. (1972)
An Efficient Algorithm for Finding the Various Intersections and Differences of Spatial Domains. Pittsburgh, Pennsylvania: Carnegie-Mellon University, Institute for Physical Planning, Research Report.

Eberhard, J.P. (1962)
"A Computer-Based Building Process: Its Potentials for Architecture." *Architectural and Engineering News,* vol. 4, no. 12 (Dec. 1962), pp. 16–18.

Echenique, M. (1972)
"Models: A Discussion," in L. Martin and L. March (eds.), *Urban Space and Structures.* Cambridge, England: Cambridge University Press.

Ehrenkrantz, E. (1975)
"Cost/Performance: The Key to Building System Approach," in D.

Hawkes (ed.), *Models and Systems in Architecture and Building.* Hornby, Lancaster, England: The Construction Press.

Eichenberger, F. (1970)
Wide Angle Perspective Systems with an Emphasis upon Cylindrical Perspective. Raleigh, North Carolina: Design Research Laboratory, School of Design, North Carolina State University.

Eilon, S., and Mathewson, S. (1973)
"A Simulation Study for the Design of an Air Terminal Building." *IEEE Transactions on Systems, Management, and Cybernetics,* vol. SMC-3, no. 4 (July 1973), pp. 308–317.

Eldar, M.S. (1973)
"Product Information: Sweet's Guidelines Structure." *Industrialization Forum,* vol. 4, no. 4, pp. 33–46.

Eldridge, H.J. (1968)
"The CIB Master List of Properties." *Building,* 14 (June 1968), pp. 155–157.

Elliott, C.E., and Fitzgerald, J.F. (1965)
"Computer Applications in Lighting." *Illuminating Engineering,* vol. 60, no. 8 (August 1965), pp. 499–505.

Ellis, T.O., Heafner, J.F., and Sibley, W.L. (1969)
The GRAIL Language and its Operations. Santa Monica, California: Rand Corporation Report RM-6001-ARPA.

Elms, D.G. (1972)
A Comprehensive Computer-Aided Building Design System. Cambridge, Mass.: MIT Department of Civil Engineering, Structures Publication no. 343, R72-32.

Engles, R.W. (1970)
A Tutorial on Data Base Organization. Poughkeepsie, New York: IBM Technical Report TR.00.2004.

Erikson, W.J. (1966)
A Pilot Study of Interactive Versus Non-Interactive Debugging. Santa Monica, California: System Development Corporation, Report TM-3296.

Evans, C.R., Purcell, P.A., and Wood, J. (1971)
An Investigation of Design Activities Using Analytic Time-Lapse Photography. Teddington, England: National Physical Laboratory, Division of Computer Science, Report Com. Sci. 50.

Evensmo, J. (1969)
"The Use of Computer Simulation in Planning the Layout and Operation of a Warehouse." *Computer-Aided Design,* Autumn 1969, pp. 32–36.

Everitt, B. (1974)
Cluster Analysis. New York: Wiley.

Fair, G.A., Flowerdew, D.J., Munro, W.G., and Rowley, D. (1966)
"Note on the Computer as an Aid to the Architect." *Computer Journal,* vol. 9 (1966), pp. 16–20.

Falk, G. (1971)
"Scene Analysis Based on Imperfect Edge Data." *Proceedings of the Second International Joint Conference on Artificial Intelligence.* London: British Computer Society.

Farnsworth, G.L. (1970)
The DIME Geocoding System. Washington, D.C.: U.S. Bureau of the Census.

Fary, I. (1948)
"On Straight Line Representation of Planar Graphs." *Acta. Sci. Math. Szeged.,* Vol. 2, pp. 229–233.

Feigenbaum, E.A. (1963)
"Artificial Intelligence Research." *IEEE Transactions on Information Theory,* vol. IT-9, no. 4 (Oct. 1963), pp. 248–261.

——— (1969)
"Artificial Intelligence: Themes in a Second Decade," in A.J.H. Morrell (ed.), *Information Processing 68,* vol. 2. Amsterdam, Holland: North-Holland Publishing Company.

Feigenbaum, E.A., and Feldman, J. (eds.) (1963)
Computers and Thought. New York: Wiley.

Feinberg, K.N. (1974)
"Use of Computer Programs to Evaluate Energy Consumption in Large Office Buildings." *ASHRAE Journal,* vol. 16, no. 1 (Jan. 1974), pp. 73–76.

Fenves, S.J. (ed.) (1965)
STRESS: A Reference Manual. Cambridge, Mass.: MIT Press.

Fetter, R.B., and Thompson, J.D. (1965)
"The Simulation of Hospital Systems." *Operations Research,* 13 (September–October), pp. 689–711.

Firschein, O., Fischler, M.A., Coles, L.S., and Tennenbaum, J.M. (1973)
"Forecasting and Assessing the Impact of Artificial Intelligence on Society." *Proceedings of the Third International Joint Conference on Artificial Intelligence.* Palo Alto, California: Stanford Research Institute.

Fishman, G.S. (1972)
Concepts and Methods in Discrete Event Digital Simulation. New York: Wiley.

Fitzgerald, D. (1971)
"Cooling Loads by Computer: Some Programs Compared." *Journal of the IHVE,* November 1971.

Fleming, J. (1973)
LIFT-A1: A Computer Simulation for the Design of Lift Installations in Buildings. Glasgow, Scotland: University of Strathclyde, ABACUS Paper 13.

Flutter, A.G., and Rolph, R.N. (1976)
"POLYSURF: An Interactive System for the Computer-Aided Design and Manufacture of Components," in *CAD 76,* Proceedings of the Second International Conference on Computers in Engineering and Building Design. Guildford, Surrey, England: IPC Science and Technology Press.

Forrest, R. (1976)
"Transformations and Matrices in Modern Descriptive Geometry," in L. March (ed.), *The Architecture of Form.* Cambridge, England: Cambridge University Press.

Forwood, B.S. (1971)
"Computer Simulated Lift Design: Analysis for Office Buildings." *Architectural Science Review,* June 1971, pp. 41–47.

Foster, C.C. (1972)
"A View of Computer Architecture." *Communications of the ACM*, vol. 15, no. 7 (July 1972), pp. 557–565.

Foxhall, W.B. (1975)
Techniques of Successful Practice for Architects and Engineers. New York: McGraw-Hill.

Frankl, P. (1968)
Principles of Architectural History. Cambridge, Mass.: MIT Press.

Frederking, M.A., and Penz, A.J. (1973)
"An Integrated Methodology for Office Building Elevator Design," in W.F.E. Preiser (ed.), *Environmental Design Research,* Proceedings of the EDRA 4 Conference. Stroudsberg, Pennsylvania: Dowden, Hutchinson, and Ross.

Freeman, H. (1961)
"On the Encoding of Arbitrary Geometric Configurations." *IEEE Transactions on Electronic Computation,* vol. EC–10, pp. 260–268.

——— (1974)
"Computer Processing of Line Drawing Images." *Computing Surveys,* vol. 6, no. 1 (March 1974), pp. 57–97.

Friend, J.K., and Jessop, W.N. (1969)
"Towards a Technology for Strategic Choice." *Local Government and Strategic Choice.* Beverly Hills: Sage Publications.

Fromboluti, C. (1971)
"The Site Plan Idea Generation System," in M. Kennedy (ed.), *Proceedings of the Kentucky Workshop on Computer Applications to Environmental Design.* Lexington, Kentucky: University of Kentucky.

Fullenwider, D.R. (1972)
"SP-1: A Computerized Model for Store Planning," in W.J. Mitchell (ed.), *Environmental Design: Research and Practice,* Proceedings of the EDRA3/AR8 Conference. Los Angeles, California: School of Architecture and Urban Planning, UCLA.

Galimberti, R., and Montanari, U. (1969)
"An Algorithm for Hidden-Line Elimination." *Communications of the ACM,* vol. 12, no. 4 (April 1969), pp. 206–211.

Gallagher, R.M., and Zienkiewicz, O.C. (1973)
Optimum Structural Design: Theory and Applications. New York: Wiley.

Gammill, R.C., and Robertson, D. (1973)
"Graphics and Interactive Systems-Design Considerations of a Software System." *Proceedings of the 1973 National Computer Conference.* Montvale, New Jersey: AFIPS Press.

Gamow, G. (1961)
One, Two, Three . . . Infinity. New York: Viking.

Gardner, M. (1958)
Logic Machines and Diagrams. New York: McGraw-Hill.

——— (1974)
"The Arts as Combinatorial Mathematics, or How to Compose Like Mozart with Dice." *Scientific American,* December 1974, p. 132.

GENESYS Center (1973)
GENESYS Reference Manual. Loughborough, England: Loughborough University of Technology, GENESYS Center.

Gerken, B.L. (1968)
An Information System for Institutional Space Inventory and Utilization. Unpublished M.Sc. thesis, Department of Civil Engineering, MIT.

Gero, J.S. (1973)
The Application of Operations Research to Architecture: A Review. Sydney, Australia: University of Sydney, Department of Architectural Science, Computer Report CR21.

——— (1975)
"Architectural Optimization: A Review." *Engineering Optimization,* vol. 1, no. 3, pp. 189–199.

——— (1976)
"Specifications by Computer." *Architectural Science Review,* vol. 19, no. 1, pp. 10–13.

——— (1976)
Dynamic Programming in Architecture. Sydney, Australia: University of Sydney, Department of Architectural Science, Computer Report CR 26.

Gero, J.S., and James, B. (1972)
"An Experiment in a Computer-Aided Constraint-Oriented Approach to the Design of Home Units," in W.J. Mitchell (ed.), *Environmental Design: Research and Practice,* Proceedings of the EDRA3/AR8 Conference. Los Angeles, California: School of Architecture and Urban Planning, UCLA.

Gero, J.S., and Julian, W.G. (1975)
"Interaction in the Planning of Buildings," in C.M. Eastman (ed.), *Spatial Synthesis in Computer-Aided Building Design.* New York: Wiley.

Gero, J.S., and Sharma, L. (1976)
Optimal Design of Roof Trusses. Sydney, Australia: University of Sydney, Department of Architectural Science.

Gibson, J.E. (1975)
Computers in Structural Engineering. London: Applied Science Publishers.

Gildersleeve, T.R. (1971)
Design of Sequential File Systems. New York: Wiley.

Gilford, M. (1972)
"Second Generation Computer Specifications." *Progressive Architecture,* May 1972, p. 127.

Gilmore, P.C. (1961)
"Optimal and Suboptimal Algorithms for the Quadratic Assignment Problem." *Journal of the Society for Industrial and Applied Mathematics,* vol. 12, no. 5 (Sept./Oct. 1961).

Gips, J. (1975)
Shape Grammars and their Uses. Basel, Switzerland: Birkhauser-Verlag.

Girardi, M.V. (1972)
"Computer Augmented Drafting System," in W.J. Mitchell (ed.), *Environmental Design: Research and Practice,* Proceedings of the EDRA3/AR8 Conference. Los Angeles, California: School of Architecture and Urban Planning, UCLA.

Givoni, B. (1976)
Man, Climate and Architecture. 2d ed. London: Elsevier.

Golomb, S.W. (1965)
Polyominoes. New York: Scribner's.

Goodman, R.V. (1967)
"The Use of Secondary Storage," in D. Roos (ed.), *ICES System: General Description.* Cambridge, Mass.: MIT Department of Civil Engineering Report R67-49.

Gordon, G.R., Pressman, I., and Milliken, R.A. (1975)
"Planning Urban Health Facilities: A Computer Simulation Approach to Delivery Room Utilization." *Computers and Urban Society,* vol. 1, no. 2–4 (Dec. 1975), pp. 169–178.

Gott, B. (1973)
"The Scope of Computer-Aided Design," in J. Vleitstra and R.F. Weilinga (eds.), *Computer-Aided Design.* Amsterdam, Holland: North-Holland Publishing Co.

Gourand, H. (1971)
Computer Display of Curved Surfaces, Salt Lake City, Utah: University of Utah, Computer Science Department Report UTEC-CSC-71-113.

Grant, E.E., and Sackman, H. (1967)
"An Exploratory Investigation of Programmer Performance under On-Line and Off-Line Conditions." *IEEE Transactions on Human Factors in Electronics,* vol. HFE-8, no. 1, pp. 33–48.

Grason, J. (1970)
Methods for the Computer-Implemented Solution of a Class of 'Floor Plan' Design Problems. Unpublished Ph.D. thesis, Department of Electrical Engineering, Carnegie-Mellon University, Pittsburgh, Pennsylvania.

Graves, G.W., and Whinston, A.B. (1970)
"An Algorithm for the Quadratic Assignment Problem." *Management Science,* vol. 16, pp. 453–471.

Grawoig, D.E. (1967)
Decision Mathematics. New York: McGraw-Hill.

Gray, J.C. (1970)
Fundamental Concepts in Computer-Aided Architecture: 1, Storage and Data Structure. Cambridge, England: Cambridge University Center for Land Use and Built Form Studies, Working Paper 49.

——— (1975)
"Automatic Hospital Layout," in D. Hawkes (ed.), *Models and Systems in Architecture and Building.* Hornby, Lancaster, England: The Construction Press.

Green, B.F., Wolf, A.K., Chomsky, C., and Laughery, K. (1961)
"Baseball: An Automatic Question Answerer." *Proceedings of the Western Joint Computer Conference.* New York: Institute of Radio Engineers.

Green, J.P.B. (1966)
"Guide to SfB Building Filing Manual." *RIBA Journal,* May 1966, pp. 208–213.

Greenberg, D.P. (1974)
"Computer Graphics in Architecture." *Scientific American*, May 1974, pp. 98–105.

Gregory, S.A. (1969)
"Morphological Analysis: Some Simple Explorations," in G. Broadbent and A. Ward (eds.), *Design Methods in Architecture.* New York: Wittenborn.

Griffin, C.W. (1972)
Development Building: The Team Approach. New York: Halsted Press.

Groner, G.F., Clark, R.L., Berman, R.A., and Deland, E.C. (1971)
"BIOMOD: An Interactive Graphics System for Modeling." *Proceedings of the 1971 Fall Joint Computer Conference.* Montvale, New Jersey: AFIPS Press.

Guadet, J. (1894)
Éléments et Théorie de l'Architecture. Paris: Librairie de la Construction Moderne.

Gupta, C.L. (1970)
"A Systematic Approach to Optimum Thermal Design." *Building Science,* vol. 5, pp. 165–173.

Gupta, C.L., Spencer, J., and Muncey, R. (1971)
"A Conceptual Survey of Computer-Oriented Thermal Calculation Methods," in T. Kusuda (ed.), *Use of Computers for Environmental Engineering Related to Buildings.* Washington, D.C.: National Bureau of Standards.

Haggett, P., and Chorley, R.J. (1969)
Network Analysis in Geography. London: Edward Arnold.

Guzman, A. (1969)
"Decomposition of a Visual Scene into Three-Dimensional Bodies," in A. Grasselli (ed.), *Automatic Interpretation and Classification of Images.* London: Academic Press.

Hale, R.E. (1968)
"Experience of the Use of Computers During the Design and Production of Components on a Large Scale." *Information Flow in the Building Process: Classification and Coding for Computer Use.* Oslo, Norway: Norwegian Building Research Institute.

Hamer, J.M. (1973)
Computer-Aided Architectural Design: A Discussion and Application. Unpublished M. Arch. thesis, School of Architecture and Urban Planning, UCLA, Los Angeles, California.

——— (1976)
"Design Notes for Environmental Design Data Structures," in G. Kunszt (ed.), *Computer Languages in Building,* Proceedings of a CIB Symposium by Correspondence. Budapest, Hungary: Hungarian Institute for Building Science.

Hamer, J.M., Milne, M.A., Mitchell, W.J., Teague, L.C., and Robinson, J.H. (1972)
Computer-Aided Design System (CADS): Program Documentation. Los Angeles, California: School of Architecture and Urban Planning, UCLA.

Hamilton, S.B. (1952)
"The Historical Development of Structural Theory." *Proceedings of the Institution of Civil Engineers,* vol. 1, pt. 3, Structural Paper no. 31.

Hanan, M., and Kurtzberg, J.M. (1972)
"A Review of the Placement and Quadratic Assignment Problems." *SIAM Review,* vol. 14, no. 2 (April 1972), pp. 324–342.

Hand, J.E., Aguilar, R.J., and Gonzalez (1971)
"Optimality in Industrial Park Development: A Systems Approach," in M. Kennedy (ed.), *Proceedings of the Kentucky Workshop on Computer Applications to Environmental Design.* Lexington, Kentucky: University of Kentucky.

Hankins, R.P. (1969)
"Using the Computer for Lighting Computation." *Heating, Piping, and Air Conditioning,* October 1969, pp. 59–62.

Harary, F. (1968)
Graph Theory. Reading, Mass.: Addison-Wesley.

Harary, F., Jessop, N., Luckman, J., and Stringer, J. (1965)
"Analysis of Interconnected Decision Areas: An Algorithm for Project Development." *Nature,* 3 (April 1965), p. 118.

Harmon, T.G. (1973)
Planning and Cost Evaluation Program for Comparing Preliminary Design Schemes for Highrise Apartments. Washington, D.C.: National Technical Information Service NSF-GK-25510X-13.

Harper, G.N. (1966)
"AUTOSPEC: Automated Preparation of Specifications." *Journal of the Structural Division, ASCE,* December 1966, pp. 45–53.

Harper, G.N. (ed.) (1968)
Computer Applications in Architecture and Engineering. New York: McGraw-Hill.

Harper, G.N. (1968)
"BOP: An Approach to Building Optimization." *Proceedings of the ACM National Conference.* New York: Association for Computing Machinery.

Harrison, H.B. (1973)
Computer Methods in Structural Analysis. Englewood Cliffs, New Jersey: Prentice-Hall.

Hartigan, J.A. (1975)
Clustering Algorithms. New York: Wiley.

Hartkopf, V. (1973)
"An Economy Model for Generating, Evaluating, and Selecting Architectural Design Alternatives," in W.F.E. Preiser (ed.), *Environmental Design Research,* Proceedings of the EDRA 4 Conference. Stroudsberg, Pennsylvania: Dowden, Hutchinson and Ross.

Harvey, J. (1972)
The Medieval Architect. London: Wayland.

Hawkes, D. (1971)
The Development of An Environmental Model. Cambridge, England: Cambridge University, Center for Land Use and Built Form Studies, Working Paper 55.

——— (1975)
"Environmental Models: Past, Present and Future," in D. Hawkes (ed.), *Models and Systems in Architecture and Building.* Hornby, Lancaster, England: The Construction Press.

——— (1976)
"Modeling the Environmental Performance of Built Forms," in L. March (ed.), *The Architecture of Form.* Cambridge, England: Cambridge University Press.

Hawkes, D., and Stibbs, R. (1969)
The Environmental Evaluation of Buildings. Cambridge, England: Cambridge University, Center for Land Use and Built Form Studies, Working Papers 15, 27, 28, 29, 30, 31.

Hayward, P. (1975)
"Building Descriptions for Data Processing," in D. Hawkes (ed.), *Models and Systems in Architecture and Building.* Hornby, Lancaster, England: The Construction Press.

Hernandez, A. (1969)
"J.N.L. Durand's Architectural Theory." *Perspecta,* vol. 12, pp. 153–160.

Higgin, J. and Jessop, N. (1965)
Communications in the Building Industry. London: Tavistock Publications.

Hilbertz, W.H. (1971)
"Cybernetic Architecture, A Teleological Process," in M. Kennedy (ed.), *Proceedings of the Kentucky Workshop on Computer Applications to Environmental Design.* Lexington, Kentucky: University of Kentucky.

——— (1973)
"Ice City 73." *Man-Environment Systems,* vol. 3, no. 2 (March 1973), pp. 129–135.

Hillier, F.S. (1963)
"Quantitative Tools for Plant Layout Analysis." *Journal of Industrial Engineering,* vol. 14, no. 1 (Jan./Feb. 1963), pp. 33–40.

Hillier, F.S., and Connors, M.M. (1966)
"Quadratic Assignment Problem Algorithms and the Location of Indivisible Facilities." *Management Science,* vol. 13, no. 1 (Sept. 1966), pp. 42–57.

Hitchner, L.E. (1968)
A Comparative Investigation of the Computational Efficiency of Shortest Path Algorithms. Berkeley, California: University of California, Operations Center.

Hoagland, A.S. (1972)
"Mass Storage: Past, Present, and Future." *Proceedings of the 1972 Fall Joint Computer Conference.* Montvale, New Jersey: AFIPS Press.

Hobson, R., and Kohn, I. (1973)
"Utility Ratings and 0-1 Programming in Housing Design," in W.F.E. Preiser (ed.), *Environmental Design Research,* Proceedings of the EDRA 4 Conference. Stroudsberg, Pennsylvania: Dowden, Hutchinson and Ross.

Hoover, T.E. (1972)
"Decision Aids for the Planning and Development of University Facilities," in H.S. Brinkers (ed.), *Decision Making.* Columbus, Ohio: Ohio State University Press.

Hopkinson, R.G., Petherbridge, P., and Longmore, J. (1966)
Daylighting. London: Heinemann.

Hormann, A.M. (1972)
"Machine-Aided Evaluation of Alternative Designs," in W.J. Mitchell

(ed.), *Environmental Design: Research and Practice,* Proceedings of the EDRA3/AR8 Conference. Los Angeles, California: School of Architecture and Urban Planning, UCLA.

Hoskins, E.M. (1972)
"OXSYS: An Integrated Computer-Aided Building System for Oxford Method." *Proceedings of the International Conference on Computers in Architecture.* London: British Computer Society.

——— (1973)
Computer-Aided Building: A Study of Current Trends. Cambridge, England: Applied Research of Cambridge.

——— (1973)
"Computer Aids for System Building." *Industrialization Forum,* vol. 4, no. 5, pp. 27–42.

Hoskins, E.M., and Bott, M.F. (1972)
"DHSS: Development Planning System and Production Documentation System." *Proceedings of the International Conference on Computers in Architecture.* London: British Computer Society.

Huffman, D.A. (1971)
"Impossible Objects as Nonsense Sentences," in D. Michie and B. Meltzer (eds.), *Machine Intelligence 6.* Edinburgh, Scotland: Edinburgh University Press.

IBM Corporation (1970)
S/360 Generalized Information System Application Description Manual. White Plains, New York: IBM Manual GH20-0574-1.

IBM Corporation (1971)
General Purpose Simulation System/360: Introductory Users' Manual. White Plains, New York: IBM Corporation.

Illuminating Engineering Society (1972)
The Use of Computers in Lighting. London: Illuminating Engineering Society.

IPC (1976)
CAD 76, Proceedings of the Second International Conference on Computers in Engineering and Building Design. Guildford, Surrey, England: IPC Science and Technology Press.

Jackson, J.N. (1970)
Building Data Management System. Cambridge, Mass.: MIT Civil Engineering Systems Laboratory Report 70-55.

Jackson, P.C. (1974)
Introduction to Artificial Intelligence. New York: Petrocelli/Charter.

Jacobsberg, J. (1975)
"Computer Design Aids for Large Modular Buildings," in D. Hawkes (ed.), *Models and Systems in Architecture and Building.* Hornby, Lancaster, England: The Construction Press.

Jantsch, E. (1967)
Technological Forecasting in Perspective. Paris: OECD.

Jardine, N., and Sibson, R. (1971)
Mathematical Taxonomy. New York: Wiley.

Johnson, T.E. (1963)
"SKETCHPAD 3: A Computer Program for Drawing in 3-Dimensions." *Proceedings of the 1963 Spring Joint Computer Conference.* Baltimore, Maryland: Spartan Books.

Jones, G.W. (ed.) (1973)
Computer-Aided Draughting Systems. Guildford, Surrey, England: IPC Science and Technology Press.

Jordon, J.A. (1970)
"The Conference on Holography and the Computer." *IBM Journal of Research and Development,* vol. 14, no. 5 (Sept. 1970), pp. 476–477.

Joseph, E.C. (1972)
"Future Computer Architecture: Polysystems." *Compcom-72 Digest of Papers.* New York: IEEE Computer Society.

Kahan, B.C. (1972)
"Simulation Models Potentially Applicable to Design." *Proceedings of the International Conference on Computers in Architecture.* London: British Computer Society.

Kamnitzer, P. (1968)
Cityscape. 16 mm. sound movie. Available from School of Architecture and Urban Planning, UCLA, Los Angeles, California.

Kamnitzer, P., and Hoffman, S. (1970)
"Intuval: An Interactive Computer Graphics Aid for Design and Decision Making in Urban Planning," in J. Archea and C. Eastman (eds.), *EDRA 2,* Proceedings of the Environmental Design Research Association Conference. Pittsburgh, Pennsylvania: Carnegie-Mellon University.

Katzan, H. (1970)
APL Programming and Computer Techniques. New York: Van Nostrand Reinhold.

——— (1975)
Computer Data Management and Data Base Technology. New York: Van Nostrand Reinhold.

Kaufman-Diamond, S. (1972)
"On Evaluation of Man-Computer Problem Working Systems," in W.J. Mitchell (ed.), *Environmental Design: Research and Practice,* Proceedings of the EDRA3/AR8 Conference. Los Angeles, California: School of Architecture and Urban Planning, UCLA.

Kaye, B. (1960)
The Development of the Architectural Profession in Britain. London: Allen and Unwin.

Kemeny, J.G., and Kurtz, T.E. (1967)
BASIC Programming. New York: Wiley.

Kenney, J.G., and Murray, G.R. (1971)
"Computer Models Evaluate Alternative Methods." *Industrial Engineering,* December 1971, pp. 20–55.

Kiviat, P.J., Villaneuva, R., and Markowitz, H. (1969)
The Simscript II Programming Language. Englewood Cliffs, New Jersey: Prentice-Hall.

Knuth, D.E. (1973)
Sorting and Searching. Reading, Mass.: Addison-Wesley.

Koopmans, T.C., and Beckman, M. (1957)
"Assignment Problems and the Location of Economic Activities." *Econometrica,* vol. 25, no. 1 (January 1957), pp. 53–76.

Krauss, R.I., and Myer, T.H. (1968)
"Computer-Aided Cost-Estimating Techniques," in G.N. Harper (ed.), *Computer Applications in Architecture and Engineering.* New York: McGraw-Hill.

Krejcirik, M. (1969)
"Computer-Aided Plant Layout." *Computer-Aided Design.* Autumn 1969, pp. 7–19.

Kruskal, J.B. (1964)
"Multidimensional Scaling by Optimizing Goodness of Fit to a Nonmetric Hypothesis." *Psychometrika,* vol. 29, pp. 1–27.

——— (1964)
"Nonmetric Multidimensional Scaling." *Psychometrika,* vol. 29, pp. 115–129.

Kuester, J.L., and Mize, J.H. (1973)
Optimization Techniques with FORTRAN. New York: McGraw-Hill.

Kulsrud, H.E. (1968)
"A General-Purpose Graphic Language." *Communications of the ACM,* vol. 11, no. 4 (April 1968), pp. 247–254.

Kuratowski, K. (1930)
"Sur le Probleme des Courbes Gauches en Topologie." *Fund. Math.,* vol. 15, pp. 271–283.

Lafue, G. (1976)
Recognition of Shapes from their Orthographic Projections. Pittsburgh, Pennsylvania: Carnegie-Mellon University, Institute for Physical Planning.

Laios, D. (1974)
A Growth Model with Applications in Architecture. Unpublished M. Arch. thesis, School of Architecture and Urban Planning, UCLA, Los Angeles, California.

Lasswitz, K. (1958)
"The Universal Library," in C. Fadiman (ed.), *Fantasia Mathematica.* New York: Simon and Schuster.

Lawrence, A. (1970)
Architectural Acoustics. New York: American Elsevier.

Lee, K. (1973)
"Computer Assisted Working Drawing Production." Paper presented at Seminar on Developing Successful Construction Details for Effective Working Drawings (reprinted in Lee below, 1974).

Lee, K. (ed.) (1973)
Computer-Aided Architectural Design: 16 ARK-2 Articles. Boston, Mass.: Center for Environmental Research.

Lee, K. (ed.) (1974)
Computer Programs in Environmental Design. Boston, Mass.: Environmental Design Research Center (5 volumes).

Lee, R.C., and Moore, J.M. (1967)
"CORELAP Computerized Relationship Layout Planning." *Journal of Industrial Engineering,* vol. 18, no. 3 (March 1967), pp. 195–200.

Levens, A.S. (1962)
Graphics, With an Introduction to Conceptual Design. New York: Wiley.

Lever, P.D. (1973)
"A Photomontage System for Site Planning." *Computer-Aided Design,* vol. 5, no. 2 (April 1973), pp. 103–104.

Levin, P.H. (1964)
"Use of Graphs to Decide the Optimum Layout of Buildings." *Architects' Journal,* Oct. 7, 1964, pp. 809–815.

Lee, I.P., and Brown, P.H. (1970)
"Evaluation and Modification of CRAFT for an Architectural Methodology," in G.T. Moore (ed.), *Emerging Methods in Environmental Design and Planning.* Cambridge, Mass.: MIT Press.

Licklider, J.C.R. (1960)
"Man-Computer Symbiosis." *IRE Transactions on Human Factors,* vol. HFE–1, no. 1 (March 1960), pp. 4–11.

Leibman, J.S., Reuter, J.A., and Reuter, L. F. (1972)
"Using a Computer Simulation to Evaluate Ambulatory Care Alternatives." *Bulletin of the Operations Research Society of America,* vol. 20 (Spring 1972), p. B194.

Liggett, R.S. (1972)
"Floor Plan Layout by Implicit Enumeration," in W.J. Mitchell (ed.), *Environmental Design: Research and Practice,* Proceedings of the EDRA3/AR8 Conference. Los Angeles, California: School of Architecture and Urban Planning, UCLA.

Lindsay, R.K. (1963)
"A Program for Parsing Sentences and Making Inferences about Kinship Relations," in A.C. Hoggatt and F.E. Balderston (eds.), *Symposium on Simulation Models: Methodology and Applications to the Behavioral Sciences.* Cincinnati, Ohio: South Western Publishing Co.

Logcher, R.D. (1970)
"ICES STRUDL: An Integrated Approach to a Computer System for Structural Engineering," in G.T. Moore (ed.), *Emerging Methods in Environmental Design and Planning.* Cambridge, Mass.: MIT Press.

Logcher, R.D., and Jackson, J.N. (1969)
ICES TABLE-II: An ICES File Storage Subsystem: Engineering User's Manual. Cambridge, Mass.: MIT Department of Civil Engineering, Report R69–34.

Lokmanhekim, M. (1971)
"Calculation of Energy Requirements with the Proposed ASHRAE Algorithms for U.S. Postal Buildings," in T. Kusuda (ed.), *Use of Computers for Environmental Engineering Related to Buildings.* Washington, D.C.: U.S. National Bureau of Standards.

Loutrel, P.P. (1970)
"A Solution to the Hidden Line Problem for Computer-Drawn Polyhedra." *IEEE Transactions on Computers,* March 1970.

Lozar, R.C. (1974)
"A Methodology for the Computer Simulation of Behavior-Environment Interactions in Dining Halls," in D. Carson (ed.), *Proceedings of the EDRA 5 Conference.* Stroudsberg, Pennsylvania: Dowden, Hutchinson, and Ross.

Luce, R.D., and Raiffa, H. (1957)
Games and Decisions. New York: Wiley.

Luckman, J. (1969)
"An Approach to the Management of Design," in G. Broadbent and A. Ward (eds.), *Design Methods in Architecture.* New York: Wittenborn.

Luenberger, D.G. (1973)
Introduction to Linear and Non-Linear Programming. Reading, Mass.: Addison-Wesley.

——— (1971)
"Counting Polyominoes," in A.O.L. Atkin and B.J. Birch (eds.), *Computers in Number Theory.* London: Academic Press.

Lunnon, W.F. (1972)
"Counting Hexagonal and Triangular Polyominoes," in R. Read (ed.), *Graph Theory and Computing.* New York: Academic Press.

Lumsdaine, A.A., and Glaser, R. (eds.) (1960)
Teaching Machines and Programmed Learning. Washington, D.C.: National Education Association.

McCarthy, J. (1956)
"The Inversion of Functions Defined by Turing Machines," in C.E. Shannon and J. McCarthy (eds.), *Automata Studies.* Princeton, New Jersey: Princeton University.

McCue, G.M., Ewald, W.R., and The Midwest Research Institute (1970)
Creating the Human Environment. Chicago, Illinois: University of Chicago Press.

McGovern, I.E. (1976)
Non-Linear Optimization Theory Applied to Floor Plan Design. Unpublished M.Sc. thesis, Graduate School of Management, UCLA, Los Angeles, California.

McGuinness, W.J. (1967)
"Computer Designs Elevators." *Progressive Architecture,* vol. 48, no. 12 (Dec. 1967), p. 144.

McKay, H.N. (1973)
A Computer-Assisted Lighting Design System. Unpublished M.Arch. thesis, School of Architecture and Urban Planning, UCLA, Los Angeles, California.

MacLane, S. (1937)
"A Structural Characterization of Planar Combinatorial Graphs." *Duke Mathematical Journal,* vol. 3, pp. 340–372.

March, L. (1972)
"Elementary Models of Built Forms," in L. Martin and L. March (eds.), *Urban Space and Structures.* Cambridge, England: Cambridge University Press.

——— (1976)
"The Logic of Design and the Question of Value," in L. March (ed.), *The Architecture of Form.* Cambridge, England: Cambridge University Press.

——— (1976)
"A Boolean Description of a Class of Built Forms," in L. March (ed.), *The Architecture of Form.* Cambridge, England: Cambridge University Press.

March, L. (ed.) (1976)
The Architecture of Form. Cambridge, England: Cambridge University Press.

March, L., and Matela, R. (1974)
"The Animals of Architecture: Some Census Results on N-Omino Populations for N=6, 7, 8." *Environment and Planning B,* vol. 1, no. 2 (Dec. 74), pp. 193–216.

March, L., and Steadman, P. (1974)
The Geometry of Environment. Cambridge, Mass.: MIT Press.

Markus, T.A., Whyman, P., Morgan, J., Whitton, D., Maver, T., Canter, D., and Fleming, J. (1972)
Building Performance. New York: Halsted Press.

Martin, J. (1975)
Computer Data-Base Organization. Englewood Cliffs, New Jersey: Prentice-Hall.

Martin, W.A. (1971)
"Sorting." *Computing Surveys,* vol. 3, no. 4 (Dec. 1971), pp. 147–174.

Masterman, M. (1971)
"Computerized Haiku," in J. Reichardt (ed.), *Cybernetics, Art and Ideas.* Greenwich, Connecticut: New York Graphic Society.

Masterson, C. (1972)
"A Computer-Based Code System." *Industrialization Forum,* vol. 3, no. 3, pp. 13–21.

Matsuka, H., Kawai, T., and Uno, S. (1975)
"Integrated Designer's Activity Support System for Architecture." *Proceedings of the 1975 Design Automation Conference.* New York: Association for Computing Machinery.

Maver, T.W. (1970)
TRAFIK: A Program Package for the Study of Circulation in Building Design. Glasgow, Scotland: Strathclyde University, ABACUS, Paper no. 5.

——— (1971)
Building Services Design. London: RIBA Publications.

——— (1971)
"Computer as an Aid to Architectural Design: Present and Future," in R. Burgess (ed.), *Progress in Construction Science and Technology.* London: Asia Publishing House.

Meads, J.A. (1972)
"A Terminal Control Language," in F. Nake and A. Rosenfeld (eds.), *Graphic Languages.* Amsterdam, Holland: North Holland Publishing Co.

Meager, M.A. (1972)
"Computer Aids in Hospital Building." *Proceedings of the International Conference on Computers in Architecture.* London: British Computer Society.

——— (1973)
"The Application of Computer Aids to Hospital Building," in J. Vlietstra

and R.F. Wielinga (eds.), *Computer-Aided Design.* Amsterdam, Holland: North-Holland Publishing Co.

Mealy, A.H. (1968)
"Another Look at Data." *Proceedings of the 1968 Fall Joint Computer Conference.* Montvale, New Jersey: AFIPS Press.

Michie, D., Fleming, J.G., and Oldfield, J.V. (1968)
"A Comparison of Heuristic, Interactive, and Unaided Methods of Solving a Shortest Route Problem," in D. Michie (ed.), *Machine Intelligence 3.* Edinburgh, Scotland: Edinburgh University Press.

Miller, W.R. (1969)
"Matrix Method for Grouping an Interrelated Set of Elements," in H. Sanoff and S. Cohn (eds.), *Proceedings of the First EDRA Conference.* Chapel Hill, North Carolina: North Carolina State University.

Milne, M.A. (1969)
Computer Graphics in Architecture and Design. New Haven, Connecticut: Yale Cooperative Corporation.

——— (1970)
"CLUSTR: A Structure-Finding Algorithm," in G.T. Moore (ed.), *Emerging Methods in Environmental Design and Planning.* Cambridge, Mass.: MIT Press.

——— (1971)
"CLUSTR: A Program for Structuring Design Problems." *Proceedings of the Design Automation Workshop.* New York: Association for Computing Machinery.

Minsky, M. (1961)
"Steps Toward Artificial Intelligence." *Proceedings of the IRE,* vol. 49, pp. 8–30.

Minsky, M. (ed.) (1968)
Semantic Information Processing. Cambridge, Mass.: MIT Press.

Mitchell, W.J. (1974)
"Computer-Aided Design and the Architecture Student in the United States." *DMG-DRS Journal,* vol. 8, no. 4 (Oct./Dec. 74), pp. 210–217.

——— (1975)
"An Approach to Automated Generation of Minimum Cost Dwelling Unit Plans." *International Technical Cooperation Center Review* (Tel-Aviv, Israel), vol. 4, no. 3 (July 1975), pp. 116–139.

——— (1975)
"Automated Generation of Minimum Energy Cost Building Designs," in B. Honikman (ed.), *Responding to Social Change.* New York: Halsted Press.

Mitchell, W.J., and Dillon, R. (1972)
"A Polyomino Assembly Procedure for Architectural Floor Planning," in W.J. Mitchell (ed.), *Environmental Design: Research and Practice,* Proceedings of the EDRA3/AR8 Conference. Los Angeles, California: School of Architecture and Urban Planning, UCLA.

Mitchell, W.J., Steadman, P., and Liggett, R.S. (1976)
"Synthesis and Optimization of Small Rectangular Floor Plans." *Environment and Planning B,* vol. 3, no. 1 (June 1976), pp. 37–70.

Mitroff, I.A., and Featherinham, T.R. (1974)
"On Systemic Problem Solving and the Error of the Third Kind." *Behavioral Science*, vol. 19, pp. 383–393.

Mogel, R.L. (1969)
Cost Models for Urban Building Systems. Cambridge, Mass.: MIT Department of Civil Engineering, Report R69–33.

Monk, K.W., and Dunstone, P.H. (1968)
"Quantity Surveying by Computer: 1961–68." *Building*, 31 (May 1968), pp. 67–68.

Moore, J.M. (1973)
"Computer-Aided Facilities Design: An International Survey." *Proceedings of the 2nd International Conference on Production Research.* Copenhagen, Denmark: Technical University of Denmark.

Morrison, P., and Morrison, E. (eds.) (1961)
Charles Babbage and His Calculating Engines: Selected Writings by Charles Babbage and Others. New York: Dover.

Morse, S.P. (1968)
"A Mathematical Model for the Analysis of Contour Line Data." *Journal of the ACM*, vol. 15, pp. 205–220.

Moseley, L. (1963)
"Rational Design Theory for Planning Buildings Based on the Analysis and Solution of Circulation Problems." *Architects' Journal*, (Sept. 1963), pp. 525–537.

Mumford, E., and Banks, O. (1967)
The Computer and the Clerk. London: Routledge and Kegan Paul.

Muther, R.D. (1974)
Systematic Layout Planning. Boston, Mass.: Cahner's.

Muther, R.D., and McPherson, K. (1970)
"Four Approaches to Computerized Layout Planning." *Industrial Engineering*, February 1970, pp. 39–42.

Nadel, E. (1967)
"Parameter Cost Estimates for Apartment Buildings." *Engineering News Record*, 16 (March 1967), pp. 112–124.

Negroponte, N. (1970)
The Architecture Machine. Cambridge, Mass.: MIT Press.

Negroponte, N. (1973)
"Recent Advances in Sketch Recognition." *Proceedings of the National Computer Conference.* Montvale, New Jersey: AFIPS Press.

Negroponte, N., (ed.) (1975)
Computer Aids to Design and Architecture. New York: Petrocelli/Charter.

Negroponte, N. (1975)
"A Computational Paradigm for Personalized Searching." *Journal of Architectural Education*, vol. 29, no. 2, pp. 26–29.

Negroponte, N., and Groisser, L.B. (1970)
"URBAN 5: A Machine that Discusses Urban Design," in G.T. Moore (ed.), *Emerging Methods in Environmental Design and Planning.* Cambridge, Mass.: MIT Press.

Negroponte, N., Groisser, L.B., and Taggart, J. (1972)
"HUNCH: An Experiment in Sketch Recognition," in W.J. Mitchell (ed.), *Environmental Design: Research and Practice,* Proceedings of the EDRA3/AR8 Conference. Los Angeles, California: School of Architecture and Urban Planning, UCLA.

Nelson, T.H. (1971)
"Halftone Image Synthesis." *Computer Decisions,* May 1971, pp. 13–14.

Nevill, G.E., and Crowe, R.A. (1974)
"Computer Augmented Conceptual Design," in W.R. Spillers (ed.), *Basic Questions of Design Theory.* Amsterdam, Holland: North-Holland Publishing Co.

Newell, A. (1955)
"The Chess Machine: An Example of Dealing with a Complex Task by Adaptation." *Proceedings of the Western Joint Computer Conference.* New York: Institute of Radio Engineers.

——— (1969)
"Heuristic Programming: Ill-Structured Problems," in J. Aronofsky (ed.), *Progress in Operations Research,* vol. 3. New York: Wiley.

——— (1973)
"Artificial Intelligence and the Concept of Mind," in R.C. Schank and K.M. Colby (eds.), *Computer Models of Thought and Language.* San Francisco, California: W.H. Freeman.

Newell, A., Shaw, J.C., and Simon, H.A. (1957)
"Empirical Foundations of the Logic Theory Machine: A Case Study in Heuristics." *Proceedings of the 1957 Western Joint Computer Conference.* New York: Institute of Radio Engineers.

Newell, A., and Simon, H.A. (1972)
Human Problem Solving. Englewood Cliffs, New Jersey: Prentice-Hall.

Newell, M.E., Newell, R.G., and Sancha, T.L. (1972)
"A New Approach to the Shaded Picture Problem." *Proceedings of the National Computer Conference.* Montvale, New Jersey: AFIPS Press.

Newman, M.H.A. (1954)
Elements of the Topology of Plane Sets of Points. Cambridge, England: Cambridge University Press.

Newman, W.M. (1966)
"An Experimental Program for Architectural Design." *Computer Journal,* vol. 9 (1966), pp. 21–26.

——— (1973)
"An Informal Graphics System Based on the LOGO Language." *Proceedings of the 1973 National Computer Conference.* Montvale, New Jersey: AFIPS Press.

Newman, W.M., Gouraud, H., and Oestreicher, D.R. (1970)
Programmer's Guide to PDP-10 EULER. Salt Lake City, Utah: University of Utah, Department of Computer Science Report UTEC-CSC-70-105.

Newman, W.M., and Sproull, R.F. (1973)
Principles of Interactive Computer Graphics. New York: McGraw-Hill.

——— (1974)
"An Approach to Graphics System Design." *Proceedings of the IEEE,* vol. 62, no. 4 (April 1974), pp. 471–483.

Nickerson, R.S. (1969)
"Man-Computer Interaction: A Challenge for Human Factors Research." *Ergonomics,* vol. 12, no. 4, pp. 501–517.

Nilsson, N.J. (1969)
"A Mobile Automaton: An Application of Artificial Intelligence Techniques," in D.E. Walker and L.M. Norton (eds.), *Proceedings of the International Joint Conference on Artificial Intelligence.* Washington, D.C.: Mitre Corporation.

——— (1971)
Problem-Solving Methods in Artificial Intelligence. New York: McGraw-Hill.

Nilsson, N.J., and Raphael, B. (1967)
"Preliminary Design of an Intelligent Robot," in J.T. Tou (ed.), *Computer and Information Sciences II.* New York: Academic Press.

Noll, A.M. (1971)
"Scanned Display Computer Graphics." *Communications of the ACM,* vol. 14, no. 3 (March 1971), pp. 143–150.

Norris, K.W. (1963)
"The Morphological Approach to Engineering Design," in J.C. Jones and D.G. Thornley (eds.), *Conference on Design Methods.* Oxford, England: Pergamon Press.

North Carolina Fund (1967)
Integrated Building Industry System for the Cost and Construction Analysis of Low-Income Housing. Washington, D.C.: National Technical Information Service, no. PB-185-722.

Nuffield Provincial Hospitals Trust (1955)
Studies in the Function and Design of Hospitals. Oxford, England: Oxford University Press.

Nugent, C.E., Vollmann, T.E., and Ruml, J. (1968)
"An Experimental Comparison of Techniques for Assignment of Facilities to Locations." *Operations Research,* 16 (January/February 1968), pp. 150–173.

Owen, C.L. (1970)
"DCMPOS: An Algorithm for the Decomposition of Nondirected Graphs," in G.T. Moore (ed.), *Emerging Methods in Environmental Design and Planning.* Cambridge, Mass.: MIT Press.

Page, E.S., and Wilson, L.B. (1973)
Information Representation and Manipulation in a Computer. Cambridge, England: Cambridge University Press.

Palmer, A.C. (1968)
"Optimal Structural Design by Dynamic Programming." *Proceedings of the ASCE,* vol. 94, no. ST8, pp. 1887–1906.

Paradis, A.R. (1971)
"An Insight into Three Dimensional Graphics," in T. Kusuda (ed.), *Use of Computers for Environmental Engineering Related to Buildings.* Washington, D.C.: National Bureau of Standards.

Parkin, A. (1968)
"How to Draw a Ball," in J. Reichardt (ed.), *Cybernetic Serendipity.* New York: Praeger.

Parkin, P.H., and Humphreys, H.R. (1967)
Acoustics, Noise and Buildings. Revised edition. London: Faber and Faber.

Parlow, H. (1966)
"Lift Operation and Computers." *Architects' Journal,* 23 March 1966, pp. 747–753.

Paterson, J.W. (1972)
"Aids to Improve the Designer's Control of Cost and Performance of Buildings, and to Speed the Pre-Contract and Post-Contract Processes," in W.J. Mitchell (ed.), *Environmental Design: Research and Practice,* Proceedings of the EDRA3/AR8 Conference. Los Angeles, California: School of Architecture and Urban Planning, UCLA.

——— (1974)
"An Integrated CAD System for an Architect's Department." *Computer-Aided Design,* vol. 6, no. 1 (Jan. 1974), pp. 25–31.

Paul, C.K., and Landini, A.J. (1975)
Final Report: LUMIS. Pasadena, California: Jet Propulsion Laboratory.

Pennington, R.P.G. (1967)
"Computerized Product Selection by Performance." *Architecture Canada,* June 1967, pp. 33–37.

Penz, A.J. (1971)
"Computer Simulation of Elevator Systems." *Proceedings of the Design Automation Workshop.* New York: Association for Computing Machinery.

Pereira, L.M., Portas, N., Monteiro, L.F., and Pereira, F. (1973)
"Interactive Dimensional Layout of Schemes from Adjacency Graphs." *Proceedings of the Design Activity International Conference.* London: Design Research Society.

Perlis, A.J. (1972)
Introduction to Computer Science. New York: Harper and Row.

Peters, B. (1972)
"Computer Applications in the Design and Build Process by West Sussex County Council." *Proceedings of the International Conference on Computers in Architecture.* London: British Computer Society.

Peterson, J.J., and Veit, S.A. (1971)
Survey of Computer Networks. Washington, D.C.: Mitre Corporation.

Peucker, T.K. (1972)
Computer Cartography. Washington, D.C.: Association of College Geographers, Commission on College Geography, Resource Paper 17.

——— (1974)
Geographical Data Structure: Report after Year 1. Vancouver, Canada: Simon Fraser University.

Peucker, T.K., and Chrisman, N. (1974)
Cartographic Data Structures. Cambridge, Mass.: Laboratory for Computer Graphics and Spatial Analysis, Harvard Graduate School of Design.

Pevsner, N. (1976)
A History of Building Types. Princeton, New Jersey: Princeton University Press.

Pfefferkorn, C.E. (1975)
"The Design Problem Solver: A System for Designing Equipment or Furniture Layouts," in C.M. Eastman (ed.), *Spatial Synthesis in Computer-Aided Building Design.* New York: Wiley.

Phong, B.T. (1975)
"Illumination for Computer-Generated Pictures." *Communications of the ACM,* vol. 18, no. 6 (June 1975), pp. 311–317.

Plant, C.G.H., and Archer, D.W. (1972)
"A Lighting Prediction Method for Complex Environments." *Lighting Research and Technology,* vol. 4, no. 2, pp. 102–104.

Pohl, J.G. (1975)
"Computers in Architectural Education." *Proceedings of the National Computer Conference.* Montvale, New Jersey: AFIPS Press.

Pollack, M., and Wiebenson, W. (1960)
"Solutions of the Shortest-Route Problem: A Review." *Operations Research,* vol. 8, no. 2 (March–April 1960), pp. 224–230.

Popper, K.R. (1972)
The Logic of Scientific Discovery. London: Hutchinson.

Porter, W., Lloyd, K., and Fleischer, A. (1970)
"Discourse: A Language and System for Computer-Aided City Design," in G.T. Moore (ed.), *Emerging Methods in Environmental Design and Planning.* Cambridge, Mass.: MIT Press.

Portlock, P.C., and Whitehead, B. (1970)
"A Program for Practical Layout Planning." *Building Science,* 6, 1970, pp. 213–220.

Powell, J.A. (1973)
"Use of a Simple Methodology in the Compilation of a Computerized Acoustic Design Package for Architects and Builders." *Bulletin of Computer-Aided Architectural Design,* no. 12 (July 1973).

Prest, A.R., and Turvey, R. (1965)
"Cost Benefit Analysis: A Survey." *Economic Journal,* December 1965.

Prince, M.D. (1971)
Interactive Graphics for Computer-Aided Design. London: Addison-Wesley.

Progressive Architecture
"Computer Drafting Speeds Motel Design." *Progressive Architecture,* September 1968, pp. 150–153.

PSAE (undated)
This Is Masterspec. Washington, D.C.: American Institute of Architects.

Purcell, P.A. (1975)
"Computer-Aided Architecture in the United Kingdom," in N. Negroponte (ed.), *Computer Aids to Design and Architecture.* New York: Petrocelli/Charter.

Raiffa, H. (1968)
Decision Analysis. London: Addison-Wesley.

Raphael, B. (1976)
The Thinking Computer. San Francisco: W.H. Freeman.

Rapkin, M.D., and Abu-Gheida, O.M. (1968)
"Stand-Alone/Remote Graphic System." *Proceedings of the 1968 Fall Joint Computer Conference.* Washington, D.C.: Thompson.

Rapoport, A. (1966)
Two-Person Game Theory. Ann Arbor, Michigan: University of Michigan Press.

——— (1970)
N-Person Game Theory. Ann Arbor, Michigan: University of Michigan Press.

Ray, K. (1975)
"Activity Modeling in Hospitals," in D. Hawkes (ed.), *Models and Systems in Architecture and Building.* Hornby, Lancaster, England: The Construction Press.

Ray-Jones, A. (1968)
"Computer Development in West Sussex." *Architects' Journal,* 12 February 1968, p. 42.

Ray-Jones, A., and McCann, W. (1968)
"SfB in Great Britain, 1961–68." *Information Flow in the Building Process: Classification and Coding for Computer Use.* Oslo, Norway: Norwegian Building Research Institute, CIB Report 13B.

Reggini, H.C. (1974)
"A Computer Program for Generating Non-Classical Perspectives." *CAD 74,* Proceedings of the Conference on Computers in Engineering and Building Design. Guildford, Surrey, England: IPC Science and Technology Press (Microfiche).

Reitman, W.R. (1965)
Cognition and Thought. New York: Wiley.

Resch, R.D. (1974)
"Portfolio of Shaded Computer Images." *Proceedings of the IEEE,* vol. 62, no. 4 (April 1974), pp. 496–502.

Reuleaux, F. (1876)
The Kinematics of Machinery. London: Macmillan.

Rhynsburger, D. (1973)
"Analytic Delineation of Thiessen Polygons." *Geographical Analysis,* vol. 5, no. 2 (April 1973), pp. 133–144.

Richens, P. (1974)
OXSYS: Computer-Aided Building for Oxford Method. Cambridge, England: Applied Research of Cambridge.

——— (1975)
"Geometry and Numbers in Building Systems," in D. Hawkes (ed.), *Models and Systems in Architecture and Building.* Hornby, Lancaster, England: The Construction Press.

——— (1976)
OXSYS System. Cambridge, England: Applied Research of Cambridge.

Ridyard, J. (1970)
"Queue Simulation for the Architect." *Architectural Science Review,* vol. 13, no. 1 (March 1970), pp. 33–39.

Rittel, H.W. (1970)
"Comment: Theories of Cell Configurations," in G.T. Moore (ed.), *Emerging Methods in Environmental Design and Planning.* Cambridge, Mass.: MIT Press.

Rittel, H.W., and Webber, M.M. (1973)
"Dilemmas in a General Theory of Planning." *Policy Sciences,* vol. 4, pp. 155–169.

Ritzman, L.P. (1972)
"The Efficiency of Computer Algorithms for Plant Layout." *Management Science,* vol. 18, no. 5 (Jan 1972), pp. 240–248.

Roberts, L.G. (1963)
"Machine Perception of Three-Dimensional Solids." Lexington, Mass.: Lincoln Laboratory Report TR 315.

Roberts, L.G. (1966)
"The Lincoln Wand." *Proceedings of the 1966 Fall Joint Computer Conference.* Washington, D.C.: Spartan Books.

Roberts, R.D. (1972)
"COMPUCON: Computer-Aided Information System for Component Construction," in W.J. Mitchell (ed.), *Environmental Design: Research and Practice,* Proceedings of the EDRA3/AR8 Conference. Los Angeles, California: School of Architecture and Urban Planning, UCLA.

Roberts, S.D. (1969)
Computerized Facilities Design: An Evaluation. Gainesville, Florida: University of Florida, Department of Industrial Engineering, Report no. 30.

Rogers, D.F., and Adams, J.A. (1976)
Mathematical Elements for Computer Graphics. New York: McGraw-Hill.

Romney, G.W., Watkins, G.S., and Evans, D.C. (1969)
"Real-Time Display of Computer Generated Half-Tone Perspective Pictures," in A.J.H. Morrell (ed.), *Proceedings of the 1968 IFIP Conference.* Amsterdam, Holland: North-Holland Publishing Co.

Roos, D. (1967)
ICES System: General Description. Cambridge, Mass.: MIT Department of Civil Engineering, Report R67-49.

Rosen, H.J. (1971)
"Computer Specifications Programs." *Progressive Architecture,* September 1971, p. 168.

——— (1974)
Construction Specifications Writing. New York: Wiley.

Rosenfeld, A. (1969)
Picture Processing by Computer. New York: Academic Press.

Ross, D.T. (1967)
"The AED Approach to Generalized Computer-Aided Design." *Proceedings of the ACM National Conference.* New York: Association for Computing Machinery.

Rougelot, R.S. (1969)
"The General Electric Color TV Display," in M. Faiman and J. Nievergelt (eds.), *Pertinent Concepts in Computer Graphics.* Urbana, Illinois: University of Illinois Press.

Royal Institution of Chartered Surveyors (1967)
Computer Techniques. London: Royal Institution of Chartered Surveyors.

Sackman, H. (1970)
Man-Computer Problem Solving. Philadelphia, Pennsylvania: Auerbach.

Sackman, H. (1974)
Rudiments of a Real-World Theory of Man-Computer Problem Solving. Santa Monica, California: Rand Corporation Report R-1491-NSF.

Safdie, M. (1970)
Beyond Habitat. Cambridge, Mass.: MIT Press.

Salzman, L.F. (1952)
Building in England Down to 1540. Oxford, England: Oxford University Press.

Sammet, J.E. (1969)
Programming Languages: History and Fundamentals. Englewood Cliffs, New Jersey: Prentice-Hall.

Sasada, T. (1974)
Sketch Recognition System (PATTERN): Program Documentation. Los Angeles, California: School of Architecture and Urban Planning, UCLA.

——— (1975)
"Computer-Aided Architecture in Japan," in N. Negroponte (ed.), *Computer Aids to Design and Architecture.* New York: Petrocelli/Charter.

Sauda, E.J. (1975)
Computer Program for the Generation of Dwelling Unit Floor Plans. Unpublished M.Arch. thesis. Los Angeles, California: School of Architecture and Urban Planning, UCLA.

Schatzoff, M., Tsao, R., and Wing, R. (1967)
"An Experimental Comparison of Time-Sharing and Batch-Processing." *Communications of the ACM,* vol. 10, no. 5, pp. 261–265.

Scher, P. (1972)
"Analysis of Building Production Drawings," in W.J. Mitchell (ed.), *Environmental Design: Research and Practice,* Proceedings of the EDRA3/AR8 Conference. Los Angeles, California: School of Architecture and Urban Planning, UCLA.

Scherr, A.L. (1966)
"Time Sharing Measurement." *Datamation,* vol. 12, no. 4 (April 1966), pp. 22–26.

Scholes, P.A. (1938)
"Composition Systems and Mechanisms." *The Oxford Companion to Music.* Oxford, England: Oxford University Press.

Schon, D.A. (1967)
Technology and Change. New York: Dell.

Schriber, T. (1972)
A GPSS Primer. Ann Arbor, Michigan: Ulrich's Books.

Schumacker, R.A., Brand, B., Gilliland, M., and Sharp, W. (1969)
Study for Applying Computer-Generated Images to Simulation. Washington, D.C.: U.S. Human Resources Laboratory Report AFHRL-TR-69-14.

Seehof, J.M., and Evans, W.O. (1967)
"Automated Layout Design Program." *Journal of Industrial Engineering,* vol. 18, no. 12 (Dec. 1967), pp. 690–695.

Selfridge, O.G. (1955)
"Pattern Recognition and Modern Computers." *Proceedings of the 1955 Western Joint Computer Conference.* New York: Institute of Radio Engineers.

Seppanen, J.J., and Moore, J.M. (1970)
"Facilities Planning with Graph Theory." *Management Science,* vol. 17, no. 4, pp. B242–B253.

Shaffer, L.H. (1965)
"Problem Solving on a Stochastic Process." *Ergonomics,* vol. 8, no. 2, pp. 182–192.

Shepard, D. (1968)
"A Two-Dimensional Interpolation Function for Irregularly Spaced Data." *Proceedings of the 23rd National Conference of the ACM.* New York: Association for Computing Machinery.

Shepard, R.N. (1962)
"The Analysis of Proximities: Multidimensional Scaling with an Unknown Distance Function." *Psychometrika,* (pt. 1) vol. 27, pp. 125–140, (pt. 2) vol. 27, pp. 219–246.

Shepard, R.N., Romney, A.K., and Nerlove, S.B. (eds.) (1972)
Multidimensional Scaling: Theory and Application in the Behavioral Sciences (2 vols.). New York: Seminar Press.

Shirey, R.W. (1969)
Implementation and Analysis of Efficient Graph Planarity Testing Algorithms. Unpublished Ph.D. thesis. University of Wisconsin.

Shirley, F. (1974)
"Circulation Analysis and Lift Placement in Hospitals." *Computer-Aided Design,* vol. 6, no. 4 (Oct. 1974), pp. 206–210.

Shubik, M. (1964)
"Game Theory and the Study of Social Behavior: An Introductory Exposition," in M. Shubik (ed.), *Game Theory and Related Approaches to Social Behavior.* New York: Wiley.

Shubnikov, A.V., and Koptsik, V.A. (1975)
Symmetry in Science and Art. New York: Plenum.

Simon, H.A. (1957)
Models of Man. New York: Wiley.

——— (1966)
The Shape of Automation. New York: Harper and Row.

——— (1967)
"The Logic of Decision and Action," in N. Rescher (ed.), *The Logic of Decision and Action.* Pittsburgh, Pennsylvania: University of Pittsburgh Press.

——— (1975)
"Style in Design," in C.M. Eastman (ed.), *Spatial Synthesis in Computer-Aided Building Design.* New York: Wiley.

Simon, J.A., and Rein, R.E. (1968)
Acoustical Design and Analysis for Speech Privacy. University Park, Pennsylvania: Pennsylvania State University, Department of Architectural Engineering.

Simpson, J.W., and Carter, D. (1973)
"Computer-Aided Luminance Design of Interiors," in R. Burgess et al (eds.), *Progress in Construction Science and Technology.* London: Medical and Technical Publishing Co.

Sinyakov, Y. (1962)
"Can a Machine Create a Design." *Moskovskaya Pravda,* 5 July 1962 (translation by Foreign Technology Division, Wright-Patterson Air Force Base, Ohio).

Slagle, J.R. (1971)
Artificial Intelligence: The Heuristic Programming Approach. New York: McGraw-Hill.

Slipchenko, P.S., and Kybasky, V.I. (1964)
"Use of Computers in USSR: Wide Applications in Industrial Construction." *Builder,* November 1964, p. 976.

Slutzah, R.P. (1971)
"Computer Assisted Examination of Building Plans." *Journal of Environmental Systems,* vol. 1, no. 1 (March 1971), pp. 81–100.

Smart, D.A. (1966)
"The Application of a Computer to Quantity Surveying." *Computer Bulletin,* 10 September 1966, pp. 24–30.

Smith, L.B. (1967)
"A Comparison of Batch Processing and Instant Turnaround." *Communications of the ACM,* vol. 10, no. 8, pp. 495–500.

Smith, M.J., MacDonald, S.L., Carr, C.S., Wehrli, R., and Smith, E.F. (1967)
Space Form: Computer-Aided Design for Architecture. Washington, D.C.: NTIS Report AD-761967.

Sneath, P.H.A., and Sokal, R.R. (1973)
Numerical Taxonomy. San Francisco, California: W.H. Freeman.

Soucek, B. (1976)
Microprocessors and Microcomputers. New York: Wiley-Interscience.

Souder, J.J., and Clark, W.E. (1963)
"Computer Technology: A New Tool for Planning." *AIA Journal,* October 1963, pp. 97–106.

——— (1964)
Planning for Hospitals: A System Approach Using Computer-Aided Techniques. Chicago: American Hospital Association.

Spillers, W.R. (1970)
"An Algorithm for Space Allocation." *Proceedings of the 5th Annual Urban Symposium.* New York: Association for Computing Machinery.

Sproull, R.F. (1973)
Omnigraph: Simple Terminal-Independent Graphics Software. Palo Alto, California: Xerox Palo Alto Research Center Report CSL-73-4.

Starr, M.K. (1963)
Product Design and Decision Theory. Englewood Cliffs, New Jersey: Prentice-Hall.

Steadman, P. (1970)
"The Automatic Generation of Minimum Standard House Plans," in J. Archea and C. Eastman (eds.), *EDRA Two,* Proceedings of the 2nd EDRA Conference. Pittsburgh, Pennsylvania: Carnegie-Mellon University.

——— (1976)
"Graph Theoretic Representation of Architectural Arrangement," in L. March (ed.), *The Architecture of Form.* Cambridge, England: Cambridge University Press.

Stender, R.C. (1970)
"The Future Role of Keyboards in Data Entry." *Datamation,* June 1970, pp. 60–72.

Stewart, C.D. (1975)
"Computer Aids to Architecture at Clifford Douglas Stewart Associates," in N. Negroponte (ed.), *Computer Aids to Design and Architecture.* New York: Petrocelli/Charter.

Stewart, C.D., and Lee, K. (1971)
"Can a 54-Year-Old Architectural Firm Find Romance and Happiness With an Interactive Computer System?" *Progressive Architecture,* July 1971, pp. 64–73.

Steyert, R.D. (1972)
"The Economics of High-Rise Apartment Buildings." *ASCE-IABSE International Conference Preprints.* Bethlehem, Pennsylvania: Lehigh University.

Stibbs, R. (1976)
"Predictions of Surface Luminances in Architectural Space," in L. March (ed.), *The Architecture of Form.* Cambridge, England: Cambridge University Press.

Stiny, G. (1975)
Pictorial and Formal Aspects of Shapes and Shape Grammars. Basel, Switzerland: Birkhauser-Verlag.

——— (1976)
"Two Exercises in Formal Composition." *Environment and Planning B,* vol. 3, no. 2, pp. 187–210.

Stone, P.A. (1966)
Building Economy: Design, Production and Organisation. London: Pergamon.

——— (1975)
Building Design Evaluation. 2d ed. London: E. and F.N. Spon.

Summerson, J. (1963)
The Classical Language of Architecture. Cambridge, Mass.: MIT Press.

Sun, T. (1968)
"Shadow Area Equations for Window Overhangs and Side Fins and Their Applications to Computer Calculation." *ASHRAE Transactions* no. 2059.

Sussman, J.M., Logcher, R.D., and Stotland, H.C. (1971)
"SPECS: A Specification Production Computer System." *Journal of the Structural Division, ASCE,* January 1971, pp. 425–437.

Sutherland, I.E. (1963)
"Sketchpad: A Man-Machine Graphical Communication System." *Proceedings of the 1963 Spring Joint Computer Conference.* Baltimore, Maryland: Spartan Books.

——— (1968)
"A Head-Mounted Three-Dimensional Display." *Proceedings of the Fall Joint Computer Conference.* Washington, D.C.: Thompson Books.

——— (1970)
"Computer Displays." *Scientific American,* June 1970, pp. 57–81.

——— (1974)
"Three-Dimensional Data Input by Tablet." *Proceedings of the IEEE,* vol. 62, no. 4 (April 1974), pp. 453–461.

Sutherland, I.E., and Hodgman, G.W. (1974)
"Reentrant Polygon Clipping." *Communications of the ACM,* vol. 17, no. 1 (Jan. 1974), pp. 32–42.

Sutherland, I.E., Sproull, R.F., and Schumacker, R.A. (1974)
"A Characterization of Ten Hidden Surface Algorithms." *Computing Surveys,* vol. 6, no. 1 (March 1974), pp. 1–56.

Sutherland, W.R., Forgie, J.W., and Morello, M.V. (1969)
"Graphics in Time-Sharing: A Summary of the TX2 Experience." *Proceedings of the 1969 Spring Joint Computer Conference. Montvale, New Jersey: AFIPS Press.*

Sweeney, J.J., and Sert, J.L. (1960)
Antoni Gaudi. New York: Praeger.

Switzer, P. (1975)
"Sampling of Planar Surfaces," in J.C. Davis and M. McCullagh (eds.), *Display and Analysis of Spatial Data.* New York: Wiley.

Tabor, P. (1970)
Traffic in Buildings. Cambridge, England: Cambridge University, Center for Land Use and Built Form Studies, Working Papers 17, 18, 19, 20.

——— (1976)
"Analyzing Route Patterns," in L. March (ed.), *The Architecture of Form.* Cambridge, England: Cambridge University Press.

——— (1976)
"Analyzing Communication Patterns," in L. March (ed.), *The Architecture of Form.* Cambridge, England: Cambridge University Press.

Taggart, J. (1975)
"Sketching: An Informal Dialogue Between Designer and Computer," in N. Negroponte (ed.), *Computer Aids to Design and Architecture.* New York: Petrocelli/Charter.

Taylor, D.R.F. (1972)
Bibliography on Computer Mapping. Monticello, Illinois: Council of Planning Librarians, Exchange Bibliography no. 263.

Teague, L.C., and Hershdorfer, A.M. (1967)
"BUILD: An Integrated System for Building Design." Seattle, Washington: Conference preprint 500, ASCE Conference.

Teague, L.C. (1970)
"Network Models of Configurations of Rectangular Parallelepipeds," in G.T. Moore (ed.), *Emerging Methods in Environmental Design and Planning.* Cambridge, Mass.: MIT Press.

Teague, L.C., and Davis, C.F. (1972)
"Information Systems for Architectural Programming," in W.J. Mitchell (ed.), *Environmental Design: Research and Practice,* Proceedings of the EDRA3/AR8 Conference. Los Angeles, California: School of Architecture and Urban Planning, UCLA.

Teicholz, E.D. (1968)
GRASP: Generation of Random Access Site Plan. Cambridge, Mass.: Harvard Graduate School of Design, Laboratory for Computer Graphics and Spatial Analysis.

Teitelman, W. (1964)
"Real-Time Recognition of Hand-Drawn Characters." *Proceedings of the 1964 Fall Joint Computer Conference.* Baltimore, Maryland: Spartan Books.

Tenenbaum, J.M. et al (1972)
"A Laboratory for Hand-Eye Research." *Information Processing 71.* Amsterdam, Holland: North-Holland Publishing Co.

Th'ng, R., and Davis, M. (1974)
SPACES: An Integral Suite of Computer Programs for Accomodation Scheduling, Layout Generation, and Appraisal of Schools. Glasgow, Scotland: University of Strathclyde, ABACUS, Paper 21.

Thompson, B., and Hughes, J. (1974)
"An Experimental Investigation of the Performance of a Computer-Aided Building Design System." *Proceedings: IFIP Congress 74.* Stockholm: Sweden.

Thompson, F.B. (1966)
"English for the Computer." *Proceedings of the 1966 Fall Joint Computer Conference.* Washington, D.C.: Spartan Books.

Thompson, J.D., and Pelletier, R.J. (1962)
"Privacy vs. Efficiency in the Inpatient Unit." *Hospitals,* 16 August 1962, pp. 53–57.

Thompson, J.D., and Goldin, G. (1975)
The Hospital: A Social and Architectural History. New Haven, Connecticut: Yale University Press.

Thomsen, C.B. (1965)
"How High to Rise." *AIA Journal,* April 1965, pp. 66–68.

Thorndike, E.L. (1931)
Human Learning. Cambridge, Mass.: MIT Press.

Tobler, W.R. (1969)
"Geographical Filters and Their Inverses." *Geographical Analysis,* vol. 1, pp. 234–253.

Tohmatsu, N. (1974)
"Computer Applications in Architecture: Review of Japan." *DMG-DRS Journal,* vol. 8, no. 4, pp. 200–206.

Tribus, M. (1969)
Rational Decisions, Descriptions, and Designs. New York: Pergamon.

Trout, R.G. (1972)
"An Interactive System for Selecting Building Products." *Proceedings of the Online 72 Conference.* Uxbridge, Middlesex, England: Online Computer Systems Ltd.

Tumarkin, J.E. (1968)
Statistical Cost Estimating Relationships for Building Construction Planning. Arlington, Virginia: Institute for Defense Analysis, Cost Analysis Group.

Turing, A.M. (1950)
"Computing Machinery and Intelligence." *Mind,* vol. 59, pp. 433–450.

Turley, R.E., Richardson, W.R., and Hanse, J.V. (1975)
"Morphological Analysis for Health Care Systems Planning." *Socio-Economic Planning Sciences,* vol. 9 (1975), pp. 83–88.

Turn, R. (1974)
Computers in the 1980's. New York: Columbia University Press.

Uhr, L. (1973)
Pattern Recognition, Learning, and Thought. Englewood Cliffs, New Jersey: Prentice-Hall.

Vacroux, A.G. (1975)
"Microcomputers." *Scientific American,* May 1975, pp. 32–40.

Van der Ryn, S. (1966)
"Problems and Puzzles." *AIA Journal,* January 1966, pp. 37–42.

Velez-Jahn, G. (1974)
A Basic Model for the Random Generation of Functionally Oriented Geometrical Configurations. Caracas, Venezuela: Universidad Central.

Vlietstra, J., and Wielinga, R.F. (eds.) (1973)
Computer-Aided Design. Amsterdam, Holland: North-Holland Publishing Co.

Vollmann, T.E., Nugent, C.E., and Zartler, R.L. (1968)
"A Computerized Model for Office Layout." *Journal of Industrial Engineering,* vol. 19, no. 7 (July 1968), pp. 321–327.

Volpel, J.H. (1969)
"Warehouse Space: How Much?" *Industrial Engineering,* January 1969, pp. 16–20.

von Neumann, J. (1958)
The Computer and the Brain. New Haven, Connecticut: Yale University Press.

Voysey, H. (1974)
"Programming Without Programmers." *New Scientist,* 15 August 1974, pp. 390–391.

Walter, R.A. (1967)
"The Generation of Problem-Oriented Languages," in D. Roos (ed.), *ICES System: General Description.* Cambridge, Mass.: MIT Department of Civil Engineering, Report R67-49.

Ward, W.S., Grant, D.P., and Chapman, A.J. (1970)
"A PL/1 Program for Architectural Space Allocation." *Proceedings of the 5th Urban Symposium.* New York: Association for Computing Machinery.

Warnock, J.E. (1969)
A Hidden-Surface Algorithm for Computer-Generated Half-Tone Pictures. Salt Lake City, Utah: University of Utah, Computer Science Department Report TR4-15.

Watkins, G.S. (1971)
A Real-Time Visible Surface Algorithm. Salt Lake City, Utah: University of Utah, Computer Science Department Report UTEC-CSC-70-101.

Weinzapfel, G.E., and Handel, S. (1975)
"IMAGE: Computer Assistant for Architectural Design," in C.M. Eastman (ed.), *Spatial Synthesis in Computer-Aided Building Design.* New York: Wiley.

Weizenbaum, J. (1963)
"Symmetric List Processor." *Communications of the ACM,* vol. 6, pp. 524–544.

——— (1966)
"Eliza: A Computer Program for the Study of Natural Language Communications Between Man and Machine." *Communications of the ACM,* vol. 9, no. 1, pp. 36–45.

——— (1967)
"Contextual Understanding by Computers." *Communications of the ACM,* vol. 10, no. 8, pp. 474–480.

——— (1976)
Computer Power and Human Reason. San Francisco, California: W.H. Freeman.

White, D.S. (1972)
"Mathematical Evaluation and Optimization of the Three-Dimensional Hospital Layout Problem," in W.J. Mitchell (ed.), *Environmental Design: Research and Practice,* Proceedings of the EDRA3/AR8 Conference. Los Angeles, California: School of Architecture and Urban Planning, UCLA.

Whitehead, B. (1970)
"The Rational Planning of School Layouts." *Build International,* December 1970, pp. 377–380.

Whitehead, B., and Eldars, M.Z. (1964)
"An Approach to the Optimum Layout of Single-Story Buildings." *Architects' Journal,* 17 June 1964, pp. 1373–1379.

Whitehead, B., and Hafez, E. (1966)
"Systematic Methods for Warehouse Design." *Journal of Productivity in Architecture, Construction and Engineering* (PACE), vol. 1, no. 1 (Jan. 1966), pp. 13–20.

Whiteside, D. (1969)
"An Illustration of a Code for the Construction Industry," in D. Bishop and K. Alsop, *A Study of Coding and Data Coordination for the Construction Industry.* London: Ministry of Building and Public Works.

Whitney, H. (1932)
"Non-Separable and Planar Graphs." *Transactions of the American Mathematical Society,* vol. 34, pp. 339–362.

——— (1933)
"Planar Graphs." *Fund. Math.,* vol. 21, pp. 73–84.

Williams, R. (1972)
"A General Purpose Graphical Language," in F. Nake and A. Rosenfeld (eds.), *Graphic Languages.* Amsterdam, Holland: North-Holland Publishing Co.

Willoughby, T.M. (1970)
"Computer-Aided Design of a University Campus." *Architects' Journal,* 25 (March 1970), pp. 753–757.

——— (1975)
"Understanding Building Plans with Computer Aids," in D. Hawkes (ed.), *Models and Systems in Architecture and Building.* Hornby, Lancaster, England: The Construction Press.

——— (1976)
"Searching for a Good Design Solution," in L. March (ed.), *The Architecture of Form.* Cambridge, England: Cambridge University Press.

Willoughby, T.M., Paterson, W., and Drummond, G. (1970)
"Computer-Aided Architectural Planning." *Operational Research Quarterly,* vol. 21, no. 1 (March 1970), pp. 91–98.

Winograd, T. (1972)
Understanding Natural Language. New York: Academic Press.

Winslow, W.F. (1972)
"Translating Individual Construction Project Information into the Resources Required for Construction," in W.J. Mitchell (ed.), *Environmental Design: Research and Practice,* Proceedings of the EDRA3/AR8 Conference. Los Angeles, California: School of Architecture and Urban Planning, UCLA.

Wirth, N., and Weber, H. (1966)
"EULER: A Generalization of Algol and its Formal Definition." *Communications of the ACM,* vol. 9, no. 1, pp. 13–25 (Pt. 1), and vol. 9, no. 2, pp. 89–99 (Pt. 2).

Wong, A.K.C., and Au, T. (1971)
"Computer Methodology for Planning at Health Care Facilities," in M. Kennedy (ed.), *Proceedings of the Kentucky Workshop on Computer Applications to Environmental Design.* Lexington, Kentucky, University of Kentucky.

——— (1971)
"Parallel Processing Approach to Bridge Planning." *Journal of the Structural Division, American Society of Civil Engineers,* January 1971, pp. 115–132.

Woodsford, P.A. (1971)
"The Design and Implementation of the GINO 3D Graphics Software Package." *Software Practice and Experience,* 1 (Oct. 1971), p. 335.

Woolacott, R.G., and Finney, A.G.G. (1976)
"Computer Generated Stereograms for Design Analysis," in *CAD 76,* Proceedings of the Second International Conference on Computers in Engineering and Building Design. Guildford, Surrey, England: IPC Science and Technology Press.

Yates, F.A. (1954)
"The Art of Ramon Lull." *Journal of the Warburg and Courtauld Institutes,* vol. 17, pp. 115–173.

Yessios, C.I. (1975)
"Formal Languages for Site Planning," in C.M. Eastman (ed.), *Spatial Synthesis in Computer-Aided Building Design.* New York: Wiley.

Yntema, D.B., and Torgerson, W.S. (1961)
"Man-Computer Cooperation in Decisions Requiring Common Sense." *IRE Transactions on Human Factors in Electronics,* vol. HFE-2, no. 1 (March 1961), pp. 20–26.

Yoeli, P. (1967)
"Mechanization of Analytical Hill Shading." *The Cartographic Journal,* vol. 4, pp. 82–88.

Zadeh, L.A. (1965)
"Fuzzy Sets." *Information and Control,* vol. 8, pp. 338–353.

Zwicky, F. (1962)
Morphology of Propulsive Power. Pasadena, California: Society for Morphological Research.

Zwicky, F. (1967)
"The Morphological Approach to Discovery, Invention, Research and Construction," in F. Zwicky and A.G. Wilson (eds.), *New Methods of Thought and Procedure.* New York: Springer-Verlag.

Index

Q

R

S

T